E
210
.N36
1988

A Nation in the womb
    of time

DATE DUE			

EARLY AMERICAN HISTORY

An eighteen volume series reproducing over three hundred of the most important articles on all aspects of the colonial experience

EDITED WITH INTRODUCTIONS BY
PETER CHARLES HOFFER
UNIVERSITY OF GEORGIA

A Garland Series

A NATION IN
THE WOMB OF TIME

Selected Articles
on the Long-Term Causes
of the American Revolution

EDITED WITH AN INTRODUCTION BY
PETER CHARLES HOFFER

Garland Publishing, Inc.
New York & London
1988

Library of Congress Cataloging-in-Publication Data

A Nation in the womb of time : selected articles on the long-term causes
of the American Revolution / edited with an introduction by Peter
Charles Hoffer.
     p. cm.—(Early American history)
          ISBN 0-8240-6245-0 (alk. paper)
  1. United States—History—Revolution, 1773–1783—Causes. I. Hoffer,
             Peter C. II. Series.
E210.N36 1988
973.3'11—dc19   87-17210
                                                                    CIP

The volumes in this series are printed on
acid-free, 250-year-life paper.

Printed in the United States of America

CONTENTS

PREFACE

In *An Inquiry Concerning Human Understanding*,[1] David Hume, the Scottish philosopher, historian, and educator, reduced long-term causation to mere constant conjunction. Our minds imputed these and other causes; there were no corporeal links between events. Relying upon custom, prejudice, learning, and reason, we assigned cause, rather than found it. In Hume's day, suspicion and conspiracy were commonly assumed to be the mainsprings of human actions.[2] Later generations of historians, following Hume's logic without perhaps realizing its full implications, attributed human events to nascent nationalism, economic self-interest, and more recently, ideological commitment. A handful of modern historians even rely on psychological theories to explain cause.

From the first generation of patriot historians, led by Mercy Otis Warren and David Ramsay, to the present, scholars have agreed that the Revolution had long term causes. No empire so vast could have fallen in so short a time, from 1763 to 1776, without deep fissures in its structure. Lawrence Henry Gipson believed that these were created by the gradual but inexorable maturation of the colonies.[3] As Benjamin Franklin wrote, it was absurd to assume that a continent could forever be ruled by an island. Edmund S. Morgan uncovered profound misunderstandings of purpose and priorities in the Stamp Act crisis, errors that grew out of deeper divisions between colonies and mother country.[4] Bernard Bailyn suggested that basic structural differences in colonial politics and imperial policies provided the idiom and the motivation for early colonial protest, and

ix

made the colonists more receptive to radical English ideologies than the English were themselves.[5]

With diligence and perspicacity historians of the early nation have researched the long-term causes of the revolution to discover the roots of republican thought. Bailyn's discussion of the true Whig ideology gave focus to two decades of investigation of "Court and Country" factions in the colonies and the mother country. Bailyn brilliantly applied to the American experience some of the conclusions of J. G. A. Pocock's and Caroline Robbins' influential studies of seventeenth and eighteenth century English political thought.[6] Pocock himself probed the American case in 1975.[7]

This intense review of the precedents for republican thought in eighteenth-century English debates over the mixed constitution, seventeenth-centry English writing on contract and civic virtue, and even sixteenth-century Florentine political and historical commentary, suggests that Americans were looking backward, to a time of public probity and private honor, rather than forward to a new world order. Joyce Appleby and Robert Shalhope have disputed this point of view, insisting that Americans looked forward to a world of flourishing commerce, personal enrichment, and social improvement, a goal which British cupidity and corruption increasingly endangered.[8]

Unlike the articles in Volume Sixteen, the present collection frankly confronts the onrushing Revolution. Such hindsight might be crippling in the hands of less skilled scholars, but here it lends urgency and vigor.

Peter Charles Hoffer
University of Georgia

Notes

1. David Hume, *An Inquiry Concerning Human Understanding* ([1748] Indianapolis, 1955), 85–86.

2. Gordon Wood, "Conspiracy and the Paranoid Style: Causality and Deceit in the Eighteenth Century,"*The William and Mary Quarterly*, 3d. ser. 39 (1982), 401–41.

3. Lawrence Henry Gipson, *The Coming of the Revolution, 1763–1775* (New York, 1954), 215.

4. Edmund S. and Helen M. Morgan, *The Stamp Act Crisis, Prologue to Revolution* (rev. ed., New York, 1962), 361–370.

5. Bernard Bailyn, *The Ideological Origins of the American Revolution* (Cambridge, Mass., 1967).

6. J. G. A. Pocock, *The Ancient Constitution and the Feudal Law* (Cambridge, Eng., 1957); Caroline Robbins, *The Eighteenth-Century Commonwealthman* (Cambridge, Mass., 1959).

7. Pocock, *The Machiavellian Moment, Florentine Political Thought and the Atlantic Republican Tradition* (Princeton, 1975).

8. Robert Shalhope, "Republicanism and Early American Historiography," *The William and Mary Quarterly*, 3d ser. 39 (1982), 334; Joyce Appleby, "Republicanism in Old and New Contexts," *WMQ*, 3d ser. 43 (1986), 20–34, and *Capitalism and a New Social Order: The Republican Vision of the 1790s* (New York, 1984), 1–24.

The Canadian
Historical Review

| VOL. XXIII | TORONTO, MARCH, 1942 | No. 1 |

THE AMERICAN REVOLUTION

THIS symposium on the causes of the American Revolution was presented at the annual meeting of the American Historical Association in Chicago on December 30 last. The papers are printed in the order in which they were given. The main papers are by Professor Lawrence A. Harper of the University of California, and Professor Winfred T. Root of the University of Iowa. The two shorter papers by Professor O. M. Dickerson of the Colorado State College of Education and Professor L. H. Gipson of Lehigh University were intended as comments on the longer papers and as an introduction to discussion.

It is planned to print in our next issue (June) some further comments, among which we expect to have one by Professor Louis M. Hacker of Columbia University, who has already consented to contribute. These varied contributions will make clear the conflict in interpretations and points of view which still exist in spite of the enormous amount of work given to the subject in the past fifty years.

The CANADIAN HISTORICAL REVIEW has always considered the American Revolution as among its principal themes of interest, and it is appropriate that this symposium should appear in these pages, especially at a time when the relations of the various parts of the English-speaking world are passing through profound changes. A generation ago the re-interpretation of the Revolution by American historians did much to remove misconceptions which had been a potent cause of friction between Britain and the United States for over a century. Seldom have the results of objective scholarship had a more far-reaching practical influence. As the Revolution recedes still further into the past, its importance in perspective tends to increase rather than diminish. It takes its place not only as an event of significance to America, but as a chapter of deep significance in the history of the modern world, and the views of our generation with regard to it will, without doubt, have a direct bearing on the solutions which are found for the baffling problems now confronting us. [EDITOR'S NOTE]

MERCANTILISM AND THE AMERICAN REVOLUTION

THE cynic who declared that history is the process whereby a complex truth becomes a simplified falsehood may have had in mind interpretations of the American Revolution. Even before the Revolution occurred, Vergennes prophesied that France's loss of Canada would eventually bring it about.[1] The

[1]George Bancroft, *History of the United States of America from the Discovery of the Continent to the Establishment of the Constitution in 1789* (1885 ed., 6 vols.), II, 564.

very document which made the severance final attributed the blame to George III, a fashion which has been generally followed, and some years ago was ardently expounded by a former mayor of this city, Big Bill Thompson. These points, however, are called to attention merely to remind us of what Professor Root will expound more fully—that there are many interpretations. Our immediate task is to concentrate upon one—the relation of English mercantilism to the American Revolution.

The term "mercantilism" is one of those words which have different meanings for different people. On the one hand, George Louis Beer claimed that English mercantilism was a well-balanced system designed for the benefit of the colonies as well as the mother country, and on the other, Sir William Ashley declared that the regulations of English mercantilism were either pious formulas nullified in the actual world of commerce by fraud and evasion, or merely a codification of commercial habits which would have been followed in any case. For reasons which have been explained more fully elsewhere[2] we shall reject Beer's claim that there was no exploitation and accept the statements of the mercantilists themselves that they planned to exploit the colonies for the benefit of the mother country. We shall deny the Ashley view that there was no actual regulation and conclude from more recent studies of the evidence that the English laws did regulate trade and commerce.

These two conclusions provide us with a working definition of English mercantilism in its colonial aspects. It had as its purpose, exploitation, and as its means, regulation. Both phases of the problem, exploitation *and* regulation, are important. To understand the relationship of mercantilism and the Revolution we must not only analyse the extent to which the colonists were exploited but also consider the skill with which they were regulated.

An analysis of how the colonists were exploited is no easy task, as any one knows who has struggled with the many statutory ambiguities involved. The calculations involved in estimating the burdens placed upon the colonial economy are complicated. They call for arithmetical computations involving duties, preferences, or drawbacks of such odd amounts as 1s. 10d. and 15 16/75 of a twentieth of a penny per pound of tobacco. They run afoul of complicated analyses of costs and close decisions about the incidence of taxation. The answer required some thousands of

[2]L. A. Harper, *The English Navigation Laws* (New York, 1939), chap. XIX.

hours of WPA and NYA labour in tabulating the necessary data and hundreds more in analysing and correlating them, the details of which have been compressed in thirty-eight rather dull pages.[1] All that can be attempted here is to state the conclusions and indicate the grounds upon which they are based. We can, however, simplify our analysis of the mercantilist code which exploited the colonies by dividing it into four parts: first, the basic provisions concerning the trans-Atlantic trade; second, the supplementary measures restricting manufactures; third, the subsidiary rules with reference to the American trade; and fourth, the much discussed measures enacted after the French and Indian War.

In examining the first part, we find that the basic provisions concerning the trans-Atlantic trade placed a heavy burden upon the colonies. By means of the Navigation Acts England attempted both to keep foreign vessels out of the colonies and to enable English merchants to share in the more profitable parts of the trans-Atlantic trade. The enumeration of key colonial exports in various Acts from 1660 to 1766 and the Staple Act of 1663 hit at colonial trade both coming and going. The Acts required the colonies to allow English middlemen to distribute such crops as tobacco and rice and stipulated that if the colonies would not buy English manufactures, at least they should purchase their European goods in England. The greatest element in the burden laid upon the colonies was not the taxes assessed. It consisted in the increased costs of shipment, trans-shipment, and middleman's profits arising out of the requirement that England be used as an entrepôt.

The burdens were somewhat lightened by legislation favouring the colonies, but not as much as usually alleged. The suppression of tobacco production in England, for example, was comparatively unimportant to the colonies since the great quantities of colonial tobacco re-exported caused its price to be determined by a world rather than an English market. Moreover, the motive was not goodwill for the colonists but fiscal, since the heavy revenues derived from tobacco could be collected more easily at the waterfront than upon the farm. Likewise, although colonial shipbuilders and shipowners approved the clauses of the Navigation Acts which eliminated Dutch rivals, they did not need such protection. They had managed to carry cargoes and

3

[1] L. A. Harper, "The Effect of the Navigation Acts on the Thirteen Colonies" (in The Era of the American Revolution, ed. by Richard B. Morris, New York, 1939).

to build ships which could be sold in the world market before the laws were enacted and they continued to do so after the Revolution.   The fact is that colonial shipowners suffered, directly, and colonial shipbuilders, indirectly, under the Navigation Acts since other clauses enabled English shipowners (as contrasted with American) to carry eighty per cent of the trade between the British Isles and the Thirteen Colonies whereas they carried only twenty per cent after the Revolution.[4]

Similarly the drawbacks, bounties, and tariff preferences, of which we are so often reminded, did not materially offset the burdens placed upon the trans-Atlantic trade.   The drawbacks paid by English customs authorities on foreign products re-exported to the colonies should not be listed as a benefit to the colonies.   There would have been no duties to be drawn back except for the requirement that the colonists purchase their European goods in England.   The portion of the duties which England retained, while less than it might have been, was obvi-

[4]*Ibid.*, 8-10, 37.   Richard Champion, *Considerations on the Present Situation of Great Britain and the United States* (London, 1784) declares at pages 27-8 that the ships in the trade between Europe and the Thirteen Colonies totalling 195,000 tons "were generally the property of British merchants, navigated by British seamen" and that they formed "no less than a sixth of our whole shipping," which had previously (p. 13) been stated to be about 1,300,000 tons.   Obviously the trans-Atlantic trade of Boston, New York, and Philadelphia included a substantial percentage of colonial-owned ships, but the *trans-Atlantic* trade of those ports was less than that of Virginia, Maryland, and South Carolina, which was overwhelmingly in the hands of British vessels.   Thus it seemed wisest to modify Champion's statement somewhat and the estimate of eighty per cent was taken as being a fairly reasonable approximation.   Subsequent analyses of the Naval Office lists show that the percentages differed radically from port to port and even within the same port during different years:

OWNERSHIP OF TONNAGE IN TRADE WITH BRITISH ISLES

Ports and years examined						
Ports	Exports for	By British	By British and colonial jointly	By colonial	By others	Total
New York.......	1754	340	550	2,585	20	3,495
" "	1764	1,362	740	2,010	100	4,212
Port York.......	1768	2,376		350		2,726
Port Hampton...	1758	2,627		465	80	3,172
" " ...	1766	3,436		1,385	35	4,856
South Carolina...	1758	8,649		1,825	670	11,144
" " ...	1766	13,982	1,691	1,205	605	17,483

An attempt was made to calculate the average for all the colonies on the assumption that the average of the New York percentages would be typical of that of the colonies north of the Mason and Dixon line, while an average of the Virginia and Charleston figures would represent that of the Southern colonies.   The averages thus derived were then weighted in accordance with the ratio of Northern (30) and Southern (70) tonnages engaged in the Anglo-American trade in 1769 (Public Record Office, London,

ously greater than nothing at all.[5] Likewise, *bounties paid upon English manufactures* exported to the colonies, were of advantage to the English producer, who received them whether his goods were exported to the colonies or anywhere else, rather than of benefit to the colonial consumer who otherwise would, and often did, buy competitive European goods.[6]

On the other hand, however, the bounties paid upon colonial products were of real advantage to the colonies. They sustained the growth of indigo in South Carolina, did much to foster the development of naval stores in North Carolina, encouraged the lumber industry in New England, and at the end of the colonial period averaged more than £65,000 a year for the Thirteen Colonies alone. Similarly the preferences granted colonial products were beneficial in so far as they operated. Although they had no effect upon such commodities as tobacco and rice and their effect upon other commodities is somewhat uncertain, colonial

Customs 16, vol. 1), with the result that the percentage of British-owned ships was found to be 74.5 per cent and that of colonial-owned ships 16.9 per cent. The procedure, however, involved other complications. Vessels listed as colonial-owned in Virginia and Charleston were listed as colonial but they were probably owned in most cases by Scottish factors who might well be classed as British. Vessels carrying rice to southern Europe were considered to be engaged in trade with the British Isles because they virtually all engaged in a triangular voyage which started and ended there. Owners listed as residing in Madeira, Rotterdam, and elsewhere (3.4 per cent) probably should have been listed as British since only ships of British subjects were allowed to trade in the colonies. Finally, there is the question of how great was the British and how great was the colonial interest in the vessels owned jointly (5.2 per cent). Thus the best estimate now possible would seem to be that the British controlled about 80 per cent of the tonnage in the Anglo-American trade under mercantilism.

[5]It is, of course, true that, if one wishes to consider the fairness of the burdens laid upon the colonists, it is relevant to remember that the allowance of drawbacks enabled them to pay lower taxes upon the same goods than the English were assessed. An analysis of the economic burdens upon the colonies, however, is concerned primarily with ascertaining how much the colonists had to pay, not with determining how fair the assessment was. If one lists the drawbacks as a colonial advantage in such an analysis, the entire tax should be calculated as a colonial burden, in which case one will attain exactly the same result reached in the calculations which follow, since the drawback has already been deducted from the gross tax and the only burden considered has been the net tax retained in Britain.

[6]The grant of the bounty did not depend upon exportation *to the colonies* in the case, of any of the bounty-paid products (cordage, corn, certain fish, beef, pork, gunpowder, linen, sailcloth, silk manufactures, and refined sugar), nor in the case of the candles, glass, hides, lace, thread and fringes, leather manufactures, paper calicoes, silks, salt, soap, and starch, the "exciseable goods" which received specified drawbacks or bounties upon exportation (Samuel Baldwin, *A Survey of the British Customs*, London, 1770, Part II, 19-22). In the case of linens the bounty was paid only for exportations to Africa, America, Spain, Portugal, Gibraltar, Minorca, and the East Indies, but those were the only regions in which British linen had an opportunity to compete successfully. It is also important to note that in the year 1773 the exports to the American colonies of bounty-paid linen totalled £348,464 (of which £168,314 went to the continental colonies), while less than £68,000 worth of bounty-paid linen was exported to the rest of the world. During the same year the continental colonies imported almost the same amount of duty-burdened linens, valued at £137,248, and similar exports to the British Carribbean amounted to £102,754 (Customs 3, vol. 73).

raw silk, naval stores, and lumber definitely benefited. Yet the total sum represented by such preferences was never great and it is doubtful whether the benefit the Thirteen Colonies thus derived amounted to even one-twentieth of that obtained by the British West Indian planters who in the year 1773 alone, pocketed £446,000, thanks to a preferential rate which enabled their sugar to hold the English market despite a five-shilling-per-hundred-weight differential in price.[7]

The uncertainties underlying many of our calculations do not permit an exact statement, but judging from calculations for the year 1773, it would seem that after all proper allowances have been made for bounties and other preferences, the net burden imposed upon the Thirteen Colonies by the restraints upon the trans-Atlantic trade was between two million and seven million dollars a year. In these days of astronomical budgets such figures do not seem especially impressive, but the annual per capita burden represented by the lower estimate would come close to meeting all the expenses of operating the national government during Washington's administration, and an annual per capita tax based upon the higher estimate would, in addition to paying the current expenses of government, have raised in twelve years (from 1790-1801) a sum sufficient to pay both the domestic and foreign debt incurred by the United States government during the Revolutionary War.[8]

When we turn to the second part of our discussion, the supplementary measures restricting manufacture, we find a difference of opinion concerning the effect of English restrictions upon manufacturing wool, hats, and iron. The earlier tendency was to dismiss the regulations as immaterial, but recently some have swung the pendulum to the other extreme and argue that the

[7]Harper, "Effect of the Navigation Acts," *passim*. As Professor Gipson points out, the British West Indies had their own burdens, such as the 4½ per cent tax in Barbados, but their increasing inability to meet world competition as shown by the decrease in re-exports of sugar from England (Frank W. Pitman, *The Development of the British West Indies*, New Haven, 1915, 156 ff.) indicates that retention of England's market was very important to them. Also one must remember that the British fleet, as well as economic interests, helped to prevent their joining the Thirteen Colonies in revolt, just as the Canadians were kept loyal to the mother country partly by their distrust of the Thirteen Colonies and partly by the profits to be derived in the fur trade from an uninterrupted supply of British manufactures.

[8]The estimate of the net burden given here has been modified slightly from that given in Harper, "The Effect of the Navigation Laws," in order to make greater allowances for the possibly beneficial effects of preferential rates on colonial products and for possible errors in estimating the ratio between the pound and the dollar.

restraints were very important.[9] Neither extreme appears to accord with the facts. In the case of hats, proximity to the source of supply of furs and the comparatively simple process of manufacturing had led to the development of an industry which appears to have been injured by the legislation,[10] but the hat industry played only a minor part in the total economy. Woollen manufactures were, of course, much more important, but there is much evidence to indicate that the English prohibitions had little material effect. The colonies found that they were handicapped by an inadequate supply of good wool when they tried to develop homespun goods at the time of the Revolution—and even as late as 1791 Hamilton found that an adequate supply of labour was one of the chief stumbling blocks to his programme for encouraging industry. It required an embargo, a war, and a protective tariff before large-scale woollen manufacturing began to develop, and it did not pass beyond the household stage until many years after being freed of English mercantilism—which, incidentally, had never forbidden the manufacture of homespun for domestic use or local distribution.[11]

In the case of iron manufactures the British legislation encouraged the development of pig and bar iron and tried to discourage the manufacture of more advanced forms, but in both respects the influence of the legislation is doubtful. Because of the proximity of iron ore to forests America had a great advantage in producing crude iron, before coke replaced charcoal, and probably did not need legislative encouragement. With such an advantage in producing crude iron it was only natural that some more advanced iron articles would be produced in the colonies, whatever thorough-going mercantilists might dream about having the crude iron sent over to England and having it returned in the form of pots, pans, and other manufactures.[12]

The various disallowances of colonial laws which were intended to foster colonial manufacturing further illustrate the English intention of discouraging it but, despite that intent, English

[9]Cf. Victor S. Clark, *History of Manufactures in the United States, 1607-1860* (2 vols., Washington, 1916-28) with Miriam Beard, *A History of the Business Man* (New York, 1938); L. M. Hacker, *The Triumph of American Capitalism* (New York, 1940) and "The First American Revolution" (*Columbia University Quarterly*, XXVII, Sept., 1935).

[10]Harper, "The Effect of the Navigation Acts," 6-7.

[11]*Report on Manufactures,* Dec. 5, 1791, in American State Papers, Finance, I, 123-44; Arthur H. Cole, *The American Wool Manufacture* (2 vols., Cambridge, Mass., 1926), *passim.*

[12]A. C. Bining, *British Regulation of the Colonial Iron Industry* (Philadelphia, 1933); *Pennsylvania Iron Manufacture in the Eighteenth Century* (Harrisburg, 1938).

mercantilism as a whole probably had a greater tendency to promote than to hinder colonial industry. The colonies' most dangerous industrial competitors were in many respects, not the English, but the Dutch, the Germans, and other Europeans—to say nothing of the natives of India—against whose competition the provisoes of the Staple Act of 1663 provided a very useful tariff barrier. Moreover, the large sums which mercantilism withheld from the colonies reduced their available cash, and probably forced many colonists to use homespun or other American products instead of buying British.[13]

The third point of our inquiry into colonial exploitation by England should not detain us long. Until the Molasses Act of 1733 the inter-American trade had been left virtually alone except for the requirement that the English colonies trade in English or colonial ships. Even after 1733, the prohibitive duties on foreign sugar, molasses, and rum were usually evaded. Such evasion required bribery, fraud, or concealment which probably served as a mildly protective tariff in favour of the British sugar islands, but the prices quoted in the Thirteen Colonies for sugar, molasses, and rum do not indicate that the legislation had any radical effect upon the trade.[14]

The fourth part of our inquiry—that relating to the period after 1763—is a different matter. The researches of Schlesinger and others have demonstrated how the British measures of that period aroused the resentment of the merchants who unleashed an avalanche of agitation which soon went beyond their control. The agitation was not directed toward revolution at first, but agitation by its very nature promotes conditions favourable for revolution—and revolution followed as a natural sequence. Yet, conceding all the irritation thus aroused, we must still face the questions: Were the measures unduly exploitive? Did they fundamentally upset the economic equilibrium? Were they fatal ills which would inevitably lead to the death of the Empire, or merely minor upsets from which the Empire might have recovered —granted otherwise favourable conditions and good luck?

In reviewing the period it does not seem fair to blame British mercantilism for prescribing regulations which were demanded by the circumstances of the time. The British currency and land

[13]Cf. Calendar of State Papers, Colonial, XXVIII, 225, July 7, 1715; XXXII, 413-14, Sept. 8, 1721; XXXVIII, 326-7, Nov. 5, 1731.
[14]See Anne Bezanson, Robert D. Gray, and Miriam Hussey, *Prices in Colonial Pennsylvania* (Philadelphia, 1935); Arthur H. Cole, *Wholesale Commodity Prices in the United States, 1700-1861*, and *Statistical Supplement* (Cambridge, Mass., 1939).

policies seem to fall under this category. The restrictions upon paper money undoubtedly distressed those who lacked funds, but they merely affirmed a truth which Americans had to learn from sad experience—that in the eighteenth century at least, no political alchemy could transmute paper into gold. Similarly the Proclamation of 1763 and the Quebec Act of 1774 essentially concerned imperial problems and American imitation of the policy after independence was not mere flattery but a tribute to its inherent soundness. The measures disappointed those who had hoped to acquire fortunes from land speculation, but what else could the British have done? Neither they nor the United States government after them could allow private individuals to stir up trouble by moving into Indian territory before the way had been prepared for settlement by negotiations which extinguished the Indians' claims to the area. In view of the British debt it was merely good fiscal policy to charge for the land, and the prices and terms of sale proposed by the British mercantilists seem very reasonable when compared with the prices and terms adopted by the federal government after 1787.[15] And what solution did the Thirteen States themselves find for the conflicting claims to the territory west of the Alleghanies except to create a new governmental unit?

To one who frankly does not profess to be an expert on the point, it is difficult to understand how British mercantilism discriminated materially against the colonists. It is true that in the manœuvering for land grants, British interests sometimes clashed with colonial interests, but we hear fully as much about clashes between different colonial groups. Both the small frontiersmen and the big speculators were charged more for land than they were accustomed to pay, but it was not as much as they were to be charged by the United States government thereafter. In the readjustments which accompanied the establish-

[15]The conditions of sale established by the British in 1774, stipulated sale by public auction and a minimum price of 6d. per acre (which however bore an annual quit-rent of 1/2d. per acre) and terms, cash (New York Colonial Documents, VIII, 410-13). The Ordinance of 1785 stipulated a 640 acre unit of purchase and a minimum price of one dollar an acre, terms, cash. The Land Act of 1796 retained the 640 acre unit of purchase but raised the minimum price to two dollars an acre and stipulated a down payment of one-half, half of the remainder within thirty days, and the balance within one year. The Harrison Land Act of 1800 reduced the unit of purchase to 320 acres but retained the minimum price of two dollars an acre and stipulated a down payment of one quarter, and the balance in four equal yearly payments. The Land Act of 1820 reduced the unit of purchase to 80 acres and the minimum price to $1.25 an acre but abolished the credit system and re-instituted cash terms (Benjamin H. Hibbard, *A History of the Public Land Policies*, New York, 1924).

ment of the new policies the fur traders of the Thirteen Colonies suffered somewhat because of the machinations of British opponents but their loss was not great, and in any event by the Revolutionary period trade in furs formed only a negligible fraction of the colonial economy.[16]

The pre-Revolutionary taxation measures, however, are a different matter, and one for which British mercantilism must bear full responsibility.[17] Yet in analysing the figures we find that the average annual revenue raised by the Sugar Acts, the Townshend Acts, and all the other taxes collected in the Thirteen Colonies by the British government amounted to only £31,000. This sum barely exceeded the indirect taxes which were collected on colonial merchandise passing through England. Moreover, both the taxes collected indirectly in England and directly in the colonies failed to equal the bounties which the British government was paying to the colonies—to say nothing of the advantages which they were deriving from preferential duties on their shipments to England. More interesting still, calculated on an annual per capita basis, the taxes collected during the Revolutionary period directly in the colonies and indirectly in England, totalled less than one-seventh of the taxes assessed at the beginning of the century.[18]

[16]According to tables compiled by Murray G. Lawson from the Inspector General's accounts (Customs 3), the imports of colonial furs decreased from 1.0 per cent of the total exports from the Thirteen Colonies to England in 1750 to 0.87 per cent in 1755, to 0.51 per cent in 1760, 0.94 per cent in 1765, 0.6 per cent in 1770, and 0.45 per cent in 1775. These percentages, however, should be further reduced because exports of the Thirteen Colonies to Scotland amounted to about one-half of the exports to England in 1769 (Customs 14, vol. 1B) and the value of exports elsewhere than Great Britain almost equalled the value of exports to Great Britain (T. Pitkin, *A Statistical View of the Commerce of the United States of America: Its Connection with Agriculture and Manufactures* . . . , Hartford, Conn., 1816, 21-3). Thus at the outbreak of the Revolution the fur trade constituted less than one-fifth of one per cent of the total exports of the Thirteen Colonies and probably had never greatly exceeded one-third of one per cent in the second half of the century. An examination of the figures in Pitkin (*ibid.*) discloses (when the £91,486 there given for the value of furs is reduced to almost one-seventh to allow for the inclusion of furs from Canada, Hudson Bay, and similar regions) that the fur trade was less important in 1770 to the Thirteen Colonies than that in spermaceti candles or in horses, to say nothing of the more important staple commodities like indigo, rice, tobacco, or provisions. The decline in importance of the fur trade dates back far before 1763. In New York, the colony most interested in the trade, furs had constituted 32 per cent of the exports to England in 1720 and had declined to 30 per cent in 1730, 23 per cent in 1740, 16 per cent in 1750, 13.8 per cent in 1755, 4.8 per cent in 1760, 10.1 per cent in 1765, 3.3 per cent in 1770, and 2.1 per cent in 1775.

[17]These taxes, of course, differed in many ways from earlier measures but they had very definite economic effects, however political some of their aims may have been. Consequently, it seemed necessary to include them if our discussion of mercantilism was to be complete.

[18]Harper, "Effect of the Navigation Acts," 27-9.

Yet even though the amount of taxation was not great, we must consider the possibility that the form of its assessment detrimentally affected colonial interests. The Tea Act, for one, definitely injured the illicit trade in tea by so reducing the price of the legal article that it lessened, if it did not eliminate, the profit from smuggling.[19] However unfair smugglers may have thought such tactics, they can hardly be said to have injured the economy of the country—especially since tea was not a pivotal commodity.

Molasses, the rum which was made from it, and the provision trade which accompanied it, however, were vital factors in colonial economy, and historians have often called attention to their importance in such books as *Rum, Romance, and Rebellion*.[20] The Sugar Act of 1764 served notice that the British government intended to make its regulations effective when it lowered the duty on foreign sugar and molasses and prohibited the importation of foreign rum entirely. The provisions concerning sugar and rum were comparatively immaterial since no great quantities were imported, but the duty of 3d. per gallon on molasses was another matter, since literally millions of gallons came from the foreign West Indies.[21] Many feared that the trade could not bear a tax of 3d. per gallon, and in response to their pleas the duty was reduced in 1766 to 1d. per gallon and the tax was assessed on both British and foreign molasses. The excitement aroused by these taxes leads one to look for evidence of the havoc which they wrought in trade, but an examination of the wholesale prices of molasses does not disclose any noticeable change attributable to the legislation.[22] And if we carry our investi-

11

[19]V. D. Harrington, *The New York Merchant on the Eve of the Revolution* (New York, 1935), 249, 344; A. M. Schlesinger, *The Colonial Merchants and the American Revolution, 1763-1776* (New York, 1918), 262-7.

[20]By Charles W. Taussig, New York, 1928.

[21]Customs 16, vol. 1 gives the following figures concerning the imports of molasses:

	FROM FOREIGN WEST INDIES	FROM BRITISH WEST INDIES
	Gallons	Gallons
1768..........	2,803,275	326,675
1769..........	3,413,367	299,678
1770..........	3,408,784	226,876

Figures for the importation of rum are not so satisfactory as we could desire, but according to Pitman (*British West Indies*, 208, n. 36) importations of foreign molasses exceeded those of foreign rum 27 to 1 in 1714, 39 to 1 in 1715, 34 to 1 in 1716, and 64 to 1 in 1717. According to the Naval Office Lists for 1764, approximately 38,000 gallons of rum were imported to Boston from the British West Indies as compared with 200 gallons from the foreign West Indies (Public Record Office, London, C.O. 58, vol. 850); at Salem and Marblehead the corresponding figures (for a half year only) were 22,000 and 1,000 (C.O. 5, vol. 850); at New Hampshire 63,000 and none (C.O. 5, vol. 969); at New York 87,000 and 5,000 (C.O. 5, vol. 1228).

[22]*Supra*, note 14.

gations further we find that the tax which the federal government placed and kept upon imports of molasses after 1790 almost equaled the 3d. per gallon placed upon foreign molasses in 1764 and materially exceeded the 1d. duty retained after 1766.[23] In brief, whatever the connection between rum and romance, the statistics of colonial trade disclose no correlation between rum and rebellion.

In so far as the statistics can be followed, the correlation between wine and rebellion is much closer. The Sugar Act of 1764 had also placed a duty upon wines which gave those imported by way of Britain a preferential rate of £3 per ton. The preference was not sufficient to enable the English to capture the trade in Madeira wine, but it enabled them to gain a flourishing trade in port which previously had been negligible.[24] Yet such an infringement of colonial taste hardly seems to justify a revolt— especially when we note that the quantity involved was not large, and that by the post-Revolutionary period Americans preferred port and other wines to Madeira.[25]

Thus, an analysis of the economic effects of British mercantilism fails to establish its exploitive aspects as the proximate cause of the Revolution. The only measures which afforded a sufficient economic grievance were the entrepôt provisions of the Navigation Acts, which governed the trans-Atlantic trade. They helped to create a fundamental economic imbalance, but cannot be connected directly with the Revolution. The colonists had lived under them for more than a century without desiring independence and even in the Revolutionary period with few exceptions the entrepôt provisions were accepted as the mother country's due for the protection which she afforded.[26] In fact, the official

[23]Adam Seybert, Statistical Annals . . . of the United States (Philadelphia, 1818), 398-9, 455-6, 469-70.

[24]In 1750 (before the new tax was placed on Madeira wine) England exported to the Thirteen Colonies 15 tons, 1 hogshead and 13 gallons of Madeira; in 1765 and 1773 (after the imposition of the new tax), the exports were only 22 tons, 1 hogshead, 62 gallons, and 23 tons, 1 hogshead, 48 gallons, respectively. In the case of port, however, England's exportations rose from only 15 tons, 2 hogsheads, and 3 gallons in 1750 to 385 tons, 53 gallons in 1765, and 860 tons, 2 hogsheads, 60 gallons in 1773 (Customs 3, vols. 50, 65, 73).

[25]Seybert, Statistical Annals, 164-9, 260.

[26]The necessity of taking considerable space to calculate the burdens laid upon the colonies by mercantilism should not be regarded as a denial that Britain had real contributions to make. The benefits of military and naval protection were very important. British merchants also probably helped the colonists to find markets for their products but it is easy to overemphasize such assistance. During the greater part of the time the entrepôt requirements were operative the Dutch were much better qualified to serve efficiently as middlemen in colonial products than the English. Similarly the flattening of the curve of the American tobacco exports after the Revolution is not as significant as it seems at first glance. The destruction wrought

representatives of the colonies were willing to guarantee the British commercial system provided that the measures of political taxation were withdrawn.[27] If there were any inexorable economic forces which were inevitably drawing the colonies toward revolution, they are hard to detect and the colonists were unaware of them.

Anyone who maintains that the Revolution resulted from the inevitable clash of competing capitalisms must reckon with several points: That burdens upon the trans-Atlantic trade were proportionately greater at the beginning of the eighteenth century than in 1776; that the restraints of the land and currency policies were basically the same as those prescribed by the federal government; and that after 1766 the taxes laid on molasses by Britain were less than those imposed by the United States after 1790. He should also explain why the surplus colonial capital alleged to be bursting its confines did not venture into the manufacturing enterprises which the law did not prohibit; why the colonists did not finance their own middlemen in England; and, finally, why they did not pay their debts.   If by a clash of expanding capitalism is meant that colonists with money were irritated because their freedom of action was restrained by outside regulation, one must immediately concede that the charge is justified; but such colonial resentment seems more properly classified as a political rather than an economic factor.   It is merely an old point dressed in new garb and was better expressed by John Adams when he declared that the American Revolution began when the first plantation was settled.[28]

When we turn, however, from the economic effects of mercantilism to its regulatory aspects, we are faced with a different story.   We can establish a direct correlation between mercantilism and the Revolution.   Although earlier English regulations had been reasonably satisfactory the regulatory technique

by the Revolution, and the interruption to the trade, first by the Revolution, and then by the wars in Europe, would appear to have done much more to discourage tobacco production than the elimination of the laws making Britain an *entrepôt*.

[27]Resolve no. 4 of the "Declaration and Resolves of the First Continental Congress, October 14, 1774" (as quoted in *Documents Illustrative of the Formation of the Union of the American States*, selected, arranged, and indexed by Charles C. Tansill, Washington, 1927, 3) contains the following statement: "But, from the necessity of the case, and a regard to the mutual interest of both countries, we cheerfully consent to the operation of such acts of the British parliament as are bona fide, restrained to the regulation of our external commerce, for the purpose of securing the commercial advantages of the whole empire to the mother country, and the commercial benefits of its respective members, excluding every idea of taxation internal or external, for raising a revenue on the subjects in America without their consent."

[28]*Works of John Adams*, ed. by Charles F. Adams (10 vols., Boston, 1856), X, 313.

of the British government under George III was pitifully defective. As a mother country, Britain had much to learn. Any modern parents' magazine could have told George III's ministers that the one mistake not to make is to take a stand and then to yield to howls of anguish. It was a mistake which the British government made repeatedly. It placed a duty of 3d. per gallon on molasses, and when it encountered opposition, reduced it to 1d. It provided for a Stamp Act and withdrew it in the face of temper tantrums. It provided for external taxes to meet the colonial objections and then yielded again by removing all except one. When finally it attempted to enforce discipline it was too late. Under the circumstances, no self-respecting child—or colonist—would be willing to yield.

Moreover, British reforming zeal came at a very bad time. The colonists were in a particularly sensitive state due to the post-war deflation and the economic distress which accompanied it. The British also attempted to exert unusual control at a time when the removal of the French from Canada had minimized the colonists' dependence upon Britain. Most important of all, the reforms followed one another too rapidly.

In social reform, irritation often is to be measured not so much by what a regulation attempts to achieve as by the extent to which it changes established habits. The early history of English mercantilism itself offers a good illustration of the point. Bitter complaints came from Virginia and Barbados when tobacco and sugar were first enumerated because those colonies had become accustomed to conditions of comparatively free trade, whereas few or no complaints were heard from Jamaica which had developed under the restrictive system.[29] The mercantilist system was geared for leisurely operation and before George III's reign succeeded by virtue of that fact. Its early restraints led to Bacon's rebellion in Virginia but fortunately for the mother country the pressure against New England was deferred until the next decade when it, too, led to an explosion in the form of revolt against Andros.[30] These uprisings were separated both geographically and chronologically so that neither attained dangerous proportions, and both were followed by a reasonably satisfactory settlement of at least some of the colonial grievances.

[29]George L. Beer, *The Old Colonial System, 1660-1754* (2 vols., New York, 1912), I, 162-3 (Virginia); I, 164-5 (Barbados); II, 83 (Jamaica); Harper, *The English Navigation Laws*, 246, n. 37.
[30]Beer, *Old Colonial System*, II, 148 ff.; Thomas J. Wertenbaker, *Torchbearer of the Revolution: The Story of Bacon's Rebellion and its Leader* (Princeton, 1940).

During the Revolutionary era, however, the tempo of reform was not leisurely. Doubtless all the colonists were not irritated by any one British reform, but each individual had his own feeling of grievance which enabled him to agree fervently with the complaints of others against British policy and thus add to the heated tempers of the time. The politician who objected to the political implications in taxation reforms found an audience in the land speculators and frontiersmen who complained that the colonists were being deprived of the reward of their blood and suffering by the Proclamation of 1763 and the Quebec Act of 1774. Debtors and inflationists chimed in to tell of the iniquities of the Currency Act; lawyers and printers could not forget the threat to their interests in the Stamp Act. On Sundays the preachers thundered against the dangers of popery in Quebec and voiced their fear that Britain planned to establish an Anglican Church in the colonies. The merchant was always ready to explain not merely how harmful British taxes were to colonial economy, but how irksome were the new administrative rules and regulations. Such chronological and geographical barriers as existed were overcome and a community of antagonisms was maintained by the Committees of Correspondence and other agitators, but such revolutionary forces could not have succeeded if the different elements of the colonies had not recently experienced a mutual sense of grievance.

In short, many of the misunderstandings which have arisen in connection with mercantilism and the American Revolution have grown out of the failure to distinguish between the two phases of mercantilism: exploitation and regulation. The fact that the colonists were exploited by English mercantilism does not necessarily mean that mercantilism caused the American Revolution. Economic forces are not magnets which inexorably move men in predetermined patterns. For better or for worse, men try to regulate their economic as well as their political destiny. A large part of governmental activity consists in attempting to mould economic conduct and to minimize the friction which results from clashes or constraints. English mercantilism was such an attempt. It succeeded rather well in minimizing friction until 1764. For the next decade it bungled badly, and the penalty was the loss of the Thirteen Colonies.

LAWRENCE A. HARPER

The University of California.

Colonial Ideas of Parliamentary Power
1764-1766[1]

Edmund S. Morgan [*]

I

THE distinction between internal and external taxes, said Charles Townshend, was "ridiculous in everybody's opinion except the Americans'."[2] The House of Commons was disposed to agree. Members had declared at the time of the Stamp Act that the distinction was meaningless. Some thought that the Americans were fools for espousing such sophistry; others thought that they were knaves, who would seize any pretext to avoid paying for their own protection. And knaves the Americans certainly appeared to be when they objected to the Townshend Duties almost as vehemently as they had to the Stamp Act. The colonists in fact seemed to be a ridiculous group of hypocrites, who capered from one pious notion of their rights to another. Their conduct was shameful and their efforts to justify it even more so. First they quibbled about external taxes and internal taxes. When this distinction failed them, they talked about taxes for regulating trade as against taxes for revenue. Before long they were denying that Parliament had any authority to tax them, and finally they concluded that they were simply not subject to Parliament at all. The frivolous way in which they skipped from one of these views to the next was sufficient evidence that they had no real devotion to any principle except that of keeping their pockets full.[3]

[*] Mr. Morgan is a member of the History Department of Brown University.

[1] This paper, in a shortened version, was read at a meeting of the American Historical Association at Cleveland on December 28, 1947. I wish to express my thanks to the members of the Association who offered comments at that time and to the members of my graduate seminar at Brown University, who criticized the paper at an earlier reading. I also wish to thank Mr. Bernhard Knollenberg, who read the manuscript and made several valuable suggestions.

[2] Quoted in J. C. Miller, *Sam Adams: Pioneer in Propaganda* (Boston, 1936), 115.

[3] See William Knox, *The Controversy between Great-Britain and her Colonies Reviewed* (London, 1769), 34-35: "When the repeal of the stamp-act was their object, a distinction was set up between internal and external taxes; they pretended not to dispute the right of parliament to impose external taxes, or port duties, upon the Colonies, whatever were the purposes of parliament in laying them on, or however productive of revenue they might be. . . . but when parliament seemed to adopt

The modern historian, who has thrown off the mantle of patriotism and Whigism for the more sober garments of impartiality, has tended to accept the Tory analysis of American resistance to taxation. He does not always cast doubt on the sincerity of the successive theories of American constitutional rights, but he agrees with Charles Townshend that it was the Americans who distinguished between internal and external taxes, that they abandoned this distinction for another, which likewise proved untenable, and so on until they reached the Declaration of Independence. Thus in the book which examines the American theories most closely, Doctor Randolph G. Adams' *Political Ideas of the American Revolution*,[4] the American advance toward independence is broken down into three stages:

In the first, the colonies admitted the right of Parliament to levy customs duties (external taxes), but denied the right of Parliament to levy excise taxes (internal taxes) upon them. In the second, the colonies conceded the right of Parliament to regulate the trade of the Empire, and hence exercise a legislative authority over the unrepresented colonies, but denied the right of Parliament to levy taxes of any kind whatever, internal or external. In the third stage of the controversy, the colonies admitted the right of Parliament to act as a quasi-imperial superintending power over them and over all the dominions, but denied that Parliament had any legislative authority over the colonies as a general proposition, on the ground that the colonies were not represented in Parliament.[5]

The first two stages of American Revolutionary thinking, as defined by Doctor Adams, have received less attention and are consequently less well understood than the last stage. My purpose is to examine the colonial ideas of Parliamentary power in the period covered by Doctor Adams' first stage, the period of the Stamp Act crisis.

---

the distinction, and waiving for the present the exercise of its right to impose internal taxes, imposed certain duties on merchandizes imported into the Colonies, . . . the distinction between internal and external taxes is rejected by the colony advocates, and a new one devised between taxes for *the regulation of trade*, and taxes for the *purpose of revenue*."

[4] New York, 1939 (second edition).

[5] P. 69. For similar views by other historians, see C. P. Nettels, *The Roots of American Civilization* (New York, 1940), 634-635; C. L. Becker, *The Declaration of Independence* (New York, 1942, 1945), 80-134; H. J. Eckenrode, *The Revolution in Virginia* (Boston and New York, 1916), 28.

It will be remembered that the Stamp Act was under discussion in the colonies from the spring of 1764 to the spring of 1766. Although it was in force for less than four months before its repeal in February, 1766, the colonists had begun to consider it as soon as they received news of the resolution passed by Parliament on March 10, 1764, the resolution which declared, "That, towards further defraying the said Expences, it may be proper to charge certain Stamp Duties in the said Colonies and Plantations."[6] The resolution was one of a series which George Grenville had introduced as the basis of his budget for the ensuing year. The others furnished the substance of the Revenue Act of 1764, the so-called Sugar Act, which became a law two months later. But the resolution for a stamp tax was phrased so as to indicate that no action would be taken on it until the next session, though its ultimate passage was almost a certainty.[7] The colonists were thus presented with two measures which threatened their prosperity and which consequently obliged them to think about the relation which they bore to the body which threatened them. They had to consider the Sugar Act, in which Parliament made use of trade regulations to raise money and which in itself would have been sufficient to set discerning minds at work on the question of Parliamentary taxation. At the same time they had to consider the Stamp Act, an act which would directly affect almost every person in the colonies. Of the two, the Stamp Act appeared to most colonists to be the more dangerous, but in formulating their ideas of Parliamentary power they could not afford to neglect either measure; they had to decide in what way their rights were affected both by the internal taxes of the Stamp Act and by the external taxes of the Sugar Act.

Under the pressure of these two acts colonial ideas reached a remarkable maturity during the period under discussion. In some regions and among some persons the theory of complete colonial autonomy was enunciated. For example a meeting of citizens at New London, Connecticut, on December 10, 1765, adopted resolutions which rehearsed the principles of

[6] *Journals of the House of Commons*, XXIX, 935.
[7] Grenville warned the colonial agents that he would bring in a bill for a stamp tax at the next session of Parliament. See the letter from Jasper Mauduit to Massachusetts, May 26, 1764 (Massachusetts Archives, XXII, 375); the letter from Charles Garth to South Carolina, June 5, 1764 (*English Historical Review*, LIV, 646-648); and the account by William Knox, agent for Georgia, in *The Claim of the Colonies to an Exemption from Internal Taxes Imposed by Authority of Parliament Examined* (London, 1765), 31-35.

government by consent, specified that the Stamp Act was a violation of
those principles, and finally declared, "That it is the Duty of every Person
in the Colonies to oppose by every lawful Means, the Execution of those
Acts imposed on them,—and if they can in no other way be relieved to
reassume their natural Rights, and the Authority the Laws of Nature and
of God have vested them with."[8] If there was any confusion in the minds
of the colonists as to how to go about reassuming natural rights, newspaper writers were ready with detailed discussions of the technique of
revolution.[9] Short of this, other writers expounded the theory which later
found more classic expression in the writings of John Adams and James
Wilson, the theory that is assumed in the Declaration of Independence,
that the colonies owe allegiance only to the king and are not bound in
any way by acts of Parliament.[10]

But in the effort to arrive at what may be called the official colonial
position during this period, one cannot rely on newspapers and pamphlets
nor on the resolutions adopted by informal gatherings of small groups, for
these may represent the views of factions or the idiosyncracies of a single
man. Fortunately it is not necessary to depend upon such partial statements, for in every colony except Georgia and North Carolina the formally elected representatives of the people produced some official statement of belief. Five of the colonies which later revolted drew up statements in 1764 while the Stamp Act was pending; nine colonies, including all of the first five, did the same in 1765 after the Act was passed; and
in the same year at the Stamp Act Congress, nine colonies combined in a
declaration which was formally approved by a tenth. These statements,
in the form of resolutions, petitions, memorials, and remonstrances, are the
safest index of colonial opinion about Parliamentary power. They were
carefully phrased by the regularly elected representatives of the voting
population and adopted, in many cases unanimously, after deliberation
and debate.

In these formal statements it is scarcely possible to discern a trace of
the ideas which the Americans are supposed to have adopted during the

[8] *Boston Post-Boy and Advertiser*, December 16, 1765.

[9] See, for example, *Boston Gazette*, December 2, 1765.

[10] *Maryland Gazette*, May 30, 1765; *Providence Gazette*, May 11, 1765; *Boston
Gazette*, February 24, March 3, March 17, 1766. Governor Bernard reported to the
Lords of Trade, November 30, 1765, that the Massachusetts politicians were claim-
ing that the colonies "have no Superiors upon Earth but the King, and him only
in the Person of the Governor, or according to the terms of the Charter." Bernard
Papers, IV, 203, Harvard College Library.

period under discussion. Almost universally the documents deny the authority of Parliament to tax the colonies at all. Nowhere is there a clear admission of the right of Parliament to levy external taxes rather than internal, and only in three cases does such a right seem to be implied. In at least one of these three, the implication which may be suggested by a partial reading is denied by a full consideration of the document and the circumstances under which it was produced.

II

20

As might be expected, the statements drawn up in 1764 while the Stamp Act was pending were generally not as explicit as those prepared a year later, when the Act had been passed and the colonists had had more time to think over its implications. The clearest of the early statements was that made by the New York Assembly in three petitions, to the King, the Lords, and the Commons, on October 18, 1764. These petitions, in objecting to both the Sugar Act and the proposed Stamp Act, claimed that the colonists should be exempt "from the Burthen of all Taxes not granted by themselves." Far from singling out internal taxes, the New York Assembly stated pointedly:

. . . since all Impositions, whether they be internal Taxes, or Duties paid, for what we consume, equally diminish the Estates upon which they are charged; what avails it to any People, by which of them they are impoverished? . . . the whole wealth of a country may be as effectually drawn off, by the Exaction of Duties, as by any other Tax upon their Estates.

In accordance with this principle New York admitted the authority of Parliament to regulate the trade of the empire for the good of the mother country, but insisted that

. . . a Freedom to drive all Kinds of Traffick in a Subordination to, and not inconsistent with, the *British* Trade; and an Exemption from all Duties in such a Course of Commerce, is humbly claimed by the Colonies, as the most essential of all the Rights to which they are intitled, as Colonists from, and connected, in the common Bond of Liberty, with the uninslaved Sons of *Great Britain*.[11]

[11] *Journal of the Votes and Proceedings of the General Assembly of the Colony of New York. Began the 8th Day of November, 1743; and Ended the 23d of December, 1765* (New York, 1766), II, 769-779.

The statement made by Virginia in 1764 was almost as plain as that of New York. The Virginia Council and House of Burgesses in a petition to the King, a memorial to the House of Lords, and a remonstrance to the Commons, claimed an exemption from all Parliamentary taxation. To the King they asserted their "Right of being governed by such laws, respecting their internal Polity and Taxation,[12] as are derived from their own Consent"; to the Lords they stated their right as British subjects to be exempt from all taxes, "but such as are laid on them by their own Consent, or by those who are legally appointed to represent them"; to the Commons they remonstrated "that laws imposing taxes on the people ought not to be made without the consent of representatives chosen by themselves," and added that they could not discern "by what Distinction they can be deprived of that sacred birthright and most valuable inheritance, by their Fellow Subjects, nor with what Propriety they can be taxed or affected in their estates by the Parliament, wherein they are not, and indeed cannot, constitutionally be represented."[13]

21

Rhode Island, Connecticut, and Massachusetts took a less precise view of their rights in 1764 than did New York and Virginia, although Massachusetts and Connecticut, at least, cleared up the uncertainty of their position in the following year. In Rhode Island the General Assembly deputed Governor Stephen Hopkins to write a statement of the colony's rights and in addition sent a petition to the King, dated November 29, 1764. Both Governor Hopkins' pamphlet and the petition ignored the constitutional question raised by the Sugar Act, the question of external taxes; they argued against the act simply as a trade regulation which would have ruinous economic consequences. Since none of the colonies at this time denied Parliament's right to regulate colonial trade, Rhode Island, in considering the Sugar Act simply as such a regulation, made no attempt to deny Parliament's right to enact it. Against the proposed Stamp Act Hopkins and the Assembly did raise the question of right. This proposal, if carried into execution, would be "a manifest violation of their just and long enjoyed rights. For it must be confessed by all men, that they who are taxed at pleasure by others, cannot possibly have any property, can

[12] For the question whether or not the adjective "internal" modifies "taxation" as well as "polity" see the discussion below of the same phrase in the Virginia Resolves of 1765.

[13] Journals of the House of Burgesses of Virginia 1761-1765 (Richmond, 1907), liv-lvii.

have nothing to be called their own; they who have no property can have no freedom, but are indeed reduced to the most abject slavery." The petition to the King recited the same objections and concluded with a request

that our trade may be restored to its former condition, and no further limited, restrained and burdened, than becomes necessary for the general good of all your Majesty's subjects; that the courts of vice admiralty may not be vested with more extensive powers in the colonies than are given them by law in Great Britain; that the colonists may not be taxed but by the consent of their own representatives, as Your Majesty's other free subjects are.[14]

Thus Rhode Island sidestepped the question of external taxes by ignoring the declared intent of the Sugar Act to raise a revenue. She took a stand upon constitutional grounds only against the proposed Stamp Act, only, in other words, against internal taxes. Yet she did not quite admit Parliament's right to levy external taxes, because she considered the Sugar Act, erroneously to be sure, as a regulation of trade and not as a tax. Her position on external taxes was ambiguous: she didn't say yes and she didn't say no.

Connecticut in 1764 was guilty of the same ambiguity. Connecticut's statement took the form of a pamphlet drawn up by a committee, consisting of Governor Fitch, Ebenezer Silliman, George Wyllys and Jared Ingersoll, deputed by the General Assembly, "to collect and set in the most advantageous light all such arguments and objections as may justly and reasonably [be] advanced against creating and collecting a revenue in America, more particularly in this Colony, and especially against effecting the same by Stamp Duties &c."[15] This committee, of which Governor Fitch was the working member, produced a pamphlet entitled *Reasons why the British Colonies in America should not be charged with Internal Taxes, by Authority of Parliament*.[16] The pamphlet came as close as any American statement to admitting the right of Parliament to levy external taxes. Like the Rhode Island statement, it confined its constitutional objections to internal taxes and failed to consider the problem, raised by the Sugar Act, of whether Parliament could make use of trade regulations as

[14] James R. Bartlett, ed., *Records of the Colony of Rhode Island and Providence Plantations* (Providence, 1861), VI, 414-427.

[15] C. J. Hoadly, ed., *Public Records of the Colony of Connecticut* (Hartford, 1881), XII, 256.

[16] New Haven, 1764. Reprinted in Hoadly, XII, 651-671.

a source of revenue. Instead, it assumed that Parliament would act for the good of the whole in its regulation of trade. "If Restrictions on Navigation, Commerce, or other external Regulations only are established," it said, "the internal Government, Powers of taxing for its Support, an Exemption from being taxed without Consent, and other Immunities, which legally belong to the Subjects of each Colony . . . will be and continue in the Substance of them whole and entire."[17] This was a rather naive view of the situation, but it did not necessarily commit the colony to a constitutional acceptance of external taxes.

The address of Massachusetts to the House of Commons, dated November 3, 1764, like the pamphlets issued by Rhode Island and Connecticut in this year, was not entirely clear on the question of external taxes. Massachusetts affirmed that the American colonists "have always judged by their representatives both of the way and manner, in which internal taxes should be raised within their respective governments, and of the ability of the inhabitants to pay them." The address concluded with the request that "the privileges of the colonies, relative to their internal taxes, which they have so long enjoyed, may still be continued to them."[18] By specifying internal taxes, the address seemed to imply that the inhabitants of Massachusetts did not object to the idea of an external tax imposed by Parliament. This implication was fortified by the rest of the document, which objected to the Sugar Act on economic rather than constitutional grounds as a measure which would ruin the trade of the colony.

Before this address is interpreted as an implied assent to external taxes the circumstances of its origin must be considered. The General Court adopted the address only because the Council refused to concur in a much more inclusive assertion of rights, originally passed by the lower house. In this version the House affirmed that "we look *upon those Duties as a Tax* [i.e. the duties imposed by the Sugar Act], and which we humbly apprehend ought not to be laid without the Representatives of the People affected by them."[19] The abandonment of this earlier version was regarded in Massachusetts as a victory for the Council under the leadership of Lieutenant-Governor Hutchinson, and the House, even though it acquiesced in the new address, did not consider it a proper state-

[17] *Ibid.*, 661.
[18] Alden Bradford, ed., *Massachusetts State Papers. Speeches of the Governors of Massachusetts from 1765 to 1775 etc.* (Boston, 1818), 21-23.
[19] Massachusetts Archives, XXII, 414.

ment of colonial rights.[20] Accordingly, when they sent it to their agent in London for presentation, they warned him that it did not represent the views of the House. "The House of Representatives," they said

were clearly for making an ample and full declaration of the exclusive Right of the People of the Colonies to tax themselves and that they ought not to be deprived of a right they had so long enjoyed and which they held by Birth and by Charter; but they could not prevail with the Councill, tho they made several Tryalls, to be more explicit than they have been in the Petition sent you . . . You will therefore collect the sentiments of the Representative Body of People rather from what they have heretofore sent you than from the present Address.[21]

What the House of Representatives had heretofore sent the agent included a long letter instructing him in the doctrine of natural rights and an explicit statement that any attempt by Parliament to tax colonial trade would be "contrary to a fundamentall Principall of our constitution vizt. That all Taxes ought to originate with the people."[22] The House had also approved and sent to the agent a pamphlet written by one of their members, James Otis, entitled *The Rights of the British Colonies asserted and proved.*[23] In this pamphlet Otis had argued against Parliament's right to tax the colonies and had stated in the most unequivocal manner that "there is no foundation for the distinction some make in England, between an internal and an external tax on the colonies."[24] It would hardly seem proper, then, to draw from the Massachusetts Address the inference that the people of the colonies accepted the right of Parliament to levy external as opposed to internal taxes.

[20] See the letters by Governor Bernard, November 17 and 18, 1764, to the Earl of Halifax, to John Pownall, and to Richard Jackson, relating the success of the Council in toning down the petition. Bernard Papers, II, 181-187, 189, 260-264.

[21] *Collections of the Massachusetts Historical Society,* LXXIV, 170-171.

[22] *Ibid.,* 39-54, 145-146.

[23] Boston, 1764. See *Journal of the Honourable House of Representatives of His Majesty's Province of the Massachusetts-Bay in New-England, Begun and held at Concord, in the county of Middlesex, on Wednesday the Thirtieth Day of May, Annoque Domini, 1764* (Boston, 1764), 66, 77.

[24] P. 42. Strangely enough these were also the private views of Lieutenant-Governor Hutchinson, who was principally responsible for suppressing the original address of the House. In a piece which he wrote in June or July, 1764, but never published, he argued against the Stamp Act on precisely the same line which was later followed by the House. He pointed out that the Sugar Act had been passed, not for the regulation of trade, but "for the sake of the money arising from the Duties,"

III

At the end of the year 1764, when the five initial colonial statements were all on the books, the colonial position was still a little obscure. New York and Virginia had been plain enough, but Rhode Island, Connecticut, and Massachusetts, while denying Parliament's right to levy a stamp tax, had evaded the question of external taxes. By the close of the following year all signs of hesitation had disappeared. The Stamp Act produced an all-but-unanimous reaction: Parliament had no right to tax the colonies.

The first declaration of rights to be made after passage of the Act was the famous set of resolves which Patrick Henry introduced into the Virginia House of Burgesses on May 30, 1765. As recorded on the Journals of the House of Burgesses there were four of these resolves which passed the House. The first two asserted the right of the inhabitants of Virginia to all the privileges of Englishmen. The third declared "that the Taxation of the People by themselves, or by Persons chosen to represent them" was a "distinguishing Characteristick of *British* Freedom, without which the ancient Constitution cannot exist." The fourth stated that the inhabitants of Virginia had always enjoyed and had never forfeited or yielded up "the inestimable Right of being governed by such Laws, respecting their internal Polity and Taxation, as are derived from their own Consent."[25]

Henry had proposed three more resolutions which either failed of passage or later were expunged from the records. The first of these merely repeated what the others had already implied, namely that the General Assembly of Virginia, in its representative capacity, had "the only exclusive right and power to lay taxes and imposts upon the inhabitants

---

and that the privileges of the people were no less affected by it than they were by an internal tax. (Massachusetts Archives, XXVI, 90-96.) Moreover, on Nov. 9, 1764, just after he had succeeded in getting the Massachusetts Address toned down, Hutchinson wrote to Ebenezer Silliman in Connecticut, criticizing the Connecticut pamphlet for neglecting to object against external taxes. He told Silliman, who was a member of the Connecticut Committee which drew up the pamphlet, that "the fallacy of the argument lies here it is your supposing duties upon trade to be imposed for the sake of regulating trade, whereas the Professed design of the duties by the late Act is to raise a revenue." (Massachusetts Archives, XXVI, 117-118.) Why Hutchinson should have objected to these views when they came from the Massachusetts House of Representatives is not apparent.

[25] *Journals of the House of Burgesses of Virginia 1761-1765*, 360.

COLONIAL IDEAS OF PARLIAMENTARY POWER

of this colony." The second, more radical, stated "That his Majesty's liege people, the inhabitants of this colony, are not bound to yield obedience to any law or ordinance whatever, designed to impose any taxation whatsoever upon them, other than the laws or ordinances of the General Assembly aforesaid." The last provided that anyone who denied the Assembly's exclusive power of taxation should be considered an enemy of the colony.[26]

The Virginia Resolves even without the inclusion of Henry's three additional clauses, constituted a clear denial of Parliament's right to tax. The only phrase which could be interpreted as distinguishing between internal and external taxes was the phrase in the third resolution "internal polity and taxation." Here it was possible to read the adjective "internal" to modify "taxation" as well as "polity." That such a reading would have been incorrect is suggested by the fact that in the version of the Resolves which was printed in the newspapers this phrase was changed to read "taxation and internal police."[27] Furthermore this was also the wording in a copy of the Resolves endorsed on the back in Patrick Henry's handwriting.[28]

The Virginia Resolves served as a model for similar declarations in most of the other colonies. Rhode Island, where the Virginia Resolves were first published, was the first to copy them. In September, 1765, the Rhode Island General Assembly passed six resolutions, three of which were adapted from those passed by the Virginia House of Burgesses, two from Henry's unsuccessful resolutions (which had been printed in the newspapers without any indication that they had failed to pass), and one

[26] *Ibid.*, lxvii. When the Resolves were printed in the newspapers, the three unsuccessful resolves were included along with the others as though they had been passed. The Resolves, so far as the incomplete newspaper records enable us to tell, were first printed in the *Newport Mercury* on June 24, 1765, and copied in the Boston papers from the version given there. The text printed in the papers, besides including the three unsuccessful resolves, omitted one of those actually passed (the third) and considerably abridged the others. The abridgment did not seriously alter the meaning of the resolves, but the wording was sufficiently changed to suggest that the newspaper text was obtained from an unofficial source, probably from some member of the assembly who had been present when the Resolves were passed. Possibly the source was Henry himself, for the newspaper version, except in its omission of resolution number 3, closely approximates a copy of the resolves which is endorsed on the back in Henry's handwriting. See *Journals of the House of Burgesses*, frontispiece and lxv.

[27] *Newport Mercury*, June 24, 1765; *Boston Post-Boy and Advertiser*, July 1, 1765; *Boston Gazette*, July 1, 1765; *Georgia Gazette*, September 5, 1765.

[28] *Journals of the House of Burgesses of Virginia, 1761-1765*, frontispiece and lxv.

original resolution which, in effect, called upon officers of government to pay no attention to the Stamp Act.[29] On the question of Parliamentary authority the Rhode Island statements, being copied from those of Virginia, were no less definite: the General Assembly of the colony had always enjoyed control over "taxation and internal police" and possessed "the only exclusive right to lay taxes and imposts upon the inhabitants of this colony."[30] Rhode Island in fact went farther than the Virginia Burgesses had been willing to go and farther than any other colony went in the next eight or nine years, by calling for direct disobedience to Parliament. She passed the measure which Virginia had rejected and declared that her inhabitants need not submit to a Parliamentary tax. Yet in so doing Rhode Island added a qualification which makes her position on the question of external taxes open to suspicion. In the fifth Rhode Island resolution it was stated that the inhabitants of the colony were "not bound to yield obedience to any law or ordinance designed to impose any internal taxation whatsoever upon them, other than the laws or ordinances of the General Assembly, aforesaid."[31] In Henry's version the word "internal" had not occurred. Rhode Island by inserting it implied that her citizens could disobey an act of Parliament imposing internal taxes but not one imposing external taxes. It should be noted that this distinction did not appear in the assertions of right contained in the preceding resolutions, where the authority of Parliament to tax the colony was denied without qualification. It was only in the summons to rebellion that the Rhode Island Assembly felt obliged to draw back a little. Though their caution on this score was boldness when compared to the stand of the other colonies, which confined themselves to declarations of right, nevertheless the appearance of the word "internal" makes one wonder whether there may not have been a moderate faction in the assembly which would have allowed Parliament a right over external taxes. If there was such a faction, it was not able to insert its views into the resolutions which defined the rights of the colony but only into the one which proposed open rebellion. Moreover, a few weeks later, on November 6, 1765, Rhode Island's popularly-elected governor, Samuel Ward, wrote to General Conway that the colonists were oppressed, because "duties and taxes" were laid upon them without their knowledge or consent.[32]

27

[29] Bartlett, *Records of the Colony of Rhode Island*, VI, 451-452.
[30] *Ibid.*, 452.
[31] *Ibid.*
[32] *Ibid.*, 473.

If the Rhode Island Resolves of 1765 still left some room for doubt on the question of external taxes, the same was not true of the other colonial statements of that year. The Maryland Assembly, on September 28, passed unanimously resolutions denying Parliament's right to tax, in which the only use of the word "internal" was in the familiar phrase "Taxes, and internal Polity."[33] Meanwhile Pennsylvania, on September 21, had drawn up its own set of Resolves, to much the same effect. The first draught of these resolves, written by John Dickinson, included one clause objecting specifically to internal taxes,[34] but in the version finally adopted by the assembly there was no mention of the word "internal." The crucial item read: "Resolved therefore, N.C.D. That the taxation of the people of this province, by any other persons whatsoever than such their representatives in assembly, is UNCONSTITUTIONAL, and subversive of their most valuable rights."[35]

Massachusetts, because of the recess of her assembly, did not take action until October, though the newspapers began to agitate for a more spirited statement of rights as soon as they received news of the Virginia Resolves.[36] Accordingly when the assembly was called together in October, it produced a set of resolutions which defined the rights of British subjects and concluded, "that all acts, made by any power whatever, other than the General Assembly of this province, imposing taxes on the inhabitants, are infringements of our inherent and unalienable rights, as men and British subjects; and render void the most valuable declarations of our charter."[37] The Connecticut Assembly likewise cleared up the ambiguity of its earlier statement by a set of resolves modeled partly on those of Virginia and affirming that an act for raising money in the colonies "by duties or taxes" was beyond the authority of Parliament. Connecticut, like Maryland and Rhode Island, included an item copied after the fourth

[33] *Maryland Gazette*, October 3, 1765.

[34] Charles J. Stillé, *The Life and Times of John Dickinson, 1732-1808* (Philadelphia, 1891), 339-340.

[35] J. Almon, ed., *A Collection of interesting, authentic papers, relative to the dispute between Great Britain and America* (London, 1777), 20-21.

[36] See, for example, the *Boston Gazette* of July 8, 1765: "The People of Virginia have spoke very sensibly, and the frozen Politicians of a more northern Government say they have spoke Treason: Their spirited Resolves do indeed serve as a perfect Contrast for a certain, tame, pusillanimous, daub'd, insipid Thing, delicately touch'd up and call'd an Address; which was lately sent from this Side the Water, to please the Taste of the Tools of Corruption on the other." The reference, of course, was to the Massachusetts Address of 1764.

[37] Bradford, *Massachusetts State Papers*, 50-51.

of the Virginia Resolves, in which once again the questionable phrase
was rendered as "taxing and internal police."[38]

South Carolina, on November 29, 1765, denied Parliament's right to
tax, in a set of eighteen resolves copied from the declarations of the Stamp
Act Congress[39] (see below). New York could scarcely state the colonial
position more explicitly than she had done the year before, but nevertheless on December 11, 1765, she adopted three more petitions to King,
Lords, and Commons, restating the case with the same clarity.[40] New Jersey in the meantime had adopted eleven resolutions copied principally
from those of the Stamp Act Congress, with nothing said about internal
taxes;[41] and New Hampshire, which did not participate in the Congress,
had given formal approval to all the resolutions and petitions of that
body.[42]

The Stamp Act Congress had met in New York during October, attended by delegates from Massachusetts, Rhode Island, Connecticut, New
York, New Jersey, Pennsylvania, Delaware, Maryland, and South Carolina. These delegates had produced a set of resolutions and three petitions,
to the King, the Lords, and the Commons, all denying the authority of
Parliament to tax the colonies.[43] Here as in the other formal colonial statements of this year there is no distinction made between internal and external taxes. The Stamp Act Congress has frequently been treated by historians as a rather conservative body of men, possibly because it acknowledged "all due subordination" to Parliament. But as conservatives at the
time recognized, this phrase was an empty one unless you stated what
subordination was due. It is true that the conservatives, in Massachusetts
at least, had hoped to gain control of the Stamp Act Congress.[44] They ac-

[38] Hoadly, *Public Records of the Colony of Connecticut*, 421-425.
[39] John Drayton, *Memoirs of the American Revolution* (Charleston, S. C., 1821),
I, 39-41.
[40] *Journals of the Votes and Proceedings of the General Assembly of the Colony
of New York 1743-1765*, II, 795-802.
[41] *New Jersey Archives*, First Series (Paterson, 1902), XXIV, 683-684.
[42] Nathaniel Bouton, ed., *Documents and Records Relating to the Province of
New Hampshire* (Nashua, 1873), VII, 92.
[43] Hezekiah Niles, *Principles and Acts of the Revolution* (Baltimore, 1822),
457-460.
[44] Governor Bernard wrote to the Lords of Trade on July 8, 1765, that in
Massachusetts, where the proposal for the congress initiated, "It was impossible to
oppose this measure to any good purpose and therefore the friends of government
took the lead in it and have kept it in their hands in pursuance of which of the
Committee appointed by this House to meet the other Committees at New York on

tually succeeded in securing Timothy Ruggles as one of the Massachusetts delegates, and Governor Bernard wrote at least one letter to Ruggles before the convention urging him to secure submission to the Stamp Act pending its probable repeal.[45] Ruggles remained faithfully conservative, but the true character of the Congress is sufficiently indicated by the fact that, as a conservative, he refused to sign the Resolutions it adopted and was later reprimanded for his refusal by the not-so-conservative Massachusetts House of Representatives.[46] The Stamp Act Congress, in other words, was no less "radical" than the colonial assemblies which sent delegates to it. Though it acknowledged due subordination to Parliament, it denied without qualification the right of Parliament to tax the colonies.

In sum, during the period of the Stamp Act crisis, fifteen formal statements of colonial rights had been issued. Of these only the three early statements by Rhode Island, Connecticut, and Massachusetts could be interpreted as implying an assent to the constitutionality of external taxes. The statement by Massachusetts was clearly not representative of official opinion, and both the Massachusetts and the Connecticut statements were clarified the following year by resolutions which unequivocally rejected the authority of Parliament to tax the colonies at all.

IV

The question suggested by all these declarations of right is: what did the Americans mean when they admitted due subordination to Parliament and at the same time denied Parliament's right to tax them? What subordination was due? If they did not distinguish between internal and external taxes, but denied all authority to tax, what authority did they leave to Parliament?

The answer is given clearly enough in the documents: the colonists allowed the right of Parliament to legislate for the whole empire in any way that concerned the common interests of all the members of the em-

---

1st of October next. Two of the three are fast friends to government prudent and discreet men such as I am assured will never consent to any undutiful or improper application to the Government of Great Britain." (Sparks Manuscripts 43: British Manuscripts, IV, Harvard College Library).

[45] Bernard Papers, IV, 72. The letter is dated September 28, 1765.

[46] *Boston Gazette*, Feb. 17, 1766. The membership of the Stamp Act Congress has been analysed in an unpublished paper by Mr. David S. Lovejoy, in which it is indicated that of the twenty-seven members only two are known to have become Tories at the time of the Revolution.

pire (as yet they made no claim that the colonial assemblies were entirely coordinate with Parliament in legislative authority), but they denied that Parliament's legislative authority extended either to the internal polity of the colonies or to taxation. Not all the colonies insisted on exclusive control of internal polity, for Parliament at this time was not attempting to interfere in this department. The issue of the day was taxation, and what the colonies insisted on most vigorously was that Parliament's supreme legislative authority did not include the right to tax. Taxation and legislation, they said, were separate functions and historically had always been treated as such. Legislation was a function of sovereignty; and as the sovereign body of the empire, Parliament had absolute legislative authority. Under this authority Parliament was entirely justified in regulating the trade and commerce of the empire. There was, in other words, nothing unconstitutional about the Acts of Trade and Navigation. But taxes were something else. Taxes were the "free gift" of the people who paid them, and as such could be levied only by a body which represented the people. As far as Great Britain was concerned the House of Commons was a representative body and could therefore tax the people of Great Britain; but since the colonists were not, and from their local circumstances could not be, represented in Parliament, they could not be taxed by Parliament. The only body with a constitutional right to tax them was a colonial assembly, in which the people upon whom the tax would fall would be represented. Thus the Connecticut Assembly in October, 1765, resolved,

That, in the opinion of this House, an act for raising money by duties or taxes differs from other acts of legislation, in that it is always considered as a free gift of the people made by their legal and elected representatives; and that we cannot conceive that the people of Great Britain, or their representatives, have right to dispose of our property.[47]

According to this distinction the power to levy taxes even in Great Britain was limited to the House of Commons, the representative part of Parliament. The petition from the General Assembly of New York to the House of Commons, December 11, 1765, while expressing "all due submission to the supreme Authority of the *British* Legislature," affirmed

That all parliamentary Aids in *Great-Britain*, are the free Gifts of the People

[47] *Public Records of the Colony of Connecticut*, XII, 423.

31

by their Representatives, consented to by the Lords, and accepted by the Crown, and therefore every Act imposing them, essentially differs from every other Statute, having the Force of a Law in no other Respect than the Manner thereby prescribed for levying the Gift.

That agreeable to this Distinction, the House of Commons has always contended for and enjoyed the constitutional Right of originating all Money Bills, as well in Aid of the Crown, as for other Purposes.

That all Supplies to the Crown being in their Nature free Gifts, it would, as we humbly conceive, be unconstitutional for the People of *Great-Britain*, by their Representatives in Parliament, to dispose of the Property of Millions of his Majesty's Subjects, who are not, and cannot be there represented.[48]

It was this distinction which the members of the Stamp Act Congress had in mind when they acknowledged "due subordination" to Parliament, for they asked in their petition to the House of Commons,

Whether there be not a material Distinction in Reason and sound Policy, at least, between the necessary Exercise of Parliamentary Jurisdiction in general Acts, for the Amendment of the Common Law, and the Regulation of Trade and Commerce through the whole Empire, and the Exercise of that Jurisdiction by imposing Taxes on the Colonies.[49]

V

Most members of Parliament would have answered this query with a flat denial that the power of taxation could be distinguished from that of legislation. Taxation, they would have said, was inseparable from sovereignty. But there were some members willing to speak in favor of the colonial view. In the debate on the Declaratory Act in the House of Commons the question arose over a motion made by Colonel Barré to omit from the act the phrase "in all cases whatsoever." This motion was intended to exclude Parliament's authority to tax the colonies, and in the debate which followed, Barré and William Pitt the elder argued for the motion in much the same terms as were used in the colonial statements. Visitors were not admitted to Parliament during this session, so that few

[48] *Journal of the Votes and Proceedings of the General Assembly of the Colony of New York 1743-1765*, II, 800.

[49] *Proceedings of the Congress at New York* (Annapolis, 1766), 23. The reprint of the proceedings in Niles, *Principles and Acts of the Revolution* is inaccurate at this point.

accounts of the debate have been preserved, but according to Charles
Garth, member for Devizes borough, Wiltshire, and agent for several of
the southern colonies, the speakers for Barré's motion contended: "That
the Principles of Taxation as distinguished from Legislation were as distinct Principles and Powers as any two Propositions under the Sun."
The speakers cited the precedents of the counties palatine of Chester and
Durham which had been subject to Parliament's legislative authority but
had not been taxed until they were represented. The clergy, it was pointed
out, taxed themselves separately but did not have separate legislative
power. Another indication that the two functions were separate was that
taxes were the free gift of the Commons, and tax bills could not be considered by the Lords or the King until the Commons had made a grant.
Other bills remained in the Upper House for the King's signature, but
tax bills were sent back to the Commons, whose speaker presented them
to the King as the free gift of the Commons. All this, it was said, showed
that Parliament might legislate as the supreme authority of the realm
but that it taxed only in its representative capacity. Since the colonies
were not represented in Parliament, they could not constitutionally be
taxed by Parliament.[50] In the House of Lords, Lord Camden argued the
case to the same effect.[51]

In spite of these arguments Parliament decided by an overwhelming
majority[52] to include the words "in all cases whatsoever," and thereby, as
far as Parliament was concerned, it was concluded that taxation and legislation were not separate functions and that Parliament's authority over
the colonies included the right to tax. But strangely enough the Declaratory Act did not include any explicit statement of the right to tax, so that
the colonists could not have recognized that Parliament was denying
their position. What the act said was that the King in Parliament had
"full power and authority to make laws and statutes of sufficient force
and validity to bind the colonies and people of *America*, subjects of the
crown of *Great Britain*, in all cases whatsoever."[53] Though the members

33

[50] Garth's account is in *Maryland Historical Magazine*, VI, 287-305. Another account is in *American Historical Review*, XVII, 565-574.
[51] *Archives of Maryland* (Baltimore, 1895), XIV, 267-268.
[52] *Maryland Historical Magazine*, VI, 300; *Archives of Maryland*, XIV, 280; Sir
John Fortescue, ed., *The Correspondence of King George the Third* (London,
1927), I, 254.
[53] Danby Pickering, ed., *The Statutes at Large* (Cambridge, England, 1767),
XXVII, 20.

of Parliament knew that the words "in all cases whatsoever" meant in cases of taxation, there is nothing in the act itself to give the words that meaning. Nor was the ambiguity entirely accidental. When the act was being drawn up, Charles Yorke, the attorney general, suggested that the crucial phrase should read "as well in cases of Taxation, as in all other cases whatsoever." But when he submitted this suggestion to Rockingham, who was then prime minister, Rockingham thought it impolitic to make any mention of the word "taxation." "I think I may say," he wrote to Yorke, "that it is our firm Resolution in the House of Lords— I mean among ourselves—that that word must be resisted."[54] Thus the omission of any mention of taxation was deliberate. By supporting the act as it stood, with the resounding but ambiguous phrase "in all cases whatsoever," the Rockingham government could gain support in Parliament by encouraging the members to beat the drum of Parliamentary power —behind closed doors—without giving offense to the colonies.

The colonies can hardly be blamed then for not getting the point of the Declaratory Act. They had not generally been informed of the debate which had taken place over the words "in all cases whatsoever,"[55] and since the act was accompanied by the repeal of Parliament's most conspicuous attempt to tax them, they might very well interpret it as a simple assertion of legislative authority with no necessary implication of a right to tax. They knew that the Declaratory Act was a copy of the earlier statute of 6 George I regarding Ireland. And they knew also that in spite of this statute Ireland had not been taxed by Parliament. The Massachusetts Assembly even before passage of the Stamp Act had argued from the example of Ireland that the colonies might be dependent on England without allowing England a right to tax them.[56] After passage of the Declaratory Act the Massachusetts agent in London, Richard Jackson, encouraged Massachusetts to believe that the same reasoning was still valid, for he wrote to Governor Bernard that the act would

[54] British Museum Additional Manuscripts 35430, ff. 37-38 (Rockingham's letter). The exchange of correspondence between Yorke and Rockingham is printed, in part in George Thomas, Earl of Albemarle, *Memoirs of the Marquis of Rockingham* (London, 1852), I, 285-288. The date of Yorke's letter is not given. Rockingham's letter is dated January 25, 1766.

[55] So far as I have been able to discover Garth's account was the only one sent to the colonies, and it was not published at the time.

[56] Massachusetts Archives, XXII, 415. The argument is made in the petition to the King passed by the House of Representatives on October 22, 1764, and non-concurred by the Council.

probably affect the colonies as little "as the Power we claim in Ireland, the manner of exercising which you are acquainted with."[57] The same view was expressed by Daniel Dulany of Maryland in a letter to General Conway. According to Dulany the Declaratory Act could not imply a power to tax, because if it did, then the act of 6 George I must give authority to tax Ireland, and such authority had never been claimed or exercised.[58] Thus the fact, so often remarked by historians, that the colonists took little notice of the Declaratory Act does not mean that the colonists were indifferent to the question of principle. They simply did not recognize the Act as a challenge to their views. They could acquiesce in it with a clear conscience and without inconsistency, unaware that their interpretation differed radically from that held in Parliament.[59]

35

VI

Unfortunately this misunderstanding on the part of the Americans was matched by a similar misunderstanding on the part of many people in England with regard to the colonial position. We have seen that the American protests against the Stamp Act did not distinguish between internal and external taxes but denied that Parliament had any right to tax the colonies. Yet some Englishmen, at least, thought that the American protests were directed only against internal taxes. The American misunderstanding of the Declaratory Act is explicable by the vagueness of the act itself, the absence of any official interpretation of it, and the fact that the Parliamentary debate on it had been closed to the public. But the colonial statements had all been communicated to the British government by the beginning of the year 1766, before Parliament began to consider repeal of the Stamp Act. Why then did Englishmen suppose that the Americans distinguished between internal and external taxes?

Of course not all Englishmen did suppose so; those who took the trouble to read the colonial statements knew better. But apparently many Englishmen, including members of Parliament, did not take that trouble.

[57] *Ibid.*, f. 458. The letter is dated March 3, 1766.

[58] Sparks Manuscripts 44, bundle 7, ff. 10-11. The letter is not dated.

[59] George Grenville wrote that the Americans were justified in rejoicing at the repeal of the Stamp Act "especially if they understand by it, as they justly may, notwithstanding the Declaratory Bill passed at the same time, that they are thereby exempted for ever from being taxed by Great Britain for the public support even of themselves." William J. Smith, ed., *The Grenville Papers* (London, 1853), III, 250.

It should be remembered that the colonial petitions were never formally considered by Parliament. Those sent before passage of the Stamp Act were thrown out because of the procedural rule against receiving petitions on money bills. Those sent for repeal of the Act were excluded for other procedural reasons and because they called the authority of Parliament into question. Thus although the contents of the statements could doubtless have been learned by anyone who wished to discover them, they were never given a regular hearing in Parliament.[60]

In the absence of any direct acquaintance with the colonial statements the average member of Parliament must have gained his impressions from one of two sources: either from the multitude of pamphlets dealing with the Stamp Act or from speeches in Parliament. It is possible but not probable that the authors of pamphlets against the Stamp Act were responsible for creating the impression that the Americans did not object to external taxes. We have already observed an ambiguity in the two pamphlets by Stephen Hopkins and John Fitch which received the approval of Rhode Island and Connecticut respectively in 1764. Both these pamphlets used the phrase "internal taxes" in such a way as to suggest that external taxes might be constitutionally acceptable, though neither Hopkins nor Fitch explicitly said as much. Two other pamphlets, which enjoyed a wide circulation though not a formal legislative approval, also used the words "internal taxes" in a way which may have helped to bring about a misunderstanding of the American position. Richard Bland in *An Inquiry into the Rights of the British Colonies*[61] demonstrated that the colonists could not constitutionally be subjected to an internal tax by act of Parliament. Anyone reading Bland's conclusions without reading the argument leading to them might get the impression that Bland would have agreed to Parliament's collection of a revenue from customs duties levied in the colonies; but Bland's demonstration of his conclusion showed that Parliament could not constitutionally charge duties in the colony upon either imports or exports. In fact, he even argued that the Navigation Acts were unconstitutional. Bland evidently included in the phrase "internal taxes" the very duties which other people called "external taxes."

Another pamphlet which objected specifically to internal taxes was Daniel Dulany's *Considerations on the Propriety of imposing Taxes in*

[60] *Collections of the Connecticut Historical Society,* XVIII, 332-335; *Maryland Historical Magazine,* VI, 282-288.
[61] Williamsburg, 1766.

the British Colonies.[62] This probably had a wider circulation than any other pamphlet against the Stamp Act, and it has frequently been cited as the source of the distinction between internal and external taxes. Although the greater part of Dulany's pamphlet was devoted to general arguments against the constitutionality of Parliamentary taxation, there were a few paragraphs in which he implied that internal taxes alone were unconstitutional. Thus he argued, on page 33, that before the Stamp Act, Parliament had never "imposed an internal Tax upon the Colonies *for the single Purpose of Revenue.*" He went on to deny the contention, which he attributed to the proponents of the Stamp Act, "That no Distinction can be supported between one Kind of Tax and another, an Authority to impose the one extending to the other." Contrary to this erroneous view, he said, "It appears to me, that there is a clear and necessary Distinction between an Act imposing a Tax *for the single Purpose of Revenue,* and those Acts which have been made for the Regulation of Trade, and have produced some Revenue in *Consequence of their Effect* and Operation as *Regulations of Trade.*" According to this distinction Parliament had the right to regulate trade by the imposition of duties, even though those duties should incidentally produce some revenue. Dulany closed the discussion of this point by affirming: "a Right to impose an internal Tax on the Colonies without their consent, *for the single Purpose of Revenue,* is denied; a Right to regulate their Trade without their Consent is admitted."

It will be observed that in the course of this discussion, which occupied two pages of the pamphlet, Dulany had not made entirely clear what he regarded as constitutional and what he considered unconstitutional. He said that internal taxes for the purpose of revenue were unconstitutional, and he said that duties on trade for the purpose of regulation were constitutional, even though an incidental revenue might attend them, but he failed to say explicitly how he regarded duties on trade for the single purpose of revenue. He failed, in other words, to say how he stood on external taxes; in fact he did not even use the words "external tax" at any point in the pamphlet. His readers would perhaps have been justified in thinking that Dulany admitted external taxes as constitutional, since he explicitly objected only to internal taxes. Yet, unless Dulany was simply confused about the matter, it would appear that in his use of the phrase

[62] Annapolis, 1765 (second edition). The succeeding quotations are taken from pp. 30-35.

37

"internal tax" he included all duties levied in the colonies for the single purpose of revenue. In no other way does Dulany's argument make sense, for he contrasted what he called an internal tax for the single purpose of revenue with duties for the purpose of regulation from which an incidental revenue might arise. The context indicates clearly that the point of the contrast was not the difference between internal taxes as opposed to duties on trade but the difference between an imposition for the purpose of regulation and one for the purpose of revenue. Dulany emphasized the contrast by italicising the phrases: *single purpose of revenue, incidental Revenue*, and *Regulations of Trade*. The whole force of the contrast is lost unless the phrase "internal tax" is taken to include duties on trade collected in the colonies for the purpose of revenue. That this was Dulany's understanding of the term is further indicated in the two paragraphs which follow those summarized above. Here Dulany demonstrated that the duties on trade which had hitherto been collected in the colony had been levied not for the purpose of revenue but for the purpose of regulating trade. The argument which he used to carry this point was drawn from the fact that the customs duties collected in North America brought only £1,900 a year into the treasury while they cost £7,600 a year to collect. Dulany had taken these figures from a pamphlet by Grenville himself. He concluded with some justice that

It would be ridiculous indeed to suppose, that the Parliament would raise a Revenue by Taxes in the Colonies to defray Part of the national Expence, the Collection of which Taxes would increase that Expence to a Sum more than three Times the Amount of the Revenue; but, the Impositions being considered in their true Light, as Regulations of Trade, the Expence arising from an Establishment necessary to carry them into Execution, is so far from being ridiculous, that it may be wisely incurred.

Thus Dulany demonstrated that Parliament could not levy what he called an internal tax for the purpose of revenue by showing that Parliament had never levied an external tax for the purpose of revenue. The conclusion seems inescapable that he used the phrase "internal tax" in a loose sense, to cover all taxes collected in the colonies, whether excise taxes or customs duties levied for the single purpose of revenue. That this was his meaning is also suggested by the remainder of the pamphlet, in which he argued against Parliamentary taxation in general terms, as when he stated that "the Inhabitants of the Colonies claim an Exemption from *all* Taxes not imposed by their own Consent." (The italics are Dulany's.)

Dulany's pamphlet, though it was widely acclaimed as a defense of colonial rights, certainly employed a confusing terminology, and it would not be surprising if Englishmen at the time had gained the impression that there was some sort of distinction in it between the constitutionality of internal taxes as opposed to that of customs duties. Though Dulany never used the phrase "external tax" and though most of the pamphlet will make sense only if his use of the phrase "internal tax" is taken to include all taxes collected in the colonies, yet if American historians have derived the impression that he distinguished between internal and external taxes, it is not unreasonable to suppose that contemporary Englishmen received the same impression.

What does seem unlikely, however, is that British statesmen would have assumed, as American historians frequently seem to do, that Daniel Dulany was the proper spokesman for all the colonies. His pamphlet was only one of many, and the others ranged in attitude from complete submission to the authority of Parliament (as in Martin Howard's *Letter from a Gentleman at Halifax, to His Friend in Rhode Island*[63]) to complete defiance of Parliament (as in the *Considerations upon the Rights of the Colonists to the Privileges of British Subjects*[64]). Most of the pamphlets against the Stamp Act refrained from discussing the question of constitutional right and argued on the grounds of inexpediency or equity.[65] Those which concerned themselves with the constitutional aspects of the question devoted a major part of their attention to the doctrine of virtual representation.[66] This was an easy target, and in centering

39

[63] Newport, 1765.

[64] New York, 1766.

[65] See for example: John Dickinson's *The Late Regulations Respecting the British Colonies on the Continent of America Considered* (London, 1765); *A Letter to a Member of Parliament, Wherein the Power of the British Legislature, and the Case of the Colonists, Are briefly and impartially considered* (London, 1765); *The True Interest of Great Britain, with respect to her American Colonies, Stated and Impartially Considered* (London, 1766); *The Importance of the Colonies of North America, and the Interest of Great Britain with regard to them, considered* (London, 1766); *The Necessity of Repealing the American Stamp Act Demonstrated* (London, 1766); *The Late Occurrences in North America, and Policy of Great Britain, Considered* (London, 1766); and Benjamin Franklin's *The General Opposition of the Colonies to the Payment of the Stamp Duty; and the Consequence of Enforcing Obedience by Military Measures; Impartially Considered* (London, 1766).

[66] See for example: Samuel Cooper, *The Crisis. Or, a Full Defense of the Colonies* (London, 1766), 3-30; Maurice Moore, *The Justice and Policy of Taxing the*

the constitutional controversy upon it the American protagonists gained a tactical victory; for when their opponents argued that the Americans might be taxed because they were virtually represented, this was tantamount to admitting that the power to tax depended upon representation. Daniel Dulany put his finger on the weakness of the ministerial position when he wrote to General Conway,

If the right to tax and the right to regulate had been imagined by Mr. Grenville to be inseparable why did he tax his ingenuity to find out a virtual Representation, why did not some able friend intimate to him his Hazard on the slippery ground, he chose, when the all powerful Sovereignty of Parliament might have afforded so safe a footing? [67]

In other words Grenville himself, by arguing for virtual representation (as he did in *The Regulations Lately Made concerning the Colonies, and the Taxes Imposed upon Them, considered* [68]), had admitted that taxation was not a function of sovereignty but rather, as the colonies were contending, the prerogative of a representative body.

There was no reason why the pamphleteers on the American side should have made a distinction between internal and external taxes when arguing the case against virtual representation; and it is not surprising that with the possible exception of those discussed above, none of them seems to have employed the distinction for purposes of argument. The distinction did appear in some of the literature in support of the Stamp Act, where it served as a whipping boy. It was attributed to the Americans and then demolished under the heavy gunfire of constitutional history.[69] It hardly seems likely that the defenders of the Stamp Act would have attributed the distinction to the Americans simply in order to discredit the colonial position. It is much more likely that they and the members of Parliament really believed that the colonists did distinguish be-

---

American Colonies, in Great Britain, Considered (Wilmington, N. C., 1765), 7-14; Richard Bland, *An Inquiry into the Rights of the British Colonies* (Williamsburg, 1766), 5-12. Daniel Dulany, *Considerations on the Propriety of imposing Taxes in the British Colonies* (Annapolis, 1765), 5-14.

[67] Sparks Manuscripts 44, bundle 7, f.10.

[68] London, 1765.

[69] See *The Rights of Parliament Vindicated, On Occasion of the late Stamp-Act. In which is exposed the conduct of the American Colonists* (London, 1766); *An Examination of the Rights of the Colonies upon Principles of Law* (London, 1766).

tween internal and external taxes. The question remains as to how they gained this impression.

The source from which, in all probability, it was derived was the speeches made in Parliament by friends of the colonies during the debates on repeal of the Stamp Act and afterwards, not excepting the brilliant interview given at the bar of the House of Commons by Benjamin Franklin. The member of Parliament who heard that carefully rehearsed performance (or who read it afterwards in print) might very justly have concluded that the Americans had no objection to external taxes, for Franklin, the arch-American, at several points had stated that the Americans objected only to internal taxes.[70] When a member had pointed out that the objection to internal taxes could with equal justice be applied to external taxes, Franklin had replied that the Americans did not reason in that way at present but that they might learn to do so from the English. The wit of Franklin's tongue obscured the fact that he was wrong, but the average member could scarcely have known that. Laughing at Franklin's clever answers, he would probably have forgotten the rather pertinent question put by a member of the opposition: "Do not the resolutions of the Pennsylvania Assembly say, all taxes?" This question was evidently asked by a member who knew something about Pennsylvania's attitude. Franklin's answer to it was not as sprightly as his replies to some of the other questions. The best he could say was that if the Pennsylvania resolutions said all taxes, they meant only internal taxes. Actually it would have been impossible to tell from Franklin's testimony exactly what he thought the constitutional position of the Americans to be. At times he seemed to be saying that the Americans assented to external taxes; at other times he implied that they consented only to the regulation of trade. The performance was a good piece of lobbying for repeal of the Stamp Act, but it gave no clear indication of the American position and certainly could have contributed to the idea that the Americans were willing to accept external taxes.

The speeches of Franklin's friend Richard Jackson, member of Parliament for Weymouth, and agent at various times for Pennsylvania, Connecticut, and Massachusetts, may also have contributed to a false impression of the colonial position. Jackson believed that Parliament had a clear right to tax the colonies by duties on trade. Since Parliament by its ad-

41

[70] William Cobbett, ed., *Parliamentary History of England, from the Earliest Period to the Year 1803* (London, 1813), XVI, 137-160.

mitted right to regulate trade could prohibit any branch of colonial trade, he reasoned, Parliament could also tax any branch of colonial trade.[71] Jackson, moreover, had searched the precedents thoroughly and found that Parliament in the past had imposed external taxes on the trade of Chester and Durham and Wales before those areas were represented in Parliament. At the same time Parliament had refrained from taxing them internally until they were granted representation. When Jackson rehearsed these views before Parliament,[72] he must have been listened to as a man of some authority; for he had the reputation of being extraordinarily learned,[73] and he was, besides, the official agent for several colonies. The average member of Parliament could not have known that he had been elected agent for Massachusetts by the political maneuvers of the royal governor,[74] nor that the Connecticut Assembly had written him a letter deploring his insufficient insistence upon colonial rights,[75] nor that he owed his appointment in Pennsylvania to his friend Benjamin Franklin, who had also misrepresented the colonial position.[76]

What must also have impressed the uninformed member was the famous speech by William Pitt, when the Great Commoner had come out of his retirement to urge the repeal of the Stamp act. On this occasion, Pitt had risen to a statement by George Grenville in which the latter had complained that he could not understand the distinction between internal and external taxes. "If the gentleman does not understand the difference between internal and external taxes," said Pitt, "I cannot help it."[77] Pitt's reply, if left there, might have been somewhat misleading. Anyone who listened to the whole of what he had to say would have known that Pitt, like the colonists, was distinguishing, not between internal and external taxes but between taxation and legislation. In an earlier speech he had stated that "Taxation is no part of the governing or legislative power,"[78] and now he went on to argue that "there is a

[71] Carl Van Doren, ed., *Letters and Papers of Benjamin Franklin and Richard Jackson 1753-1785* (Philadelphia, 1947), 123-124, 138-139.

[72] *Ibid.*, 194-196; *Collections of the Connecticut Historical Society*, XVIII, 316; Bradford, *Massachusetts State Papers*, 72-73.

[73] Van Doren, *Letters and Papers of Benjamin Franklin and Richard Jackson*, 1-2.

[74] Bernard Papers, III, 277-283.

[75] *Collections of the Connecticut Historical Society*, XVIII, 366-367.

[76] Van Doren, *Letters and Papers of Benjamin Franklin and Richard Jackson*, 87, 100.

[77] *Parliamentary History*, XVI, 105.

[78] *Ibid.*, 99.

plain distinction between taxes levied for the purposes of raising a revenue, and duties imposed for the regulation of trade, for the accomodation of the subject; although, in the consequences, some revenue might incidentally arise from the latter."[79] Pitt was following the argument of Dulany, whom he had read and admired;[80] and if historians have misunderstood Dulany's argument, it is not unlikely that the members of Parliament may have misunderstood Pitt's. Though there was a manifest difference between Pitt's and Dulany's acceptance of trade regulations which might incidentally produce a revenue and Jackson's and Franklin's acceptance of external taxes as such, nevertheless all four men were arguing in behalf of the colonies. The average member may have lumped them all together and come out with the simple conclusion that Americans accepted external taxes.

43

This conclusion would have been strengthened a little later by a speech of Thomas Pownall. Pownall, speaking with some authority as the former governor of Massachusetts, said explicitly that the colonists *"never objected to external taxes*—to imposts, subsidies and duties. They know that the express conditions of their settlements and establishments were, that they should pay these—and therefore they never have had any disputes with government on this head—but have always found reason to be satisfied *in the moderation with which government hath exercised this power."*[81] Pownall had apparently never read any of the colonial statements. Perhaps he derived some of his ideas from his friend Benjamin Franklin.[82] Certainly his authority to represent the views of the colonists was long since out of date. But how was the average member to know that? All the friends of America in Parliament seemed to be of opinion that the Americans were resigned to external taxes.

Why the colonial advocates in Parliament should have joined in con-

[79] *Ibid.*, 105.

[80] W. S. Taylor and J. H. Pringle, eds., *The Chatham Correspondence* (London, 1838-40), III, 192; Moses C. Tyler, *The Literary History of the American Revolution 1763-1783* (New York, 1941), 111 and n.

[81] *The Speech of Th-m-s P-n-ll, Esq* . . . *in the H—se of C—m-ns, in favor of America* (Boston, 1769), 12.

[82] Pownall cooperated with Franklin on a scheme for raising money in the colonies by interest-bearing paper currency. This scheme was proposed by Franklin as a substitute for the Stamp Tax. For details see V. W. Crane, "Benjamin Franklin and the Stamp Act" *Publications of the Colonial Society of Massachusetts*, XXXII, 56-78. On Pownall's participation, see Pownall's letter to Hutchinson, Dec. 3, 1765, in Massachusetts Archives, XXV, 113.

veying so false an impression of the colonial position is not entirely clear. A number of reasons might be offered why Pownall or Jackson or Pitt argued as they did: Pownall may have been misinformed;[83] Jackson may have been speaking for himself rather than for the colonies; and Pitt was misunderstood. But Franklin's testimony is more difficult to explain, for Franklin must have been better acquainted with the colonial declarations than he appeared to be. Why should he have contributed to the general misunderstanding? Furthermore why should all the proponents of colonial rights have misrepresented the colonies in the same way?

In the absence of direct information one can only suggest that political circumstances in 1766 required that every friend of the colonies in England refrain from urging the extreme claims put forward by the colonial assemblies and join in representing the colonies as more moderate than they actually were. The immediate object in 1766 was the repeal of the Stamp Act, and repeal was not to be attained by blunt denials of Parliament's authority. Though the colonists seemed to be unaware of this fact and continued on their intransigent course, their friends in England had to seek support where they could find it. They found it in the Rockingham administration, and consequently when they argued for repeal of the Stamp Act, they argued in Rockingham's terms. Now Rockingham's terms, to judge from at least one account, were a recognition of the distinction between internal and external taxes. According to Charles Garth the administration refused to hear the petition of the Stamp Act Congress, because "it tended to question not only the Right of Parliament to impose internal Taxes, but external Duties."[84] Rockingham, it would appear, was prepared to settle the colonial issue by leaving internal taxes to the colonial assemblies. Though this was not as much as the colonies demanded, it was more than the rest of Parliament was willing to give, for most members were as ready to assert Parliament's right to levy all taxes as the colonists were to deny it.[85] Rockingham in fact was unable to repeal the

[83] That Pownall was an unreliable source of information is suggested by the fact that he himself had suggested a stamp tax in his book *The Administration of the Colonies*. Dennys De Berdt later wrote that he was "as irresolute as the Wind, in one days debate a friend to America the next quite with the Ministry." (*Publications of the Colonial Society of Massachusetts*, XIII, 377-378.)

[84] *Maryland Historical Magazine*, VI, 285.

[85] This fact was reported to the colonists in several letters. See, for example, that of Jared Ingersoll in *Collections of the Connecticut Historical Society*, XVIII, 317-326, and that of Richard Jackson in *ibid.*, 349-351.

Stamp Act on the basis of the distinction between internal and external taxes. Instead he was obliged to agree to the Declaratory Act, though worded in the ambiguous terms already noticed.[46] Rockingham, it is plain, needed all the support he could get, for he could not carry the rest of Parliament even as far as he and his own group were willing to go. In these circumstances it would have been undiplomatic, not to say reckless, for the friends of the colonies to embarrass him by insisting on the politically impossible claims of the colonial declarations. It seems unlikely that there was any formal agreement between the Rockingham group and the other colonial protagonists, whereby the latter agreed to soft-pedal the colonial claims to exclusive powers of taxation, but the pressure of politics undoubtedly dissuaded the friends of the colonies from giving publicity to the colonial declarations, and probably led them to co-operate with Rockingham in adopting a distinction which the colonists would never have allowed.

45

One conclusion in any case is clear: it was not the Americans who drew the line between internal and external taxes. It was recognized in America at the time by such diverse political personalities as James Otis and Thomas Hutchinson that the distinction was an English one. Otis, as already noticed, in the pamphlet approved by the Massachusetts assembly in 1764, scouted the distinction as one that "some make in England."[47] Hutchinson, in the third volume of his history of Massachusetts, gave credit for it to Pitt. Though it is clear that Pitt did not originate it, Hutchinson evidently thought that he did and was equally certain that the Americans did not accept it; for he averred that in levying the Townshend duties, "government in England too easily presumed, that Mr. Pitt's distinction between internal and external taxes would be favourably received in America."[48] There were members of Parliament in England, too, who realized that the distinction was not an American one, for in the debates on the Declaratory Act, Hans Stanley, the member for Southampton, em-

[46] Dennys De Berdt wrote to Samuel White at the time of repeal that there were three parties in Parliament so far as the Stamp Act was concerned, one for enforcing, one for repeal with a declaration of right, and one for repeal without a declaration. According to De Berdt the administration favored the last view but was obliged to take the middle position in order to gain a majority. (*Publications of the Colonial Society of Massachusetts*, XIII, 311-312.)

[47] *The Rights of the British Colonies asserted and proved* (Boston, 1764), 42.

[48] L. S. Mayo, ed., *History of the Province of Massachusetts Bay* (Cambridge, Mass., 1936), III, 130.

barrassed the Rockingham administration by pointing out that "The Americans have not made the futile Distinction between internal and external taxes,"[89] and Lord Lyttelton did the same thing in the House of Lords in the debate on the repeal of the Stamp Act, when he stated that "The Americans themselves make no distinction between external and internal taxes."[90] The colonial agents also realized that the colonists were talking bigger at home than their friends in England would admit, and the agents repeatedly requested their constitutents to be less noisy about their rights. The colonists in return instructed the agents to be more noisy about them.[91]

46

The colonists were bumptious, blunt, and lacking in diplomacy, but they were not guilty of the constitutional frivolity with which they have been charged. When they objected to the Townshend Duties in 1767, they had in no way changed the conception of Parliamentary power which they avowed at the time of the Stamp Act: they still admitted the authority of Parliament to regulate trade and to legislate in other ways for the whole empire; they still denied that Parliament had a right to tax them. These views they continued to affirm until the 1770's when they advanced to the more radical position of denying the authority of Parliament to legislate as well as to tax. Though this denial was generally accompanied by an allowance of Parliamentary legislation as a matter of convenience, there can be no question that the later position was constitutionally different from the earlier one. But that the colonists were guilty of skipping from one constitutional theory to another, like so many grasshoppers, is a Tory libel that has too readily been accepted by modern historians. American Revolutionary thought went through two stages, not three; the supposed first stage never existed. If anyone took a more advanced position because of the passage of the Townshend Duties, it was not the colonists. They were already there.

[89] *American Historical Review*, XVII, 566.
[90] *Parliamentary History*, XVI, 167.
[91] *Collections of the Connecticut Historical Society*, XVIII, 349-351, 366-367; *Collections of the Massachusetts Historical Society*, LXXIV, 39-54, 145-146; Massachusetts Archives, XXII, 361-363; *Publications of the Colonial Society of Massachusetts*, XIII, 332-333, 335, 337, 354.

THE AMERICAN REVOLUTION AS AN AFTERMATH
OF THE GREAT WAR FOR THE EMPIRE, 1754–1763

REAT wars in modern times have too frequently been the breeders of revolution. The exhausting armed struggles in which France became engaged in the latter half of the eighteenth century led as directly to the French Revolution as did the First World War to the Russian Revolution; it may be said as truly that the American Revolution was an aftermath of the Anglo-French conflict in the New World carried on between 1754 and 1763. This is by no means to deny that other factors were involved in the launching of these revolutionary movements. Before proceeding with an analysis of the theme of this paper, however, it would be well to consider the wording of the title given to it.*

Words may be used either to disguise or to distort facts as well as to clarify them, but the chief task of the historian is to illuminate the past. He is faced, therefore, with the responsibility of using only such words as will achieve this broad objective of his calling and to reject those that obscure or defeat it. For this reason " the French and Indian War ", as a term descriptive of the conflict to which we have just referred, has been avoided in this essay as well as in the writer's series on the *British Empire before the American Revolution*. This has been done in spite of the fact that it has been employed by most Americans ever since the early days of our Republic and therefore has the sanction of long usage as well as the sanction of American national tradition assigning, as does the latter, to the Revolutionary War a position of such commanding importance as to make all other events in American history, preceding as well as following it, quite subordinate to it. In contrast to this traditional interpretation of our history one may affirm that the Anglo-French conflict settled nothing less than the incom-

* This paper was read before the colonial history section of the American Historical Association in December 1948 at the Annual Meeting held in Washington.

parably vital question as to what civilization—what complex
cultural patterns, what political institutions—would arise in the
great Mississippi basin and the valleys of the rivers draining it, a
civilization, whatever it might be, surely destined to expand to
the Pacific seaboard and finally to dominate the North American continent. The determination of this crucial issue is perhaps the most momentous event in the life of the English-
speaking people in the New World and quite overshadows in
importance both the Revolutionary War and the later Civil
War, events which, it is quite clear, were each contingent upon
the outcome of the earlier crisis.

A struggle of such proportions, involving tremendous stakes,
deserves a name accurately descriptive of its place in the history
of the English-speaking people, and the title " the French and
Indian War ", as suggested, in no way fulfills this need. For
the war was not, as the name would seem to imply, a conflict
largely between English and French New World colonials and
their Indian allies, nor was it localized in North America to the
extent that the name would appear to indicate. In contrast, it
was waged both before and after an open declaration of war by
the British and French nations with all their resources for nine
years on three oceans, and much of the land washed by the
waters of them, and it ultimately brought in both Spain, allied
to France, and Portugal, allied to Great Britain. While it involved, it is true, as the name would connote, wilderness fighting, yet of equal, if not of greater, importance in assessing its
final outcome was the pouring forth of Britain's financial resources in a vast program of shipbuilding, in the equipment and
support of the British and colonial armies and the royal navy,
and in the subsidization both of allies on the European continent and of the colonies in America. If it also involved the
reduction of the fortress of Louisbourg, Fort Niagara, Fort Du-
quesne, Quebec and Montreal in North America, each in turn
to fall to British regulars aided by American provincial troops,
these successes, of great significance, were, in fact, really contingent upon the resounding British naval victories in the Medi-
terranean, off the Strait of Gibraltar, in the Bay of Biscay, and
elsewhere, that brought about the virtual extinction of the
French navy and merchant marine and thereby presented to

France—seeking to supply her forces in Canada and elsewhere with adequate reinforcements and matériel—a logistical problem so insoluble as to spell the doom of her North American empire and of her possessions in India and elsewhere.

If the term " the French and Indian War " meets none of the requirements of accurate historical nomenclature, neither does the term "the Seven Years' War "—a name appropriately enough employed by historians to designate the mighty conflict that raged for seven years in Germany before its conclusion in the Treaty of Hubertusburg in 1763. The principals in this war were Prussia, allied with Great Britain, Hanover, Brunswick and Hesse, facing Austria, most of the Holy Roman Empire, Russia and Sweden, all allied with France and receiving subsidies from her. Although George II, as King of Great Britain and Elector of Hanover, in the treaty of 1758 with Frederick of Prussia, promised not to conclude peace without mutual agreement with the latter, and although large subsidies were annually paid to Prussia as well as to the other continental allies out of the British treasury and troops were also sent to Germany, it must be emphasized that these aids were designed primarily for the protection of the King's German Electorate. In other words, the British alliance in no way supported the objectives of the Prussian King, when he suddenly began the German war in 1756 by invading Saxony—two years after the beginning of the Anglo-French war. In this connection it should be borne in mind that throughout the Seven Years' War in Germany Great Britain remained at peace with both Russia and Sweden and refused therefore to send a fleet into the Baltic in spite of the demands of Frederick that this be done; nor were British land troops permitted to assist him against Austria, but only to help form a protective shield for Hanover against the thrusts of the French armies. For the latter were determined not only to overrun the Electorate—something that they succeeded in doing —but to hold it as a bargaining point to be used at the conclusion of hostilities with Great Britain, a feat, however, beyond their power of accomplishment. Closely related and intertwined as were the two wars, they were, nevertheless, distinct in their beginning and distinct in their termination.

49

Indeed, while British historians at length were led to adopt the nomenclature applied by German and other continental historians to all hostilities that took place between 1754 and 1763 in both the Old and New Worlds, American historians, by and large in the past, have rejected, and rightly so, it seems, the name " the Seven Years' War " to designate specifically the struggle during these years in North America with the fate of that continent at stake; so likewise many of them have rejected, as equally inadmissible, the name " the French and Indian War ". Instead, the late Professor Osgood employed the title " the Fourth Intercolonial War ", surely not a good one; George Bancroft called the war " the American Revolution: First Phase ", still more inaccurate in some respects than the names he sought to avoid; Francis Parkman, with the flare of a romanticist, was at first inclined to call it " the Old French War " but finally, under the influence of the great-man-in-history thesis, gave to his two remarkable volumes concerned with it the totally misleading name, *Montcalm and Wolfe;* finally, John Fiske, the philosopher-historian, as luminous in his views as he was apt to be careless in the details of historical scholarship, happily fastened upon the name " the Great War ". In the series on the *British Empire before the American Revolution* the writer has built upon Fiske's title and has called it " the Great War for the Empire " in order to emphasize not only the fact that the war was a very great conflict both in its scope and in its lasting effects, as Fiske saw it with clearness, but also, as a war entered into specifically for the defense of the British Empire, that it was by far the most important ever waged by Great Britain to this end.

It may be pointed out that later charges, especially by American writers, that the war was begun by Great Britain with less worthy motives in mind, are not supported by the great mass of state papers and the private correspondence of British statesmen responsible for making the weighty decisions at the time— materials now available to the student which the writer has attempted to analyze in detail in the two volumes of his series that appeared under the title of *Zones of International Friction, 1748–1754.* In other words, the idea that the war was started as the result of European balance-of-power politics or by British mercantilists for the purpose of destroying a commercial rival and for conquering Canada and the French West Indies, and for expelling the French from India, rather than for the much more limited and legitimate objective of affording the colonies and particularly the new province of Nova Scotia and the Old Dominion of Virginia protection against the aggressive aims of France, must be dismissed by students brought face to face with impressive evidence to the contrary.

The development of the war into one for the military mastery of the North American continent came with the growing conviction on the part of the British ministers that nothing short of this drastic step would realize the primary aims of the government in arriving at the determination, as the result of appeals from the colonies for assistance, to challenge the right of French troops to be planted well within the borders of the Nova Scotia peninsula and at the forks of the Ohio. One may go as far as to state that the acquisition of Canada—as an objective sought by mercantilists to contribute to the wealth of Great Britain—would have seemed fantastic to any contemporary who had the slightest knowledge of the tremendous financial drain that that great possession had been on the treasury of the French King for over a century before 1754. Moreover, the motives that ultimately led, after much searching of heart, to its retention after its conquest by Great Britain were not commercial but strategic and had primarily in view the security and welfare generally of the older American colonies.

In view of these facts, not to be confused with surmises, the name " the Great War for the Empire " seems to the writer not only not inappropriate but among all the names heretofore applied to the war in question by far the most suitable that can be used by one concerned with the history of the old British Empire, who seeks earnestly to maintain that standard of exactness in terminology, as well as in other respects, which the public has a right to demand of him.

The description just given of the motives that led to the Great War for the Empire, nevertheless, runs counter, as suggested, to American national tradition and most history that has

51

been written by American historians in harmony with it. This tradition had a curious beginning. It arose partly out of Pitt's zealous efforts to energize the colonies to prosecute the war most actively; but there also was another potent factor involved in its creation. Before the conclusion of hostilities in 1763 certain powerful commercial interests—centered particularly at Newport, Rhode Island, Boston, New York City, and to a less extent in Philadelphia—in a desire to continue an enormously lucrative trade with the French West Indies, and therefore with the enemy, all in the face of Pitt's determination to keep supplies from the French armed forces operating in the New World, began to express themselves in terms that implied that the war was peculiarly Great Britain's war and only incidentally one that concerned her colonies and that the French, really friendly to the aspirations of British colonials, were opposed only to the mercantilistic ambitions of the mother country. By 1766—just twelve years after the beginning of the war and three years after its termination—this extraordinary tradition had become so well established that Benjamin Franklin, astonishingly enough, could actually assert in his examination before a committee of the House of Commons:

> I know the last war is commonly spoke of here as entered into for the defence, or for the sake of the people of America; I think it is quite misunderstood. It began about the limits between Canada and Nova Scotia, about territories to which the crown indeed laid claim, but were not claimed by any British colony . . . . We had therefore no particular concern or interest in that dispute. As to the Ohio, the contest there began about your right of trading in the Indian country, a right you had by the Treaty of Utrecht, which the French infringed . . . they took a fort which a company of your merchants, and their factors and correspondents, had erected there to secure that trade. Braddock was sent with an army to retake that fort . . . and to protect your trade. It was not until after his defeat that the colonies were attacked. They were before in perfect peace with both French and Indians. . . .

By the beginning of 1768 the tradition had been so extended that John Dickinson—voicing the popular American view in

his highly important *Letters from a Farmer in Pennsylvania,*
No. VIII—felt that he not only could affirm, as did Franklin,
that the war was strictly Britain's war and fought for selfish
purposes, but could even insist that the acquisition of territory
in North America as the result of it " is greatly injurious to
these colonies " and that they therefore were not under the
slightest obligation to the mother country.

But to return to the last phases of the Great War for the Empire. The British customs officials—spurred into unusual activity in the face of Pitt's demand for the strict enforcement of
the Trade and Navigation Acts in order to break up the pernicious practice of bringing aid and comfort to the enemy—were
led to employ writs of assistance for the purpose of laying their
hands upon goods landed in American ports and secured in exchange for American provisions sent for the most part either
directly or indirectly to the French West Indies. Although in
the midst of hostilities, most of the merchants in Boston showed
bitter opposition to the writs and equally ardent support of
James Otis' declaration made in open court in 1761 that Parliament, acting within the limits of the constitution, was powerless
to extend the use of these writs to America, whatever its authority might be in Great Britain. The importance of this declaration lies not so much in its immediate effect but rather in
the fact that it was indicative of the line of attack that not only
Otis would subsequently follow but also the Adamses, Hawley,
Hancock, and other popular leaders in the Bay colony during
the developing crisis, in the laying down of constitutional restrictions upon the power of Parliament to legislate for America.
Further, it is clear that, even before the Great War for the Empire had been terminated, there were those in the province who
had begun to view Great Britain as the real enemy rather than
France.

Just as definitely as was the issue over writs of assistance related to the war under consideration was that growing out of
the twopenny acts of the Virginia Assembly. In search of funds
for maintaining the frontier defensive forces under the command of Colonel George Washington, the Assembly was led to
pass in 1755 and 1758 those highly questionable laws as favor-

53

able to the tobacco planters as they were indefensively unjust
to the clergy. Even assuming the fact that these laws were war
measures, and therefore in a sense emergency measures, it was
inconceivable that the Privy Council would permit so palpable
a violation of contractual relations as they involved. The royal
disallowance of the laws in question opened the way for Patrick
Henry, the year that hostilities were terminated by the Peace
of Paris, not only to challenge in the Louisa County courthouse
the right of the King in Council to refuse to approve any law
that a colony might pass that in its judgment was a good law,
but to affirm that such refusal was nothing less than an act of
tyranny on the part of the King. It was thus resentment at the
overturning of Virginia war legislation that led to this attack
upon the judicial authority of review by the Crown—an authority exercised previously without serious protest for over a
century. It should also be noted that the Henry thesis helped
to lay the foundation for the theory of the equality of colonial
laws with those passed by Parliament, a theory of the constitution of the empire that most American leaders in 1774 had come
to accept in arguing that if the King could no longer exercise
a veto over the acts of the legislature of Great Britain, it was
unjust that he should do so over those of the colonial assemblies.

But the most fateful aftermath of the Great War for the
Empire, with respect to the maintenance of the historic connection between the mother country and the colonies, grew out of
the problem of the control and support not only of the vast
trans-Appalachian interior, the right to which was now confirmed by treaty to Great Britain, but of the new acquisitions
in North America secured from France and Spain. Under the
terms of the royal Proclamation of 1763, French Canada to the
east of the Great Lakes was organized as the Province of Quebec; most of old Spanish Florida became the Province of East
Florida; and those areas, previously held by Spain as well as by
France to the west of the Apalachicola and to the east of New
Orleans and its immediate environs, became the Province of
West Florida. The Proclamation indicated that proper inducements would be offered British and other Protestants to establish themselves in these new provinces. With respect to the

trans-Appalachian region, however, it created there a temporary but vast Indian reserve by laying down as a barrier the crest of the mountains beyond which there should be no white settlement except by specific permission of the Crown.

The Proclamation has been represented not only as a blunder, the result largely of carelessness and ignorance on the part of those responsible for it, but also as a cynical attempt by the British ministry to embody mercantilistic principles in an American land policy that in itself ran counter to the charter limits of many of the colonies and the interests in general of the colonials. Nevertheless, this view of the Proclamation fails to take into account the fact that it was the offspring of the war and that the trans-Appalachian aspects of it were an almost inevitable result of promises made during the progress of hostilities. For both in the Treaty of Easton in 1758 with the Ohio Valley Indians, a treaty ratified by the Crown, and in the asseverations of such military leaders as Colonel Bouquet, these Indians were assured that they would be secure in their trans-Appalachian lands as a reward for deserting their allies, the French. As a sign of good faith, the lands lying within the bounds of Pennsylvania to the west of the mountains, purchased by the Proprietors from the Six Nations in 1754, were solemnly released. Thus committed in honor in the course of the war, what could the Cabinet Council at its termination do other than it finally did in the Proclamation of 1763? But this step not only was in opposition to the interests of such groups of land speculators as, for example, the Patrick Henry group in Virginia and the Richard Henderson group in North Carolina, both of whom boldly ignored the Proclamation in negotiating with the Cherokee Indians for land grants, but also led to open defiance of this imperial regulation by frontiersmen who, moving beyond the mountains by the thousands, proceeded to settle within the Indian reserve—some on lands previously occupied before the beginning of the late war or before the great Indian revolt in 1763, and others on new lands.

The Proclamation line of 1763 might have become an issue, indeed a most formidable one, between the government of Great Britain and the colonials, had not the former acquiesced in the

55

inevitable and confirmed certain Indian treaties that provided
for the transfer of much of the land which had been the particular object of quest on the part of speculators and of those
moving westward from the settled areas to establish new homes.
Such were the treaties of Hard Labor, Fort Stanwix, Lochaber,
and the modification of the last-named by the Donelson agreement with the Cherokees in 1771. Nor did the regulation of
the trans-Appalachian Indian trade create serious colonial irritation, especially in view of the failure of the government to
implement the elaborate Board of Trade plan drawn up in 1764.
The same, however, cannot be said of the program put forward
by the ministry and accepted by Parliament for securing the
means to maintain order and provide protection for this vast
area and the new acquisitions to the north and south of it.

Theoretically, it would have been possible for the government
of Great Britain to have dropped onto the lap of the old continental colonies the entire responsibility for maintaining garrisons
at various strategic points in North America—in Canada, about
the Great Lakes, in the Ohio and Mississippi valleys, and in East
and West Florida. In spite, however, of assertions made by some
prominent colonials, such as Franklin, in 1765 and 1766, that
the colonies would be able and were willing to take up the
burden of providing for the defense of America, this, under the
circumstances, was utterly chimerical, involving, as it would
have, not only a vast expenditure of funds but highly complicated inter-colonial arrangements, even in the face of the most
serious inter-colonial rivalry such as that between Pennsylvania
and Virginia respecting the control of the upper Ohio Valley.
The very proportions of the task were an insuperable obstacle
to leaving it to the colonies; and the colonies, moreover, would
have been faced by another impediment almost as difficult to
surmount—the utter aversion of Americans of the eighteenth
century, by and large, to the dull routine of garrison duty.
This was emphasized by the Massachusetts Bay Assembly in
1755 in its appeal to the government of Great Britain after
Braddock's defeat to send regulars to man the frontier forts of
that province; the dispatches of Colonel George Washington in
1756 and in 1757 respecting the shameful desertion of militia-

men, ordered to hold the chain of posts on the western frontier of Virginia in order to check the frightful French and Indian raids, support this position, as does the testimony in 1757 of Governor Lyttelton of South Carolina, who made clear that the inhabitants of that colony were not at all adapted to this type of work. The post-war task of garrison duty was clearly one to be assumed by regulars held to their duty under firm discipline and capable of being shifted from one strategic point to another as circumstances might require. Further, to be effective, any plan for the defense of the new possessions and the trans-Appalachian region demanded unity of command, something the colonies could not provide. Manifestly this could be done only through the instrumentalities of the mother country.

The British ministry, thus confronted with the problem of guaranteeing the necessary security for the extended empire in North America, which it was estimated would involve the annual expenditure of from three to four hundred thousand pounds for the maintenance of ten thousand troops—according to various estimates made by General Amherst and others in 1764 and to be found among the Shelburne Papers—was impelled to raise the question: Should not the colonials be expected to assume some definite part of the cost of this? In view of the fact that it was felt not only that they were in a position to do so but that the stability of these outlying possessions was a matter of greater concern and importance generally to them, by reason of their proximity, than to the people of the mother country three thousand miles away, the answer was in the affirmative. The reason for this is not hard to fathom. The nine years of war had involved Britons in tremendous expenditures. In spite of very heavy taxation during these years, the people were left saddled at the termination of hostilities with a national debt of unprecedented proportions for that day and age of over one hundred and forty million pounds. It was necessary not only to service and to retire this debt, in so far as was possible, but also to meet the ordinary demands of the civil government and to maintain the navy at a point of strength that would offer some assurance that France and Spain would have no desire in the future to plan a war to recover their territorial losses. In addition to all this, there was now the problem of meeting the charges necessary for keeping the new possessions in North America under firm military control for their internal good order and for protection from outside interference.

It may be noted that before the war the British budget had called for average annual expenditures of six and a half million pounds; between the years 1756 and 1766 these expenditures mounted to fourteen and a half million pounds a year on the average and from the latter date to 1775 ranged close to ten million pounds. As a result, the annual per capita tax in Great Britain, from 1763 to 1775, without considering local rates, was many times the average annual per capita tax in even those American colonies that made the greatest contribution to the Great War for the Empire, such as Massachusetts Bay and Connecticut—without reference to those colonies that had done little or nothing in this conflict, and therefore had accumulated little in the way of a war debt, such as Maryland and Georgia. The student of the history of the old British Empire, in fact, should accept with great reserve statements to the contrary— some of them quite irresponsible in nature—made by Americans during the heat of the controversy, with respect to the nature of the public burdens they were obliged to carry in the years preceding the outbreak of the Revolutionary War. In this connection a study of parliamentary reimbursement of colonial war expenses from 1756 to 1763 in its relation to public debts in America between the years 1763 and 1775 is most revealing. As to American public finance, all that space will here permit is to state that there is abundant evidence to indicate that, during the five-year period preceding the outbreak of the Revolutionary War, had the inhabitants of any of the thirteen colonies, which therefore included those of Massachusetts Bay and Virginia, been taxed in one of these years at the average high per capita rate that the British people were taxed from 1760 to 1775, the proceeds of that one year's tax not only would have taken care of the ordinary expenditures of the colony in question for that year but also would have quite liquidated its war debt, so little of which remained in any of the colonies by 1770. Well may John Adams have admitted in 1780 what was equally true in 1770: "America is not used to great taxes, and the people there are not yet disciplined to such enormous taxation as in England."

Assuming, as did the Grenville ministry in 1764, the justice of expecting the Americans to share in the cost of policing the new possessions in North America, the simplest and most obvious way, it might appear, to secure this contribution to a common end so important to both Americans and Britons was to request the colonial governments to make definite grants of funds. This was the requisition or quota system that had been employed in the course of the recent war. But the most obvious objections to it were voiced that same year by Benjamin Franklin, who, incidentally, was to reverse himself the following year in conferring with Grenville as the Pennsylvania London agent. In expressing confidentially his personal, rather than any official, views to his friend Richard Jackson on June 25, 1764 he declared: "Quota's would be difficult to settle at first with Equality, and would, if they could be made equal at first, soon become unequal, and never would be satisfactory." Indeed, experience with this system in practice, as a settled method of guaranteeing even the minimum essential resources for the end in view, had shown its weakness and utter unfairness. If it could not work equitably even in war time, could it be expected to work in peace? It is, therefore, not surprising that this method of securing even a portion of the funds required for North American security should have been rejected in favor of some plan that presented better prospects of a definite American revenue.

The plan of last resort to the ministry was therefore to ask Parliament to act. That Grenville, however, was aware that serious objections might be raised against any direct taxation of the colonials by the government of Great Britain is indicated by the caution with which he approached the solution of the problem of securing from America about a third of the total cost of its defense. The so-called Sugar Act first of all was passed at his request. This provided for import duties on certain West Indian and other products. Colonial import duties imposed by Parliament, at least since 1733, were no innovation.

59

But the anticipated yield of these duties fell far short of the desired one hundred thousand pounds. He therefore, in introducing the bill for the above Act, raised the question of a stamp duty but requested postponement of parliamentary action until the colonial governments had been consulted. The latter were thereupon requested to make any suggestions for ways of raising an American fund that might seem more proper to the people than such a tax. Further, it would appear—at least, according to various London advices published in Franklin and Hall's *Pennsylvania Gazette*—that proposals were seriously considered by the Cabinet Council during the fall of 1764 for extending to the colonies representation in Parliament through the election of members to the House of Commons by various colonial assemblies. However, it is quite clear that by the beginning of 1765 any such proposals, as seem to have been under deliberation by the ministry, had been put aside when Grenville at length had become convinced that representation in Parliament was neither actively sought nor even desired by Americans. For the South Carolina Commons House of Assembly went strongly on record against this idea in September 1764 and was followed by the Virginia House of Burgesses in December. In fact, when in the presence of the London colonial agents the minister had outlined the objections raised by Americans to the idea of such representation, no one of them, including Franklin, was prepared to deny the validity of these objections. That he was not mistaken in the opposition of Americans at large to sending members to Parliament, in spite of the advocacy of this by James Otis, is clear in the resolutions passed both by other colonial assemblies than the ones to which reference has been made and by the Stamp Act Congress in 1765. Indeed, in 1768 the House of Representatives of Massachusetts Bay went so far in its famous Circular Letter framed in opposition to the Townshend duties as to make clear that the people of that colony actually preferred taxation by Parliament without representation to such taxation with representation.

When—in view of the failure of the colonial governments to suggest any practicable, alternate plan for making some contribution to the post-war defensive program in North America—

Grenville finally urged in Parliament the passage of an American stamp bill, he acted on an unwarranted assumption. This assumption was—in paraphrasing the minister's remarks to the colonial agents in 1765—that opposition to stamp taxes, for the specific purpose in mind, would disappear in America both in light of the benefits such provision would bring to colonials in general and by reason of the plain justice of the measure itself; and that, in place of opposition, an atmosphere of mutual good-will would be generated by a growing recognition on the part of Americans that they could trust the benevolence of the mother country to act with fairness to all within the empire. Instead, with the news of the passage of the act, cries of British tyranny and impending slavery soon resounded throughout the entire eastern Atlantic American seaboard. What would have been the fate of the empire had Grenville remained in office to attempt to enforce the act, no one can say. But as members of the opposition to the Rockingham ministry, he and his brother, Earl Temple, raised their voices—one as a commoner, the other as a peer—in warning that the American colonies would inevitably be lost to the empire should Parliament be led to repeal the act in the face of colonial resistance and the pressure of British merchants. Had Parliament determined, in spite of violence and threats of violence, to enforce the act, it might have meant open rebellion and civil war, ten years before it actually occurred. Instead, this body decided to yield and, in spite of the passing of the so-called Declaratory Act setting forth its fundamental powers to legislate on all matters relating to the empire, suffered a loss of prestige in the New World that was never to be regained.

But the Stamp Act was not the sole object of attack by colonials. To many of them not only the Sugar Act of 1764 but the whole English pre-war trade and navigation system was equally, if not actually more, obnoxious. Indeed, the unusual energy displayed by the navy and the customs officials, spurred into action by Pitt during the latter years of the war—bringing with it the condemnation in courts of vice-admiralty of many American vessels whose owners were guilty of serious trade violations, if not greater crimes—generated a degree of antagonism against the whole body of late seventeenth- and early

61

eighteenth-century restrictions on commercial intercourse such as never had previously existed. It is not without significance that the greatest acts of terrorism and destruction during the great riot of August 1765 in Boston were directed not against the Massachusetts Bay stamp distributor but against those officials responsible for encouraging and supporting the enforcement, during the late war, of the various trade acts passed long before its beginning in 1754. The hatred also of the Rhode Island merchants, as a group, against the restrictions of the navigation system as well as against the Sugar Act of 1764, remained constant. Moreover, in December 1766 most of the New York merchants, over two hundred in number, showed their repugnance to the way that this system was functioning by a strongly worded petition to the House of Commons in which they enumerated an impressive list of grievances that they asked to be redressed. Even Chatham, the great friend of America, regarded their petition " highly improper: in point of time most absurd, in the extent of their pretensions, most excessive; and in the reasoning, most grossly fallacious and offensive." In fact, all the leading men in Great Britain supported the system of trade restrictions.

Nevertheless, the determination of the government—in view especially of the great financial burdens that the late war had placed upon the mother country—to enforce it now much more effectively than had been done before 1754, and to that end in 1767 to pass appropriate legislation in order to secure funds from the colonies by way of import duties so that public officials in America might be held to greater accountability when paid their salaries by the Crown, could have only one result: the combined resistance of those, on the one hand, opposed to any type of taxation that Parliament might apply to America and of those, on the other, desiring to free the colonies of hampering trade restrictions.

The suggestion on the part of the Continental Congress in 1774 that Americans would uphold the British navigation system, if exempted from parliamentary taxation, while a shrewd gesture to win support in England, had really, it would seem, no other significance. For it is utterly inconceivable that the Congress itself, or the individual colonial governments, could have set up machinery capable of preventing violations of the system at will on the part of those whose financial interests were adversely affected by its operation.   Moreover, it is obvious that, by the time the news had reached America that Lord North's ministry had secured the passage of the coercive acts—for the most part directed against Massachusetts Bay for the defiant destruction of the East India Company's tea—leading colonials, among them Franklin, had arrived at the conclusion that Parliament possessed powers so very limited with respect to the empire that without the consent of the local assemblies it could pass neither constitutional nor fiscal legislation that affected Americans and the framework of their governments.   It is equally obvious that this represented a most revolutionary position when contrasted with that held by Franklin and the other delegates to the Albany Congress twenty years earlier.   For it was in 1754 that the famous Plan of Union was drawn up there and approved by the Congress—a plan based upon the view that Parliament, and not the Crown, had supreme authority within the empire, an authority that alone was adequate in view of framers of the Plan to bring about fundamental changes in the constitutions of the colonies in order legally to clothe the proposed union government with adequate fiscal as well as other powers.

In accounting for the radical change in attitude of many leading colonials between the years 1754 and 1774 respecting the nature of the constitution of the empire, surely among the factors that must be weighed was the truly overwhelming victory achieved in the Great War for the Empire. This victory not only freed colonials for the first time in the history of the English-speaking people in the New World from dread of the French, their Indian allies, and the Spaniards, but, what is of equal significance, opened up to them the prospect, if given freedom of action, of a vast growth of power and wealth with an amazing westward expansion.   Indeed, it is abundantly clear that a continued subordination of the colonies to the government of Great Britain was no longer considered an asset in the eyes of many Americans by 1774, as it had been so judged by them to be in 1754, but rather an onerous liability.   What, pray tell, had the debt-ridden mother country to offer in 1774 to the now geographically secure, politically mature, prosperous,

63

dynamic, and self-reliant offspring along the Atlantic seaboard, except the dubious opportunity of accepting new, as well as retaining old, burdens?   And these burdens would have to be borne in order to lighten somewhat the great financial load that the taxpayers of Great Britain were forced to carry by reason of obligations the nation had assumed both in the course of the late war and at its termination.   If many Americans thought they had a perfect right to profit personally by trading with the enemy in time of war, how much more deeply must they have resented in time of peace the serious efforts made by the home government to enforce the elaborate restrictions on commercial intercourse?   Again, if, even after the defeat of Colonel Washington at Great Meadows in 1754, colonials such as Franklin were opposed to paying any tax levied by Parliament for establishing a fund for the defense of North America, how much more must they have been inclined to oppose such taxation to that end with the passing in 1763 of the great international crisis?

At this point the question must be frankly faced: If France had won the war decisively and thereby consolidated her position and perfected her claims in Nova Scotia, as well as to the southward of the St. Lawrence, in the Great Lakes region, and in the Ohio and Mississippi valleys, is it at all likely that colonials would have made so fundamental a constitutional issue of the extension to them of the principle of the British stamp tax? Would they have resisted such a tax had Parliament imposed it in order to provide on an equitable basis the maximum resources for guaranteeing their safety, at a time when they were faced on their highly restricted borders by a militant, victorious enemy having at its command thousands of ferocious redskins? Again, accepting the fact of Britain's victory, is it not reasonable to believe that, had Great Britain at the close of the triumphant war left Canada to France and carefully limited her territorial demands in North America to those comparatively modest objectives that she had in mind at its beginning, there would have been no very powerful movement within the foreseeable future toward complete colonial autonomy—not to mention American independence?   Would not Americans have continued to feel the need as in the past to rely for their safety and welfare upon British sea power and British land power, as well as upon British resources generally? In other words, was Governor Thomas Hutchinson of Massachusetts Bay far mistaken when, in analyzing the American situation late in 1773, he affirmed in writing to the Earl of Dartmouth:

> Before the peace [of 1763] I thought nothing so much to be desired as the cession of Canada. I am now convinced that if it had remained to the French none of the spirit of opposition to the Mother Country would have yet appeared & I think the effects of it [that is, the cession of Canada] worse than all we had to fear from the French or Indians. 65

In conclusion, it may be said that it would be idle to deny that most colonials in the eighteenth century at one time or another felt strongly the desire for freedom of action in a wider variety of ways than was legally permitted before 1754. Indeed, one can readily uncover these strong impulses even in the early part of the seventeenth century. Yet Americans were, by and large, realists, as were the British, and under the functioning of the imperial system from, let us say, 1650 to 1750 great mutual advantages were enjoyed, with a fair division, taking everything into consideration, of the financial burdens necessary to support the system. However, the mounting Anglo-French rivalry in North America from 1750 onward, the outbreak of hostilities in 1754, and the subsequent nine years of fighting destroyed the old equilibrium, leaving the colonials after 1760 in a highly favored position in comparison with the taxpayers of Great Britain. Attempts on the part of the Crown and Parliament to restore by statute the old balance led directly to the American constitutional crisis, out of which came the Revolutionary War and the establishment of American independence. Such, ironically, was the aftermath of the Great War for the Empire, a war that Britons believed, as the Earl of Shelburne affirmed in 1762 in Parliament, was begun for the " security of the British colonies in N. America. . . ."

LAWRENCE HENRY GIPSON

LEHIGH UNIVERSITY

Planter Indebtedness and the Coming of the Revolution in Virginia

Emory G. Evans*

I

A T the outbreak of the American Revolution colonial indebtedness to Great Britain exceeded five million pounds. The southern colonies were most heavily encumbered; among them Virginia stood first with a debt of over two million pounds.[1] Historians have
long been intrigued by the possible influence of this indebtedness on the
coming of the American Revolution. Preoccupied with the importance of
economic forces during the long flirtation with economic determinism
through much of the period between 1910 and 1950, a number of scholars
viewed indebtedness as one of the central causes of the Revolution. Thus
Charles A. Beard suggested in 1915 that it "is generally known, the debts
due to British merchants and other private citizens constituted one of the
powerful causes leading to the Revolution,"[2] and a decade later Isaac S.

* Mr. Evans is a member of the Department of History, the University of Pittsburgh. The research for this article was made possible by grants from Colonial Williamsburg, Inc., the American Philosophical Society, and the University of Pittsburgh.
Special thanks should be extended to Dr. Edward M. Riley, Director of Research
for Colonial Williamsburg, Inc., whose kindness and co-operation were especially
helpful. A version of this article was presented at the annual meeting of the Southern Historical Association, Chattanooga, Nov. 9, 1961.

[1] Jefferson estimated that Virginia's debts were "certainly . . . two millions
sterling." Julian P. Boyd and others, eds., *The Papers of Thomas Jefferson* (Princeton,
1950————), X, 27; James Monroe said that "Our debt to B. merchants I am well informed amounts to about 2.800.000 £." Monroe to Benjamin Harrison, Mar. 26, 1784,
ibid., VII, 48. The claims against Virginians of the British mercantile community in
1790 substantiate these estimates. They amounted to £2,305,408.19/2 out of an
American total of £4,984,655.5/8. This sum included 14 years interest and may
have been somewhat inflated, but debts paid between 1783 and 1790 do not, of
course, appear in the total. List of debts due by the Citizens of the United States
of America to the Merchants and Traders of Great Britain contracted previous to the
year 1776 with interest on the same to 1 January 1790, Chatham Papers, Public
Record Office, Gifts and Deposits, Ser. 30, VIII, 343, Public Record Office, London.

[2] Charles A. Beard, *Economic Origins of Jeffersonian Democracy* (New York,
1915), 270.

Harrell in *Loyalism in Virginia* sought to provide documentary support for Beard's suggestion. Building his case on the Virginia plan of 1774 to halt debt payment and the sequestration law of 1777 which enabled Virginians to pay debts in depreciated currency, Harrell argued that "with their plantations, slaves, and sometimes household furnishings hypothecated, the planters were in an almost inextricable position in 1775; it seemed that nothing less than virtual repudiation would relieve them." The heavy debt and the actions of Virginians between 1774 and 1790 to escape payment seemed to Harrell to point clearly to indebtedness as the key to Virginia's discontent in the decade before the Revolution and led him irresistibly to the conclusion that revolution and independence simply provided a convenient release from an inextricable economic situation.[3]

That the evidence was *post hoc* and circumstantial did not keep a number of later scholars from accepting to varying extents the Beard-Harrell argument.[4] Quite recently, Lawrence Henry Gipson has sought to reinforce this argument by studying Virginia indebtedness during the Seven Years' War. Examining the operation of the Virginia laws between 1749 and 1763 that set the exchange rate between Virginia currency and sterling, Gipson shows that the legal rate never kept pace with the actual rate, suggests that British merchants lost heavily as a result, and implies that indebted Virginians purposely created this situation to enable them legally to write off a portion of the debt. Although the Currency Act of 1764 solved the immediate problem by forbidding payment of sterling debts in paper money, these early Virginia actions to avoid payment, Gipson strongly implies, suggest a state of mind which made independence attractive as a means of debt repudiation.[5] A close look at existing evidence,

67

[3] Isaac S. Harrell, *Loyalism in Virginia: Chapters in the Economic History of the Revolution* (Durham, 1926), 26-28.

[4] For examples of those accepting the Harrell-Beard argument see Oscar T. Barck, Jr., and Hugh T. Lefler, *Colonial America* (New York, 1958), 596; William B. Hesseltine and David L. Smiley, *The South in American History* (Englewood Cliffs, N. J., 1960), 73; Merrill Jensen, *The Articles of Confederation* . . . (Madison, 1940), 23-24. Others deny that Virginians were repudiationists, but still insist that indebtedness was a major factor. See Curtis P. Nettels, *The Roots of American Civilization* (New York, 1938), 620; Harry J. Carman, Harold C. Syrett, Bernard W. Wishy, *A History of the American People,* 2d ed. rev. (New York, 1960), I, 172; Harold U. Faulkner, *American Economic History,* 5th ed. (New York, 1943), 127-128; John C. Miller, *Origins of the American Revolution* (New York, 1943), 16. For an opposite point of view see Hamilton J. Eckenrode, *The Revolution in Virginia* (New York, 1916), 38-40; and Thomas P. Abernethy, *Western Lands and the American Revolution* (New York, 1937), 160-161.

[5] Lawrence Henry Gipson, "Virginia Planter Debts Before the American Revolu-

however, indicates that neither Harrell nor Gipson has stated the case accurately.

II

Both the Gipson and Harrell accounts suffer from the same deficiencies. They rely more heavily upon deduction, inference, and circumstance than upon evidence. Neither has made any systematic investigation of the abundant sources for the crucial years between 1764 and 1775, when the Revolution was actually developing, and such evidence as they present relates to periods other than the one in question, Gipson relying on the years before 1763 and Harrell the period after 1775. Moreover, both—Harrell explicitly and Gipson implicitly—assume, without offering supporting evidence, that Virginians consciously shaped their political course to avoid debt payment. At the root of their interpretations must be the questionable assumptions that men are moved largely by economic considerations and that abstractions and statements of principle are merely masks of more basic economic interests.

Strongly influenced by the traditional nineteenth-century view that all paper money is not only inherently bad but also a form of conspiracy to enable debtors to pay their obligations in depreciated currency, Gipson has built his case almost entirely upon the testimony of merchants and interested officials in Britain. British merchants originally protested because the actual rate of exchange between Virginia money and sterling fluctuated about 4 per cent above the legal rate during the period between 1748 and 1755. Although the Virginia legislature—upon the recommendation of the Board of Trade—passed a measure in 1755 to remedy the situation by enabling the courts to alter the legal rate to keep pace with the actual rate of exchange,[6] the emission of a large number of legal tender paper bills (ultimately £440,000) to meet war expenses between 1755 and 1763 and a simultaneous inflationary trend produced considerable alarm among

tion," *Virginia Magazine of History and Biography*, LXIX (1961), 259-277; *The Triumphant Empire: Thunder-Clouds Gather in the West, 1763-1766* (New York, 1961), chap. 8. See also Professor Gipson's *The Coming of the Revolution, 1763-1775* (New York, 1954), chap. 4.

[6] William Waller Hening, ed., *The Statutes at Large: Being a Collection of All the Laws of Virginia* . . . (Richmond, 1809-23), V, 540; VI, 478. Table XVI, Average Annual Rate of Exchange, Virginia Currency on Sterling, prepared by John M. Hemphill, in James Soltow, The Economic Role of Williamsburg (unpubl. research report, Colonial Williamsburg, Inc., Research Library, 1956).

the merchants, who proposed that the paper bills be accepted at their discretion and at the rate they thought proper. They assumed—as does Gipson—that the paper emissions were responsible for the inflation and argued that they depreciated so rapidly that exchange rates settled by the courts were always, except at the moment they were set, lower than the actual rate, to the detriment of the merchant.[7] There was and is considerable disagreement with this position. Governor Francis Fauquier argued at the time and several recent scholars have agreed that it was Virginia's increasing demand for imported goods that produced an excess of imports over exports which, by creating a seller's market, influenced merchants to raise their prices, and not the paper money issues per se that produced the inflation of the 1750's and 1760's.[8] The paper currency, then, as Yorktown merchant William Nelson pointed out in 1768, influenced the exchange rate only to the extent that it encouraged Virginians to think they were more affluent than they really were and thus to indulge in greater extravagances.[9] According to this argument, then, it was the merchants' taking advantage of the extravagance of Virginians and not the legislature's emission of paper that was largely responsible for the rising exchange rate.

69

[7] See Memorial of London Merchants to Board of Trade, June 21, 1758, Dec. 22, 1762, C.O. 5/1329 and C.O. 5/1330; Richard Corbin to John Robert, July 29, 1762, and to Robert Cary, Aug. 22, 1762, Richard Corbin Letter book, 1758-1768, Colonial Williamsburg, Inc., Research Library, Williamsburg, Va.; and Gipson, "Virginia Planter Debts," 264-265. A critique of the view that fiat money is inherently bad can be found in Leslie Van Horn Brock, The Currency of the American Colonies, 1700-1764: A Study of Colonial Finance and Imperial Relations (unpubl. Ph.D. diss., University of Michigan, 1941); and E. James Ferguson, The Power of the Purse: A History of American Public Finance, 1776-1790 (Chapel Hill, 1961), 24. Ferguson points to the need for a circulating medium in colonial America and suggests that "the efforts of the American provinces to create a medium of exchange . . . hardly constitute a 'dark and disgraceful picture,' nor, on the whole, a record of failure. Most colonies handled their currency with discretion and were successful in realizing the purposes associated with its use."

[8] Fauquier said "there is a much more fundamental Cause of the rise, to wit, the Increase of the Imports, to such a Height that the Crops of Tobacco will not pay for them." Fauquier to the Board of Trade, Nov. 3, 1762, C.O. 5/1330; Samuel M. Rosenblatt, The House of John Norton & Sons: A Study of the Consignment Method of Marketing from Virginia to England (unpubl. Ph.D. diss., Rutgers University, 1960), 107-114. See also James H. Soltow, "The Role of Williamsburg in the Virginia Economy, 1750-1775," William and Mary Quarterly, 3d Ser., XV (1958), 475. In partial support of their position, Rosenblatt and Soltow are able to show, through a comparison of the rate of exchange with the emission of paper money, that the rate of exchange continued to rise, in the period 1762-64, after the supply of currency was diminishing.

[9] William Nelson to Capel and Osgood Hanbury, Feb. 27, 1768, William and Thomas Nelson Letter book, 1766-1775, Virginia State Library, Richmond.

Even if one rejects this interpretation he cannot be certain that the merchants actually lost much money as a result of the difference between the legal and actual exchange rates. On the contrary, there is considerable evidence to support the assertion of Scottish merchant Charles Steuart that the merchants were merely protesting "against imaginary losses and ill-founded apprehensions."[10] A comparison between the judgments obtained by British merchants in the Virginia General Court between 1757 and 1763 and the actual rate of exchange reveals that the merchants lost an average of no more than 2 per cent on the original debt,[11] hardly enough to warrant their outraged cries. Such a loss undoubtedly cut into the merchants' profits, but a recent study of one London firm shows that despite such a loss profits would still have been very high.[12]

Moreover, Virginia political leaders certainly were convinced that they were acting with reasonable justice to the merchants and that existing arrangements were fairer to all concerned than those proposed by the merchants. The committee of correspondence wrote to London agent Edward Montague that it seemed more just "that the difference of Exchange be settled by the determination of disinterested judges than to leave it to the arbitrary will of the Creditor." The committee also pointed out that the merchants' greatest losses came about as a result of the "Ignorance or inadvertancy of some Factors who while bringing suits have too hastily received said debts before the Exchange was either settled by the purchasers of Bills or the Court." Moreover, the legislature argued that to remove the legal tender clause as the merchants requested would be unjust to the many people who had accepted the notes with the guarantee that they were a tender in payment of all obligations.[13]

There would seem to be no direct evidence on which to question the sincerity of the committee's statement or to support Gipson's assumption that Virginians consciously shaped their policies to enable them to avoid

[10] Charles Steuart to James Parker, Jan. 29, 1764, Parker Papers, Liverpool Record Office, Liverpool, Eng., quoted in Rosenblatt, The House of Norton, 107.

[11] "A List of Judgments for Sterling Money Obtained in the General Court of Virginia by Persons Residing in Great Britain [1757-1763]," *Va. Mag. of Hist. and Biog.*, XII (1904-5), 1-4; Table XVI, Soltow, The Economic Role of Williamsburg.

[12] See Rosenblatt, The House of Norton, chap. 5.

[13] The committee also argued that in time of deflation it was the debtor who suffered because the value of money appreciated and he would inevitably pay more when fulfilling his obligations. Virginia Committee of Correspondence to Agent, June 16, 1763, *Va. Mag. of Hist. and Biog.*, XI (1903-4), 345-349; Representation of Virginia Burgesses, May 1763, Stevens Transcripts, I, No. 1, Additional Manuscripts, 42257, British Museum, London.

part of their debt. Had they had such goals in mind it is doubtful that they would have so willingly consented to permit the General Court to adjust the exchange rate as they did in 1755. Gipson's conclusion that Virginia's actions between 1750 and 1763 indicate an inclination toward repudiation at a later date is not only in itself ahistorical but also a projection of an interpretation that both ignores Virginia's side of the case and relies almost entirely upon merchant accusations and circumstantial evidence.

The same objections can be raised to Harrell's account. There is no denying Harrell's argument that Virginians enacted measures to enable payment of British debts in depreciated currency to the state government during the Revolution and that their record on debt payment was extremely poor after the war.[14] But to use these facts as evidence that Virginians had repudiation in mind prior to 1776 is questionable. That Virginians acted a certain way in 1777 or 1787 does not necessarily mean that they were thinking in similar terms in 1774. Moreover, Harrell's conclusion ignores the particular conditions surrounding later events. The sequestration act of 1777—which permitted people to pay off British debts by payments into the state loan office—was not simply a bald and blatant attempt at debt repudiation. It was, in fact, demanded by the exigencies of the situation and was in large part an effort to stabilize Virginia's finances and to shore up the state's shaky credit.[15] Furthermore, it must be remembered that in 1777 the British were Virginia's enemies, as they had not been before 1775, and that many private individuals assumed that the state accepted responsibility for all debts paid to the loan office.[16] Similarly,

71

---

[14] Harrell devotes the first of five chapters to the period prior to 1774. Even in this chapter he devotes little space to pre-1770 factors. For the Act for Sequestering British Property, see Hening, ed., *Statutes at Large*, IX, 377-380. The evidence on the failure of Virginians to pay their debts after the war is extensive. For example see William Hay to James Baird, July 14, 1784, same to same, Aug. 11 [1789?], Claims of John Hay & Co., Treasury Papers, Ser. 79, XXVII, Public Record Office; and Statement of William Hay #2, Richmond, Feb. 19, 1798, *ibid.*

[15] For a discussion of this aspect of the sequestration law see Boyd and others, eds., *Papers of Jefferson*, II, 170-171n.

[16] In 1788 the State declared that it was liable for the amount paid into the loan office only when it was reduced by a scale of depreciation with 6 per cent interest added. At the same time no judgment was made as to whether the payment into the loan office was a valid payment of the debt. This decision was left up to the courts. Hening, ed., *Statutes at Large*, XII, 529-530. In 1793 George Wythe ruled in the case of Carter Page, executor of Archibald Cary, vs. Edmund Pendleton and Peter Lyons, administrators of John Robinson, that payment into the loan office did

it should not be forgotten that Virginia's poor postwar record on debt payment was in great part caused by extremely unfavorable economic conditions in the decade after 1783 which made it virtually impossible for most people to meet their obligations.[17] Moreover, to have forced immediate payment would have ruined both debtor and creditor. "There are two circumstances of difficulty in the paiment of these debts," Jefferson explained. "To speak of the particular state with which you and I are best acquainted, we know that it's debt is ten times the amount of it's circulating cash. To pay that debt at once then is a physical impossibility. Time is requisite. Were all the creditors to rush to judgment together, a mass of two millions of property would be brought to market where there is but the tenth of that sum of money in circulation to purchase it. Both debtor and creditor would be ruined, as debts would be thus rendered desperate which are in themselves good."[18]

The post-1775 situation is, then, much more complicated than Harrell suggests and by no means points even circumstantially to the conclusion that Virginians consciously pushed for independence as a convenient means to repudiate their debts. Any understanding of the relation between indebtedness and the coming of the Revolution in Virginia will have to rest upon a thorough examination of the large amount of material on the question for the crucial years between 1763 and 1776. The picture that emerges from such an examination modifies considerably the conclusions of earlier writers.

III

Indebtedness was such a constant companion of the Virginia planter that it seemed to be almost endemic to the plantation economy. Dependent

not discharge debts due British creditors. *Virginia Reports* (Charlottesville, 1903), Wythe, 211-218.

[17] For example see David Ross to Hercules Ross, Aug. 22, 1783, Hercules Ross vs. Daniel Ross, U. S. Circuit Court, Virginia District (1806), Virginia State Library, Richmond. I was allowed to see the Circuit Court Records through the kindness of Mr. William J. Van Schreeven, Archivist of the State of Virginia. Peter Lyons to Samuel Gist, Aug. 4, 1784, Virginia Claims G(II), Samuel Gist, Audit Office Papers, Ser. 13, XXX, Public Record Office; John Syme to Archibald Hamilton, Mar. 31, 1785, Loyalist, Part I, A.O. 13/85; William Allason to Robert Allason, May 18, 1785, William Allason Letter book, 1770-1789, Virginia State Library; Ralph Wormeley, Jr., to Welch & Son, Sept. 20, 1785, same to [?], Mar. 5, 1792, Wormeley Letter book, Alderman Library, University of Virginia, Charlottesville.

[18] Thomas Jefferson to Alexander McCaul, Mar. 19, 1786, in Boyd and others, eds., *Papers of Jefferson*, IX, 388.

upon unpredictable tobacco crops and markets 3,000 miles away, few planters after 1660 had managed to stay entirely free of debts during their lifetimes. But beginning in the 1740's there was a marked increase both in the size of the debt and in the number of those indebted—an increase all out of proportion to population growth. Moreover, the trend seemed to accelerate as the Revolution approached, despite higher tobacco prices that might have enabled the planters to extricate themselves.

There is no simple explanation for this indebtedness. It was distributed throughout Virginia society, though the large planters were most heavily obligated. The involvement of smaller planters and yeomen was a relatively recent development. The consignment method of marketing tobacco that had prevailed before 1750 had primarily involved the larger producers, but during the twenty-five years prior to the Revolution the Scots had sent resident factors to buy tobacco and sell goods on the spot to all classes of tobacco growers through an elaborate system of stores. This system not only resulted in the predominance of the Scots in the tobacco trade but also led to the indebtedness of all elements in society.[19] After the Revolution one observer estimated that the majority of debts were under one hundred dollars, and an examination of the books of the Glasgow firm of William Cuninghame and Co., which in 1784 claimed a total debt of £95,000, tends to confirm the validity of this estimate.[20]

But the explanation for the increasing indebtedness is not to be found simply in the fact that more and more people were becoming indebted; it is also to be explained by the extravagance of the Virginia gentry. The gentry's increase in wealth and its assumption of political and social leadership had been accompanied by a desire for the refinements of the more cultivated existence enjoyed by its counterpart in Britain. Trouble came when this desire outran income. By the 1750's and 1760's few commen-

[19] Calvin B. Coulter, The Virginia Merchant (unpubl. Ph.D. diss., Princeton University, 1944); Jacob M. Price, "The Rise of Glasgow in the Chesapeake Tobacco Trade, 1707-1775," Wm. and Mary Qtly., 3d Ser., XI (1954), 179-199; Robert P. Thomson, The Merchant in Virginia, 1700-1775 (unpubl. Ph.D. diss., University of Wisconsin, 1955); Robert P. Thomson, "The Tobacco Export of the Upper James River Naval District, 1773-1775," Wm. and Mary Qtly., 3d Ser., XVIII (1961), 393-407; James H. Soltow, "Scottish Traders in Virginia, 1750-1775," Economic History Review, 2d Ser., XII (1959-60), 83-98.

[20] Claim of William Cuninghame, Mar. 15, 1784, A.O. 13/29; Statement of William Hay #2, Richmond, Feb. 19, 1798, Claim of John Hay & Co., T. 79/27. Cuninghame claimed that £14,940 was owed the firm in Maryland. See also list of debts claimed by Buchanan, Hastie & Co. at their Charlotte County Store and Eilbeck, Chambre, Ross & Co. at their Petersburg store, T. 79/95.

tators failed to mention the extravagant, luxurious, and even ostentatious tastes and habits of the large Virginia planters. Writing in 1766, John Wayles observed that in 1740 a debt of £1,000 seemed tremendous, but that "Ten times that sum is now spoke of with Indifference and thought no great burthen on some Estates. Indeed in that series of time property is become more valuable and Estates have increased more than ten fold. But then Luxury and expensive living have gone hand in hand with the increase in wealth. In 1740 I don't remember to have seen such a thing as a turkey carpet in the Country except a small thing in a bedchamber. Now nothing are so common as Turkey or Wilton Carpetts, the whole furniture, Roomes, Elegant and every appearance of opulence."[21] In 1762 Governor Fauquier expressed alarm at the tendency of imports to exceed exports but despaired of reform. Truth was so disagreeable to Virginians, he wrote, that "the generality . . . obstinately shut their Eyes against it."[22] "Extravagance," wrote William Nelson, "hath been our Ruin"; and Receiver-General Richard Corbin recognized that if "Luxury Still prevails and Extravagance continues all hopes of . . . recovery will be lost for this generation." The only "Recipe that can be prescribed at this juncture," declared Nathaniel Savage, "is Frugality and Industry, which is a potion scarcely to be swallowed by Virginians brought up from their cradles in Idleness Luxury and Extravagance."[23] But it was easier to suggest the remedy than to apply it, for, as George Washington explained, the "extravagant and expensive man" was "ashamed" to alter his "system of . . . living" because it would create suspicions of a decay in his fortune. Thus, ego and pride interacted with extravagant tastes to drive the planter further and further into debt with the all too frequent result, Washington remarked, that the planter lost his estate in "consequence of his preseverance in error."[24]

The planters' optimism was almost as important as their extravagance in increasing their indebtedness. They always expected that the next crop would bail them out of debt. Consequently, they did not let their indebtedness deter them from ordering large amounts of British goods. John Syme

[21] John Wayles to John T. Warre, Aug. 30, 1766, American Loyalist Claims, T. 79/30.
[22] Fauquier to Board of Trade, Nov. 3, 1762, C.O. 5/1330.
[23] William Nelson to Capel and Osgood Hanbury, Feb. 27, 1768, Nelson Letter book, 1766-1775; Richard Corbin to Phillip Ludwell, Aug. 13, 1764, Corbin Letter book, 1758-1768; Nathaniel Savage to John Norton, July 22, 1766, Norton-Dixon-Savage Papers, Henry E. Huntington Library, San Marino, Calif.
[24] Washington to George Mason, Apr. 5, 1769, in John C. Fitzpatrick, ed., Writings of George Washington (Washington, 1931-44), II, 503.

of Hanover County, writing in 1753 to the Bristol concern of Lidderdale, Harmer and Farrell, apologized for drawing so "largely on you" but "I have a Probability of making an hundred hogsheads this year, which shall be sent to your house on good usage." The following year he was still in trouble and still optimistic, expecting that an increase in slaves and the amount of "genuine sweetscented" tobacco under cultivation would cover his debts and his bills of exchange. The pattern continued until 1757, when the firm refused to honor his demands. Syme's reaction clearly pinpointed the psychology of the indebted planter. "It gives me much concern, to have my bills protested," he wrote, for "the shortness of the crop was what I could not forsee." In return for shipping the firm his entire crop, Syme expected a continued extension of credit: "I am truly sensible, Gentlemen, the Debt I owe you is large, but then I pay interest for it, and with tolerable Success, I shall be now able, to send you Yearly, considerably above an Hundred hogsheads, and you may Depend, I shall not by any means Exceed £300 a year, both in Bills and Goods till I have payed the Old Score." At Syme's demand the firm permitted the debt to continue piling up until it amounted in 1766 to a "Prodigious Sum." But he was still asking for credit to buy Negroes so that he could produce more tobacco to pay his debts. The vicious circle of unfulfilled hopes and rising debts continued until at the outbreak of the Revolution Syme owed £8,000.[28]

Nor was Syme's case atypical. Robert Beverley of Blandford, grandson of the historian, wrote English merchant John Bland in 1761 soon after taking over the management of the family estate not to "conclude that I am *embracing* those Maxims so generally *embraced* in this Country; viz. that of being in Debt and making great promises for the future; Those, Sir, are Notions, which I condemn as much as you can, and though at this Time I desire you to be a little in advance, it is only because I propose to make you a large consignment which will fully reimburse you, and hereafter when I send for anything, I will take care to lodge cash for those

[28] See Letters of John Syme to Lidderdale, Harmer and Farrell (Farrell and Jones after 1760) between 1753 and 1774, especially June 9, 1753, May 27, 1754, Feb. 9, 1757, June 2, 1760, May 10, 1763, May 21, 1763, Nov. 15, 1764, June 20, 1766, May 25, 1768, Mar. 29, 1769, May 28, 1769, Aug. 4, 1773, Mar. 4, 1774, in Jones Exors. vs. John Syme, U. S. Circuit Court, Virginia District, Ended Cases (1797). In 1763, while protesting that he would make no more purchases, Syme asked the firm to send him a stud since "it is impossible to do without one for my mares" as well as a good plowman and seedman to help do things in "a Farmer like way, besides, such as one would do to take care of the Horse on his Passage."

Purposes." Despite these protestations, Beverley was writing the following year for more goods, which "will leave me in your Debt, but as I design to ship the above mentioned Tobacco, I am in Hopes that the Ballance will be nearly equal." By 1763 he owed Bland £1,800 and was trying to borrow £300 more while protesting that this would be the "Last time I will Ask any Man for Money. For thank God I have a very fine Estate, which even with the Crop I have alread[y] made will put me in a State of Perfect Independence." Two years later, however, he was still heavily in debt.[26] Like Syme and Beverley, John Baylor, who in 1764 excluded himself from that group which he called "indolent or extravagant," found himself in 1768 in debt £700 to London merchant John Norton. Norton complained that, although the tobacco Baylor sent would only pay a fraction of the debt, Baylor requested his annual supply of wine, drew on Norton for his son's expenses in England, sent a large family invoice for goods, and added "without apology" that he intended to "draw a bill to the Mississippi Company." Two years later Baylor's indebtedness to Norton had doubled, and to make matters worse Baylor had also become indebted to Liverpool merchant John Backhouse, whom he was trying to put off by saying that as soon as his son's education was completed "in a year or two more" he would send "every pound of tobacco I make," a promise that was never fulfilled.[27]

The planter had come to expect leniency because the merchant was so heavily involved that consciously or not he tended to encourage it. He expected the merchant to honor his bills of exchange when he had no balance, to ship goods on the promise that next year's tobacco would be sent, and to be extremely patient when his debts were long overdue.[28]

[26] Robert Beverley to John Bland, Nov. 16, 1761; same to same, June 1762; Beverley to Samuel Athawes, Nov. 18, 1763; Beverley to Bland, Aug. 18, 1765, Robert Beverley Letter book, 1761-1793, Library of Congress, Washington, D. C. In all fairness to Beverley it should be said that he was the exception among Virginians in that he seems to have been able eventually to surmount his financial difficulties.
[27] John Baylor to John Norton, Sept. 18, 1764, in Frances Norton Mason, ed., *John Norton & Sons, Merchants of London and Virginia* . . . (Richmond, 1937), 12; John Norton to John Hatley Norton, Oct. 25, 1768, Norton-Dixon-Savage Papers; List of Foreign Debtors to John Norton & Son, July 30, 1770, Norton Papers, Colonial Williamsburg, Inc., Research Library; John Baylor to John Backhouse, July 21, 1769, Backhouse Admx, vs. Baylors Exors., U. S. Circuit Court, Virginia District, Ended Cases (1798).
[28] For example see William Davies to John Norton, Oct. 6, 1773, Norton Papers; Robert Carter to James Buchanan & Co., Jan. 1, 1761, Robert Carter Letter book, 1760, Virginia Historical Society, Richmond; Richard Corbin to Robert Dinwiddie,

Historically, the relationship between merchant and planter had been based partly on mutual trust between the participants,[29] and despite the traditional picture of the grasping merchant it should not be forgotten that he was nearly as dependent on the planter as the planter was on him.[30] The merchant needed Virginia tobacco, and with his customer 3,000 miles and six to eight weeks distant it was essential that he handle the planter carefully. In an economy where the large shippers were limited to a relatively small number of people whose relationships were close, the merchant had to tread lightly. If he were reticent in advancing credit, he might find that the planters would not consign him their tobacco. William Nelson advised merchant Edward Hunt of this fact in 1766, remarking that "You are the proper Judge in matters of this sort . . . but it hurts me to have your ship go out without being fully loaded."[31]

77

Once credit had been extended, overzealous attempts to gain payment could easily bring about the loss of a customer; the planters were extremely sensitive to any sort of pressure, regarding it as an affront to their honor. Thus Thomas Jones, on being pressed for payment, replied that his feelings were "as delicate as any Mans living," intimated that the debt was the result of the poor price for his tobacco, and warned that he might break off his correspondence and discharge the debt by shipping his tobacco where the prices were more favorable.[32] This was no idle threat, and it was not

---

Sept. 20, 1758, Corbin Letter book, 1758-1768; Augustine Smith to John Norton, Aug. 13, 1769, Norton Papers.

[29] Robert Beverley expressed Virginia opinion well when he told Samuel Athawes that, though he would sometimes become indebted to him, he did not think that Athawes would be a loser, for he paid him interest and consigned him his tobacco. He explained that it was a "mutual intercourse of good offices, conducted with Honor and Candor, which produces Friendships and tis such an Intercourse, which I should wish should subsist between you and myself." Beverley to Athawes [1773?], Beverley Letter book, 1761-1793; see also Beverley to Athawes, Oct. 17, 1770, ibid.; Landon Carter Diary, Mar. 23, 1770, Alderman Library, University of Virginia; William Davies to John Norton, Oct. 6, 1773, Norton Papers; Louis B. Wright, The First Gentlemen of Virginia: Intellectual Qualities of the Early Colonial Ruling Class (San Marino, Calif., 1940), 178; an outstanding treatment of the consignment trade and merchant-planter relations can be found in Rosenblatt, The House of Norton.

[30] A convincing revision of the idea that the merchant exploited the planter can be found in Rosenblatt, The House of Norton, chap. 6.

[31] William Nelson to Edward Hunt, Sept. 11, 1766, Nelson Letter book, 1766-1775.

[32] Thomas Jones to Mr. Molleson, July 1774, Jones Family Papers, Lib. Cong.; see also Robert Beverley to Samuel Athawes, Sept. 6, 1769, Beverley Letter book, 1761-1793; John Baylor to John Norton, Sept. 18, 1764, Norton Papers.

unusual for a merchant to find himself in the position of Londoner James Pratt, who complained "of the Ungenerous Treatment" he had "met with f[rom] Mr. D. J. who instead of making me Rem[ittances] agreeable to his promise has as I am . . . informed opened a correspondence with . . . Flowerdue."[33] Even in distressed times, and despite heavy involvement, the planter seemed to be able to find other merchants who were willing to do business with him. "The misfortune," wrote Robert Carter Nicholas during the panic of 1773, "is that, if one Merchant will not comply with their Desires, they fly to another."[34]

Furthermore, if the merchant earned the displeasure of one planter, relationships were so close among the large Virginia planters that he could easily find himself in bad odor among other customers. When Samuel Athawes failed to ship all the goods that a customer ordered because, as he explained in what was termed an "uncivil" letter, the order exceeded the customer's balance, William Nelson reported that it "was much the subject of conversation" and no little disgust.[35] John Wayles explained the merchant's problem well when he remarked in a letter to a British firm he was representing that the Harrison family was "somehow or other so connected with your Other Friends, that, where the debt is not in danger, indulgences are unavoidable."[36] Similarly, the merchant hesitated to resort to legal action because to do so was to demonstrate a loss of faith in the customer—an action that did not help his reputation in Virginia. Besides, such proceedings were always long, drawn out, and expensive.[37] Merchants were, therefore, usually more indulgent than was prudent, and the planters, encouraged by this indulgence and overoptimistic about their ability to meet their obligations, sank deeper and deeper into debt.

To make matters worse, there was a significant inflation in credit in the

[33] James Pratt to Col. Thomas Jones, May 20, 1754, Jones Family Papers.
[34] Robert Carter Nicholas to John Norton, July 30, 1773, quoted in Rosenblatt, The House of Norton, 126.
[35] William Nelson to Samuel Athawes, Nov. 15, 1768, Nelson Letter book, 1766-1775.
[36] John Wayles to [John T. Warre for Farrell and Jones?], Aug. 30, 1766, American Loyalist Claims, T. 79/30.
[37] See Harry Piper to Dixon and Lidderdale, Aug. 10, 1768, Apr. 15, 1769, Harry Piper Letter book, 1767-1776, Alderman Library, University of Virginia; Richard Corbin to Edmund Jenings, Mar. 15, 1759, Oct. 8, 1760, Corbin Letter book, 1758-1768; John Tazewell to John Norton, July 12, 1770, June 4, 1771, Norton Papers; Rosenblatt, The House of Norton, 129-131; George L. Chumbley, Colonial Justice in Virginia . . . (Richmond, 1938), chap. 12.

decade prior to the Revolution.[38] Thus the £11,000 owed to John Norton in 1769 had increased to £18,000 in 1770 and £40,000 in 1773.[39] The easy manner in which credit could be obtained in these years can be seen in the case of Rappahannock River merchants John and George Fowler. In 1769 the Fowlers wrote the Liverpool firm of Dobson, Daltera and Walker for £1,000 in goods on credit to open a store, and in 1770 they submitted two additional requests for goods amounting to £1,500 and £1,200. They promised to pay for each order promptly but did not actually make a remittance until the fall of 1772, when they sent only £950, or about one-fourth of the sum owed. Nonetheless, the firm continued to give the Fowlers credit, and by 1776 they owed it £14,384.[40] No wonder Virginians came to expect extensive credit and to protest, as did Thomas Nelson, that unless "a Merchant will upon occasion advance 3 or 4,000 he is not a man for me."[41]

To complicate the situation further, the planter mistakenly believed that as a last resort he could always sell part of his estate to pay his debts. As planter-merchant Roger Atkinson remarked to an English correspondent, land "is the best security" for "by the Laws of this Country, both Lands and Slaves are liable for English Debts." Calm in the belief that if worse came to worse his large estate would protect him from ruin,[42] the planter did not reckon with the real scarcity of a circulating medium in Virginia in the ten years prior to the Revolution,[43] and, when the financial

79

[38] William Allason to James Dunlop, Feb. 24, 1763, and to Alexander Walker, June 24, 1764, Allason Letter book, 1757-1770; Robert Beverley to Samuel Athawes [1773?], Beverley Letter book, 1761-1793; James Parker to Charles Steuart, May 19, 1773, Charles Steuart Papers, 1773-1774, National Library of Scotland, Edinburgh; Charles M. Andrews, *The Colonial Backgrounds of the American Revolution* (New Haven, 1924), 101-102; Rosenblatt, The House of Norton, 183-192.

[39] John Norton to John Hatley Norton, Jan. 25, 1769, Sept. 4, 1773, and List of Foreign Debtors to John Norton & Son, July 31, 1770, July 30, 1773, Norton Papers.

[40] See John and George Fowler to Dobson, Daltera and Walker, Nov. 12, 1769, Dec. 4, 1769, Feb. 30, 1770, June 1770, Sept. 20, 1770, Jan. 1, 1771, Oct. 20, 1772, Feb. 21, 1773, Oct. 25, 1774, June 1, 1775, Sept. 4, 1775, as well as numerous bills of lading and accounts in Dobson & Daltera vs. Fowler Svg. Ptr., U. S. Circuit Court, Virginia District, Ended Cases (1798).

[41] Thomas Nelson to Rowland Hunt, June 29, 1773, Nelson Letter book, 1766-1775.

[42] Roger Atkinson to John Gale, July 22, 1771, Roger Atkinson Letter book, 1769-1776, Alderman Library, University of Virginia; see also John Syme to Farrell and Jones, Mar. 29, 1769, Aug. 4, 1773, Jones Exors vs. Syme, U. S. Circuit Court, Virginia District, Ended Cases (1797); John Page to Duncan Campbell, June 14, 1773, Notarial Copies of Letters to Duncan Campbell, American Loyalist Claims, T. 79/12.

[43] Francis Fauquier to Secretary of State, June 14, 1765, C.O. 5/1345; Harry

crisis of 1773 resulted in a scarcity of money and English creditors pressed for payment, he found few buyers for his land. Thus, along with credit inflation, which increased indebtedness, the scarcity of money made it increasingly difficult for the planter to pay his debts. This situation had been coming on for some time, but most Virginians were not aware of their dilemma until the economic crisis of 1773. Thereafter, there is evidence to suggest the gradual development of considerable frustration. "I want exceedingly to pay the Wh[ite]haven People," wrote Atkinson in 1773, "but there is no such thing as selling land now for ready money." Thomas Adams wrote from Williamsburg of the "distress of Numbers of worthy People which don't know which way to turn themselves for Want of Money to pay their just debts." John Page stated that he would like to sell part of his estate to pay his debts, "but from the present scarcity of Money here I should not expect to get near the value of it." Thomas Nelson, both a debtor and a creditor, bemoaned his inability to pay, but explained that "our Country is at present in so deplorable a situation that a person who may have thousands due to him can command no more than he who has little or I may say nothing." In 1776 Roger Atkinson expressed the opinion of many Virginians when he said "I know it a stale Apology, the Cant of every villain, as well as honest Man-The Times-The Times."[44]

80

Piper to Dixon and Lidderdale, Jan. 7, 1769, Piper Letter book, 1767-1776; Agent to William Cuninghame & Co., Oct. 10, 1772, Agents Letter book, Cuninghame & Co., National Library of Scotland, Edinburgh; Richard Randolph to Farrell and Jones, Jan. 25, 1773, Sept. 15, 1773, Copies of Letters from Richard Randolph to Farrell and Jones, American Loyalist Claims, T. 79/30. Randolph remarked in Sept. 1773 that there was not more than £80,000 currency in circulation, that £10,000 of that was to be retired in Oct., and that this sum was insufficient in a country which required "near five hundred thousand pounds to support a proper medium." See also Charles Yates to Dixon and Lidderdale, July 3, 1773, and to Gales and Fearon, Sept. 3, 1773, Charles Yates Letter book, 1773-1783, Alderman Library, University of Virginia; Rosenblatt, The House of Norton, chap. 3. For a general discussion of the Currency Act and its effect on the Revolutionary movement see Jack P. Greene and Richard M. Jellison, "The Currency Act of 1764 in Imperial-Colonial Relations, 1764-1776," *Wm. and Mary Qtly.*, 3d Ser., XVIII (1961), 485-518.

[44] Roger Atkinson to Benson Fearon, Mar. 1, 1773, Atkinson Letter book, 1769-1776; Thomas Adams to Mrs. Cocke, May 5, 1773, Robert Carter Papers, 1772-1785, Va. Hist. Soc.; John Page to Duncan Campbell, June 14, 1773, Notarial Copies of Letters to Duncan Campbell, American Loyalist Claims, T. 79/12; Thomas Nelson to Robert Cary & Co., Aug. 19, 1773, Nelson Letter book, 1766-1775; Roger Atkinson to Samuel Pleasants, Nov. 20, 1776, Atkinson Letter book, 1769-1776.

IV

In this general economic and social situation the difficulties with Britain began and developed, and as a result it has been easy for some historians to suggest that Virginians welcomed the controversy and ultimately sought independence to escape payment of their debts. Of course, Virginians never included complaints about economic conditions in their protests against British actions, and those who have emphasized indebtedness as a causative factor have relied largely upon the circumstances of the situation and charges by people after 1775 to support their view. This is not to indicate that a few contemporaries did not make the connection between indebtedness and the protest against Britain. As early as 1769 James Parker, a Norfolk merchant of loyalist sympathies, wrote on a copy of the Virginia Association Resolves of that year that of all the signers there were but seven who "could obtain credit for One Shilling . . . in England." Included in the list were most of Virginia's leading patriots.[45] Repeatedly during the crucial years prior to 1776 Parker voiced the opinion that "generally speaking the more a man is in debit, the greater patriot he is" and that "calling a man a patriot" in Virginia "is saying that he is in bad circumstances."[46] But too much weight should not be given to Parker's views, for he was so pro-British that he joined forces with Lord Dunmore and ultimately left Virginia.

However, few of Parker's contemporaries shared his suspicions for the good reason that difficulty in collecting debts in Virginia was nothing new. Merchants had always complained about the problem of collecting debts, and they continued to do so in the period from 1763 to 1776.[47] Of course, complaints became more intense as indebtedness increased, and agitation against Virginians reached new heights immediately before

[45] See copy of Virginia Association Resolves, May 17, 1769, Parker Papers, Liverpool Record Office.

[46] James Parker to Charles Steuart, June 7, 1774, Steuart Papers, 1773-1774. See also Parker to Steuart, Aug. 2, 1770, Aug. 5, 1770, May 17, 1774, Feb. 14, 1775, *ibid.*

[47] See, for instance, the remark of merchant George Bogle in 1731: "By all means . . . Endeavor and make it your Business to Leave as few Debts in the Country [Virginia] as you can or rather none at all for you know that when at Home what Immense Difficulty there is of Raising them when at such a Distance." George Bogle to Matthew Bogle, Oct. 20, 1731, Bogle Papers, 1696-1777, Mitchell Library, Glasgow, Scotland. See also the charge of Richard Corbin in 1762 that so few Virginians had "just notions of Credit, that it renders the Collection of Money troublesome and Irksome." Richard Corbin to Capel and Osgood Hanbury, Oct. 8, 1762, Corbin Letter book, 1758-1768.

the Revolution. But in their complaints the merchants rarely expressed any fear that Virginians might seek to repudiate their debts by political revolution. Nor did agents of British firms in Virginia such as William Carr, Charles Yates, Harry Piper, and William Allason anticipate more than mere dilatory tactics to postpone payment.[48]

Despite the heavy indebtedness and the considerable frustration it produced, there does not seem to have been any important connection between the debts and the Revolutionary movement in Virginia before 1774. The passage of a law in 1770 to limit the jurisdiction of the Hustings Court in Williamsburg to Williamsburg cases may well have constituted a delaying action. This court was noted for its speedy action in debt cases, and the new law restricted suits for debt, outside of Williamsburg, to either the county courts or the General Court, where judgments sometimes required three or four years. Although the House of Burgesses passed this measure only by a slim majority of two, it does not seem to have caused much furor on either side of the Atlantic. In fact, only one adverse reaction appears in the mass of mercantile correspondence for the period.[49] But even if the law was intended to slow down the process of collecting debts, there is no evidence that it had any direct relationship with the debate with Britain.

The Coercive Acts of 1774 greatly altered this situation. In reaction to those measures, Virginia patriots, among other things, closed the courts, thus preventing actions for debt and encouraging a great many citizens to refuse to pay their debts. This development has been an important element in the case for indebtedness as a cause of the Revolution. But what is either forgotten or ignored is that the Virginians had learned at the time of the Stamp Act just how powerful a weapon closing the courts could be in the fight with Britain. In 1765 the courts had been closed because of lack of stamps, and the action had been a major factor in deciding

[48] Admittedly, aside from the correspondence of London merchant John Norton and that of one or two Scottish firms such as the Cuninghames, extant letters of British merchants are limited. The correspondence of their agents is more extensive. The letters of Yates, Piper, and Allason have already been mentioned in the footnotes. William Carr served London merchant James Russell, whose papers can be found at the firm of Coutts & Co., Bankers, London, Eng.

[49] Hening, ed., *Statutes at Large*, VIII, 401-402; John Tazewell to John Norton, July 12, 1770, June 4, 1771, Norton Papers. Tazewell asked Norton to use his influence to get the Board of Trade to recommend disallowance of the act. As a result the act was disallowed in 1772. Rind's *Virginia Gazette* (Williamsburg), May 22, 1772.

British creditors, alarmed at their inability to sue for debt, to press Parliament to repeal the Stamp Act. "The true Reason . . . for the Repeal was the great sums owing by Americans to great Britain," wrote a Scot in 1766. "The Town of Glasgow was Reckoned Itself to have owing them near £1,000,000 sterling."[50] The impact of such action was not lost upon Virginians, and the closing of the courts in 1774 cannot be understood except as a weapon to secure repeal of the Coercive Acts. Most of the mercantile community understood very well that Virginia leaders had no other aim in mind. Harry Piper explained that "it is . . . proposed to stop all proceedings in the Courts of Justice with regard to the recovery of Debts so that you see the Merchants are to be distressed at all events in order to make them active in getting the Acts Repealed." Piper fumed about the Boston Port Bill—"that Confounded Act of Parliament"—and predicted that if Britain persisted in her course it would lead to the ruin of both her and the colonies. "Americans," he wrote, "will undergo many hardships before they will part with their liberty."[51] What Piper was implying was that nonpayment of debts had become a patriotic act. True, as one contemporary put it, nonpayment was "a mode so pleasant and agreeable to those indebted," but it was still an act of patriotism suggested and undertaken to secure political ends.[52] Virginians, merchant Charles Yates dryly remarked, "have determined it takes Patriotism not to pay anybody."[53] Even Lord Dunmore, who was far from being a disinterested bystander, recognized that the desire to put pressure on British creditors to join the "clamor" against the Coercive Acts was equally important in the decision to close the courts as the wish to delay debt payment.[54]

83

[50] Journal of J. Brown, Feb. 1766, Bogle Papers, 1696-1777. See also Edmund S. and Helen M. Morgan, *The Stamp Act Crisis: Prologue to Revolution* (Chapel Hill, 1953), chaps. 10, 15.

[51] Harry Piper to Dixon and Lidderdale, June 9, 1774, Piper Letter book, 1767-1776; see also Charles Yates to Henry Ellison, July 21, 1774, Yates Letter book, 1773-1783; William Allason to Robert Allason, Dec. 8, 1774, Allason Letter book, 1770-1789.

[52] See William Carr to James Russell, May 26, 1774, Russell Papers, #2.

[53] Charles Yates to Samuel and William Vernon, Oct. 5, 1774, Yates Letter book, 1773-1783.

[54] Lord Dunmore to Secretary of State, Dec. 24, 1774, C.O. 5/1353. The British merchants, by this time, understood their role very well, for as London merchant James Russell wrote planter Thomas Jones "we have not yet received the resolves of the General Congress [but] when they come I shall endeavor to get a petition presented to the new Parliament praying a redress of the Hardships America suffers by the late Acts, I hope to get many of the most eminent Merchants here to join in

In their search for economic motives historians have either overlooked or tended to minimize the seriousness of Virginia resentment against British policy. That Virginians were deeply and sincerely concerned about not only past infringements on what they considered their constitutional rights but also the threat of future encroachments is evident even from a casual reading of the sources for the period. Because of the Coercive Acts, William Carr remarked in 1774, the "People . . . will go naked rather than have any commerce or connection with Great Brittain. . . . I never expected to see such a spirit of opposition and resistance as now prevails amongst all sorts of People indeed it appears to me that they are ready for Battle."[55] William Reynolds wrote in a similar vein, "The Common people in this Country and I believe all through the Colony are so much inflamed that they publickly declare they will sacrifice their lives rather than submit to the Tyrannical oppression of a Corrupt Minister."[56] In a speech to his fellow justices of the peace in Richmond County, Landon Carter put the case for suspending actions for debt succinctly. Because the people of Great Britain did not seem to be concerned about "the Arbitrary Proceeding[s] of their Parliament," he declared, it "behooved" Virginians "to have as little commerce with them as Possible and farther to refuse to do them the service to determine their suits for debts since they had consented to a manifest violation of our whole Constitution."[57]

That the decision to close the courts did not mean that Virginians planned to avoid the eventual payment of their debts is clearly indicated in their exchanges with British merchants. Richard Randolph was infuriated when the Bristol firm of Farrell and Jones suggested that he might not meet his obligations. He expressed his regret that his "Honour" was held "in so little Esteem" and his determination to meet his obligations as soon as it was in his "Power." However, Randolph made it clear that payment would be delayed until the Coercive Acts had been repealed, observ-

---

that Petition it will give me real pleasure to do everyhing in my power to promote the interest of the colonies." James Russell to Thomas Jones, Nov. 25, 1774, Jones Family Papers.

[55] William Carr to James Russell, Oct. 23, 1774, Russell Papers, #2.

[56] William Reynolds to John Norton, Aug. 6, 1774, William Reynolds Letter book, 1771-1779, Lib. Cong.; see also John Taylor to Duncan Campbell, July 20, 1774, Notarial Copies of sundry letters to Duncan Campbell, American Loyalist Claims, T. 79/12; Thomas Nelson to Samuel Athawes, Aug. 7, 1774, Nelson Letter book, 1766-1775.

[57] Landon Carter Diary, June 8, 1774.

ing that "there is not a man amongst us that entertains the least Idea of giving up the point in dispute between us and our Parent State." At the same time, he urged his correspondents not to worry about his debts, for he had provided in his will, in case of his death, that they would be paid out of his estate—an arrangement which would make it easy for them "to repossess what you have so generously advanced." This fact, he added, would give him great pleasure in his last moments, "as I have very abominated the sin of ingratitude."[58] Such a statement may sound insincere, but Randolph and many others felt exactly that way. Perhaps the consensus of opinion was expressed by Burges Ball, who wrote merchant Duncan Campbell that "you may rely that no private advantage shall be thought of by me, and I hope that matters will ee'r long be friendly determined."[59]

At the same time, there was a real division of opinion among Virginians on the justice of using nonpayment as a political weapon. George Washington felt that nonpayment should be used only in "the last extremity,"[60] and Robert Beverley thought such action "full of Cruelty and Injustice." "Our Dispute is not with this Set of Men [merchants]," he said.[61] James Parker reported that debates among patriot leaders over the

[58] Richard Randolph to Farrell and Jones, May 15, 1775, Copies of Letters of Richard Randolph to Farrell and Jones, American Loyalist Claims, T. 79/30. In fairness to Farrell and Jones, it must be said that neither Randolph nor his heirs paid his debts until they were forced to by court judgment in 1797. But time, bitterness engendered by the war, and economic conditions during the 1780's made people less willing and less able to pay their just debts after the war. I hope to treat the postwar problem of debts in a subsequent article. For the story of the failure of Randolph and his heirs to pay their debts see Richard Hanson to [Farrell and Jones], July 5, 1786, Sept. 3, 1787, June 2, 1797, Extracts of letters of Richard Hanson as relate to Richard Randolph's accounts, American Loyalist Claims, T. 79/30.

[59] Burges Ball to Duncan Campbell, Aug. 7, 1774, Notarial Copies of letters to Duncan Campbell, T. 79/12. It should perhaps be asked of those who consider indebtedness as a major factor in the coming of the Revolution in Virginia that if Virginians were repudiationists, whom did they plan to trade with once the difficulties were over? The question is of course silly, for Virginians did not contemplate breaking off their commercial relations with their English correspondents until political events pushed them into such a course, and once the war was over they planned to renew their connections. Even if Virginians had considered repudiation seriously, replacing nine-tenths of their trade would have given them serious pause. See for example William Clayton to John Norton, June 2, 1775, John Hart to John Norton, Aug. 16, 1775, Archibald Ritchie to John Norton, Aug. 16, 1775, Thomas Everard to John Norton, Aug. 24, 1775, in Mason, ed., Norton & Sons, 379, 384, 386, 387; Roger Atkinson to Richard Hanson, May 1, 1779, T. 79/17.

[60] George Washington to Bryan Fairfax, July 4, 1774, July 20, 1774, in Fitzpatrick, ed., Writings of Washington, III, 229-234.

[61] Robert Beverley to Landon Carter, Aug. 28, 1774, Robert Beverley Letters, 1763-1774, Alderman Library, University of Virginia.

proper course to pursue were violent, George Mason, Patrick Henry, Richard Henry Lee, and Robert Carter Nicholas supporting nonpayment of debts and Paul Carrington, Carter Braxton, Edmund Pendleton, Thomas Nelson, Jr., and Peyton Randolph opposing it.[62] All of these men were patriots, and the question at issue was not repudiation, but whether or not temporary nonpayment was a proper device by which to bring Britain to heel. George Washington and Landon Carter were in agreement about the seriousness of the British challenge and their indebtedness was relatively small. Yet Washington opposed nonpayment because it was unjust to the merchants, while Carter thought that paying the debts was "Hypocrisy to America," the measure of a "half Patriot."[63]

Despite such differences, it is highly probable that a majority of Virginians were in favor of nonpayment; and unquestionably the heavy indebtedness of the planter encouraged him to pursue such a course. It would be naïve to suggest that many planters were not delighted with the prospect of having a respite from the dunning of their creditors. There were some who took advantage of the situation to escape their obligations, as had been the case during the Stamp Act crisis. Governor Fauquier remarked at that time that "People are daily going out to settle beyond the . . . Mountains. They flock there just now more than usual, as all Debtors are in dred of the opening of the Courts on the Repeal of the Stamp Act."[64] Similarly, after 1774, some "men of bad Principles" acted, if not in the same manner, with the same end in mind.[65] But most planters were not thinking of repudiation. They considered themselves honorable men and intended eventually to meet their obligations.[66] Consequently, the initial closing of the courts in 1774 and the resulting nonpayment of debts must be viewed as an attempt to force England to repeal the Coercive Acts, rather than as a first step on a consciously-plotted route to independence and debt repudiation.

V

That closing the courts was an important part in the chain of events that led ultimately to war in 1775, independence in 1776, and temporary repudiation of debts during the war years and, in many cases, well into the

[62] James Parker to Charles Steuart, June 17, 1774, Charles Steuart Papers.
[63] Landon Carter Diary, Aug. 8, 1774, Sept. 20, 1775.
[64] Francis Fauquier to Board of Trade, May 22, 1766, C.O. 5/1331.
[65] See William Carr to James Russell, May 14, 1776, Russell Papers, #2.
[66] For example see Roger Atkinson to Richard Hanson, May 1, 1779, T. 79/17.

1790's does not mean that the desire to postpone debt payment was the fountainhead of the whole series of events. Virginians did, in fact, continue to hope that nonpayment would force Parliament to back down until the outbreak of hostilities in April 1775. Thus Richard Randolph wrote his British creditors in March 1775, "We are endeavoring as much as ever for a Crop of Tobacco in hopes of a favourable measure being adopted by your Rulers respecting the Colonys as we sincerely wish to continue in the Old Chanel having the greatest aversion to the new mode lately prescribed by them."[67] After Lexington and Concord, the debt question became hopelessly submerged in the whole dynamic of the Revolution. There was, thereafter, no further hope that nonpayment would in itself produce a change in British policy; similarly, there was no possibility that the planters would seriously consider paying their debts to citizens of a country with whom they were at war.

The facts that more than a few indebted Virginians opposed independence,[68] that independence was not the signal for the immediate and wholesale—or, for that matter, even eventual—repudiation of debts, and that British threats to Virginia constitutional rights—according to existing evidence[69]—loomed much larger than indebtedness in Virginia conscious-

87

[67] Richard Randolph to Farrell & Jones, Mar. 8, 1775, T. 79/30; see also William Reynolds to George F. Norton, Apr. 20, 1775, Reynolds Letter book, 1771-1779. It should be pointed out that Robert Polk Thomson in a recent article in the *Wm. and Mary Qtly.* (see n. 19) has shown that in 1775 exports of tobacco from private planters in Virginia were significantly lower than in 1774. He asks if this decline might not be evidence that Virginians did not make an honest effort to reduce their debts, "after nonimportation had begun, but before the Continental nonexportation agreement took effect." (pp. 400-401) Unquestionably, the fact that the nonexportation agreement was to go into effect in Aug. of 1775 had some influence in that it limited the time for exportation. For those with slight debts, or none at all, there was not much point in shipping tobacco if you could not import goods in return. More importantly, without the threat of court action hanging over their heads, the planters hoped that by holding on to their tobacco they would be able to force the price up and make a better profit. See William Carr to James Russell, Mar. 11, 1775, Russell Papers; Charles Yates to Dixon and Lidderdale, Apr. 4, 1775, and Yates to Gales and Fearon, Aug. 29, 1775, Yates Letter book, 1773-1783; Harry Piper to Dixon and Lidderdale, Apr. 7, 1775, and May 10, 1775, Piper Letter book, 1767-1776.
[68] Keith B. Berwick, Loyalties in Crisis: A Study of the Attitudes of Virginians in the Revolution (unpubl. Ph.D. diss., University of Chicago, 1959), especially chaps. 1-3.
[69] The best analysis of the causes of the Revolution in Virginia is Thad W. Tate, "The Coming of the Revolution in Virginia: Britain's Challenge to Virginia's Ruling Class, 1763-1776," *Wm. and Mary Qtly.*, 3d Ser., XIX (1962), 323-343.

ness right down to independence seriously undermine the Harrell-Beard view that indebtedness operated as a conscious element in the Virginia decisions to oppose British policy after 1763 and to declare independence in 1776. If indebtedness had any relationship to the coming of the Revolution other than as a political weapon to secure a change in British policy, it was certainly as no more than an unconscious and unarticulated conditioning element that helped to make Virginians more receptive to rebellion and independence.

88

Borrowed Rhetoric:
The Massachusetts Excise Controversy of 1754

Paul S. Boyer*

W

HEN John Quincy Adams in 1823 expressed his concern that the United States might become a mere cockboat in the wake of the British man-of-war, he vented a fear which Americans have frequently felt. As we seem at last to be acquiring a certain degree of confidence in our national distinctiveness, now is perhaps a propitious time for a closer examination of those occasions when the direction of the American cockboat through uncharted seas was, in fact, determined by the course of the British vessel out ahead. We may drop the nautical metaphor, but instances of the relationship which it suggests occur frequently throughout our history. Just as historians of the national period recognize that such diverse phenomena as the antislavery movement, William Graham Sumner, Hull House, and New Deal economics cannot be fully understood without a look at William Wilberforce, Herbert Spencer, Toynbee Hall, and John Maynard Keynes, so colonial historians find that events of their period frequently come more sharply into focus when British history on a similar subject is examined. Such an event is a little-known controversy over a liquor excise bill which shook Massachusetts in 1754. This dispute illuminates several aspects of colonial Massachusetts's history: the conflict between the rural interior and the mercantile coast; the political sagacity of Governor William Shirley (a quality which John Schutz and others have remarked)[1]; the use of London agents in the resolution of colonial squabbles; and the development of constitutional theory in the pre-Revolutionary generation—but its most interesting feature is the way it was decisively conditioned by a similar

89

* Mr. Boyer is a Ph.D. candidate at Harvard.

[1] John A. Schutz, *William Shirley, King's Governor of Massachusetts* (Chapel Hill, 1961); George A. Wood, *William Shirley, Governor of Massachusetts, 1741-1756* (New York, 1920). Schutz mentions the 1754 excise controversy only briefly (pp. 179-180); the single volume in Wood's unfinished biography does not reach 1754.

upheaval which had occurred in Great Britain two decades earlier.

An understanding of the sources of the 1754 dispute requires a brief look at the history of the liquor excise in Massachusetts. Such an excise was imposed early in the history of the colony and had remained in force down through the years. The law, however, contained some serious loopholes. It applied only to wine and spirits sold through licensed inns and taverns in quantities of less than thirty gallons. As time passed, these loopholes had been increasingly exploited by the merchants of Boston and other coastal towns who imported for their own use expensive wine upon which no excise was collected, as it was never sold at retail. Further, a number of merchants of Boston and surrounding towns, particularly Medford, were engaged in importing molasses, distilling it into rum, and shipping it directly to a variety of outlets within Massachusetts from which it flowed directly to the consumer, avoiding the licensed channels and the excise. Evidence of this practice crops up in the correspondence of Boston merchants and distillers. For example, in 1754 an Eastham tenant of the Boston distiller Melatiah Bourne added a postscript to a letter dealing with other matters: "[B]e pleased to send me a Barrel of Rum and I will send you the money as soon as I have drawed the rum."[2] And in the same year a baker of Ipswich wrote to Nathaniel Holmes, a large rum merchant of Boston: "I have sent you by Capt. Harris . . . a Empty barril pray send me a recpt. and a Barril of Rum."[3] Sir William Pepperrell and his son-in-law Nathaniel Sparhawk, the important merchants of Kittery (on the Atlantic coast fifty miles north of Boston), were key figures in this direct sale of rum. Much of the rum for the Maine settlements was obtained by Pepperrell and Sparhawk from William Tyler, a Boston merchant associated with Thomas Hancock.[4]

That a significant quantity of rum was being sold in avoidance of the excise was indicated in 1754 by an advocate of a stricter law who wrote of "those vast Quantities of Rum, that are consumed in the Eastern Parts of this Province [i.e., Maine]," adding, "Scarce a Coaster goes a Trip without carrying a Barrel of Rum, not one in a Hundred of which pays any Excise; not to mention the great Quantities of *French* Wines of late con-

[2] Theophilus Paine to Bourne, May 25, 1754, Bourne Papers, I, Houghton Library, Harvard University.

[3] Edmund Heard to Holmes, Dec. 18, 1754, Bourne Papers, VII.

[4] Byron Fairchild, *Messrs. William Pepperrell: Merchants at Piscataqua* (Ithaca, 1954), 90-91, 138, 196.

sumed in those Parts. . . ."[5] The evasion of the excise was so flagrant that as early as 1726 the Massachusetts General Court was forced to admit that the purpose of the law was "in a great measure frustrated."[6] A related complaint was that much of the rum and wine was smuggled into the province in the first place, thereby avoiding Massachusetts's import duties as well. Thomas Hancock, for example, was deeply engaged in smuggling.[7] An indication of the Assembly's concern over the evasion of the provincial import duties is the fact that in 1748 tax collectors were authorized to search the ships of suspected smugglers.[8]

This wholesale flouting of the various liquor taxes by the merchants was a source of continual irritation to the General Court. The small farmers and landholders of the interior were heavily overrepresented in the General Court (due to the town unit basis of representation), and their interest in keeping land and property taxes low made them receptive to any plan for increasing the tax share borne by the mercantile group. It was natural, then, for members of the General Court to agitate for tightening the excise law. At first they attempted to force all wine and rum to flow through licensed outlets by prescribing, from 1715 on, lashings and jail terms for violators, but the increasing severity of the punishments prescribed as the century progressed is a measure of the degree to which the law was being successfully avoided.[9]

Gradually attention turned to the root of the trouble: the merchants and distillers who were conniving in the untaxed consumption of liquor. In 1748 the General Court talked of imposing a rum excise payable directly by the distillers, but the idea was stillborn.[10] Again in 1751 "after a long Debate" a committee was chosen to prepare an excise bill which would provide for a direct tax on the distillers, but once more the plan was dropped and a second committee was instructed to prepare an excise

91

[5] Rusticus, *The Good of the Community Impartially Considered.* . . . (Boston, 1754), 36.
[6] Act of May 25, 1726, in *Acts and Resolves, Public and Private, of the Province of the Massachusetts Bay* (Boston, 1869-1922), II, 400-403.
[7] William T. Baxter, *The House of Hancock: Business in Boston, 1724-1775* (Cambridge, Mass., 1945), 87.
[8] James Truslow Adams, *Revolutionary New England, 1691-1776* (Boston, 1923), 271.
[9] Acts of July 29, 1721, June 29, 1725, and July 7, 1737, in *Acts and Resolves*, II, 204, 400, 849.
[10] June 1, 1748, in *Journals of the House of Representatives of Massachusetts . . .* (Boston, 1919—), XXV, 25; hereafter cited as *House Journals*.

bill "in the usual Way."[11] By 1754, however, the atmosphere was favorable for another attempt to tighten the excise law. War with the French was impending and funds were needed for ambitious military undertakings. In his message to the Assembly on May 30, 1754, Governor William Shirley urged that taxation be "in the most easy and equal manner" and that the tax laws be tightened to "secure to the publick the full revenue which every fund is capable of producing."[12] The Assembly interpreted this message to be a green light for the long talked-of excise revision, and in the new tax bill a section was added which began: "Every person consuming, using or any way expending in his or her house, family, apartment or business, any rum or other distilled spirits, or wine, except they purchased the same of a taverner, innholder or retailer in this province, and in a quantity less than thirty gallons, shall pay the duties following." The duties then imposed were fourpence for a gallon of rum and sixpence for a gallon of wine.[13] Teeth were given this new provision by the requirement that each resident of the province annually report to the excise collector, *under oath* if so required, all unlicensed liquor imbibed in his household the previous twelvemonth and pay the required excise.

In a message to the Governor's Council regarding the new provision, the Assembly succinctly stated its purpose: in order that "all that consumed spiritous Liquors, the Rich as well as the Poor; those who consumed them for Luxury, as well as those who consumed the same for Necessity, might pay an Excise therefor." A hint of the mood pervading the General Court during the numerous long debates on this proposal is found in the complaint of Assemblyman William Fletcher of Cambridge who told the Assembly on June 18 that a "Report was spread Abroad" that in the excise debates he had "reflected on the Merchants as a Sett of Men who had no Regard for the Good of their Country, and that no Regard ought to be given to any Thing they said."[14] The fact that the Assembly promptly absolved Fletcher of having intimated any such dastardly thing is perhaps less significant than the fact that the report had been spread abroad in the first place.

On June 13, 1754, the excise measure, with its new provision that

[11] June 4, 5, and 13, 1751, *ibid.*, XXVIII, 13, 17, 32.
[12] William Shirley to House of Representatives, May 30, 1754, Massachusetts Archives, CVIII, State House, Boston.
[13] Act of Dec. 21, 1754, in *Acts and Resolves*, III, 787-788.
[14] June 15 and 18, 1754, in *House Journals*, XXXI, 43, 48.

"the Rich as well as the Poor" should bear the liquor tax burden, passed the Assembly. Only seventeen votes were mustered in opposition. They came from Boston itself (two votes), other coastal mercantile towns (eleven votes), and towns in the Pepperrell trading area in Maine (four votes). As these votes suggest, the opposition to the proposed excise revision arose in the coastal areas where merchants, distillers, and unlicensed distributors were persuaded that it was an agrarian scheme to increase their tax burden. Evidence of the strength and concentration of the opposition to the new tax arrangement is provided by a strongly worded petition submitted to the Massachusetts General Court in December 1755 (after the events about to be described had run their course), making a final appeal for a relaxation of the new excise system. Of the 131 legible signatures, about eighty are identifiable as those of merchants, distillers, or men with close mercantile ties. The rest remain unidentified. The first name on the petition is Thomas Hancock's, followed by the names of a variety of his business associates and relatives.[15] But however formidable the economic strength of the opposition, it was hopelessly weak in the Assembly where fifty-two "Yeas," drawn from towns scattered throughout the hinterland, swept aside the seventeen feeble "Nays," and the bill proceeded to the Governor's Council in its journey toward enactment.[16]

The Governor's Council, a twenty-eight member body elected annually by the Assembly and the outgoing Council, was not in these years a potent political force. Wholly dependent upon the favor of the Assembly for their office, the Councilors could not afford repeated opposition to Assembly measures. And yet there were men on the Council at this time, particularly Thomas Hutchinson, Andrew Oliver, and the aging Sir William Pepperrell himself, who in some respects represented the merchant group. For a time it appeared their view might prevail when the Council refused its approval of the new measure and manfully announced its opposition to the Assembly. The larger body at once returned the bill to the Council, however, with a strongly worded message expressing "great Surprise" at the Council's action and including a veiled threat that further Council balkiness might lead the Assembly to abandon the whole attempt to levy taxes. The following day, taking advantage of the absence

[15] Sundry Gentlemen, Merchants and Other Inhabitants of Boston to the General Assembly, Dec. 11, 1755, Mass. Archives, CXVII, fol. 51.

[16] June 13, 1754, in *House Journals*, XXXI, 38.

93

of four Councilors who had opposed the measure the day before, the Council hastily voted to reconsider, and this time approved the measure.[17] On June 15 the new excise measure was placed upon the desk of William Shirley for what was normally a final formality for fiscal measures: the Governor's signature.

On the basis of Shirley's May 30 message to the Assembly calling for a tightening of the tax laws one would conclude that the Assembly and the Governor were in full accord on the proposed change in the excise-collecting system. On June 17, however, Shirley informed the Assembly of his refusal to sign the new proposal. He defended his decision in a lengthy message in which, after assuring the Assemblymen of his "real Desire to lighten the Tax upon the Polls and Estates of your Constituents," he ignored fiscal matters altogether and raised ideological issues. He denounced the provision in the bill requiring individuals to report their liquor consumption under oath as "inconsistent with the *natural Rights* of every private Family" and "altogether unprecedented in the *English* Government." If passed, he warned, the measure would result in "general Discontent" as the people found it *"grievous"* and *"unconstitutional."* Despite the heat of his attack, Shirley did not simply veto the measure, as was his right. Rather, resorting to a complicated expedient, he announced an adjournment until October and requested that copies of the bill be sent to all Massachusetts towns during the summer for the citizens to express their considered judgment upon it in town meeting. If the legislators should pass the measure once more upon reconvening in October after fully informing themselves of the sentiments of their constituents, he concluded, "I shall think my self more at Liberty to pass it."[18] Receiving this curious message the Assembly ordered the bill circulated among the various towns and stood adjourned until October.

Governor Shirley had thus provided a four month period during which opponents of the excise revision could mount their campaign. Yet he washed his hands of any direct responsibility for the final defeat of the popular measure by his tacit promise to sign it into law if it were passed again in October. His message, carefully treading between conflicting factions, suggests the action of a man drawn by mutually contradictory obligations and interests. This is, indeed, the case. In 1741 Shirley had unseated Governor Jonathan Belcher after a struggle involving a tangle

---

[17] June 15 and 17, 1754, *ibid.*, 43, 45-47.
[18] *Ibid.*, 45-47.

of issues including New Hampshire timber rights, resentment over the British invalidation of the Land Bank, British patronage, and personal intrigue.[19] The significant fact is that without the support of a number of key merchants such as Elisha Cooke, Charles Apthorp, Benning Wentworth, Peter Faneuil, and especially Samuel Waldo, Shirley's campaign for the governorship would have been fatally weakened. Recognition of this fact had led him very nearly to mortage his political future to them. In 1739, writing to Waldo (who was then in London), Shirley, promising money to help finance the anti-Belcher campaign, had added: "I do assure you, I think you entitled to all the possible good Consequences of it [the governorship] . . . having ever exerted from the first knowledge of me an open, disinterested and sincere Friendship for me; And the pleasure which I shall ever take in making you returns of Friendship will be a sufficient recompence to me for any Service I can do for you."[20] The names Wentworth, Apthorp, Hancock, Faneuil, Waldo, and Cooke all appear on the anti-excise petition of 1755. The Boston merchants in the forefront of the opposition to the excise revision had strong, not to say overriding, claims upon William Shirley.

Yet the Governor also had powerful reasons for wishing to remain in the good graces of the General Court. There was, of course, the perennial quarrel over the Chief Executive's salary, but Shirley's ambitions encompassed more than just drawing a salary for amiable inactivity: he had military dreams. In 1745, after the successful Louisbourg expedition, he had received warm popular acclaim as welcome as it was unusual for colonial governors, and now in 1754 when conflict with the French was entering a new active phase, opportunities for further glory emerged. This "lifelong 'tory imperialist' "[21] was full of plans for expeditions—to Crown Point, Fort Beauséjour, Fort Niagara, Fort Frontenac. But such ventures depended upon the willingness of the people of Massachusetts, as voiced in the General Court, to vote necessary funds and muster colonial regiments. The Assembly, moreover, was showing signs of balking, hoping to shift the economic burden to London, and all Shirley's political acumen was needed.[22]

[19] Wood, *Shirley*, 63-89; John A. Schutz, "Succession Politics in Massachusetts, 1730-1741," *William and Mary Quarterly*, 3d Ser., XV (1958), 508-520, esp. 515-516.
[20] Shirley to Waldo, Apr. 15, 1739, in "Document: William Shirley to Samuel Waldo," *American Historical Review*, XXXVI (1930-31), 351.
[21] Fairchild, *Pepperrell*, 171.
[22] Thomas Hutchinson, *The History of the Province of Massachusetts Bay* (London, 1828), III, 29.

Thus, with the merchants opposing the excise revision and the Assembly strongly backing it, Shirley was indeed in a delicate position, and his solution, that of giving some encouragement and support to each side, follows the classic course of the ambitious man caught between two hostile interest groups: he avoided total identification with either group, tried to maintain the good will of each, and kept his personal goals firmly in the fore.

The merchants demonstrated their gratitude to the Governor for his delaying action by arranging for his portrait to be hung in Faneuil Hall,[23] and then quickly proceeded to organize a campaign against the proposed tax revision. The magnitude of their task was apparent in the lopsided vote by which the measure had been approved in the General Court. It would indeed require a major effort to defeat a proposal that had such wide support. Strong and persuasive issues were needed to divert attention from the obvious inequities the proposed revision was designed to correct and focus it rather on supposed evils inherent in the scheme. But what evils? As opponents of the measure pondered this problem their thoughts turned to Great Britain and a well-known occasion when the merchant gentlemen of London had faced, and successfully overcome, a very similar challenge.

In 1731, the ministry of Sir Robert Walpole, in an effort to quiet the grumbling of the landed gentry, had cut the land tax by one half. In 1733, to compensate for this lost revenue, Walpole proposed that an excise be imposed upon wine and tobacco, with a concomitant reduction in the import duties on these commodities, since these duties were being avoided by wholesale smuggling. Walpole's plan had much to recommend it. Rather than requiring payment upon landing, as did the import law, it would have allowed merchants to store their wine and tobacco imports in bonded warehouses and pay the excise only when the products were actually sold. It has been argued that the proposal would not only have secured an additional £500,000 in revenue lost through smuggling but that the free warehousing proposal would also have in effect made London a free port for those commodities and a center of the world market.[24]

---

[23] *A Report of the Record Commissioners of the City of Boston Containing the Boston Town Records, 1742 to 1757* (Boston, 1885), 261.
[24] W. E. H. Lecky, *A History of England in the Eighteenth Century*, 3d ed., I (London, 1883), 331; Arthur L. Cross, *A Shorter History of England and Greater Britain* (New York, 1920), 477.

96

The apparent wisdom of the plan notwithstanding, the merchants of London, many of whom had been evading the less closely regulated import duties, saw it as a threat and opposed it "almost to a man."[25] Despite an initial parliamentary majority, Walpole had withdrawn his proposal in the face of violent opposition. The whole episode had been interpreted by Londoners and the nation as a great political victory for the London merchant interests. A typical broadside published after Walpole's surrender was entitled "The London Merchants Triumphant" and a ballad reviewing the event was dedicated to "the Courage and Loyalty of the Citizens of LONDON."[26]

News of the 1733 incident had doubtless been followed closely by the Massachusetts merchants, as was all news from Great Britain. In 1754 the earlier London controversy, and the extensive literature it had generated, suddenly took on renewed interest. The lead article in an August 1754 issue of the *Boston Evening-Post* was a verbatim reprint of an article in a December 1733 issue of *The London Magazine*.[27] Alexander Pope's famous jibe at the 1733 excise proposal, "Shortly no lad shall chuck [play ball] or lady vole [play cards], But some excising courtier will have toll,"[28] began to be quoted in Boston. Admiring references to the London of 1733 were made. "The City of *London*, as it was first in the Opposition to [Walpole's excise] so first began the Triumph at its Overthrow," writes the schoolmaster John Lovell, after recounting the story of 1733 in a pamphlet, while another author speaks of the "patriotick Struggles" of the anti-excise leaders of 1733.[29] The obvious, if not wholly valid, analogy was soon made: the excise facing Boston in 1754 was simply

97

---

[25] William T. Laprade, *Public Opinion and Politics in Eighteenth Century England to the Fall of Walpole* (New York, 1936), 342. The chief pamphleteer and Parliamentary spokesman for the anti-excise forces was Walpole's great political enemy, William Pulteney. See Principal A. W. Ward in *DNB* s.v. "Pulteney, William."

[26] *The London Merchants Triumphant (or Sturdy Beggars are Brave Fellows) being a sketch of the rejoyceings in the citty, etc. occasioned by the excize bill being postponed* (London, 1733). A copy of this broadside is interleaved between pages 404 and 405 of Vol. II of the special edition of William Coxe, *Memoirs of the Life and Administration of Sir Robert Walpole, Earl of Orford*, 3 vols. (London, 1798) in Houghton Library; *The Sturdy Beggars, A New Ballad Opera* (London, 1733), iv.

[27] *Boston Evening-Post*, Aug. 19, 1754.

[28] *The Works of Alexander Pope*, new ed., III (London, 1881), 438. Quoted in Samuel Cooper, *The Crisis* (Boston, 1754), 5.

[29] John Lovell, *Freedom the First of Blessings* (Boston, 1754), 2; Cooper, *The Crisis*, 4.

another outcropping of that rural insolence toward urban mercantile activities which the Londoners had faced and vanquished in 1733. Walpole's excise "was but a Bawble in Comparison of that now in Question among us," they concluded.[30]

Still, the problem of *how* to duplicate the earlier successful anti-excise campaign remained, and as the opponents of the scheme cast about for the specific means of generating the desired reversal of public opinion, the experience of the Londoners in 1733 again was instructive.

The spokesmen for the London merchants had aroused mass opposition to the proposal by the shrewd circulation of popular pamphlets, broadsides, and ballads which ridiculed the proposed tax and carefully avoided the major issue, which was the flagrant smuggling under the then-existing system. In the words of Walpole's biographer, William Coxe, these pamphlets and ballads "delineated such a hideous picture of the EXCISE, as raised among the people the most terrible apprehensions." "When we called for an *Argument,* they repeated *a Song,* and to enforce this produced *a Picture,*" sourly observed one ministerial writer. As a result, "while he still had a small though decreasing majority for his bill, Walpole, yielding to the popular clamor, quietly withdrew it; for he regarded it as impolitic to cross the will of the people, even for their good."[31]

With these events in mind, the Massachusetts opponents of the excise proposal launched their own pamphlet campaign, hoping they too could arouse such a popular outcry that the Assembly would be forced to back down. Governor Shirley had provided the opportunity,[32] and the printers of Boston (doubtless aware that at the peak of the 1733 campaign the principal anti-excise organ, *The Craftsman,* had sold an estimated twelve thousand copies weekly)[33] were eager to co-operate. Anti-excise pamphlets

[30] Lovell, *Freedom,* 2.

[31] Coxe, *Walpole,* II, 378; [Horatio Walpole], THE RISE AND FALL *of the late Projected* EXCISE, *Impartially Consider'd* . . . (London, 1733), 23; Cross, *England,* 477.

[32] It seems a likely possibility that Shirley had the 1733 episode in mind when he acted as he did in 1754. Both his father and his father-in-law had been London merchants while he himself was a London barrister in the period immediately preceding the 1733 incident. Though his coming to Boston in 1731 precluded his direct participation in the London struggle he was doubtless thoroughly familiar with it, and all ties of family and profession would suggest opposition to Walpole. Wood, *Shirley,* chap. 1.

[33] Laprade, *Public Opinion,* 335. *The Craftsman* (London) was founded in 1726 by William Pulteney. Lecky, *England in the Eighteenth Century,* I, 375.

were soon rolling from the presses. The brief titles of eleven extant pamphlets, in the approximate order of their publication from June 1754 to around May 1755, are as follows: *The Crisis; The Monster of Monsters ...; The Voice of the People; A Plea for the Poor and Distressed ...; Freedom, the First of Blessings; Some Observations on the [Excise] Bill ...; A Letter from a Gentleman to His Friend ...; The Relapse; The Cub New-Lick'd ...; The Eclipse;* and *The Review.* The only two acknowledged authors are the Reverend Mr. Samuel Cooper of the merchant-oriented Brattle Square Church of Boston, who wrote *The Crisis,* and John Lovell, master of a Boston grammar school and a member of the Brattle Square Church, who wrote *Freedom, the First of Blessings.* Authorship of the most celebrated of the pamphlets, *The Monster of Monsters,* is uncertain. The Boston merchant Royall Tyler was subsequently accused by the Massachusetts General Court of having written it, but other names have been suggested.[34] As for the other eight pamphlets, the passage of two centuries has only deepened the anonymity their authors preferred.

That the propagandists of 1754 should have turned with such a vengeance to the pamphleteering tactics which had succeeded in 1733 is not in itself remarkable. The eighteenth was the century of pamphlets par excellence, and every controversy spawned its quota of evanescent scribblers. What is striking, however, is the manner in which the substance of the 1754 pamphlets, in broad outline and minute detail, closely parallels that of the 1733 efforts. In the response to criticism, in the arguments promulgated, and even in the images, metaphors, and slogans employed, these similarities repeatedly emerge.

The accusation that the anti-excise forces had ulterior motives was a common one in 1733 and 1754, and the arguments replying to these accusations in 1754 were reminiscent of the earlier responses. In 1733 the Walpole forces had repeatedly charged that their proposal was opposed

---

[34] Isaiah Thomas (1749-1831) who grew up in the home of Zechariah Fowle, brother of the printer of *The Monster of Monsters,* later wrote that the manuscript had been given to Zechariah Fowle by "a number of gentlemen who were in opposition to the General Court." Charles Evans attributes it to Samuel Waterhouse as he is known to have used the "Thomas Thumb" pseudonym in later writings, but Evans also mentions three other men to whom it has been attributed. Isaiah Thomas, *The History of Printing in America* ... (American Antiquarian Society, *Transactions and Collections,* V [Albany, 1874]), I, 130, 133; Charles Evans, ed., *American Bibliography,* III (Chicago, 1905), 93.

solely by a small cabal of powerful merchants, primarily wine and tobacco smugglers who were fearful they would be forced to pay legitimate taxes that they had theretofore avoided. "The most part of the people concerned in those clamours did not speak their own sentiments," Walpole later charged bitterly in Parliament; "they were played by others like so many puppets: it was not the puppets that spoke, it was those behind the curtain that played them, and made them speak whatever they had a mind."[35] The London opposition had countered with the repeated assertion that the outcry was nationwide and arose from constitutional concerns rather than from an attempt to avoid legitimate taxation. *The Craftsman* averred that the opposition represented the view of *"a whole trading People"* and not of "any particular Body of Men" and, in a later issue, that the opponents of the measure "did not object to this project ... as an additional Tax upon *Trade,* but to the grievous Method of *collecting* it."[36]

Similarly in 1754 the proponents of the excise revision charged that the anti-excise outcry was simply the work of a knot of merchants evading their fair share of taxes. A writer in the *Boston Gazette* charged that the basis of opposition was the belief that "the Rich ought not to pay as well as the Poor"; and that "The lower Sort of People are but a Degree above Slavery." Another newspaper, the *Boston Evening-Post,* published a letter charging that the "Cry of Liberty" was no more than a smoke screen thrown up by the opposition to conceal their true interest which was "the saving their Money."[37] Realizing the weight of such charges, the excise opponents sought to portray their cause as a popular and spontaneous movement, just as their predecessors of 1733 had done. The excise is "universally the Subject of Censure" argued one pamphleteer, while another protested that "the Reasons of the Opposition are not confined to a *few,*—they are *general.*"[38] As they stressed the supposed colony-wide nature of the opposition, the pamphleteers, again paralleling the London dispute, vigorously asserted that their cause was wholly disinterested and involved no desire merely to avoid taxes. "I have not the least Objection to the Duties laid by this Bill," wrote one in words very similar to the

[35] Mar. 9, 1733, in *Parliamentary History of England, from the Earliest Period to the Year 1803* ... (London, 1806—), VIII, 1305.

[36] *The Craftsman,* X (Mar. 17, 1732/33), 181; XI (May 12, 1733), 21.

[37] *Boston Gazette, or, Weekly Advertiser,* Dec. 31, 1754; *Boston Evening-Post,* Oct. 21, 1754.

[38] Lovell, *Freedom,* 1; *Some Observations on the* [*Excise*] *Bill* . . . (Boston, 1754), 7.

1733 *Craftsman* article. "It is . . . this Method of collecting the Duties, so inconsistent with the *natural Rights* of every private Family, that I oppose."[39]

When they turned from refuting the accusations of their opponents to building a positive case against the excise revision, the 1754 pamphleteers continued to draw upon the literature of the 1733 dispute. In 1733 the cornerstone of the opposition case had been the charge that the excise proposal threatened personal liberty. Walpole in Parliament had been forced to defend his scheme against the charge that it was an infringe-ment of liberty; in the same debate an opponent of the excise declaimed, the supposed advantages of the excise "will be purchased at too dear a rate, if they are purchased at the expence of the liberty of the meanest of his Majesty's subjects."[40] A ballad circulated in 1733 had praised the opponents of the excise for their efforts to "Maintain English Rights, and our Liberties guard."[41] *The Craftsman* similarly denounced the proposal as "contrary to the *native Right of Englishmen*" because it would "dis-franchise every *freeborn Englishman*." After Walpole bowed before the storm *The Craftsman* noted with pleasure "that the *Spirit of Liberty* is not yet extinct in this Kingdom."[42] The issue of personal liberty was like-wise made the focus of the 1754 campaign, as the title of one pamphlet, *Freedom, the First of Blessings,* suggests. "[T]he most pernicious Attack upon *English Liberty* that ever was attempted," Lovell charged. "[T]he Extension of the E[xcis]e A[c]t will deprive us of Part of our Liberty," Cooper agreed.[43]

A companion to this argument was the plea that the memory of ancestors who fought for these threatened liberties not be desecrated. Re-calling the Glorious Revolution, one 1733 pamphlet says, "There was a publick Spirit in the Nation in those Days which was not to be tamed by Oppression," while a Member of Parliament declaimed, "There are some still alive, who bravely ventured their lives and fortunes in defence of the liberties of their country. . . . Let it never be said, that the sons of such men wantonly gave up those liberties for which their fathers had risked

101

[39] *Some Observations on the [Excise] Bill. . . ,* 4. See also, Cooper, *The Crisis,* 10-11, and Lovell, *Freedom,* 1, for statements of this argument.

[40] *Parliamentary History,* VIII, 1281, 1285.

[41] *London Merchants Triumphant,* broadside.

[42] *The Craftsman,* X (Nov. 4, 1732), 11; (Jan. 20, 1732/33), 116; (Apr. 21, 1733), 211. See also, *Observations Upon the Laws of Excise* (London [1733]), 16.

[43] Lovell, *Freedom,* 1; Cooper, *The Crisis,* 4.

so much."[44] The appeal to filial piety was picked up by the 1754 pamphleteers. "Where is that Spirit of Freedom that flamed in the Breasts of our Ancestors?" rhetorically asked one while another echoed earlier appeals when he asked, "And how can we bear that the fair Patrimony of Freedom should not descend as full and ample to our Children, as it was conveyed to us by our Fathers?"[45]

Another major object of attack in both anti-excise campaigns was the excise collector. The pamphleteers of 1733 had attempted to discredit the excise proposal by exaggerating the number of new excisemen it would require and luridly speculating on their probable rascalities. "Pert Rascal[s]" one pamphlet called them. "A standing army" added another. "Locusts" chimed in *The Craftsman*, adding elsewhere that the merchant would be at the mercy of excisemen "who are not his *Equals*, or *Neighbours*."[46] The Boston pamphleteers appropriated this line of attack with gusto and outdid their predecessors in heaping epithets upon the excise collectors: "Publicans," "little pestilent Creature," "dregs and scum," *"little dirty Fellow,"* "dirty miscreants," "the meanest and worst of the People," and *"Petty Understrappers* of authority" were some of the terms employed.[47]

In exploiting and exacerbating dislike of excisemen, the London pamphleteers had invented the bogey of the lecherous excise collector sullying the virtue of English womankind. This motif appears particularly in the ballads which were widely sold and sung by hawkers who catered to the tastes of street crowds. "An Excise Elegy" is a typical example:

> No new EXCISE
> With five hundred Eyes,
> Shall henceforth your Wives or your Daughters surprize;
> For if they had Licence to gage all your *Stocks*,
> May also pretend to gage under their Smocks.

And another, "BRITANNIA Excisa," described the dragon "Excise":

[44] *Observations Upon the Laws of Excise*, 22; *Parliamentary History*, VIII, 1297.

[45] *The Relapse* (Boston [1755]), 3; *The Eclipse* (Boston [1755]), 8.

[46] E. R. Turner, "The Excise Scheme of 1733," *English Historical Review*, XLII (1927), 53; *Parliamentary History*, VIII, 1289; *The Craftsman*, X (Nov. 4, 1732), 13.

[47] *The Relapse*, 2; *Some Observations on the [Excise] Bill*, 5; *The Voice of the People* (Boston, 1754), 3; *Boston Gazette, or, Weekly Advertiser*, July 16, 1754.

> Then sometimes he stoops
> To take up the Hoops
> Of your Daughters as well as your Barrels.[48]

Less poetically, but no less suggestively, the New England opponents of the 1754 excise picked up this theme and exploited it to the fullest. "The good Women of *New England*," warned one pamphleteer, "would do well to take Care ... for by the Bill I find Mr. *Exciseman* is to have the Examination of them too."[49] Another described a fanciful scene in which an evil exciseman throws an honest yeoman in jail and then basely suggests to the distraught wife that she barter her virtue for her husband's freedom. The story concludes in a flood of bathos: "The poor Woman, who always intended Honestly, and now had rather continue so than otherwise; yet, to prevent what she feared would be a worse Evil, consents or submits to sacrifice her Virtue to the letcherous Humour of a brawny Deputy-Exciseman."[50]

A final major argument (one which quite contradicted the claim that the excise bill was opposed by the whole population) was introduced in 1733 and reappears in 1754. At both times there was a veiled reminder of the economic power of the merchants and the danger of crossing their interests. In 1733 this was expressed in such comments as this in *The Craftsman:* "[W]ill not This [the excise proposal] look as if We intended to provoke Them [the merchants] by all possible Methods, to withdraw from us, and settle in those Countries where They can carry on their Traffick with more Freedom?"[51] In 1754 the argument is repeated in a sentence which reads as though the writer had *The Craftsman* open on his desk as he wrote. "Will it not have a Tendency to drive Persons of Stock and Reputation into other Governments, where they may enjoy the Fruits of their honest Industry, without these unsufferable[*sic*] Burdens?"[52] This threat, rather half-hearted in 1733, had a particularly ominous ring in 1754 because the support of the merchants was essential to the defense plans of Massachusetts. None could fail to catch the import of the warning in one Boston pamphlet that if the proposed excise be

103

---

[48] *An Excise Elegy: or, the Dragon Demolish'd, a New Ballad* (London, 1733), 5, Houghton Library; *Britannia Excisa: Britain Excis'd, a New BALLAD to be Sung in Time, and to Some Tune* (London, 1733), 6, Houghton Library.
[49] Lovell, *Freedom,* 3.
[50] *A Plea for the Poor and Distressed* ... (Boston, 1754), 13.
[51] *The Craftsman,* X (Nov. 4, 1732), 15.
[52] *The Voice of the People,* 4.

adopted "the Hearts of the People will fail . . . and they will not be willing *to Risque their Lives, or Fortunes*," or another which noted that "if any Thing in earnest is designed Against the *French*" an excise opposed by those "who are chiefly expected to exert themselves in such a Cause" ought not be contemplated.[53]

Perhaps the most striking evidence of the dependence of the Massachusetts propagandists upon their counterparts of an earlier day is the wholesale borrowing of the slogans, metaphors, and images of the 1733 campaign by the Boston pamphleteers. In 1733 one of the most common methods of influencing the popular mind had been to portray Walpole's excise as a monster. When Walpole defended his proposals in Parliament with the sarcastic comment, "this is the monster, the many headed monster, which was to devour the people,"[54] he referred to such ballads as "An Excise Elegy: or the Dragon Demolished" which describes the "Monster Excise" with a penchant for gobbling up little children, and "Brittania Excisa" which pictures on its cover a monster hitched to a chariot in which a rotund Walpole rides, hoarding a steady flow of gold coins that the monster generates from the wine, tobacco, and other products he devours as he lumbers along. A third ballad calls the excise bill "the ill-shaped Monster" while yet another contains the lines:

Saint GEORGE, as they say,
The DRAGON did slay,
But our *Kn[igh]t*, both *older* and *wiser*,
To keep us all *Quiet*,
Prescribes a LOW DIET,
And lets loose the *fell Dragon*, EXCISE, Sir.

In the British ballads the monster had "a *Sting* in his Tail," "sharp Claws," and an insatiable desire to "cram us into his wide Jaws."[55]

The monster image was enthusiastically appropriated by the Boston pamphleteers in 1754. Perhaps the most famous pamphlet to emerge from the American anti-excise campaign was *The Monster of Monsters*, an allegory in which the monster excise with "terrible *Claws*," a fearsome tail, and that old familiar urge to "cram his merciless and insatiable Maw

---

[53] *Some Observations on the [Excise] Bill*, 10; *The Eclipse*, 5.
[54] *Parliamentary History*, VIII, 1281.
[55] *An Excise Elegy*, 6; *Britannia Excisa*, 4; *The Sturdy Beggars*, vi; *The Congress of Excise-Asses* (London, 1733), 8.

with our very Blood, and Bones, and Vitals" terrifies the populace.[56] In
1733 the suggestion had been made that those who found the monster
appealing (i.e., those who supported Walpole's excise) were perversely
fascinated by the revolting. One ballad included the stanza:

> Behold here the Creature,
> Contemplate each Feature,
> And if you are charm'd with his Beauty
> Elect his false Tribe.

Similarly the 1754 allegory describes a group of ladies (the Massachusetts
General Court) who admit the monster to their presence and are "greatly
pleased with the Creature."[57]

105

The deceptive Trojan Horse had been another popular creature in
1733. "I cannot conclude better than by putting my readers in mind of
the Trojan Horse," said a writer in *The Craftsman* at the close of an
article on the excise.[58] In one of the ballads the excise monster was compared with the

> Great *Trojan* Horse, which contain'd in his Belly,
> Twice thirty-five *Greeks*, at the least, let me tell y'.[59]

In 1754 the Attic nag came galloping 'round the track once móre, though
with its martial innards considerably augmented: "The *Trojan Horse*,
when armed *Greeks* burst by Thousands from his Belly, did not cause
half so much Terror," says *The Monster of Monsters*.[60]

In 1733, the pamphleteers and balladeers had been almost embarrass-
ingly successful. Unruly crowds had besieged Parliament. Walpole himself had been mobbed and his protectors manhandled. When Walpole
withdrew the excise proposal because, as he told his ministers, "he would
not be the minister to enforce taxes, at the expence of blood," his decision
had been greeted with violent celebrations in London and other commercial towns. At the height of the controversy Walpole had been burned

[56] Thomas Thumb, *The Monster of Monsters* . . . (Boston, 1754), 19, 20.
[57] *Britannia Excisa*, 8; *The Monster of Monsters*, 4.
[58] *The Craftsman*, X (Jan. 27, 1732/33), 129.
[59] *An Excise Elegy*, 6. See also *The Congress of Excise-Asses*, 4.
[60] *The Monster of Monsters*, 16.

in effigy amid scenes of drunken disorder.[61] In fact, the pamphlet campaign had gotten out of hand. The good-humored, if somewhat ribald, tone of the ballads and pamphlets had given way to a more dangerous and incendiary note. "Burn him, burn him," screams a character in an anti-excise "ballad opera" when a Walpole effigy is brought on the scene; while a pamphlet called *The Vinter and Tobacconist's Advocate* says of Walpole's proposal: "I remember to have read of some state, wherein it was the custom that if any one should propose a new law, he must do it with a rope about his neck, that in case it were judged prejudicial, he might very fairly be hanged up for his pains without further ceremony. I heartily wish that law had been in force amongst us."[62] Even the more restrained *Craftsman* had warned Walpole to exercise more discretion in his proposals if he wished to sleep "without being haunted with continual Dreams of *Murder* and *Assassination*."[63]

With such things being bandied about, and such events taking place, *The Craftsman* and the anti-excise pamphleteers had come in for severe censure. Though William Pulteney, the anti-excise leader, professed to believe Walpole's fears were exaggerated and wrote blandly of the burnings in effigy that "this *imaginary Execution* . . . hath done Him no bodily Hurt. He rather comes more purifyed out of the Flames, like *Gold* seven Times tryed,"[64] the ministerial spokesmen did not take so lighthearted a view. Walpole charged in Parliament that the pamphleteers were "stirring up the people to mutiny and sedition," while others denounced the attacks upon him as a "deep laid scheme for assassination" and an effort to form "a Party of Ruffians to butcher the PRINCIPAL MINISTER."[65] This fearful reaction had gone beyond mere verbal denunciations. Richard Francklin, publisher of *The Craftsman*, was arrested on several different occasions and spent a period of time in prison.[66]

[61] Laprade, *Public Opinion*, 344; Cross, *England*, 477; Coxe, *Walpole*, II, 404.

[62] *The Sturdy Beggars*, 60; Lord Mahon [Philip Henry Stanhope], *History of England from the Peace of Utrecht to the Peace of Versailles, 1713-1783*, I (London, 1853), 251.

[63] *The Craftsman*, X (Apr. 21, 1733), 214.

[64] [William Pulteney], *A REVIEW OF THE EXCISE-SCHEME; In Answer to a PAMPHLET intitled "The Rise and Fall of the late projected EXCISE, impartially Considered"* (London, 1733), 52.

[65] *Parliamentary History*, VIII, 1269; Reginald R. Sharpe, *London and the Kingdom . . .*, III (London, 1895), 37; *REMARKS ON FOG'S Journal, of FEBRUARY 10, 1732/33. Exciting the PEOPLE to an ASSASSINATION* (London, 1733), 7.

[66] Laprade, *Public Opinion*, 295, 323, 326, 331.

Aware that events had taken this ominous turn in 1733, the Boston merchants of 1754 were careful to dissociate themselves from any suggestion of mob violence. A number of pamphlets, while urging the case against the excise, carefully warn against any resort to force or violence. "THE VOICE OF THE PEOPLE has been distinctly heard, not in rude Clamours, not in calumnious Invectives—not in outragious [sic] Declamations, but in the sober Strains of Reason and Argument," says one pamphlet, while another declares its "Detestation of *Mob* Principles."[67]

Despite the efforts of the Massachusetts pamphleteers to avoid the pitfalls of the 1733 campaign, however, the General Assembly saw the parallel clearly, and played its role accordingly. One of its first items of business upon reconvening in October was to order that a copy of *The Monster of Monsters* be burned by the common hangman and that Daniel Fowle, the printer, and Royall Tyler, the suspected author, be arrested. These men were interrogated in two acrimonious Assembly sessions and thrown into jail on the slim legal authority of writs signed by the Speaker.[68] The Assembly soon realized, however, that despite the many similarities, 1754 was not 1733. The violent, incendiary spirit which had so frightened Walpole had not been aroused in the Boston populace in 1754. Tyler was released somewhat sheepishly after two days with the officious demand that he be "forthcoming when required," but he was never required. Fowle was released after five days, apparently being detained that long only because the Assembly preferred to release him quietly at night while the printer demanded that his release come at a time when more of his friends could conveniently attend.[69] Fowle promptly instituted suit for £1,000. After prolonged litigation he was awarded £20 by the Superior Court in 1766 "on account of the sufferings mentioned."[70]

Soon after his release Fowle published a pamphlet, *A Total Eclipse of Liberty*, which describes his incarceration in lurid detail and compares his fate with that of Socrates and Saint Paul, among others.[71] In an "Appendix" to this work, published in 1756, Fowle used the legal irregularities of his imprisonment as the basis for a discussion of the nature and

[67] Cooper, *The Crisis*, 1; *The Voice of the People*, 8.
[68] October 24, 1754, in *House Journals*, XXXI, 63-64.
[69] Daniel Fowle, *A Total Eclipse of Liberty* . . . (Boston, 1755), 23-24.
[70] Clyde A. Duniway, *The Development of Freedom of the Press in Massachusetts* (New York, 1906), 117, 173.
[71] Fowle, *Total Eclipse*, 18, 24.

limitations of government, which in general follows John Locke. Despite his weakness for melodrama, Fowle's genuine concern about the issues he raised is apparent. He concluded his pamphlet movingly: "The Power of the People has a kind of Eternity with respect to Politick Duration: Parliaments may cease, but the People remain; for them they were originally made, by them they are continued and renewed, from them they receive their Power." [72]

The Monster of Monsters, Fowle's imprisonment, and his subsequent pamphlets are the best-known aspects of this entire excise controversy. Frequently historians have stressed the innocuous nature of *The Monster of Monsters* to heighten the sense of the injustice done to Fowle. "As harmless as any tea table conversations by old ladies," one has called it. [73] Yet, in 1754 *The Monster of Monsters* and the other pamphlets stirred frightening memories in the minds of the Assemblymen. When one understands what happened in London in 1733 the Assembly's actions in the Massachusetts struggle two decades later become more comprehensible.

While an awareness of the British precedent of the 1754 dispute is essential for a full understanding of it, one important distinction between the two episodes must be drawn. In 1733 the intellectual level of the pamphlets and ballads had seldom risen above that of a public brawl, and even *The Craftsman* had tended to substitute rhetoric for reason. Slogans and epithets had replaced sober analysis. This was also true of most of the Massachusetts pamphlets, with one important exception. *The Good of the Community Impartially Considered,* the only known pamphlet published in favor of the proposed excise revision, is a sober and closely reasoned document fifty pages long. The author styled himself "Rusticus," but the sophisticated level of argument indicates he was no simple son of the soil. *The Good of the Community,* in fact, deals in a somewhat attenuated form with a number of the constitutional and political issues which were soon to occupy the minds of a whole generation of Americans.

Rusticus pays scant attention to most of the arguments the pamphleteers had raised against the excise, dismissing them as designed only for

---

[72] Daniel Fowle, *An Appendix to the Late Total Eclipse of Liberty* . . . (Boston, 1756), 24.

[73] Samuel G. Drake, *The History and Antiquities of Boston* . . . (Boston, 1856), 635. See Leonard W. Levy, *Legacy of Suppression: Freedom of Speech and Press in Early American History* (Cambridge, Mass., 1960), 39-41, for a brief discussion of Fowle's imprisonment.

"terrifying the weak and unthinking Part of the Community."[74] However, the anti-excise argument that the provision for a personal report of liquor consumption was contrary to natural rights leads him to assert that in fact there is no appeal from within an organized society to natural rights unless one is willing to return to a state of nature, which to Rusticus means simply anarchy. The very idea of society assumes as a corollary that certain natural rights have been forever forsworn. As to the crucial question *which* natural rights must be abandoned for the well-being of a specific society, this is left by Rusticus wholly to the majority will as expressed through designated representatives. "[T]hose intrusted with the Power of making Laws, are to be Judges of what Laws are necessary for the Good of the Community," he flatly declares.[75] Thus, in ruling out appeals either to a state of nature antedating society or to any source within society beyond majoritarianism, Rusticus has built a logically tight argument making the acceptance of all laws, even unpleasant excises, mandatory and automatic.

At this point his argument is theoretically complete, but Rusticus cannot resist showing *why* a consumption tax on imported goods is a legitimate and valuable tax for society to levy. He uses as his point of departure the argument raised by some anti-excise forces that if imported wine and rum are excised, home brewed beer and cider (consumed widely in those rural areas dominant in the Assembly) should likewise be taxed. Rusticus attacks this argument by postulating that the first object of society, once the anarchistic state of nature is abandoned, is to secure itself from external invasion. This is done by maintaining a favorable military power balance in relation to other societies. For military power, wealth is necessary. The accumulation of wealth in a trading country demands that more goods be exported than are imported. All consumption of imported goods decreases the "trading stock" of a state, thus reducing its wealth, thus reducing its capacity for military strength, thus making its power balance less favorable, thus rendering it more liable to invasion, thus defeating the first object of society. Hence, after this labored demonstration, Rusticus again reaches the predictable conclusion that the proposed excise is justified and valuable.[76]

Rusticus's rejection of natural rights as a valid arbiter of political dis-

[74] Rusticus, *Good of the Community*, 46.
[75] *Ibid.*, 32, 33.
[76] *Ibid.*, 33-35, 9-12.

putes suggests the position later taken by reluctant revolutionaries such as John Dickinson who based their opposition to the British revenue measures on the colonists' rights as *British subjects* and recoiled from the appeal to nature embodied in the Declaration of Independence, fearing that such drastic tampering with the established body politic would shatter the foundation of society. Similarly, Rusticus's elevation of majoritarianism as the sole means of legitimatizing political action reveals how the American experience was being translated into constitutional theories that would cause such difficulties for Madison, Jefferson, Adams, and others as they wrestled with the problem of faction and the means whereby the general welfare could be determined. The fact that Rusticus proceeds to introduce arguments based on the "good of the community" suggests that he himself was aware that pure and simple majoritarianism leaves something to be desired. Rusticus here emerges as the proponent of a strong, activist government working in a positive way for the general welfare of the state, with a stress on economic development and military power: in short, a proto-Hamiltonian. Thus a controversy which in many respects harked back to events, slogans, and arguments of the past, did generate one pamphlet which anticipated a number of the important issues of the years which lay ahead.

The concluding phases of the dispute may be briefly told. The pamphleteers had sought to bring about the popular rejection of the excise revision in the informal town-meeting referendum Governor Shirley had called for. This objective, however, was not achieved. A check of town records, histories, and other sources has revealed the way twenty-one Massachusetts towns voted on the proposed revision. Sixteen voted against the measure and five supported it. On the face of it, this would appear to be a preponderant opposition vindicating the pamphleteers' efforts; but of the sixteen towns opposing the measure all but two (Lunenburg and Stoughton) were coastal and commercial towns, and their negative vote simply represents a further extension of the mercantile opposition centered in Boston. All five of the towns which supported the proposal were away from the coast.[77] As for the other inland towns whose votes

[77] Towns opposing the excise proposal: Amesbury, Newbury, Ipswich, Lunenburg, Gloucester, Salem, Marblehead, Medford, Boston, Dorchester, Braintree, Weymouth, Stoughton, Plymouth, Eastham, Nantucket. Towns supporting the proposal: Hardwick, Lancaster, Weston, Watertown, Cambridge. Mass. Archives, CXIX, foll. 674, 675, 675a; *Boston Gazette, or, Weekly Advertiser,* July 9, Aug. 20, Sept. 17,

are not recorded, a writer in the *Boston Gazette* sensibly concluded in December 1754 that a majority of the towns supported the excise bill "if we take for granted, as in all Reason we ought, that those Towns were for the Bill that would not so much as meet upon it."[78]

The opposition forces had, in fact, fought a losing battle. They did not persuade the citizenry that Massachusetts's freedom was threatened by the excise, that New England womankind was in danger, or that the merchants would stage a mass exodus if the excise passed into law. They had, in short, failed to repeat the success of their London mentors. The dragons and monsters which had such a popular success in 1733 suffered a sharp diminution of vigor in the Atlantic crossing. When the Assembly reconvened it refused even to receive the resolutions passed by the various coastal towns, and on December 19, 1754, the excise measure, substantially the same as the June version, was passed once more.[79] The Council approved and Governor Shirley promptly signed the excise proposal into law, as he had indicated he would.

Now only a final expedient, one which had not been available to the Londoners of 1733, remained for the opponents of the new law: an appeal to England. On December 30 a group of merchants submitted a petition to the Boston Selectmen calling for a town meeting, which was promptly scheduled for three days later.[80] At this meeting, January 3, 1755, John Phillips, Esq., was in the chair. After "some debate" the meeting voted unanimously to appoint the London merchant Christopher Kilby to "Use his utmost Endeavours to prevent said Acts obtaining the Royal Assent."[81]

111

1754; Joseph Merrill, *History of Amesbury* . . . (Haverhill, 1880), 220; Samuel A. Bates, ed., *Records of the Town of Braintree, 1640 to 1793* (Randolph, 1886), 336-337; Lucius R. Paige, *History of Hardwick, Massachusetts* . . . (Boston, 1883), 47; Abijah P. Marvin, *History of the Town of Lancaster, Massachusetts* . . . (Lancaster, 1879), 266; *The Early Records of the Town of Lunenburg, Massachusetts* . . . (Fitchburg, 1896), 166; Samuel Roads, *The History and Traditions of Marblehead* (Boston, 1880), 63; Alexander Starbuck, *History of Nantucket* . . . (Boston, 1924), 107; Joshua Coffin, *A Sketch of the History of Newbury, Newburyport and West Newbury, from 1635 to 1845* (Boston, 1845), 221; *Records of the Town of Plymouth*, III (Plymouth, 1903), 64; Joseph B. Felt, *The Annals of Salem* . . . (Salem, 1827), 444; *Watertown Records Comprising the Fifth Book of the Town Proceedings 1745 to 1769 and the Sixth Book of Town Proceedings 1769 to 1792* (Newton, 1928), 147.

[78] *Boston Gazette, or, Weekly Advertiser*, Dec. 31, 1754.

[79] *House Journals*, XXXI, 160.

[80] *A Report of the Record Commissioners of the City of Boston Containing the Selectmen's Minutes from 1754 through 1763* (Boston, 1887), 17.

[81] *Boston Town Records, 1742-1757*, 265. Furthermore, the town meeting made

While the Bostonians were thus organizing their campaign for a royal disallowance, however, the Assembly did not remain inactive. On December 28 it voted that a letter be sent to Bollan providing him with ammunition with which to defend the excise proposal before the Board of Trade.[82]

On June 17, 1755, the great confrontation before the Board of Trade finally took place. Kilby spoke first, raising "sixteen different Objections to the Act, stating them so briefly as scarce to allow time sufficient to take the shortest notes of them." Bollan then responded, "fully considering and answering every Point in the best manner that I could." Bollan's remarks concluded, Kilby "said very little, upon the reply, and in Effect gave up the matter."[83] Bollan's arguments prevailed, and on August 12 a formal proclamation was sent to Massachusetts by the Board of Trade stating that the excise measure had been examined and found acceptable.[84]

Thus, over a year after the struggle had begun, the opponents of the excise proposal were finally defeated in their persistent and resourceful attempts to defeat a measure favored by a majority of the province. An examination of the pamphlet campaign of 1754 reveals the crucial role the British excise controversy of 1733 played in the formulation of the terms of the 1754 dispute, and demonstrates once more in what varied ways the intellectual bond linking America and Great Britain in the colonial period could make its presence manifest.

Kilby's appointment permanent: "Said Christopher Kilby . . . hereby is appointed Agent for the Town . . . to Conduct himself according to such directions and Instructions as he may from time to time receive from the Town. . . ." This appointment, growing out of the excise controversy, meant that the nominal agent for Massachusetts, William Bollan, now in fact represented only the dominant agrarian interest in the General Court, while Kilby spoke with equal if not more weight as agent for the Boston merchants. Kilby was a transplanted Bostonian who in 1754 was in London engaged in the American trade. His American associate and close friend Thomas Hancock had been seeking for some time Kilby's selection as Massachusetts's agent in London and used the excise dispute as a means of furthering this goal. Thomas Hancock to Kilby, Jan. 16, 1755, Hancock Papers, TH-4, Baker Library, Harvard Business School.

[82] *House Journals*, XXXI, 185.

[83] William Bollan to the Speaker of the Massachusetts House of Representatives, Aug. 18, 1755, Mass. Archives, XXI, fol. 324. This is Bollan's own version of the meeting and doubtless puts his own performance in the best possible light.

[84] *Ibid.*, fol. 314.

Notes and Documents

The Colonists Discover America:
Attention Patterns in the Colonial Press, 1735-1775

Richard L. Merritt *

THE extent to which the eighteenth-century American colonists comprised an integrated political community, that is, one based on a high degree of mutual contacts together with expectations of peaceful relations among its members, is a moot point among historians and political scientists. On the one hand writers such as Evarts Boutell Greene, John C. Ranney, and Kenneth Wheare have suggested that the colonies, prior to their unification, were separate communities, more interested in their connections to the Mother Country than in intercolonial affairs.[1] On the other hand James Truslow Adams, Charles M. Andrews, Oscar Handlin, Michael Kraus, and others have argued that the steady growth of intercolonial contacts led to a sense of political community among the colonists long before the outbreak of the Revolution.[2] Most students of the colonial era are, to be sure, somewhere between these two positions, often pointing to specific events, such as the War of Jenkins' Ear, the French and Indian

* Mr. Merritt is a member of the Department of Political Science and Director of the Political Science Research Library, Yale University.

[1] See, for example, Evarts Boutell Greene, *The Revolutionary Generation, 1763-1790* (New York, 1943); John C. Ranney, "The Bases of American Federalism," *William and Mary Quarterly*, 3d Ser., III (1946), 1-35; and Kenneth C. Wheare, "Federalism and the Making of Nations," in Arthur W. Macmahon, ed., *Federalism, Mature and Emergent* (Garden City, New York, 1955), 28-43.

[2] See James Truslow Adams, *The March of Democracy: The Rise of the Union* (New York and London, 1932); Charles M. Andrews, "The American Revolution: An Interpretation," *American Historical Review*, XXXI (1925-26), 219-232; Oscar Handlin, *This was America: True Accounts of People and Places, Manners and Customs, as Recorded by European Travelers to the Western Shore in the Eighteenth, Nineteenth and Twentieth Centuries* (Cambridge, Mass., 1949); and Michael Kraus, *Intercolonial Aspects of American Culture on the Eve of the Revolution, With Special Reference to the Northern Towns* (New York, 1928).

War, or the Stamp Act crisis, as the main source producing an awareness
of common bonds among the colonists.[3]

In this essay I should like to consider one of the most essential features
of the process by which political communities are formed out of separate
entities: the emergence of communication or attention patterns focusing
upon the community, that is, the growth of community self-awareness.
In one sense self-awareness is a quantitative concept. Over a certain period
of time a member or potential member of a community devotes more, less,
or about the same amount of its attention to other members or to the
community as a whole. In another sense, however, self-awareness is a
qualitative concept. That American statesmen and writers discuss the
Soviet Union more now than they did during the 1930's is by no means
an indication that the two countries are drawing closer together into some
form of political community. Equally important in the process of com-
munity-building is a high ratio of rewarding or mutually beneficial transactions to the total number of transactions. When the individual colonies
threw their spotlights of attention upon one another, did they like what
they saw? Did the Southerners, for example, perceive the New Englanders
as "the Goths and Vandals of America," as did the loyalist Jonathan
Boucher?[4] Or were they more captivated by the view of the Northerners
as brethren oppressed by the redcoats stationed in Boston? Did the image
that the colonists had of each other become more or less friendly as the
colonial years passed? How favorable were intercolonial attention patterns
as opposed to those between the colonies and Great Britain?

Although I shall have something to say about the qualitative side of
colonial self-attention patterns, I shall concentrate upon the quantitative
aspects. To what extent were the colonists aware of or interested in places
and events American during the pre-Revolutionary decades? How did
their patterns of attention change during these years? Did attention paid
to the Mother Country increase or decline relative to that devoted to
America?

In attempting to answer such questions I analyzed the focus of attention of one of the more popular and enduring communication media in
colonial America, the newspapers. These journals, I would suggest, shared

[3] See Albert Harkness, Jr., "Americanism and Jenkins' Ear," *Mississippi Valley
Historical Review*, XXXVII (1950-51), 61-90; Carl Lotus Becker, *Beginnings of the
American People* (Boston, 1915); and Allan Nevins, *The American States During
and After the Revolution, 1775-1789* (New York, 1924).

[4] Jonathan Boucher, *Reminiscences of an American Loyalist, 1738-1789* . . . (Boston, 1925), 132-133; cited in Max Savelle, *Seeds of Liberty: The Genesis of the
American Mind* (New York, 1948), 563-564.

and to a large measure helped to shape the images and attention patterns of the politically relevant strata of colonial society.[5] Systematically examining the news columns of four randomly selected issues per year of newspapers from each of five colonial population centers—Boston, New York, Philadelphia, Williamsburg, and Charleston in South Carolina—I counted each appearance of place-name symbols (such as "Boston," "the Carolinas," "Warwickshire," "Europe," or other names of actual places) during the forty-one years from 1735 to 1775.[6] I then categorized these place-name symbols into three broad groups: American symbols, comprising references to the area that later became the United States of America; British symbols, including the British possessions of Minorca and Gibraltar in Europe as well as the British Isles; and other symbols, consisting in Canadian, Caribbean, South American, European, Asian, and African place names.

115

This essay will concentrate upon three aspects of the quantitative distribution of place-name symbols in the colonial press. First of all, by finding the average attention pattern of the newspapers from the five towns,[7] we may analyze changes in the composite picture of the colonial focus of attention. Second, to determine which colonies led in focusing attention upon American events, we may consider the five sets of newspapers separately, to see how they differed from the average or composite attention patterns. Finally, since it turned out that the five-year period from 1762 to 1766 was extremely significant in terms of the growth of attention paid to American symbols, we may examine symbol usage during those years somewhat more closely.

[5] See Richard L. Merritt, "Public Opinion in Colonial America: Content Analyzing the Colonial Press," *Public Opinion Quarterly*, XXVII (1963), 356-371.

[6] The newspapers were: *The Boston News-Letter* (issues from 1735 to 1775) and *The Boston-Gazette, and Country Journal* (1762-75); *The New-York Weekly Journal* (1735-51) and *The New-York Mercury* (1752-75); *The Pennsylvania Gazette* (1735-75); the various *Virginia Gazettes* (under William Parks from 1736 to 1750, and under William Hunter and his successors from 1751 to 1775); and *The South-Carolina Gazette* (1735-75). On the use of content analysis in historical research, as well as for more details on the research design of the present project, see Richard L. Merritt, *The Growth of American Community, 1735-1775* (New Haven: Yale University Press, forthcoming).

[7] This is found by dividing the total number of symbols in each category by the total number of symbols in all categories appearing each year in all of the newspapers together. Thus the composite is the mean of the actual occurrence of symbols rather than the mean of the percentage distributions for each newspaper. The symbol distribution of the *Boston Gazette* will not be included in the composite picture, since the analysis of that newspaper covered but 14 years, from 1762 to 1775; its symbol distribution is sufficiently different from the others that its inclusion for 14 of the 41 years would distort the composite picture of the colonial newspapers.

I

At a first glance a curve representing the composite percentage distribution of place-name symbols in the colonial press (Figure 1) seems to show

FIGURE 1

THE FOCUS OF ATTENTION OF THE COLONIAL PRESS, 1735-1775
Composite Percentage Distribution of Place-Name Symbols by Year

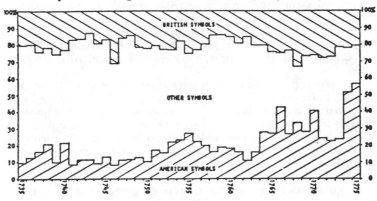

116

a high degree of correlation between levels of interest in America on the one hand and, on the other, some of the more spectacular events of the colonial era. Except for two peak years in 1738 and 1740 (the latter of which corresponds to a critical year in the War of Jenkins' Ear), the curve remained low until the outbreak of the French and Indian War in 1754. The highest point of the ensuing cycle occurred in the year of Braddock's defeat, 1755. In the next years, as the scene of battle in North America began to shift from American to Canadian fields, the percentage share of American symbols dropped off by more than 60 per cent. The period from 1764 to 1766, which encompassed the announcement, enactment, and repeal of the Stamp Act, was one of heightened attention paid by the newspapers to colonial events; for the first time they devoted more than one third of their symbol space to American symbols. The next decade saw three more peak years in the curve representing interest in colonial events: 1768, when opposition to the Townshend Acts was mounting; 1770, the year of the Boston Massacre; and 1774-75, the tension-filled years of the Intolerable Acts, the First Continental Congress, the Association, and the Second Continental Congress. In these latter two years the news-papers devoted over one half of their symbol space to American events.

A similar if not so marked pattern occurred in the distribution of British symbols. The high points of the two rather shallow cycles of the twenty-five years prior to 1760 appeared in 1739 and 1755—the early years of the War of Jenkins' Ear and of the French and Indian War respectively—while the troughs, from 1743 to 1748 (with the exception of the year 1746) and from 1758 to 1760, were time periods coincidental with the intensively European phases of the War of the Austrian Succession and the Seven Years' War. In the year 1746, the most noticeable aberration from the trend of shallow cycles, the Royal Army defeated the Pretender's forces at Culloden, ending the Second Jacobite Rebellion. In 1759 began another cycle that reached its peak in 1768 before dropping off to a level not too different from that of the 1730's and 1740's.

117

There is another aspect of the total picture, however, one tempering the conclusion that the focus of attention in the colonial press changed solely in response to single, spectacular events. A consideration of just the American share of the total symbol count reveals three interesting points.

First, the essentially cyclical pattern representing the emphasis upon American symbols in the colonial press, with its low points in 1735 (or earlier), 1744-46, 1762, and 1772, and its peaks in 1740, 1755, 1766, and 1775 (or possibly later), appears in sharp relief. I have already noted that the peaks in the curves were years of important and dramatic events in colonial history. It is probably not accidental, nor is it particularly sur-prising, that the newspapers gave heavy emphasis to American symbols during those years. More significant are the first years of increasing atten-tion to America—1747, 1763, and 1773—following troughs in the cycles. What was it during those years that arrested a declining interest in Ameri-can events, sending the curve upwards? We might also ask why the curves dropped off sharply immediately after the spectacular events of the peak years.

Second, the cycles of attention to American symbols became progres-sively shorter over time. A time span of fifteen years divided the first two peaks, eleven years passed between 1755 and 1766, and nine years between the latter date and 1775. A similar pattern marked the cycles' visibly low points of 1744-46, 1762, and 1772.

Third, and related to the ever shorter cycles, the general trend of the curve was upwards. This can be easily seen by drawing a line connecting the peaks of the cycles, or even their low points. The low year of 1762 was on a plane higher than the previous low period of 1744-46, while the lowest point of the next cycle, 1772, was on an even higher level. In the period from 1764 to 1775 there were but three years in which the American share of the symbol distribution dropped to a plane slightly below the 1755 peak. During only six of the twenty-nine years from 1735 to 1763 did American self-awareness reach the 20 per cent level; afterwards it never fell below that level.[8] In a metaphorical sense, the trend toward shorter and higher cycles is similar to an automobile's motor being started on a cold day: with each new contact the motor is more responsive and turns over more quickly, until finally it begins to run smoothly. The data found in the present inquiry suggest that the cycles of increasing and decreasing interest in American events had turned into a smooth pattern of self-awareness and self-interest by 1774.

There is still another point of importance in the distribution of the broad categories of symbols: the ratio of American to British symbols. As may be seen in Figure 1, attention to British symbols fluctuated around the 20 per cent level during the entire forty-one years. From 1735 to 1753 there was not a single year in which the number of American symbols was greater than the number of British symbols. The ten years of the French and Indian War (1754-63) comprised a transitional period, during which American symbols appeared more often in the colonial press than did British symbols one half of the time. Only three times during the next twelve years did British symbols take precedence over American symbols; and by 1775 there were almost three American symbols for each British. British and American symbols combined accounted for roughly one out of every three (34.9 per cent) symbols in the colonial newspapers from 1735 to 1763. In the twelve years after 1763 one out of three (34.0 per cent) was American. Thus, by the time of the decade prior to the Revolution, it might be said that the American political community alone had taken over the space in the colonial press previously allocated to the entire Anglo-American community.

II

Curves representing the American share of the total symbol count are roughly similar for each of the newspapers included in the analysis. This is not to say that the curves are identical in all respects, or even that they

[8] On the basis of these data, some interesting (although a posteriori) parabolic curves could be constructed, showing the progressively shorter and steadily rising cycles. For future studies of the pre-Revolutionary era in America, such curves showing the rise of American community sentiments might be projected and tested. These data, if verified through additional empirical tests, would seem to contradict the theory of revolution proposed by James C. Davies, "Toward a Theory of Revolution," *American Sociological Review*, XXVII (1962), 5-19.

118

are on the same level. The American share of symbols in the *Massachusetts Gazette*, for example, was above the average or composite distribution curve 90 per cent of the time—in twenty-five of the first twenty-nine years, and in each of the last twelve years of the period. The *South-Carolina Gazette* paid a greater than average amount of attention to America about one half (51.7 per cent) of the time between 1735 and 1763, and in ten of the twelve years from 1764 to 1775 (an over-all average of 61.0 per cent). For the twenty-eight years for which the *Virginia Gazette* is currently available, the percentage of space devoted to American symbols was below the average in twenty-one (or 75.0 per cent) of them; the curve for the *Pennsylvania Gazette* was below the composite curve almost four times in five (78.0 per cent); while the New York newspapers gave a greater than average share of attention to American events only 34.1 per cent of the time. The *Boston Gazette*'s curve was higher than the composite in each of the fourteen years analyzed. In spite of these variations, however, it is significant that, in terms of the share of symbol space devoted to American symbols, the degree of difference among the newspapers declined during the course of the forty-one-year period.[9]

The basic similarity as well as the marginal dissimilarities of the distribution curves for the various newspapers can be shown most clearly and simply by linear regressions or trend lines. Such trend lines smooth out all fluctuations into single, straight lines, the slopes of which, that is, the average yearly percentage change for the period as a whole, provide means for accurate comparisons.[10] Figures 2-A and 2-B reveal that for both the entire forty-one-year period (1735-75) and the crucial fourteen years leading up to the outbreak of the Revolution (1762-75) the secular trend of attention to American events rose. In no newspaper did the share of

119

[9] In terms of the share of symbol space devoted to American symbols, the degree of correlation among the 10 pairs of newspapers in the period 1764-75 was more than twice as high as in the 1735-63 period. Using the nonparametric Spearman rank correlation coefficient r_s, the average coefficient of correlation for the 10 pairs of newspapers for the earlier period was $r_s = .24$. The coefficient of correlation was significant at the .05 level (using a one-tailed test) for only three of the ten pairs, and was not significant at that level for the average or mean coefficient. For the 12 years from 1764 to 1775, the average coefficient of correlation was $r_s = .57$. The mean coefficient as well as those for 7 of the 10 pairs were significant at the .05 level. For a more extensive discussion of this test, see Sidney Siegel, *Nonparametric Statistics for the Behavioral Sciences* (New York, 1956), 202-213.

[10] For a discussion of this technique, see Harold T. Davis, *Political Statistics* (Evanston, Illinois, 1954), 168-169. In Table 1, a correlation coefficient of .95 means that a trend line will rise 0.95 per cent each year.

FIGURE 2
TRENDS IN AMERICAN SYMBOL USAGE, BY NEWSPAPER

KEY:
——— Composite (excluding <u>Boston Gazette</u>)
— — — Massachusetts Gazette   ——— Virginia Gazette
▬▬▬ N.-Y. Weekly Journal/Mercury   ——— South-Carolina Gazette
·—·—·— Pennsylvania Gazette   •—·—•—• Boston Gazette

A. LINEAR TRENDS, 1735-1775

120

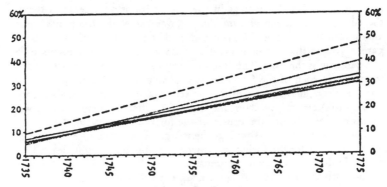

B. LINEAR TRENDS, 1762-1775

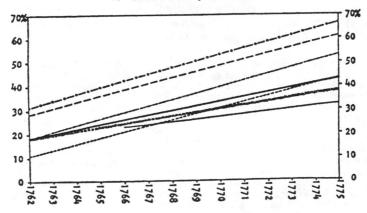

American symbols decrease generally from 1735 or 1762 to 1775. The differences in the slopes of the individual trend lines are shown in Table 1.

TABLE I

SLOPES OF TREND LINES SHOWING ATTENTION TO AMERICAN SYMBOLS, BY NEWSPAPER 1735-1775 and 1762-1775

Newspaper	1735-1775	1762-1775
Massachusetts Gazette	.95	2.51
South-Carolina Gazette	.86	2.60
Virginia Gazette	.82	1.00
New-York Weekly Journal/Mercury	.66	1.53
Pennsylvania Gazette	.60	2.49
Boston Gazette		2.74
Composite*	.67	1.90

*Excludes *Boston Gazette*

Figures 2-A and 2-B indicate that for both the longer and the shorter time periods the New England newspapers not only started at a point well above the average but, with one exception, also rose at a steeper angle of incline than did the others. The *South-Carolina Gazette* did not lag far behind: for the forty-one-year period the slope of its trend line, which crossed the composite trend line in the late 1740's, was nine tenths as great as that of the *Massachusetts Gazette*; from 1762 to 1775 its annual percentage increase in attention to American events was second only to that of the *Boston Gazette*. While the trend lines from 1735 to 1775 for the Virginia, New York, and Pennsylvania newspapers were all below the composite trend line, only that of the New York journals rose more sharply than the composite. Perhaps most surprising of all was the rapid increase in the amount of attention that the *Pennsylvania Gazette* paid to American symbols from 1762 to 1775. Although still less steep than the slopes of the trend lines for the Massachusetts and South Carolina newspapers, the trend line for the *Pennsylvania Gazette* for the 1762-75 period was more than four times as steep as its slope for the 1735-75 period as a whole.

If the colonial newspapers became increasingly unified as to the amount of attention that they paid to American symbols, their patterns of attention to British symbols diverged increasingly.[11] Their general congruence

[11] In terms of the share of symbol space devoted to British symbols, using the Spearman rank correlation coefficient discussed in n. 9 above, the mean coefficient

is nonetheless remarkable. With the single exception of the *Pennsylvania Gazette,* all of them presented a greater than average amount of news about the Mother Country between one half and two thirds of the time. The Philadelphia journal did so in only nine of the forty-one years (22.0 per cent). It was the *Virginia Gazette,* however, that deviated most significantly from the composite curve—once, in 1753, by more than 25 percentage points.[12] It is also interesting to note that, as a general rule, again with the exception of the Virginia newspaper, the journals that devoted a greater than average amount of symbol space to American events tended also to pay a greater than average amount of attention to Britain.

Particularly important in assessing the interests of the individual newspapers are the varying ratios of American to British symbols. In the twenty-nine-year period from 1735 to 1763, the *Massachusetts Gazette* had more American than British symbols in twelve different years (41.4 per cent), the New York and South Carolina newspapers seven years (24.1 per cent), the *Pennsylvania Gazette* six years (20.7 per cent), and the *Virginia Gazette* only four years of the eighteen (22.2 per cent) of that period for which Virginia newspapers are extant. For the twelve years from 1764 to 1775, the *Massachusetts Gazette* printed more American than British symbols every single year, the *South-Carolina Gazette* in ten of the twelve years (83.3 per cent), the *New-York Mercury* in seven years (58.3 per cent), the *Pennsylvania Gazette* one half of the time, and the *Virginia Gazette* in four of the ten years available. Each of the fourteen years from 1762 to 1775 saw the *Boston Gazette* devoting more space to American symbols than to British symbols. Over the entire forty-one-year period, as shown in Table 2 (p. 280), only the Virginia and Pennsylvania newspapers gave more prominence to British than to colonial events.

What do all of these figures tell us about variations among the colonial newspapers in the distribution of their news space. The first and most obvious point is that the two Boston newspapers—the *Massachusetts Gazette* and the *Boston Gazette*—were far and away the leaders in reporting both colonial and British events, and more inclined to give precedence to the former. This was particularly true during the dozen years immediately prior to the outbreak of revolution, when both prints devoted about one

for the 1735-63 period was $r_s = .29$, significant at the .10 level (using a one-tailed test), while the correlation coefficients for 4 of the 10 pairs were significant at the .05 level. The mean coefficient for the 1764-75 period was $r_s = .27$, which is not significant even at the .10 level. None of the 10 pairs was significant at the .05 level (using a one-tailed test).

[12] The apparently erratic curves of the Virginia newspapers may in part be due to the incompleteness of the files of these journals—and hence of the sample used in this study—for the middle years of the 41-year period.

122

TABLE 2

TOTAL SYMBOL DISTRIBUTION, BY NEWSPAPER, OVER
ENTIRE PERIOD, 1735-1775

Newspapers	American Symbols	British Symbols	Other Symbols	Total Symbols
Massachusetts Gazette	28.8%	22.5%	48.8%	100.1%
South-Carolina Gazette	25.4	21.5	53.1	100.0
N.-Y. Weekly Journal/Mercury	21.2	21.1	57.7	100.0
Virginia Gazette	19.9	26.4	53.7	100.0
Pennsylvania Gazette	18.2	19.2	62.5	99.9
*Boston Gazette**	48.8	25.4	25.7	99.9
Composite†	22.4	21.5	56.1	100.0

* Figures include fourteen years (1762–1775) only
† Composite figures do not include *Boston Gazette*

123

quarter of their news space to British symbols and almost twice as much to occurrences in the colonies.

The second point is related to the first: although the Whiggish *Boston Gazette* devoted more space to American symbols and presented a higher ratio of American to British symbols for the fourteen years from 1762 to 1775 than did the Tory-oriented *Massachusetts Gazette*, the two New England newspapers differed from one another in these respects to a far lesser extent than either of them differed from the New York, Pennsylvania, Virginia, or South Carolina journals. This fact certainly argues for the case that, whatever the political biases of the newspapers, there was a common shift of attention toward the discussion of American news and problems in their columns.

Third, the newspapers of the middle colonies—the *Pennsylvania Gazette*, the *New-York Weekly Journal*, and the *New-York Mercury*—presented a fairly congruent picture of interest in American news. Their growing tendency to print American symbols was not essentially dissimilar from, although a bit below, the composite trend line (Figure 2-A); and while the New York prints had a higher ratio of American to British symbols in fourteen of the forty-one years (that is, in 34.1 per cent of the years), those of Philadelphia had a higher ratio in only nine (22.0 per cent). As Table 2 indicates, over the entire period each of them printed roughly as many American as British symbols. The major difference between them, and the difference that sets the *Pennsylvania Gazette* off from all of the colonial newspapers included in this study, is that that newspaper was generally much more preoccupied with European (and to a lesser extent Caribbean and Canadian) events than was any of the others. If any laggard in interest in American news and symbols existed, it was the *Virginia Gazette*. In only eight of the twenty-eight years (28.6 per cent) for which that newspaper is available did it print more American than British symbols; it was above average in giving symbol space to Britain about two thirds of the time, and below average in its share of American symbols three years in four. Over the entire 41-year period, as may be seen in Table 2, the Virginia newspapers devoted a third again as many symbols to the Mother Country as to the colonies. It would seem that, from the point of view of its communications and focus of attention, the Old Dominion retained closer ties to England throughout the last four decades of the colonial period than did the other provinces in America.[18]

Finally, in spite of some fairly extreme fluctuations, the *South-Carolina Gazette* was second only to the Massachusetts newspapers in giving space to American symbols. Its slope of rising interest in colonial news was even steeper during the last fourteen years of the colonial era than was that of the *Massachusetts Gazette*. Thus, in an era when its geographic core area was more concerned with British than with American events, the population centers at either end of the chain of American colonies were focusing their attention more upon American than upon British events. It was the geographic periphery rather than the core area of eighteenth-century America that led in the symbolic revolution of shifting images and focuses of attention.

III

The analysis of the forty-one-year period from 1735 to 1775 revealed that the sharpest incline in the percentage of symbol space devoted to American symbols occurred during the five-year period from 1762 to 1766. As shown in Figure 1, the American share of the total composite symbol count rose from 10.7 per cent in 1762 to 42.2 per cent in 1766—an increase of three hundred per cent. Moreover, the sharp rise in the American percentage occurred during this time period for all of the newspapers analyzed, with the most marked change in the *Boston Gazette*, which rose from 12.6 per cent in 1762 to 54.7 per cent in 1765 and fell off slightly in the following year. A similar, though not quite so dramatic, trend occurred in the distribution curve of British symbols: the most sustained period of incline during the years from 1759 to 1768 came during these same five years.

[18] On the ties of Virginia to Great Britain during the later colonial years, see Carl Bridenbaugh, *Seat of Empire: The Political Role of Eighteenth-Century Williamsburg* (Williamsburg, 1950), 7-10.

The more intensive analysis of the years 1762-66 followed the methodology outlined above, except for the size of the sample and the newspapers selected. Using a standard technique for random sampling, an independent sample of one issue per month for each of the five years (or sixty issues in all) was drawn from each of two newspapers—the *Boston Gazette* and the *New-York Mercury*. These journals were selected as representative of newspapers paying, respectively, more and less than average attention to American events. As far as the manner of presenting the data is concerned, the extreme fluctuations in the symbol distributions from month to month (Figure 3) become more readable and perhaps more meaningful through the use of trend lines (Figure 4) produced by the method of "moving averages."[14] Such trend lines also enable the clear presentation of another dimension of the data, the role of the Stamp Act crisis in changing colonial attention patterns.

125

COMPOSITE DISTRIBUTION OF SYMBOLS, 1762–1766

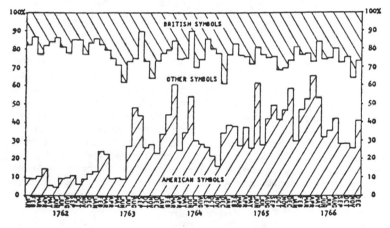

[14] A "moving averages" curve smooths out extreme fluctuations in a year-by-year curve (such as Figure 3), and presents a curved line that may serve to indicate the trend of symbol usage. To find the "moving average" for any single year, it is necessary merely to find the mean average of the symbol usage for the year itself, the year preceding, and the year following. While a "moving averages" curve is quite useful for showing trends, it cannot be used to show the precise symbol distribution for any single year.

FIGURE 4

COMPOSITE "MOVING AVERAGES" DISTRIBUTION OF SYMBOLS,

1762–1766

126

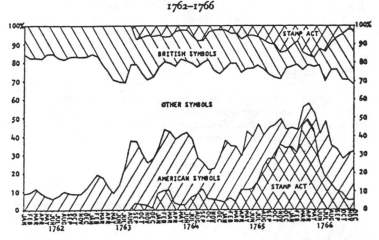

Generally speaking, the results of the intensive analysis were rather close to those of the general study, as shown in Table 3 (p. 284). In both analyses the American share of the total symbol count rose from about 10 per cent to 40 per cent over the five years, while the British share rose from approximately 16 per cent to about 25 per cent. The most important differences in the year-by-year comparison of the two samples lay in the patterns of the growth of American symbol usage: the monthly sample revealed a steady rise culminating in a peak in 1765, and dropping off slightly in the following year; while the quarterly sample showed a slower rise until 1764, a decline in 1765, and a very sharp rise in 1766. Statistical tests designed to determine the extent to which two independent samples of the same body of data differ suggest that there was no significant difference between the sample of four issues per year and the sample of twelve issues per year 90 per cent of the time.[15] The monthly analysis, however, presents a picture more sensitive to the changes in the colonial newspapers' focuses of attention.

[15] Statistically speaking, in 9 of 10 cases (that is, two different sets of newspapers, each for five separate years), nonparametric tests did not reject a null hypothesis asserting that there was no significant difference between the sample of 4 and the

TABLE 3

COMPARISON OF COMPOSITE SYMBOL DISTRIBUTIONS, 1762-1766
FOR QUARTERLY-SAMPLE AND MONTHLY-SAMPLE ANALYSES

Symbol Categories	1762	1763	1764	1765	1766
Quarterly Sample*					
American symbols	10.7%	15.4%	27.5%	26.7%	42.2%
British symbols	15.4	20.5	20.5	24.4	24.9
Other symbols	73.9	64.1	52.0	48.9	32.9
Total	100.0	100.0	100.0	100.0	100.0
Monthly Sample†					
American symbols	8.8%	20.3%	33.7%	41.1%	40.5%
British symbols	17.0	24.4	21.3	23.8	24.2
Other symbols	74.2	55.3	45.0	35.1	35.3
Total	100.0	100.0	100.0	100.0	100.0

127

* Mean average annual distribution of symbols in four issues per year of the *Massachusetts Gazette*, the *New-York Mercury*, the *Pennsylvania Gazette*, the *Virginia Gazette*, and the *South-Carolina Gazette*.

† Mean average annual distribution of symbols in twelve issues per year (one per month) of the *Boston Gazette* and the *New-York Mercury*.

Looking at the composite monthly distribution of symbols as a whole (Figure 4), it may be seen that there were two major cycles in the curve representing the American share of the total symbol count. The first of these started in May of 1763 and ended in October of the following year, while the second started at the latter date and continued for two years. The structure and composition of these two cycles are of considerable importance in our discussion and evaluation of the development of self-awareness processes in colonial America.

The most significant revolution in symbol usage during these five years, the most crucial period of the forty-one years prior to the outbreak of the Revolution, occurred during the summer of 1763. From June until August of that year the share of American symbols rose almost fivefold (Figure 3) and, after a decline during the autumn, rose to new heights in the following spring and early summer. A similar pattern appeared in the curves of American symbol usage for both the *New-York Mercury*

independent sample of 12 issues. For the *New-York Mercury* in 1765, the test rejected the null hypothesis at a significance level of .05 for a two-tailed test. For a discussion of this test—the Mann-Whitney *U* test—see Siegel, *Nonparametric Statistics*, 116-127.

and the *Boston Gazette*. Indeed, the curve of the latter suggests that for Bostonians the height of American self-interest came during this period, for between January and July of 1764 the *Gazette* devoted more than seven out of ten place-name symbols to American affairs.

While the second cycle in the composite curve reached a higher point —in the spring of 1766, when it rose above the 50 per cent level—it is perhaps not quite so dramatic in that it seems merely to have been a continuation of the previous cycle. Considered as a unity, the two cycles present a picture of increasing interest in American affairs, building to a climax in the months when the joyous colonists received word from the Mother Country that their opposition had forced Parliament to repeal the Stamp Act—probably the most spectacular and important event of the 1760's for the Americans.

But how important was the Stamp Act crisis in these cycles of increased American self-awareness? To ascertain this it was necessary to divide the content of the American share of symbols into two categories: one category comprising news directly or indirectly related to the Stamp and Sugar Acts—their announcement, enactment, and repeal—as well as all forms of colonial opposition, such as trade associations, decisions to simplify funeral clothing, colonial versions of the "buy American" principle, and the Stamp Act Congress; the other category consisting in news not in the least pertaining to these acts. The cross-hatched portion of Figure 4 shows the trend in the share of symbols in the first category.

Such an analysis reveals that, although the climax of the Stamp Act crisis coincided with the culminating point of interest in American events, it was not the news of the trade restrictions that touched off the aroused interest. The trend toward increased interest in American events and news was well under way before information about trade restrictions began to appear regularly in the colonial press. Prior to the fall of 1764 the only news items pertaining to the Sugar and Stamp Acts were scattered bits in the *New-York Mercury* echoing colonial disgruntlement at trade restrictions already existing, and reporting rumors about parliamentary intentions vis-à-vis colonial trade. And it was not until a year later that symbols found in news of the Stamp Act crisis consistently began to outnumber symbols relating to other events. In the issues that reported the repeal of the Stamp Act, about nine in ten symbols referring to America pertained more or less directly to the parliamentary tax measures.

As a triggering event of American self-awareness, if we may judge from symbol usage in the *Boston Gazette*, the Stamp Act crisis was particularly irrelevant in Boston. The American share of the total symbol count reached its climax months before the *Gazette* began to discuss the

128

trade restrictions. As the crisis mounted, to be sure, Bostonian interest in it grew rapidly, until by the spring of 1766 the *Gazette's* focus of attention upon American events and news was absorbed almost totally by items on the Stamp Act and its repeal.

There is another point to be mentioned before leaving the discussion of the intensive analysis of the *New-York Mercury* and the *Boston Gazette:* the relative unimportance of the Stamp Act crisis as an influence on the distribution of British symbols. It is of course true that the period from January of 1762 to December of 1766 saw the British share of the total symbol count gradually increasing (Figure 4); and during the height of the crisis itself most of the British symbols appearing in the two newspapers were related to the trade measures. But the peak months shown by the trend lines occurred either before or after the bulk of the news pertaining to the Stamp Act crisis. And the British share of the symbols was higher during the summer of 1763 than at any point prior to the fall of 1766, when the Stamp Act crisis itself was no longer of great moment.

129

IV

From the quantitative point of view, the colonists' focus of attention (or at the very least that of their newspapers) shifted dramatically during the four decades before the outbreak of the War of Independence. Of only marginal interest during the 1730's and 1740's, American news and events became the major concern of the newspapers by the end of the colonial era. I would suggest, on the basis of evidence from the newspapers themselves, that the "take-off" point of increased interest in America came during the early summer of 1763—before news of Pontiac's uprising reached the inhabitants of the towns along the Atlantic seaboard, before the announcement of the Royal Proclamation restricting the settling and trading patterns of the colonists, before the beginning of agitation about British mercantile policies. Meanwhile the colonists became less absorbed in European wars and other events outside the Anglo-American community, while maintaining a fairly steady interest in the Mother Country. It is important to add, however, that, although British news generally occupied about one fifth of the newspapers' columns throughout the entire forty-one years, its share declined sharply relative to the space given over to American symbols.

But what about the qualitative side of colonial attention patterns? It is a commonplace in the many studies of American history that, on the whole, the quality of communication transactions among the colonies improved during the decades prior to 1775, particularly in contrast to those transactions between the colonies and England. Those who argue that the colonists had no sense of community awareness before that date most often base their case on indifference rather than fear and mutual distrust, on parochialism rather than hate. A brief test applied to the place-name symbols appearing in samples of colonial newspapers for 1738 and 1768 tends to bear out this commonplace. Following the general sampling procedure outlined above and a standard procedure for indicating the quality of symbol usage, I examined the contexts in which the symbols referring to American and British place names occurred. It seems to have been characteristic of the colonial press that few such symbols appeared in contexts clearly approving or disapproving of the place name represented by the symbol. According to the sample, however, American symbols appeared in more favorable contexts in 1768 than in 1738, while the reverse was the case for British symbols.[16]

130

Individually, each of the newspapers included in this analysis followed essentially the same changing pattern in the distribution of its news space. If, on the one hand, the New England and South Carolina prints were far more interested in colonial events than were the others, the communication ties of Virginia, on the other hand, seem to have been strongest with the Mother Country. Pennsylvania, and to a lesser extent New York, remained generally more interested in European news than were newspapers from other colonies. Not until 1774 did the entire colonial group finally accept the pattern of interest in America advanced by the Massachusetts and South Carolina press. The Revolutionary War followed upon the heels of this revolution in symbol usage.

[16] Using the method described by Ithiel de Sola Pool (with the collaboration of Harold D. Lasswell, Daniel Lerner, and others, *Symbols of Democracy* [Stanford, 1952], 14), I subtracted the number of American symbols appearing in unfavorable contexts from the number of such symbols appearing in favorable contexts, and divided the remainder by the sum of all American symbols appearing in the sample of newspapers for each year. The formula for this is $F-U$ over $F + U + N$, where F is the number of symbols appearing in favorable contexts, U the number appearing in unfavorable contexts, and N the number appearing in neutral contexts. I then performed the same test for British symbols during these two years. For American symbols in 1738, the quality of symbol usage was $-.013$; by 1768 it had gone up to $\pm.000$. The change in the quality of British symbol usage was from $+.079$ in 1738 to $+.004$ in 1768. The low scores result primarily from the high number of symbols appearing in neutral contexts.

PAUL A. VARG
Michigan State University

The Advent of Nationalism, 1758-1776

IN A SERMON PREACHED AT GLOUCESTER, MASSACHUSETTS, ON NOVEMBER 29, 1759, Samuel Chandler spoke of "British America," of "the People of this Land," of "This America." [1] In another sermon of thanksgiving for recent victories over the French, Samuel Cooper focused his attention on His Majesty's "American Dominions." [2]

The term "America," seldom used until this time, found frequent employment and a new meaning during the public festivities in the autumn of 1759. In the closing years of the Seven Years War George Fisher, preparing the twelfth edition of his book, gave it the title *The American Instructor* and in the preface explained that "many Things of little or no Use in these Parts of the World" had been omitted and "in their Room many other Matters inserted, more immediately useful to us Americans." In October 1760 William Adams, of New London, wrote:

> The years *seventeen hundred fifty nine and sixty,* will shine with distinguish'd lustre, in the *British and American* annals, for the numerous and surprising victories and conquests gained therein, and which have exceeded, even our most sanguine hopes and expectations.[3]

Prior to 1759 British settlers in North America took the name of their province or simply referred to themselves as "British colonists." The term "American colonies" was used by Englishmen at home, but it carried no

1 Samuel Chandler, *A Sermon Preached at Gloucester, Thursday, Nov. 29, 1759. Being the Day of the Provincial Anniversary Thanksgiving* (Boston, 1759).

2 Samuel Cooper, *A Sermon Preached before His Excellency Thomas Pownall; Captain-General and Governor in Chief, Oct. 16, 1759* (Boston, 1759).

3 William Adams, *A Discourse Delivered at New London October 23d. A.D. 1760. On the Thanksgiving For the Success of the British Arms, in the reduction of Montreal, and the conquest of all Canada* (New London, Conn., 1760).

more than a geographical meaning. In the fall of 1759, during the celebrations of the conquest of Quebec, the name "Americans" became
something more than a geographical expression. The use of the term
suggests the development of nascent nationalism.

We are prone to seek in the developments of the quarter-century preceding the break with the mother country the causes of the separation.
It is not the purpose of this article to establish any causal connection between the development of nationalism and the revolution; the only aim
is to examine the process by which this nationalism came into being. Probably because nationalism connotes a bit more than what had developed,
historians have usually steered clear of using that term. They refer vaguely
to the quality but refuse to name it, but Edmund Cody Burnett, editor of
the letters of the members of the Continental Congress, called it "nationalism in a stage of gestation." [4] However, it is more fruitful not to quibble
about the term. In this case we may define it as no more than a self-
conscious awareness of unity and separateness growing out of a common
historical background and ideology. Our task is no more than to indicate
the beginnings of this awareness and its various expressions. Nor is it our
purpose to show its chronological development; that must wait for a fuller
treatment covering a larger span of time. In the brief period of 1758 to
1776 the awareness was only in the first stage of becoming; it had no
clearly defined character and therefore the new dimensions which it did
assume are of less importance than the fact of its presence.

British nationalism preceded the American variety and endowed it
with some of its major characteristics. During the Seven Years War the
Americans bore the name of Briton with pride. Celebrations of victory
rang with praise of the mother country.[5] Identification of themselves as
Englishmen owed much to the French encirclement of the colonies. To
the normal fear of a rival imperialist power was added the highly charged
prejudice against France as the citadel of Roman Catholicism and mon-

[4] Edmund Cody Burnett, *The Continental Congress* (New York, 1941), p. 3. Burnett
went no further than to say that the elements of national beginnings were present and
he was of the opinion that a genuine national spirit did not come into being until long
after the establishment of the new government in 1789. Max Savelle, in *Seeds of Liberty
The Genesis of the American Mind*, frankly uses the term nationalism and presents a
most able discussion of its bases.

[5] A great many public addresses can be cited in support of this statement. Aaron Burr,
President of the College of New Jersey, called on his hearers, " 'Tis high Time to awake,
to call up all the *Briton* in us, every Spark of *English* Valour; cheerfully to offer our
Purses, our Arms, and our Lives, to the Defence of our Country, our holy Religion, our
excellent Constitution, and invaluable Liberties." See Aaron Burr, *A Discourse Delivered
at New-Ark, in New Jersey*, January 1, 1755. See also the resolution passed by the Con-
gregational clergy in New Hampshire, *Provincial Papers Documents and Records Relating to the Province of New Hampshire from 1749 to 1763* (Manchester, 1872), VI, 783-84.

archical absolutism. The Americans, overwhelmingly Protestant, inter-preted history in terms of a never ending struggle between freedom and absolutism, enlightenment and superstition, light and darkness. Catholi-cism was, of course, identified with persecution, reactionary rule and super-stition. The Reverend Jonathan Mayhew expressed a common view when he said: "It were next to madness to imagine that the nation could ever be safe and happy under a Roman Catholic prince." Hundreds of sermons expressed the same feelings.

Dread of the French, however, was only one factor in the ardent British feelings of the colonists.[6] The almost daily allusions to "glorious British liberties" symbolized the fact that Englishmen at home and Englishmen in the colonies shared a common political ideology. Absolutism had triumphed on the continent during the seventeenth century while the British bled and died to curb the Stuart kings and to establish rule by "King, Lords, and Commons." The colonists, in many cases refugees from the Stuart reigns, naturally took delight in the Glorious Revolution. The political principles established by the revolution became the alpha and omega of their political theory. It gave to the colonists a sense of oneness with Englishmen at home.

133

But the lusty growth of British nationalism in the new world was not simply a matter of common political principles. As the Americans under-stood those principles, they meant that Englishmen on both sides of the ocean enjoyed government by consent and agreement. The cohesive ele-ment provided by this political system constituted the basis of nationalism both in the mother country and in the colonies. Herein, in very large part, lies the explanation of praise of the mother country. A few years after the Glorious Revolution Cotton Mather declared: "It is no Little Blessing of God, that we are a part of the *English Nation.*" "There is no *English man,*" said Mather, "but what has for his *Birthright* those *Liberties,* which are a rich *Inheritance:* When all the Nations of *North-ern Europe* of late years foolishly Lost their *Liberties,* the brave English

---

[6] Some may question how loyal the colonists really were in view of the frequent charges that they engaged in trading with the enemy and failed to contribute both men and money in the degree expected of them by the Crown. The present writer would question this conclusion. Certainly there was considerable trading with the enemy by many American and British merchants, but one may question whether this is an accurate measure of loyalty. Secondly, the debates over appropriations in several of the legislative assemblies suggest that the delays were due in considerable part to questions concerning how troops were to be employed and related questions rather than to lack of conviction that the war was necessary or to any hostility toward the mother country. It should also be kept in mind that in an agrarian community the sending of fathers and sons to war imposed special difficulties. Those who criticize the effort of the colonists usually cite British complaints. These should be compared with deeply held convictions among the colonists that they had made a most creditable showing.

(tho' with struggle enough, against the *Unnatural Conspiracies* of the *Late Reigns*) have still preserved Theirs. . . ." [7]

In a notable exposition of political theory the Reverend John Barnard, in 1734, affirmed "that form of Civil Government is best for us, which we are under, I mean the *British Constitution.*" He did not know "of a single true *New England* Man, in the whole Province, but what readily subscribes to these Sentiments, and hopes we shall continue to be the genuine Members of that glorious Constitution, thro'out all Ages." [8]

British liberties continued to win the praise of the colonists down to the very eve of the Declaration of Independence. In an election day sermon in 1758, Benjamin Throop admonished his listeners that "the World knows not a more just and happy Constitution, or a more mild and faithful Administration than ours is." [9] Jonathan Mayhew wrote: "The British government and laws, by which the subject's life and liberty, his property and religion, are so well secured to him, are blessings, very extensive in their nature, and will ever be accounted invaluable, by all who have a just conception of what the happiness of civil society consists in; . . ." [10]

The constant appeal to the British Constitution and to the charters in all colonial disputes was based on the faith that they offered firm guarantees of personal liberties. The interests of the colonies were similarly secure because of the balance of power within the British government. The colonists referred to this check and balance system as rule by "King, Lords, and Commons." John Barnard spelled it out as rule by the blending of monarchy, nobility and democracy. Only under such a system could the passions of individuals and groups be controlled. Americans held no illusions concerning the seething ambitions that tended to tear society apart or to erect themselves into arbitrary domination of other interests under the banners of justice or concern for the public welfare.

And because all groups were represented and could defend their interests, the British government ruled by consent and agreement. No group, including the colonists, need fear "Encroachments of Sovereignty" by any

---

[7] Cotton Mather, *A Pillar of Gratitude* (Boston, 1700).

[8] John Barnard, *The Throne Established By Righteousness. A Sermon Preach'd Before His Excellency Jonathan Belcher, Esq.; His Majesty's Council, and the Representatives of the Province of the Massachusetts-Bay in New England, May 29, 1734, Being the Day for the Electing His Majesty's Council There* (Boston, 1734).

[9] Benjamin Throop, *Religion and Loyalty, The Duty And Glory Of A People; Illustrated In A Sermon. From 1, Peter 2, 17. Preached Before The General Assembly Of The Colony of Connecticut at Hartford, On The Day Of the Anniversary Election. May 11th, 1758* (New London, Conn., 1758).

[10] Jonathan Mayhew, *Dr. Mayhew's Two Thanksgiving Discourses November 23rd, 1758* (Boston, 1758).

other group if each exercised a zealous regard for its own interests and an unceasing vigilance in checking the ambitions of others. This feature of British government, duplicated in the colonial governments, assured the colonists that even they were important members of the political order, that they "belonged." And because they counted in the scheme of things, they looked upon England as *their* country.

The prevailing religious thought reinforced the ideal of a government of checks and balances. Few sermons failed to stress the sinful nature of man. The individual was by nature jealous, vengeful, self-seeking, full of pride and vanity, and not to be trusted with the liberty of others. Man must by his very nature view all matters in terms of his own interests and could never rise to a position of impartiality when these were involved. This view of human nature gave rise to a querulous state of mind that put every man on guard against exploitation.

Liberty was, in fact, only to be preserved where different parts of the body politic maintained a jealous watch over each other. Government, said the Reverend Andrew Eliot in an election sermon in May 1765, originated in the imperfect state of human nature. The facts of human behavior, facts that "originated with him who is the author of nature," made unlimited freedom unbearable. The jungle of cross purposes had made it necessary to give up absolute freedom. Men had surrendered this freedom for the common good. But only as each individual and each interest jealously kept an eye on the government to assure that it served the common welfare, could government be kept to its original function.[11]

The Pennsylvania farmer, John Dickinson, expressed the same basic faith when he condemned apathy and praised an almost peevish questioning. A good disposition toward the rulers is amiable, he warned, but it could only be indulged at great danger. Dickinson, like the clergy, laid it down as a first principle that "all men are subject to the frailties of nature; and therefore whatever regard we entertain for the *persons* of those who govern us, we should always remember that their conduct, as *rulers,* may be influenced by human infirmities."

This was the nature of British nationalism. At its core was the theory of government by consent and agreement. Rule by force in the shape of standing armies was so horrendous a thought to Englishmen on both sides of the Atlantic that the aversion to a standing army became a political first principle. So pathetic in strength of numbers was the British army during the eighteenth century that there was a considerable reliance on the use of foreign mercenaries.

[11]Andrew Eliot, *A Sermon Preached Before His Excellency Francis Bernard, Esq.; Governor, The Honorable His Majesty's Council and The Honorable House of Representatives, Of The Province of The Massachusetts-Bay In New England, May 29th, 1765.*

Implicit for the Americans in this whole body of thought was a position of equality within the empire. It was an illusion they could easily entertain although the idea that colonies were to be governed wholly by consent and agreement entered the minds of few Englishmen at home. The authorities in London were too busy with civil strife in the seventeenth century to give much thought to the colonies, but the policy of salutary neglect was not based on any idea that the colonies were not subordinate.

This discussion of the roots of British nationalism is necessary if we are to understand the beginnings of American nationalism. Once the Americans discovered that a common political theory did not mean that the authorities in London meant to apply it to the British plantations, that colonies were not in the category of equals, that government by consent and agreement was to be limited to minor local matters, loyalty to the mother country increasingly gave way to a sense of separateness. The colonists now assumed the role of defenders of what they had assumed to be the meaning of the British constitution, and their interpretation of it became the warp and woof of a new nationalism.

This American nationalism would not have come into being so easily had not the colonists already developed strong convictions of their own importance in the world. They did not fail to note that both Frenchmen and Englishmen said that whoever controlled the colonies would control Europe. Colonists quickly seized and expanded upon this flattering estimate of their own importance.[12] As early as 1754 William Clarke maintained that British trade, wealth and naval power depended upon the colonies. The loss of the colonies to France, he warned, would reduce Great Britain "to an absolute Subjection to the *French Crown* and she would be nothing more than a *Province of France*."[13] William Livingston gave a similar assessment of the "inexhaustible magazine of wealth" in the colonies and held that without them "Great Britain must not only lose her former lustre, but, dreadful even in thought! cease to be any longer an independent power."[14] When Samuel Cooper addressed the Massachusetts assembly in the autumn of 1759, he gave thanks to

12 Gerald Stourzh, *Benjamin Franklin and American Foreign Policy* (Chicago, 1954), p. 113.

13 William Clarke, *Observations on the late and present Conduct of the French, with Regard to their Encroachments upon the British Colonies in North America. Together With Remarks on the Importance of these Colonies to Great Britain* (Boston, 1755).

14 William Livingston, *A Review of the Military Operations in North America from the Commencement of the French Hostilities on the Frontier of Virginia in 1753, to the Surrender of Oswego, on the 14th of August, 1756. Interspersed With Various Observations, Characters, and Anecdotes; Necessary To Give Light into The Conduct of American Transactions in General; And More Especially Into The Political Management of Affairs In New York. In A Letter to A. Nobleman* (London, 1758).

the King who had manifested "a peculiar Concern for His American Dominions," and then added: "with the safety of which, the Dignity of his Crown, and the Power and Commerce of *Great-Britain* are so closely connected." [15] Benjamin Franklin wrote to Lord Kames, the British philosopher: "I have long been of opinion, that the *foundations of the future grandeur and stability of the British empire lie in America;* and though, like other foundations, they are low and little seen, they are, nevertheless, broad and strong enough to support the greatest political structure human wisdom ever yet erected." [16] Both Franklin and John Adams believed it highly probable that the seat of the empire would some day be moved to the new world because it was there that the nation's future greatness lay.

137

The colonists' boasting, so characteristic of national movements in their early stages, had a considerable basis in fact. In his book *Cities in Revolt* Carl Bridenbaugh has documented in detail the phenomenal growth that took place between 1743 and 1776. The five leading cities increased in population from 72,881 in 1760 to 104,000 by 1775, an increase of 33 per cent in fifteen years.[17] Only London among English cities surpassed Philadelphia in size at the eve of the Revolution. The foreign commerce of the colonies reached impressive proportions. In 1774 Philadelphia alone exported commodities valued at £720,135 sterling.[18] All these cities had groups of merchants whose sumptuous houses, dress and manners impressed European visitors as superior. Cultural life was nourished by libraries, schools, great numbers of bookstores, and concerts. America had developed an urban life that compared favorably with that of Europe.

A survey of the members at the opening of the second Continental Congress reveals the great wealth, the growth of the professions and the rise of a highly successful merchant class. Of the 55 delegates, 28 were lawyers, 12 were merchants and almost all had held public office. Others were successful planters. Henry Middleton, at one time president of the Congress, owned nearly 20 plantations with a total of 50,000 acres and about 800 slaves.

The gathering of the revolutionaries in Philadelphia was one of prosperous lawyers, merchants and planters who lived in style. John Adams has left a picture of the social life of the Congress, of elaborate dinners, of sumptuous homes and gay entertainment.

Nationalism as a self-conscious phenomenon was stimulated by the British challenge of the colonists' illusion of equal status and their con-

[15] Samuel Cooper, *op. cit.*   [16] Gerald Stourzh, *op. cit.*
[17] Carl Bridenbaugh, *Cities in Revolt Urban Life in America, 1743-1776* (New York, 1955), p. 216.
[18] *Ibid.*, p. 257.

fidence in their future role. It expressed itself in resentment at the British habit of referring to the colonists as subjects, in the political argument and in a new emphasis on the history of the colonies.

What really injured the Americans was the British assumption of superiority. Pocketbooks were undoubtedly touched by the new taxes and the restraints of trade, but it was the self assurance, the sense of great achievement, the sense of equality within the empire that explains the querulous spirit of the colonists. Feelings involving pride and status suffered greater injury than did financial interests. These feelings did not add up to a full-blown nationalism in 1763 but they were sufficiently strong so that when offended they matured into full-scale intercolonial cooperation, bleached the formerly virile British nationalism until it was ready for a new shading, and brought into sharper focus the fact that the American environment had transformed British political institutions so that the differences between the mother country and America encouraged a sense of uniqueness among the Americans who had previously so easily identified themselves with Englishmen at home.

America had made England great. England would need America more than America would need England, warned Franklin. Scotland and Ireland must depend upon England, he wrote, "But America, an immense territory, favored by nature with all advantages of climate, soils, great navigable rivers, lakes, etc., must become a great country, populous and mighty; and will, in less time than is generally conceived, be able to shake off any shackles that may be imposed upon her, and perhaps place them on the imposers." [19] Oxenbridge Thacher, of Boston, expressed the set of mind in 1764 when he said:

> Great Britain, at this day, is arrived to an height of glory and wealth, which no European nation hath ever reached, since the decline of the Roman empire. Everybody knows, that it is not indebted to itself alone, for this envied power: That it's colonies, placed in a distant quarter of the earth, have had their share of efficiency, in it's late successes; as indeed they have also contributed to the advancing and increasing its grandeur from their very first beginnings.
>
> In the forming and settling therefore the internal polity of the kingdom; these have reason to expect, that *their* interest should be considered and attended to; that *their* rights, if they have any, should be preserved to them: and that *they* should have no reason to complain, that they have been lavish of their blood and treasure in the late war, only to bind the shackles of slavery on themselves and their children. [20]

[19] *The Works of Benjamin Franklin*, ed. John Bigelow (New York, 1904), IV, 286.
[20] Oxenbridge Thacher, *The Sentiments of a British American* (Boston, 1764).

138

The cocksureness of the colonists found repeated expression in the controversy with Great Britain, and the controversy itself nurtured their self confidence. Nicholas Ray, a former resident of New York who moved to London, outlined what the new relationship must be. The colonies, wrote Ray, were more important than many of the kingdoms of Europe and the Americans felt their strength. Therefore, he said, America could only be bound to Great Britain by friendship and discretion.[21] It appeared to the Americans that Parliament was intent on enacting legislation that served no good purpose other than pinning on them the badge of parliamentary supremacy. And such an assertion now appeared unreasonable. A Boston town meeting in 1772 passed a resolution which asked: "Can it be said with any Colour of Truth and Justice, that this Continent of three Thousand Miles in Length, and of a Breadth as yet unexplored, in which however, it is supposed, there are five Millions of People, has the least Voice, Vote, or Influence in the Decisions of the British Parliament?" And, said the resolution, by the nature of the situation, the colonists could not be represented and therefore must legislate for themselves. The Bostonians undoubtedly felt exactly as their resolution indicated.

139

> The Inhabitants of this Country, in all Probability, in a few Years, will be more numerous than those of Great Britain and Ireland together. Yet it is absurdly expected, by the Promoters of the present Measures, that these, with their Posterity to all Generations, should be easy, while their Property shall be disposed of by a House of Commons at Three Thousand Miles distance from them. . . .[22]

The more impulsive spirits among the Sons of Liberty spoke more bluntly of what was involved. At the dedication of the Tree of Liberty at Providence in 1768, the speaker complained that a "new system of politics hath been adopted in Great Britain and the common people there claim a sovereignty over us although they be only fellow subjects." The weight of his argument against the mother country, if it can be called an argument, was against the inference of an inferior status. In dedicating the Tree of Liberty he said little about liberty but much about the causes for resentment. What was really galling was the language "of every paltry scribler, even of those who pretend friendship for us in some things. . . ." These Britishers wrote in "this lordly stile, *our colonies—our western dominions—our plantations—our islands—our subjects in America—our authority—our government* with many more of the like *imperious expres-*

21 Nicholas Ray, *The Importance of the Colonies* (New York, 1766).
22 *Boston The Votes and Proceedings of the Freeholders and other Inhabitants October 28, 1772* (Boston, 1772).

sions." "Strange doctrine," he thought, "that we should be the subjects of subjects, and liable to be controuled at their will!" [23]

The question, said William Hicks in his pamphlet *The Nature and Extent of Parliamentary Power,* was that of subordination. Parliament was, he said, determined to put the colonies in their place, and to make clearer the motive of the ministry, he cited how New York had in fact met the overall requirements of the Quartering Act. To remind the New Yorkers of their subordinate role the ministry had suspended the legislature simply because it had not adhered to the most minor of specifications as to exactly what food and drink should be provided.[24] Actually the New York legislature met all specifications of the act immediately before Parliament suspended it, and the issue had little practical importance. Other writers pointed to the Declaratory Act as evidence of the British intent to bring about a subordination. The Stamp tax had been rescinded due to a prudent concern over trade, but Parliament had maintained the principle. When the Townshend duties on paint, paper and glass were repealed, the duty on tea was retained simply because the right to tax had to be maintained. The theory employed by the colonists in support of their rights need not concern us here, but the constant inference that their own importance made subordination unreasonable testifies that their self awareness was nourished by the exhilarating controversy.

Benjamin Franklin showed how in his own pride in America he resented what he termed British haughtiness. He wrote to the British press:

> Give me leave, Master John Bull, to remind you, that you are related to all mankind; and therefore it less becomes you than anybody to affront and abuse other nations. But you have mixed with your many virtues a pride, a haughtiness, and an insolent contempt for all but yourself, that, I am afraid, will, if not abated, procure you one day or other a handsome drubbing.[25]

In the years down to 1776 the nationalism of the colonists exhibited a dual nature, loyalty to the mother country and an increasing awareness of their separateness and importance. The former nationalism that had focused on the British constitution was undergoing a subtle shift whereby a high degree of autonomy for themselves was becoming the center of their attention.

[23] *Discourse, Delivered in Providence, in the Colony of Rhode-Island, upon the 25th Day of July, 1768 at The Dedication of the Tree of Liberty, From the Summer House in the Tree by a Son of Liberty* (Providence, 1768).
[24] William Hicks, *The Nature and Extent of Parliamentary Power* (Philadelphia, 1768).
[25] *The Writings of Benjamin Franklin,* ed. Albert Henry Smyth (New York, 1907), IV, 398.

Among all the able political disquisitions of the time, perhaps none surpassed in perspicuity Daniel Dulany's *Considerations on the Propriety of Imposing Taxes in the British Colonies, for the Purpose of raising a Revenue, by an Act of Parliament*. Dulany, very significantly, wrote in terms of the interests of all the colonies. He used the term "American" repeatedly, the first pamphleteer to do so with any frequency, and he connoted by this the existence of an intercolonial interest that surpassed all local interests. Finally he delineated with clarity an American interest as opposed to an English interest.

Dulany repeated what was at the very heart of the emerging American self awareness, the importance of the colonies to England. The mother country had fought the Seven Years War, not out of a spirit of generosity to the Americans, but because the war involved her own interests and was "necessary to the *Defence of Great Britain* herself." Great Britain, he contended, "could not long subsist as an independent Kingdom after the loss of the Colonies." [26]

The broader issue of taxation provided the opportunity for the colonists to express the idea that they constituted a separate entity. At the Stamp Act Congress Americans discovered that all held one principle in common: namely, that the power of the purse must reside with the people. Allegiance to this principle provided the unfolding nationalism with a cardinal political dogma. The British probably did not see in whole but they did see in part that the colonists had developed a sense of separate identity which made the controversy over taxes a path to independence. Ingersoll, who met with Grenville and many members of the House of Commons during the debate over the bill to levy a stamp tax, noted that the best friends of America were all agreed on the necessity of upholding that power for "if they have not that Power over America, they have none, and then America is at once a Kingdom of itself." [27]

Important though it was, nationalism was developing a base that was broader than the common sharing of one political principle. In the summer of 1775 Congress debated a proposal for reconciliation made by Lord North the preceding February. The British ministry proposed to substitute for the system of taxes an agreement whereby the colonies would vote annual gifts and these would be subject to the approval of Parliament. A committee headed by Thomas Jefferson drew up a report that made clear for all to see the issue behind the long debate over taxes. The report charged that Lord North's latest proposition "seems to have been held up

141

---

[26] Daniel Dulany, *Considerations on the Propriety of Imposing Taxes in the British Colonies, For the Purpose of raising a Revenue, by Act of Parliament* (Annapolis, 1765), p. 17.

[27] *Mr. Ingersoll's Letters Relating to the Stamp Act* (New Haven, 1766).

to the world, to deceive it into a belief that there was nothing in dispute between us but the mode of levying taxes. . . ." [28] Behind the question of taxes lay the demand for a recognition of the colonial view that while they were loyal Britishers, they were entitled to equal and separate treatment.

The rise of nationalism is also evident in the appeal to history that found its way into so much of the American writing of the period. There were fewer references now to the glories of the struggle against the Stuarts and many more to the founding fathers, who left England when that country fell into ways of oppression. They had endured all sorts of miseries, starvation, the hard work of carving a home in the wilderness, battles with the treacherous Indians. Without any assistance from the government at home, they had built colonies that from the first brought both glory and wealth to the mother country. The first settlers had come in the hope that they would be able to enjoy the blessings of freedom. They had lived and labored in the expectation that the blessings of freedom would be the inheritance of their posterity. Now the heritage of the forefathers was being threatened.

The clergy invoked the lessons of history and reminded their listeners of their obligations to the freedom-loving and pious generation of pioneers. Often they went further and likened the Americans to the Israelites, the chosen people of God. Charles Chauncy, after tracing the great hardships endured by the forefathers, concluded:

> In a word, our fathers, as they trusted in God, were favored with many deliverances from great dangers, and heavily pressing difficulties; and in manner, sometimes, peculiarly striking and surprising. Perhaps it cannot be said of any deliverance, wrought out for people, those excepted which God wrought out for his Israel of old, that they were more signally great and glorious than those, in which he made his arm bare for the salvation of our fathers in this land. [29]

Chauncy went on to portray the decline that had taken place in England and the trials facing the Americans. "The restraints we are under as to the exercise of some of our rights and privileges are grievous"; he said, "and the more so, as they were the purchase of our fathers at the risque of every thing near and dear to them, their lives not excepted." [30]

The analogy of the Israelites was a popular one. The Reverend Judah Champion, of Litchfield, Connecticut, used as his text for two sermons the final words of Moses reminding his people "of the wonderful things

---

[28] Burnett, *The Continental Congress*, p. 96.
[29] Charles Chauncy, *Trust in God* (Boston, 1770), p. 21.
[30] *Ibid.*, p. 23.

God had done for them." Just as God had extended his compassionate regards and tokens of distinguishing respect to the offspring of Abraham, Isaac and Jacob, so He had guided the founding fathers. "God took Abraham from his father's house, from his kindred and country;—sent him to set up God's true worship in a strange land." In the same manner, said the Litchfield clergyman, "the Almighty took our fathers from their native land, when the nation was in confusion, and they groaned under spiritual tyranny, being extremely harrass'd, some cast into prisons, others beset in their houses for worshipping God according to the dictates of their own consciences, which was then prohibited."[31]

The sense that Americans were the chosen people of God, that he had guided them through the wilderness and made of them a great people was indeed an intoxicating idea, but it is an idea not uncommon in the history of nationalism.

143

There was something that can appropriately be called nationalism in the period prior to the Revolution. The attachment to the colony and, after the War for Independence, attachment to the state remained strong, but in the face of the challenge from London, the union of the colonies was nothing short of remarkable. Once the War for Independence had been won this intercolonial unity appeared to dissolve. The apparent absence of any concern for the Union in the immediate postwar years and even a willingness to see it disappear from history raises questions about the genuineness of the prewar article we have called nationalism.

That it should have flowered so luxuriantly under the stimulus of a foreign challenge and then wilted is only an indication that nationalism involves the innermost feelings and loyalties and is therefore subject to setbacks when the immediate stimulus is withdrawn. It is not achieved in a short span of years. The plant that seemed on the point of withering away after peace had been negotiated soon took on new life once the foreign challenge reappeared. Neither is the presence of a strong localism or the strife betweeen vested interests inconsistent with the existence at the same time of national feeling. Few would deny that there is an American nationalism today simply because local, sectional or economic interests exhibit an undiminished vitality. It should also be noted that an essential ingredient of American nationalism was the idea of greater freedom for the individual. The absence of restraints encouraged both sectional and economic interests to flex their muscles.

---

[31] Judah Champion, *A Brief View of the Distresses, Hardships, and Dangers Our Ancestors Encounter'd, In Settling New England — The Privileges We Enjoy, And Our Obligations Thence Arising; With Moral Reflections Thereupon* (Hartford, Conn., 1770).

Rhetoric and Reality in the American Revolution

Gordon S. Wood[*]

144

IF any catch phrase is to characterize the work being done on the American Revolution by this generation of historians, it will probably be "the American Revolution considered as an intellectual movement."[1] For we now seem to be fully involved in a phase of writing about the Revolution in which the thought of the Revolutionaries, rather than their social and economic interests, has become the major focus of research and analysis. This recent emphasis on ideas is not of course new, and indeed right from the beginning it has characterized almost all our attempts to understand the Revolution. The ideas of a period which Samuel Eliot Morison and Harold Laski once described as, next to the English revolutionary decades of the seventeenth century, the most fruitful era in the history of Western political thought could never be completely ignored in any phase of our history writing.[2]

It has not been simply the inherent importance of the Revolutionary ideas, those "great principles of freedom,"[3] that has continually attracted the attention of historians. It has been rather the unusual nature of the Revolution and the constant need to explain what on the face of it seems inexplicable that has compelled almost all interpreters of the Revolution, including the participants themselves, to stress its predominantly intellectual character and hence its uniqueness among Western revolutions. Within the context of Revolutionary historiography the one great effort to disparage the significance of ideas in the Revolution—an effort which dominated our history writing in the first half of the twentieth century—

[*] Mr. Wood is a Fellow at the Institute of Early American History and Culture at Williamsburg, and a member of the Department of History, the College of William and Mary.

[1] This is the title of a recent essay by Edmund S. Morgan in Arthur M. Schlesinger, Jr., and Morton White, eds., *Paths of American Thought* (Boston, 1963), 11-33.

[2] Samuel E. Morison, ed., "William Manning's *The Key of Libberty*," *William and Mary Quarterly*, 3d Ser., XIII (1956), 208.

[3] Edmund S. Morgan, "The American Revolution: Revisions in Need of Revising," *Wm. and Mary Qtly.*, 3d Ser., XIV (1957), 14.

becomes something of an anomaly, a temporary aberration into a deterministic social and economic explanation from which we have been retreating for the past two decades. Since roughly the end of World War II we have witnessed a resumed and increasingly heightened insistence on the primary significance of conscious beliefs, and particularly of constitutional principles, in explaining what once again has become the unique character of the American Revolution. In the hands of idealist-minded historians the thought and principles of the Americans have consequently come to repossess that explanative force which the previous generation of materialist-minded historians had tried to locate in the social structure.

Indeed, our renewed insistence on the importance of ideas in explaining the Revolution has now attained a level of fullness and sophistication never before achieved, with the consequence that the economic and social approach of the previous generation of behaviorist historians has never seemed more anomalous and irrelevant than it does at present. Yet paradoxically it may be that this preoccupation with the explanatory power of the Revolutionary ideas has become so intensive and so refined, assumed such a character, that the apparently discredited social and economic approach of an earlier generation has at the same time never seemed more attractive and relevant. In other words, we may be approaching a crucial juncture in our writing about the Revolution where idealism and behaviorism meet.

I

It was the Revolutionaries themselves who first described the peculiar character of what they had been involved in. The Revolution, as those who took stock at the end of three decades of revolutionary activity noted, was not "one of those events which strikes the public eye in the subversions of laws which have usually attended the revolutions of governments." Because it did not seem to have been a typical revolution, the sources of its force and its momentum appeared strangely unaccountable. "In other revolutions, the sword has been drawn by the arm of offended freedom, under an oppression that threatened the vital powers of society."[4] But this seemed hardly true of the American Revolution. There was none of the legendary tyranny that had so often driven desperate peoples into

[4] [William Vans Murray], *Political Sketches, Inscribed to His Excellency John Adams* (London, 1787), 21, 48.

revolution. The Americans were not an oppressed people; they had no crushing imperial shackles to throw off. In fact, the Americans knew they were probably freer and less burdened with cumbersome feudal and monarchical restraints than any part of mankind in the eighteenth century. To its victims, the Tories, the Revolution was truly incomprehensible. Never in history, said Daniel Leonard, had there been so much rebellion with so "little real cause." It was, wrote Peter Oliver, "the most wanton and unnatural rebellion that ever existed."[5] The Americans' response was out of all proportion to the stimuli. The objective social reality scarcely seemed capable of explaining a revolution.

Yet no American doubted that there had been a revolution. How then was it to be justified and explained? If the American Revolution, lacking "those mad, tumultuous actions which disgraced many of the great revolutions of antiquity," was not a typical revolution, what kind of revolution was it? If the origin of the American Revolution lay not in the usual passions and interests of men, wherein did it lay? Those Americans who looked back at what they had been through could only marvel at the rationality and moderation, "supported by the energies of well weighed choice," involved in their separation from Britain, a revolution remarkably "without violence or convulsion."[6] It seemed to be peculiarly an affair of the mind. Even two such dissimilar sorts of Whigs as Thomas Paine and John Adams both came to see the Revolution they had done so much to bring about as especially involved with ideas, resulting from "a mental examination," a change in "the minds and hearts of the people."[7] The Americans were fortunate in being born at a time when the principles of government and freedom were better known than at any time in history. The Americans had learned "how to define the rights of nature,—how to search into, to distinguish, and to comprehend, the principles of physical, moral, religious, and civil liberty," how, in short, to discover and

146

[5] [Daniel Leonard], *The Origin of the American Contest with Great Britain* . . . [by] *Massachusettensis* . . . (New York, 1775), 40; Douglass Adair and John A. Schutz, eds., *Peter Oliver's Origin and Progress of the American Rebellion: A Tory View* (San Marino, 1963), 159.

[6] Simeon Baldwin, *An Oration Pronounced Before the Citizens of New-Haven, July 4th, 1788* . . . (New Haven, 1788), 10; [Murray], *Political Sketches*, 48; David Ramsay, *The History of the American Revolution* (Philadelphia, 1789), I, 350.

[7] Thomas Paine, *Letter to the Abbé Raynal* . . . (1782) in Philip S. Foner, ed., *The Complete Writings of Thomas Paine* (New York, 1945), II, 243; John Adams to H. Niles, Feb. 13, 1818, in Charles Francis Adams, ed., *The Works of John Adams* (Boston, 1850-56), X, 282.

resist the forces of tyranny before they could be applied. Never before in history had a people achieved "a revolution by reasoning" alone.[8]

The Americans, "born the heirs of freedom,"[9] revolted not to create but to maintain their freedom. American society had developed differently from that of the Old World. From the time of the first settlements in the seventeenth century, wrote Samuel Williams in 1794, "every thing tended to produce, and to establish the spirit of freedom." While the speculative philosophers of Europe were laboriously searching their minds in an effort to decide the first principles of liberty, the Americans had come to experience vividly that liberty in their everyday lives. The American Revolution, said Williams, joined together these enlightened ideas with America's experience. The Revolution was thus essentially intellectual and declaratory: it "explained the business to the world, and served to confirm what nature and society had before produced." "All was the result of reason. . . ."[10] The Revolution had taken place not in a succession of eruptions that had crumbled the existing social structure, but in a succession of new thoughts and new ideas that had vindicated that social structure.

147

The same logic that drove the participants to view the Revolution as peculiarly intellectual also compelled Moses Coit Tyler, writing at the end of the nineteenth century, to describe the American Revolution as "preeminently a revolution caused by ideas, and pivoted on ideas." That ideas played a part in all revolutions Tyler readily admitted. But in most revolutions, like that of the French, ideas had been perceived and acted upon only when the social reality had caught up with them, only when the ideas had been given meaning and force by long-experienced "real evils." The American Revolution, said Tyler, had been different: it was directed "not against tyranny inflicted, but only against tyranny anticipated." The Americans revolted not out of actual suffering but out of reasoned principle. "Hence, more than with most other epochs of revolutionary strife, our epoch of revolutionary strife was a strife of ideas: a long warfare of political logic; a succession of annual campaigns in which

---

[8] William Pierce, *An Oration, Delivered at Christ Church, Savannah, on the 4th of July, 1788* . . . (Providence, [1788]), 6; Enos Hitchcock, *An Oration; Delivered July 4th, 1788* . . . (Providence, [1788]), 11.
[9] Petition to the King, Oct. 1774, in Worthington C. Ford, ed., *Journals of the Continental Congress, 1774-1789* (Washington, 1904-37), I, 118.
[10] Samuel Williams, *The Natural and Civil History of Vermont* . . . (Walpole, New Hamp., 1794), vii, 372-373; Pierce, *Oration . . . 4th July, 1788*, p. 8.

the marshalling of arguments not only preceded the marshalling of armies, but often exceeded them in impression upon the final result."[11]

II

It is in this historiographical context developed by the end of the nineteenth century, this constant and at times extravagant emphasis on the idealism of the Revolution, that the true radical quality of the Progressive generation's interpretation of the Revolution becomes so vividly apparent. For the work of these Progressive historians was grounded in a social and economic explanation of the Revolutionary era that explicitly rejected the causal importance of ideas. These historians could scarcely have avoided the general intellectual climate of the first part of the twentieth century which regarded ideas as suspect. By absorbing the diffused thinking of Marx and Freud and the assumptions of behaviorist psychology, men had come to conceive of ideas as ideologies or rationalizations, as masks obscuring the underlying interests and drives that actually determined social behavior. For too long, it seemed, philosophers had reified thought, detaching ideas from the material conditions that produced them and investing them with an independent will that was somehow alone responsible for the determination of events.[12] As Charles Beard pointed out in his introduction to the 1935 edition of *An Economic Interpretation of the Constitution*, previous historians of the Constitution had assumed that ideas were "entities, particularities, or forces, apparently independent of all earthly considerations coming under the head of 'economic.'" It was Beard's aim, as it was the aim of many of his contemporaries, to bring into historical consideration "those realistic features of economic conflict, stress, and strain" which previous interpreters of the Revolution had largely ignored.[13] The product of this aim was a generation or more of historical writing about the Revolutionary period (of which Beard's was but the most famous expression) that sought to explain the Revolution and the formation of the Constitution in terms of socio-economic relationships and interests rather than in terms of ideas.[14]

[11] Moses Coit Tyler, *The Literary History of the American Revolution, 1763-1783* (New York, 1897), I, 8-9.
[12] For a bald description of the assumptions with which this generation of historians worked see Graham Wallas, *Human Nature in Politics*, 3d ed. (New York, 1921), 5, 45, 48-49, 83, 94, 96, 118, 122, 156.
[13] Charles A. Beard, *An Economic Interpretation of the Constitution* (New York, 1935), x, viii.
[14] While the Progressive historians were attempting to absorb and use the latest

Curiously, the consequence of this reversal of historical approaches was not the destruction of the old-fashioned conception of the nature of ideas. As Marx had said, he intended only to put Hegel's head in its rightful place; he had no desire to cut it off. Ideas as rationalization, as ideology, remained—still distinct entities set in opposition to interests, now however lacking any deep causal significance, becoming merely a covering superstructure for the underlying and determinative social reality. Ideas therefore could still be the subject of historical investigation, as long as one kept them in their proper place, interesting no doubt in their own right but not actually counting for much in the movement of events.

Even someone as interested in ideas as Carl Becker never seriously considered them to be in any way determinants of what happened. Ideas fascinated Becker, but it was as superstructure that he enjoyed examining them, their consistency, their logic, their clarity, the way men formed and played with them. In his *Declaration of Independence: A Study in the History of Political Ideas* the political theory of the Americans takes on an unreal and even fatuous quality. It was as if ideas were merely refined tools to be used by the colonists in the most adroit manner possible. The entire Declaration of Independence, said Becker, was calculated for effect, designed primarily "to convince a candid world that the colonies had a moral and legal right to separate from Great Britain." The severe indictment of the King did not spring from unfathomable passions but was contrived, conjured up, to justify a rebellion whose sources lay elsewhere. Men to Becker were never the victims of their thought, always the masters of it. Ideas were a kind of legal brief. "Thus step by step, from 1764 to 1776, the colonists modified their theory to suit their needs."[15] The assumptions behind Becker's 1909 behaviorist work on New York politics in the Revolution and his 1922 study of the political ideas in the Declaration of Independence were more alike than they at first might appear.

Bringing to their studies of the Revolution similar assumptions about the nature of ideas, some of Becker's contemporaries went on to expose starkly the implications of those assumptions. When the entire body of

scientific techniques of the day nonbehaviorists in government departments and others with a traditional approach to political theory—men like Andrew C. McLaughlin, Edwin S. Corwin, William S. Carpenter, Charles M. McIlwain, and Benjamin F. Wright—were writing during this same period some of the best work that has ever been done on Revolutionary constitutional and political thought. However, because most of them were not, strictly speaking, historians, they never sought to explain the causes of the Revolution in terms of ideas.

[15] Carl L. Becker, *The Declaration of Independence: A Study in the History of Political Ideas* (New York, 1922), 203, 207, 133.

Revolutionary thinking was examined, these historians could not avoid being struck by its generally bombastic and overwrought quality. The ideas expressed seemed so inflated, such obvious exaggerations of reality, that they could scarcely be taken seriously. The Tories were all "wretched hirelings, and execrable parricides"; George III, the "tyrant of the earth," a "monster in human form"; the British soldiers, "a mercenary, licentious rabble of banditti," intending to "tear the bowels and vitals of their brave but peaceable fellow subjects, and *to wash the ground with a profusion of innocent blood*."[16] Such extravagant language, it seemed, could be nothing but calculated deception, at best an obvious distortion of fact, designed to incite and mold a revolutionary fervor. "The stigmatizing of British policy as 'tyranny,' 'oppression' and 'slavery,'" wrote Arthur M. Schlesinger, the dean of the Progressive historians, "had little or no objective reality, at least prior to the Intolerable Acts, but ceaseless repetition of the charge kept emotions at fever pitch."[17]

Indeed, so grandiose, so overdrawn, it seemed, were the ideas that the historians were necessarily led to ask not whether such ideas were valid but why men should have expressed them. It was not the content of such ideas but the function that was really interesting. The Revolutionary rhetoric, the profusion of sermons, pamphlets, and articles in the patriotic cause, could best be examined as propaganda, that is, as a concerted and self-conscious effort by agitators to manipulate and shape public opinion. Because of the Progressive historians' view of the Revolution as the movement of class minorities bent on promoting particular social and economic interests, the conception of propaganda was crucial to their explanation of what seemed to be a revolutionary consensus. Through the use of ideas in provoking hatred and influencing opinion and creating at least "an appearance of unity," the influence of a minority of agitators was out of all proportion to their number. The Revolution thus became a display of extraordinary skillfulness in the manipulation of public opinion. In fact, wrote Schlesinger, "no disaffected element in history has ever risen more splendidly to the occasion."[18]

Ideas thus became, as it were, parcels of thought to be distributed

[16] Quoted in Philip Davidson, *Propaganda and the American Revolution, 1763-1783* (Chapel Hill, 1941), 141, 373, 150.

[17] Arthur M. Schlesinger, *Prelude to Independence: The Newspaper War on Britain, 1764-1776* (New York, 1958), 34. For examples of the scientific work on which the propagandist studies drew, see note one in Sidney I. Pomerantz, "The Patriot Newspaper and the American Revolution," in Richard B. Morris, ed., *The Era of the American Revolution* (New York, 1939), 305.

[18] Davidson, *Propaganda*, 59; Schlesinger, *Prelude to Independence*, 20.

and used where they would do the most good. This propaganda was not of course necessarily false, but it was always capable of manipulation. "Whether the suggestions are to be true or false, whether the activities are to be open or concealed," wrote Philip Davidson, "are matters for the propagandist to decide." Apparently ideas could be turned on or off at will, and men controlled their rhetoric in a way they could not control their interests. Whatever the importance of propaganda, its connection with social reality was tenuous. Since ideas were so self-consciously manageable, the Whigs were not actually expressing anything meaningful about themselves but were rather feigning and exaggerating for effect. What the Americans said could not be taken at face value but must be considered as a rhetorical disguise for some hidden interest. The expression of even the classic and well-defined natural rights philosophy became, in Davidson's view, but "the propagandist's rationalization of his desire to protect his vested interests."[19]

151

With this conception of ideas as weapons shrewdly used by designing propagandists, it was inevitable that the thought of the Revolutionaries should have been denigrated. The Revolutionaries became by implication hypocritical demagogues, "adroitly tailoring their arguments to changing conditions." Their political thinking appeared to possess neither consistency nor significance. "At best," said Schlesinger in an early summary of his interpretation, "an exposition of the political theories of the anti-parliamentary party is an account of their retreat from one strategic position to another." So the Whigs moved, it was strongly suggested, easily if not frivolously from a defense of charter rights, to the rights of Englishmen, and finally to the rights of man, as each position was exposed and became untenable. In short, concluded Schlesinger, the Revolution could never be understood if it were regarded "as a great forensic controversy over abstract governmental rights."[20]

III

It is essentially on this point of intellectual consistency that Edmund S. Morgan has fastened for the past decade and a half in an attempt to bring down the entire interpretive framework of the socio-economic argument. If it could be shown that the thinking of the Revolutionaries

[19] Davidson, *Propaganda*, xiv, 46.
[20] Schlesinger, *Prelude to Independence*, 44; Arthur M. Schlesinger, *New Viewpoints in American History* (New York, 1923), 179.

was not inconsistent after all, that the Whigs did not actually skip from one constitutional notion to the next, then the imputation of Whig frivolity and hypocrisy would lose its force. This was a central intention of Morgan's study of the political thought surrounding the Stamp Act. As Morgan himself has noted and others have repeated, "In the last analysis the significance of the Stamp Act crisis lies in the emergence, not of leaders and methods and organizations, but of well-defined constitutional principles." As early as 1765 the Whigs "laid down the line on which Americans stood until they cut their connections with England. Consistently from 1765 to 1776 they denied the authority of Parliament to tax them externally or internally; consistently they affirmed their willingness to submit to whatever legislation Parliament should enact for the supervision of the empire as a whole."[21] This consistency thus becomes, as one scholar's survey of the current interpretation puts it, "an indication of American devotion to principle."[22]

It seemed clear once again after Morgan's study that the Americans were more sincerely attached to constitutional principles than the behaviorist historians had supposed, and that their ideas could not be viewed as simply manipulated propaganda. Consequently the cogency of the Progressive historians' interpretation was weakened if not unhinged. And as the evidence against viewing the Revolution as rooted in internal class-conflict continued to mount from various directions, it appeared more and more comprehensible to accept the old-fashioned notion that the Revolution was after all the consequence of "a great forensic controversy over abstract governmental rights." There were, it seemed, no deprived and depressed populace yearning for a participation in politics that had long been denied; no coherent merchant class victimizing a mass of insolvent debtors; no seething discontent with the British mercantile system; no privileged aristocracy, protected by law, anxiously and insecurely holding power against a clamoring democracy. There was, in short, no internal class upheaval in the Revolution.[23]

[21] Edmund S. Morgan, "Colonial Ideas of Parliamentary Power, 1764-1766," *Wm. and Mary Qtly.*, 3d Ser., V (1948), 311, 341; Edmund S. and Helen M. Morgan, *The Stamp Act Crisis: Prologue to Revolution*, rev. ed. (New York, 1963), 369-370; Page Smith, "David Ramsay and the Causes of the American Revolution," *Wm. and Mary Qtly.*, 3d Ser., XVII (1960), 70-71.

[22] Jack P. Greene, "The Flight From Determinism: A Review of Recent Literature on the Coming of the American Revolution," *South Atlantic Quarterly*, LXI (1962), 257.

[23] This revisionist literature of the 1950's is well known. See the listings in

If the Revolution was not to become virtually incomprehensible, it must have been the result of what the American Whigs always contended it was—a dispute between Mother Country and colonies over constitutional liberties. By concentrating on the immediate events of the decade leading up to independence, the historians of the 1950's have necessarily fled from the economic and social determinism of the Progressive historians. And by emphasizing the consistency and devotion with which Americans held their constitutional beliefs they have once again focused on what seems to be the extraordinary intellectuality of the American Revolution and hence its uniqueness among Western revolutions. This interpretation, which, as Jack P. Greene notes, "may appropriately be styled neo-whig," has turned the Revolution into a rationally conservative movement, involving mainly a constitutional defense of existing political liberties against the abrupt and unexpected provocations of the British government after 1760. "The issue then, according to the neo-whigs, was no more and no less than separation from Britain and the preservation of American liberty." The Revolution has therefore become "more political, legalistic, and constitutional than social or economic." Indeed, some of the neo-Whig historians have implied not just that social and economic conditions were less important in bringing on the Revolution as we once thought, but rather that the social situation in the colonies had little or nothing to do with causing the Revolution. The Whig statements of principle iterated in numerous declarations appear to be the only causal residue after all the supposedly deeper social and economic causes have been washed away. As one scholar who has recently investigated and carefully dismissed the potential social and economic issues in pre-Revolutionary Virginia has concluded, "What remains as the fundamental issue in the coming of the Revolution, then, is nothing more than the contest over constitutional rights."[24]

In a different way Bernard Bailyn in a recent article has clarified and reinforced this revived idealistic interpretation of the Revolution. The accumulative influence of much of the latest historical writing on the character of eighteenth-century American society has led Bailyn to the

---

Bernard Bailyn, "Political Experience and Enlightenment Ideas in Eighteenth-Century America," *American Historical Review*, LXVII (1961-62), 341n; and in Greene, "Flight From Determinism," 235-259.

[24] Greene, "Flight From Determinism," 237, 257; Thad W. Tate, "The Coming of the Revolution in Virginia: Britain's Challenge to Virginia's Ruling Class, 1763-1776," *Wm. and Mary Qtly.*, 3d Ser., XIX (1962), 323-343, esp. 340.

same insight expressed by Samuel Williams in 1794. What made the Revolution truly revolutionary was not the wholesale disruption of social groups and political institutions, for compared to other revolutions such disruption was slight; rather it was the fundamental alteration in the Americans' structure of values, the way they looked at themselves and their institutions. Bailyn has seized on this basic intellectual shift as a means of explaining the apparent contradiction between the seriousness with which the Americans took their Revolutionary ideas and the absence of radical social and institutional change. The Revolution, argues Bailyn, was not so much the transformation as the realization of American society.

154

The Americans had been gradually and unwittingly preparing themselves for such a mental revolution since they first came to the New World in the seventeenth century. The substantive changes in American society had taken place in the course of the previous century, slowly, often imperceptibly, as a series of small piecemeal deviations from what was regarded by most Englishmen as the accepted orthodoxy in society, state, and religion. What the Revolution marked, so to speak, was the point when the Americans suddenly blinked and saw their society, its changes, its differences, in a new perspective. Their deviation from European standards, their lack of an established church and a titled aristocracy, their apparent rusticity and general equality, now became desirable, even necessary, elements in the maintenance of their society and politics. The comprehending and justifying, the endowing with high moral purpose, of these confusing and disturbing social and political divergences, Bailyn concludes, was the American Revolution.[25]

Bailyn's more recent investigation of the rich pamphlet literature of the decades before Independence has filled out and refined his idealist interpretation, confirming him in his "rather old-fashioned view that the American Revolution was above all else an ideological-constitutional struggle and not primarily a controversy between social groups undertaken to force changes in the organization of society." While Bailyn's book-length introduction to the first of a multivolumed edition of Revolutionary pamphlets makes no effort to stress the conservative character of the Revolution and indeed emphasizes (in contrast to the earlier article) its radicalism and the dynamic and transforming rather than the rationalizing and declarative quality of Whig thought, it nevertheless represents the culmination of the idealist approach to the history of the

[25] Bailyn, "Political Experience and Enlightenment Ideas," 339-351.

Revolution. For "above all else," argues Bailyn, it was the Americans' world-view, the peculiar bundle of notions and beliefs they put together during the imperial debate, "that in the end propelled them into Revolution." Through his study of the Whig pamphlets Bailyn became convinced "that the fear of a comprehensive conspiracy against liberty throughout the English-speaking world—a conspiracy believed to have been nourished in corruption, and of which, it was felt, oppression in America was only the most immediately visible part—lay at the heart of the Revolutionary movement." No one of the various acts and measures of the British government after 1763 could by itself have provoked the extreme and violent response of the American Whigs. But when linked together they formed in the minds of the Americans, imbued with a particular historical understanding of what constituted tyranny, an extensive and frightening program designed to enslave the New World. The Revolution becomes comprehensible only when the mental framework, the Whig world-view into which the Americans fitted the events of the 1760's and 1770's, is known. "It is the development of this view to the point of overwhelming persuasiveness to the majority of American leaders and the meaning this view gave to the events of the time, and not simply an accumulation of grievances," writes Bailyn, "that explains the origins of the American Revolution."[26]

155

It now seems evident from Bailyn's analysis that it was the Americans' peculiar conception of reality more than anything else that convinced them that tyranny was afoot and that they must fight if their liberty was to survive. By an empathic understanding of a wide range of American thinking Bailyn has been able to offer us a most persuasive argument for the importance of ideas in bringing on the Revolution. Not since Tyler has the intellectual character of the Revolution received such emphasis and never before has it been set out so cogently and completely. It would seem that the idealist explanation of the Revolution has nowhere else to go.[27]

[26] Bernard Bailyn, ed., assisted by Jane N. Garrett, *Pamphlets of the American Revolution, 1750-1776* (Cambridge, Mass., 1965—), I, viii, 60, x, 20. The 200-page general introduction is entitled, "The Transforming Radicalism of the American Revolution."
[27] This is not to say, however, that work on the Revolutionary ideas is in any way finished. For examples of the re-examination of traditional problems in Revolutionary political theory see Richard Buel, Jr., "Democracy and the American Revolution: A Frame of Reference," *Wm. and Mary Qtly.*, 3d Ser., XXI (1964), 165-190;

IV

Labeling the recent historical interpretations of the Revolution as "neo-whig" is indeed appropriate, for, as Page Smith has pointed out, "After a century and a half of progress in historical scholarship, in research techniques, in tools and methods, we have found our way to the interpretation held, substantially, by those historians who themselves participated in or lived through the era of, the Revolution." By describing the Revolution as a conservative, principled defense of American freedom against the provocations of the English government, the neo-Whig historians have come full circle to the position of the Revolutionaries themselves and to the interpretation of the first generation of historians.[28] Indeed, as a consequence of this historical atavism, praise for the contemporary or early historians has become increasingly common.

But to say "that the Whig interpretation of the American Revolution may not be as dead as some historians would have us believe" is perhaps less to commend the work of David Ramsay and George Bancroft than to indict the approach of recent historians.[29] However necessary and rewarding the neo-Whig histories have been, they present us with only a partial perspective on the Revolution. The neo-Whig interpretation is intrinsically polemical; however subtly presented, it aims to justify the Revolution. It therefore cannot accommodate a totally different, an opposing, perspective, a Tory view of the Revolution. It is for this reason that the recent publication of Peter Oliver's "Origin and Progress of the American Rebellion" is of major significance, for it offers us—"by attacking the hallowed traditions of the revolution, challenging the motives of the founding fathers, and depicting revolution as passion, plotting, and violence"—an explanation of what happened quite different from what we have been recently accustomed to.[30] Oliver's vivid portrait of the Revolutionaries with his accent on their vicious emotions and interests seriously disturbs the present Whiggish interpretation of the Revolution. It is not that Oliver's description of, say, John Adams as madly ambitious

---

and Bailyn's resolution of James Otis's apparent inconsistency in *Revolutionary Pamphlets*, I, 100-103, 106-107, 121-123, 409-417, 546-552.

[28] Smith, "Ramsay and the American Revolution," 72.

[29] Morgan, "Revisions in Need of Revising," 13.

[30] Adair and Schutz, eds., *Peter Oliver's Origin*, ix. In the present neo-Whig context, Sidney S. Fisher, "The Legendary and Myth-Making Process in Histories of the American Revolution," in American Philosophical Society, *Proceedings* LI (Philadelphia, 1912), 53-75, takes on a renewed relevance.

and consumingly resentful is any more correct than Adams's own description of himself as a virtuous and patriotic defender of liberty against tyranny. Both interpretations of Adams are in a sense right, but neither can comprehend the other because each is preoccupied with seemingly contradictory sets of motives. Indeed, it is really these two interpretations that have divided historians of the Revolution ever since.

Any intellectually satisfying explanation of the Revolution must encompass the Tory perspective as well as the Whig, for if we are compelled to take sides and choose between opposing motives—unconscious or avowed, passion or principle, greed or liberty—we will be endlessly caught up in the polemics of the participants themselves. We must, in other words, eventually dissolve the distinction between conscious and unconscious motives, between the Revolutionaries' stated intentions and their supposedly hidden needs and desires, a dissolution that involves somehow relating beliefs and ideas to the social world in which they operate. If we are to understand the causes of the Revolution we must therefore ultimately transcend this problem of motivation. But this we can never do as long as we attempt to explain the Revolution mainly in terms of the intentions of the participants. It is not that men's motives are unimportant; they indeed make events, including revolutions. But the purposes of men, especially in a revolution, are so numerous, so varied, and so contradictory that their complex interaction produces results that no one intended or could even foresee. It is this interaction and these results that recent historians are referring to when they speak so disparagingly of those "underlying determinants" and "impersonal and inexorable forces" bringing on the Revolution. Historical explanation which does not account for these "forces," which, in other words, relies simply on understanding the conscious intentions of the actors, will thus be limited. This preoccupation with men's purposes was what restricted the perspectives of the contemporaneous Whig and Tory interpretations; and it is still the weakness of the neo-Whig histories, and indeed of any interpretation which attempts to explain the events of the Revolution by discovering the calculations from which individuals supposed themselves to have acted.

No explanation of the American Revolution in terms of the intentions and designs of particular individuals could have been more crudely put than that offered by the Revolutionaries themselves. American Whigs, like men of the eighteenth century generally, were fascinated with what

157

seemed to the age to be the newly appreciated problem of human motivation and causation in the affairs of the world. In the decade before independence the Americans sought endlessly to discover the supposed calculations and purposes of individuals or groups that lay behind the otherwise incomprehensible rush of events. More than anything else perhaps, it was this obsession with motives that led to the prevalence in the eighteenth century of beliefs in conspiracies to account for the confusing happenings in which men found themselves caught up. Bailyn has suggested that this common fear of conspiracy was "deeply rooted in the political awareness of eighteenth-century Britons, involved in the very structure of their political life"; it "reflected so clearly the realities of life in an age in which monarchical autocracy flourished, [and] in which the stability and freedom of England's 'mixed' constitution was a recent and remarkable achievement."[31] Yet it might also be argued that the tendency to see conspiracy behind what happened reflected as well the very enlightenment of the age. To attribute events to the designs and purposes of human agents seemed after all to be an enlightened advance over older beliefs in blind chance, providence, or God's interventions. It was rational and scientific, a product of both the popularization of politics and the secularization of knowledge. It was obvious to Americans that the series of events in the years after 1763, those "unheard of intolerable calamities, spring not of the dust, come not causeless." "Ought not the PEOPLE therefore," asked John Dickinson, "to watch? to observe facts? to search into causes? to investigate designs?"[32] And these causes and designs could be traced to individuals in high places, to ministers, to royal governors, and their lackeys. The belief in conspiracy grew naturally out of the enlightened need to find the human purposes behind the multitude of phenomena, to find the causes for what happened in the social world just as the natural scientist was discovering the causes for what happened in the physical world.[33] It was a necessary consequence of the search for

[31] Bailyn, *Revolutionary Pamphlets*, I, 87, ix.

[32] [Moses Mather], *America's Appeal to the Impartial World* . . . (Hartford, 1775), 59; [John Dickinson], *Letters from a Farmer in Pennsylvania to the Inhabitants of the British Colonies* (1768), in Paul L. Ford, ed., *The Life and Writings of John Dickinson* (Historical Society of Pennsylvania, *Memoirs*, XIV [Philadelphia, 1895]), II, 348. Dickinson hinged his entire argument on the ability of the Americans to decipher the "intention" of parliamentary legislation, whether for revenue or for commercial regulation. *Ibid.*, 348, 364.

[33] See Herbert Davis, "The Augustan Conception of History," in J. A. Mazzeo, ed., *Reason and the Imagination: Studies in the History of Ideas, 1600-1800* (New

connections and patterns in events. The various acts of the British government, the Americans knew, should not be "regarded according to the simple force of each, but as parts of a system of oppression."[34] The Whigs' intense search for the human purposes behind events was in fact an example of the beginnings of modern history.

In attempting to rebut those interpretations disparaging the colonists' cause, the present neo-Whig historians have been drawn into writing as partisans of the Revolutionaries. And they have thus found themselves entangled in the same kind of explanation used by the original antagonists, an explanation, despite obvious refinements, still involved with the discovery of motives and its corollary, the assessing of a personal sort of responsibility for what happened. While most of the neo-Whig historians have not gone so far as to see conspiracy in British actions (although some have come close),[35] they have tended to point up the blundering and stupidity of British officials in contrast to "the breadth of vision" that moved the Americans. If George III was in a position of central responsibility in the British government, as English historians have recently said, then, according to Edmund S. Morgan, "he must bear most of the praise or blame for the series of measures that alienated and lost the colonies, and it is hard to see how there can be much praise." By seeking "to define issues, fix responsibilities," and thereby to shift the "burden of proof" onto those who say the Americans were narrow and selfish and the empire was basically just and beneficent, the neo-Whigs have attempted

159

York, 1962), 226-228; W. H. Greenleaf, *Order, Empiricism and Politics: Two Traditions of English Political Thought, 1500-1700* (New York, 1964), 166; R. N. Stromberg, "History in the Eighteenth Century," *Journal of the History of Ideas,* XII (1951), 300. It was against this "dominant characteristic of the historical thought of the age," this "tendency to explain events in terms of conscious action by individuals," that the brilliant group of Scottish social scientists writing at the end of the 18th century directed much of their work. Duncan Forbes, "'Scientific' Whiggism: Adam Smith and John Millar," *Cambridge Journal,* VII (1954), 651, 653-654. While we have had recently several good studies of historical thinking in 17th-century England, virtually nothing has been done on the 18th century. See, however, J. G. A. Pocock, "Burke and the Ancient Constitution—A Problem in the History of Ideas," *The Historical Journal,* III (1960), 125-143; and Stow Persons, "The Cyclical Theory of History in Eighteenth Century America," *American Quarterly,* VI (1954), 147-163.

[34] [Dickinson], *Letters from a Farmer,* in Ford, ed., *Writings of Dickinson,* 388.

[35] Bailyn has noted that Oliver M. Dickerson, in chap. 7 of his *The Navigation Acts and the American Revolution* (Philadelphia, 1951), "adopts wholesale the contemporary Whig interpretation of the Revolution as the result of a conspiracy of 'King's Friends.'" Bailyn, *Revolutionary Pamphlets,* I, 724.

to redress what they felt was an unfair neo-Tory bias of previous explanations of the Revolution;[36] they have not, however, challenged the terms of the argument. They are still obsessed with why men said they acted and with who was right and who was wrong. Viewing the history of the Revolution in this judicatory manner has therefore restricted the issues over which historians have disagreed to those of motivation and responsibility, the very issues with which the participants themselves were concerned.

The neo-Whig "conviction that the colonists' attachment to principle was genuine"[37] has undoubtedly been refreshing, and indeed necessary, given the Tory slant of earlier twentieth-century interpretations. It now seems clearer that the Progressive historians, with their naive and crude reflex conception of human behavior, had too long treated the ideas of the Revolution superficially if not superciliously. Psychologists and sociologists are now willing to grant a more determining role to beliefs, particularly in revolutionary situations. It is now accepted that men act not simply in response to some kind of objective reality but to the meaning they give to that reality. Since men's beliefs are as much a part of the given stimuli as the objective environment, the beliefs must be understood and taken seriously if men's behavior is to be fully explained. The American Revolutionary ideas were more than cooked up pieces of thought served by an aggressive and interested minority to a gullible and unsuspecting populace. The concept of propaganda permitted the Progressive historians to account for the presence of ideas but it prevented them from recognizing ideas as an important determinant of the Americans' behavior. The weight attributed to ideas and constitutional principles by the neo-Whig historians was thus an essential corrective to the propagandist studies.

Yet in its laudable effort to resurrect the importance of ideas in historical explanation much of the writing of the neo-Whigs has tended to return to the simple nineteenth-century intellectualist assumption that history is the consequence of a rational calculation of ends and means, that what happened was what was consciously desired and planned. By supposing "that individual actions and immediate issues are more important than underlying determinants in explaining particular events," by em-

---

[36] Morgan, "Revisions in Need of Revising," 7, 13, 8; Greene, "Flight From Determinism," 237.

[37] Edmund S. Morgan, *The Birth of the Republic, 1763-89* (Chicago, 1956), 51.

phasizing conscious and articulated motives, the neo-Whig historians have
selected and presented that evidence which is most directly and clearly ex-
pressive of the intentions of the Whigs, that is, the most well-defined, the
most constitutional, the most reasonable of the Whig beliefs, those found
in their public documents, their several declarations of grievances and
causes. It is not surprising that for the neo-Whigs the history of the
American Revolution should be more than anything else "the history of
the Americans' search for principles."[38] Not only, then, did nothing
in the Americans' economic and social structure really determine their
behavior, but the colonists in fact acted from the most rational and calculated of motives: they fought, as they said they would, simply to defend
their ancient liberties against British provocation.

161

By implying that certain declared rational purposes are by themselves an adequate explanation for the Americans' revolt, in other words
that the Revolution was really nothing more than a contest over constitutional principles, the neo-Whig historians have not only threatened to deny
what we have learned of human psychology in the twentieth century, but
they have also in fact failed to exploit fully the terms of their own idealist approach by not taking into account all of what the Americans
believed and said. Whatever the deficiencies and misunderstandings of the
role of ideas in human behavior present in the propagandist studies of
the 1930's, these studies did for the first time attempt to deal with the
entirety and complexity of American Revolutionary thought—to explain
not only all the well-reasoned notions of law and liberty that were so
familiar but, more important, all the irrational and hysterical beliefs that
had been so long neglected. Indeed, it was the patent absurdity and im-
plausibility of much of what the Americans said that lent credence and
persuasiveness to their mistrustful approach to the ideas. Once this exaggerated and fanatical rhetoric was uncovered by the Progressive historians,
it should not have subsequently been ignored—no matter how much it
may have impugned the reasonableness of the American response. No
widely expressed ideas can be dismissed out of hand by the historian.

In his recent analysis of Revolutionary thinking Bernard Bailyn has
avoided the neo-Whig tendency to distort the historical reconstruction
of the American mind. By comprehending "the assumptions, beliefs, and
ideas that lay behind the manifest events of the time," Bailyn has attempted

[38] Greene, "Flight From Determinism," 258; Morgan, *Birth of the Republic*, 3.

to get inside the Whigs' mind, and to experience vicariously all of what they thought and felt, both their rational constitutional beliefs and their hysterical and emotional ideas as well. The inflammatory phrases, "slavery," "corruption," "conspiracy," that most historians had either ignored or readily dismissed as propaganda, took on a new significance for Bailyn. He came "to suspect that they meant something very real to both the writers and their readers: that there were real fears, real anxieties, a sense of real danger behind these phrases, and not merely the desire to influence by rhetoric and propaganda the inert minds of an otherwise passive populace."[39] No part of American thinking, Bailyn suggests—not the widespread belief in a ministerial conspiracy, not the hostile and vicious indictments of individuals, not the fear of corruption and the hope for regeneration, not any of the violent seemingly absurd distortions and falsifications of what we now believe to be true, in short, none of the frenzied rhetoric—can be safely ignored by the historian seeking to understand the causes of the Revolution.

Bailyn's study, however, represents something other than a more complete and uncorrupted version of the common idealist interpretations of the Revolution. By viewing from the "interior" the Revolutionary pamphlets, which were "to an unusual degree, *explanatory,*" revealing "not merely positions taken but the reasons why positions were taken," Bailyn like any idealist historian has sought to discover the motives the participants themselves gave for their actions, to re-enact their thinking at crucial moments, and thereby to recapture some of the "unpredictable reality" of the Revolution.[40] But for Bailyn the very unpredictability of the reality he has disclosed has undermined the idealist obsession with explaining why, in the participants' own estimation, they acted as they did. Ideas emerge as more than explanatory devices, as more than indicators of motives. They become as well objects for analysis in and for themselves, historical events in their own right to be treated as other historical events are treated. Although Bailyn has examined the Revolutionary ideas subjectively from the inside, he has also analyzed them objectively from the outside. Thus, in addition to a contemporary Whig perspective, he presents us with a retrospective view of the ideas—their complexity, their development, and their consequences—that the actual participants did not have. In effect his essay represents what has been called "a Namierism of

162

[39] Bailyn, *Revolutionary Pamphlets,* I, vii, ix.
[40] *Ibid.,* vii, viii, 17.

the history of ideas,"[41] a structural analysis of thought that suggests a conclusion about the movement of history not very different from Sir Lewis Namier's, where history becomes something "started in ridiculous beginnings, while small men did things both infinitely smaller and infinitely greater than they knew."[42]

In his *England in the Age of the American Revolution* Namier attacked the Whig tendency to overrate "the importance of the conscious will and purpose in individuals." Above all he urged us "to ascertain and recognize the deeper irrelevancies and incoherence of human actions, which are not so much directed by reason, as invested by it *ex post facto* with the appearances of logic and rationality," to discover the unpredictable reality, where men's motives and intentions were lost in the accumulation and momentum of interacting events. The whole force of Namier's approach tended to squeeze the intellectual content out of what men did. Ideas setting forth principles and purposes for action, said Namier, did not count for much in the movement of history.[43]

In his study of the Revolutionary ideas Bailyn has come to an opposite conclusion: ideas counted for a great deal, not only being responsible for the Revolution but also for transforming the character of American society. Yet in his hands ideas lose that static quality they have commonly had for the Whig historians, the simple statements of intention that so exasperated Namier. For Bailyn the ideas of the Revolutionaries take on an elusive and unmanageable quality, a dynamic self-intensifying character that transcended the intentions and desires of any of the historical participants. By emphasizing how the thought of the colonists was "strangely reshaped, turned in unfamiliar directions," by describing how the Americans "indeliberately, half-knowingly" groped toward "conclusions they could not themselves clearly perceive," by demonstrating how new beliefs and hence new actions were the responses not to desire but to the logic of developing situations, Bailyn has wrested the explanation of the Revolution out of the realm of motivation in which the neo-Whig historians had confined it.

With this kind of approach to ideas, the degree of consistency and devotion to principles become less important, and indeed the major issues

[41] J. G. A. Pocock, "Machiavelli, Harrington, and English Political Ideologies in the Eighteenth Century," *Wm. and Mary Qtly.*, 3d Ser., XXII (1965), 550.
[42] Sir Lewis Namier, *England in the Age of the American Revolution*, 2d ed. (London, 1961), 131.
[43] *Ibid.*, 129.

of motivation and responsibility over which historians have disagreed become largely irrelevant. Action becomes not the product of rational and conscious calculation but of dimly perceived and rapidly changing thoughts and situations, "where the familiar meaning of ideas and words faded away into confusion, and leaders felt themselves peering into a haze, seeking to bring shifting conceptions somehow into focus." Men become more the victims than the manipulators of their ideas, as their thought unfolds in ways few anticipated, "rapid, irreversible, and irresistible," creating new problems, new considerations, new ideas, which have their own unforeseen implications. In this kind of atmosphere the Revolution, not at first desired by the Americans, takes on something of an inevitable character, moving through a process of escalation into levels few had intended or perceived. It no longer makes sense to assign motives or responsibility to particular individuals for the totality of what happened. Men were involved in a complicated web of phenomena, ideas, and situations, from which in retrospect escape seems impossible.[44]

By seeking to uncover the motives of the Americans expressed in the Revolutionary pamphlets, Bailyn has ended by demonstrating the autonomy of ideas as phenomena, where the ideas operate, as it were, over the heads of the participants, taking them in directions no one could have foreseen. His discussion of Revolutionary thought thus represents a move back to a deterministic approach to the Revolution, a determinism, however, which is different from that which the neo-Whig historians have so recently and self-consciously abandoned. Yet while the suggested determinism is thoroughly idealist—indeed never before has the force of ideas in bringing on the Revolution been so emphatically put—its implications are not. By helping to purge our writing about the Revolution of its concentration on constitutional principles and its stifling judicial-like preoccupation with motivation and responsibility, the study serves to open the way for new questions and new appraisals. In fact, it is out of the very completeness of his idealist interpretation, out of his exposition of the extraordinary nature—the very dynamism and emotionalism—of the Americans' thought that we have the evidence for an entirely different, a behaviorist, perspective on the causes of the American Revolution.

[44] Bailyn, *Revolutionary Pamphlets*, I, 90, x, 169, 140. See Hannah Arendt, *On Revolution* (New York, 1963), 173: "American experience had taught the men of the Revolution that action, though it may be started in isolation and decided upon by single individuals for very different motives, can be accomplished only by some joint effort in which the motivation of single individuals . . . no longer counts. . . ."

164

Bailyn's book-length introduction to his edition of Revolutionary
pamphlets is therefore not only a point of fulfillment for the idealist approach to the Revolution, it is also a point of departure for a new look at
the social sources of the Revolution.

V

It seems clear that historians of eighteenth-century America and the
Revolution cannot ignore the force of ideas in history to the extent that
Namier and his students have done in their investigations of eighteenth-
century English politics. This is not to say, however, that the Namier approach to English politics has been crucially limiting and distorting.
Rather it may suggest that the Namier denigration of ideas and principles
is inapplicable for American politics because the American social situation in which ideas operated was very different from that of eighteenth-
century England. It may be that ideas are less meaningful to a people in a
socially stable situation. Only when ideas have become stereotyped reflexes
do evasion and hypocrisy and the Namier mistrust of what men believe
become significant. Only in a relatively settled society does ideology become a kind of habit, a bundle of widely shared and instinctive conventions, offering ready-made explanations for men who are not being compelled to ask any serious questions. Conversely, it is perhaps only in a
relatively unsettled, disordered society, where the questions come fas-
ter than men's answers, that ideas become truly vital and creative.[45]

165

Paradoxically it may be the very vitality of the Americans' ideas, then,
that suggests the need to examine the circumstances in which they
flourished. Since ideas and beliefs are ways of perceiving and explaining
the world, the nature of the ideas expressed is determined as much by the
character of the world being confronted as by the internal development of
inherited and borrowed conceptions. Out of the multitude of inherited
and transmitted ideas available in the eighteenth century, Americans selected and emphasized those which seemed to make meaningful what
was happening to them. In the colonists' use of classical literature, for
example, "their detailed knowledge and engaged interest covered only
one era and one small group of writers," Plutarch, Livy, Cicero, Sallust,
and Tacitus—those who "had hated and feared the trends of their

[45] See Sir Lewis Namier, *The Structure of Politics at the Accession of George III*,
2d ed. (London, 1961), 16; Sir Lewis Namier, "Human Nature in Politics," in
Personalities and Power: Selected Essays (New York, 1965), 5-6.

own time, and in their writing had contrasted the present with a better past, which they endowed with qualities absent from their own, corrupt era."[46] There was always, in Max Weber's term, some sort of elective affinity between the Americans' interests and their beliefs, and without that affinity their ideas would not have possessed the peculiar character and persuasiveness they did. Only the most revolutionary social needs and circumstances could have sustained such revolutionary ideas.[47]

When the ideas of the Americans are examined comprehensively, when all of the Whig rhetoric, irrational as well as rational, is taken into account, one cannot but be struck by the predominant characteristics of fear and frenzy, the exaggerations and the enthusiasm, the general sense of social corruption and disorder out of which would be born a new world of benevolence and harmony where Americans would become the "eminent examples of every divine and social virtue."[48] As Bailyn and the propaganda studies have amply shown, there is simply too much fanatical and millennial thinking even by the best minds that must be explained before we can characterize the Americans' ideas as peculiarly rational and legalistic and thus view the Revolution as merely a conservative defense of constitutional liberties. To isolate refined and nicely-reasoned arguments from the writings of John Adams and Jefferson is not only to disregard the more inflamed expressions of the rest of the Whigs but also to overlook the enthusiastic extravagance—the paranoiac obsession with a diabolical Crown conspiracy and the dream of a restored Saxon era—in the thinking of Adams and Jefferson themselves.

The ideas of the Americans seem, in fact, to form what can only be called a revolutionary syndrome. If we were to confine ourselves to examining the Revolutionary rhetoric alone, apart from what happened politically or socially, it would be virtually impossible to distinguish the American Revolution from any other revolution in modern Western his-

---

[46] Bailyn, *Revolutionary Pamphlets,* I, 22. The French Revolutionaries were using the same group of classical writings to express their estrangement from the *ancien régime* and their hope for the new order. Harold T. Parker, *The Cult of Antiquity and the French Revolutionaries: A Study in the Development of the Revolutionary Spirit* (Chicago, 1937), 22-23.

[47] The relation of ideas to social structure is one of the most perplexing and intriguing in the social sciences. For an extensive bibliography on the subject see Norman Birnbaum, "The Sociological Study of Ideology (1940-60)," *Current Sociology,* IX (1960).

[48] Jacob Duché, *The American Vine, A Sermon, Preached . . . Before the Honourable Continental Congress, July 20th, 1775 . . .* (Philadelphia, 1775), 29.

tory. In the kinds of ideas expressed the American Revolution is remarkably similar to the seventeenth-century Puritan Revolution and to the
eighteenth-century French Revolution: the same general disgust with
a chaotic and corrupt world, the same anxious and angry bombast, the
same excited fears of conspiracies by depraved men, the same utopian
hopes for the construction of a new and virtuous order.[49] It was not that
this syndrome of ideas was simply transmitted from one generation
or from one people to another. It was rather perhaps that similar, though
hardly identical, social situations called forth within the limitations of inherited and available conceptions similar modes of expression. Although
we need to know much more about the sociology of revolutions and
collective movements, it does seem possible that particular patterns of
thought, particular forms of expression, correspond to certain basic social
experiences. There may be, in other words, typical modes of expression,
typical kinds of beliefs and values, characterizing a revolutionary situation, at least within roughly similar Western societies. Indeed, the types
of ideas manifested may be the best way of identifying a collective movement as a revolution. As one student of revolutions writes, "It is on the
basis of a knowledge of men's beliefs that we can distinguish their behaviour from riot, rebellion or insanity."[50]

It is thus the very nature of the Americans' rhetoric—its obsession with
corruption and disorder, its hostile and conspiratorial outlook, and its millennial vision of a regenerated society—that reveals as nothing else apparently can the American Revolution as a true revolution with its
sources lying deep in the social structure. For this kind of frenzied rhetoric could spring only from the most severe sorts of social strain. The
grandiose and feverish language of the Americans was indeed the natural,
even the inevitable, expression of a people caught up in a revolutionary
situation, deeply alienated from the existing sources of authority and

[49] For recent discussions of French and Puritan revolutionary rhetoric see Peter
Gay, "Rhetoric and Politics in the French Revolution," *Amer. Hist. Rev.*, LXVI
(1960-61), 664-676; Michael Walzer, "Puritanism as a Revolutionary Ideology,"
History and Theory, III (1963), 59-90. This entire issue of *History and Theory* is
devoted to a symposium on the uses of theory in the study of history. In addition to
the Walzer article, I have found the papers by Samuel H. Beer, "Causal Explanation
and Imaginative Re-enactment," and Charles Tilly, "The Analysis of a Counter-
Revolution," very stimulating and helpful.

[50] Bryan A. Wilson, "Millennialism in Comparative Perspective," *Comparative
Studies in Society and History*, VI (1963-64), 108. See also Neil J. Smelser, *Theory
of Collective Behaviour* (London, 1962), 83, 120, 383.

vehemently involved in a basic reconstruction of their political and social order. The hysteria of the Americans' thinking was but a measure of the intensity of their revolutionary passions. Undoubtedly the growing American alienation from British authority contributed greatly to this revolutionary situation. Yet the very weakness of the British imperial system and the accumulating ferocity of American antagonism to it suggests that other sources of social strain were being fed into the revolutionary movement. It may be that the Progressive historians in their preoccupation with internal social problems were more right than we have recently been willing to grant. It would be repeating their mistake, however, to expect this internal social strain necessarily to take the form of coherent class conflict or overt social disruption. The sources of revolutionary social stress may have been much more subtle but no less severe.

Of all of the colonies in the mid-eighteenth century, Virginia seems the most settled, the most lacking in obvious social tensions. Therefore, as it has been recently argued, since conspicuous social issues were nonexistent, the only plausible remaining explanation for the Virginians' energetic and almost unanimous commitment to the Revolution must have been their devotion to constitutional principles.[51] Yet it may be that we have been looking for the wrong kind of social issues, for organized conflicts, for conscious divisions, within the society. It seems clear that Virginia's difficulties were not the consequence of any obvious sectional or class antagonism, Tidewater versus Piedmont, aristocratic planters versus yeomen farmers. There was apparently no discontent with the political system that went deep into the social structure. But there does seem to have been something of a social crisis within the ruling group itself, which intensely aggravated the Virginians' antagonism to the imperial system. Contrary to the impression of confidence and stability that the Virginia planters have historically acquired, they seemed to have been in very uneasy circumstances in the years before the Revolution. The signs of the eventual nineteenth-century decline of the Virginia gentry were, in other words, already felt if not readily apparent.

The planters' ability to command the acquiescence of the people seems extraordinary compared to the unstable politics of the other colonies. But in the years before independence there were signs of increasing anxiety among the gentry over their representative role. The ambiguities in the relationship between the Burgesses and their constituents erupted

[51] Tate, "Coming of the Revolution in Virginia," 324-343.

into open debate in the 1750's. And men began voicing more and more concern over the mounting costs of elections and growing corruption in the soliciting of votes, especially by "those who have neither natural nor acquired parts to recommend them."[52] By the late sixties and early seventies the newspapers were filled with warnings against electoral influence, bribery, and vote seeking. The freeholders were stridently urged to "strike at the Root of this growing Evil; be influenced by Merit alone," and avoid electing "obscure and inferior persons."[53] It was as if ignoble ambition and demagoguery, one bitter pamphlet remarked, were a "Daemon lately come among us to disturb the peace and harmony, which had so long subsisted in this place."[54] In this context Robert Munford's famous play, *The Candidates*, written in 1770, does not so much confirm the planters' confidence as it betrays their uneasiness with electoral developments in the colony, "when coxcombs and jockies can impose themselves upon it for men of learning." Although disinterested virtue eventually wins out, Munford's satire reveals the kinds of threats the established planters faced from ambitious knaves and blockheads who were turning representatives into slaves of the people.[55]

169

By the eve of the Revolution the planters were voicing a growing sense of impending ruin, whose sources seemed in the minds of many to be linked more and more with the corrupting British connection and the

[52] Robert E. and B. Katherine Brown, *Virginia, 1705-1786: Democracy or Aristocracy?* (East Lansing, Mich., 1964), 236; Alexander White to Richard Henry Lee, 1758, quoted in J. R. Pole, "Representation and Authority in Virginia from the Revolution to Reform," *The Journal of Southern History*, XXIV (1958), 23.

[53] Purdie and Dixon's *Virginia Gazette* (Williamsburg), Apr. 11, 1771; Rind's *Virginia Gazette*, Oct. 31, 1771. See Lester J. Cappon and Stella F. Duff, eds., *Virginia Gazette Index, 1736-1780* (Williamsburg, 1950), I, 351, for entries on the astounding increase in essays on corruption and cost of elections in the late 1760's and early 1770's.

[54] *The Defence of Injur'd Merit Unmasked; or, the Scurrilous Piece of Philander Dissected and Exposed to Public View. By a Friend to Merit, wherever found* (n.p., 1771), 10. Robert Carter chose to retire to private life in the early 1770's rather than adjust to the "new system of politicks" that had begun "to prevail generally." Quoted in Louis Morton, *Robert Carter of Nomini Hall: A Virginia Tobacco Planter of the Eighteenth Century* (Williamsburg, 1941), 52.

[55] Jay B. Hubbell and Douglass Adair, "Robert Munford's *The Candidates*," *Wm. and Mary Qtly.*, 3d Ser., V (1948), 246, 238. The ambivalence in Munford's attitude toward the representative process is reflected in the different way historians have interpreted his play. Cf. *ibid.*, 223-225, with Brown, *Virginia*, 236-237. Munford's fear of "men who aim at power without merit" was more fully expressed in his later play, *The Patriots*, written in 1775 or 1776. Courtlandt Canby, "Robert Munford's *The Patriots*," *Wm. and Mary Qtly.*, 3d Ser., VI (1949), 437-503, quotation from 450.

Scottish factors, but for others frighteningly rooted in "our Pride, our Luxury, and Idleness."[56] The public and private writings of Virginians became obsessed with "corruption," "virtue," and "luxury." The increasing defections from the Church of England, even among ministers and vestrymen, and the remarkable growth of dissent in the years before the Revolution, "so much complained of in many parts of the colony," further suggests some sort of social stress. The strange religious conversions of Robert Carter may represent only the most dramatic example of what was taking place less frenziedly elsewhere among the gentry.[57] By the middle of the eighteenth century it was evident that many of the planters were living on the edge of bankruptcy, seriously overextended and spending beyond their means in an almost frantic effort to fulfill the aristocratic image they had created of themselves.[58] Perhaps the importance of the Robinson affair in the 1760's lies not in any constitutional changes that resulted but in the shattering effect the disclosures had on that virtuous image.[59] Some of the planters expressed openly their fears for the future, seeing the products of their lives being destroyed in the reckless gambling and drinking of their heirs, who, as Landon Carter put it, "play away and play it all away."[60]

The Revolution in Virginia, "produced by the wantonness of the Gentleman," as one planter suggested,[61] undoubtedly gained much of its force from this social crisis within the gentry. Certainly more was expected from the Revolution than simply a break from British imperialism, and it was not any crude avoidance of British debts.[62] The Revolution-

[56] [John Randolph], *Considerations on the Present State of Virginia* ([Williamsburg], 1774), in Earl G. Swem, ed., *Virginia and the Revolution: Two Pamphlets, 1774* (New York, 1919), 16; Purdie and Dixon's *Virginia Gazette*, Nov. 25, 1773.

[57] Rind's *Virginia Gazette*, Sept. 8, 1774; Brown, *Virginia*, 252-254; Morton, *Robert Carter*, 231-250.

[58] See George Washington to George Mason, Apr. 5, 1769, in John C. Fitzpatrick, ed., *The Writings of George Washington* (Washington, 1931-44), II, 502; Carl Bridenbaugh, *Myths and Realities: Societies of the Colonial South* (New York, 1963), 5, 10, 14, 16; Emory G. Evans, "Planter Indebtedness and the Coming of the Revolution in Virginia," *Wm. and Mary Qtly.*, 3d Ser., XIX (1962), 518-519.

[59] Rind's *Virginia Gazette*, Aug. 15, 1766. See Carl Bridenbaugh, "Violence and Virtue in Virginia, 1766: or The Importance of the Trivial," Massachusetts Historical Society, *Proceedings*, LXXVI (1964), 3-29.

[60] Quoted in Bridenbaugh, *Myths and Realities*, 27. See also Morton, *Robert Carter*, 223-225.

[61] John A. Washington to R. H. Lee, June 20, 1778, quoted in Pole, "Representation and Authority in Virginia," 28.

[62] Evans, "Planter Indebtedness," 526-527.

ary reforms, like the abolition of entail and primogeniture, may have signified something other than mere symbolic legal adjustments to an existing reality. In addition to being an attempt to make the older Tidewater
plantations more economically competitive with lands farther west, the
reforms may have represented a real effort to redirect what was believed
to be a dangerous tendency in social and family development within the
ruling gentry. The Virginians were not after all aristocrats who could afford having their entailed families' estates in the hands of weak or inef-
fectual eldest sons. Entail, as the preamble to the 1776 act abolishing it
stated, had often done "injury to the morals of youth by rendering
them independent of, and disobedient to, their parents."[63] There was too
much likelihood, as the Nelson family sadly demonstrated, that a single
wayward generation would virtually wipe out what had been so pains-
takingly built.[64] George Mason bespoke the anxieties of many Virginians
when he warned the Philadelphia Convention in 1787 that "our own
Children will in a short time be among the general mass."[65]

Precisely how the strains within Virginia society contributed to the
creation of a revolutionary situation and in what way the planters expected independence and republicanism to alleviate their problems, of
course, need to be fully explored. It seems clear, however, from the very
nature of the ideas expressed that the sources of the Revolution in Virginia were much more subtle and complicated than a simple antagonism
to the British government. Constitutional principles alone do not explain
the Virginians' almost unanimous determination to revolt. And if the
Revolution in the seemingly stable colony of Virginia possessed internal
social roots, it is to be expected that the other colonies were experiencing
their own forms of social strain that in a like manner sought mitigation
through revolution and republicanism.

171

[63] Julian P. Boyd and others, eds., *The Papers of Thomas Jefferson* (Princeton,
1950—), I, 560. Most of our knowledge of entail and primogeniture in Virginia stems
from an unpublished doctoral dissertation, Clarence R. Keim, Influence of Primogeniture and Entail in the Development of Virginia, (University of Chicago, 1926).
Keim's is a very careful and qualified study and conclusions from his evidence—
other than the obvious fact that much land was held in fee simple—are by no means
easy to make. See particularly pp. 56, 60-62, 110-114, 122, 195-196.
[64] Emory S. Evans, "The Rise and Decline of the Virginia Aristocracy in the
Eighteenth Century: The Nelsons," in Darrett B. Rutman, ed., *The Old Dominion:
Essays for Thomas Perkins Abernethy* (Charlottesville, 1964), 73-74.
[65] Max Farrand, ed., *The Records of the Federal Convention of 1787* (New
Haven, 1911), I, 56; Bridenbaugh, *Myths and Realities*, 14, 16.

It is through the Whigs' ideas, then, that we may be led back to take up where the Progressive historians left off in their investigation of the internal social sources of the Revolution. By working through the ideas—by reading them imaginatively and relating them to the objective social world they both reflected and confronted—we may be able to eliminate the unrewarding distinction between conscious and unconscious motives, and eventually thereby to combine a Whig with a Tory, an idealist with a behaviorist, interpretation. For the ideas, the rhetoric, of the Americans was never obscuring but remarkably revealing of their deepest interests and passions. What they expressed may not have been for the most part factually true, but it was always psychologically true. In this sense their rhetoric was never detached from the social and political reality; and indeed it becomes the best entry into an understanding of that reality. Their repeated overstatements of reality, their incessant talk of "tyranny" when there seems to have been no real oppression, their obsession with "virtue," "luxury," and "corruption," their devotion to "liberty" and "equality"—all these notions were neither manipulated propaganda nor borrowed empty abstractions, but ideas with real personal and social significance for those who used them. Propaganda could never move men to revolution. No popular leader, as John Adams put it, has ever been able "to persuade a large people, for any length of time together, to think themselves wronged, injured, and oppressed, unless they really were, and saw and felt it to be so."[66] The ideas had relevance; the sense of oppression and injury, although often displaced onto the imperial system, was nonetheless real. It was indeed the meaningfulness of the connection between what the Americans said and what they felt that gave the ideas their propulsive force and their overwhelming persuasiveness.

It is precisely the remarkable revolutionary character of the Americans' ideas now being revealed by historians that best indicates that something profoundly unsettling was going on in the society, that raises the question, as it did for the Progressive historians, why the Americans should have expressed such thoughts. With their crude conception of propaganda the Progressive historians at least attempted to grapple with the problem. Since we cannot regard the ideas of the Revolutionaries as simply propaganda, the question still remains to be answered. "When 'ideas' in full cry drive past," wrote Arthur F. Bentley in his classic behavioral

[66] John Adams, "Novanglus," in Charles F. Adams, ed., *The Works of John Adams* (Boston, 1851), IV, 14.

study, *The Process of Government,* "the thing to do with them is to accept them as an indication that something is happening; and then search carefully to find out what it really is they stand for, what the factors of the social life are that are expressing themselves through the ideas."[67] Precisely because they sought to understand both the Revolutionary ideas and American society, the behaviorist historians of the Progressive generation, for all of their crude conceptualizations, their obsession with "class" and hidden economic interests, and their treatment of ideas as propaganda, have still offered us an explanation of the Revolutionary era so powerful and so comprehensive that no purely intellectual interpretation will ever replace it.

[67] Arthur F. Bentley, *The Process of Government: A Study of Social Pressures* (Chicago, 1908), 152.

The Puritan Ethic and the American Revolution

Edmund S. Morgan*

T HE American Revolution, we have been told, was radical and conservative, a movement for home rule and a contest for rule at home, the product of a rising nationality and the cause of that nationality, the work of designing demagogues and a triumph of statesmanship. John Adams said it took place in the minds and hearts of the people before 1776; Benjamin Rush thought it had scarcely begun in 1787. There were evidently many revolutions, many contests, divisions, and developments that deserve to be considered as part of the American Revolution. This paper deals in a preliminary, exploratory way with an aspect of the subject that has hitherto received little attention.[1] Without pretending to explain the whole exciting variety of the Revolution, I should like to suggest that the movement in all its phases, from the resistance against Parliamentary taxation in the 1760's to the establishment of a national government and national policies in the 1790's was affected, not to say guided, by a set of values inherited from the age of Puritanism.

These values or ideas, which I will call collectively the Puritan Ethic,[2] were not unconscious or subconscious, but were deliberately and openly expressed by men of the time. The men who expressed them were not Puritans, and few of the ideas included in the Puritan Ethic were actually new. Many of them had existed in other intellectual contexts before Puritanism was heard of, and many of them continue to exist today, as they did in the Revolutionary period, without the support of Puritanism. But Puritanism

* Mr. Morgan is a member of the Department of History, Yale University.

[1] The author is engaged in a full-scale study of this theme. The present essay is interpretative, and citations have for the most part been limited to identifying the sources of quotations.

[2] I have chosen this term rather than the familiar "Protestant Ethic" of Max Weber, partly because I mean something slightly different and partly because Weber confined his phrase to attitudes prevailing while the religious impulse was paramount. The attitudes that survived the decline of religion he designated as the "spirit of capitalism." In this essay I have not attempted to distinguish earlier from later, though I am concerned with a period when the attitudes were no longer dictated primarily by religion.

wove them together in a single rational pattern, and Puritans planted the pattern in America. It may be instructive, therefore, to identify the ideas as the Puritans defined and explained them before going on to the way in which they were applied in Revolutionary America after they had emerged from the Puritan mesh.

The values, ideas, and attitudes of the Puritan Ethic, as the term will be used here, clustered around the familiar idea of "calling." God, the Puritans believed, called every man to serve Him by serving society and himself in some useful, productive occupation. Before entering on a trade or profession, a man must determine whether he had a calling to undertake it. If he had talents for it, if it was useful to society, if it was appropriate to his station in life, he could feel confident that God called him to it. God called no one to a life of prayer or to a life of ease or to any life that added nothing to the common good. It was a "foul disorder in any Commonwealth that there should be suffered rogues, beggars, vagabonds." The life of a monk or nun was no calling because prayer must be the daily exercise of every man, not a way for particular men to make a living. And perhaps most important, the life of the carefree aristocrat was no calling: "miserable and damnable is the estate of those that being enriched with great livings and revenues, do spend their days in eating and drinking, in sports and pastimes, not employing themselves in service for Church or Commonwealth."[3]

175

Once called to an occupation, a man's duty to the Maker Who called him demanded that he labor assiduously at it. He must shun both idleness, or neglect of his calling, and sloth, or slackness in it. Recreation was legitimate, because body and mind sometimes needed a release in order to return to work with renewed vigor. But recreation must not become an end in itself. One of the Puritans' objections to the stage was that professional players made recreation an occupation and thereby robbed the commonwealth of productive labor. The emphasis throughout was on productivity for the benefit of society.

In addition to working diligently at productive tasks, a man was supposed to be thrifty and frugal. It was good to produce but bad to consume any more than necessity required. A man was but the steward of the possessions he accumulated. If he indulged himself in luxurious living, he would have that much less with which to support church and society. If

³ William Perkins, *Workes* (London, 1626-31), I, 755-756.

he needlessly consumed his substance, either from carelessness or from sensuality, he failed to honor the God who furnished him with it.

In this atmosphere the tolerance accorded to merchants was grudging. The merchant was suspect because he tended to encourage unnecessary consumption and because he did not actually produce anything; he simply moved things about. It was formally recognized that making exchanges could be a useful service, but it was a less essential one than that performed by the farmer, the shoemaker, or the weaver. Moreover, the merchant sometimes demeaned his calling by practicing it to the detriment rather than the benefit of society: he took advantage of his position to collect more than the value of his services, to charge what the market would bear. In short, he sometimes engaged in what a later generation would call speculation.

As the Puritan Ethic induced a suspicion of merchants, it also induced, for different reasons, a suspicion of prosperity. Superficial readers of Max Weber have often leapt to the conclusion that Puritans viewed economic success as a sign of salvation. In fact, Puritans were always uncomfortable in the presence of prosperity. Although they constantly sought it, although hard work combined with frugality could scarcely fail in the New World to bring it, the Puritans always felt more at ease when adversity made them tighten their belts. They knew that they must be thankful for prosperity, that like everything good in the world it came from God. But they also knew that God could use it as a temptation, that it could lead to idleness, sloth, and extravagance. These were vices, not simply because they in turn led to poverty, but because God forbade them. Adversity, on the other hand, though a sign of God's temporary displeasure, and therefore a cause for worry, was also God's means of recalling a people to Him. When God showed anger man knew he must repent and do something about it. In times of drought, disease, and disaster a man could renew his faith by exercising frugality and industry, which were good not simply because they would lead to a restoration of prosperity, but because God demanded them.

The ambivalence of this attitude toward prosperity and adversity was characteristic of the Puritans: it was their lot to be forever improving the world, in full knowledge that every improvement would in the end prove illusory. While rejoicing at the superior purity of the churches they founded in New England, they had to tell themselves that they had often enjoyed more godliness while striving against heavy odds in England. The experience caused Nathaniel Ward, the "simple cobbler of Aggawam," to lament the declension that he was sure would overtake the Puritans in England after they gained the upper hand in the 1640's: "my heart hath mourned, and mine eyes wept in secret, to consider what will become of multitudes of my dear Country-men [in England], when they shall enjoy what they now covet."[4] Human flesh was too proud to stand success; it needed the discipline of adversity to keep it in line. And Puritans accordingly relished every difficulty and worried over every success.

This thirst for adversity found expression in a special kind of sermon, the Jeremiad, which was a lament for the loss of virtue and a warning of divine displeasure and desolation to come. The Jeremiad was a rhetorical substitute for adversity, designed to stiffen the virtue of the prosperous and successful by assuring them that they had failed. Nowhere was the Puritan Ethic more assiduously inculcated than in these laments, and it accordingly became a characteristic of the virtues which that ethic demanded that they were always seen to be expiring, if not already dead. Industry and frugality in their full vigor belonged always to an earlier generation, which the existing one must learn to emulate if it would avoid the wrath of God.

177

These ideas and attitudes were not peculiar to Puritans. The voluminous critiques of the Weber thesis have shown that similar attitudes prevailed widely among many groups and at many times. But the Puritans did have them, and so did their descendants in the time of the Revolution and indeed for long after it. It matters little by what name we call them or where they came from. "The Puritan Ethic" is used here simply as an appropriate shorthand phrase to designate them, and should not be taken to imply that the American Revolutionists were Puritans.

The Puritan Ethic as it existed among the Revolutionary generation had in fact lost for most men the endorsement of an omnipresent angry God. The element of divinity had not entirely departed, but it was a good deal diluted. The values and precepts derived from it, however, remained intact and were reinforced by a reading of history that attributed the rise and fall of empires to the acquisition and loss of the same virtues that God had demanded of the founders of New England. Rome, it was learned, had risen while its citizens worked at their callings and led lives of simplicity and frugality. Success as usual had resulted in extravagance and luxury. "The ancient, regular, and laborious life was relaxed and sunk in Idleness,"

⁴Nathaniel Ward, *The Simple Cobbler of Aggawam in America* (London, 1647), 41.

and the torrent of vices thus let loose had overwhelmed the empire. In modern times the frugal Dutch had overthrown the extravagant Spanish.[5] The lesson of history carried the same imperatives that were intoned from the pulpit.

Whether they derived their ideas from history thus interpreted or from the Puritan tradition or elsewhere, Americans of the Revolutionary period in every colony and state paid tribute to the Puritan Ethic and repeated its injunctions. Although it was probably strongest among Presbyterians and Congregationalists like Benjamin Rush and Samuel Adams, it is evident enough among Anglicans like Henry Laurens and Richard Henry Lee and even among deists like Franklin and Jefferson. Jefferson's letters to his daughters sometimes sound as though they had been written by Cotton Mather: "It is your future happiness which interests me, and nothing can contribute more to it (moral rectitude always excepted) than the contracting a habit of industry and activity. Of all the cankers of human happiness, none corrodes it with so silent, yet so baneful a tooth, as indolence." "Determine never to be idle. No person will have occasion to complain of the want of time, who never loses any. It is wonderful how much may be done, if we are always doing."[6] And Jefferson of course followed his own injunction: a more methodically industrious man never lived.

The Puritan Ethic whether enjoined by God, by history, or by philosophy, called for diligence in a productive calling, beneficial both to society and to the individual. It encouraged frugality and frowned on extravagance. It viewed the merchant with suspicion and speculation with horror. It distrusted prosperity and gathered strength from adversity. It prevailed widely among Americans of different times and places, but those who urged it most vigorously always believed it to be on the point of expiring and in need of renewal.

The role of these ideas in the American Revolution—during the period, say, roughly from 1764 to 1789—was not explicitly causative. That is, the important events of the time can seldom be seen as the result of these ideas and never as the result solely of these ideas. Yet the major developments, the resistance to Great Britain, independence, the divisions among the successful Revolutionists, and the formulation of policies for the new nation,

[5] Purdie and Dixon's *Virginia Gazette* (Williamsburg), Sept. 5, 1771. Cf. *Pennsylvania Chronicle* (Philadelphia), Feb. 9-16, May 4-11, 1767; *Newport Mercury*, Mar. 7, 1774; and *Boston Evening Post*, Nov. 30, 1767.

[6] To Martha Jefferson, Mar. 28, May 5, 1787, in Julian Boyd *et al.*, eds., *The Papers of Thomas Jefferson* (Princeton, 1950-), XI, 250, 349.

178

were all discussed and understood by men of the time in terms derived from the Puritan Ethic. And the way men understood and defined the issues before them frequently influenced their decisions.

I. *The Origins of American Independence*

In the first phase of the American Revolution, the period of agitation between the passage of the Sugar Act in 1764 and the outbreak of hostilities at Lexington in 1775, Americans were primarily concerned with finding ways to prevent British authority from infringing what they considered to be their rights. The principal point of contention was Parliament's attempt to tax them; and their efforts to prevent taxation, short of outright resistance, took two forms: economic pressure through boycotts and political pressure through the assertion of political and constitutional principles. Neither form of protest required the application of the Puritan Ethic, but both in the end were affected by it.

179

The boycott movements were a means of getting British merchants to bring their weight to bear on Parliament for the specific purpose of repealing tax laws. In each case the boycotts began with extralegal voluntary agreements among citizens not to consume British goods. In 1764-65, for instance, artisans agreed to wear only leather working clothes. Students forbore imported beer. Fire companies pledged themselves to eat no mutton in order to increase the supply of local wool. Backed by the nonconsumers, merchants of New York, Philadelphia, and Boston agreed to import no British goods until the repeal of the Stamp Act. The pressure had the desired effect: the Stamp Act was repealed and the Sugar Act revised. When the Townshend Acts and later the Coercive Acts were passed, new nonconsumption and nonimportation agreements were launched.[7]

From the outset these colonial boycott movements were more than a means of bringing pressure on Parliament. That is to say, they were not simply negative in intent. They were also a positive end in themselves, a way of reaffirming and rehabilitating the virtues of the Puritan Ethic. Parliamentary taxation offered Americans the prospect of poverty and adversity, and, as of old, adversity provided a spur to virtue. In 1764, when Richard Henry Lee got news of the Sugar Act, he wrote to a friend in London: "Possibly this step of the mother country, though intended to oppress and keep us low, in order to secure our dependence, may be

[7] Arthur M. Schlesinger, *The Colonial Merchants and the American Revolution, 1763-1776* (New York, 1918), remains the best account of these movements.

subversive of this end. Poverty and oppression, among those whose minds are filled with ideas of British liberty, may introduce a virtuous industry, with a train of generous and manly sentiments. . . ."[8] And so it proved in the years that followed: as their Puritan forefathers had met providential disasters with a renewal of the virtue that would restore God's favor, the Revolutionary generation met taxation with a self-denial and industry that would hopefully restore their accustomed freedom and simultaneously enable them to identify with their virtuous ancestors.

The advocates of nonconsumption and nonimportation, in urging austerity on their countrymen, made very little of the effect that self-denial would have on the British government. Nonimportation and nonconsumption were preached as means of renewing ancestral virtues. Americans were reminded that they had been "of late years insensibly drawn into too great a degree of *luxury* and *dissipation*."[9] Parliamentary taxation was a blessing in disguise, because it produced the nonimportation and nonconsumption agreements. "Luxury," the people of the colonies were told, "has taken deep root among us, and to cure a people of luxury were an Herculean task indeed; what perhaps no power on earth but a British Parliament, in the very method they are taking with us, could possibly execute."[10] Parliamentary taxation, like an Indian attack in earlier years, was thus both a danger to be resisted and an act of providence to recall Americans from declension: "The Americans have plentifully enjoyed the delights and comforts, as well as the necessaries of life, and it is well known that an increase of wealth and affluence paves the way to an increase of luxury, immorality and profaneness, and here kind providence interposes; and as it were, obliges them to forsake the use of one of their delights, to preserve their liberty."[11] The principal object of this last homily was tea, which, upon being subjected to a Parliamentary duty, became luxurious and enervating. Physicians even discovered that it was bad for the health.[12]

In these appeals for self-denial, the Puritan Ethic acquired a value that had been only loosely associated with it hitherto: it became an essential

---

[8] To [Unknown], May 31, 1764, in James C. Ballagh, ed., *The Letters of Richard Henry Lee* (New York, 1911), I, 7.
[9] *Boston Evening Post,* Nov. 16, 1767.
[10] *Va. Gazette* (Purdie and Dixon), June 1, 1769 (reprinted from *New York Chronicle*).
[11] *Newport Mercury,* Dec. 13, 1773.
[12] *Ibid.,* Nov. 9, 1767, Nov. 29, 1773, Feb. 14, 28, 1774.

condition of political liberty. An author who signed himself "Frugality" advised the readers of the *Newport Mercury* that "We may talk and boast of liberty; but after all, the industrious and frugal only will be free,"[13] free not merely because their self-denial would secure repeal of Parliamentary taxes, but because freedom was inseparable from virtue, and frugality and industry were the most conspicuous public virtues. The Americans were fortunate in having so direct and easy a way to preserve liberty, for importations, it now appeared, were mainly luxuries, "Baubles of Britain," "foreign trifles."[14] By barring their entrance, "by consuming *less* of what we are not really in want of, and by industriously cultivating and improving the natural advantages of our own country, we might save our *substance, even our lands,* from becoming the property of others, and we might effectually preserve our *virtue* and our *liberty,* to the latest posterity." Americans like Englishmen had long associated liberty with property. They now concluded that both rested on virtue: while liberty would expire without the support of property, property itself could not exist without industry and frugality. "Our enemies," they were assured, "very well know that dominion and property are closely connected; and that to impoverish us, is the surest way to enslave us. Therefore, if we mean still to be free, let us unanimously lay aside foreign superfluities, and encourage our own manufacture. SAVE YOUR MONEY AND YOU WILL SAVE YOUR COUNTRY!"[15]

There was one class of Americans who could take no comfort in this motto. The merchants, on whom nonimportation depended, stood to lose by the campaign for austerity, and it is not surprising that they showed less enthusiasm for it than the rest of the population. Their lukewarmness only served to heighten the suspicion with which their calling was still viewed. "Merchants have no country," Jefferson once remarked. "The mere spot they stand on does not constitute so strong an attachment as that from which they draw their gains."[16] And John Adams at the Continental Congress was warned by his wife's uncle that merchants "have no Object but

181

[13] *Ibid.,* Feb. 28, 1774.

[14] *Boston Evening Post,* Nov. 9, 16, 1767; To Arthur Lee, Oct. 31, 1771, in H. A. Cushing, ed., *The Writings of Samuel Adams* (New York, 1904-08), II, 267.

[15] *Boston Evening Post,* Nov. 16, 1767; *Pennsylvania Journal* (Philadelphia), Dec. 10, 1767.

[16] To Horatio Spafford, Mar. 17, 1817, quoted in Boyd, ed., *Jefferson Papers,* XIV, 221.

their own particular Interest and they must be Contrould or they will ruin any State under Heaven."[17]

Such attitudes had been nourished by the merchants' behavior in the 1760's and 1770's. After repeal of the Stamp Act, Silas Downer, secretary of the Sons of Liberty in Providence, Rhode Island, wrote to the New York Sons of Liberty that "From many observations when the Stamp Act was new, I found that the Merchants in general would have quietly submitted, and many were zealous for it, always reciting the Difficulties their Trade would be cast into on Non Compliance, and never regarding the Interest of the whole Community. . . ."[18] When the Townshend Acts were passed, it was not the merchants but the Boston town meeting that took the lead in promoting nonimportation, and after the repeal of the Acts the merchants broke down and began importing while the duty on tea still remained. Samuel Adams had expected their defection to come much sooner for he recognized that the nonimportation agreements had "pressed hard upon their private Interest" while the majority of consumers could participate under the "happy Consideration that while they are most effectually serving their Country they are adding to their private fortunes."[19]

The merchants actually had more than a short-range interest at stake in their reluctance to undertake nonimportation. The movement, as we have seen, was not simply a means of securing repeal of the taxes to which merchants along with other colonists were opposed. The movement was in fact anticommercial, a repudiation of the merchant's calling. Merchants, it was said, encouraged men to go into debt. Merchants pandered to luxury. Since they made more on the sale of superfluous baubles than on necessities, they therefore pressed the sale of them to a weak and gullible public. What the advocates of nonimportation demanded was not merely an interruption of commerce but a permanent reduction, not to say elimination, of it. In its place they called for manufacturing, a palpably productive, useful calling.

The encouragement of manufacturing was an accompaniment to all the nonimportation, nonconsumption movements. New Yorkers organized a society specifically for that purpose, which offered bounties for the

182

[17] Cotton Tufts to John Adams, Apr. 26, 1776, in L. H. Butterfield et al., eds., *Adams Family Correspondence* (Cambridge, Mass., 1963-), I, 395.
[18] Letter dated July 21, 1766, Peck Manuscripts, III, 3, Rhode Island Historical Society, Providence.
[19] To Stephen Sayre, Nov. 16, 1770, in Cushing, ed., *Writings of Samuel Adams*, II, 58.

production of native textiles and other necessaries. The nonconsumption of mutton provided new supplies of wool, which housewives turned into thread in spinning matches (wheelwrights did a land-office business in spinning wheels). Stores began selling American cloth, and college students appeared at commencement in homespun. Tories ridiculed these efforts, and the total production was doubtless small, but it would be difficult to underestimate the importance of the attitude toward manufacturing that originated at this time. In a letter of Abigail Adams can be seen the way in which the Puritan Ethic was creating out of a Revolutionary protest movement the conception of a self-sufficient American economy. Abigail was writing to her husband, who was at the First Continental Congress, helping to frame the Continental Association for nonimportation, nonexportation, and nonconsumption:

183

If we expect to inherit the blessings of our Fathers, we should return a little more to their primitive Simplicity of Manners, and not sink into inglorious ease. We have too many high sounding words, and too few actions that correspond with them. I have spent one Sabbeth in Town since you left me. I saw no difference in respect to ornaments, etc. etc. but in the Country you must look for that virtue, of which you find but small Glimerings in the Metropolis. Indeed they have not the advantages, nor the resolution to encourage their own Manufactories which people in the country have. To the Mercantile part, tis considerd as throwing away their own Bread; but they must retrench their expenses and be content with a small share of gain for they will find but few who will wear their Livery. As for me I will seek wool and flax and work willingly with my Hands, and indeed their is occasion for all our industry and economy.[20]

In 1774 manufacture retained its primitive meaning of something made by hand, and making things by hand seemed a fitting occupation for frugal country people who had always exhibited more of the Puritan Ethic than high-living city folk. Abigail's espousal of manufactures, with its defiant rejection of dependence on the merchants of the city, marks a step away from the traditional notion that America because of its empty lands and scarcity of people was unsuited to manufactures and must therefore obtain them from the Old World. Through the nonimportation movements the colonists discovered that manufacturing was a calling not beyond the capacities of a frugal, industrious people, however few in number, and that importation of British manufactures actually menaced frugality

[20] Oct. 16, 1774, in Butterfield, ed., *Adams Family Correspondence*, I, 173.

and industry. The result of the discovery was to make a connection with Britain seem neither wholly necessary nor wholly desirable, so that when the thought of independence at last came, it was greeted with less apprehension that it might otherwise have been.

Nonimportation had produced in effect a trial run in economic self-sufficiency. The trial was inconclusive as a demonstration of American economic capacity, but it carried immense significance intellectually, for it obliged the colonists to think about the possibility of an economy that would not be colonial. At the same time it confirmed them in the notion that liberty was the companion not only of property but of frugality and industry, two virtues that in turn fostered manufactures. The Puritan Ethic had shaped a protest movement into affirmations of value in which can be seen the glimmerings of a future national economic policy.

While engaged in their campaign of patriotic frugality, Americans were also articulating the political principles that they thought should govern free countries and that should bar Parliament from taxing them. The front line of defense against Parliament was the ancient maxim that a man could not be taxed except by his own consent given in person or by his representative. The colonists believed this to be an acknowledged principle of free government, indelibly stamped on the British Constitution, and they wrote hundreds of pages affirming it. In those pages the Puritan Ethic was revealed at the very root of the constitutional principle when taxation without representation was condemned as an assault on every man's calling. To tax a man without his consent, Samuel Adams said, was "against the plain and obvious rule of equity, whereby the industrious man is intitled to the fruits of his industry."[21] And the New York Assembly referred to the Puritan Ethic when it told Parliament that the effect of the sugar and stamp taxes would be to "dispirit the People, abate their Industry, discourage Trade, introduce Discord, Poverty, and Slavery."[22] In slavery, of course, there could be no liberty and no property and so no motive for frugality and industry. Uncontrolled Parliamentary taxation, like luxury and extravagance, was an attack not merely on property but on industry and frugality, for which liberty and property must be the expected re-

[21] [*Boston Gazette*, Dec. 19, 1768] in Cushing, ed., *Writings of Samuel Adams*, I, 271.
[22] E. S. Morgan, ed., *Prologue to Revolution: Sources and Documents on the Stamp Act Crisis, 1764-1766* (Chapel Hill, 1959), 13.

wards. With every protest that British taxation was reducing them to slavery, Americans reaffirmed their devotion to industry and frugality and their readiness to defy the British threat to them. Students of the American Revolution have often found it difficult to believe that the colonists were willing to fight about an abstract principle and have sometimes dismissed the constitutional arguments of the time as mere rhetoric. But the constitutional principle on which the colonists rested their case was not the product either of abstract political philosophy or of the needs of the moment. In the colonists' view, it was a means, hallowed by history, of protecting property and of maintaining those virtues, associated with property, without which no people could be free. Through the rhetoric, if it may be called that, of the Puritan Ethic, the colonists reached behind the constitutional principle to the enduring human needs that had brought the principle into being.

185

We may perhaps understand better the urgency both of the constitutional argument and of the drive toward independence that it ultimately generated, if we observe the growing suspicion among the colonists that the British government had betrayed its own constitution and the values which that constitution protected. In an earlier generation the colonists had vied with one another in praising the government of England. Englishmen, they believed, had suffered again and again from invasion and tyranny, had each time recovered control of their government, and in the course of centuries had developed unparalleled constitutional safeguards to keep rulers true to their callings. The calling of a ruler, as the colonists and their Puritan forbears saw it, was like any other calling: it must serve the common good; it must be useful, productive; and it must be assiduously pursued. After the Glorious Revolution of 1688, Englishmen had fashioned what seemed a nearly perfect instrument of government, a constitution that blended monarchy, aristocracy, and democracy in a mixture designed to avoid the defects and secure the benefits of each. But something had gone wrong. The human capacity for corruption had transformed the balanced government of King, Lords, and Commons into a single-minded body of rulers bent on their own enrichment and heedless of the public good.

A principal means of corruption had been the multiplication of officeholders who served no useful purpose but fattened on the labors of those who did the country's work. Even before the dispute over taxation began, few colonists who undertook trips to England failed to make unflattering comparisons between the simplicity, frugality, and industry that prevailed in the colonies and the extravagance, luxury, idleness, drunkenness, poverty, and crime that they saw in the mother country. To Americans bred on the values of the Puritan Ethic, England seemed to have fallen prey to her own opulence, and the government shared heavily in the corruption. In England, the most powerful country in the world, the visitors found the people laboring under a heavy load of taxes, levied by a government that swarmed with functionless placeholders and pensioners. The cost of government in the colonies, as Professor Gipson has shown, was vastly lower than in England, with the per capita burden of taxation only a fraction of that which Englishmen bore.[23] And whatever the costs of maintaining the empire may have contributed to the British burden, it was clear that the English taxpayers supported a large band of men who lived well from offices that existed only to pay their holders. Even an American like George Croghan, who journeyed to London to promote dubious speculative schemes of his own, felt uncomfortable in the presence of English corruption: "I am Nott Sorry I Came hear," he wrote, "as it will Larn Me to be Contented on a Litle farm in amerrica. . . . I am Sick of London and harttily Tierd of the pride and pompe. . . ."[24]

In the 1760's Americans were given the opportunity to gain the perspective of a Croghan without the need for a trip abroad. The Townshend Acts called for a reorganization of the customs service with a new set of higher officials, who would perforce be paid out of the duties they extracted from the colonists. In the establishment of this American Board of Customs Commissioners, Americans saw the extension of England's corrupt system of officeholding to America. As Professor Dickerson has shown, the Commissioners were indeed corrupt.[25] They engaged in extensive "customs racketeering" and they were involved in many of the episodes that heightened the tension between England and the colonies: it was on their request that troops were sent to Boston; the Boston Massacre took place before their headquarters; the *Gaspée* was operating under their orders. But it was not merely the official actions of the Commissioners that offended Americans. Their very existence seemed to pose a threat both to

[23] L. H. Gipson, *The British Empire Before the American Revolution* . . . (New York, 1936-   ), X, 53-110; Gipson, *The Coming of the Revolution 1763-1775* (New York, 1954), 116-161.

[24] Quoted in T. P. Abernethy, *Western Lands and the American Revolution* (New York, 1937), 24.

[25] O. M. Dickerson, *The Navigation Acts and the American Revolution* (Philadelphia, 1951), 208-265.

the Puritan Ethic and to the conscientious, frugal kind of government that went with it. Hitherto colonial governments had been relatively free of the evils that had overtaken England. But now the horde of placeholders was descending on America.

From the time the Commissioners arrived in Boston in November 1767, the newspapers were filled with complaints that "there can be no such thing as common good or common cause where mens estates are ravaged at pleasure to lavish on parasitical minions."[26] Samuel Adams remarked that the commissioners were "a useless and very expensive set of officers" and that they had power to appoint "as many officers under them as they please, for whose Support it is said they may sink the whole revenue."[27] American writers protested against the "legions of idle, lazy, and to say no worse, altogether useless customs house locusts, catterpillars, flies and lice."[28] They were "a parcel of dependant tools of arbitrary power, sent hither to enrich themselves and their Masters, on the Spoil of the honest and industrious of these colonies."[29] By 1774, when the debate between colonies and Parliament was moving into its final stages, town meetings could state it as an intolerable grievance "that so many unnecessary officers are supported by the earnings of honest industry, in a life of dissipation and ease; who, by being *properly* employed, might be useful members of society."[30]

The coming of the Customs Commissioners showed the colonists that the ocean barrier which had hitherto isolated them from the corruption of Britain was no longer adequate. Eventually, perhaps, Englishmen would again arise, turn out the scoundrels, and recall their government to its proper tasks. And Americans did not fail to support Englishmen like John Wilkes whom they thought to be working toward this end. But meanwhile they could not ignore the dangers on their own shores. There would henceforth be in their midst a growing enclave of men whose lives and values denied the Puritan Ethic; and there would be an increasing number of lucrative offices to tempt Americans to desert ancestral standards and join the ranks of the "parasitical minions." No American was sure that his countrymen would be able to resist the temptation. In 1766, after repeal of the Stamp Act, George Mason had advised the merchants of London that

[26] *Boston Evening Post*, Nov. 30, 1767.
[27] To Dennys De Berdt, May 14, 1768, in Cushing, ed., *Writings of Samuel Adams*, I, 216.
[28] *Newport Mercury*, June 21, 1773.
[29] *Ibid.*, July 13, 1772.
[30] Resolves of Bristol, R. I., *ibid.*, Mar. 21, 1774.

Americans were "not yet debauched by wealth, luxury, venality and corruption."[31] But who could say how long their virtue would withstand the closer subjection to British control that Whitehall seemed to be designing? Some Americans believed that the British were deliberately attempting to undermine the Puritan Ethic. In Boston Samuel Adams observed in 1771 that "the Conspirators against our Liberties are employing all their Influence to divide the people, . . . introducing Levity Luxury and Indolence and assuring them that if they are quiet the Ministry will alter their Measures."[32] And in 1772 Henry Marchant, a Rhode Island traveler in England wrote to his friend Ezra Stiles: "You will often hear the following Language—Damn those Fellows we shall never do any Thing with Them till we root out that cursed puritanick Spirit—How is this to be done?—keep Soldiers amongst Them, not so much to awe Them, as to debauch their Morals—Toss off to them all the Toies and Baubles that genius can invent to weaken their Minds, fill Them with Pride and Vanity, and beget in them all possible Extravagance in Dress and Living, that They may be kept poor and made wretched. . . ."[33]

By the time the First Continental Congress came together in 1774, large numbers of leading Americans had come to identify Great Britain with vice and America with virtue, yet with the fearful recognition that virtue stands in perennial danger from the onslaughts of vice. Patrick Henry gave voice to the feeling when he denounced Galloway's plan for an intercolonial American legislature that would stand between the colonies and Parliament. "We shall liberate our Constituents," he warned, "from a corrupt House of Commons, but thro[w] them into the Arms of an American Legislature that may be bribed by that Nation which avows in the Face of the World, that Bribery is a Part of her System of Government."[34] A government that had succeeded in taxing seven million Englishmen (with the consent of their supposed representatives), to support an army of placeholders, would have no hesitation in using every means to corrupt the representatives of two and one half million Americans.

When the Second Congress met in 1775, Benjamin Franklin, fresh from

---

[31] Morgan, *Prologue to Revolution*, 160.

[32] To Arthur Lee, Oct. 31, 1771, in Cushing, ed., *Writings of Samuel Adams*, II, 266-267.

[33] Quoted in E. S. Morgan, *The Gentle Puritan: A Life of Ezra Stiles, 1727-1795* (New Haven, 1962), 265.

[34] Sept. 28, 1774, in L. H. Butterfield *et al.*, eds., *Diary and Autobiography of John Adams* (Cambridge, Mass., 1961), II, 143.

London, could assure the members that their contrast of England and America was justified. Writing back to Joseph Priestley, he said it would "scarce be credited in Britain, that men can be as diligent with us from zeal for the public good, as with you for thousands per annum. Such is the difference between uncorrupted new states, and corrupted old ones."[35] Thomas Jefferson drew the contrast even more bluntly in an answer rejecting Lord North's Conciliatory Proposal of February 20, 1775, which had suggested that Parliament could make provisions for the government of the colonies. "The provisions we have made," said Jefferson, "are such as please our selves, and are agreeable to our own circumstances; they answer the substantial purposes of government and of justice, and other purposes than these should not be answered. We do not mean that our people shall be burthened with oppressive taxes to provide sinecures for the idle or the wicked...."[36]

189

When Congress finally dissolved the political bands that had connected America with England, the act was rendered less painful by the colonial conviction that America and England were already separated as virtue is from vice. The British Constitution had foundered, and the British government had fallen into the hands of a luxurious and corrupt ruling class. There remained no way of preserving American virtue unless the connection with Britain was severed. The meaning of virtue in this context embraced somewhat more than the values of the Puritan Ethic, but those values were pre-eminent in it. In the eyes of many Americans the Revolution was a defense of industry and frugality, whether in rulers or people, from the assaults of British vice. The Puritan Ethic, in the colonists' political as in their economic thinking, prepared the way for independence.

II. *Who Should Rule at Home*

Virtue, as everyone knew, was a fragile and probably fleeting possession. Even while defending it from the British, Americans worried about their own uneasy hold on it and eyed one another for signs of its departure. The war, of course, furnished the conditions of adversity in which virtue could be expected to flourish. On the day after Congress voted independence, John Adams wrote exultantly to Abigail of the difficulties ahead: "It may be the Will of Heaven that America shall suffer Calamities

---

[35] July 6, 1775, in E. C. Burnett, ed., *Letters of Members of The Continental Congress* (Washington, 1921-36), I, 156.

[36] July 31, 1775, in Boyd, ed., *Jefferson Papers*, I, 232.

still more wasting and Distresses yet more dreadfull. If this is to be the Case, it will have this good Effect, at least: it will inspire Us with many Virtues, which We have not, and correct many Errors, Follies, and Vices, which threaten to disturb, dishonour, and destroy Us.—The Furnace of Affliction produces Refinement, in States as well as Individuals."[37] Thereafter, as afflictions came, Adams welcomed them in good Puritan fashion. But the war did not prove a sufficient spur to virtue, and by the fall of 1776 Adams was already observing that "There is too much Corruption, even in this infant Age of our Republic. Virtue is not in Fashion. Vice is not infamous."[38] Sitting with the Congress in Philadelphia, he privately yearned for General Howe to capture the town, because the ensuing hardship "would cure Americans of their vicious and luxurious and effeminate Appetites, Passions and Habits, a more dangerous Army to American Liberty than Mr. Howes."[39]

Within a year or two Americans would begin to look back on 1775 and 1776 as a golden age, when vice had given way to heroic self-denial, and luxury and corruption had not yet raised their heads. In revolutionary America as in Puritan New England the virtues of the Puritan Ethic must be quickened by laments for their loss.

Many of these eighteenth-century lamentations seem perfunctory— mere nostalgic ritual in which men purged their sins by confessing their inferiority to their fathers. But in the years after 1776 the laments were prompted by a genuine uneasiness among the Revolutionists about their own worthiness for the role they had undertaken. In the agitation against Britain they had repeatedly told themselves that liberty could not live without virtue. Having cast off the threat posed to both liberty and virtue by a corrupt monarchy, they recognized that the republican governments they had created must depend for their success on the virtue, not of a king or of a few aristocrats, but of an entire people. Unless the virtue of Americans proved equal to its tasks, liberty would quickly give way once again to tyranny and perhaps a worse tyranny than that of George III.

As Americans faced the problems of independence, the possibility of failure did not seem remote. By recalling the values that had inspired the resistance to British taxation they hoped to lend success to their venture in republican government. The Puritan Ethic thus continued to occupy their

[37] July 3, 1776, in Butterfield, ed., *Adams Family Correspondence*, II, 28.
[38] John to Abigail Adams, Sept. 22, 1776, *ibid.*, II, 131.
[39] Same to same, Sept. 8, 1777, *ibid.*, II, 338. Cf. pp. 169-170, 326.

consciousness (and their letters, diaries, newspapers, and pamphlets) and to provide the framework within which alternatives were debated and sides taken.

Next to the task of defeating the British armies, perhaps the most urgent problem that confronted the new nation was to prove its nationality, for no one was certain that independent Americans would be able to get on with one another. Before the Revolution there had been many predictions, both European and American, that if independence were achieved it would be followed by bloody civil wars among the states, which would eventually fall prostrate before some foreign invader. The anticipated civil war did not take place for eighty-five years. Americans during those years were not without divisions, but they did manage to stay together. Their success in doing so, exemplified in the adoption of the Constitution of 1787, demonstrated that the divisions among them were less serious than they themselves had realized. Without attempting to examine the nature of the debates over the Constitution itself, I should like to show how the Puritan Ethic, while contributing to divisions among Americans, also furnished both sides with a common set of values that limited the extent and bitterness of divisions and thus helped to make a United States Constitution possible.

191

In the period after 1776 perhaps the most immediate threat to the American union was the possibility that the secession of the United States from Great Britain would be followed by a secession of the lower Mississippi and Ohio valleys from the United States. The gravity of the threat, which ended with the fiasco of the Burr Conspiracy, is difficult to assess, but few historians would deny that real friction between East and West existed.

The role of the Puritan Ethic in the situation was characteristic: each side tended to see the other as deficient in the same virtues. To westerners the eastern-dominated governments seemed to be in the grip of speculators and merchants determined to satisfy their own avarice by sacrificing the interests of the industrious farmers of the West. To easterners, or at least to some easterners, the West seemed to be filling up with shiftless adventurers, as lazy and lawless and unconcerned with the values of the Puritan Ethic as were the native Indians. Such men were unworthy of a share in government and must be restrained in their restless hunt for land and furs; they must be made to settle down and build civilized communities where industry and frugality would thrive.

The effects of these attitudes cannot be demonstrated at length here, but may be suggested by the views of a key figure, John Jay. As early as 1779, the French Ambassador, Conrad Alexandre Gérard, had found Jay one of the most reasonable members of Congress, that is, one of the members most ready to fall in with the Ambassador's instructions to discourage American expansion. Jay belonged to a group which suggested that Spain ought to close the Mississippi to American navigation in order to keep the settlers of the West "from living in a half-savage condition." Presumably the group reasoned that the settlers were mostly fur traders; if they were prevented from trading their furs through New Orleans, they might settle down to farming and thus achieve "an attachment to property and industry."[40] Whatever the line of reasoning, the attitude toward the West is clear, and Jay obliged the French Ambassador by volunteering the opinion that the United States was already too large.[41]

In 1786 Jay offered similar opinions to Jefferson, suggesting that settlement of the West should be more gradual, that Americans should be prevented from pitching their tents "through the Wilderness in a great Variety of Places, far distant from each other, and from those Advantages of Education, Civilization, Law, and Government which compact Settlements and Neighbourhood afford."[42] It is difficult to believe that Jay was unaffected by this attitude in the negotiations he was carrying on with the Spanish envoy Gardoqui over the right of the United States to navigate the Mississippi. When Jay presented Congress with a treaty in which the United States agreed to forego navigation of the Mississippi in return for commercial concessions in Spain, it seemed, to westerners at least, that the United States Secretary for Foreign Affairs was willing to sacrifice their interests in favor of his merchant friends in the East.

Fortunately the conflict was not a lasting one. Jay was misinformed about the West, for the advance wave of fur traders and adventurers who pitched their tents far apart occupied only a brief moment in the history of any part of the West. The tens of thousands of men who entered Kentucky and Tennessee in the 1780's came to farm the rich lands, and they carried

[40] John J. Meng, ed., *Despatches and Instructions of Conrad Alexandre Gérard* . . . (Baltimore, 1939), 531. Gérard reported of this group in February, 1779, "qu'ils desiroient fortement que Sa Majesté Catholique tint la clef du Mississippi de sorte que personne n'entrat du Mississippi dans l'Ocean ni de l'Ocean dans ce fleuve; mais qu'il falloit du Commerce aux peuplades dont il s'agit; que par là seulement on pourroit les empêcher de demeurer à demi Sauvages en les attachant à la propriété et à l'industrie."

[41] *Ibid.*, 433-434, 494.

[42] Dec. 14, 1786, in Boyd, ed., *Jefferson Papers*, X, 599.

the values of the Puritan Ethic with them. As this fact became apparent, conflict subsided. Throughout American history, in fact, the West was perpetually turning into a new East, complete with industrious inhabitants, spurred by adversity, and pursuing their callings with an assiduity that the next generation would lament as lost.

Another sectional conflict was not so transitory. The South was not in the process of becoming northern or the North southern. And their differing interests were already discernible in the 1780's, at least to an astute observer like James Madison, as the primary source of friction among Americans. The difference arose, he believed, "principally from the effects of their having or not having slaves."[43]

The bearing of the Puritan Ethic on slavery, as on many other institutions, was complex and ambivalent. It heightened the conflict between those who did and those who did not have slaves. But it also, for a time at least, set limits to the conflict by offering a common ground on which both sides could agree in deploring the institution.

The Puritans themselves had not hesitated to enslave Indian captives or to sell and buy slaves. At the opening of the Revolution no state prohibited slavery. But the institution obviously violated the precepts of the Puritan Ethic: it deprived men of the fruits of their labor and thus removed a primary motive for industry and frugality. How it came into existence in the first place among a people devoted to the Puritan Ethic is a question not yet solved, but as soon as Americans began complaining of Parliament's assault on their liberty and property, it was difficult not to see the inconsistency of continuing to hold slaves. "I wish most sincerely," Abigail Adams wrote to her husband in 1774, "there was not a Slave in the province. It allways appeard a most iniquitous Scheme to me—fight ourselfs for what we are daily robbing and plundering from those who have as good a right to freedom as we have."[44] Newspaper articles everywhere made the same point. As a result, slavery was gradually abolished in the northern states (where it was not important in the economy), and the self-righteousness with which New Englanders already regarded their southern neighbors was thereby heightened.

Although the South failed to abolish slavery, southerners like northern-

193

[43] In Convention, June 30, 1787, in C. C. Tansill, ed., *Documents Illustrative of the Formation of the Union of the American States* (Washington, 1927), 310.
[44] Sept. 22, 1774, in Butterfield, ed., *Adams Family Correspondence*, I, 162.

ers recognized the threat it posed to the values that all Americans held. Partly as a result of that recognition, more slaves were freed by voluntary manumission in the South than by legal and constitutional abolition in the North. There were other reasons for hostility to slavery in both North and South, including fear of insurrection, humanitarianism, and apprehension of the wrath of God; but a predominant reason, in the South at least, was the evil effect of slavery on the industry and frugality of both master and slave, but especially of the master.

A perhaps extreme example of this argument, divested of all considerations of justice and humanity, appeared in a Virginia newspaper in 1767. The author (who signed himself "Philanthropos"!) proposed to abolish slavery in Virginia by having the government lay a prohibitory duty on importation and then purchase one tenth of everyone's slaves every year. The purchase price would be recovered by selling the slaves in the West Indies. Philanthropos acknowledged that slaves were "used with more barbarity" in the West Indies than in Virginia but offered them the consolation "that this sacrifice of themselves will put a quicker period to a miserable life." To emancipate them and leave them in Virginia would be fatal, because they would probably "attempt to arrive at our possessions by force, rather than wait the tedious operation of labour, industry and time." But unless slavery was abolished in Virginia, the industry and frugality of the free population would expire. As it was, said Philanthropos, when a man got a slave or two, he sat back and stopped working. Promising young men failed to take up productive occupations because they could get jobs as overseers. By selling off their slaves in the West Indies, Virginians would get the money to import white indentured servants and would encourage "our own common people, who would no longer be diverted from industry by the prospect of overseers places, to [enter] agriculture and arts."[45]

Few opponents of slavery were so callous, but even the most humane stressed the effect of slavery on masters and the problems of instilling the values of industry in emancipated slaves. Thomas Jefferson hated slavery, but he hated idleness equally, and he would not have been willing to abolish slavery without making arrangements to preserve the useful activity it exacted from its victims. He had heard of one group of Virginia slaves who had been freed by their Quaker owners and kept as tenants on

[45] Reprinted in Pa. Chronicle, Aug. 31-Sept. 7, 1767. The Virginia paper in which it originally appeared has not been found.

the land. The results had been unsatisfactory, because the ex-slaves had
lacked the habits of industry and "chose to steal from their neighbors
rather than work." Jefferson had plans to free his own slaves (after he
freed himself from his creditors) by a gradual system which provided
means for educating the Negroes into habits of industry.[46] But Jefferson
never put his scheme into practice. He and most other Southerners continued to hold slaves, and the result was as predicted: slavery steadily
eroded the honor accorded work among southerners.

During the Revolutionary epoch, however, the erosion had not yet proceeded far enough to alienate North from South. Until well into the nineteenth century Southerners continued to deplore the effects of slavery on
the industry and frugality at least of the whites. Until the North began to
demand immediate abolition and the South began to defend slavery as a
permanent blessing, leaders of the two sections could find a good deal of
room for agreement in the shared values of the Puritan Ethic.

The fact that Americans of different sections could remain united came
as something of a surprise. Even more surprising, so surprising that for a
long time few could believe it, was the fact that party divisions in politics,
instead of hindering, actually helped the cause of union. Parties or "factions" had been everywhere denounced in the eighteenth century. When
men disagreed on political issues, each side was likely to accuse the other of
being a party. Advocates of any measure preceded their arguments by dis-
claiming adherence to a party. And the last thing that the architects of the
American national government wanted or anticipated was that it would
fall into the hands of parties. But that of course is precisely what happened,
and the result proved to be a blessing.

The unexpected success of the American party system has been the subject of continuous comment and congratulation among historians and political scientists ever since. Success, it seems clear, has depended in large
part on the absence of any clear ideological difference between the major
parties. It would be difficult, for example, for any but the most experienced historian, if presented with the Republican and Democratic plat-
forms of the past hundred years, to distinguish one from the other. Our
political disputes are peaceful, because both parties espouse similar principles and objectives and neither feels itself severely threatened by the
other. And yet in any given issue or election neither side has difficulty

[46] To Edward Bancroft, Jan. 26, 1788, in Boyd, ed., *Jefferson Papers*, XIV, 492.

in identifying friends and enemies. The members of any party recognize their own kind.

This situation has prevailed in American national politics from the outset. In the Continental Congress and in the first Congresses under the new Constitution, political divisions were unorganized. In the Continental Congress, partly because of rotation in office, groupings were transitory. But one finds the same absence of ideological difference and the same recognition by political partisans of their own kind. In the absence of party organization, one can see in these early divisions, even more clearly than in later ones, the forces that led some men to join one side and others another.[47]

The first serious division in national politics after independence occurred in 1778 and 1779 over the conduct of the American envoy to France, Silas Deane; and the men who voted together in the divisions on that question often voted together on other seemingly unrelated questions. On each side, in other words, a kind of party was formed. If we examine the men on each side, together with their avowed principles and their application of those principles, if we examine the way a man regarded men on his own side and men on the other side, we will discover, I believe, that the Puritan Ethic, in this period at least, helped both to create political parties and to limit the differences between them.

The facts in the case of Silas Deane will probably never be fully known.[48] The question at issue was whether Deane had used public

[47] A work of major importance is Herbert James Henderson, Party Politics in the Continental Congress, 1774-1783 (unpubl. Ph.D. diss., Columbia University, 1962). I arrived at the conclusions presented in the succeeding pages of this section, about the nature of the divisions in Congress in 1778 and 1779, by reading in the letters and papers of the members and then examining votes on specific issues. Dr. Henderson, who kindly allowed me to read his manuscript after my own investigation was completed, had independently studied the divisions in Congress during its first ten years, starting from an exhaustive statistical analysis of the voting. His study, which goes far beyond what I have attempted here, will greatly advance our understanding both of the American Revolution and of the origins of American political parties.

[48] The complexity of the problems involved can be appreciated by anyone who reads the Deane Papers, published by the New-York Historical Society in its Collections for 1886-1890. Important aspects of the case are presented in Thomas P. Abernethy, "Commercial Activities of Silas Deane in France," American Historical Review, XXXIX (1933-34), 477-485; Samuel F. Bemis, "British Secret Service and the French-American Alliance," ibid., XXIX (1923-24), 474-495; and Julian P. Boyd, "Silas Deane: Death by a Kindly Teacher of Treason?" William and Mary Quarterly, 3d Ser., XVI (1959), 165-187, 319-342, 515-550.

funds and public office for private gain, as was charged by another American agent abroad, Arthur Lee. When challenged by Congress, Deane was unable to produce vouchers to account for his expenditures, but he consistently maintained that the money had been spent on legitimate public business; and in the private papers that have survived he never admitted, even to himself, that he had done anything wrong. We know now a good deal more about him than the members of Congress did. We know, for example, that his close associate, Edward Bancroft, was a double agent. We know that Deane did engage in private speculation while in public office. But we still do not know that his transactions were any more dubious than those of, say, Robert Morris, who also mingled public and private funds and by so doing emerged as the financier of the Revolution. The members of Congress in 1778 and 1779, knowing even less than we do, were obliged to decide whether to honor Silas Deane's accounts. In a series of votes on questions relating to this issue the members had to make up their minds with very little to go on. Under the circumstances, it would not be surprising if they lined up according to the way in which Silas Deane struck them as a man. Those who found him to be their sort of person would take one side; those who distrusted that sort of person would take the other side.

197

What sort of person, then, was Silas Deane? He was, to begin with, an able man. He made a good impression at the First Continental Congress, and when Connecticut dropped him from its delegation, Congress sent him to France. In France he was indubitably successful in securing the supplies that made possible the success of the American armies at Saratoga. After Congress dismissed him and refused to honor his accounts, Deane became disillusioned with the patriot cause and in a series of letters to friends in Connecticut, unfortunately intercepted by the British, he argued that the war and the French alliance had corrupted his countrymen and that independence would consequently prove a curse instead of a blessing. In his native Connecticut he said, he had seen "thousands of industrious youth forced from the plough and other useful, homely occupations, and prematurely destroyed by the diseases, wants, and sufferings of a military life, whilst the survivors, by exchanging their plain morals and honest industry for the habits of idleness and vice, appeared more likely to burthen than to benefit their country hereafter."[49] Silas Deane could avow his attachment to the values of the Puritan Ethic as ardently as any man.

[49] To Jesse Root, May 20, 1781, in *Deane Papers*, IV, 350.

But avowing the values was not quite the same as exemplifying them, and Deane as a person exhibited none of the moral austerity that ardent practitioners of the Puritan Ethic demanded. John Adams, always sensitive in these matters, was Deane's successor in the American mission to France. There he observed with distaste that Deane had taken extravagant lodgings in Paris in addition to his quarters with Benjamin Franklin at Passy.[50] Adams, though he always found Franklin's company trying, preferred to put up with it rather than cause the United States extra expense. Adams later recalled Deane as "a person of a plausible readiness and Volubility with his Tongue and his Pen, much addicted to Ostentation and Expence in Dress and Living but without any deliberate forecast or reflection or solidity of Judgment, or real Information."[51] Deane, on the other hand, found Adams absurdly spartan. "This man," he wrote, "who may have read much, appears to have retained nothing, except law knowledge and the fierce and haughty manners of the Lacedemonians and first Romans. These he has adopted as a perfect model to form a modern republican by."[52] If Adams could have read the criticism, he would have taken it as a tribute.

Adams, of course, was not a member of Congress when the Deane case was under debate, but Deane's characterization of Adams could easily have applied to the three men who led the fight against Deane: Samuel Adams of Massachusetts, Richard Henry Lee of Virginia, and Henry Laurens of South Carolina.

Samuel Adams thought of the Revolution as a holy war to save America from British corruption, and corruption to Adams meant luxury, extravagance, and avarice. During the nonimportation crusade he had worried about such weaknesses in the merchant battalion; and after independence merchants still failed to live up to the standards he expected of Americans. In 1778, detecting a spirit of avarice in Boston, he remarked, "but it rages only among the few, because perhaps, the few only are concerned at present in trade."[53] Even a little avarice was too much, however, for Adams, who had visions of Boston as the Sparta of America. Writing from Philadelphia to a Boston friend, he expressed concern about reports that the city had become exceedingly gay in appearance. "I would fain hope," he said, "this is confind to Strangers. Luxury and Extravagance are

198

[50] Apr. 1778, in Butterfield, ed., *Diary and Autobiography of John Adams*, IV, 42.
[51] Nov.-Dec. 1775, *ibid.*, III, 340.
[52] To John Jay, Nov. 1780, in *Deane Papers*, IV, 262.
[53] To Francis Lee [?] 1778, in Cushing, ed., *Writings of Samuel Adams*, IV, 19.

in my opinion totally destructive of those Virtues which are necessary for the Preservation of the Liberty and Happiness of the People. Is it true that the Review of the Boston Militia was closd with an expensive Entertainment? If it was, and the Example is followed by the Country, I hope I shall be excusd when I venture to pledge myself, that the Militia of that State will never be put on such a Footing as to become formidable to its Enemies."[54]

Richard Henry Lee, a brother of the man who first accused Deane, was a Virginia gentleman planter but not so strange an ally for Samuel Adams, as he might at first seem to be. The two had been in correspondence even before the First Continental Congress, and there they had sided together from the beginning. Although Lee was an Anglican and a slaveowner, he had spoken out against slavery (condemning it for its ill effect on industriousness) and by 1779 he was contemplating retirement to Massachusetts. "The hasty, unpersevering, aristocratic genius of the south," he confessed, "suits not my disposition, and is inconsistent with my ideas of what must constitute social happiness and security."[55] Lee never carried out his intention of retiring to Massachusetts and probably would not have been happy if he had, but he sometimes must have struck his contemporaries as a New Englander manqué. The French Ambassador Gérard not surprisingly mistook him for a Presbyterian, for he had, according to Gérard, "the severity of manners, and the gravity that is natural to Presbyterians."[56]

Lee had begun his attacks on political corruption in 1764 by sniffing out a scandal in the Virginia government: the Speaker of the House of Burgesses, John Robinson, who was also Treasurer, had been lending vast amounts in public funds to his political friends, and his friends included some of the best families in Virginia. The people involved were able to hush things up, but they did not forgive Lee for demanding an investigation.[57] The Deane affair, then, was not the first time he had caught men in high office with their fingers in the public till.

Henry Laurens, like Lee, was an Anglican, but the description of him

---

[54] To Samuel Savage, Oct. 6, 1778, ibid., IV, 67-68.

[55] Burnett, ed., Letters of Members, II, 155.

[56] ". . . la sévérité des moeurs, et la gravité naturelle aux Presbytériens." Meng, ed., Despatches of Gérard, 569.

[57] Burton J. Hendrick, The Lees of Virginia: Biography of a Family (Boston, 1935), 101-105; David J. Mays, Edmund Pendleton, 1721-1803: A Biography (Cambridge, Mass., 1952), I, 174-208.

by a fellow South Carolinian, David Ramsay, who knew him well, makes
Laurens, too, sound like a Puritan: "In the performance of his religious
duties Mr. Laurens was strict and exemplary. The emergency was great
which kept him from church either forenoon or afternoon, and very great
indeed which kept him from his regular monthly communion. With the
bible he was intimately acquainted. Its doctrines he firmly believed, its
precepts and history he admired, and was much in the habit of quoting
and applying portions of it to present occurrences. He not only read the
scriptures diligently to his family, but made all his children read them also.
His family bible contained in his own hand-writing several of his remarks
on passing providences." Ramsay also tells us that Laurens frowned on
cardplaying and gambling. On some occasions in Charleston society when
he could not avoid playing cards without being rude, he promptly paid if
he lost, "but uniformly refused to receive what he won, esteeming it
wrong to take any man's money without giving an equivalent."[58]

Laurens had himself been a merchant and a very methodical and assiduous one. After making a fortune, he transferred his activities from trade
to planting. He seldom slept more than four hours a day, and he had a low
opinion of gentlemen of leisure. Like Richard Henry Lee he had had a
brush with corruption in high places earlier in his career when the customs
officers in Charleston seized a ship of his on a flimsy pretext. They had
offered to release the ship in return for a bribe. Laurens had indignantly
refused, and the officers, in collusion with a judge of the Admiralty Court,
had succeeded in having the ship condemned and sold. Laurens had then
written and published an account of the whole affair, including the attempt to shake him down.[59]

It was this episode that converted Laurens from staunch support of
British authority to a deep suspicion of British corruption. But avarice
among his own countrymen perturbed him even more. At the time when
the Deane case came up, Laurens was serving as president of the Continental Congress. He had already denounced the "sacrilegious Robberies of
public Money" by congressmen and military officers carrying on private
trade in army supplies.[60] A little later he observed that many members of

200

[58] David Ramsay, *The History of South Carolina from its first Settlement in
1670 to the Year 1808* (Charleston, 1809), II, 484, 485.
[59] David D. Wallace, *The Life of Henry Laurens* . . . (New York, 1915);
Dickerson, *Navigation Acts,* 224-231.
[60] Laurens to Rawlins Lowndes, May 17, 1778, in Burnett, ed., *Letters of
Members,* III, 248.

Congress, doubtless because they were themselves engaged in such practices, were ready to defend them, so that "he must be a pitiful rogue indeed, who, when detected, or suspected, meets not with powerful advocates among those, who in the present corrupt time, ought to exert all their
powers in defence and support of these friend-plundered, much injured,
and I was almost going to say, sinking States."[61]

Although Laurens was a merchant, he was so shocked by the activities
of other merchants in and out of Congress that he wrote in despair in 1779:
"Reduce us all to poverty and cut off or wisely restrict that bane of patriotism, Commerce, and we shall soon become Patriots, but how hard is it for
a rich or covetous Man to enter heartily into the Kingdom of Patriotism?"[62] When Congress voted what Laurens considered too high salaries
for the secretaries of its ministry abroad and elected Laurens's son to one of
these positions, Laurens protested and informed his son that "men who
are sincerely devoted to the service of their Country will not accept of
Salaries which will tend to distress it."[63]

It is impossible to examine here the rank and file of Deane's opponents,
but perhaps enough has been said to suggest what sort of person disliked
Deane. It will come as no surprise that Deane's supporters were men more
like himself. A principal supporter, of course, was Robert Morris, who had
engaged deeply in trading enterprises with Deane but whose commercial
empire extended throughout the country. At the outset of Deane's mission
to France, Morris had directed him in both his private and his public in-
vestments and had advised him that "there never has been so fair an op-
pertunity of making a large Fortune. . . ."[64] At the time of the Deane affair,
Morris was not a member of Congress, but he remained in Philadelphia,
served in the Pennsylvania Assembly, and helped to marshal support for
Deane. Deane's other defenders, like his opponents, were too numerous to
bear examination in detail here, but they included men from the same
states as his principal opponents.

In Massachusetts John Hancock was a Deane man, and it was Hancock who had provided the expensive entertainment for the militia which
so disturbed Samuel Adams. Indeed Hancock, when inaugurated as Governor of Massachusetts in 1780, scandalized Adams by sponsoring a whole

[61] Laurens to John Houstoun, Aug. 27 [1778], *ibid.*, III, 385.
[62] Laurens to William Livingston, Apr. 19 [1779], *ibid.*, IV, 163.
[63] H. Laurens to John Laurens, Oct. 5, 1779, *ibid.*, IV 467.
[64] From Robert Morris, Aug. 11, 1776, in *Deane Papers*, I, 176.

series of balls and parties. By introducing such "Scenes of Dissipation and
Folly" Adams believed that Hancock endangered public virtue, and when
virtue departed, liberty would accompany it. Adams accordingly considered Hancock a peril to the republic, as dangerous as the British.[65]

In Virginia Deane's supporters included most of the congressional delegates, apart from the Lees. Benjamin Harrison's position can be anticipated from John Adams's characterization of him at the Second Continental Congress as "an indolent, luxurious, heavy Gentleman," and as
"another Sir John Falstaff, excepting in his Larcenies and Robberies, his
Conversation disgusting to every Man of Delicacy or decorum, Obscaene,
profane, impious, perpetually ridiculing the Bible, calling it the Worst
Book in the World...."[66] In Congress Harrison associated frequently with
Hancock. He was also engaged in business with Robert Morris. When he
got his son made Deputy Paymaster General of the Southern District, the
son made a secret agreement with Morris to charge a premium of 2 per
cent on any bills that either drew on the other in connection with public
business.[67]

Carter Braxton, another supporter of Deane from Virginia was discovered in 1778 to have made a dubious deal with Morris and in 1779 was
censured by Congress for sponsoring a privateer which captured a Portuguese vessel, an act that amounted to piracy, since the United States was
not at war with Portugal and in fact was seeking Portuguese trade.[68]
Braxton had been one of the many Virginians involved in the Robinson
scandal.[69] The Lees tried to exclude such men from representing Virginia
in Congress by securing passage in the Virginia legislature of a law requiring delegates to swear that they were not engaged and would not
engage in trade.[70] But the delegates who took the oath evidently interpreted
their business dealings as something other than trade.

From South Carolina Deane's advocate was William Henry Drayton,
a man with whom Henry Laurens regularly disagreed. Their different

[65] Cushing, ed., *Writings of Samuel Adams,* IV, 208, 210, 227-230, 236-238, 241-
242, 244-248; John C. Miller, *Sam Adams: Pioneer in Propaganda* (Boston, 1936),
359-369.
[66] Feb., Mar. 1776, in Butterfield, ed., *Diary and Autobiography of John Adams,*
III, 367, 371.
[67] Abernethy, *Western Lands,* 159-160.
[68] *Ibid.,* 215, 232.
[69] Mays, *Pendleton,* I, 180, 359.
[70] From Meriwether Smith, July 6, 1779, in Boyd, ed., *Jefferson Papers,* III, 28-
29, 29n.

characters were significantly revealed in an insignificant episode, when
Drayton in 1779 urged Congress to authorize the celebration of Independence Day by an elaborate display of fireworks. In what Laurens called
"a funny declamation," Drayton praised the Olympic games and other
festivities by which nations celebrated their nativity. Laurens, outraged by
the extravagance of celebrations in general, answered that "the Olympic
Games of Greece and other fooleries brought on the desolation of Greece."
When Drayton won approval for his motion and pointed out that the
Olympic games "were calculated for improving bodily strength, to make
men athletic and robust," Laurens was left to reflect in his diary, "Is
drinking Madeira Wine from 5 to 9 o'clock, then sallying out to gaze at
fire works, and afterwards returning to Wine again, calculated to make
men athletic and robust?"[71]

Two years earlier on the first anniversary of independence, Congress
had also celebrated and there had also been a dissenter, William Williams
of Connecticut, who wrote on July 5, 1777, to his friend Governor Trumbull: "Yesterday was in my opinion poorly spent in celebrating the anniversary of the Declaration of Independence . . . a great expenditure of
Liquor, Powder etc. took up the Day, and of candles thro the City good
part of the night."[72] By an interesting coincidence, William Williams was
also an early opponent of Silas Deane. He had opposed Deane's election as
a delegate to Congress; he had warned his friend Samuel Adams, as early
as July 30, 1774, before the first Congress met, that Deane would be likely
to place private interests above patriotism; and he had finally secured
Deane's dismissal from the Connecticut delegation in 1775. Williams's own
record in the Revolution, like Laurens's, was one of financial sacrifice.[73]

It would be impossible to prove conclusively that all the opponents of
Silas Deane were frugal, industrious, and devoted to the common good or
that all his advocates were addicted to trade, speculation, and profiteering.
Men on both sides proclaimed their belief in the same values, but it seems
likely that men like Adams, Lee, and Laurens recognized one another as
kindred spirits and that men like Morris, Harrison, and Braxton did the
same.[74] In the Continental Congress the turnover of delegates (required

[71] Laurens, Notes, July 2, 1779, Burnett, ed., *Letters of Members*, IV, 293-294.
[72] *Ibid.*, II, 401.
[73] Oscar Zeichner, *Connecticut's Years of Controversy, 1750-1776* (Chapel Hill,
1949), 322.
[74] Other active opponents of Deane included William Whipple of New Hampshire, James Lovell of Massachusetts, Roger Sherman of Connecticut, Nathaniel

by the Articles of Confederation) prevented the formation of any durable parties, but in 1779 the groups that formed over the Deane issue tended to act together also in other divisions, such as the dispute over half pay for army officers and the dispute over war aims. In the latter dispute, for example, the French Ambassador found the friends of Deane far more amenable than the Adams-Lee-Laurens group, many of whom felt a sense of shame that the United States had been unable to fight its own battles without French financial and military assistance.[76]

204

The party divisions of 1778-79 seem to indicate that although most Americans made adherence to the Puritan Ethic an article of faith, some Americans were far more assiduous than others in exemplifying it. Since such men were confined to no particular section, and since men active in national politics could recognize their own kind from whatever section, political divisions in the early years of the republic actually brought Americans from all over the country into working harmony within a single group. And parties, instead of destroying the union, became a means of holding it together.

Recent studies have shown that there was no continuity in the political divisions of the 1770's, 1780's, and 1790's, by demonstrating that the split between Federalists and Republicans in the 1790's cannot be traced to the preceding splits between reluctant and ardent revolutionaries of 1776 or between Federalists and Antifederalists of 1789. The continuity that a previous generation of historians had seen in the political history of these years has thus proved specious. It is tempting, however, to suggest that there may have been a form of continuity in American political history hitherto unnoticed, a continuity based on the attitudes we have been exploring. Although the divisions of 1778-79 did not endure, Americans of succeeding years continued to show differing degrees of attachment to the values of the Puritan Ethic. By the time when national political parties were organized in the 1790's, a good many other factors were involved in attracting men to one side or the other, far too many to permit discussion here. But the Puritan Ethic remained a constant ingredient, molding the

---

Scudder of New Jersey, and James Searle and William Shippen of Pennsylvania. Other advocates of Deane included Gouverneur Morris and John Jay of New York, Cyrus Griffin and Meriwether Smith of Virginia, William Carmichael of Maryland, and Henry Wynkoop of Pennsylvania.

[76] The solidity of the division is perhaps exaggerated in the extended reports on it by *Gérard* in Meng, ed., *Despatches of Gérard,* esp. pp. 429-918, *passim.* On the half pay issue R. H. Lee parted from his anti-Deane allies.

style of American politics not only in the 1790's but long afterwards. Men on both sides, and seemingly the whole population, continued to proclaim their devotion to it by mourning its decline, and each side regularly accused the other of being deficient in it. It served as a weapon for political conflict but also as a tether which kept parties from straying too far apart. It deserves perhaps to be considered as one of the major reasons why American party battles have generally remained rhetorical and American national government has endured as a workable government.

III. An Economic Interpretation of the Constitution

As the Puritan Ethic helped to give shape to national politics, so too it helped to shape national policy, especially in the economic sphere. Before 1776 the economic policy of the American colonies had been made for them in London: they had been discouraged from manufacturing, barred from certain channels of trade, and encouraged to exploit the natural resources of the continent, especially its land. After 1776 the independent states were free to adopt, singly or collectively, any policy that suited them. At first the exigencies of the war against England directed every measure; but as the fighting subsided, Americans began to consider the economic alternatives open to them.

There appeared to be three possible kinds of activity: agriculture, manufacturing, and commerce. Of these, agriculture and commerce had hitherto dominated the American scene. Americans, in accepting the place assigned them under the British Navigation Acts, had seen the force of their own environment operating in the same direction as British policy: as long as the continent had an abundance of unoccupied land and a scarcity of labor, it seemed unlikely that its inhabitants could profitably engage in manufacturing. The nonimportation agreements had done much to dispel this opinion in America; and the war that followed, by interdicting trade in some regions and hindering it in others, had given a further spur to manufactures. By the time peace came numerous observers were able to point out fallacies in the supposition that manufacturing was not economically feasible in the United States. From England, Richard Price reminded Americans that their country contained such a variety of soils and climates that it was capable of "producing not only every *necessary*, but every *convenience* of life," and Americans were quick to agree.[76] They acknowl-

[76] Richard Price, *Observations on the Importance of the American Revolution*

edged that their population was small by comparison with Europe's and the numbers skilled in manufacturing even smaller. But they now discovered reasons why this deficiency was no insuperable handicap. People without regular employment, women and children for example, could be put to useful work in manufacturing. Moreover, if Americans turned to manufactures, many skilled artisans of the Old World, losing their New World customers, would move to America in order to regain them. Immigrants would come in large numbers anyhow, attracted by the blessings of republican liberty. And scarcity of labor could also be overcome by labor-saving machinery and by water and steam power.[77]

A few men like Thomas Jefferson continued to think manufacturing neither feasible nor desirable for Americans, but the economic vicissitudes of the postwar years subdued the voices of such men to a whisper. No one suggested that the country should abandon its major commitment to agriculture in favor of manufacturing, but it became a commonplace that too many Americans were engaged in commerce and that the moral, economic, and political welfare of the United States demanded a greater attention to manufacturing. The profiteering of merchants during the war had kept the old suspicions of that calling very much alive, so that long before the fighting stopped, people were worried about the effects of an unrestrained commerce on the independent United States. A Yale student reflected the mood in a declamation offered in July 1778. If the country indulged too freely in commerce, he warned, the result would be "Luxury with its train of the blackest vices, which will debase our manliness of sentiment, and spread a general dissolution of manners thro the Continent. This extensive Commerce is the most direct method to ruin our country, and we may affirm that we shall exist as an empire but a short space, unless it can be circumscribed within narrow limits."[78]

The prophecy seemed to be on the way to swift fulfillment within a year or two of the war's end. As soon as the peace treaty was signed,

---

. . . (London, 1785), 75. Cf. *New Haven Gazette and Connecticut Magazine*, Nov. 16, 23, 1786; *American Mercury* (Hartford), Aug. 13, 1787.

[77] Hugh Williamson, *Letters from Sylvius to the Freemen Inhabitants of the United States* . . . (New York, 1787); Tench Coxe: *An Address to an Assembly of the Friends of American Manufactures* . . . (Philadelphia, 1787); *An Enquiry into the Principles on which a commercial system for the United States of America should be founded* . . . (Philadelphia, 1787); and *Observations on the Agriculture, Manufactures and Commerce of the United States* . . . (New York, 1789).

[78] Declamation, July 18, 1778, Yale University Archives, New Haven, Conn.

American merchants rushed to offer Americans the familiar British goods which they had done without for nearly a decade. The British gladly supplied the market, extending a liberal credit, and the result was a flood of British textiles and hardware in every state. As credit extended from merchant to tradesman to farmer and planter, Americans were caught up in an orgy of buying. But at the same time Britain barred American ships from her West Indies possessions, where America cattle, lumber, and foodstuffs had enjoyed a prime market. The British could now buy these articles in the United States at their own prices and carry them in their own ships, depriving the American merchant and farmer alike of accustomed profits. Hard cash was rapidly drained off; debts grew to alarming proportions; and the buying boom turned to a sharp depression.[79]

Casting about for a remedy, some states turned to the old expedient of paper money. But to many Americans this was a cure worse than the disease and no real cure anyhow. The root of the trouble, they told themselves, was their own frivolity. Newspapers and pamphlets from one end of the continent to the other lamented the lost virtues that had inspired resistance to tyranny a few short years before. While Rome had enjoyed a republican simplicity for centuries, the United States seemed to have sunk into luxury and decay almost as soon as born. And who indulged this weakness, who coaxed Americans into this wild extravagance? It was the merchants. Shelves bulging with oversupplies of ribbons, laces, and yard goods, the merchants outdid themselves in appealing to every gullible woman and every foolish fop to buy. There was an oversupply, it seemed, not merely of ribbons and laces but of merchants, a breed of men, according to Hugh Williamson of North Carolina, "too lazy to plow, or labour at any other calling."[80] "What can we promise ourselves," asked another writer, "if we still pursue the same extensive trade? What, but total destruction to our manners, and the entire loss of our virtue?"[81]

The basic remedy must be frugality. The laments over luxury were a summons to Americans to tighten their belts, as they had done before in the face of adversity. And as they had also done in the earlier campaigns, they again linked frugality with nonimportation and with manufacturing for themselves, but this time with somewhat more confidence in the result.

207

[79] This picture of the economic history of the 1780's seems to have been universally accepted at the time. A typical statement is in Coxe, *Observations*, 59-64.
[80] Williamson, *Letters from Sylvius*, 30.
[81] *The American Museum*, I (Feb. 1787), 124.

Manufacturing was now freed of the restrictions formerly imposed by the British; if once firmly established in the United States, it would help protect the very virtues that fostered it. An industrious, frugal people would manufacture for themselves, and in turn "Manufactures will promote industry, and industry contributes to health, virtue, riches and population."[82] Although the riches thus gained might constitute a danger to the virtues that begot them, they would not be as great a danger as riches arising from trade or speculation: "the evils resulting from opulence in a nation whose inhabitants are habituated to industry from their childhood, will never be so predominant as in those nations, whose riches are spontaneously produced, without labour or care...."[83]

208

As manufactures were linked to virtue, so both were linked to the independent republican government for which Americans had been fighting. "America must adopt [a] new policy," David Ramsay insisted in 1785, "or she never will be independent in reality. We must import less and attend more to agriculture and manufactures."[84] It was now possible to see a new significance in England's old restraints on colonial manufacturing. Why had she prevented Americans from "working up those materials that God and nature have given us?" The answer was clear to a Maryland writer: because England knew "it was the only way to our real independence, and to render the habitable parts of our country truly valuable. What countries are the most flourishing and most powerful in the world? Manufacturing countries. It is not hills, mountains, woods, and rivers that constitute the true riches of a country. It is the number of industrious mechanic and manufacturing as well as agriculturing inhabitants. That a country composed of agricultivators and shepherds is not so valuable as one wherein a just proportion of the people attend to arts and manufactures, is known to every politician in Europe: And America will never feel her importance and dignity, until she alters her present system of trade, so ruinous to the interests, to the morals, and to the reputation of her citizens."[85]

Britain's extension of credit to American merchants, it now seemed, was only part of a perfidious plan to undermine through trade the independence she had acknowledged by treaty. Samuel Adams had once detected a British plan to destroy American liberty by introducing luxury

[82] *Am. Mercury,* Aug. 13, 1787.
[83] *New Haven Gazette and Conn. Mag.,* Nov. 23, 1786.
[84] R. L. Brunhouse, ed., *David Ramsay, 1749-1815, Selections from his writings,* American Philosophical Society, *Transactions,* LV, Pt. 4 (1965), 87.
[85] *Am. Museum,* I (Feb. 1787), 124-125.

and levity among the people. Having been thwarted in 1776, the British were now on the verge of success. As a South Carolina writer charged, they had let loose, "as from Pandora's box, a ruinous luxury, speculation, and extravagance, vitiated our taste, corrupted our manners, plunged the whole state into a private debt, never before equalled, and thro' the means of their trade, luxury, influence, and good things, brought the Republic into a dilemma, an example of which has not before happened in the world."[86] From France, where he was serving as ambassador, Thomas Jefferson could see that Britain by her liberal credits had put the whole United States in the same economic thralldom in which her merchants had held (and still held) the Virginia tobacco planters. From economic thralldom back to political thralldom was only a step. Unless the United States could break the grip, her experiment in independence was over.

Jefferson, while joining in the hymns to frugality (he thought extravagance a "more baneful evil than toryism was during the war"),[87] had a peculiar prejudice against manufacturing and hoped to break the British grip and achieve economic independence by gaining new commercial treaties with other countries.[88] But few of his countrymen shared his prejudice. In every state they told themselves to manufacture. Even if it cost more to make a coat or a pair of shoes or a plow or a gun in America, the price of foreign imports was independence. "No man," warned Hugh Williamson, drawing upon another precept of the Puritan Ethic, "is to say that a thing may be good for individuals which is not good for the public, or that our citizens may thrive by cheap bargains, while the nation is ruined by them." Considered in the light of the national interest, "every domestic manufacture is cheaper than a foreign one, for this plain reason, by the first nothing is lost to the country, by the other the whole value is lost—it is carried away never to return."[89]

Williamson, like many others, welcomed the economic depression as the kind of adversity that brings its own cure. Poverty might induce Americans of necessity to manufacture for themselves. Societies for the pro-

---

[86] [Anonymous], *A Few Salutary Hints, pointing out the Policy and Consequences of Admitting British Subjects to Engross our Trade and Become our Citizens* (Charleston printed, New York reprinted, 1786), 4.

[87] To John Page, May 4, 1786, in Boyd, ed., *Jefferson Papers*, IX, 445.

[88] These views are scattered throughout Jefferson's letters during his stay in France. See Boyd, ed., *Jefferson Papers*, VIII-XV. For a typical statement see letter to Thomas Pleasants, May 8, 1786, *ibid.*, IX, 472-473.

[89] Williamson, *Letters from Sylvius*, 13-14.

motion of arts and manufactures sprang up everywhere, as they had in the 1760's and 1770's, and in Boston there was even a new nonimportation agreement.[90] But Americans as an independent nation were no longer confined to such informal and extralegal methods either in bringing pressure on the British or in encouraging their own manufactures. The states could now levy duties and prohibitions against foreign importations, and several did so. But the results served only to remind Americans of the importance of union. The old nonimportation agreements against the Townshend duties had foundered when the merchants of one colony gave way. In the 1780's the uncoordinated actions of individual states in penalizing foreign trade did not break the British grip on the American market, did not end the drainage of specie, and did not lead Britain to restore trading privileges in the West Indies, but they did become an unexpected source of bitterness and disunion. When states tried individually to regulate commerce, they often failed to discern the harmful repercussions of their measures in other states. As John Sullivan confessed, concerning the New Hampshire law, "it was a blow aimed at Britain but wounds us and our friends."[91]

The advocates of frugality and manufacturing did not conclude from such failures that trade needed no regulation or that it could not be regulated. "If we Americans do not choose to regulate it," one of them warned, "it will regulate us, till we have not a farthing left in our land. . . . unless we shortly regulate and correct the abuses of our trade by lopping off its useless branches, and establishing manufactures, we shall be corrected, perhaps even to our very destruction."[92] Even Thomas Jefferson, who had been impressed by Adam Smith's advocacy of free trade, thought that Smith's policy could not be adopted unilaterally.[93] As long as the other nations of the world continued to regulate trade, the United States could not survive without doing likewise. What the failure of individual state regulation showed was not that regulation was wrong but that it must be nationwide. As James Madison wrote to Jefferson in March 1786, "The

210 (margin)

---

[90] *Am. Mercury*, Nov. 18, 1786.
[91] From John Sullivan, Mar. 4, 1786, in Boyd, ed., *Jefferson Papers*, IX, 314.
[92] *Am. Museum*, I (Mar. 1787), 213.
[93] To G. K. van Hogendorp, Oct. 13, 1785, in Boyd, ed., *Jefferson Papers*, VIII, 633. While Smith argued for free trade, he based his arguments on a new conception of the wealth of nations that stressed the achievement of maximum productivity. With this conception and with Smith's palpable hostility to merchants and their efforts to influence policy, the Americans could readily agree.

States are every day giving proofs that separate regulations are more likely
to set them by the ears, than to attain the common object."[94]

Harmony in commercial regulations was needed not simply in order to
promote American trade by united retaliation against British restrictions.
Although merchants might look toward an increase in national authority
with this end in view, farseeing observers had much larger goals: not
merely to strike at British commerce in favor of American, but to strike at
all commerce that threatened the nation's economic independence. The
support that merchants gave the movement for a stronger central government has often blinded us to the larger aims of men like Madison and
Hamilton who, as the latter put it, thought "continentally." What they
wanted was to transform the still-colonial economy of the United States by
directing the industry and productivity of its citizens toward a balanced
self-sufficiency. The country, they knew, would remain predominantly
agricultural for some years to come; and they also knew that it could support its own merchant class, as it had done under British rule. But merchants and farmers were not enough to give the nation true independence;
and the merchants, if left to themselves, could easily bring ruin to the
country. To attain true independence, the United States must achieve a
balance in which manufacturing would find its place beside commerce and
agriculture. When they demanded a national regulation of trade, con-
tinentally-minded Americans had in mind as much the restraint as the
encouragement of trade. They wanted not a southern economy or a New
England economy, but an American economy, of the kind described some
decades later by Henry Clay.

The possibility of such a harmonious economy did not seem visionary
in 1789. Southerners already acknowledged that New Englanders would
excel in manufacturing. The climate, the compact settlements, the absence
of slavery all favored them. But it was pointed out that the New Englanders, as they turned their efforts to manufactures, would buy raw materials and foodstuffs from the South. Nationally-minded southerners like
Madison even spoke up for a national navigation act to confine American
trade to American vessels, though they knew that in shipbuilding and
commerce as in manufactures the New Englanders would surpass them.[95]

211

[94] *Ibid.*, IX, 334.
[95] Jan. 22, 1786, Nov. 14, 1785, *ibid.*, IX, 198, 203-204; Williamson, *Letters from
Sylvius, passim; A Jew Salutary Hints, passim;* St. George Tucker, *Reflections on
the Policy and Necessity of Encouraging the Commerce of the Citizens of the
United States of America* ... (Richmond, 1785), *passim.*

Manufacturing, commerce, and agriculture were all necessary to an independent nation, and all three might need encouragement and protection, not only from foreign sources but from each other. Tench Coxe (who argued strongly for restraining commerce in favor of manufactures) expressed the larger concern for economic co-ordination when he warned that trade regulations must be phrased with great care, so as not to injure the various agricultural activities which occupied the bulk of the people throughout the country.[96] There was widespread agreement that economic co-ordination must be accomplished and that only a national, rather than a local, regulation of trade could do the job.[97] Not everyone who supported national regulation was moved by a large view of the national interest. Doubtless many merchants were looking merely for better trading opportunities, farmers for higher prices, would-be manufacturers for protection. But because national regulation could offer something to everyone, and because the appeal of the ancient virtues could also be harnessed to it, men who did see its larger implications for national independence were able to enlist powerful support behind it.

There were, of course, many forces working simultaneously toward the establishment of an effective national government in the 1780's, and perhaps economic forces were not the most important. It has been shown that Charles Beard's interpretation of the economic forces leading to the Constitution was without adequate foundation, and economic interpretations thus far advanced in place of Beard's have been only more complex versions of his. But another economic interpretation of the Constitution may be suggested: Americans from the time of their first nonimportation agreements against England had been groping toward a national economic policy that would bestow freedom from domination by outsiders. Long before the country had a national government capable of executing it, the outlines of that policy were visible, and the national government of 1789 was created, in part at least, in order to carry it out. Only an independent national economy could guarantee the political independence that Americans had declared in 1776, and only an independent national economy could preserve the virtue, the industry, frugality, and simplicity that Americans had sought to protect from the luxury and corruption of Great

---

[96] Coxe, *An Enquiry into the Principles, passim.*
[97] Examples will be found in *A Few Salutary Hints,* 16; Tucker, *Reflections,* 16; William Barton, *The True Interest of the United States, and Particularly of Pennsylvania, Considered* . . . (Philadelphia, 1786).

Britain. By 1787 it had become clear that none of these objectives could be attained without a national government empowered to control trade—and through trade all other parts of the national economy.

It is altogether fitting that the United States, which first acted as a government when the Continental Congress undertook the nonimportation, nonexportation, nonconsumption Association of 1774, gained a permanent effective government when Americans again felt an urgent need to control trade. There was in each case an immediate objective, to bring pressure on the British, and in each case a larger objective, to build American economic and moral strength. As the Philadelphia Convention was drafting its great document, Tench Coxe expressed a hope which many members of that body cherished equally with the members of the First Continental Congress, that the encouragement of manufacturing would "lead us once more into the paths of virtue by restoring frugality and industry, those potent antidotes to the vices of mankind and will give us real independence by rescuing us from the tyranny of foreign fashions, and the destructive torrent of luxury."[98] Patriotism and the Puritan Ethic marched hand in hand from 1764 to 1789.

213

The vicissitudes of the new national government in carrying out a national economic policy form another story, and one full of ironies. Alexander Hamilton, the brilliant executor of the policy, had scarcely a grain of the Puritan Ethic in him and did not hesitate to enroll the merchant class in his schemes. Hamilton, for purely economic and patriotic reasons, favored direct encouragement of manufactures by the national government; but the merchants whom he had gathered behind him helped to defeat him. Thomas Jefferson, devoted to the values of the Puritan Ethic but prejudiced against manufactures, fought against governmental support of them, yet in the end adopted the measures that turned the country decisively toward manufacturing.

The Puritan Ethic did not die with the eighteenth century. Throughout our history it has been there, though it has continued to be in the process of expiring. One student of the Jacksonian period has concluded that politics in the 1830's and 1840's was dominated by an appeal for restoration of the frugality and simplicity which men of that generation thought had pre-

---

[98] Coxe, *An Address to Friends of Manufactures*, 29-30. Coxe was not a member of the Convention. He was addressing, in Philadelphia, a group "convened for the purpose of establishing a Society for the Encouragement of Manufactures and the Useful Arts."

vailed in the preceding one. The most popular analysis of American society after the second World War was a lament for the loss of inner-directedness (read simplicity, industry, frugality) which had been replaced by other-directedness (read luxury, extravagance). The Puritan Ethic has always been known by its epitaphs. Perhaps it is not quite dead yet.

214

THE CAUCUS AND DEMOCRACY IN COLONIAL BOSTON

G. B. WARDEN

IN the history of political institutions, New England is famous for two inventions: the town meeting, the purest
form of democratic local government since the Greek *polis*,
and the Boston Caucus, America's first urban political "machine" which, expanded and modified, became the ancestor of
modern party conventions and organization. In general, both
historians and New Englanders have ignored the curious, implicit contradiction between the democratic practices of the
town meeting in early Boston and the secretive, exclusive, not-
so-democratic control exercised by the Caucus during the colonial period.

Such an oversight about the Caucus and democracy is easy
to understand. Conclusive evidence about early Boston politics
is sadly lacking, mainly because such activities are usually
carried on by conversation in the proverbial smoke-filled rooms
rather than by writing. Colonists also feared factionalism, and
the members of a faction took great pains to subdue any hints
or accusations of privately manipulating public decisions. Historians, therefore, must rely on meager written evidence, circumstantial elements, patterns of clues, educated guesses, and
frankly speculative hypotheses in their attempts to illustrate
the origins, membership, and operations of the Caucus. Today,
it is taken for granted that relatively restrictive leadership and
organization are necessary complements of democratic politics,
but it is by no means certain why this is so or how this seemingly antithetical conjunction of interests began in the Caucus'
control of the town meeting. Still, the historian must at least
attempt to answer such questions about the Caucus as: Did it
exist? When? Who was in it? How did it operate? And, most
important, how did it affect democratic practices in colonial
Boston?

The first frustrating puzzle about the Caucus is the origin

of the word itself. Among the alternatives proposed are corruptions of words like "Caucasus," the mythological meeting-place of ancient gods; "caulkers," the men who tarred the seams of ships and may have been active members of Boston's first political organization; "cau-cau-asu," an Indian verb meaning "to confer," referring to the Caucus' role in drawing up a slate of candidates before elections; "Cooke's house," the residence on the present site of the old City Hall where Elisha Cooke, Jr., presumably managed the town's politics; and "kaukos," the Greek word for "wine bowl" suggesting the importance of alcohol in winning friends and influencing voters. Of these, I prefer "kaukos," if only because Oxenbridge Thacher and others sometimes referred to the Caucus as the "corkus," a phonetic spelling once again suggesting the connection between bottles and ballots.[1]

Whatever the origin of the word may be, the second problem about the Caucus is the curious lack of references to it in contemporary sources. John Adams reported hearsay evidence about the Caucus in 1763 and named six of its leaders. In 1788 the often unreliable historian, William Gordon, said that the Caucus had been operating fifty years before the Revolution, placing its origin in the 1720's. The arch-Tory Peter Oliver condemned the Caucus' nefarious influence and its enormous expenses for liquor in the 1720's. The appendix to E. H. Goss's *Life of Colonel Paul Revere* provides a list of members and resolutions of the North End Caucus in 1772, and reveals that at a late date there was a Caucus for the South End and one for the middle of town. Aside from five or six items in letters and

---

[1] *The Diary and Autobiography of John Adams* in *The Adams Papers*, edited by Lyman H. Butterfield *et al.* (Cambridge, Mass., 1961), I, 239n.; Samuel A. Drake, *Old Boston Taverns and Tavern Clubs* (Boston, 1917), 45; John C. Miller, *Samuel Adams, Pioneer in Propaganda* (Stanford, Cal., 1936), 8; *Oxford English Dictionary* (Oxford, 1933), II, 191; William V. Wells, *The Life and Public Services of Samuel Adams* (Boston, 1865), I, 3; Annie H. Thwing, *The Crooked and Narrow Streets of Boston* (Boston, 1920), 110; Carl Bridenbaugh, *Cities in the Wilderness, 1643-1743* (New York, 1960), 358; Oxenbridge Thacher to Benjamin Prat, Boston, 1762, Oxenbridge Thacher Collection, Massachusetts Historical Society, Boston.

newspapers, there is no other explicit evidence that the Caucus existed before 1776.[2]

Historians who like ironclad proof and absolute certainty might stop here and dismiss the Caucus as an insoluble enigma or exaggerated suspicion. Yet two men of different biases, Gordon and Oliver, agreed at least that the Caucus existed in the 1720's. What happened then that might indicate the existence of the Caucus at that time?

Certainly, after 1719 Elisha Cooke led a persistent campaign against the powers of the Governor and the King's feudal rights to the forests of Maine. Cooke caused so much trouble and brought the province so close to rebellion that royal officials had to issue an explanatory charter to settle the major conflicts in Massachusetts. In Cooke's campaign the instructions of the Boston town meeting in 1721 spelled out the major objectives and thus became Massachusetts' first modern political platform.[3] But, important as these events were, they offer little evidence of organized political machinery in Boston.

217

2 Adams, *Diary*, I, 238; William Gordon, *History of the Rise, Progress and Establishment of the Independence of the United States of America* (London, 1788), I, 365n.; Peter Oliver, *The Origins and Progress of the American Rebellion*, edited by Douglass Adair and John A. Schutz (San Marino, Cal., 1961), 26; Edward H. Goss, *The Life of Colonel Paul Revere* (Boston, 1891), II, 635-636, 638; David Jeffries reported a great change under the leadership of Elisha Cooke in 1719, David Jeffries to John Usher, May 26, 1719, Jeffries Papers, XVIII, Mass. Hist. Soc.; a letter by "J. C." described a group with great influence which possibly was the Caucus, Aug. 22, 1729, Miscellaneous Bound Collection, IX, Mass. Hist. Soc.; *The New England Weekly Journal*, April 10 and 17, 1727; *Boston Gazette*, May 12, 1760; *Boston Evening Post*, March 21, 1763 and May 14, 1764; a long, undated poem satirized powerful leaders in Boston and referred to a "public Cabal" in the 1750's, Misc. Bound Coll., XII, Mass. Hist. Soc.; in 1767 Governor Bernard said the faction against him was the same that attacked his distant relative, Governor Samuel Shute, in the 1720's, Francis Bernard to the Earl of Shelburne, Jan. 24, 1767, Bernard Letters, IV, Sparks Collection, Houghton Library, Harvard University; for an imaginative reconstruction of the Caucus, see Esther Forbes, *Paul Revere and the World He Lived In* (Boston, 1942), 119-125.

3 Thomas Hutchinson, *History of the Colony and Province of Massachusetts Bay*, edited by Lawrence S. Mayo (Cambridge, Mass., 1936), II, 169-241; Samuel Sewall, *Diary*, III, in Mass. Hist. Soc. *Collections*, 5th Series, VII (1882), 187, 189, 235; Boston Registry Department, *Records Relating to the Early History of Boston* (Boston, 1876-1909), VIII, 154-155 (hereafter BRC).

One indication of an organized political group is its success in getting officials elected over a long period of time. The records of elections in Boston do reveal an extraordinary amount of continuity, an apparent process of promotion, and a structural hierarchy suggesting the efforts of an organized group in the background. The elections for three offices—Representative, Selectman, and Assessor—reveal an unusual pattern after 1719.[4] Bostonians could elect four Representatives to the General Court, and incumbents won 63 per cent of the elections between 1692 and 1719. But in 1719 three of the four incumbents were not reelected, being replaced by Elisha Cooke, Oliver Noyes, and William Clark. Cooke and Noyes had been elected Representatives in 1715 and 1716, when they had tried and failed to create a private bank to manage finances in the province. Cooke was chosen for the Governor's Council in 1717 but rejected by the Governor on the advice of the Dudleys, who had been enemies of the Cooke family since 1692 and probably earlier.[5] After 1719 Cooke was reelected to the House each year until his death in 1737, except for two years when he was the House's agent in England protesting the Governor's powers. William Clark was reelected five times after 1719. John Clark replaced Noyes in 1721 and served until his death in 1725. Among other long terms after 1720, Ezekiel Lewis served from 1723 to 1731. Thomas Cushing was elected nine times after 1721, rose to the Council and was replaced by his son who served for sixteen more years in the House. Although incumbents won 63 per cent of the elections before 1719, incumbents won 82 per cent of the elections for Representative in Boston between 1719 and 1775, a substantial increase, to say the least. The long terms of Cooke and Cushing and the relatively continuous terms of their associates after 1719 provide one indication of the perennial support which an organized group like the Caucus might create.

218

---

[4] All of the information on office-holding in this paper comes from Robert F. Seybolt, *The Town Officials of Colonial Boston, 1632-1775* (Cambridge, Mass., 1939).

[5] Hutchinson, *History*, I, 348, 412; II, 102, 166; Sewall, *Diary*, II, 41.

Another possible indication that an organized political force began operating in 1719 is the fact that six of the seven incumbent Selectmen failed to be reelected that year. Three of the new Selectmen were Cooke, Noyes, and William Clark, an unusual coincidence since Bostonians had previously been averse to letting the same men act as Representatives and Selectmen simultaneously. Cooke and Clark served five more years as Selectmen while they were in the House. Another of the new Selectmen in 1719 was the elder Thomas Cushing, who served for eight more years and was Representative for four of them. When Ezekiel Lewis became Representative in 1723, he also became Selectman and served five years in the two posts. Before 1719 less than a third of the Selectmen became Representatives, but between 1719 and 1729 half of the Selectmen rose to Representative, suggesting a more rapid process of promotion under the influence of an organized group like the Caucus.

219

Elections of Assessors do not show a sharp break in 1719, but the continuity resembles the pattern in higher offices. For example, Daniel Farnham, Joshua Loring, and Daniel Powning regularly served as Assessors after 1715. Although tax officials are rarely popular in towns, Farnham was reelected ten times until 1725, while Loring and Powning served until 1728. Samuel Adams, Sr., first served as Assessor in 1724, as Selectman from 1729 to 1734, and later became a Representative. According to Gordon, the elder Adams was a leader of the Caucus and, after serving as a Director of the Land Bank in 1740, paved the way for the political talents of his more famous son.[6]

Despite the intrinsic problems of the office, Assessors continued to be popular in Boston. Joshua Loring was replaced by his son Daniel who served from 1729 to 1741. Jonas Clark served as Assessor from 1728 to 1735 and then served six terms

6 Miller. *Adams*, 9-19; George A. Billias, "The Massachusetts Land Bankers of 1740," *University of Maine Studies*, 2d Ser., No. 74 (1959). 19; Andrew MacF. Davis, "The Land Bank of 1740," *American Antiquarian Society Proceedings*, New Ser., XI, 92-143 (1896-1897).

as Selectman. Richard Bulkley served thirteen years as Assessor. During the 1740's when the town's finances were in chaos and complaints increased about the Assessors' incompetence, they still remained popular; only ten men were elected as Assessors from 1740 to 1750, although the seven posts were up for election each year.[7] The record for longevity as Assessor went to William Fairfield, who served for twenty-eight years from 1742 to his death in 1770; Fairfield was a brother-in-law of Samuel Adams, Sr., young Samuel's uncle, and headed the list of Caucus members in John Adams' report of 1763. The traitor Benjamin Church probably entered the secret councils of the Sons of Liberty because of his long service as Assessor in the 1750's and 1760's. In a town with annual elections and a large, shifting population noted for its hatred of taxation, the number of men who served extremely long terms is remarkable and important in the town's political leadership. Of all the factors which could explain the extraordinary continuity in office, the influence of an organized system like the Caucus seems most likely.

220

The same conjecture could apply to another difficult but influential office, that of tax collector. Bostonians first started electing Collectors in 1733. In the following years at least three Collectors were elected each March, and the two most popular choices were Nathaniel Barber and Daniel Packer who served six terms until 1739 when they were both promoted to Assessor. In the 1740's and 1750's John Ruddock, young Samuel Adams, Jonathan Payson, and Jonathan Scutt served unusually long terms. Ruddock served from 1747 to 1763, when he was promoted to Selectman.[8] He and Adams were among the leaders of the Caucus in 1763. Like the Assessors, the Collectors were far from competent. They fell behind in their collections as early as 1736. In 1750 one Collector was still trying to collect taxes levied in 1734. Almost everyone is familiar with Samuel

[7] For Boston's economic difficulties, see note 26 below; BRC, XVIII, 93; XIV, 61, 70, 93, 281.

[8] Francis Bernard to [?], Dec. 23, 1769, Bernard Letters, III, Sparks Coll., Houghton Library, Harvard.

Adams' arrears as Collector, but his colleagues were equally notorious for not collecting taxes.[9] Despite defaults and numerous complaints, the Collectors remained powerful and popular; even after the most serious warnings and censures, the Collectors held their jobs and even got salary increases.

After 1719 unusual continuity prevailed in offices other than those of Representative, Selectman, Assessor, and Collector. When he was not in England, Elisha Cooke served as the Moderator of town meetings for every election and important vote from 1719 to 1737. In what looks like a concerted plan, Samuel Checkley, a relative of the Adamses, served as Town Clerk from 1721 to 1734. Joseph Wadsworth served as Town Treasurer from 1721 to 1749, when he was replaced by David Jeffries who served from 1750 until the 1780's. Ezekiel Goldthwait replaced Checkley as Town Clerk in 1742 and served until 1760. He was replaced by William Cooper who served for forty more years, the longest in the town's history. Cooper was one of the Caucus leaders mentioned by John Adams in 1763. In contrast to the frequent rotation of officeholders which one might expect in annual elections, the continuity of Representatives, Selectmen, Assessors, Collectors, and other important officials indicates the possibility of an organized system developing in Boston.

Although circumstantial, the record of elections in Boston seems to justify Oliver and Gordon in their assertions that the Caucus began influencing elections in the 1720's and perhaps as early as 1719. But who was in the Caucus? What bonds united its members? And how did the Caucus influence other groups in Boston? The leadership and membership of the Caucus at various times remain mysterious problems. But it seems likely that Elisha Cooke, Oliver Noyes, Thomas Cushing, John Clark, and William Clark formed the nucleus of the Caucus at its beginning. All but William Clark were Harvard graduates. All but Cushing were physicians, although without medical degrees.[10] Although education seems to have played no

9 BRC, XII, 52, 123, 301; XIV, 177; XVI, 201.

10 John L. Sibley and Clifford K. Shipton, *Biographical Sketches of Graduates of Harvard College* (Cambridge, Mass., 1879-   ), I, 520-525; III, 375-379; IV, 260-

great part in Boston's politics, doctors remained extremely influential until the days of Drs. Joseph Warren, Thomas Young, and Benjamin Church before the Revolution. Geographically, the elder Cushing and the Clarks lived in the North End, but Cooke, Noyes, and the younger Cushing lived in the South End; until the days of Paul Revere, South Enders like the Adamses seem to have dominated the Caucus, although the North End provided the workers and small tradesmen necessary for minor roles in a political machine. One possible reason for this odd division of leadership arose in the 1690's when the Cookes of the South End vehemently opposed the province's new charter which was supported by the Mathers of the Old North Church and their parishioner, Governor Sir William Phips. No North Ender was elected to high office in Boston between 1692 and 1708.[11] Perhaps this division lingered long enough to allow South Enders to dominate the Caucus until a late date.

As for economic ties among the leaders and members of the Caucus, it is doubtful that Drs. Cooke, Noyes, and Clark received any great financial benefits from their medical practice. Economically, they were landlords and property-owners. In addition to houses, mills, shops, and warehouses in Boston, Cooke and Noyes had enormous tracts of land in Maine, the major source of Boston's firewood, barrel staves, building lumber, and ship timbers. Cooke, however, could attract the support of Boston's financial and commercial leaders because of

---

264, 349-356. Elisha Cooke and his father must have been great conversationalists, for only a few of their letters exist.

11 Everett Kimball, *The Public Life of Joseph Dudley* (New York, 1911), 14; Perry Miller, *The New England Mind: From Colony to Province* (Cambridge, Mass., 1953), 191, 208; Hutchinson, *History*, II, 109, 129; Edmund S. Morgan, "A Boston Heiress and Her Husbands: A True Story," Colonial Society of Massachusetts *Publications*, XXXIV, 508-511 (1937-1942); for the influence of the medical profession in Boston, see John Cary, *Joseph Warren* (Urbana, Ill., 1961), 26; J. S. Loring, *One Hundred Boston Orators* (Boston, 1852), I, 37-78; Herbert H. Edes, "A Memoir of Dr. Thomas Young," Col. Soc. Mass. *Pubs.*, XI, 6-37 (1906-1907); for the absence of North Enders from high office, compare Seybolt, *Town Officials*, with lists in A. B. Ellis, *History of the First Church in Boston* (Boston, 1881), I, 140-178, *Historical Catalogue of the Old South Church* (Boston, 1883), 3-27, 260-349, and H. A. Hill, *History of the Old South Church* (Cambridge, Mass., 1890), 279-341.

his monopoly of salt production and land development on Boston Neck. Noyes had a large share in another monopolistic venture important to the merchants: the Long Wharf at the foot of King Street.[12] Most important, Cooke and Noyes were the leaders of the private bank scheme in 1715. One of their associates in that venture, John Colman, promoted the Land Bank in 1740, in which Samuel Adams, Sr., was a Director. Young Samuel Adams achieved his earliest popularity in Boston by his efforts to forestall the county sheriff's efforts to auction the Adamses' property after the Land Bank's demise. Apparently, many of the Caucus' leaders were incipient capitalists, chafing at royal restrictions. Their long efforts to control currency, oppose customs rules, establish a bank, create insurance companies, promote local manufacturing, and build a Charles River bridge finally bore fruit in the days of John Hancock during and after the Revolution.[13]

223

Of course, not all of the members of the Caucus or the men whom the Caucus influenced were entrepreneurs. Before the Revolution many craftsmen like Paul Revere, tradesmen,

12 Although the merchants were important in Boston's economy and province politics, distrust lingered about their sense of public welfare; for example, in 1690, John Nelson was not elected to the General Court because "he was a merchant and therefore not to be trusted," Mass. Hist. Soc. *Proceedings*, xvi, 103-108 (1878); see also Thomas Hutchinson, *Collection of Original Papers Relative to the History of the Colony of Massachusetts Bay* (Boston, 1769), 569-570; BRC, vii, 242-244; viii, 7; ix, 5; Sewall, *Diary*, ii, 280-281, 384; BRC, ix, 194, 196; Thomas Coram to Benjamin Colman, July 9, 1737, Colman Coll., ii, Mass. Hist. Soc.; for another view, see Bernard Bailyn, *The New England Merchants in the Seventeenth Century* (Cambridge, Mass., 1955), 195-197.

For the interests of Boston's politicians in Maine Lands from the days of Elisha Cooke to Samuel Adams, James Otis and John Hancock, see Roy Akagi, *The Town Proprietors of the New England Colonies* (Philadelphia, 1924), 211, 243, 246, 248; Miller, *Adams*, 59. For the salt monopoly, see "Copy of the Salt Act," Dec. 14, 1695, Photostat Coll., Box 32, Mass. Hist. Soc. For the Long Wharf project, see list dated Jan. 26, 1715, Photostat Coll., Box 37, and account book, 1711-1718, David S. Greenough Papers, Folder 1, Mass. Hist. Soc. For other connections among Cooke's associates, see Caleb Snow, *History of Boston* (Boston, 1828), 209; Drake, *Old Boston Taverns*, 38-40; Bridenbaugh, *Cities in the Wilderness*, 171; and Andrew MacF. Davis, *Colonial Currency Reprints* (Boston, 1910), ii, 377-429.

13 See note 6 above and Wells, *Adams*, i, 27; Bridenbaugh, *Cities in the Wilderness*, 161; A. E. Brown, *John Hancock, His Book* (Boston, 1898), 50; Andrew MacF. Davis, *Tracts Relating to the Currency of Massachusetts Bay, 1682-1720* (New York, 1902), 173-175, 245.

workers, distillers, professional men, and minor officials were as important to the Caucus as land barons like Cooke or merchant princes like John Hancock. Without further evidence about the people involved in the Caucus no one can say absolutely just what the true economic origins and interests of the Caucus were.

The same doubts remain about how the Caucus operated in influencing voters and the many townspeople who did not vote. According to John Adams, the Caucus met before elections to choose a slate of candidates to be approved by the voters. Presumably the Caucus also met before other important town meetings. Adams reported, too, that the Caucus in 1763 coordinated its slate of candidates with the Merchants' Club, a select group of ship owners and wholesalers who joined together in 1751 to protest the oppressive tactics of royal customs officials. Actually, cooperation between the merchants and the leaders of the town meeting began around 1740; at that time, when Boston was suffering from an economic depression and the Collectors were behind in their accounts, the Town Treasurer with public approval began to borrow funds for immediate expenses from merchants until tax revenues could pay off the debt.[14] After 1760, when James Otis and John Adams moved to Boston, lawyers played an influential part in developing policy and legal tactics to coincide with economic measures and political methods already created by the Merchants' Club and the Caucus.

Aside from attracting the influence of merchants and lawyers, the town's political leaders operated by keeping in close touch with important tradesmen like Paul Revere. Royall Tyler, a wellborn fop and successful vote getter, made a point just before elections of calling Boston's leading carpenters, masons, coopers, and other craftsmen to do "repairs" on his house to win their influence in return for his business.[15] Guilds

[14] Charles McL. Andrews, "Boston Merchants and the Non-importation Movement," Col. Soc. Mass. *Pubs.*, XIX, 160 (1916-1917); BRC, XII, 268, 272, 276; XIV, 61, 159, 235, 258.

[15] *Conversation of Two Persons under a Window on Monday Evening the 23d of March* [Boston, 1765].

did not exist in Boston, but tradesmen often met regularly for a stroll down King Street or a mug of ale at one of the many local taverns. In the 1720's newspapers in Boston denounced the superfluity of tavern clubs as cheap, pretentious copies of London clubs, but by 1760 there were so many clubs that the diarist John Rowe hardly spent an evening at home. The clubs had interlocking memberships, so that a decision by the Caucus or Merchants' Club easily filtered through all parts of Boston; during the important discussions of non-importation in the late 1760's, the overlapping influence of social organizations became so great that royal officials complained about the preponderance of lawyers and workers at the meetings of the Merchants' Club.[16]

225

Anyone familiar with the operation of elections in England or Virginia in the eighteenth century knows that voting depended as much on liquor as on formal campaigning, appeals to reason or careful discussion of issues. Boston's political leaders were not exceptional in relying on liquor at social clubs and taverns before elections to persuade voters. Peter Oliver said that in the 1720's the Boston Caucus spent the huge sum of £9000 sterling on liquor to attract votes and reward supporters. Even if Oliver exaggerated the amount, still, Elisha Cooke's land company spent over half of its budget in 1721 at taverns. According to John Colman, Cooke himself was overly fond of the bottle to the extent of flying into vicious rages and falling over furniture.[17] A complete alcoholic history of colonial America remains to be written, but it is perhaps signifi-

16 *Boston Newsletter*, April 18, 1720; *Gazette*, Jan. 15, 1722; *New England Courant*, Sept. 4, 1721, Feb. 12, 1722, Jan. 7, 1723, Feb. 26, 1726; *New England Weekly Journal*, April 10 and 17, 1727; *Letters and Diary of John Rowe, 1759-1779*, edited by A. R. Cunningham (Boston, 1903), 35-37, 72; Adams, *Diary*, I, 269-270, 299; Miller, *Adams*, 37-38; Andrew Oliver to Francis Bernard, Nov. 21, 1769, Andrew Oliver Letterbook, Mass. Hist. Soc.; Thomas Hutchinson to Thomas Whatley, April 30, 1770, Massachusetts Archives, xxv, 399-400, State House, Boston; "Report of Town Meeting," Jan. 17, 1770, Chalmers Papers, III, Sparks Coll., Houghton Library, Harvard. For the Masons in Boston, see Cary, *Warren*, 55-59.

17 Oliver, *Origins*, 26; Lincolnshire Associates Account, Dec. 20, 1720, Photostat Coll., Box 38, and John Colman to Benjamin Colman, March 20, 1725, and Feb. 4, 1726, Colman Coll., I, Mass. Hist. Soc.

cant that conflict in Boston often coincided with such events as
the Molasses Act of 1733, the Excise Act of 1754, the Sugar Act
of 1764, and the *Liberty* case in 1768 involving smuggled wine.
Rich men like Elisha Cooke and John Hancock could afford
the liquor for influencing Boston's thirsty voters. And it is perhaps no accident that the Sons of Liberty in 1765 included a
distiller who provided the group's meeting place and that the
North End Caucus met regularly at the Green Dragon Tavern.[18] With the influence of professional groups, tradesmen
and social clubs, liquor provided an important means by which
the Caucus might win the loyalty of the townspeople.

The connection between liquor and social organization appeared in the activities of another important group in the
town, perhaps for peripheral political purposes. Most of Boston's thirstiest drinkers seem to have been in the fire companies. Volunteer fire companies originated in Boston around
the time of the Caucus' probable beginning in 1719. Although
fires often destroyed large parts of Boston, the volunteer fire
companies and the public engine companies elected in each
ward after 1733 were little more than drinking clubs which
met monthly and occasionally appeared at fires. The firemen,
however, were more important than the votes which they
might cast. Some suspicious events suggest that the firemen did
not restrict their public exertions to voting and drinking.
They were trained to work quickly in the dark with axes and
hooks provided by the town for pulling down buildings in the
path of fires. When Jonathan Loring refused to remove his
barn to make way for a street in 1732, a mob levelled the building one night before the Constables could arrive. A few years
later the South Enders failed to get formal approval to lay out
a bowling green where an old garrison house stood on the top
of Fort Hill. After legal means failed, the Constables reported
that unknown persons were dismantling the fort log by log at
night; then, the remains of the fort mysteriously caught on fire,

226

[18] The impressment riot of 1747 and the Tea Party of 1773 are, of course,
notable exceptions. Drake, *Old Boston Taverns*, 45; Francis S. Drake, *Tea Leaves*
(Boston, 1884), lxvii; Adams, *Diary*, I, 294.

the firemen were suspiciously late in arriving at the scene, and the South Enders finally got a site for their bowling green. In 1737 a mob disguised as clergymen turned out one wintry night, sawed through the supports of the public market in the North End, and completely demolished the market house in Dock Square. In 1740 Peter Faneuil took the precaution of building a market hall in brick, but, after repeated attempts to close the hall's market facilities, a mysterious fire gutted the building in 1762, and in 1765 a mob took only fifteen minutes to pull down a brick building that supposedly was to be used as a Stamp Office.[19] The Caucus and the Sons of Liberty may have provided the policies and liquor for influencing votes in the town meeting, but the firemen seem to have provided the muscle for mob action.

227

One advantage of the fire companies was that they were organized by wards, as were Boston's Constables. In the later colonial period tithingmen, firewards, and other officials were elected for each of the twelve wards in Boston. The ward system provided a ready-made means of organizing political activity, supplementing the organization provided by occupations and social clubs. Many of these lowly ward posts were held by important politicians with other connections in the town. In 1768, for example, Selectman John Rowe, Representative Samuel Adams, Selectman John Hancock, Town Clerk William Cooper, and six militia officers were Firewards, presumably for reasons other than their knowledge of fire fighting. The group of militia officers included Thomas

19 Bridenbaugh, *Cities in the Wilderness*, 210, 265-272, 367; Samuel G. Drake, *History and Antiquities of Boston* (Boston, 1856), 557, 607; Mass. Hist. Soc. *Colls.*, 2d Ser., I, 81-83 (1814); Edmund S. and Helen M. Morgan, *The Stamp Act Crisis: Prologue to Revolution* (Chapel Hill, N. C., 1953), 121; BRC, xv, 171, 216; xii, 248, 257; xiv, 5; Jonathan Belcher to the Duke of Newcastle, April 14, 1737, State Papers, xi, Gay Transcripts, Mass. Hist. Soc.; *Newsletter*, April 1 and 21, 1737; Bridenbaugh, *Cities in Revolt, 1743-1776* (New York, 1955), 295; John Avery to John Collins, Aug. 14, 1765, Photostat Coll., Box 43, Mass. Hist. Soc.; *Gazette*, Aug. 11, 1766; *New England Historical and Genealogical Register* (hereafter NEHGR), LXXXIV, 156 (1930). Fires served other purposes in Boston; in 1711 someone stole the records of the Admiralty Court during a disastrous fire, *Newsletter*, Jan. 26, 1711; John Mein accused Samuel Adams of burning the Land Bank records during a fire at the old State House in 1747, *Boston Chronicle*, Oct. 26, 1769.

Dawes, the Adjutant of the Boston regiment, who, according to John Adams, let the Caucus use his garret as a meeting place. Naturally, ward officials, social clubs, militia companies, the Ancient and Honorable Artillery Company, and the Corps of Cadets (commanded by Colonel John Hancock) provided possible means by which the town's political leaders might influence the citizenry for voting and mob activity.[20]

In addition to social clubs, professions, and ward groups, churches also offered a weekly meeting place and forum for political ideas, and Boston's ministers were not shy about meddling in politics. Elisha Cooke, Sr., who opposed the Mathers, was a brother-in-law of Samuel Willard of the Old South. After many political manoeuvers, Willard replaced Increase Mather as President of Harvard College and in 1707 was replaced by John Leverett, another brother-in-law of the elder Cooke.[21] Benjamin Colman, the pastor of the Brattle Street Church, was the brother of young Cooke's partner John Colman, and the Colmans' brother-in-law John Staniford served as a Tax Collector and was the major promoter of a bridge over the Charles River. For four decades the Reverend Mr. Colman corresponded with politicians in Boston and England on highly secular matters.[22] He was succeeded at Brattle Street by Samuel Cooper, brother of the Town Clerk, and one of the "black regiment" of clergymen denounced by Peter Oliver for their politi-

228

20 A comparison between the lists of Seybolt, *Town Officials*, Goss, *Revere*, II, 635-636, Drake, *Tea Leaves*, 95-171, and Zachariah G. Whitman, *History of the Ancient and Honorable Artillery Company* (Boston, 1842) show little, if any, class distinctions among political activists and high officials. In "Economic Development and Social Structure in Colonial Boston," *William and Mary Quarterly*, 3d Ser., XXII, 89-90 (1965), James A. Henretta says that the correlation between wealth and high office was "almost exact" and "nearly perfect" based on an "integrated economic and political hierarchy" in the "hands of a broad elite, entry into which was conditioned by commercial achievement and family background"; "By the seventh decade of the eighteenth century, in a mature economic environment, the merchant prince had replaced the man of action at the apex of the social order." For the truly elite Corps of Cadets, see Herbert S. Allan, *John Hancock, Patriot in Purple* (New York, 1948), 151. For McIntosh, see note 30 below and for Warren, see Cary, *Warren*, 46-47.

21 Hutchinson, *History*, II, 53, 96; Miller, *Colony to Province*, 191-208.

22 Bridenbaugh, *Cities in the Wilderness*, 319; see the correspondence in Colman Coll., I, Mass. Hist. Soc.; *Gazette*, March 12, 1729; BRC, XII, 224, 234, 281; Sibley and Shipton, *Harvard Graduates*, IV, 120-129.

cal power. Cooper, Jonathan Mayhew of West Church, Andrew Eliot of the New North, and Charles Chauncy of the First Church were willing allies of Boston's rebels in attacking kings and bishops.[23] Puritanism and religion may have declined in Boston, but the town's ministers maintained strong political influence throughout the eighteenth century.

The political combination of the ward system, liquor, social clubs, militia, churches, fire companies, and trades might, of course, rest on historical accidents or a fortuitous combination of coincidences common to developing urban communities and not on the conscious influence of a central organization like the Caucus. Unfortunately, there has been no extensive research about towns comparable to Boston in size and political organization, and the evidence from smaller, rural towns in New England does not seem applicable to Boston. Political cohesion and continuity are fairly prevalent in small, isolated towns dominated by a few families; in a larger, more diverse and more unstable community like Boston, other, more sophisticated explanations must be made. In Boston the coincidences are combined in such a systematic way, involve such a common group of leaders, and fit so closely with the available literary references and patterns of elections that it is hard to ignore the conclusion that the Caucus did exist and operated with the techniques usually associated with urban politics. The question may never be answered satisfactorily, but, of all the possible alternative explanations, it seems more reasonable and accurate to view events in Boston as the result of an organized political group than as the products of accidents.

It would be a mistake, however, to say that the Caucus always succeeded in organizing popular support and in dominating public decisions. Especially in the 1740's and 1750's, popular politics in Boston was chaotic and lacked the cohesive

229

23 Oliver, Origins, 42-44; C. A. W. Pownall, Thomas Pownall (London, 1908), 88; John A. Schutz, Thomas Pownall (Glendale, Cal., 1951), 220; William Tudor, Life of James Otis (Boston, 1823), 152; Philip Davidson, Propaganda in the American Revolution (Chapel Hill, N. C., 1943), 22; Ellis, First Church, 190; Davis, Reprints, II, 134; Miller, Colony to Province, 305-322; the Hollis Papers, Andrews-Eliot Letters and "The Boston Ministers," 1774, Photostat Coll., Box 45, Mass. Hist. Soc.; and Carl Bridenbaugh, Mitre and Sceptre (New York, 1962).

leadership and uniformity of support that marked the 1720's when Elisha Cooke brought the province to the brink of rebellion, or the 1760's when Samuel Adams was in power. Important issues did appear between Cooke's death in 1737 and the rise of Adams and Hancock in 1764, but the interim leaders lacked their power and fortunes. Cooke squandered a fortune on liquor. Hancock and his wealthy aunt in 1771 had £30,000 lent at interest to grateful voters when the assessed value of real property in Boston was only £39,000, had nearly 1,000 families dependent on his generosity and even spent £1,000 for one dinner uniting the North and South End mobs in 1765.[24] Without such wealthy patrons between 1737 and 1764 the Caucus faced a crisis of leadership. The crisis coincided with the worst depression in Boston's history. How could the Caucus operate without a wealthy patron during a long period of economic distress?

No one in Boston could ignore the town's serious financial problems. While almost every other community in America doubled in size every twenty-five years, the population in Boston between 1730 and 1775 stayed the same and may even have declined. Aside from the birth rate, death rate, and growth of suburbs,[25] the town meeting in the 1730's began to report the factors which for several years had plagued the town. By 1750 shipbuilding orders in Boston dwindled from twenty to two a year. Twenty-five of the town's thirty butchers left. The distilling business declined by 66 per cent. In the war years of 1742 to 1745 over £200,000 of property was lost at sea. From

---

[24] Mass. Archives, cxxxii, 92-147, State House, Boston; Allan, *Hancock*, 92.

[25] Bridenbaugh, *Cities in the Wilderness*, 143n., 303, and *Cities in Revolt*, 216. The only vaguely reliable figures for Boston's death, marriages and births, averaged per year in ten-year groups are:

	Deaths	Marriages	Births
1704-1713	314.8	136.3	261.1
1714-1723	435.2	181.1	288.4
1724-1733	489.5	170.9	293.7

Mass. Hist. Soc. *Colls.*, 1st Ser., IV, 213-215 (1795); BRC, xxiv, xxviii. As for the move to the suburbs in 1690, there were 954 men in the Boston regiment and 1,139 in the Suffolk regiment, but in 1751 there were 2,786 taxpayers in Boston and 4,732 elsewhere in Suffolk County, "Muster List" May 13, 1690, State Papers, vii, Gay Transcripts, and "Evaluation of Suffolk, 1751," Misc. Bound Coll., xii, Mass. Hist. Soc.

1738 to 1748 the number of taxpayers fell from 3,400 to 2,400. One thousand of the town's 15,000 inhabitants were poor widows dependent on public charity. Every year the list of evils grew longer.[26] Whatever the cause of Boston's distress, the results were apparent and made the Bostonians hypersensitive to issues involving taxation and currency.

Even if the Bostonians exaggerated their woes, the town certainly lost the eminence and prosperity of earlier days, creating problems for Elisha Cooke's successors. To be sure, Bostonians led the demand for more paper money and after 1763 the opposition to Parliament's new taxes. These appeals by themselves might explain how the leaders of the Caucus gained support among the suffering citizens. But for many years Bostonians elected hard-money men and failed to prevent adverse legislation like the Tea Act of 1750 and the Excise Act of 1754. The possible leaders, patrons, or important candidates after 1740 apparently had their own problems to worry about and left actual management to second-rate people. Samuel Adams, Sr., Cooke's probable successor, had to pay off the debts of the Land Bank. His son failed as a maltster. Thomas Hancock, John's wealthy uncle, was too busy getting war contracts from royal officials to take Cooke's place. The Caucus leaders from the 1740's whom John Adams later mentioned—Assessor William Fairfield and Collector John Ruddock—did not have the personal wealth to lubricate the political machinery with liquor. James Allen, a fiery popular figure of the 1740's, was the son of a former Province Treasurer but was more important for his flamboyant actions than for wealth or man-

231

---

[26] Henretta, "Economic Development," 88, bases his hypotheses about wealth and political power on Boston's "increase of wealth and resources" and on the town's developing prosperity. For the depression in Boston, see BRC, xii, 119-123, 177-178, 198, 225-229; xiv, 12-14, 98-100, 238-240, 277, 302-303; xv, 368; xxix, v, and Mass. Archives, cxvii, 51-68, 399, State House, Boston. See also Bridenbaugh, *Cities in Revolt*, 43; Henry W. Foote, *Annals of King's Chapel* (Boston, 1882), i, 522; ii, 19; Justin Winsor et al., *The Memorial History of Boston* (Boston, 1880-1882), ii, 443, 447; Rufus K. Wilson, editor, *Burnaby's Travels through North America* (New York, 1904), 142-143; Joseph Bennett, "History of New England in 1740," 160-161, Houghton Library, Harvard; NEHGR, lxxxiv, 153 (1930); Francis Bernard to the Lords Commissioners of Trade and Plantations, April 8, 1765, Bernard Letters, iii, Sparks Coll., Houghton Library, Harvard.

agerial skill.[27] Presumably in those troubled years, the Caucus had to get along without a patron or first-rate political leader and to use non-economic means of persuasion. Yet the dismal depression coincided with the extraordinarily long terms of the Assessors and Collectors, the same people whom one would expect to be extremely unpopular in times of financial distress. If the town was in dire financial straits and the Caucus had no patron, how can one explain the unusual continuity, popularity, and influence of the Assessors and Collectors, who presumably would have had few friends among the impoverished citizens?

The Assessors' and Collectors' longevity in office, their triumph over numerous complaints and adverse conditions, and young Samuel Adams' amazing political success despite being behind £8,000 in his collection demand explanation. Unfortunately, no one has found any complete tax records for Boston between 1687 and 1771, so that there is no way of telling how the Collectors operated or who failed to pay taxes.

One possible hypothesis to explain the Collectors' and Assessors' popularity during the depression is that they used tax abatements to gain support and votes for the Caucus. A fragment of an account book kept by Treasurer David Jeffries in 1763 shows that Samuel Adams made no collections that year until after the May elections.[28] Perhaps Adams delayed his collections on the theory that numerous demands for taxes before elections might harm his popularity and ability to win votes for the Caucus' candidates. If he did go on his rounds, he might possibly have offered to abate a potential supporter's tax in exchange for his vote. The default could be justified legally by the Assessors' power of abatement and by any reason of sudden poverty that the voter could muster. If, however, a voter fell behind in his tax payments, the Collectors had a powerful means of "persuasion" to influence his vote; by law the Collectors could seize a defaulting taxpayer's property without trial

[27] See note 6 above; Miller, *Adams*, 17; Sibley and Shipton, *Harvard Graduates*, IV, 159-164; Allan, *Hancock*, 51; John A. Schutz, *William Shirley* (Chapel Hill, N. C., 1961), 72.

[28] Jeffries Papers, XXII, Mass. Hist. Soc.

and auction it off to pay the debt. This method was rarely used to collect taxes, and in a very few cases the Collectors started civil suits for debt against obstinate defaulters.[29] The threat of possible seizure or civil suit could be as powerful as an abatement in winning over a voter. To pursue the conjecture further, it is perhaps no accident that Samuel Adams listed Ebenezer McIntosh as a tax defaulter in 1763 just before his meteoric rise as a mob leader in Boston's political circles during the Stamp Act riots.[30]

The Assessors and Collectors might get away with not collecting taxes and manipulating voters indefinitely or, at least, as long as merchants lent money to pay the town's necessary public expenses. Tax deficits were carried from year to year until the Province Treasurer began to complain, but by then Boston managed to get a much-needed reduction of its share of the province's tax burden.[31] The Assessors repeatedly refused to let anyone examine their books, and perhaps a little juggling might have transferred some of the deficits to those citizens who could afford to pay; after 1740 Bostonians no longer had to submit annual lists of taxable property and income and were assessed by rough estimate, so that a rich man might never even know he was being assessed for other people's taxes.[32] Some

233

---

[29] See "Ruggles v. Doane" in *The Legal Papers of John Adams*, edited by L. Kinvin Wroth and Hiller B. Zobel (Cambridge, Mass., 1965), I, 42, and "Grant v. Hornsby," Sept. 16, 1760, Richard Henry Dana Papers, Mass. Hist. Soc.

[30] "A List of outstanding Taxes due to Samuel Adams late Collector lodged by him with the Selectmen, to be laid before the Town," [1767], Loose Papers, City Clerk's Office, Old City Hall, Boston; in March, 1765, McIntosh was elected to be a Sealer of Leather, a month after being tried for manslaughter in the death of a boy during the Pope's Day fight in Nov., 1764, Rowe, *Diary*, 76, and Col. Soc. Mass. *Pubs.*, XXVI, 20-49, 350-358 (1923-1924).

[31] For the Collectors' deficits and problems, see BRC, XII, 301; XIV, 20, 61, 94, 109, 112, 138, 160, 168; John Ruddock to Samuel Phillips Savage, March 15, 1762, Samuel Phillips Savage Papers, II, Mass. Hist. Soc.; to get the rebate, Bostonians even used a lobbyist, "A list of subscribers for paying John Rowe . . . for his expenses in the next Assembly," Nov. 13, 1759, William Gardner Papers, Box I, Mass. Hist. Soc.

[32] E. Ames and Abner C. Goodell, editors, *The Acts and Resolves, Public and Private, of the Province of Massachusetts Bay* (Boston, 1869), II, 1073; III, 47, 63. For protests of assessments see "Account of Real and Personal Estate," Feb. 9, 1753, Melatiah Bourn Letterbook, Bourn Papers, I, Houghton Library, Harvard, and "Complaint of Henry Sewall," Aug. 27, 1753, Misc. Bound Coll., XII, Mass.

wealthy men did challenge their assessments and got lower rates, but the town's finances were in such chaos that an over-evaluation could be explained as a clerical error. Without further evidence, of course, such a hypothesis that taxation was used for political purposes must remain only speculative, but it does seem to be the only reasonable way of explaining the sorry state of the town's treasury, the Assessors' and Collectors' unusual popularity, and how the Caucus may have operated during the town's long depression.

234

The mysteries about the origins, leaders, members, organization, and methods of the Caucus may never be solved to everyone's satisfaction. But, in truth, they are of secondary importance to the central question about the relation between the Caucus and democratic institutions in the town. The very existence of a small group of men selecting candidates and managing votes seems to minimize the importance of popular participation in elections, officeholding, and direction of local affairs. The New England town meeting was America's most democratic invention, but the exclusiveness and secrecy implicit in the operations of the Caucus obviously require careful qualifications about the extent of popular participation in Boston's politics.

It is necessary, of course, to consider the familiar problem of the size of Boston's electorate. At the most, only about 15 per cent of the town's one thousand taxpayers in 1687 had sufficient property to qualify as voters in town or province elections under the rules imposed in 1692. By some mysterious means, however, the number of voters rose from 150 in 1692 to about 350 in 1698.[33] Until 1771 there are no tax records for Boston and no way of knowing how many of the adult males were eligible voters. Yet a list of 1752 recorded 2,786 taxpayers in Boston,

Hist. Soc. For the intricacies of assessment and its confusion, see John Higginson to S. Gardner, Salem, July 28, 1755, John Higginson Coll., Mass. Hist. Soc.

[33] BRC, I, 21-133; William MacDonald, editor, *Select Charters and Other Documents Illustrative of American History, 1606-1775* (New York, 1906), 208; T. McClure Peters, *A Picture of Town Government in the Massachusetts Bay Colony at the Middle of the Seventeenth Century as Illustrated by the Town of Boston* (New York, n.d.), 7.

and a bill in that year charged the town for printing 1,800 tickets to be distributed to the eligible voters.[34] With these figures a little arithmetic shows that a maximum of 66 per cent of the adult males were eligible to vote, lower perhaps than the province average but probably normal for a crowded seaport. By 1771 the eligible voters probably amounted to 78 per cent of the adult males.[35] Despite a long depression the electorate in Boston was becoming more democratic along with the development of the Caucus.

Actual attendance at elections and town meetings is another indication of democratic participation. The record of votes cast is more complete but does not reveal truly democratic participation. Throughout most of the eighteenth century, the number of voters actually in attendance varied between 200 and 600, a relatively small proportion of the probable number of potential voters. Only rarely did more than a third of the eligible voters bother to exercise their suffrage. Even in the most important votes on the eve of the Revolution only about half of the potential voters appeared.[36] Either the voters were apathetic, or they were content to let the Caucus and its regular supporters manage public affairs.

The number of potential or actual voters, however, is not the only measure of democracy; the support of large numbers in dictatorships does not necessarily mean democracy. The most important indication of democracy in a political institution is whether or not it serves the people and their needs on a wide scale free from arbitrary restrictions. Despite the relatively small number of eligible voters, the low number of actual voters, and the tiny number of political managers, Boston's town meeting remained a democratic institution in its actions.

235

[34] "List of Smallpox Inoculations, Boston," July 24, 1752, Misc. Bound Coll., XII, Mass. Hist. Soc.; Edes & Gill to Town Treasurer, April 11, 1752, Loose Papers, City Clerk's Office, Old City Hall, Boston.

[35] Robert E. Brown, *Middle-Class Democracy and the Revolution in Massachusetts, 1691-1780* (Ithaca, N. Y., 1955), 21-37; Henretta, "Economic Development," 82.

[36] Sewall, *Diary*, I, 425, 480, 496; II, 74, 77, 253, 385; BRC, XIV, 17, 45, 72, 93, 115, 148, 153, 161, 176; XVIII, 21, 53, 78, 129, 166, 190.

For example, throughout the eighteenth century, Bostonians consistently refused to make the town into an incorporated borough along the lines of New York, Philadelphia, and most large English communities. Rather than put the town officially under the control of a small, self-perpetuating group of mayors, aldermen, and burgesses, the Bostonians kept the town meeting system until 1822 when the population reached 40,000.[37] In another continued effort to avoid arbitrary restrictions, the Bostonians refused to establish regulated public markets, except for three years in the 1730's. The townspeople preferred the chaos, haggling, and occasionally fraudulent practices of buying and selling in the streets at all hours to a guild system or restriction of marketing to limited hours and places; this preference for freedom in trade even went to the extent of refusing to allow the newspapers to print lists of prices current. Despite the justified popularity of Faneuil Hall as a political forum, the townspeople persistently refused to let its market facilities operate under tight regulations.[38]

The townspeople's fear of restrictive rules created great and continuing distrust of English customs and pretensions of aristocracy and privilege. Opposition to the province charter in the 1690's was one symptom of this anglophobia. Even young Cooke with his popularity could not get the Bostonians to approve his proposals for a private bank which would have dominated the province's economy. Having learned that lesson, Cooke led the fight against the Governor, the King, and the hard-money policies of the Governor's friends.[39] In the 1720's popular feeling ran high against the Anglican church, duelling, public dancing on royal holidays, and the loose

---

[37] Col. Soc. Mass. *Pubs.*, x, 353-354 (1904-1906); Bridenbaugh, *Cities in the Wilderness*, 144, and *Cities in Revolt*, 7; Snow, *History*, 207; Thomas Hutchinson wanted to have Parliament incorporate Boston as a borough, Thomas Hutchinson to Thomas Whatley, May 24, 1771, Mass. Arch., xxvii, 171-173, State House, Boston.

[38] Abram E. Brown, *Faneuil Hall* (Boston, 1900), 69, 71; Bridenbaugh, *Cities in the Wilderness*, 192; Winsor, *Memorial History*, ii, 462-466; *Gazette*, Dec. 21, 1719 and Jan. 4, 1720; Davis, *Reprints*, i, 390; Davis, *Tracts*, 226; *Some Considerations against the Setting Up of a Market*, Boston, 1733, Mass. Hist. Soc.

[39] Davis, *Tracts*, 112-132; Hutchinson, *History*, ii, 156, 166.

morals of the Franklins' Hell-Fire Club.[40] Bostonians for many years refused to let the Selectmen have an annual dinner at public expense in imitation of the practice in English boroughs.[41] In the 1750's public hatred turned against royal customs officials, their corrupt and devious methods. In times of economic crisis the importation of English fashions and fads was denounced. The resentment against powerful families like the Dudleys, Hutchinsons, and Olivers began long before the Revolutionary era.[42]

Almost everyone in Boston shuddered at the thought of "levelling" tendencies in a pure democracy, but the townspeople's anglophobia and fear of restrictions contributed greatly to the decay of arbitrary traditional distinctions in society and to the gradual development of popular practices in the town.[43] Although the suffrage was not universal, everyone in Boston was still eligible for holding office, and often the number of officials in the town outnumbered the actual voters at town meetings. Despite the exclusiveness and continuity of officeholding under the reign of the Caucus, the number of officeholders in Boston increased from 133 in 1709 to 228 in 1733 and remained near 200 until 1776, so that almost every adult male probably had the chance to serve in public office at least once if he showed any willingness. The practice also persisted from the seventeenth century of allowing anyone, even strangers and those without the franchise, to attend town meetings, make proposals, and debate issues. Since most questions were decided by voice vote and since it was almost impossible to sort out the voices, most adult males in the town probably had an opportunity to share in the management of public

237

---

[40] Newsletter, Aug. 14 and 28, 1721, March 9 and Sept. 7, 1727; Bridenbaugh, Cities in the Wilderness, 277, and Mitre and Sceptre, 27; Foote, King's Chapel, I, 285-376; Brown, Faneuil Hall, 59-63; Snow, History, 219; Hutchinson, History, II, 180; Sewall, Diary, II, 419, and Letters, Mass. Hist. Soc. Colls., 5th Ser., II, 30 (1887).

[41] BRC. xv, 226, 237.

[42] Davis, Reprints, II, 283, and Tracts, 176, 331; Ellen Brennan, Plural Officeholding in Massachusetts, 1760-1780 (Chapel Hill, N. C., 1945), 31-34.

[43] Gazette, Jan. 1, 1733, and Jan. 2, 1771.

affairs or, at least, in the approval of the Caucus' management. Then, too, any decisions could be reviewed or repealed at subsequent town meetings, and the citizens could demand an accounting from any official suspected of dangerous conduct. It is little wonder that, among other reasons, the Bostonians performed their most overt acts of rebellion in 1689 and 1775 after the town meeting system had been threatened and that the institution survived until the late date of 1822.[44]

If the Bostonians thought that the Caucus posed any threat to the open practices of the town meeting, they did not often show it. A few pamphlets and newspaper articles lodged vague and infrequent complaints against secret influences in elections and public decisions, but it is not clear if these charges were directed against the Caucus or at the Governor's friends who looked on the town meeting with fear and disdain.[45] Although the inherent exclusiveness of the Caucus could possibly threaten the practices and very existence of the town meeting, for nearly one hundred years the Caucus served as a complement to gradually developing democratic practices in Boston.

A skeptic or extreme idealist might minimize the value of the Caucus and its relation to the town meeting because they appear to be devoid of any redeeming political principles and operated only for the mundane purpose of achieving materialistic goals. Yet the practices of the town meeting represented actual applications of such principles as popular sovereignty, consent, direct representation, responsibility, freedom of assembly, freedom of speech, the right of petition, and many others. The Caucus did not really interfere with these principles, and the Caucus' leaders knew full well that their power rested ultimately on the people's enjoyment of traditional rights and privileges.

Far from being an inchoate assembly dedicated only to political expediency, the town meeting had an extraordinary

---

[44] Peters, *Town Government*, 25-26; "A memorial to explain the articles of the Declaration of April 18, 1689," Misc. Bound Coll., III, Mass. Hist. Soc.

[45] See the newspaper articles in note 16 above.

political philosophy expressed in two pamphlets which appeared around the time of the Caucus' probable beginning.[46] The purpose of the pamphlets was to oppose incorporation and regulated markets. The pamphlets not only expressed the fundamental ideas and benefits of the town meeting; in the argument, the anonymous authors made astounding, sophisticated remarks about English and American society, revealing an early awareness that in thought and in practice the colonists had deviated from the feudal and limiting traditions of Europe.

239

Both writers agreed that the town meeting system avoided the "Needless, Childish and troublesome Formalities" involved in the fees and ceremonies of borough governments and was "the least burthensome to the Inhabitants." The expenses required to enter guilds, rent market stalls, and pay feudal dues in borough corporations were not simply a prohibitive burden on the people's economic freedom to follow whatever calling suited them; according to the pamphleteers, these endless fees created an arbitrary division in society between the rich and the poor. The most significant requirement in English boroughs was that a resident had to "buy" the "freedom of the borough" in order to enjoy the privileges of membership in the corporation. As one writer pointed out, this fee implied a totally different view of political man in England from the idea that prevailed in the town meetings of New England; in England a man was implicitly similar to a slave who could become a part of the community only by buying freedom, while in a New England town, there was no such distinction made between a man in his natural and civil roles. This distinction between English and American definitions of man in the civil state is worth volumes about the development of an independent American mentality.

The writers not only expressed a provocatively new value of the American man; they also provided an elaborate, sophisti-

---

[46] Col. Soc. Mass. *Pubs.*, x, 345-352 (1904-1906); similar expressions are in Davis, *Reprints*, iii, 145, and *Tracts*, 134-136.

cated sociological explanation of the origin of America's developing identity. Among other arguments, the most significant hypothesis rested on the premises that in England wealth was the only source of social and political power and that land was the principal standard of wealth. But the population in England exceeded the available amount of land, so that the majority of the population was prevented from having the tangible means to gain wealth and power. According to the writer of one pamphlet, this restriction weighed most heavily on lawyers, scholars, and the younger sons of the gentry, all of whom were so numerous that the supply exceeded the demand for their talents and, consequently, they had no outlet for their social energies except in artificial, superfluous creations like municipal boroughs where wealth and power could be won without land. The pamphleteer ignored some of the fallacies of his argument and went on to say that in New England land was plentiful enough for anyone to possess it, that scholars were in demand at all times to fill country pulpits, schools, and Indian missions, and that almost everyone could read a statute and defend himself in court. Honest labor, not land, was the primary means to wealth and social power in the colonies. Conditions in America, therefore, differed so much from England's that a town like Boston needed no municipal corporations or feudal restrictions.

The pamphleteers may not have won any prizes for accuracy, rhetoric or logic. What is important is their belief that the profound difference between America and England contributed to distinctive values of man and society in America, and provided justification for the town meeting. With this philosophy and the direction of the Caucus, the town meeting survived and flourished in Boston. Despite its exclusiveness, the Caucus supplemented the power of the town meeting, providing the methods and ideas inherent in the Sons of Liberty, the Committee of Correspondence, and later political parties. Paradoxically, because of and not in spite of the Caucus, politics in Boston perpetuated an essential democratic element of basic

240

American pragmatism; as one pamphleteer put it, "If you would have your work well done, do it yourself."[47]

[47] Modern theorists in political science and sociology are, of course, familiar with the co-existence of democracy and leadership or elitism, their compatibility, and their conflicts. Colonial historians have concentrated perhaps too much on the question of democracy *versus* aristocracy, even though the colonists themselves accommodated both in their ideas of "mixed" government. Recent research and theory have transcended a simplistic either/or conceptual framework and, taking for granted the co-existence of democratic and elitist tendencies, have tried to analyze and distinguish functional relationships and processes. The characteristics and methods attributed to the Caucus in the essay above should indicate some of the distinctive qualities of that group, as compared or contrasted with elites associated with the governor in any colony, with Philadelphia merchants or with Virginia gentlemen. For a survey of various modern hypotheses of this problem, see Peter Bachrach, *The Theory of Democratic Elitism: A Critique* (Boston, 1967).

241

THE MEANING OF COLONIZATION IN
AMERICAN REVOLUTIONARY THOUGHT

BY MICHAEL KAMMEN*

One of the most enduring and intriguing inquiries in American intellectual history concerns the nature and development of revolutionary ideas between 1763 and 1776. In the many constitutional, political, philosophical, and literary studies that have appeared, the historical assumptions of Americans in these years have been a secondary, if not marginal, consideration. Those assumptions have usually been regarded as incidental to the central thrust of an emerging ideology which tended to be ahistorical or primarily whiggish in its reading of the past.[1] My purpose here, therefore, is to consider pre-revolutionary American attitudes toward colonial origins, particularly colonization before 1652.[2] Such attitudes were inextricably intertwined with the better known political ideas of these years, but their relationship has not hitherto been fully explored.

Students of American thought in the revolutionary era have generally presupposed the importance and inevitability of intellectual change as colonials groped for secure and tenable ground in the Great Debate. In 1922 Arthur M. Schlesinger characterized such change as "a strategic retreat," and his view was accepted and adopted by many others.[3]

242

*An earlier version of this paper was read before the Southern Historical Association, Nov. 10, 1967, in Atlanta, Georgia.

[1] There are two significant exceptions. Wesley F. Craven, *The Legend of the Founding Fathers* (N.Y., 1956), ch. 2, is concerned with tradition as a force that shaped the developing contest with England, and especially with the extent to which the colonists' case depended upon an appeal to their own history. H. Trevor Colbourn, *The Lamp of Experience: Whig History and the Intellectual Origins of the American Revolution* (Chapel Hill, 1965) concentrates on books the provincials read, particularly English history. The author gives much attention to their reading of Saxon history and the Norman conquest, but then skims down to the later seventeenth century. While displaying the colonists' distaste for the Stuarts generally, Colbourn devotes little space to the Stuarts' historic role in New World colonization. See also Richard M. Gummere, *The American Colonial Mind and the Classical Tradition* (Cambridge, Mass., 1963), ch. 6.

[2] In New England the concern with colonization concentrated on the years 1620–1640. In Virginia the years 1584–1624 were only slightly more important than 1624–1652. Craven, *Legend of the Founding Fathers*, 54, 56.

[3] *New Viewpoints in American History* (N.Y., 1922), 179; also Carl L. Becker, *The Declaration of Independence: A Study in the History of Political Ideas* (N.Y., 1922), 133; Randolph G. Adams, *Political Ideas of the American Revolution* (Durham, N.C., 1922), *passim*; Charles F. Mullett, *Fundamental Law and the American Revolution, 1760–1776* (N.Y., 1933), 79, though Mullett feels there were some who took a consistent stand through the whole polemic. Max Beloff's Introduction to *The Debate on the*

In 1948 Edmund S. Morgan rejected the notion "that the colonists were guilty of skipping from one constitutional theory to another, like so many grasshoppers." Nevertheless he saw a growth in radicalism after 1770, and admitted that "American revolutionary thought went through two stages, [if] not three."[4] In recent years historians have abandoned the attempt to reconstruct revolutionary thought as a kind of three-stage rocket. Whether they regard the changes as a liberating progression of propulsive discoveries, or as a "strategic retreat," all join in viewing the intellectual history of these years as a matter of flux. In the main they are right to do so, for the patterns of change are by now well-documented. Nonetheless their emphasis has tended to obscure the most constant consideration in the colonial mind: the historical meaning of early colonization.

243

What emerges from an examination of pre-revolutionary writings, private as well as public, is a cluster of preliminary observations on the importance of provincial origins in American thought. First, there was an interpretative debate of significant proportions on this issue, conducted on both sides of the Atlantic. Second, the patriots' completely Lockean position helped to sustain their faith in the justness of their cause. Third, it led them to question and challenge parliamentary sovereignty as early as 1765. Fourth, the patriot position utterly infuriated their opponents. And finally, it constituted a major line of consistency and continuity in revolutionary political thought. Until the fullest implications of the meaning of colonization became clear after 1772, and reliance upon this argument was augmented, Americans of very diverse political persuasions shared a common body of historical assumptions: John Dickinson, William Smith, *and* their opponent Benjamin Franklin in Pennsylvania; Samuel Adams, James Otis, *and* Thomas Hutchinson in Massachusetts; Richard Bland, George Wythe, *and* Arthur Lee in Virginia.

The two most striking tendencies in early American historical thought and writing seem oddly paired: an emphasis upon colonizing origins coupled with a desire to explicate "the present state" of a given colony. To some extent this juxtaposition encouraged a foreshortening of the intervening narrative, as well as an inability to develop fully both the inherent continuities and patterns of change. Not surprisingly, by the 1760's, the century since Cromwell and the Restoration

---

American Revolution, 1761-1783 (London, 1949) refers to "the shifting of the grounds of the discussion as it proceeded" (8).

[4]"Colonial Ideas of Parliamentary Power 1764-1766," *William and Mary Qtly.*, ser. 3, V (July 1948), 341. I agree with Morgan that the patriot position was more advanced in 1764-66 than most historians have recognized. In analyzing the colonists' rejection of Parliament's right to tax, however, Morgan does not treat the historical basis of their argument.

had been intellectually telescoped and blurred. Yet there were advantages in doing so, for during that century the colonies, however inadvertently, had seemed·to acquiesce in parliamentary sovereignty. This might have been a much greater source of embarrassment after 1765 had not the first generations *already* been staked out by writers on the past as constitutionally determinative. Just where "the first generations" ended is not clear; but the years 1641-52 formed a twilight zone beyond which most patriotic Americans of the revolutionary period were reluctant to reach. And with good reason. After 1641 all "dominions of the Crown" had effectively become part of "the Commonwealth of England and the dominions and territories thereunto belonging," though that terminology would not become official until 1649 when Parliament passed the Act establishing the Commonwealth, an indivisible entity ruled absolutely by a Parliament of the English nation. The full exercise of Parliament's power over her colonies came in 1651 with passage of the first Navigation Act on October 9th.[5] Some provincial historians and polemicists would wind their accounts through the years after 1652; but most preferred to confine their investigations to the earlier decades.

244

After 1763, when the prolonged controversy with Parliament made arguments based upon the original character of English colonization politically useful, the best documented part of that polemic involved Puritan New England. Michael Wigglesworth's vision of the purpose and nature of early settlement had become widely read after 1662 in "God's Controversy With New England." The following generation added such laments as Joshua Scottow's *Narrative of the Planting of the Massachusetts Colony* (1694) and Cotton Mather's *Magnalia Christi Americana* at the turn of century. John Callender's centennial work on Rhode Island (1738) focused on that colony's origins, hoping thereby to develop provincial self-consciousness through the use of history. Thomas Prince's purpose in compiling his narrative was partially to show that Puritan colonization had been the true culmination of the Protestant Reformation.[6]

In contrast, the earliest historical treatments of colonial origins in New York were not used to praise the pious and exhort the impious, but rather to justify conflicting Dutch and later Anglo-Dutch claims. From Adriaen van der Donck's *Representation of New Netherland* (1650) until the *History* of William Smith, Jr. (1757), Yorkers examined their provincial genesis with a critical eye. Smith's title page

[5]C. H. McIlwain, *The American Revolution: A Constitutional Interpretation* (N.Y., 1923), 21, 28, 44, 108, 110, 112-13.

[6]Callender, *An Historical Discourse on the Civil and Religious Affairs of the Colony of Rhode-Island*, R.I. Hist. Soc. *Collections*, IV (1838); Prince, *Chronological History of New England in the Form of Annals* (Boston, 1736).

quoted from James Thomson's *Liberty* five lines emblematic of the meaning of colonization accepted well before the revolutionary crisis unfolded.

> Lo! Swarming o'er the new discover'd World,
> Gay Colonies extend; the calm Retreat
> Of undeserv'd Distress. . . . .
> . . . . Bound by social Freedom, firm they rise;
> Of *Britain's* Empire the Support and Strength.

In Virginia William Stith's long history (1747) was essentially devoted to clarifying the historical circumstances of Chesapeake colonization—an effort to rectify Captain John Smith's misleading story. Samuel Smith's bulky *History of the Colony of . . . New Jersey*, published in 1765 but written earlier, followed the well-established doctrine: the first Americans had emigrated to seek or preserve civil and religious liberty.[7]

For more than a century then, as Carl Bridenbaugh has shown, "the colonists had been constructing the version of history employed during the debate of the 'sixties.''[8] In all of these narratives, whether Robert Beverley's Virginia, Provost Smith's Pennsylvania, or Thomas Hutchinson's Bay Colony, the legal arrangements and charter provisions of colonization received great attention alongside the hardships and motivations for migrating. Meanwhile such historical discussions were paralleled by the political writings of the pre-revolutionary years. By 1760 the surviving charters had long been consulted as special documents of higher law inextricably involved in the circumstances of colonization. New England received her charters, according to Jeremiah Dummer in 1721, in order to settle colonies: "to strip the country of their charters after the service has been so successfully performed is abhorrent from all reason, equity and justice."[9]

In 1728 the elder Daniel Dulany insisted that the first settlers of Maryland were Englishmen entitled to the benefits of English statutes as well as the common law. His argument, rooted in the earliest circumstances of colonization, stressed the reciprocal nature of allegiance and protection. A decade later a dispute in South Carolina elicited from Maurice Lewis the view that "the Common Law and the Principles of our Constitution immediately take Place upon the forming of

245

---

[7]*The History of the First Discovery and Settlement of Virginia* (Williamsburg, 1747), 329; *History of . . . New Jersey . . . to the Year 1721* (Burlington, 1765), xi.

[8]*Mitre and Sceptre: Transatlantic Faiths, Ideas, Personalities, and Politics, 1689–1775* (N.Y., 1962), 172–78.

[9]Dummer, *A Defence of the New-England Charters* (Boston, 1721, 1745, 1765), 7–8; Perry Miller, *The New England Mind from Colony to Province* (Cambridge, Mass., 1953), 389.

a new Colony of British Subjects, and . . . no Usage or Royal Instructions can take away the Force of it in America." Once again the colonists would cherish and defend "a fundamental Right . . . handed down to us from our Ancestors."[10] In New York during the 1740's, Cadwallader Colden, a learned Newtonian and conservative Scot, devoted to the Crown, depicted the earliest history of New England in terms that would be repeated again and again by patriots a quarter century later.

246

The first settlers of New England at First underwent great difficulties having little assistance from their Mother Country & became in a great measure independent of it. It is probable that without that enthusiastic zeal which animated the first planters they must have succumbed under the difficulties they met with in a wilderness destitute not only of all the comforts of life but even of necessaries otherwise than by hard labour and a penurious manner of liveing. By Voluntarly subjecting themselves to the strictest discipline in the performance of all religeous civil & military duties they established a numerous & flowrishing colony with little or no assistance from their mother country.[11]

Thus by the time of the Seven Years' War a consistent and well-developed view of colonial origins had been in common use for decades. Portents of trouble ahead, however, lay in the rather different understanding held by imperial administrators, such as Arthur Dobbs or Benjamin Martyn. As Secretary to the Trustees of Georgia, Martyn was deeply involved in administrative aspects of colonization in the 1730's. To his mind colonies were unquestionably dependencies, fully subject to imperial authority from the very outset. Governor Dobbs believed that the establishment of colonies was due to overpopulation and the lust for dominion. Because land had been grabbed in America by greedy settlers regardless of the rights of the natives, much trouble had ensued, not to mention great expense incurred by the Crown in protecting her colonies. Nothing could have been farther from the patriot view of colonization adumbrated with growing intensity after 1764.[12]

The patriot view during the pre-revolutionary decade essentially comprised answers to five questions: why had the first English settlers

[10]*The Right of the Inhabitants of Maryland to the Benefit of the English Laws* (Annapolis, 1728); M. Eugene Sirmans, *Colonial South Carolina: A Political History, 1663-1763* (Chapel Hill, 1966), 203-4; J. H. Easterby and R. S. Green, eds., *The Colonial Records of South Carolina: the Journals of the Commons House of Assembly* (8 vols., Columbia, S.C., 1951-61), 1736-1739, p. 720.

[11]Colden, "Account of the Government of the New England Colonies" [c. 1742], in N.Y. Hist. Soc. *Collections*, LXVIII (N.Y., 1937), 247-48.

[12]Albert B. Saye, "The Genesis of Georgia Reviewed," *Georgia Historical Quarterly*, L (June 1966), 159 and n22; Caroline Robbins, *The Eighteenth-Century Commonwealthmen* (Cambridge, Mass., 1961), 151-52.

emigrated? under what circumstances? what had become of their relationship to England after settling here? what constitutional and
social consequences of lasting importance ensued? and finally, why
were all of these matters significant a century and a half later?
The first of these queries was the most simply answered. At a
critical point in the history of England and Liberty, the colonizers
had escaped an arbitrary reign, marked by oppression and bad legislation, in order to enjoy civil and religious liberties undisturbed and
pass such cherished treasures on to their posterity.[13] More important were the circumstances of their coming, for as Samuel Adams
noted in 1765, they "emigrated at their own Expence, & not the
Nations; As it was their own & not a National Act; so they came to
& settled a Country which the Nation had no sort of Right in." They
brought with them all the privileges, immunities, and rights of Englishmen—rights assured in the future by virtue of royal charters.
"By all these charters," wrote Stephen Hopkins, "it is in the most
express and solemn manner granted, that these adventurers, and
their children after them forever, should have and enjoy all the freedom and liberty that the subjects in *England* enjoy."[14]
The first settlers brought with them the "full and absolute power
of governing all the people of this place, by men chosen from among
themselves," because when men "withdraw themselves from their
country, they recover their natural Freedom and Independence: The
Jurisdiction and Sovereignty of the State they have quitted ceases;
and if they unite, and by common Consent take possession of a new
country, and form themselves into a political Society, they become a
Sovereign State, independent of the State from which they separated."[15] This view of Richard Bland's, written in Virginia in 1766,
was reiterated in 1768 by William Hicks of Philadelphia, in 1774 by
Peter Whitney of Boston, and throughout these years by countless
others. The colonizers had brought with them the spirit of English
government, and assumed that "they should be allowed to make such
regulations as might answer the purposes of their emigration." Once
colonial governments were organized (with the concurrence of Crown

247

[13]James Lovell, *An Oration Delivered April 2d. 1771* (Boston, 1771), 13-14; Oliver
Noble, *Some Strictures upon the . . . Book of Esther . . .* (Newburyport, 1775), 21n.
    [14]Harry A. Cushing, ed., *The Writings of Samuel Adams,* I (N.Y., 1904), 27-28;
[Stephen Hopkins], *The Rights of Colonies Examined* (Providence, 1765), 5, 8-9;
[Daniel Dulany], *Considerations on the Propriety of Imposing Taxes* ([An-
napolis], 1765), 14-15, 29-30.
    [15]Cf. John Locke, *Two Treatises of Government: A Critical Edition With an Intro-
duction and Apparatus Criticus,* by Peter Laslett (2nd ed., Cambridge, Eng., 1967),
363-64.

officials), Hicks observed, they "totally disclaim[ed] all *subordination* to, and dependence upon, the two inferior estates of their Mother country."[16]

Because only the King, and not Parliament, had entered into compacts with the first settlers, he alone retained any sort of relationship to "all the lands in America." "The great enquiry, therefore," as young Alexander Hamilton put it, "is concerning the terms on which these lands were really dispensed."[17] The responses to this enquiry were not of a piece. Most essayists agreed that the colonizers had passed through a "state of nature" in coming, that (Blackstone to the contrary notwithstanding) the colonies were not obtained by Crown conquest, and that if anyone had conquered the New World it had been the patriot's forebears.[18]

But insisting that the colonizers had been conquerors rather than conquered, like the Irish, raised embarrassing questions about the Americans' just title to the soil—in the eyes of God as well as man. Consequently the preferred and popular argument persisted that the early settlers had duly purchased their land from the Indians and then elected (quite voluntarily) to become subjects of the English King by subscribing to a compact. Additional lands had been added later through defensive wars. Therefore the Crown had never had any legal right to grant these lands, "for they were not seized of them, and consequently had no property in them." The crucial factor was that the land had previously been inhabited. The charters could not so much grant the land as merely convey a royal assurance that the colonizers would not be disturbed in their enjoyment of it once tenure had been legitimately secured.[19] By cultivating "the barren soil by their incessant labour," and by instituting provincial legislatures which were complete in themselves, the colonizers established and legitimized their total independence of Parliament. Even the Crown

[16]Bland, *An Inquiry Into the Rights of the British Colonies* (Williamsburg, 1766), 14, 20-22; [William Hicks], *The Nature and Extent of Parliamentary Power Considered* (Philadelphia, 1768), 5-8; Peter Whitney, *The Transgression of a Land* (Boston, 1774), 48.

[17]*The Farmer Refuted* (N.Y., 1775) in Harold C. Syrett, ed., *The Papers of Alexander Hamilton*, I (N.Y., 1961), 108.

[18][John Allen], *The American Alarm* (Boston, 1773), 22; [James Wilson], *Considerations on the Nature and the Extent of the British Parliament* (Philadelphia, 1774), 14, 25-26, 29; [John Dickinson], *An Essay on the Constitutional Power of Great-Britain* (Philadelphia, 1774), 97-98. Cf. Locke, *Two Treatises of Government*, 295-96, 402-03.

[19]Noble, *Some Strictures*, 21n; William Stearns, *A View of the Controversy* (Watertown, 1775), 12-15; Samuel Webster, *The Misery and Duty of an Oppress'd and Enslav'd People* (Boston, 1774), 21-22.

became more symbolic than real as an effective bond and source of original authority.[20]

The social consequences of colonization were less complicated, though scarcely less important. Americans were decidedly not descended from the scum of Europe, but rather from her substantial and better families. Consequently they deserved rights and privileges consistent with their social origins. William Livingston of New York, for whom American beginnings held a compelling fascination, felt that the several generations of colonials had been pious, and had given due attention to social institutions in an effort to maintain a flourishing culture despite great hardships. Although some writers envisioned the earliest environment as "a howling wilderness," while others depicted "an uncultivated desert," all were agreed on the strong moral fibre of the people who had surmounted the environment.[21]

249

Most revolutionaries had no doubts whatever about the enduring significance of colonization in the American experience. As their fathers and grandfathers had, they turned for reassurance and strength to the founders' intentions and relevant provisions of early governmental documents. For those canny enough to see through the mist of myth and historic obfuscation, it mattered little "whether the Colonists were invested with a *Right* to these liberties and privileges that ought not to be wrested from them, or whether they were not; tis the truth of fact, that they really *thought* they were." Joseph Warren could thus look back in 1775, just as Charles Chauncy had in 1766, in order to rationalize the non-rational, and clarify the obscure circumstances of American origins.[22]

As early as the Stamp Act crisis, then, the colonists' understanding of their seventeenth-century origins contributed significantly to the widening chasm of contrasting conceptions and positions that made it so difficult for Americans and Englishmen to communicate meaningfully with one another. Moreover, the Americans' reading of provincial history helped to clarify their quest for identity during the long crisis by establishing securely who they were and how they had come to be there. By defining the nature of the great migrations in essen-

[20]Joseph Warren, *An Oration Delivered March 5th, 1772* (Boston, 1772), 7-8; [Silas Downer], *A Discourse Delivered in Providence* (Providence, 1768), 6.

[21][Arthur Lee], *An Essay in Vindication of the Continental Colonies of America* (London, 1764); William Livingston, *A Letter to the . . .Bishop of Landaff* (N.Y., 1768), 5-6, 8.

[22]J. R. Pole, *Political Representation in England and the Origins of the American Republic* (N.Y., 1966), 269; Charles Chauncy, *A Discourse on "the Good news From a Far Country"* (Boston, 1766), 14-15 (my italics); Joseph Warren, *An Oration Delivered March Sixth, 1775* (Boston, 1775), 6-8.

tially Lockean terms, such pamphleteers as Richard Bland established their own peculiar criteria for judging the colonists' obligation to obey the laws of England. Thus Bland's view of the original settlement of Virginia, and especially of the origins and powers of the colonial assembly, helped to shape and reinforce the provincial repudiation of the English concept of virtual representation.[23]

As early as 1765 the colonists had begun to relate their particular origins to a more general conception of the history of colonization. In so doing they elevated their appeal to a higher level of abstraction and universal justice. When Stephen Hopkins examined *The Rights of Colonies*, he included a brief survey since antiquity of "what hath generally been the condition of colonies with respect to their freedom." Not surprisingly, Hopkins and his contemporaries found that "colonies in general, both ancient and modern, have always enjoyed as much freedom as the mother state from which they went out." Surely then Britain's American possessions would not be "an exception to this general rule?"[24] With the whole history of human colonization to bolster their cause, and with axioms of constitutional propriety extrapolated therewith, the colonists might well feel secure in their historical heritage and future forensic fights.

After 1772, as the related issues of taxation and representation gave way to a stark problem of sovereignty, the whole historical question took on a new urgency, causing colonists to look to their books more intensively in search of definitive answers. In 1773 George Mason of Virginia made elaborate extracts from the Virginia charters with his own commentaries appended. For Mason,

every clause relating to the people and inhabitants in general . . . under the Faith of which our Ancestors left their native land, and adventured to settle an unknown country, operated and inures to the benefit of their posterity forever, notwithstanding the dissolution of the Virginia Company, had such dissolution been ever so legal. . . . When America was discovered, the sending abroad colonies had been unknown in Europe from the times of the ancient Greeks and Romans. . . . To the people of Great Britain the scene then opening was entirely new; and altho' the people removing from thence, to settle Colonies in America, under the auspices and protection and for the benefit of Great Britain, would by the laws of Nature and Nations, have carried with them the Constitution of the Country they came from, and consequently been entitled to all its advantages, yet not caring to trust altogether to general principles applied to a new subject, and anxious to secure to themselves and

[23]Bernard Bailyn, ed., *Pamphlets of the American Revolution, 1750–1776* (Cambridge, Mass., 1965), I, 319, 321, 323; Bland, *An Inquiry Into the Rights of the Colonies,* 9–10, 13–14, 20–22.

[24][Hopkins], *Rights of Colonies Examined,* in Bailyn, ed., *Pamphlets of the American Revolution,* I, 508–10.

their posterity, by every means in their power, the rights and privileges of their beloved laws and Constitution, they entered into a solemn compact with the Crown for that purpose. Under the faith of these compacts, at their own private expense and Hazard, amidst a thousand Difficulties and Dangers, our Ancestors explored and settled a New World: their posterity have enjoyed these rights and privileges from time Immemorial; and have thereby (even if the Charters had been originally defective) acquired a legal Title. It ought to wear well; for it has been dearly earned.[25]

Mason had been driven to research and analysis by critics of the colonial position whom we shall discuss below. In Massachusetts that same year a confrontation flared up directly. In January 1773 Governor Hutchinson spoke to the General Court in terms that body could not stomach. He informed them that both colonizers and Crown early in the seventeenth century had assumed they would remain subject to the supreme authority of Parliament. The response of the Court's committee, drafted by John Adams and reported by Samuel, analyzed the history of American colonization, especially its constitutional and legal aspects. What emerged was not so much new in substance as more comprehensive in its implications and thrust. The New Englanders relied heavily on Virginia origins and even upon the late sixteenth-century voyages and patents. The meaning of colonization in revolutionary thought had thus come to transcend the provincial bounds of experience. Patriots borrowed freely from one colony's narrative or another in buttressing arguments. The significance of colonization by 1773 was that it had an *American* application.[26]

Nowhere was this more true than in New York and Jamaica, which *had* in fact been conquered provinces. A century earlier the second Jamaican Assembly had declared "the laws of England in force in this island," thereby hoping to ensure the enjoyment of constitutional liberties. In 1678-80 an attempt to apply the Poynings' system of control to Jamaica as a conquered colony failed once and for all in the face of determined opposition by the planters.[27] In New York, however, such ambiguities were not early put to rest, and by mid-eighteenth century haunted some Yorkers and perplexed others. Where the constitutional implications of English conquest in 1664 were not ignored altogether, authors were obliged to make concessions or modifications

251

[25]Kate M. Rowland, *The Life of George Mason, 1725-1792* (N.Y., 1892), I, 393-414. The quotation appears on 398-99.
[26]*The Speeches of His Excellency Governor Hutchinson* (Boston, 1773), 4, 19, 36-37 *et passim*; Cushing, *The Writings of Samuel Adams*, II, 403-9, 415-23; Silas Deane to Patrick Henry, Jan. 2, 1775, in *Collections of the New York Historical Society for the Year 1886; Deane Papers*, I (New York, 1887), 37-41.
[27]Frederick G. Spurdle, *Early West Indian Government* (Palmerston North, N.Z., [n.d.]), 27, 222n4.

not required elsewhere: colonizers had been lured to New York by extraordinary concessions from the Crown; they had not been banished from Britain, however, and they brought with them both the allegiances and rights of Englishmen. Colonial disputes had been decided by the Privy Council, patriots admitted; but, they contended, that body had eventually usurped more power than it was justly entitled to.[28]

Despite such glibness, and given New York's hybrid history, Parliament's power over the province could not be so easily disregarded as in other colonies. In 1770, however, William Livingston's *America: or, a Poem on the Settlement of the British Colonies* anticipated the common direction of colonial thought after 1773.

252

> Forc'd from the pleasures of their native soil,
> Where Liberty had lighten'd every toil;
> Forc'd from the arms of friends and kindred dear,
> With scarce the comfort of one parting tear . . .
>
> To these far-distant climes our fathers came,
> Where blest NEW-ENGLAND boasts a parent's name,
> With Freedom's fire their gen'rous bosoms glow'd,
> Warm for the truth, and zealous for their God; . . .
>
> Penn led a peaceful train to that kind clime,
> Where Nature wantons in her liveliest prime, . . .
>
> Brave Oglethorpe in Georgia fix'd his feat,
> And deep distress there found a calm retreat.

Livingston's own ancestry was as mixed as his colony's, and he was very much a Yorker; but he drew upon the experience of New England, Pennsylvania, and Georgia, in short, upon American origins generally in composing his patriotic paean. (Four years later his brother Philip took a more cautious view of colonization than most colonial patriots, but with some cause. Contested lands along the Massachusetts border were adjacent to the Livingston estates. Steadily after 1767 the family petitioned for a favorable settlement; but their arguments were contingent upon the conquest of 1664 and the extent of Dutch claims acquired by the Duke of York. Hence the muted tones of both Livingstons on the colonization question.)[29]

[28]James Fenimore Cooper, *Satanstoe; or, the Littlepage Manuscripts. A Tale of the Colony* (N.Y., 1845), 218; Britannus Americanus, *Liberty, Property and No Stamps* (N.Y., 17 Dec. 1765) [Evans #10041]; *Considerations Upon the Rights of Colonists to the Privileges of British Subjects* (N.Y., 1766), 4, 9–10.

[29][William Livingston], *America: or, a Poem on the Settlement of the British Colonies* (New Haven, [1770]), 4–5; [Philip Livingston], *The Other Side of the Question: Or, A Defense of the Liberties of North America* (N.Y., 1774), 16; Irving Mark, *Agrarian Conflicts in Colonial New York, 1711–1775* (N.Y., 1940), 51–56; "William Livingston," *Dictionary of American Biography*.

In 1774 Samuel Seabury offered whiggish New Yorkers a challenge by contending that legislation was not an inherent right in colonies. He examined many colonial charters in support of this view, and then taunted his readers by pointing out that New York lacked a charter altogether. To this Alexander Hamilton, still a college student, responded in ways the Livingstons must have quietly applauded. Hamilton was obliged to concede New York's particular deficiency; but following Mason in Virginia and the General Court's committee in Massachusetts, he insisted that he could, "with justice, plead the *common* principles of colonization: for, it would be unreasonable, to seclude one colony, from the enjoyment of the most important privileges of the rest." With that established, Hamilton had an easy time examining the general history of colonial settlement and charters, finally rejecting any parliamentary dependency.[30]

253

By the eve of independence, then, the meaning of colonization in American revolutionary thought had been enunciated with consistency in sermons, pamphlets, private correspondence, and public documents. After 1773 the traditional refrain swelled into a crescendo that would be sustained for more than two years by a chorus of American patriots.[31] All that was needed was a director to set the refrain in measured, dignified cadences heard beyond the seas. They found two in fact: Thomas Jefferson and John Adams.

The Stamp Act had led Adams to see in the original settlement of the colonies "the opening of a grand scene and design in providence for the illumination of the ignorant and the emancipation of the slavish part of mankind all over the earth." In the subsequent decade he embellished and enlarged this view; but he did not change it. His fear of any combination of civil and ecclesiastical tyranny underlay his understanding of American history and forged links in his mind between the earliest settlements and his own time. "British liberties are not the grants of princes or parliaments," he proclaimed in 1765, "but original rights, conditions of original contracts." Because the first settlers had not been a conquered people, feudalism had no place in America. Adams's ancestors had *chosen* to hold their land from the Crown, he

---

[30][Seabury], *A View of the Controversy Between Great-Britain and Her Colonies: Including a Mode of Determining their Present Disputes* (N.Y., 1774), 9, 11-14; [Hamilton], *The Farmer Refuted* (N.Y., 1775) in Syrett, *Papers of Hamilton,* I, 91, 104, 108-09, 114, 121-22 (italics mine).

[31]In addition to titles already cited, see Roger Clap, *Memoirs of Capt. Roger Clap* (Boston, 1774), 15; Joseph Bean, *A Sermon Delivered at Wrentham* (Boston, 1774), 9; *A Brief Review of the Rise, Progress, Services and Sufferings of New England* (Norwich, Conn., 1774), 5, 10; [Arthur Lee], *An Appeal to the Justice and Interests of the People of Great Britain* (N.Y., 1775), 11; [Moses Mather], *America's Appeal to the Impartial World* (Hartford, 1775), 6-7, 24; Samuel Webster, *Rabshakeh's Proposals Considered* (Boston, 1775), 20-22.

declared in the *Dissertation*. Ten years later his *Novanglus* pursued
the same theme: those ancestors were entitled to as much of the common law as they chose to adopt upon emigration; moreover they could
have erected any form of government they wished in the wilderness.
Finally, "their children would not have been born within the king's allegiance, would not have been natural subjects, and consequently not
entitled to protection, or bound to the King." Adams drew upon the
Chesapeake story as well as New England to support his view that the
early inhabitants had been in full accord on their proper relationship
to England.[32]

254

Jefferson, eight years Adams's junior, emerged in 1774 with the
most comprehensive American statement concerning the meaning of
colonization: the *Summary View*, written in July 1774 as draft instructions for Virginia's delegates to the Continental Congress. It was not,
as historians have suggested, an especially radical breakthrough in
colonial political thought, and certainly not in historical thought. To
summarize the *Summary View*'s historical perspective would be to
recapitulate the essence of this paper: our earliest ancestors were free
inhabitants of Britain; they had a perfect right to emigrate, colonize,
and establish good laws; their Saxon ancestors had done likewise centuries before; if America *had* been conquered it was by colonizers
rather than the British State; Crown treasuries never helped the
colonies until long after they were established; the emigrants *chose* to
accept English law and continue in political union with Britain by
submitting to a common sovereign; the colonizers were victimized by
English politicians, and their hard earned lands were parcelled out to
various favorites and followers of the court. Despite some new emphases (and an admirable clarity of exposition), like the Declaration of
Independence, it basically summed up what had been said and was
being said by patriots everywhere.[33]

Jefferson's understanding of the motives and circumstances of
colonization had not gone much beyond Richard Bland's in 1766. The
future president's research was more comprehensive, for he had carefully worked through Virginia's early records, and his coverage included New England. But the basic historical contentions are the
same: the pact of 1651 had been accepted voluntarily; there had been
no conquest; and the 1652 articles of surrender remained determinative
(as they had been for Bland) because they specifically acknowledged
that the surrender was "a voluntary act not forced nor constrained by a

[32]*The Works of John Adams*, ed. Charles F. Adams (Boston, 1851), III, 452, 463;
IV, 108-12, 121-24, 126, 173-77.
[33]Julian P. Boyd, ed., *The Papers of Thomas Jefferson*, I (Princeton, 1950), 121-24,
133, 136n5.

conquest upon the countrey." Professors Dumas Malone and Elisha Douglass properly credit Jefferson with an ingenious but unhistorical composition. Like his contemporaries Jefferson was making history the handmaiden of politics; but unlike many English counterparts he was not *re*-writing history to suit the occasion. If *A Summary View* was not a faithful rendering of the history of English colonization, it was at least the traditional rendering, familiar to generations of Americans.[34] Jefferson's concern with colonial origins remained a vital one. During the summer of 1775 he recapitulated all the familiar arguments in writing the *Declaration of the Causes and Necessity for Taking Up Arms:* why the forefathers had emigrated, what they had done upon arrival, the constitutional consequences, and subsequent assumptions of parliamentary power by Great Britain. When George III's speech upon the convening of Parliament in October 1775 dwelled upon England's nurturing the colonies with great tenderness, news of such a declaration stung Jefferson into renewing his documentary research into the history of colonization. Early in 1776 he completed those efforts with conclusions that would form part of his early draft of the Declaration of Independence.

255

This short narration of facts, extracted principally from Hakluyt's voiages, may enable us to judge of the effect which the charter to Sr. Walter Ralegh may have on our own constitution and also on those of the other colonies within its limits, to which it is of equal concernment. It serves also to expose the distress of those ministerial writers, who, in order to prove that the British parliament may of right legislate for the colonies, are driven to the necessity of advancing this palpable untruth that 'the colonies were planted and nursed at the expence of the British nation': an untruth which even majesty itself, descending from it's dignity, has lately been induced to utter from the throne.

These lengthy investigations were never published as such, but they colored the outlook of the founders at a critical juncture. They were communicated to Ebenezer Hazard of Pennsylvania for his *Historical Collections,* and in an abstract and highly idealized form they may be found embodied in Thomas Paine's *Common Sense.*[35]

[34]Dumas Malone, *Jefferson the Virginian* (Boston, 1948), 182-86; Elisha P. Douglass, *Rebels and Democrats, The Struggle for Equal Political Rights and Majority Rule During the American Revolution* (Chapel Hill, 1955), 291-92; A. M. Lewis, "Jefferson's Summary View as a Chart of Political Union," *William and Mary Quarterly*, ser. 3, V (Jan. 1948), 34-51; Colbourn, *Lamp of Experience*, 161-63; Craven, *Legend of the Founding Fathers*, 55-57.

[35]Declaration of the Causes and Necessity for Taking Up Arms, Boyd, *Papers of Jefferson*, I, 199; Refutation of the Argument that the Colonies were Established at the Expense of the British Nation, *ibid.*, 283-84; correspondence with Hazard and memoranda, *ibid.*, 144-48, 164; Becker, *Declaration of Independence*, 122-23, 191; William M. Van der Weyde, ed., *The Life and Works of Thomas Paine* (New Rochelle, N.Y., 1921), II, 98-101.

American opponents of the dominant view we have been describing emerged rather slowly. Martin Howard, for example, was one of the few in 1765 who regarded the original charters as restrictive rather than permissive grants of authority. Nor did he directly oppose the traditional understanding of colonial origins. By 1773, however, potential Loyalists, such as Thomas Hutchinson, had changed their minds considerably on the constitutional circumstances of colonization. Not until 1774, however, did whole-hearted critiques of the patriot stand appear.[36]

256

Jonathan Boucher agreed that the early history of the colonists might be important, but wondered whether their ancestors' status and rights had been clearly understood or asserted: "even these legal constitutional Privileges were encumbered with a Thousand legal Customs, which they patiently submitted to." John Mein found that the patriot assertions were based on the most extravagant and impudent absurdities. An inhabitant of Middlesex might move to the Isle of Man without being outside the British dominions; why therefore would an Englishman in North America be so since that country "appertained" to the Crown? Mein cleverly twisted the knife several times, noting the blatant intolerance of provincials who had emigrated to escape oppression, and the attempt by Massachusetts to exert authority over Connecticut because settlers there had formerly resided in the Bay Colony. Isaac Hunt divided colonization into two sorts of enterprises: discovery and purchase on the one hand, and conquest on the other. In the former case the laws of England unquestionably took effect immediately upon discovery and settlement, while in the latter not until the conqueror so declared. But in both situations acts of Parliament bound the colonies where they were specifically named.[37]

In England contempt for the settlers, and especially for their devious descendants, had long been in evidence. By 1763 it was manifest to imperial bureaucrats in London that colonization was somehow a subversive process viewed altogether differently by men living on opposite sides of the Atlantic.[38] By the time of the Stamp Act crisis such men searched the annals of Greek and Roman colonization to

[36][Martin Howard], *A Letter from a Gentleman at Halifax* (Newport, 1765), 8–10, 14–15; Becker, *Declaration of Independence*, 84; Hutchinson, *The History of the Colony and Province of Massachusetts Bay*, ed. Lawrence S. Mayo (Cambridge, Mass., 1936), III, 266; McIlwain, *American Revolution*, 123–29.

[37][Boucher], *A Letter from a Virginian to the Members of the Congress* ([New York], 1774), 9–10; [Mein], *Sagittarius's Letters* (Boston, 1775), 5–6, 10, 22–24, 32; Hunt, *The Political Family* (Philadelphia, 1775), 8–9.

[38]Sydney W. Jackman, *Man of Mercury. An Appreciation of the Mind of Henry St. John, Viscount Bolingbroke* (London, 1965), 136; Thomas C. Barrow, ed., "A Project for Imperial Reform: 'Hints Respecting the Settlement for our American Provinces,' 1763," *William and Mary Quarterly*, ser. 3, XXIV (Jan. 1967), 114, 117.

support the assertion that colonies were, always had been, and always would be subordinate to the laws of the mother country. The first Anglo-Americans had gone abroad "under the authority of the state . . . to remain Subject to, and under the Power and Dominion of the Kingdom of England." One placeman spelled out such a view for George Grenville in 155 manuscript pages. Charles Townshend, meanwhile, voiced the commonplace conception of "children planted by our care," and debated the issue with Isaac Barré in the House of Commons early in 1765.[39]

In 1769 Israel Mauduit, sometime agent and general placeman, published *A Short View of the History of the Colony of Massachusetts Bay,* which in subsequent expansions became a general *History of the New England Colonies, With Respect to Their Charters and Constitutions.* The Pilgrims, he declared, had been totally subject to the authority of England, while the 1620 grant to some Dorsetshire patentees had *not* included an exemption from parliamentary jurisdiction. In Mauduit's view colonial writers

who talk so arrogantly about the original Terms of Colonization, would do well to ask themselves, whether they really think, that Mr. *Matthew Cradock* and Mr. *Thomas Goff,* and 18 other Gentlemen living in *London,* could send over by Mr. *John Endicott* to the Rev. Mr. *Conant,* and a Number of poor Creatures in *America,* who were starving, and wanting to come home again, a Right of Independence on the Parliament *of England.*

With very ill Grace must these Men now upbraid us with their original Terms of Colonization; or set up what they call their constitutional Rights against the Authority of Parliament, when their first Charter and their original Constitution in New England knew nothing of any House of Representatives at all.

Whatever Privileges therefore can now be claimed as original Charter Rights, or Motives of their first Settlement, or Covenants of Colonization, as they now call them, ought to be produced from Grants or Charters prior to this Period. For since that no new Settlements were made, and all the after Enlargements were only Continuations of the old.

American Whigs were simply deluded, he argued, and had distorted their own constitutional history.[40]

By 1775 Britons had hardened their historical outlook. The Rev. Andrew Burnaby, a reasonably sympathetic visitor to the colonies, believed "they settled in America under the charters, which expressly

---

[39][James Abercromby], *De Jure Coloniarum,* or An Inquiry into the Nature and the Rights of Colonies Ancient and Modern [c. 1765-66], MS in the John Carter Brown Library, Providence, R.I., esp. pp. 9, 84; Ian Christie, *Crisis of Empire. Great Britain and the American Colonies, 1754-1783* (London, 1966), 52-53.

[40]Editions of Mauduit's book appeared in London in 1769, 1774 twice, and the 1776 edition which I have used (pp. 8-13, 14, 16, 20-22, 30).

reserved to the British Parliament the authority . . . now asserted."
Dr. Samuel Johnson, unsympathetic as ever, described the colonization
process in terms that made sense to every true Englishman.

An English colony is a number of persons, to whom the king grants a charter,
permitting them to settle in some distant country, and enabling them to constitute a corporation enjoying such powers as the charter grants. . . . As a
corporation they make laws for themselves; but as a corporation subsisting by
a grant from higher authority, to the control of that authority they continue
subject. . . . If their ancestors were subjects, they acknowledged a sovereign;
if they had a right to English privileges, they were accountable to English
laws; and, what must grieve the lover of liberty to discover, had ceded to the
king and parliament, whether the right or not, at least, the power of dispos-
ing, "without their consent, of their lives, liberties, and properties."[41]

258

Writing that same year, William Knox echoed Johnson's sentiments.
The right to American soil had inhered in the Crown before English
subjects settled there. From the very outset planters carried grants
from the King, who had every right to prescribe conditions for those
who received such rights. Adventurers had been assisted in many ways
by fellow subjects at home, and the power of the state had been exercised in their behalf. Finally, no act passed by Parliament since the
beginning of colonization had ever distinguished between a man born
in England and one born in America.[42]

In 1760 David Hume admonished Benjamin Franklin for using
such a peculiar word as "colonize" in his Canada pamphlet. The word
was already an accepted part of American usage; owing to the forthcoming debate over the meaning of colonization it would soon gain
currency even in the King's English.[43] Such an etymological discrepancy was symptomatic of a larger gap. Just when Americans
were coming to glorify colonization as a great era in the history of
freedom, Britons were regarding it as a period of waste, suffering,
and tyranny over heathen natives. By 1775 the two conceptions of
colonization were counterpoised: the noble purposes of emigration as
against the ignoble processes of settlement.[44] The patriot conception

[41]Burnaby, *Travels Through the Middle Settlements in North America* (Ithaca,
N.Y., 1960), x; Samuel Johnson, *Taxation No Tyranny; An Answer to the Resolutions
and Address of the American Congress* (London, 1775) in *The Works of Samuel
Johnson* (Troy, N.Y., 1903), xiv, 107-9, 114.

[42][Knox], *The Interest of the Merchants and Manufacturers of Great Britain in
the Present Contest* [London, 1775], 3-6.

[43]Franklin to Hume, 27 Sept. 1760, Leonard W. Labaree, ed., *The Papers of
Benjamin Franklin*, IX (New Haven, 1966), 95, 229.

[44]See David Brion Davis, *The Problem of Slavery in Western Culture* (Ithaca, N.Y.,
1966), 423-24, 431-32.

reinforced the Americans' view of themselves as a people peculiarly descended and chosen for a special destiny. By the 1770's a sense of *American*, as opposed to provincial history, was born of the inevitable borrowing by essayists and politicians. Especially was this true in New York, where William Livingston, Alexander Hamilton and others adopted the more congenial history of other colonies as part of their own heritage.[45]

The historic sense of the significance and meaning of colonization shared by most Americans was neither sound nor even consistent. But it at least antedated the controversy that had fired it with a glaze of glowing lustre. On this account it had a greater measure of persuasiveness during the revolutionary crisis, and perhaps more integrity than the utterly contrived whig history produced during the most troubled years of Stuart England.[46] Despite the absence of substantiating evidence, despite Poyning's Law (1495), the Declaratory Act of 1719, and other evidence to the contrary, Irish nationalists would persistently foster the myth of Henry II's grant to John of an independent kingdom in Ireland. By contrast, the Puritan leaders of the Massachusetts Bay Company had *indeed* tried to eliminate the Crown by insisting that, in approving the grant of the charter in 1629, the Crown had divested itself of all right to interfere in the affairs of the new colony. The Puritans *had* shrugged off the authority of Parliament by asserting that the statute law of England did not concern them. And Roger Williams, moreover, *had* denied the right of Charles I to grant lands that he did not properly own. To be sure, there was sophistry and casuistry in these early American arguments. But they endured, so that after five or six generations of repetition they had a certain ring of integrity and familiarity.

When the colonists' sense of their past was reinforced by persuasive currents of Enlightenment thought, the resulting ideology acquired

259

---

[45]William Smith, Jr. of New York had a serious interest in colonial origins; but he was also shrewd and forthright enough to recognize that "the Empire, long after the Constitution was formed, acquired a *new, adventitious* State. And the question therefore is not, what the Constitution was, or is, but what, present Circumstances considered, it ought to be." Robert M. Calhoon, ed., "William Smith Jr.'s Alternative to the American Revolution," *William and Mary Quarterly*, ser. 3, XXII (Jan. 1965), 113. In 1777, while simultaneously revising his *History of the late Province of New-York* and agonizing over his allegiances, Smith noted that "our ancestors claimed every social benefit not injurious to the Mother Country, nor inconsistant with their loyalty to the Crown or their dependence upon Great Britain." MS marginalia on p. 109 of Smith's copy of his *History*, Philip H. and A. S. W. Rosenbach Foundation, Philadelphia.

[46]Quentin Skinner, "History and Ideology in the English Revolution," *Historical Journal*, VIII (1965), 151–78; J. G. A. Pocock, *The Ancient Constitution and the Feudal Law: A Study of English Historical Thought in the Seventeenth Century* (Cambridge, 1957).

both momentum and a certain self-righteousness. The very essence of Lockeanism, for example, seemed to confirm the significance of the seventeenth-century migration in the American mind, and the two became intertwined in revolutionary thought. Locke's understanding of the origins of society presented a clear picture of persons emigrating with their property and then contracting together for its preservation. Locke had said that men are naturally in a state of nature, "and remain so, till by their own Consents they make themselves Members of some Politick Society." The Great Philosopher had also observed that "many have mistaken the force of Arms, for the consent of the People; and reckon Conquest as one of the Originals of Government. But *Conquest* is as far from setting up any Government, as demolishing an House is from building a new one in the place." Here was special comfort and sustenance for colonists in New York and Jamaica.[47]

More important than Locke's chapters on "The State of Nature" and "Conquest," however, was his long section "Of the Beginning of Political Societies." Lawful government derived *only* from "the consent of any number of Freemen capable of a majority;" and when such a society had been joined, its members "might set up what form of Government they thought fit." Each man who gave his consent to such a community put "himself under an Obligation" to every other member. Therefore the colonist's greatest allegiance must have been to his immediate community, and not to such larger political abstractions as the English constitution or Empire. The Lockean axiom most relevant to the colonists' understanding of colonial origins, however, came in chapter 116 of *The Second Treatise*. There Locke rejected the notion that birth into one polity restrained the individual's ability to give consent to another. " 'Tis true, that whatever Engagements or Promises any one has made for himself, he is under the Obligation of them, but *cannot* by any *Compact* whatsoever, bind *his Children* or Posterity."[48] The seventeenth-century settlers, therefore, had simply left a corrupt country and created a new "Politick Society" in America. Their descendants cherished this simple truth and used it to underpin maxims of their natural rights philosophy during the revolutionary crisis.

It is ironic, if not surprising, that English conceptions of the state of nature were changing during the 1760's and 1770's. Just when the colonists were finding analytical uses for Locke's abstract state of

260

---

[47] Pole, *Political Representation and the American Republic*, 25; Locke, *Two Treatises of Government*, 295-96, 362, 402-403.

[48] Locke, *Two Treatises of Government*, 350-31, 355, 363-64. Cf. John Adams's view, cited above from *Novanglus*.

nature and Rousseau's state of nature as a historical condition, English writers—especially the antiradicals—were ridiculing both conceptions and thereby drifting away from the traditional Lockean domination of British political ideas. Surely this trend, occurring quite independently of the debate on the colonial-constitutional question, contributed to Anglo-American misunderstanding. The Americans' Lockean view of the seventeenth-century migration simply did not fit into most advanced English schema; and they, in turn, were irrelevant to the colonists' quest for a rational past. There was consequently no possible hope for a meeting of minds where colonial origins and political theory were concerned.[49]

In addition to the colonists' very obvious Lockeanism, their views of Stuart colonization must also have been buttressed by their deeply ingrained Protestantism. Martin Luther's *Open Letter to the Christian Nobility*, for example, had described the process whereby colonizers create viable instruments of self control in response to their primitive needs. "If a little group of pious Christian laymen," Luther wrote, "were taken captive and set down in a wilderness, and had among them no priest consecrated by a bishop, and if there in the wilderness they were to agree in choosing one of themselves, married or unmarried, and were to charge him with the office of baptising, saying mass, absolving and preaching, such a man would be as truly a priest as though all bishops and popes had consecrated him. . . . It was in the manner aforesaid that Christians in olden days chose from their number bishops and priests."[50] The sermon literature of the pre-revolutionary decade contains numerous echoes of these thoughts, and similar sentiments designed to justify the historical understanding of colonization, which I have described above.[51]

It is important to realize that patriotic Americans were not in complete agreement on every aspect and detail of the seventeenth-

261

[49]H. V. S. Ogden, "The State of Nature and the Decline of Lockian Political Theory in England, 1760–1800," *American Historical Review*, XLVI (1940), 21–44.

[50]*An Open Letter to the Christian Nobility of the German Nation Concerning the Reform of the Christian Estate* (Wittenberg, 1520), in C. M. Jacobs, ed., *Works of Martin Luther* (Philadelphia, 1915), II, 67–68.

[51]Amos Adams, *A Concise Historical View of the Perils . . . Which Have Attended the Planting and Progressive Improvements of New England* (Boston, 1769), 7–9, 13, 51–52, 63–64; Judah Champion, *A Brief View of the Distresses, Hardships and Dangers Our Ancestors Encounter'd in Settling New-England* (Hartford, 1770), 10–19; James Dana, *A Century Discourse* (New Haven, [1770]), 22 ff.; Gad Hitchcock, *A Sermon Preached at Plymouth December 22d, 1774* (Boston, 1775), 5–6, 17, 36; Samuel Baldwin, *A Sermon, Preached at Plymouth, December 22, 1775* (Boston, 1776), 16–17, 24; Samuel Williams, *A Discourse on the Love of Our Country* (Salem, 1775), 15; Joseph Montgomery, *A Sermon Preached at Christiana Bridge* (Philadelphia, 1775), 23–24.

century migration and its meaning. In 1774, for example, John Adams, Benjamin Franklin, and Thomas Jefferson differed over whether their forefathers had had a perfect right to leave England. (Adams believed the King's permission was required; Franklin and Jefferson felt that it was not.)[52] But they all—Calvinists and Liberals—read the same broad lessons from the history of colonization, and saw the same constitutional implications.[53] Hence the emphatic meaning behind the sixth resolution of the First Continental Congress: "That they [the colonies] are entitled to the benefit of such of the English statutes, as existed at the time of their colonization; and which they have by experience, respectively found to be applicable to their several local and other circumstances."[54]

In the years from 1764 until 1776 Americans were simultaneously obliged to understand the present and anticipate the future in terms consonant with their past. Unlike the moderate reformers in England who simply wished to wash away the corruption that had eaten into the system since 1688, and unlike the Old Whigs who looked back to a fictive Gothic constitution which had been overthrown by the Normans, colonial patriots concentrated on an intermediate period of English history: the first half of the seventeenth century. These variant historical emphases would lead to divergent interpretations of the present, thereby weakening the bonds among segments of the trans-Atlantic community.[55] New Englanders especially "paid tribute to their ancestors and themselves simultaneously by identifying their own cause—political and religious liberty—as the one that had animated the founding of New England." But to patriots generally, it became a commonplace that overseas territories had long been the natural sanctuaries for liberty and virtue, especially when they were suffering "at home" from corruption and authoritarianism.[56]

In 1776 and the years following, when intellectual energies in the new states were applied to creating new sets of constitutional arrangements, the history and meaning of colonization—less relevant for the moment—faded temporarily into the background. In England, however,

---

[52]Cf. *Works of John Adams*, IV, 121-22; *Papers of Thomas Jefferson*, I, 121; Verner W. Crane, *Benjamin Franklin, Englishman and American* (Baltimore, 1936), 117.

[53]Alan Heimert, *Religion and the American Mind from the Great Awakening to the Revolution* (Cambridge, Mass., 1966) 98, 245-46, 358-59, 429, 438, 450n2, 462, 470.

[54]*Journals of the American Congress: From 1774 to 1778* (Washington, 1823), I, 21.

[55]Pole, *Origins of the American Republic*, 427-28.

[56]Edmund S. Morgan, "The Historians of Early New England," in *The Reinterpretation of Early American History: Essays in Honor of John Edwin Pomfret*, Ray A. Billington, ed. (San Marino, California, 1966), 43. See also Bernard Bailyn, *The Ideological Origins of the American Revolution* (Cambridge, Mass., 1967), 140-41.

the interest in colonization that had been stimulated by the Great Debate was diverted eastward to the new imperial outposts, and after 1776 to scholarship; so that the modern scholarly study of ancient colonization dates from the late 1770's.[57]

Cornell University.

[57]Richard W. Van Alstyne, *Empire and Independence; The International History of the American Revolution* (N.Y., 1965), 45–46; [William Barron], *A History of the Colonization of the Free States of Antiquity, applied to the present contest between Great Britain and her American colonies* (London, 1777); John Symonds, *Remarks upon an essay entitled the History of the Colonization of the Free States of Antiquity* (London, 1778); A. J. Graham, *Colony and Mother City in Ancient Greece* (Manchester, Eng., 1964), xvii–xviii.

Popular Uprisings and Civil Authority in Eighteenth-Century America

Pauline Maier*

I T is only natural that the riots and civil turbulence of the past decade and a half have awakened a new interest in the history of American mobs. It should be emphasized, however, that scholarly attention to the subject has roots independent of contemporary events and founded in long-developing historiographical trends. George Rudé's studies of pre-industrial crowds in France and England, E. J. Hobsbawm's discussion of "archaic" social movements, and recent works linking eighteenth-century American thought with English revolutionary tradition have all, in different ways, inspired a new concern among historians with colonial uprisings.[1] This discovery of the early American mob promises to have a significant effect upon historical interpretation. Particularly affected are the Revolutionary struggle and the early decades of the new nation, when events often turned upon well-known popular insurrections.

* Mrs. Maier is a member of the Department of History, University of Massachusetts.

[1] See the following by George Rudé: *The Crowd in the French Revolution* (Oxford, 1959); "The London 'Mob' of the Eighteenth Century," *The Historical Journal*, II (1959), 1-18; *Wilkes and Liberty: A Social Study of 1763 to 1774* (Oxford, 1962); *The Crowd in History: A Study of Popular Disturbances in France and England, 1730-1848* (New York, 1964). See also E. J. Hobsbawm, *Primitive Rebels: Studies in Archaic Forms of Social Movement in the 19th and 20th Centuries* (New York, 1959), esp. "The City Mob," 108-125. For recent discussions of the colonial mob see: Bernard Bailyn, *Pamphlets of the American Revolution* (Cambridge, Mass., 1965), I, 581-584; Jesse Lemisch, "Jack Tar in the Street: Merchant Seamen in the Politics of Revolutionary America," *William and Mary Quarterly*, 3d Ser., XXV (1968), 371-407; Gordon S. Wood, "A Note on Mobs in the American Revolution," *Wm. and Mary Qtly.*, 3d Ser., XXIII (1966), 635-642, and more recently Wood's *Creation of the American Republic, 1776-1787* (Chapel Hill, 1969), *passim*, but esp. 319-328. Wood offers an excellent analysis of the place of mobs and extralegal assemblies in the development of American constitutionalism. Hugh D. Graham and Ted R. Gurr, *Violence in America: Historical and Comparative Perspectives* (New York, 1969) primarily discusses uprisings of the 19th and 20th centuries, but see the chapters by Richard M. Brown, "Historical Patterns of Violence in America," 45-84, and "The American Vigilante Tradition," 154-226.

Eighteenth-century uprisings were in some important ways different
than those of today—different in themselves, but even more in the political context within which they occurred. As a result they carried different
connotations for the American Revolutionaries than they do today. Not
all eighteenth-century mobs simply defied the law: some used extralegal
means to implement official demands or to enforce laws not otherwise
enforceable, others in effect extended the law in urgent situations beyond its technical limits. Since leading eighteenth-century Americans
had known many occasions on which mobs took on the defense of the
public welfare, which was, after all, the stated purpose of government,
they were less likely to deny popular upheavals all legitimacy than are
modern leaders. While not advocating popular uprisings, they could still
grant such incidents an established and necessary role in free societies,
one that made them an integral and even respected element of the
political order. These attitudes, and the tradition of colonial insurrections on which they drew, not only shaped political events of the
Revolutionary era, but also lay behind many laws and civil procedures
that were framed during the 1780's and 1790's, some of which still have a
place in the American legal system.

I

Not all colonial uprisings were identical in character or significance.
Some involved no more than disorderly vandalism or traditional brawls
such as those that annually marked Pope's Day on November 5, particularly in New England. Occasional insurrections defied established
laws and authorities in the name of isolated private interests alone—
a set of Hartford County, Connecticut, landowners arose in 1722, for
example, after a court decision imperiled their particular land titles. Still
others—which are of interest here—took on a broader purpose, and
defended the interests of their community in general where established
authorities failed to act.[2] This common characteristic linked otherwise
diverse rural uprisings in New Jersey and the Carolinas. The insurrec-
tionists' punishment of outlaws, their interposition to secure land titles
or prevent abuses at the hands of legal officials followed a frustration

[2] Carl Bridenbaugh, *Cities in the Wilderness: The First Century of Urban Life
in America, 1625-1742* (New York, 1964), 70-71, 223-224, 382-384; and Carl Bridenbaugh, *Cities in Revolt: Urban Life in America, 1743-1776* (New York, 1964), 113-
118; Charles J. Hoadly, ed., *The Public Records of the Colony of Connecticut . . .*
(Hartford, 1872), VI, 332-333, 341-348.

with established institutions and a belief that justice and even security had to be imposed by the people directly.³ The earlier Virginia tobacco insurrection also illustrates this common pattern well: Virginians began tearing up young tobacco plants in 1682 only after Governor Thomas Culpeper forced the quick adjournment of their assembly, which had been called to curtail tobacco planting during an economic crisis. The insurrections in Massachusetts a little over a century later represent a variation on this theme. The insurgents in Worcester, Berkshire, Hampshire, Middlesex, and Bristol counties—often linked together as members of "Shays's Rebellion"—forced the closing of civil courts, which threatened to send a major portion of the local population to debtors' prison, only until a new legislature could remedy their pressing needs.⁴

This role of the mob as extralegal arm of the community's interest emerged, too, in repeated uprisings that occurred within the more densely settled coastal areas. The history of Boston, where by the mid-eighteenth century "public order . . . prevailed to a greater degree than anywhere else in England or America," is full of such incidents. During the food shortage of 1710, after the governor rejected a petition from the Boston selectmen calling for a temporary embargo on the exportation of foodstuffs one heavily laden ship found its rudder cut away, and fifty men sought to haul another outward bound vessel back to shore. Under similar circumstances Boston mobs again intervened to keep foodstuffs in the colony in 1713 and 1729. When there was some doubt a few years later whether or not the selectmen had the authority to seize a barn lying in the path of a proposed street, a group of townsmen, their faces

---

³ See particularly Richard M. Brown, *The South Carolina Regulators* (Cambridge, Mass., 1963). There is no published study of the New Jersey land riots, which lasted over a decade and were due above all to the protracted inability of the royal government to settle land disputes stemming from conflicting proprietary grants made in the late 17th century. See, however, "A State of Facts concerning the Riots and Insurrections in New Jersey, and the Remedies Attempted to Restore the Peace of the Province," William A. Whitehead *et al.*, eds., *Archives of the State of New Jersey* (Newark, 1883), VII, 207-226. On other rural insurrections see Irving Mark, *Agrarian Conflicts in Colonial New York, 1711-1775* (New York, 1940), Chap. IV, V; Staughton Lynd, "The Tenant Rising at Livingston Manor," *New-York Historical Society Quarterly*, XLVIII (1964), 163-177; Matt Bushnell Jones, *Vermont in the Making, 1750-1777* (Cambridge, Mass., 1939), Chap. XII, XIII; John R. Dunbar, ed., *The Paxton Papers* (The Hague, 1957), esp. 3-51.

⁴ Richard L. Morton, *Colonial Virginia* (Chapel Hill, 1960), I, 303-304; Jonathan Smith, "The Depression of 1785 and Daniel Shays' Rebellion," *Wm. and Mary Qtly.*, 3d Ser., V (1948), 86-87, 91.

blackened, levelled the structure and the road went through. Houses of ill fame were attacked by Boston mobs in 1734, 1737, and 1771; and in the late 1760's the *New York Gazette* claimed that mobs in Providence and Newport had taken on responsibility for "disciplining" unfaithful husbands. Meanwhile in New London, Connecticut, another mob prevented a radical religious sect, the Rogerenes, from disturbing normal Sunday services, "a practice they . . . [had] followed more or less for many years past; and which all the laws made in that government, and executed in the most judicious manner could not put a stop to."[8]

Threats of epidemic inspired particularly dramatic instances of this community oriented role of the mob. One revealing episode occurred in Massachusetts in 1773-1774. A smallpox hospital had been built on Essex Island near Marblehead "much against the will of the multitude" according to John Adams. "The patients were careless, some of them wantonly so; and others were suspected of designing to spread the smallpox in the town, which was full of people who had not passed through the distemper." In January 1774 patients from the hospital who tried to enter the town from unauthorized landing places were forcefully prevented from doing so; a hospital boat was burned; and four men suspected of stealing infected clothes from the hospital were tarred and feathered, then carted from Marblehead to Salem in a long cortege. The Marblehead town meeting finally won the proprietors' agreement to shut down the hospital; but after some twenty-two new cases of smallpox broke out in the town within a few days "apprehension became general," and some "Ruffians" in disguise hastened the hospital's demise by burning the nearly evacuated building. A military watch of forty men were needed for several nights to keep the peace in Marblehead.[9]

A similar episode occurred in Norfolk, Virginia, when a group of

267

---

[8] Bridenbaugh, *Cities in Revolt*, 114; Bridenbaugh, *Cities in the Wilderness*, 196, 383, 388-389; Edmund S. and Helen M. Morgan, *The Stamp Act Crisis*, rev. ed. (New York, 1963), 159; Anne Rowe Cunningham, ed., *Letters and Diary of John Rowe, Boston Merchant, 1759-1762, 1764-1779* (Boston, 1903), 218. On the marriage riots, see *New-York Gazette* (New York City), July 11, 1765—and note, that when the reporter speaks of persons "concern'd in such unlawful Enterprises" he clearly is referring to the husbands, not their "Disciplinarians." On the Rogerenes, see item in *Connecticut Gazette* (New Haven), Apr. 5, 1766, reprinted in Lawrence H. Gipson, *Jared Ingersoll* (New Haven, 1920), 195, n. 1.

[9] John Adams, "Novanglus," in Charles F. Adams, ed., *The Works of John Adams* (Boston, 1850-1856), IV, 76-77; Salem news of Jan. 25 and Feb. 1, 1774, in *Providence Gazette* (Rhode Island), Feb. 5, and Feb. 12, 1774.

wealthy residents decided to have their families innoculated for smallpox. Fears arose that the lesser disease brought on by the innoculations would spread and necessitate a general innoculation, which would cost 'more money than is circulating in Norfolk" and ruin trade and commerce such that "the whole colony would feel the effects." Local magistrates said they could not interfere because "the law was silent in the matter." Public and private meetings then sought to negotiate the issue. Despite a hard-won agreement, however, the pro-innoculation faction persisted in its original plan. Then finally a mob drove the newly innoculated women and children on a five-mile forced march in darkness and rain to the common Pest House, a three-year old institution designed to isolate seamen and others, particularly Negroes, infected with smallpox.[7]

These local incidents indicate a willingness among many Americans to act outside the bounds of law, but they cannot be described as antiauthoritarian in any general sense. Sometimes in fact—as in the Boston bawdy house riot of 1734, or the Norfolk smallpox incident—local magistrates openly countenanced or participated in the mob's activities. Far from opposing established institutions, many supporters of Shays's Rebellion honored their leaders "by no less decisive marks of popular favor than elections to local offices of trust and authority."[8] It was above all the existence of such elections that forced local magistrates to reflect community feelings and so prevented their becoming the targets of insurrections. Certainly in New England, where the town meeting ruled, and to some extent in New York, where aldermen and councilmen were annually elected, this was true; yet even in Philadelphia, with its lethargic closed corporation, or Charleston, which lacked municipal institutions, authority was normally exerted by residents who had an immediate sense of local sentiment. Provincial governments were also for the most part kept alert to local feelings by their elected assemblies. Sometimes,

[7] Letter from "Friend to the Borough and county of Norfolk," in Purdie and Dixon's *Virginia Gazette Postscript* (Williamsburg), Sept. 8, 1768, which gives the fullest account. This letter answered an earlier letter from Norfolk, Aug. 6, 1768, available in Rind's *Va. Gaz. Supplement* (Wmsbg.), Aug. 25, 1768. See also letter of Cornelius Calvert in Purdie and Dixon's *Va. Gaz.* (Wmsbg.), Jan. 9, 1772. Divisions over the innoculation seemed to follow more general political lines. See Patrick Henderson, "Smallpox and Patriotism, The Norfolk Riots, 1768-1769," *Virginia Magazine of History and Biography*, LXXIII (1965), 413-424.

[8] James Madison to Thomas Jefferson, Mar. 19, 1787, in Julian P. Boyd, ed., *The Papers of Thomas Jefferson* (Princeton, 1950-), XI, 223.

of course, uprisings turned against domestic American institutions—as in Pennsylvania in 1764, when the "Paxton Boys" complained that the colony's Quaker assembly had failed to provide adequately for their defense against the Indians. But uprisings over local issues proved *extra-institutional* in character more often than they were anti-institutional; they served the community where no law existed, or intervened beyond what magistrates thought they could do officially to cope with a local problem.

The case was different when imperial authority was involved. There legal authority emanated from a capital an ocean away, where the colonists had no integral voice in the formation of policy, where governmental decisions were based largely upon the reports of "king's men" and sought above all to promote the king's interests. When London's legal authority and local interest conflicted, efforts to implement the edicts of royal officials were often answered by uprisings, and it was not unusual in these cases for local magistrates to participate or openly sympathize with the insurgents. The colonial response to the White Pines Acts of 1722 and 1729 is one example. Enforcement of the acts was difficult in general because "the various elements of colonial society . . . seemed inclined to violate the pine laws—legislatures, lumbermen, and merchants were against them, and even the royal governors were divided." At Exeter, New Hampshire, in 1734 about thirty men prevented royal officials from putting the king's broad arrow on some seized boards; efforts to enforce the acts in Connecticut during the 1750's ended after a deputy of the surveyor-general was thrown in a pond and nearly drowned; five years later logs seized in Massachusetts and New Hampshire were either "rescued" or destroyed.[9] Two other imperial issues that provoked local American uprisings long before 1765 and continued to do so during the Revolutionary period were impressment and customs enforcement.

As early as 1743 the colonists' violent opposition to impressment was said to indicate a "Contempt of Government." Some captains had been mobbed, the Admiralty complained, "others emprisoned, and afterwards held to exorbitant Bail, and are now under Prosecutions carried on by

269

---

[9] Bernhard Knollenberg, *Origin of the American Revolution: 1759-1766* (New York, 1965), 126, 129. See also, Robert G. Albion, *Forests and Sea Power* (Cambridge, Mass., 1926), 262-263, 265. Joseph J. Malone, *Pine Trees and Politics* (Seattle, 1964), includes less detail on the forceful resistance to the acts.

Combination, and by joint Subscription towards the expense." Colonial governors, despite their offers, furnished captains with little real aid either to procure seamen or "even to protect them from the Rage and Insults of the People." Two days of severe rioting answered Commodore Charles Knowles's efforts to sweep Boston harbor for able-bodied men in November 1747. Again in 1764 when Rear Admiral Lord Alexander Colville sent out orders to "procure" men in principal harbors between Casco Bay and Cape Henlopen, mobs met the ships at every turn. When the *St. John* sent out a boat to seize a recently impressed deserter from a Newport wharf, a mob protected him, captured the boat's officer, and hurled stones at the crew; later fifty Newporters joined the colony's gunner at Fort George in opening fire on the king's ship itself. Under threat to her master the *Chaleur* was forced to release four fishermen seized off Long Island, and when that ship's captain went ashore at New York a mob seized his boat and burned it in the Fields. In the spring of 1765 after the *Maidstone* capped a six-month siege of Newport harbor by seizing "all the Men" out of a brigantine from Africa, a mob of about five hundred men similarly seized a ship's officer and burned one of her boats on the Common. Impressment also met mass resistance at Norfolk in 1767 and was a major cause of the famous *Liberty* riot at Boston in 1768.[10]

Like the impressment uprisings, which in most instances sought to protect or rescue men from the "press," customs incidents were aimed at impeding the customs service in enforcing British laws. Tactics

[10] Admiralty to Gov. George Thomas, Sept. 26, 1743, in Samuel Hazard *et al.*, eds., *Pennsylvania Archives* (Philadelphia, 1852-1949), I, 639. For accounts of the Knowles riot, see Gov. William Shirley to Josiah Willard, Nov. 19, 1747, Shirley's Proclamation of Nov. 21, 1747, and his letter to the Board of Trade, Dec. 1, 1747, in Charles H. Lincoln, ed., *The Correspondence of William Shirley . . . 1731-1760* (New York, 1912), I, 406-419; see also Thomas Hutchinson, *History of the Province of Massachusetts Bay*, ed. Lawrence S. Mayo (Cambridge, Mass., 1936), II, 330-333; and *Reports of the Record Commissioners of Boston* (Boston, 1885), XIV, 127-130. David Lovejoy, *Rhode Island Politics and the American Revolution, 1760-1776* (Providence, 1958), 36-39, and on the *Maidstone* in particular see "O. G." in *Newport Mercury* (Rhode Island), June 10, 1765. Bridenbaugh, *Cities in Revolt*, 309-311; documents on the *St. John* episode in *Records of the Colony of Rhode Island and Providence Plantations* (Providence, 1856-1865), VI, 427-430. George G. Wolkins, "The Seizure of John Hancock's Sloop 'Liberty,'" *Massachusetts Historical Society, Proceedings* (1921-1923), LV, 239-284. See also Lemisch, "Jack Tar," *Wm. and Mary Qtly.*, 3d Ser., XXV (1968), 391-393; and Neil R. Stout, "Manning the Royal Navy in North America, 1763-1775," *American Neptune*, XXIII (1963), 179-181.

varied, and although incidents occurred long before 1764—in 1719, for example, Caleb Heathcote reported a "riotous and tumultuous" rescue of seized claret by Newporters—their frequency, like those of the impressment "riots," apparently increased after the Sugar Act was passed and customs enforcement efforts were tightened. The 1764 rescue of the *Rhoda* in Rhode Island preceded a theft in Dighton, Massachusetts, of the cargo from a newly seized vessel, the *Polly*, by a mob of some forty men with blackened faces. In 1766 again a mob stoned a customs official's home in Falmouth (Portland), Maine, while "Persons unknown and disguised" stole sugar and rum that had been impounded that morning. The intimidation of customs officials and of the particularly despised customs informers also enjoyed a long history. In 1701 the South Carolina attorney general publicly attacked an informer "and struck him several times, crying out, this is the Informer, this is he that will ruin the country." Similar assaults occurred decades later, in New Haven in 1766 and 1769, and New London in 1769, and were then often distinguished by their brutality. In 1771 a Providence tidesman, Jesse Saville, was seized, stripped, bound hand and foot, tarred and feathered, had dirt thrown in his face, then was beaten and "almost strangled." Even more thorough assaults upon two other Rhode Island tidesmen followed in July 1770 and upon Collector Charles Dudley in April 1771. Finally, customs vessels came under attack: the *St. John* was shelled at Newport in 1764 where the customs ship *Liberty* was sunk in 1769—both episodes that served as prelude to the destruction of the *Gaspée* outside Providence in 1772.[11]

271

[11] Heathcote letter from Newport, Sept. 7, 1719, *Records of the Colony of Rhode Island*, IV, 259-260; Lovejoy, *Rhode Island Politics*, 35-39. There is an excellent summary of the *Polly* incident in Morgan, *Stamp Act Crisis*, 59, 64-67; and see also *Providence Gaz.* (R. I.), Apr. 27, 1765. On the Falmouth incident see the letter from the collector and comptroller of Falmouth, Aug. 19, 1766, Treasury Group 1, Class 453, Piece 182, Public Records Office. Hereafter cited as T. 1/453, 182. See also the account in Appendix I of Josiah Quincy, Jr., *Reports of the Cases Argued and Adjudged in the Superior Court of Judicature of the Province of Massachusetts Bay, between 1761 and 1772* (Boston, 1865), 446-447. W. Noel Sainsbury *et al.*, eds., *Calendar of State Papers, Colonial Series, America and the West Indies* (London, 1910), *1701*, no. 1042, xi, a. A summary of one of the New Haven informer attacks is in Willard M. Wallace, *Traitorous Hero: The Life and Fortunes of Benedict Arnold* (New York, 1954), 20-23. Arnold's statement on the affair which he led is in Malcolm Decker, *Benedict Arnold, Son of the Havens* (Tarrytown, N. Y., 1932), 27-29. Gipson, in *Jared Ingersoll*, 277-278, relates the later incidents. For the New London informer attacks, see documents of July 1769 in T.

Such incidents were not confined to New England. Philadelphia witnessed some of the most savage attacks, and even the surveyor of Sassafras and Bohemia in Maryland—an office long a sinecure, since no ships entered or cleared in Sassafras or Bohemia—met with violence when he tried to execute his office in March 1775. After seizing two wagons of goods being carried overland from Maryland toward Duck Creek, Pennsylvania, the officer was overpowered by a "licentious mob" that kept shouting "Liberty and Duck Creek forever" as it went through the hours-long rituals of tarring and feathering him and threatening his life. And at Norfolk, Virginia, in the spring 1766 an accused customs informer was tarred and feathered, pelted with stones and rotten eggs, and finally thrown in the sea where he nearly drowned. Even Georgia saw customs violence before independence, and one of the rare deaths resulting from a colonial riot occurred there in 1775.[12]

272

1/471. On the Saville affair see Saville to collector and comptroller of customs in Newport, May 18, 1769, T. 1/471, and *New York Journal* (New York City), July 6, 1769. On later Rhode Island incidents see Dudley and John Nicoll to governor of Rhode Island, Aug. 1, 1770, T. 1/471. Dudley to commissioners of customs at Boston, Newport, Apr. 11, 1771, T. 1/482. On the destruction of the *Liberty* see documents in T. 1/471, esp. comptroller and collector to ʾthe governor, July 21, 1769.

[12] On Philadelphia violence see William Sheppard to commissioners of customs, Apr. 21, 1769, T. 1/471; Deputy Collector at Philadelphia John Swift to commissioners of customs at Boston, Oct. 13, 1769, *ibid.;* and on a particularly brutal attack on the son of customsman John Hatton, see Deputy Collector John Swift to Boston customs commissioners, Nov. 15, 1770, and related documents in T. 1/476. See also Alfred S. Martin, "The King's Customs: Philadelphia, 1763-1774," *Wm. and Mary Qtly.*, 3d Ser., V (1948), 201-216. Documents on the Maryland episode are in T. 1/513, including the following: Richard Reeve to Grey Cooper, Apr. 19, 1775; extracts from a Council meeting, Mar. 16, 1775; deposition of Robert Stratford Byrne, surveyor of His Majesty's Customs at Sassafras and Bohemia, and Byrne to customs commissioners, Mar. 17, 1775. On the Virginia incident see William Smith to Jeremiah Morgan, Apr. 3, 1766, Colonial Office Group, Class 5, Piece 1331, 80, Public Record Office. Hereafter cited as C. O. 5/1331, 80. W. W. Abbot, *The Royal Governors of Georgia, 1754-1775* (Chapel Hill, 1959), 174-175. These customs riots remained generally separate from the more central intercolonial opposition to Britain that emerged in 1765. Isolated individuals like John Brown of Providence and Maximilian Calvert of Norfolk were involved in both the organized intercolonial Sons of Liberty and in leading mobs against customs functionaries or informers. These roles, however, for the most part were unconnected, that is, there was no radical program of customs obstruction *per se*. Outbreaks were above all local responses to random provocations and, at least before the Townshend duties, usually devoid of explicit ideological justifications.

White Pines, impressment, and customs uprisings have attracted
historians' attention because they opposed British authority and so seemed
to presage the Revolution. In fact, however, they had much in common
with many exclusively local uprisings. In each of the incidents violence
was directed not so much against the "rich and powerful"[13] as against
men who—as it was said after the Norfolk smallpox incident—"in
every part of their conduct . . . acted very inconsistently as good
neighbors or citizens." The effort remained one of safeguarding not the
interests of isolated groups alone, but the community's safety and welfare.
The White Pines Acts need not have provoked this opposition had they
applied only to trees of potential use to the Navy, and had they been
framed and executed with concern for colonial rights. But instead the
acts reserved to the Crown all white pine trees including those "utterly
unfit for masts, yards, or bowsprits," and prevented colonists from using
them for building materials or lumber exportation even in regions where
white pine constituted the principal forest growth. As a result the acts
"operated so much against the convenience and even necessities of the
inhabitants," Surveyor John Wentworth explained, that "it became almost
a general interest of the country" to frustrate the acts' execution. Impressment offered a more immediate effect, since the "press" could quickly
cripple whole towns. Merchants and masters were affected as immediately
as seamen: the targeted port, as Massachusetts' Governor William
Shirley explained in 1747, was drained of mariners by both impressment
itself and the flight of navigation to safer provinces, driving the wages
for any remaining seamen upward. When the press was of long duration,
moreover, or when it took place during a normally busy season, it could
mean serious shortages of food or firewood for winter, and a general at-
trition of the commercial life that sustained all strata of society in trading towns. Commerce seemed even more directly attacked by British
trade regulations, particularly by the proliferation of customs procedures
in the mid-1760's that seemed to be in no American's interest, and by
the Sugar Act with its virtual prohibition of the trade with the foreign
West Indies that sustained the economies of colonies like Rhode Island.
As a result even when only a limited contingent of sailors participated
in a customs incident officials could suspect—as did the deputy collector

273

---

[13] Hobsbawm, *Primitive Rebels*, 111. For a different effort to see class division
as relevant in 18th century uprisings, see Lemisch, "Jack Tar," *Wm. and Mary
Qtly.*, 3d Ser., XXV (1968), 387.

at Philadelphia in 1770—that the mass of citizens "in their Hearts" approved of it.[14]

Because the various uprisings discussed here grew out of concerns essential to wide sections of the community, the "rioters" were not necessarily confined to the seamen, servants, Negroes, and boys generally described as the staple components of the colonial mob. The uprising of Exeter, New Hampshire, townsmen against the king's surveyor of the woods in 1754 was organized by a member of the prominent Gillman family who was a mill owner and a militia officer. Members of the upper classes participated in Norfolk's smallpox uprising, and Cornelius Calvert, who was later attacked in a related incident, protested that leading members of the community, doctors and magistrates, had posted securities for the good behavior of the "Villains" convicted of mobbing him. Captain Jeremiah Morgan complained about the virtually universal participation of Norfolkers in an impressment incident of 1767, and "all the principal Gentlemen in Town" were supposedly present when a customs informer was tarred and feathered there in 1766. Merchant Benedict Arnold admitted leading a New Haven mob against an informer in 1766; New London merchants Joseph Packwood and Nathaniel Shaw commanded the mob that first accosted Captain William Reid the night the *Liberty* was destroyed at Newport in 1769, just as John Brown, a leading Providence merchant, led that against the *Gaspée.* Charles Dudley reported in April 1771 that the men who beat him in Newport "did not come from the . . . lowest class of Men," but were "stiled Merchants and the Masters of their Vessels"; and again in 1775 Robert Stratford Byrne said many of his Maryland and Pennsylvania attackers were "from Appearance . . . Men of Property." It is interesting, too, that during Shays's Rebellion—so often considered a class uprising— "men who were of good property and owed not a shilling" were said to be "involved in the train of desperado's to suppress the courts."[15]

274

[14] "Friends to the borough and county of Norfolk," Purdie and Dixon's *Va. Gaz. Postscrpt.* (Wmsbg.), Sept. 8, 1768. Wentworth quoted in Knollenberg, *Origin of American Revolution,* 124-125. Lemisch, "Jack Tar," *Wm. and Mary Qtly.,* 3d Ser., XXV (1968), 383-385. Shirley to Duke of Newcastle, Dec. 31, 1747, in Lincoln, ed., *Shirley Correspondence,* I, 420-423. Dora Mae Clark, "The Impressment of Seamen in the American Colonies," *Essays in Colonial History Presented to Charles McLean Andrews* (New Haven, 1931), 199-200; John Swift to Boston customs commissioners, Nov. 15, 1770, T. 1/476.

[15] Malone, *White Pines,* 112. "Friends to the borough and county of Norfolk," Purdie and Dixon's *Va. Gaz. Postscrpt.* (Wmsbg.), Sept. 8, 1768; Calvert letter,

Opposition to impressment and customs enforcement in itself was not, moreover, the only cause of the so-called impressment or customs "riots." The complete narratives of these incidents indicate again not only that the crowd acted to support local interests, but that it sometimes enforced the will of local magistrates by extralegal means. Although British officials blamed the *St. John* incident upon that ship's customs and impressment activities, colonists insisted that the confrontation began when some sailors stole a few pigs and chickens from a local miller and the ship's crew refused to surrender the thieves to Newport officials. Two members of the Rhode Island council then ordered the gunner of Fort George to detain the schooner until the accused seamen were delivered to the sheriff, and "many People went over the Fort to assist the Gunner in the Discharge of his Duty." Only after this up-. rising did the ship's officers surrender the accused men.[16] Similarly, the 1747 Knowles impressment riot in Boston and the 1765 *Maidstone* impressment riot in Newport broke out after governors' request for the release of impressed seamen had gone unanswered, and only after the outbreaks of violence were the governors' requests honored. The crowd that first assembled on the night the *Liberty* was destroyed in Newport also began by demanding the allegedly drunken sailors who that after-

275

ibid., Jan. 9, 1772. Capt. Jeremiah Morgan, quoted in Lemisch, "Jack Tar," *Wm. and Mary Qtly.*, 3d Ser., XXV (1968), 391; and William Smith to Morgan, Apr. 3, 1766, C. O. 5/1331, 80. Decker, *Benedict Arnold*, 27-29; deposition of Capt. William Reid on the *Liberty* affair, July 21, 1769, T. 1/471; Ephraim Bowen's narrative on the *Gaspée* affair, *Records of the Colony of Rhode Island*, VII, 68-73; Charles Dudley to Boston customs commissioners, Apr. 11, 1771, T. 1/482, and deposition by Byrne, T. 1/513. Edward Carrington to Jefferson, June 9, 1787, Boyd, ed., *Jefferson Papers*, XI, 408; and see also Smith, "Depression of 1785," *Wm. and Mary Qtly.*, 3d Ser., V (1948), 88—of the 21 men indicted for treason in Worcester during the court's April term 1787, 15 were "gentlemen" and only 6 "yeomen."

[16] Gov. Samuel Ward's report to the Treasury lords, Oct. 23, 1765, Ward Manuscripts, Box 1, fol. 58, Rhode Island Historical Society, Providence. See also deposition of Daniel Vaughn of Newport—Vaughn was the gunner at Fort George—July 8, 1764, Chalmers Papers, Rhode Island, fol. 41, New York Public Library, New York City. For British official accounts of the affair, see Lieut. Hill's version in James Munro, ed., *Acts of the Privy Council of England, Colonial Series* (London, 1912), VI, 374-376, and the report of John Robinson and John Nicoll to the customs commissioners, Aug. 30, 1765, Privy Council Group, Class I, Piece 51, Bundle 1 (532), Public Record Office. Hill, whose report was drawn up soon after the incident, does not contradict Ward's narrative, but seems oblivious of any warrant-granting process on shore; Robinson and Nicoll—whose report was drawn up over a year later, and in the midst of the Stamp Act turmoil—claimed that a recent customs seizure had precipitated the attack upon the *St. John*.

noon had abused and shot at a colonial captain, Joseph Packwood, so they could be bound over to local magistrates for prosecution.[17]

In circumstances such as these, the "mob" often appeared only after the legal channels of redress had proven inadequate. The main thrust of the colonists' resistance to the White Pines Acts had always been made in their courts and legislatures. Violence broke out only in local situations where no alternative was available. Even the burning of the *Gaspée* in June 1772 was a last resort. Three months before the incident a group of prominent Providence citizens complained about the ship's wanton severity with all vessels along the coast and the colony's governor pressed their case with the fleet's admiral. The admiral, however, supported the *Gaspée*'s commander, Lieutenant William Dudingston; and thereafter, the *Providence Gazette* reported, Dudingston became "more haughty, insolent and intolerable, . . . personally ill treating every master and merchant of the vessels he boarded, stealing sheep, hogs, poultry, etc. from farmers round the bay, and cutting down their fruit and other trees for firewood." Redress from London was possible but time-consuming, and in the meantime Rhode Island was approaching what its governor called "the deepest calamity" as supplies of food and fuel were curtailed and prices, especially in Newport, rose steeply. It was significant that merchant John Brown finally led the Providence "mob" that seized the moment in June when the *Gaspée* ran aground near Warwick, for it was he who had spearheaded the effort in March 1772 to win redress through the normal channels of government.[18]

II

There was little that was distinctively American about the colonial insurrections. The uprisings over grain exportations during times of dearth, the attacks on brothels, press gangs, royal forest officials, and customsmen, all had their counterparts in seventeenth- and eighteenth-

[17] On the Knowles and *Maidstone* incidents see above, n. 10. On the *Liberty* affair see documents in T. 1/471, esp. the deposition of Capt. William Reid, July 21, 1769, and that of John Carr, the second mate, who indicates that the mob soon forgot its scheme of delivering the crew members to the magistrates.
[18] Malone, *White Pines*, 8-9, and *passim*. *Records of the Colony of Rhode Island*, VII, 60, 62-63, 174-175, including the deposition of Dep. Gov. Darius Sessions, June 12, 1772, and Adm. Montagu to Gov. Wanton, Apr. 8, 1772. Also, Wanton to Hillsborough, June 16, 1772, and Ephraim Bowen's narrative, *ibid.*, 63-73, 90-92. *Providence Gaz.* (R. I.), Jan. 9, 1773.

century England. Even the Americans' hatred of the customs establishment mirrored the Englishman's traditional loathing of excise men. Like the customsmen in the colonies, they seemed to descend into localities armed with extraordinary prerogative powers. Often, too, English excisemen were "thugs and brutes who beat up their victims without compunction or stole or wrecked their property" and against whose extravagances little redress was possible through the law.[19] Charges of an identical character were made in the colonies against customsmen and naval officials as well, particularly after 1763 when officers of the Royal Navy were commissioned as deputy members of the customs service,[20] and a history of such accusations lay behind many of the best-known waterfront insurrections. The Americans' complaints took on particular significance only because in the colonies those officials embodied the authority of a "foreign" power. Their arrogance and arbitrariness helped effect "an estrangement of the Affections of the People from the Authority under which they act," and eventually added an emotional element of anger against the Crown to a revolutionary conflict otherwise carried on in the language of law and right.[21]

The focused character of colonial uprisings also resembled those in England and even France where, Rudé has pointed out, crowds were remarkably single-minded and discriminating.[22] Targets were character-

277

[19] Max Beloff, *Public Order and Popular Disturbances, 1660-1714* (London, 1938), *passim;* Albion, *Forests and Sea Power,* 263; J. H. Plumb, *England in the Eighteenth Century* (Baltimore, 1961 [orig. publ., Oxford, 1950]), 66.

[20] See, for example, "A Pumkin" in the *New London Gazette* (Connecticut), May 14, 18, 1773; "O. G." in *Newport Merc.* (R. I.), June 10, 1765; *New London Gaz.* (Conn.), Sept. 22, 1769; complaints of Marylander David Bevan, reprinted in Rind's *Va. Gaz.* (Wmsbg.), July 27, 1769, and *New London Gaz.* (Conn.), July 21, 1769. Stout, "Manning the Royal Navy," *American Neptune,* XXIII (1963), 174. For a similar accusation against a surveyor-general of the king's woods, see Albion, *Forests and Sea Power,* 262.

[21] Joseph Reed to the president of Congress, Oct. 21, 1779, in Hazard *et al.,* eds., *Pennsylvania Archives,* VII, 762. Five years earlier Reed had tried to impress upon Lord Dartmouth the importance of constraining Crown agents in the colonies if any reconciliation were to be made between Britain and the colonies. See his letter to Earl of Dartmouth, Apr. 4, 1774, in William B. Reed, *Life and Correspondence of Joseph Reed* (Philadelphia, 1847), I, 56-57. For a similar plea, again from a man close to the American Revolutionary leadership, see Stephen Sayre to Lord Dartmouth, Dec. 13, 1766, Dartmouth Papers, D 1778/2/258, William Salt Library, Stafford, England.

[22] Rudé, *Crowd in History,* 60, 253-254. The restraint exercised by 18th century mobs has often been commented upon. See, for example, Wood, "A Note on Mobs," *Wm. and Mary Qtly.,* 3d Ser., XXIII (1966), 636-637.

istically related to grievances: the Knowles rioters sought only the release of the impressed men; they set free a captured officer when assured he had nothing to do with the press, and refrained from burning a boat near Province House for fear the fire would spread. The Norfolk rioters, driven by fear of smallpox, forcefully isolated the innoculated persons where they would be least dangerous. Even the customs rioters vented their brutality on customs officers and informers alone, and the Shaysite "mobs" dispersed after closing the courts which promised most immediately to effect their ruin. So domesticated and controlled was the Boston mob that it refused to riot on Saturday and Sunday nights, which were considered holy by New Englanders.[22]

When colonists compared their mobs with those in the Mother Country they were struck only with the greater degree of restraint among Americans. "These People bear no Resemblance to an English Mob," John Jay wrote of the Shaysites in December 1786, "they are more temperate, cool and regular in their Conduct—they have hitherto abstained from Plunder, nor have they that I know of committed any outrages but such as the accomplishment of their Purpose made necessary." Similar comparisons were often repeated during the Revolutionary conflict, and were at least partially grounded in fact. When Londoners set out to "pull down" houses of ill fame in 1688, for example, the affair spread, prisons were opened, and disorder ended only when troops were called out. But when eighteenth-century Bostonians set out on the same task, there is no record that their destruction extended beyond the bordellos themselves. Even the violence of the customs riots—which contrast in that regard from other American incidents—can sometimes be explained by the presence of volatile foreign seamen. The attack on the son of customsman John Hatton, who was nearly killed in a Philadelphia riot, occurred, for example, when the city was crowded by over a thousand seamen. His attackers were apparently Irish crew members of a vessel he and his father had tried to seize off Cape May, and they were "set on," the Philadelphia collector speculated, by an Irish merchant in Philadelphia to whom the vessel was consigned. One of the most lethal riots in the history of colonial America, in which rioters killed five people, occurred in a small town near Norfolk, Virginia, and was significantly perpetrated entirely by British seamen who resisted the local

278

---

[22] Joseph Harrison's testimony in Wolkins, "Seizure of Hancock's Sloop 'Liberty,'" Mass. Hist. Soc., *Proceedings*, LV, 254.

inhabitants' efforts to reinstitute peace.[24] During and immediately after the Revolutionary War some incidents occurred in which deaths are recorded; but contemporaries felt these were historical aberrations, caused by the "brutalizing" effect of the war itself. "Our citizens, from a habit of putting . . . [the British] to death, have reconciled their minds to the killing of each other," South Carolina Judge Aedanus Burke explained.[25]

To a large extent the pervasive restraint and virtual absence of bloodshed in American incidents can best be understood in terms of social and military circumstance. There was no large amorphous city in America comparable to London, where England's worst incidents occurred. More important, the casualties even in eighteenth-century British riots were rarely the work of rioters. No deaths were inflicted by the Wilkes, Anti-Irish, or "No Popery" mobs, and only single fatalities resulted from other upheavals such as the Porteous riots of 1736. "It was authority rather than the crowd that was conspicuous for its violence to life and limb": all 285 casualties of the Gordon riots, for example, were rioters.[26] Since a regular army was less at the ready for use against colonial mobs, casualty figures for American uprisings were naturally much reduced.

To some extent the general tendency toward a discriminating purposefulness was shared by mobs throughout western Europe, but within the British Empire the focused character of popular uprisings and also

[24] Jay to Jefferson, Dec. 14, 1786, Boyd, ed., *Jefferson Papers*, X, 597. Beloff, *Public Order*, 30. John Swift to Boston customs commissioners, Nov. 15, 1770, Gov. William Franklin's Proclamation, Nov. 17, 1770, and John Hatton to Boston customs commissioners, Nov. 20, 1770, T. 1/476. The last mentioned riot occurred in November 1762. A cartel ship from Havanna had stopped for repairs in October. On Nov. 21 a rumor spread that the Spaniards were murdering the inhabitants, which drew seamen from His Majesty's ship, *Arundel*, also in the harbor, into town, where the seamen drove the Spaniards into a house, set fire to it, and apparently intended to blow it up. A dignitary of the Spanish colonial service, who had been a passenger on the cartel ship, was beaten and some money and valuables were stolen from him. Local men tried to quell the riot without success. It was eventually put down by militiamen from Norfolk. See "A Narrative of a Riot in Virginia in November 1762," T. 1/476.

[25] Burke and others to the same effect, quoted in Jerome J. Nadelhaft, The Revolutionary Era in South Carolina, 1775-1788 (unpubl. Ph.D. diss., University of Wisconsin, 1965), 151-152. See also account of the "Fort Wilson" riot of October 1779 in J. Thomas Scharf and Thompson Westcott, *History of Philadelphia, 1609-1884* (Philadelphia, 1884), I, 401-403.

[26] Rudé, *Crowd in History*, 255-257.

their persistence can be explained in part by the character of law enforcement procedures. There were no professional police forces in the eighteenth century. Instead the power of government depended traditionally upon institutions like the "hue and cry," by which the community in general rose to apprehend felons. In its original medieval form the "hue and cry" was a form of summary justice that resembled modern lynch law. More commonly by the eighteenth century magistrates turned to the *posse commitatus*, literally the "power of the country," and in practice all able-bodied men a sheriff might call upon to assist him. Where greater and more organized support was needed, magistrates could call out the militia.[27] Both the *posse* and the militia drew upon local men, including many of the same persons who made up the mob. This was particularly clear where these traditional mechanisms failed to function effectively. At Boston in September 1766 when customsmen contemplated breaking into the house of merchant Daniel Malcom to search for contraband goods, Sheriff Stephen Greenleaf threatened to call for support from members of the very crowd suspected of an intent to riot; and when someone suggested during the Stamp Act riots that the militia be raised Greenleaf was told it had already risen. This situation meant that mobs could naturally assume the manner of a lawful institution, acting by habit with relative restraint and responsibility. On the other hand, the militia institutionalized the practice of forcible popular coercion and so made the formation of extralegal mobs more natural that J. R. Western has called the militia "a relic of the bad old days," and hailed its passing as "a step towards . . . bringing civilization and humanity into our [English] political life."[28]

These law enforcement mechanisms left magistrates virtually helpless whenever a large segment of the population was immediately involved in the disorder, or when the community had a strong sympathy for the rioters. The Boston militia's failure to act in the Stamp Act riots,

[27] On the "hue and cry" see Frederick Pollock and Frederic W. Maitland, *The History of English Law before the Time of Edward I* (Cambridge, Eng., 1968 [orig. publ., Cambridge, Eng., 1895]), II, 578-580, and William Blackstone, *Commentaries on the Laws of England* (Philadelphia, 1771), IV, 290-291. John Shy, *Toward Lexington: The Role of the British Army in the Coming of the American Revolution* (Princeton, 1965), 40. The English militia underwent a period of decay after 1670 but was revived in 1757. See J. R. Western, *The English Militia in the Eighteenth Century* (London, 1965).

[28] Greenleaf's deposition, T. 1/446; *Providence Gaz.* (R. I.), Aug. 24, 1765. Western, *English Militia,* 74.

which was repeated in nearly all the North American colonies, recapitulated a similar refusal during the Knowles riot of 1747.[29] If the mob's sympathizers were confined to a single locality, the governor could try to call out the militias of surrounding areas, as Massachusetts Governor William Shirley began to do in 1747, and as, to some extent, Governor Francis Bernard attempted after the rescue of the *Polly* in 1765.[30] In the case of sudden uprisings, however, these peace-keeping mechanisms were at best partially effective since they required time to assemble strength, which often made the effort wholly pointless.

When the disorder continued and the militia either failed to appear or proved insufficient, there was, of course, the army, which was used periodically in the eighteenth century against rioters in England and Scotland. Even in America peacetime garrisons tended to be placed where they might serve to maintain law and order. But since all Englishmen shared a fear of standing armies the deployment of troops had always to be a sensitive and carefully limited recourse. Military and civil spheres of authority were rigidly separated, as was clear to Lord Jeffery Amherst, who refused to use soldiers against antimilitary rioters during the Seven Years' War because that function was "entirely foreign to their command and belongs of right to none but the civil power." In fact troops could be used against British subjects, as in the suppression of civil disorder, only upon the request of local magistrates. This institutional inhibition carried, if anything, more weight in the colonies. There royal governors had quickly lost their right to declare martial law without the consent of the provincial councils that were, again, usually filled with local men.[31]

For all practical purposes, then, when a large political unit such as an

[29] Gov. William Shirley explained the militia's failure to appear during the opening stages of the Knowles riot by citing the militiamen's opposition to impressment and consequent sympathy for the rioters. See his letter to the Lords of Trade, Dec. 1, 1747, in Lincoln, ed., *Shirley Correspondence*, I, 417-418. The English militia was also unreliable. It worked well against invasions and unpopular rebellions, but was less likely to support the government when official orders "clashed with the desires of the citizens" or when ordered to protect unpopular minorities. Sir Robert Walpole believed "that if called on to suppress smuggling, protect the turnpikes, or enforce the gin act, the militia would take the wrong side." Western, *English Militia*, 72-73.

[30] Shirley to Josiah Willard, Nov. 19, 1747, Lincoln, ed., *Shirley Correspondence*, I, 407; Bernard's orders in *Providence Gaz.* (R. I.), Apr. 27, 1765.

[31] Shy, *Toward Lexington*, 39-40, 44, 47, 74. Amherst, quoted in J. C. Long, *Lord Jeffery Amherst* (New York, 1933), 124.

entire town or colony condoned an act of mass force, problems were raised "almost insoluble without rending the whole fabric of English law." Nor was the situation confined to the colonies. After describing England's institutions for keeping the peace under the later Stuarts, Max Beloff suggested that no technique for maintaining order was found until nineteenth-century reformers took on the task of reshaping urban government. Certainly by the 1770's no acceptable solution had been found—neither by any colonists, nor "anyone in London, Paris, or Rome, either," as Carl Bridenbaugh has put it. To even farsighted contemporaries like John Adams the weakness of authority was a fact of the social order that necessarily conditioned the way rulers could act. "It is vain to expect or hope to carry on government against the universal bent and genius of the people," he wrote, "we may whimper and whine as much as we will, but nature made it impossible when she made man."[32]

The mechanisms of enforcing public order were rendered even more fragile since the difference between legal and illegal applications of mass force was distinct in theory, but sometimes indistinguishable in practice. The English common law prohibited riot, defined as an uprising of three or more persons who performed what Blackstone called an "unlawful act of violence" for a private purpose. If the act was never carried out or attempted the offense became unlawful assembly; if some effort was made toward its execution, rout; and if the purpose of the uprising was public rather than private—tearing down whore houses, for example, or destroying all enclosures rather than just those personally affecting the insurgents—the offense became treason since it constituted a usurpation of the king's function, a "levying war against the King." The precise legal offence lay not so much in the purpose of the uprising as in its use of force and violence "wherein the Law does not allow the Use of such Force." Such unlawful assumptions of force were carefully distinguished by commentators upon the common law from other occasions on which the law authorized a use of force. It was, for example, legal for force to be used by a sheriff, constable, "or perhaps even . . . a private Person" who assembled "a competent Number of People, in Order with Force to suppress Rebels, or Enemies, or Rioters"; for a justice of the peace to raise the *posse* when opposed in detaining lands, or for Crown officers

282

[32] Shy, *Toward Lexington*, 44; Beloff, *Public Order*, 157-158; Bridenbaugh, *Cities in Revolt*, 297; C. F. Adams, ed., *Works of Adams*, IV, 74-75, V, 209.

to raise "a Power as may effectually enable them to over-power any . . .
Resistance" in the execution of the King's writs.[33]

In certain situations these distinctions offered at best a very uncertain
guide as to who did or did not exert force lawfully. Should a *posse*
employ more force than was necessary to overcome overt resistance, for
example, its members acted illegally and were indictable for riot. And
where established officials supported both sides in a confrontation, or
where the legality of an act that officials were attempting to enforce
was itself disputed, the decision as to who were or were not rioters
seemed to depend upon the observer's point of view. Impressment is a
good example. The colonists claimed that impressment was unlawful
in North America under an act of 1708, while British authorities and
some—but not all—spokesmen for the government held that the law
had lapsed in 1713. The question was settled only in 1775, when Parliament finally repealed the "Sixth of Anne." Moreover, supposing impressment could indeed be carried on, were press warrants from provincial
authorities still necessary? Royal instructions of 1697 had given royal
governors the "sole power of impressing seamen in any of our plantations in America or in sight of them." Admittedly that clause was dropped
in 1708, and a subsequent parliamentary act of 1746, which required the
full consent of the governor and council before impressment could be
carried on within their province, applied only to the West Indies. Nonetheless it seems that in 1764 the Lords of the Admiralty thought the requirement held throughout North America.[34] With the legality of impressment efforts so uncertain, especially when opposed by local authorities, it was possible to see the press gangs as "rioters" for trying *en masse*
to perpetrate an unlawful act of violence. In that case the local townsmen who opposed them might be considered lawful defenders of the
public welfare, acting much as they would in a *posse*. In 1770 John Adams
cited opposition to press gangs who acted without warrants as an example of the lawful use of force; and when the sloop of war *Hornet*

283

[33] The definition of the common law of riot most commonly cited—for example,
by John Adams in the Massacre trials—was from William Hawkins, *A Treatise of
the Pleas of the Crown* (London, 1716), I, 155-159. See also, Blackstone, *Commentaries*, IV, 146-147, and Edward Coke, *The Third Part of the Institutes of the Laws
of England* (London, 1797), 176.

[34] Clark, "Impressment of Seamen," *Essays in Honor of Andrews*, 198-224;
Stout, "Manning the Royal Navy," *American Neptune*, XXIII (1963), 178-179; and
Leonard W. Labaree, ed., *Royal Instructions to British Colonial Governors, 1670-
1776* (New York, 1935), I, 442-443.

swept into Norfolk, Virginia, in September 1767 with a "bloody riotous plan . . . to impress seamen, without consulting the Mayor, or any other magistrate," the offense was charged to the pressmen. Roused by the watchman, who called out *"a riot by man of war's men,"* the inhabitants rose to back the magistrates, and not only secured the release of the impressed men but also imprisoned ten members of the press gang. The ship's captain, on the other hand, condemned the townsmen as "Rioters." Ambiguity was present, too, in Newport's *St. John* clash, which involved both impressment and criminal action on the part of royal seamen and culminated with Newporters firing on the king's ship. The Privy Council in England promptly classified the incident as a riot, but the Rhode Island governor's report boldly maintained that "the people meant nothing but to assist [the magistrates] in apprehending the Offenders" on the vessel, and even suggested that "their Conduct be honored with his Majesty's royal Approbation."[35]

The enforcement of the White Pines Acts was similarly open to legal dispute. The acts seemed to violate both the Massachusetts and Connecticut charters; the meaning of provisions exempting trees growing within townships (act of 1722) and those which were "the property of private persons" (act of 1729) was contested, and royal officials tended to work on the basis of interpretations of the laws that Bernhard Knollenberg has called farfetched and, in one case, "utterly ur.tenable." The Exeter, New Hampshire, "riot" of 1734, for example, answered an attempt of the surveyor to seize boards on the argument that the authorization to seize logs from allegedly illegally felled white pine trees in the act of 1722 included an authorization to seize processed lumber. As a result, Knollenberg concluded, although the surveyors' reports "give the impression that the New Englanders were an utterly lawless lot, . . . in many if not most cases they were standing for what they believed, with reason, were their legal and equitable rights in trees growing on their own lands."[36]

[35] L. Kinvin Wroth and Hiller B. Zobel, eds., *Legal Papers of John Adams* (Cambridge, Mass., 1965), III, 253. Account of the Norfolk incident by George Abyvon, Sept. 5, 1767, in Purdie and Dixon's *Va. Gaz.* (Wmsbg.), Oct. 1, 1767. Capt. Morgan quoted in Lemisch, "Jack Tar," *Wm. and Mary Qtly.*, 3d Ser., XXV (1968), 391. Munro, ed., *Acts of the Privy Council, Colonial Series*, VI, 374; Gov. Samuel Ward to Treasury lords, Oct. 23. 1765, Ward MSS, Box 1, fol. 58.

[36] Knollenberg, *Origin of the Revolution*, 122-130; Albion, *Forests and Sea Power*, 255-258.

Occasions open to such conflicting interpretations were rare. Most often even those who sympathized with the mobs' motives condemned its use of force as illegal and unjustifiable. That ambiguous cases did arise, however, indicates that legitimacy and illegitimacy, *posses* and rioters, represented but poles of the same spectrum. And where a mob took upon itself the defense of the community, it benefited from a certain popular legitimacy even when the strict legality of its action was in doubt, particularly among a people taught that the legitimacy of law itself depended upon its defense of the public welfare.

Whatever quasi-legal status mobs were accorded by local communities was reinforced, moreover, by formal political thought. "Riots and rebellions" were often calmly accepted as a constant and even necessary element of free government. This acceptance depended, however, upon certain essential assumptions about popular uprisings. With words that could be drawn amost verbatim from John Locke or any other English author of similar convictions, colonial writers posited a continuing moderation and purposefulness on the part of the mob. "Tho' innocent Persons may sometimes suffer in popular Tumults," observed a 1768 writer in the *New York Journal*, "yet the general Resentment of the People is principally directed according to Justice, and the greatest Delinquent feels it most." Moreover, upheavals constituted only occasional interruptions in well-governed societies. "Good Laws and good Rulers will always be obey'd and respected"; "the Experience of all Ages proves, that Mankind are much more likely to submit to bad Laws and wicked Rulers, than to resist good ones." "Mobs and Tumults," it was often said, "never happen but thro' Oppression and a scandalous Abuse of Power."[37]

In the hands of Locke such remarks constituted relatively inert

[37] *N. Y. Jour.* (N. Y. C.), Aug. 18, 1768 (the writer was allegedly drawing together arguments that had recently appeared in the British press); and *N. Y. Jour. Supplement* (N. Y. C.), Jan. 4, 1770. Note also that Jefferson accepted Shays's rebellion as a sign of health in American institutions only after he had been assured by men like Jay that the insurgents had acted purposely and moderately, and after he had concluded that the uprising represented no continuous threat to established government. "An insurrection in one of the 13. states in the course of 11. years that they have subsisted amounts to one in any particular state in 143 years, say a century and a half," he calculated. "This would not be near as many as has happened in every other government that has ever existed," and clearly posed no threat to the constitutional order as a whole. To David Hartley, July 2, 1787, Boyd, ed., *Jefferson Papers*, XI, 526.

statements of fact. Colonial writers, however, often turned these pronouncements on their heads such that observed instances of popular disorder became *prima facie* indictments of authority. In 1747, for example, New Jersey land rioters argued that "from their Numbers, Violences, and unlawful Actions" it was to be "inferred that . . . they are wronged and oppressed, or else they would never *rebell agt. the Laws.*" Always, a New York writer said in 1770, when "the People of any Government" become "turbulent and uneasy," it was above all "a certain Sign of Maladministration." Even when disorders were not directly levelled against government they provided "strong proofs that something is much amiss in the state" as William Samuel Johnson put it; that—in Samuel Adams's words—the "wheels of good government" were "somewhat clogged." Americans who used this argument against Britain in the 1760's continued to depend upon it two decades later when they reacted to Shays's Rebellion by seeking out the public "Disease" in their own independent governments that was indicated by the "Spirit of Licentiousness" in Massachusetts.[88]

Popular turbulence seemed to follow so naturally from inadequacies of government that uprisings were often described with similes from the physical world. In 1770 John Adams said that there were "Churchquakes and state-quakes in the moral and political world, as well as earthquakes, storms and tempests in the physical." Two years earlier a writer in the *New York Journal* likened popular tumults to "Thunder Gusts" which "commonly do more Good than Harm." Thomas Jefferson continued the imagery in the 1780's, particularly with his famous statement that he liked "a little rebellion now and then" for it was "like a storm in the atmosphere." It was, moreover, because of the "imperfection of all things in this world," including government, that Adams found it "vain to seek a government in all points free from a possibility of civil wars, tumults and seditions." That was "a blessing denied to this life and preserved to complete the felicity of the next."[89]

[88] John Locke, *The Second Treatise of Government*, paragraphs 223-225. "A State of Facts Concerning the Riots . . . in New Jersey," *New Jersey Archives*, VII, 217. *N. Y. Jour., Supp.* (N. Y. C.), Jan. 4, 1770. Johnson to Wm. Pitkin, Apr. 29, 1768, Massachusetts Historical Society, *Collections*, 5th Ser., IX (1885), 275. Adams as "Determinus" in *Boston Gazette*, Aug. 8, 1768; and Harry A. Cushing, ed., *The Writings of Samuel Adams* (New York, 1904-1908), I, 237. Jay to Jefferson, Oct. 27, 1786, Boyd, ed., *Jefferson Papers*, X, 488.
[89] Wroth and Zobel, eds., *Adams Legal Papers*, III, 249-250; *N. Y. Jour. Supp.*

286

If popular uprisings occurred "in all governments at all times," they were nonetheless most able to break out in free governments. Tyrants imposed order and submission upon their subjects by force, thus dividing society, as Jefferson said, into wolves and sheep. Only under free governments were the people "nervous," spirited, jealous of their rights, ready to react against unjust provocations; and this being the case, popular disorders could be interpreted as "Symptoms of a strong and healthy Constitution" even while they indicated some lesser shortcoming in administration. It would be futile, Josiah Quincy, Jr., said in 1770, to expect "that pacific, timid, obsequious, and servile temper, so predominant in more despotic governments" from those who lived under free British institutions. From "our happy constitution," he claimed, there resulted as "very natural Effects" an "impatience of injuries, and a strong resentment of insults."[40]

This popular impatience constituted an essential force in the maintenance of free instutions. "What country can preserve it's [*sic*] liberties if their rulers are not warned from time to time that their people preserve the spirit of resistance?" Jefferson asked in 1787. Occasional insurrections were thus "an evil . . . productive of good": even those founded on popular error tended to hold rulers "to the true principles of their institution" and generally provided "a medecine necessary for the sound health of government." This meant that an aroused people had a role not only in extreme situations, where revolution was requisite, but in the normal course of free government. For that reason members of the House of Lords could seriously argue—as A. J. P. Taylor has pointed out—that "rioting is an essential part of our constitution"; and for that reason, too, even Massachusetts's conservative Lieutenant Governor

287

(N. Y. C.), Aug. 18, 1768; Jefferson to Abigail Adams, Feb. 22, 1787, Boyd, ed., *Jefferson Papers*, XI, 174. C. F. Adams, ed., *Works of Adams*, IV, 77, 80 (quoting Algernon Sydney).

[40] Jefferson to Edward Carrington, Jan. 16, 1787, Boyd, ed., *Jefferson Papers*, XI, 49, and Rev. James Madison to Jefferson, Mar. 28, 1787, *ibid.*, 252. Wroth and Zobel, eds., *Adams Legal Papers*, III, 250. Quincy's address to the jury in the soldiers' trial after the Boston Massacre in Josiah Quincy, *Memoir of the Life of Josiah Quincy, Junior, of Massachusetts Bay, 1744-1775*, ed. Eliza Susan Quincy, 3d ed. (Boston, 1875), 46. See also Massachusetts Assembly's similar statement in its address to Gov. Hutchinson, Apr. 24, 1770, Hutchinson, *History of Massachusetts Bay*, ed. Mayo, III, 365-366. This 18th century devotion to political "jealousy" resembles the doctrine of "vigilance" that was defended by 19th century vigilante groups. See Graham and Gurr, *Violence in America*, 179-183.

Thomas Hutchinson could remark in 1768 that "mobs a sort of them at least are constitutional."[41]

III

It was, finally, the interaction of this constitutional role of the mob with the written law that makes the story of eighteenth-century popular uprisings complexity itself.[42] If mobs were appreciated because they provided a check on power, it was always understood that, insofar as upheavals threatened "running to such excesses, as will overturn the whole system of government," "strong discouragements" had to be provided against them. For eighteenth-century Americans, like the English writers they admired, liberty demanded the rule of law. In extreme situations where the rulers had clearly chosen arbitrary power over the limits of law, men like John Adams could prefer the risk of anarchy to continued submission because "anarchy can never last long, and tyranny may be perpetual," but only when "there was any hope that the fair order of liberty and a free constitution would arise out of it." This desire to maintain the orderly rule of law led legislatures in England and the colonies to pass antiriot statutes and to make strong efforts—in the words of a 1753 Massachusetts law—to discountenance "a mobbish temper and spirit in . . . the inhabitants" that would oppose "all government and order."[43]

[41] Jefferson to William Stephen Smith, Nov. 13, 1787, Boyd, ed., *Jefferson Papers*, XII, 356, Jefferson to Carrington, Jan. 16, 1787, *ibid.*, XI, 49, Jefferson to James Madison, Jan. 30, 1787, *ibid.*, 92-93. Taylor's remarks in "History of Violence," *The Listener*, CXXIX (1968), 701. ("Members of the House of Lords . . . said . . . if the people really don't like something, then they work our carriages and tear off our wigs and throw stones through the windows of our town-houses. And this is an essential thing to have if you are going to have a free country.") Hutchinson to [John or Robert] Grant, July 27, 1768, Massachusetts Archives, XXVI, 317, State House, Boston. See also the related story about John Selden, the famous 17th century lawyer, told to the House of Commons in Jan. 1775 by Lord Camden and recorded by Josiah Quincy, Jr., in the "Journal of Josiah Quincy, Jun., During his Voyage and Residence in England from September 28th, 1774, to March 3d, 1775," Massachusetts Historical Society, *Proceedings*, L (1916-1917), 462-463. Selden was asked what lawbook contained the laws for resisting tyranny. He replied he did not know, "but I'll tell [you] what is most certain, that it has always been the custom of England—and the Custom of England is the *Law* of the *Land*."

[42] On the developing distinction Americans drew between what was legal and constitutional, see Wood, *Creation of the American Republic*, 261-268.

[43] *N. Y. Jour. Supp.* (N. Y. C.), Jan. 4, 1770; Wroth and Zobel, eds., *Adams Legal Papers*, III, 250, and C. F. Adams, ed., *Works of Adams*, VI, 151. Adams's

The problem of limiting mass violence was dealt with most intensely over a sustained period by the American Revolutionary leadership, which has perhaps suffered most from historians' earlier inattention to the history of colonial uprisings. So long as it could be maintained—as it was only fifteen years ago—that political mobs were "rare or unknown in America" before the 1760's, the Revolutionaries were implicitly credited with their creation. American patriots, Charles McLean Andrews wrote, were often "lawless men who were nothing more than agitators and demagogues" and who attracted a following from the riffraff of colonial society. It now seems clear that the mob drew on all elements of the population. More important, the Revolutionary leaders had no need to create mob support. Instead they were forced to work with a "permanent entity," a traditional crowd that exerted itself before, after, and even during the Revolutionary struggle over issues unrelated to the conflict with Britain, and that, as Hobsbawm has noted, characteristically aided the Revolutionary cause in the opening phases of conflict but was hard to discipline thereafter.[44]

289

In focusing popular exuberance the American leaders could work with long-established tendencies in the mob toward purposefulness and responsibility. In doing so they could, moreover, draw heavily upon the guidelines for direct action that had been defined by English radical writers since the seventeenth century. Extralegal action was justified only when all established avenues to redress had failed. It could not answer casual errors or private failings on the part of the magistrates, but had

---

views were altered in 1815, *ibid.*, X, 181. It is noteworthy that the Boston town meeting condemned the Knowles rioters not simply for their method of opposing impressment but because they insulted the governor and the legislature, and the Massachusetts Assembly acted against the uprising only after Gov. Shirley had left Boston and events seemed to be "tending to the destruction of all government and order." Hutchinson, *History of Massachusetts Bay*, ed. Mayo, II, 332-333. *Acts and Resolves of the Province of Massachusetts Bay*, III, 647. (Chap. 18 of the Province laws, 1752-1753, "An Act for Further Preventing all Riotous, Tumultuous and Disorderly Assemblies or Companies or Persons. . . .") This act, which was inspired particularly by Pope's Day violence, was renewed after the Boston Massacre in 1770 even though the legislature refused to renew its main Riot Act of 1751. *Ibid.*, IV, 87.

[44] Arthur M. Schlesinger, "Political Mobs and the American Revolution, 1765-1776," *Proceedings of the American Philosophical Society*, XCIX (1955), 246; Charles M. Andrews, *The Colonial Background of the American Revolution*, rev. ed. (New Haven, 1939), 176; Charles M. Andrews, "The Boston Merchants and the Non-Importation Movement," Colonial Society of Massachusetts, *Transactions*, XIX (1916-1917), 241; Hobsbawm, *Primitive Rebels*, 111, 123-124.

to await fundamental public abuses so egregious that the "whole people" turned against their rulers. Even then, it was held, opposition had to be measured so that ño more force was exerted than was necessary for the public good. Following these principles colonial leaders sought by careful organization to avoid the excesses that first greeted the Stamp Act. Hutchinson's query after a crowd in Connecticut had forced the resignation of stampman Jared Ingersoll—whether "such a public regular assembly can be called a mob"—could with equal appropriateness have been repeated during the tea resistance, or in 1774 when Massachusetts *mandamus* councillors were forced to resign.[45]

290

From the first appearance of an organized resistance movement in 1765, moreover, efforts were made to support the legal magistrates such that, as John Adams said in 1774, government would have "as much vigor then as ever" except where its authority was specifically under dispute. This concern for the maintenance of order and the general framework of law explains why the American Revolution was largely free from the "universal tumults and all the irregularities and violence of mobbish factions [that] naturally arise when legal authority ceases." It explains, too, why old revolutionaries like Samuel Adams or Christopher Gadsden disapproved of those popular conventions and committees that persisted after regular independent state governments were established in the 1770's. "Decency and Respect [are] due to Constitutional Authority," Samuel Adams said in 1784, "and those Men, who under any Pretence or by any Means whatever, would lessen the Weight of Government lawfully exercised must be Enemies to our happy Revolution and the Common Liberty."[46]

In normal circumstances the "strong discouragements" to dangerous disorder were provided by established legislatures. The measures enacted by them to deal with insurrections were shaped by the eighteenth-century understanding of civil uprisings. Since turbulence indicated above all

[45] Hutchinson to Thomas Pownall, [Sept. or Oct. 1765], Mass. Archives, XXVI, 157. Pauline Maier, From Resistance to Revolution: American Radicals and the Development of Intercolonial Opposition to Britain, 1765-1776 (unpubl. Ph.D. diss., Harvard University, 1968), I, 37-45, 72-215.

[46] C. F. Adams, ed., *Works of Adams*, IV, 51; Rev. Samuel Langdon's election sermon to third Massachusetts Provincial Congress, May 31, 1775, quoted in Richard Frothingham, *Life and Times of Joseph Warren* (Boston, 1865), 499; Samuel Adams to Noah Webster, Apr. 30, 1784, Cushing, ed., *Writings of Samuel Adams*, IV, 305-306. On Gadsden see Richard Walsh, *Charleston's Sons of Liberty* (Columbia, 1959), 87.

some shortcoming in government, it was never to be met by increasing
the authorities' power of suppression. The "weakness of authority"
that was a function of its dependence upon popular support appeared
to contemporary Americans as a continuing virtue of British institutions,
as one reason why rulers could not simply dictate to their subjects and
why Britain had for so long been hailed as one of the freest nations in
Europe. It was "far less dangerous to the Freedom of a State" to allow
"the laws to be trampled upon, by the licence among the rabble . . . than
to dispence with their force by an act of power." Insurrections were to
be answered by reform, by attacking the "Disease"—to use John Jay's
term of 1786—that lay behind them rather than by suppressing its
"Symptoms." And ultimately, as William Samuel Johnson observed in
1768, "the only effectual way to prevent them is to govern with wisdom,
justice, and moderation."[47]

In immediate crises, however, legislatures in both England and
America resorted to special legislation that supplemented the common
law prohibition of riot. The English Riot Act of 1714 was passed when
disorder threatened to disrupt the accession of George I; a Connecticut
act of 1722 followed a rash of incidents over land title in Hartford
County; the Massachusetts act of 1751 answered "several tumultuous
assemblies" over the currency issue and another of 1786 was enacted at
the time of Shays's Rebellion. The New Jersey legislature passed an act
in 1747 during that colony's protracted land riots; Pennsylvania's Riot
Act of 1764 was inspired by the Paxton Boys; North Carolina's of 1771
by the Regulators; New York's of 1774 by the "land wars" in Charlotte
and Albany County.[48] Always the acts specified that the magistrates were
to depend upon the *posse* in enforcing their provisions, and in North

291

[47] *N. Y. Jour. Supp.* (N. Y. C.), Jan. 4, 1770; Jay to Jefferson, Oct. 27, 1786,
Boyd, ed., *Jefferson Papers,* X, 488; Johnson to William Pitkin, July 23, 1768, Massachusetts Historical Society, *Collections,* 5th Ser., IX, 294-295.

[48] *The Statutes at Large* [of Great Britain] (London, 1786), V, 4-6; Hoadly,
ed., *Public Records of Connecticut,* VI, 346-348 for the law, and see also 332-333,
341-348; *Acts and Resolves of Massachusetts Bay,* III, 544-546, for the Riot Act of
1751, and see also Hutchinson, *History of Massachusetts Bay,* ed. Mayo, III, 6-7; and
Acts and Laws of the Commonwealth of Massachusetts (Boston, 1893), 87-88, for
Act of 1786; "A State of Facts Concerning the Riots . . . in New Jersey," *N. J.
Archives,* VII, 211-212, 221-222; *The Statutes at Large of Pennsylvania* . . . (n.p.,
1899), VI, 325-328; William A. Saunders, ed., *The Colonial Records of North
Carolina* (Raleigh, 1890), VIII, 481-486; *Laws of the Colony of New York in the
Years 1774 and 1775* (Albany, 1888), 38-43.

Carolina on the militia as well. They differed over the number of people who had to remain "unlawfully, riotously, and tumultuously assembled together, to the Disturbance of the Publick Peace" for one hour after the reading of a prescribed riot proclamation before becoming judicable under the act. Some colonies specified lesser punishments than the death penalty provided for in the English act, but the American statutes were not in general more "liberal" than the British. Two of them so violated elementary judicial rights that they were subsequently condemned—North Carolina's by Britain, and New York's act of 1774 by a later, Revolutionary state legislature.[49]

In one important respect, however, the English Riot Act was reformed. Each colonial riot law, except that of Connecticut, was enacted for only one to three years, whereas the British law was perpetual. By this provision colonial legislators avoided the shortcoming which, it was said, was "more likely to introduce *arbitrary Power* than even an *Army* itself," because a perpetual riot act meant that "in all future time" by "reading a Proclamation" the Crown had the power "of hanging up their Subjects wholesale, or of picking out Those, to whom they have the greatest Dislike." If the death penalty was removed, the danger was less. When, therefore, riot acts without limit of time were finally enacted—as Connecticut had done in 1722, Massachusetts in 1786, New Jersey in 1797—the punishments were considerably milder, providing, for example, for imprisonment not exceeding six months in Connecticut, one year in Massachusetts, and three years in New Jersey.[50]

Riot legislation, it is true, was not the only recourse against insurgents, who throughout the eighteenth century could also be prosecuted for treason. The colonial and state riot acts suggest, nonetheless, that American legislators recognized the participants in civil insurrections as guilty of a crime peculiarly complicated because it had social benefits as well as damages. To some degree, it appears, they shared the idea expressed well by Jefferson in 1787: that "honest republican governors" should be "so mild in their punishments of rebellions, as not to discourage them too much."[51] Even in countering riots the legislators

[49] See additional instruction to Gov. Josiah Martin, Saunders, ed., *Colonial Records of North Carolina*, VIII, 515-516; and *Laws of the State of New York* (Albany, 1886), I, 20.
[50] *The Craftsman* (London, 1731), VI, 263-264. Connecticut and Massachusetts laws cited in n. 45; and *Laws of the State of New Jersey* (Trenton, 1821), 279-281.
[51] Jefferson to Madison, Jan. 30, 1787, Boyd, ed., *Jefferson Papers*, XI, 93.

seemed as intent upon preventing any perversion of the forces of law and order by established authorities as with chastising the insurgents. Reform of the English Riot Act thus paralleled the abolition of constitutent treasons—a traditional recourse against enemies of the Crown— in American state treason acts of the Revolutionary period and finally in Article III of the Federal Constitution.[52] From the same preoccupation, too, sprang the limitations placed upon the regular army provided for in the Constitution in part to assure the continuation of republican government guaranteed to the states by Article IV, Section IV. Just as the riot acts were for so long limited in duration, appropriations for the army were never to extend beyond two years (Article I, Section viii, 12); and the army could be used within a state against domestic violence only after application by the legislature or governor, if the legislature could not be convened (Article IV, Section iv).

A continuing desire to control authority through popular action also underlay the declaration in the Second Amendment that "a well regulated Militia being necessary to the security of a free State," citizens were assured the "right . . . to keep and bear Arms." The militia was meant above all "to prevent the establishment of a standing army, the bane of liberty"; and the right to bear arms—taken in part from the English Bill of Rights of 1689—was considered a standing threat to would-be tryants. It embodied "a public allowance, under due restrictions, of the *natural right of resistance and self preservation,* when the sanctions of society and laws are found *insufficient* to restrain the *violence of oppression.*" And on the basis of their eighteenth-century experience, Americans could consider that right to be "perfectly harmless. . . . If the government be equitable; if it be reasonable in its exactions; if proper attention be paid to the education of children in knowledge, and religion," Timothy Dwight declared, "few men will be disposed to use arms, unless for their amusement, and for the defence of themselves and their country."[68]

The need felt to continue the eighteenth-century militia as a counter-

---

[52] See Bradley Chapin, "Colonial and Revolutionary Origins of the American Law of Treason," *Wm. and Mary Qtly.,* 3d Ser., XVII (1960), 3-21.

[68] Elbridge Gerry in Congressional debates, quoted in Irving Brant, *The Bill of Rights, Its Origin and Meaning* (Indianapolis, 1965), 486; Samuel Adams, quoting Blackstone, as "E. A." in *Boston Gaz.,* Feb. 27, 1769, and Cushing, ed., *Writings of Samuel Adams,* I, 317. Timothy Dwight, quoted in Daniel J. Boorstin, *The Americans: The Colonial Experience* (New York, 1958), 353.

weight to government along with the efforts to outlaw rioting and to provide for the use of a standing army against domestic insurrections under carefully defined circumstances together illustrate the complex attitude toward peacekeeping that prevailed among the nation's founders. The rule of law had to be maintained, yet complete order was neither expected nor even desired when it could be purchased, it seemed, only at the cost of forcefully suppressing the spirit of a free people. The constant possibility of insurrection—as institutionalized in the militia— was to remain an element of the United States Constitution, just as it had played an essential role in Great Britain's.

294

This readiness to accept some degree of tumultuousness depended to a large degree upon the lawmakers' own experience with insurrections in the eighteenth century, when "disorder" was seldom anarchic and "rioters" often acted to defend law and justice rather than to oppose them. In the years after independence this toleration declined, in part because mass action took on new dimensions. Nineteenth-century mobs often resembled in outward form those of the previous century, but a new violence was added. Moreover, the literal assumption of popular rule in the years after Lexington taught many thoughtful Revolutionary partisans what was for them an unexpected lesson—that the people were "as capable of despotism as any prince," that "public liberty was no guarantee after all of private liberty."[64] With home rule secured, attention focused more exclusively upon minority rights, which mob action had always to some extent imperiled. And the danger that uprisings carried for individual freedom became ever more egregious as mobs shed their former restraint and burned Catholic convents, attacked nativist speakers, lynched Mormons, or destroyed the presses and threatened the lives of abolitionists.

Ultimately, however, changing attitudes toward popular uprisings turned upon fundamental transformations in the political perspective of Americans after 1776. Throughout the eighteenth century political institutions had been viewed as in a constant evolution: the colonies' relationship with Britain and with each other, even the balance of power within the governments of various colonies, remained unsettled. Under such circumstances the imputations of governmental shortcoming that uprisings carried could easily be accepted and absorbed. But after Independence, when the form and conduct of the Americans' governments

[64] Wood, *Creation of the American Republic*, 410.

were under their exclusive control, and when those governments represented, moreover, an experiment in republicanism on which depended their own happiness and "that of generations unborn," Americans became less ready to endure domestic turbulence or accept its disturbing implications. Some continued to argue that "distrust and dissatisfaction" on the part of the multitude were "always the consequence of tyranny or corruption." Others, however, began to see domestic turbulence not as indictments but as insults to government that were likely to discredit American republicanism in the eyes of European observers. "Mobs are a reproach to Free Governments," where all grievances could be legally redressed through the courts or the ballot box, it was argued in 1783. They originated there "not in Oppression, but in Licentiousness," an "ungovernable spirit" among the people. Under republican governments even that distrust of power colonists had found so necessary for liberty, and which uprisings seemed to manifest, could appear outmoded. "There is some consistency in being jealous of power in the hands of those who assume it by birth . . . and over whom we have no controul . . . as was the case with the Crown of England over America," another writer suggested. "But to be jealous of those whom we chuse, the instant we have chosen them" was absurd: perhaps in the transition from monarchy to republic Americans had "bastardized" their ideas by placing jealousy where confidence was more appropriate.[55] In short, the assumptions behind the Americans' earlier toleration of the mob were corroded in republican America. Old and new attitudes coexisted in the 1780's and even later. But the appropriateness of popular uprisings in the United States became increasingly in doubt after the Federal Constitution came to be seen as the final product of long-term institutional experimentation, "a momentous contribution to the history of politics" that rendered even that most glorious exertion of popular force, revolution itself, an obsolete resort for Americans.[56]

Yet this change must not be viewed exclusively as a product of America's distinctive Revolutionary achievement. J. H. Plumb has

[55] Judge Aedanus Burke's Charge to the Grand Jury at Charleston, June 9, 1783, in *South-Carolina Gazette and General Advertiser* (Charleston), June 10, 1783; "A Patriot," *ibid.*, July 15, 1783; and "Another Patriot," *ibid.*, July 29, 1783; and on the relevance of jealousy of power, see a letter to Virginia in *ibid.*, Aug. 9, 1783. "Democratic Gentle-Touch," *Gazette of the State of South Carolina* (Charleston), May 13, 1784.
[56] Wood, *Creation of the American Republic*, 612-614.

pointed out, that a century earlier, when England passed beyond her revolutionary era and progressed toward political "stability," radical ideology with its talk of resistance and revolution was gradually left behind. A commitment to peace and permanence emerged from decades of fundamental change. In America as in England this stability demanded that operative sovereignty, including the right finally to decide what was and was not in the community's interest, and which laws were and were not constitutional, be entrusted to established governmental institutions. The result was to minimize the role of the people at large, who had been the ultimate arbiters of those questions in English and American Revolutionary thought. Even law enforcement was to become the task primarily of professional agencies. As a result in time all popular upheavals alike became menacing efforts to "pluck up law and justice by the roots," and riot itself gradually became defined as a purposeless act of anarchy, "a blind and misguided outburst of popular fury," of "undirected violence with no articulated goals."[57]

[57] J. H. Plumb, *The Origins of Political Stability, England 1675-1725* (Boston, 1967), xv, 187; John Adams on the leaders of Shays's Rebellion in a letter to Benjamin Hitchborn, Jan. 27, 1787, in C. F. Adams, ed., *Works of Adams*, IX, 551; modern definitions of riot in "Riot Control and the Use of Federal Troops," *Harvard Law Review*, LXXXI (1968), 643.

"Things in the Womb of Time":
Ideas of American Independence, 1633 to 1763

I N January 1776 Thomas Paine's *Common Sense* appeared, the first
thoroughly reasoned argument for immediate American independence from Great Britain. Paine was not an original thinker. His
strength as a political pamphleteer was his ability to articulate more
clearly—and in memorable, ringing phrases—what others had said and
were thinking. Paine asserted that "I have never met with a man, either
in England or America, who hath not confessed his opinion, that a
separation between the countries, would take place one time or other."[1]
Allowing for the pamphleteer's overstatement, Paine's observation of
the perception of inevitability was accurate. Indeed, even before the
crisis of the 1760s, the prospect of American independence had been a
matter of frequent comment. The discussion of separation from Britain,
especially after 1750, had provided a pool of arguments and a specification of conditions under which the event might happen, given the appropriate occasion.

In some respects, the recent insistence of historians upon the reluctance of the Americans to consider independence, coupled with the
reaction against so-called "whig" history that viewed everything in the
colonial period as prologue to revolution, has obscured the obvious.[2]
While colonial developments must be seen on their own merits and not
as acts of proto-revolution, many contemporary participants and observers regarded Anglo-American conflict leading to American independence as a central theme, particularly of the late colonial period.
Moreover, this conviction helped produce a climate of opinion that had

* Mr. Bumsted is a member of the Department of History, Simon Fraser University. He wishes to thank the Canada Council and the Simon Fraser President's
Research Fund for financial assistance that made the research and writing of this
article possible.
[1] [Thomas Paine], *Common Sense: Addressed to the Inhabitants of America*
(Philadelphia, 1776), 61.
[2] Bernhard Knollenberg, in his *Origin of the American Revolution: 1759-1766*
(New York, 1960), 16-20, vehemently denies any evidence of American separatist
intent before the 1760s. See also Bernard Bailyn, *The Ideological Origins of the
American Revolution* (Cambridge, Mass., 1967).

some influence in shaping British policy after the Peace of Paris.

The strong undercurrent of concern about, and anticipation of, eventual American separation from the Empire in the years before 1763 has seldom been properly recognized.[3] In part this is because the discussion rarely became a clearly focused debate. Instead, occasional comments of a variety of theorists, statesmen, and pamphleteers have been buried in forgotten writings. Moreover, the subject of American independence was usually raised in order to refute its likelihood. Most writers made reference to unnamed "theys," who feared such developments and then presented arguments against such anxieties. Seen in isolation, such refutations would seem to support the notion that few really believed in the eventuality.[4] Perhaps so. But the persistence of the denials, increasing in number, force, and coherence in the years immediately before 1763, suggests that many were prepared to entertain the possibility. In effect, these denials added up to little less than a prophecy waiting to be fulfilled.

Strong arguments could be adduced for eventual separation. The history of Greek and Roman colonization had suggested to men of the seventeenth century that colonies could become independent of the metropolis, and the eighteenth century added concrete areas of concern. Economic thinkers committed to mercantilistic ideas worried that colonies that ceased to remain sources of primary materials and became manufacturing centers would break their ties with the mother country. Colonial governors and British statesmen, struggling continually against the pretensions of American assemblies to legislative preeminence, feared that assemblies which were miniature Parliaments would cast off their "dependence" upon the British Parliament, and some saw independence as the result.[5] The growth of the colonies' population increased their

[3] One author who did recognize the theme was George Louis Beer, *British Colonial Policy, 1754-1765* (New York, 1907), 160-180. I am deeply indebted to his pioneer work.

[4] This, for example, is the position taken by the editors of the *Franklin Papers* in their discussion of Franklin's Canada pamphlet, *The Interest of Great Britain with Regard to her Colonies:* "While he [Franklin] discusses the argument that the retention of Canada might lead in time to the independence of the older colonies, he does so only to refute the charge, and he urges that fair and considerate treatment by Great Britain would effectively prevent any move toward separation." Leonard W. Labaree *et al.*, eds., *The Papers of Benjamin Franklin* (New Haven, Conn., 1959-   ), IX, 59.

[5] It is not clear that the many who wrote about the problems of American "dependence" all saw "independence" as the only alternative. Nor did everyone understand by "independence" what Tom Paine meant in 1776. But while the nuances of the terms are uncertain, the implication of American autonomy and separatism was clearly meant.

ability to fight their own battles, and the removal of the French threat in Canada was held by many to be fraught with danger to the imperial relationship.

In the minds of all who pondered the possibility of independence was the matter of timing. Paine was again not far wrong when he argued that "all men allow the measure, and vary only in their opinion of the time."[6] Here conceptualization played a major role. The British, after all, had not developed a very clear idea of Empire.[7] What they had were less theories than metaphors. As John Brooks has pointed out, British statesmen saw the colonial relationship in highly personalized terms.[8] The most common concept was that of the family. The metropolis became the "mother country," and the colonies her children. Most writers agreed that when the colonies had grown to "maturity," they must be treated as independent equals. This was what usually happened in the family: children grew up and made their own way in the world. Not all observers agreed, however, on the point when maturity was reached or on the stage of development of the colonies at any given time before 1763. Were they still infants? Were they now out of swaddling clothes and capable of doing some things for themselves? No one, not even Paine, argued that the colonies were full-grown, but in what stage of childhood were they?

Perhaps equally important, lurking in the background was the question of how one dealt with growing children. David Hume indicated the problem very well in his account of a conversation with Lord Bathurst in the early 1770s: "Nations, as well as Individuals, had their different Ages, which challeng'd a different Treatment. For Instance, My Lord, said I to the old Peer, you have sometimes, no doubt, given your Son a Whipping: and I doubt not, but it was well merited and did him much good: Yet you will not think proper at present to employ the Birch: The Colonies are no longer in their Infancy."[9] Hume himself thought the colonies still "in their Nonage," not yet ready for full adulthood. But given the prevalence of the metaphor, how a parent disciplined delinquent children and when they were recognized as grown were questions that, by the time of the Stamp Act, had become perhaps as vital for British statesmen as any economic or political theories.[10]

[6] *Common Sense*, 61.
[7] Richard Koebner, *Empire* (Cambridge, 1961); Klaus E. Knorr, *British Colonial Theories, 1570-1850* (Toronto, 1944).
[8] Sir Lewis Namier and John Brooke, *Charles Townshend* (London, 1964), 147.
[9] Ernest Campbell Mossner, *The Life of David Hume* (Edinburgh, 1954), 554.
[10] Edwin G. Burrows and Michael Wallace, "The American Revolution: The

Before 1763 only a few individuals on either side of the Atlantic were openly predicting American independence in a foreseeable future. Nevertheless, in the writings of imperial reformers of the 1750s and of political pamphleteers of the early 1760s, the specter had been raised, thoroughly discussed, and not laid to rest. No informed individual by 1763 could claim ignorance of the issues. Each time a writer refuted the possibility of separation, he added to the list of conditions under which it might occur. Implicit in denials that the Americans were populous enough, or powerful enough, or prosperous enough, or unhappy enough, was the thought that someday they might become so. Circumstances could change. Observers had argued in the years before 1763 that they were changing, and fear that such was the case was a central factor in British policy in the 1760s.

Almost from the first settlement of America, there had been sporadic discussion of the possibility of colonial separation, although it would take a century for scattered comments to attain some unity and coherence. As early as 1633 George Downing sought to silence English critics by categorically denying that New England would renounce Charles I, arguing that "it is a causeless fear without precedent that a colony planted in a strange land was ever so foolishly besotted as to reject the protection of their natural prince."[11] Others in the seventeenth century were less certain. Thomas Hobbes, in the *Leviathan*, described two types of "Plantations or Colonies":

They are either a Common-wealth of themselves, discharged of their subjection to their Soverain that sent them, (as hath been done by many Common-wealths, of ancient time,) in which case the Common-wealth from which they went, was called their Metropolis or Mother, and requires no more of them, than Fathers require of the Children, whom they emancipate and make free from their domestique government, which is Honour and Friendship; or else they remain united to their Metropolis, as were the Colonies of the people in Rome; and then they are no Common-wealths themselves, but Provinces, and parts of the Common-wealth that sent them.[12]

Ideology and Psychology of National Liberation," *Perspectives in American History*, VI (1972), 167-306.

[11] Beer, *British Colonial Policy*, 170.

[12] Thomas Hobbes, *Leviathan, Or the Matter, Forme and Power of a Commonwealth, Ecclesiasticall and Civil* (London, 1651), 131.

300

Also employing the metaphor of the family, James Harrington recognized in a primitive way that colonies, like children, passed through stages of development. "For the Colonies in the Indies," he wrote, "they are yet babes, that cannot live without sucking the breasts of their mother-Cities, but such as, I mistake, if when they come of age, they do not wean themselves; which causeth me to wonder at Princes that delight to be exhausted in that way."[13] Thus the two giants of English political theory in the mid-seventeenth century employed concepts of an imperial family and ultimate separation, relying upon classical precedents to support their views.

301

The question of colonial independence soon left the realm of abstract political theory and became part of the concrete course of events. Much of America, particularly the New England colonies, became virtually independent states during the English Civil War, and Oliver Cromwell and the later Stuarts alike sought to restore them to a proper dependency. A deep-seated suspicion of New England's ambitions and objectives affected the making of British colonial policy. Warnings of an independent colonial spirit came regularly from officials in both England and America.[14] Reports such as one in 1709 that in Massachusetts "some of the leading men already begin to talke of shaking off their subjection to the Crown of England" were to a large extent merely exercises in self-justification and bureaucratic paranoia.[15] In part they also reflected the real difficulties of governing colonists who were divided by an ocean from the metropolis.[16] In New York, Gov. Robert Hunter formulated such concerns as a constitutional issue that would be raised continually in the eighteenth century. New York's Assembly, wrote Hunter to the secretary of state in England, insisted upon "all the previledges of a House of Commons, and Stretching them even beyond what they were ever Imagined to be there, should the Counsill by the same Rule lay Claime to the rights and priviledges of a house of Peers, here is a body politik Coordinate with (and claiming equal powers) and Consequently Independant of the Great Counsill of the Realme."[17] Legislative in-

---

[13] James Harrington, *The Oceana of James Harrington, esq.* (Dublin, 1731), 20. This was subsequently quoted by John Adams in *Novanglus*. See Charles Francis Adams, ed., *The Works of John Adams,* IV (Boston, 1851), 104.

[14] Beer, *British Colonial Policy,* 166ff.

[15] Roger Mompesson to the earl of Nottingham, July 4, 1709, *ibid.,* 167-168.

[16] French officials had similar comments about the population of Acadia, and in 1704 one report to Paris noted that the Acadians "lived like true republicans, not acknowledging royal or judicial authority." John Bartlet Brebner, *New England's Outpost: Acadia before the Conquest of Canada* (New York, 1927), 47.

[17] Beer, *British Colonial Policy,* 166-167.

dependence seemed to Hunter and other governors quite consistent with the general colonial tendency to autonomy, and they easily became convinced that their struggles with the assemblies were part of this larger problem.[18]

Colonial officials were not alone in worrying about potential American separation. A number of British writers, particularly although not exclusively economists, devoted attention to the possibility after 1688. Charles D'Avenant, friend of Shaftesbury, self-proclaimed Old Whig, and pioneer economist, turned in one of his major works, *Discourses on the Public Revenue,* to the plantation trade and prospective colonial independence.[19] The colonies were a useful place to which to exile troublemakers, said D'Avenant, and "this can be no damage to the state, if they consist of men turbulent and unquiet at home, unless it can be made out, that they acquire abroad such riches, power and dominion, as may render them, in process of time, formidable to their mother country." He went on to contend that the colonies "are a spring of wealth to this nation," and insisted "that it must be through our own fault and misgovernment, if they become independent of England." Corrupt governors, "supine negligence," and mistaken measures "may indeed drive them, or put it into their heads to erect themselves into independent commonwealths."[20]

To assure imperial harmony and prosperity D'Avenant urged that the colonial commercial growth be encouraged and that military, especially naval, power be retained in English hands, unless its use by the colonists were absolutely necessary for their defense. Like many other British commentators, he concluded, "Colonies are a strength to their mother kingdom, while they are under good discipline, while they are strictly made to observe the fundamental laws of their original country, and while they are kept dependent on it." Although this sentence verged on the family metaphor, D'Avenant preferred to see empire in terms of the human body. If not kept dependent, colonies were "worse than members lopped from the body politic, being indeed like offensive arms wrested from a nation, to be turned against it as occasion shall serve."

---

[18] Perfectly employing the family metaphor, Hunter indicated his preference for future colonial policy: "In the Infancy of the Colonies the Crown was lavish of priviledges as necessary for their nurseing, but a full grown boy makes commonly but Indifferent use of that Indulgence requisite toward a Child." *Ibid.,* 167n.

[19] D'Avenant or Davenant (1656-1714) was a son of the poet reputed to have sheltered Milton. He served as commissioner of the excise from 1678 to 1689. *Dictionary of National Biography,* s.v. "Davenant, Charles."

[20] Charles D'Avenant, *Discourses on the Publick Revenues* (London, 1697), Pt. II, Discourse III, "On the Plantation-Trade," 8-11.

But he emphasized that he did not believe that growing and prosperous colonies were a danger to Britain, at least while they remained British in blood and trade. "Nothing," wrote D'Avenant, "but such an arbitrary power as shall make them desperate, can bring them to rebel."[21] D'Avenant did not pause to consider whether such views might contribute to putting ideas of independence into colonial heads, yet they constituted, in effect, an unintended invitation to rebellion. If the colonists became desperate—if they could demonstrate or at least convince themselves that the power of Britain was arbitrary—the unthinkable could occur.

D'Avenant anticipated much of the eighteenth-century writing on colonial policy before the Stamp Act, particularly by critics of the government. One such work—and one that the colonists were able to employ in opposing arbitrary power—was *Cato's Letters*, written between 1720 and 1723 by John Trenchard and Thomas Gordon.[22] The authors of *Cato's Letters* devoted an entire number (106) to the themes that D'Avenant had raised a generation earlier. After justifying the possession of colonies in familiar mercantilist terms, Cato moved on to indict the government for colonial mismanagement. The limitations of Cato's position were clearly stated in the opening sentence of the critique: "I would not suggest so distant a Thought, as that any of our Colonies, when they grow stronger, should ever attempt to wean themselves from us; however, I think too much Care cannot be taken to prevent it, and to preserve their Dependencies upon their Mother-Country."[23] The government's policy was wrong only because it did not maintain the plantations in a properly dependent relationship.

Employing the family metaphor, Cato recognized a potential thrust toward independence, especially when the colonial children found it to their advantage to separate from "those who use them ill." After all, wrote Cato, "All Nature points out that Course. No Creatures suck the Teats of their Dams longer than they can draw Milk from thence, or can provide themselves with better Food: Nor will any Country continue their Subjection to another, only because their Great-Grandmothers were acquainted." Cato saw two ways to keep colonies from "throwing off their Dependence." One was to keep the act out of their power

303

---

[21] *Ibid.*

[22] For Trenchard (1662-1723) and Gordon (d. 1750) see *DNB* and Caroline Robbins, *The Eighteenth-Century Commonwealthman: Studies in the Transmission, Development and Circumstance of English Liberal Thought from the Restoration of Charles II until the War with the Thirteen Colonies* (Cambridge, Mass., 1959).

[23] *Cato's Letters: Or, Essays on Liberty, Civil and Religious, and Other Important Subjects*, IV, 5th ed., corrected (London, 1748), 6.

through the use of force. The other was to keep it out of their will "by using them well" and by permitting them to become prosperous in ways not prejudicial to the mother country.[24]

Force would not do. Neatly combining the "country" objections to standing armies and political corruption, Cato observed that the maintenance of a body of troops sufficient to overawe the colonists, under the direction of governors who were out to make their fortunes, would be disastrous. Yet the mainland colonies, if not prevented by forceful methods, would naturally grow and prosper and must in a century become populous states. It was therefore essential that the interests of colonies and mother country be kept in harmony. This was no easy task, said Cato, for "the Interest of Colonies is often to gain Independency; and is always so when they no longer want Protection, and when they can employ themselves more advantageously, than in supplying Materials of Traffick to others: And the Interest of the Mother-Country is always to keep them dependent, and so employed."[25] Cato thus provided a theme for the imperial relationship of the eighteenth century, one which before 1763 was perhaps more clearly recognized by British politicians and colonial experts than by the American colonials. The fundamental interests of colonies and mother country were naturally in conflict; the two major areas of confrontation were commerce and war. Colonies remained dependent only while military and economic considerations demanded such status. When these circumstances changed, Cato implied, the colonies and the metropolis would be set on a collision course.

Like Cato, most British mercantilist writers tended to deny the likelihood of American separation, provided certain conditions were met. Joshua Gee in *The Trade and Navigation of Great-Britain Considered* (1729) worried that the colonies would "set up for themselves, and cast off the English Government" only if colonial manufacturing were encouraged. Daniel Defoe argued in *A Plan of the English Commerce* (1730) that fears of colonial independence were "preposterous" because of the economic dependence of the colonies on Great Britain. Colonial prosperity did not alarm him, because it meant increased trade and "in particular an Encrease of the Consumption of our Manufactures."[26]

<hr/>

[24] *Ibid.*, 7.
[25] *Ibid.*, 8-9.
[26] Joshua Gee, *The Trade and Navigation of Great-Britain Considered* (London, 1729), 71. Gee (1698-1748) served as agent of Pennsylvania for some years and was active in colonial speculations. [Daniel Defoe], *A Plan of the English Commerce. Being a Compleat Prospect of the Trade of this Nation, as Well the Home Trade as the Foreign* (London, 1728), 361-363.

Nevertheless, both Gee and Defoe found concern over colonial separatism sufficiently widespread to require detailed refutation.[27]

The few colonials who dealt with the independence issue before the 1740s concentrated, like their British counterparts, on denial. Jeremiah Dummer in 1721 defended his native New England against charges that "their encreasing Numbers and Wealth, join'd to their great Distance from Britain, will give them an Opportunity in the Course of some Years, to throw off their Dependence on the Nation, and declare themselves a free State, if not curb'd in Time, by being made entirely subject to the Crown."[28] Dummer was responding to a periodic rethinking of colonial administration that had culminated in 1721 in a major report to the Board of Trade.[29] Significantly, the report, like most such official productions, argued for greater dependence without openly raising the question of independence. But Dummer, who was close to several officials on the Board of Trade, recognized that the Board's efforts to secure greater dependence rested implicitly on concern about potential independence. Dummer ridiculed such fears, arguing that poverty and differences among the colonies "in their Forms of Government, in their religious Rites, in their Emulation of Trade, and consequently in their Affections," made it impossible for them "to unite in so dangerous an Enterprize." Turning to the family image, he went on to add, "I may say, without being ludicrous, that it would not be more absurd to place two of his Majesty's Beef-Eaters to watch an Infant in the Cradle, that it don't rise and cut its Father's Throat, than to guard these weak infant Colonies, to prevent their shaking off the British Yoke."[30]

305

[27] In 1729 Martin Bladen (1680-1746), the leading voice on the Board of Trade, had argued in a memorandum to the duke of Newcastle that Nova Scotia settlement would provide defense against French encroachments and would "drain great Numbers of Inhabitants from New England, where they are daily aiming at an independency and very much Interfere with the Trade of their Mother Kingdom." A few years later Bladen defended the sugar duties in Parliament as something near absolute prohibition, "for in the way the northern colonies are, they raise the French islands at the expense of ours, and raise themselves also to[o] high, even to an independency." James A. Henretta, "Salutary Neglect": Colonial Administration under the Duke of Newcastle (Princeton, N. J., 1972), 96.

[28] Jeremiah Dummer, A Defence of the New-England Charters (Boston, 1721), 36-37. For information on Dummer (1681-1739) see Sheldon S. Cohen, "The Diary of Jeremiah Dummer," William and Mary Quarterly, 3d Ser., XXIV (1967), 397-422, and Charles L. Sanford, "The Days of Jeremy Dummer, Colonial Agent" (Ph.D. diss., Harvard University, 1952).

[29] E. B. O'Callaghan and Berthold Fernow, eds., Documents Relative to the Colonial History of the State of New York (Albany, N. Y., 1856-1887), V, 592-630.

[30] Dummer, Defence of the Charters, 36-37.

A decade after the publication of Dummer's *A Defence of the New-England Charters*, another colonial, James Logan of Pennsylvania, produced a lengthy manuscript essay on the state of the British plantations in America. Logan had long years of American experience in government and commerce which he attempted to impart to Robert Walpole, who was "too busily employ'd another way to mind Such Trifles." Although Logan's "Memorial"—an insightful analysis of the imperial relationship by a knowledgeable colonial—was mainly concerned with French encroachments on British territory, it concluded with a critique of British colonial policy in terms of the possibility of American separation. Logan saw the very multiplicity of colonial governments as a product of Britain's "Natural Policy to keep the several Colonies under distinct and independant Commands, the more effectually to Secure them from a Revolt from the Crown." This was one of the earliest arguments that colonial disunity was deliberately fostered by imperial policy. But, continued Logan, "those who Apprehend any probability of [revolt] for Several Ages to come, or while the Mother Countrys in Europe Maintain their Power at Home, indulge their Political Speculations without any just foundation." America would remain dependent for some time, so long as the colonies were "treated with Tenderness and Humanity and not Considered only as Slavishly Subservient to the Interest of the Countrey they came from." Only oppression to the point of making them incapable of self-support, wrote Logan, could provoke the desperation that would fuel rebellion.[31]

Logan offered interesting reasons to support his confidence in continued colonial loyalty. In the British plantations there were no noble and ancient families to lead a rebellion, and no large revenues to finance one. Moreover, he added, "while Canada is so near, they cannot Rebel." Emphasizing the French threat, Logan held that "it will Probably be the true Interest of both Britain and France to have each other's Colonies on the Continent Supported as the most Effective Check that could be thought of, to retain them on both sides in a sight of their Duty." Cato and others in England had stressed colonists' need for British military protection, but Logan gave a new twist to the argument. In so doing he added yet another condition to the list of those that might make separation possible. If French Canada were conquered, a substantial reason for subservience would be removed. Thus introduced

---

[31] Joseph C. Johnson, "A Quaker Imperialist's View of the British Colonies in America: 1732," *Pennsylvania Magazine of History and Biography*, LX (1936), 100, 127.

306

into the discussion of independence, the Gallic question would emerge as critical after the conquest of Canada in 1759.[32]

The decade of the 1730s was one of relative peace for England and her colonies, quieting many of the issues that had raised concern about independence. Conflict with assemblies, commercial rivalry, and military maneuvering did not cease, but the absence of great international struggle made them seem less urgent. In times of peace, assemblies could defy governors, and merchants break the navigation acts, without endangering the security of the Empire. Although Walpole's policies were not directly designed to pacify the colonists and their critics, they had such an effect. But the warhawks in Britain eventually triumphed, and the Empire entered a period of almost uninterrupted warfare that would unmistakably reveal and continually exacerbate the many strains between colonies and mother country.[33] Increasingly, men contemplated the possibility of American independence, and their anxieties, formerly expressed in scattered comments, acquired more coherent form, sharper focus, and far greater force.

307

In the 1740s the connection between the exigencies of war and eventual American independence became more clearly articulated. The governor of New York in 1741 reminded a recalcitrant Assembly that some in England thought the colonies eager for independence, leading the Assembly to answer that "We dare Vouch That not one single Person in it [the Assembly] has any such Thoughts or Desire, for under what Government can we be better Protected, or our Liberties and Properties so well secured?"[34] In Massachusetts, Gov. William Shirley warned the Board of Trade that illicit trade with the French "must be highly destructive . . . and finally weakening the Dependance which the British Northern Colonies ought to have upon their Mother Country."[35] Two years later Shirley attempted to gain British support for the New England attack on Louisbourg by arguing that if the colonies became restless and wanted independence, the Cape Breton fortress would be a useful check upon them. He added the disclaimer that

---

[32] *Ibid.*, 127-128. Benjamin Franklin, one of the major participants in the latter debate, made a copy of Logan's "Memorial" and was familiar with its arguments.

[33] A point made generally in Lawrence Henry Gipson, "The American Revolution as an Aftermath of the Great War for the Empire, 1754-1763," *Political Science Quarterly*, LXV (1950), 86-104.

[34] Beer, *British Colonial Policy*, 171n.

[35] Thomas C. Barrow, *Trade and Empire: The British Customs Service in Colonial America 1660-1775* (Cambridge, Mass., 1967), 153.

independence "seems to me from the observation I have been able to make up on the Spot, at the Distance of some Centuries farther off than, I have heard, it does to Some Gentlemen at home."[36] Yet Shirley unwittingly advanced arguments for the gentlemen at home. One such Cassandra at the center of British policy-making was the duke of Bedford, who expostulated to Newcastle in 1746 that it would be undesirable for colonial troops, so successful at Louisbourg, to take Canada on their own. An American conquest, said the duke, would create an "independence . . . in those provinces towards their mother country, when they shall see within themselves so great an army possessed in their own right by conquest, of so great an extent of country."[37] When the British decided not to employ their own troops, the invasion was cancelled.[38]

After Aix-la-Chapelle had restored the territorial status quo in America, the problem of American separatism focused in discussions by Josiah Tucker, one of the most influential economic thinkers of the mid-century in England, who predicted in 1749 that the British colonies in America would revolt if the time should come when they felt themselves economically self-sufficient. For the present, however, he thought the imperial relationship mutually beneficial.[39] About the same time, the Massachusetts-born Otis Little produced *The State of Trade in the Northern Colonies Considered*. In Britain to lobby for Nova Scotia settlement and a hard-money currency, Little argued for Nova Scotia in terms of expanding colonial markets: "By enlarging the Trade, and increasing the Number of Inhabitants in the Northern Colonies, their Demand and Abilities to pay for *British* goods would be proportionable." Almost as a matter of course, Little met the objection to colonial prosperity, that "great Care ought to be taken, lest those Colonies grow too powerful, and set up a Government of their own," by denying the existence of any such colonial ambition "whilst they enjoy the Freedom of *English* Subjects under so happy a Constitution."[40]

[36] Beer, *British Colonial Policy*, 171n.
[37] George Arthur Wood, *William Shirley, Governor of Massachusetts, 1741-1756: A History* (New York, 1920), 318.
[38] Arthur Buffinton, "The Canadian Expedition of 1746: Its Relation to British Politics," *American Historical Review*, XL (1939-1940), 552-580.
[39] Josiah Tucker, *Essay on Trade* . . . , 3d ed. (London, 1749), 93-96. For Tucker (1712-1799) see Robert Livingston Schuyler, ed., *Josiah Tucker: A Selection from His Economic and Political Writings* (New York, 1931), and Walter E. Clark, *Josiah Tucker, Economist* (New York, 1903).
[40] (London, 1748), 13, 11. For Little (1711/12-ca. 1754) see my biographical sketch in *Dictionary of Canadian Biography*, III, forthcoming.

Not everyone was as sanguine as Little about the constitutional happiness of the colonies. George Clinton, governor of New York, struggling with his Assembly, told the legislators in a speech written by Cadwallader Colden that in demanding "all the Privileges and Rights, of the House of Commons of *Great Britain*" they not only assumed the right to be a branch of the kingdom's legislature but denied "Dependence and Subjection on the Crown and Parliament." Clinton added that the Assembly must either admit the authority of Parliament over it or "you must think yourselves independent of the Crown of *Great-Britain*."[41] Governor James Glen of South Carolina was less theoretical in letters to the duke of Bedford. "Here," wrote Glen, "levelling principles prevail; the frame of civil government is unhinged; a governor, if he would be idolized, must betray his trust; . . . to preserve the dependence of America in general, the Constitution must be new modelled."[42] In its report on New York affairs to the Privy Council in 1751, the Board of Trade echoed Clinton and Glen: "There is nothing so essentially necessary to the preservation of his Maj'ty's Govern't in the American provinces, as the careful and strickt maintenance of the just prerogative, which is the only means by which those Colonies can be kept dependant on the mother Country, or the Governors themselves representing the Crown, maintain any power over their Assemblies, or any agreement with them."[13] The Board of Trade offered no solutions beyond "maintenance of the just prerogative," but the concern that its report represented produced a new round of attempts by colonial experts, mostly self-styled, to remodel the colonial constitution. War, reform, and American separatism were inextricably bound together in these efforts.

Proposals for constitutional reform in the colonies were hardly novel or unusual.[44] What was different in the 1750s was the clear articulation of the choice facing the British: institute reform (usually by strengthening the prerogative) or risk American separation. In two pamphlets of 1750 and 1751 Archibald Kennedy of New York called for British

[41] G. Clinton to New York Assembly, Oct. 13, 1747, in O'Callaghan and Fernow, eds., *N. Y. Col. Docs.*, VI, 630-631. For Colden's authorship see Alice Mapelsden Keys, *Cadwallader Colden: A Representative Eighteenth Century Official* (New York, 1906), 176.

[42] Eugene Irving McCormac, *Colonial Opposition to Imperial Authority during the French and Indian War*, University of California Publications in History, I (Berkeley, Calif., 1914), 9.

[43] O'Callaghan and Fernow, eds., *N. Y. Col. Docs.*, VI, 614.

[44] For examples see Albert Bushnell Hart and Edward Channing, eds., "Plans of Union, 1696-1780," *American History Leaflets*, 14 (1894), and Robert M. Calhoon, "William Smith Jr.'s Alternative to the American Revolution," *WMQ*, 3d Ser., XXII (1965), 105n.

action. The first of these, *Observations on the Importance of the Northern Colonies under Proper Regulations*, urged improved trade and, while not very specific about means, made explicit the consequences of inaction. If the British did not improve American trade, the colonies would have to manufacture, and "where People in such Circumstances are numerous and free, they will push what they think is for their Interest, and all restraining Laws will be thought Oppression; especially such Laws, as according to the Conceptions we have of *English Liberty*, they have no Hand in the contriving or making." Kennedy opposed restrictions on trade, for *"Liberty and Encouragement are the Basis of Colonies."*[45] He concluded his pamphlet by reprinting almost in entirety the passages from *Cato's Letters* on potential American independence. The following year Kennedy called for colonial union by act of Parliament in a pamphlet misleadingly entitled *The Importance of Gaining and Preserving the Friendship of the Indians to the British Interest, Considered*. His intent, he wrote, was to offer hints for improving the constitution of the colonies in hopes that there "are those amongst us, of Capacity, Leisure and publick Spirit, sufficient to model them into a proper Shape, for the perusal" of Parliament.[46] An appended anonymous letter from Philadelphia, written by Benjamin Franklin, endorsed Kennedy's call for colonial union but preferred a voluntary one "entered into by the Colonies themselves" to "one impos'd by Parliament."[46] Franklin's letter testified to the close contact many of the American reformers had with one another.[47]

Kennedy's efforts at colonial reform tended to employ the carrot rather than the stick, as his use of Cato suggests. But in his recognition of the possibility of American separatism he was well in tune with many who were less tolerant of American sensitivities. James Abercromby, for example, concluded his reform proposals of 1752 (circulated in manuscript in Britain) by arguing that the colonies were too divided to throw off their dependency, but might do so if measures were not taken to settle the question "whether they are to remain subjects or become confederates."[48] Perhaps the clearest synthesis of these warnings and

---

[44] Charles M. Andrews, *The Colonial Period of American History*, IV (New Haven, Conn., 1938), 411.

[45] [Archibald Kennedy], *Observations on the Importance of the Northern Colonies under Proper Regulations* (New York, 1750), 10, 12.

[46] [Archibald Kennedy], *The Importance of Gaining and Preserving the Friendship of the Indians to the British Interest, Considered* (New York, 1751), 7, 28. For an analysis of Kennedy's career see Milton M. Klein, "Archibald Kennedy: Imperial Pamphleteer," in Lawrence H. Leder, ed., *The Colonial Legacy*, Vol. II: *Some Eighteenth-Century Commentators* (New York, 1971), 75-105.

[47] The circle of acquaintanceship and correspondence included William Douglass in Boston, Kennedy and Colden in New York, Franklin in Philadelphia, and John Mitchell in Virginia. Except for Franklin, all were Scotsmen. Douglass, Colden, and Mitchell had attended the University of Edinburgh.

counsels in the 1750s was provided by Henry McCulloh, a Scotsman who had spent many years in government service in America, mostly in South Carolina. As a lower official involved in collecting a colonial revenue, McCulloh had found himself constantly squeezed between the complaints of governors whom he regarded as incompetent and the demands of colonial legislatures which he thought pretentious. Under fire from several directions, he had retired to Britain to recoup his position.[49] At the close of 1751 he submitted to the earl of Halifax a lengthy manuscript on colonial affairs, summarizing his thoughts and expressing his grievances.[50] Halifax seemed a particularly likely patron, since he was president of the Board of Trade and known to be interested in many of the problems the treatise considered. Halifax apparently brushed McCulloh away, but the manuscript ultimately appeared as four separate pamphlets in 1754, 1755, and 1757.[51] The original essay is perhaps more worthy of detailed consideration than the pamphlets, for it is more coherent and better organized.

311

McCulloh's main theme was that in the English colonies, unlike the French, there was "a continuing Clashing of Interest" and "alternatively both the Rights of the Crown and the liberties and properties of the Subject invaded and that in too many Cases without a possibility of redress." His aim was to reform colonial administration "so as to have an immediate dependance on their mother Country," while bridling governors and officers of the crown. Denying that he sought either "to

Charles G. Sellers, Jr., "Private Profit and British Colonial Policy: The Speculations of Henry McCulloh," *WMQ*, 3d Ser., VIII (1951), 535-551; James High, "Henry McCulloh, Progenitor of the Stamp Act, *North Carolina Historical Review*, XXIX (1952), 24-38; John Cannon, "Henry McCulloch and Henry McCulloh," *WMQ*, 3d Ser., XV (1958), 71-73. McCulloh was more than simply an abused civil servant; he was deeply involved in land speculation and political maneuvering in South Carolina and London. His patron was Martin Bladen.

Additional Manuscripts, 11514, 1-220, British Museum. I have in preparation a more detailed study of the pamphleteering activities of McCulloh briefly summarized here.

Lord John Russell, ed., *Correspondence of John, Fourth Duke of Bedford*, II (London, 1842), 150. McCulloh was recommended to Bedford by William Beckford, later Pitt's chief London lieutenant in the Commons. The pamphlets were *General Thoughts on the Construction, Use and Abuse of the Great Offices: with a View to Some Further Discourses on the Same Subject* (London, 1754); *The Wisdom and Policy of the French in the Construction of their Great Offices, So as Best to Answer the Purposes of Extending their Trade and Commerce, and Enlarging their Foreign Settlements. With Some Observations in Relation to the Disputes Now Subsisting between the English and French Colonies in America* (London, 1755); *A Miscellaneous Essay Concerning the Courses Pursued by Great Britain in the Affairs of the Colonies: With Some Observations on the Great Importance of Our Settlements in America, and the Trade Thereof* (London, 1755); *Proposals for Uniting the English Colonies on the Continent of America. So as to Enable Them to Act with Force and Vigour Against their Enemies* (London, 1757). Although published anonymously, all the pamphlets include large sections from the 1751 manuscript known to be by McCulloh.

invade the Liberties of his Majestys American Subjects or to restrain the
prerogatives of the Crown," McCulloh declared that "the only Design
of this Essay is to demonstrate the necessity of keeping the Colonies
within due Bounds and in a proper dependence on their Mother Country . . . and to the protecting of the Subjects from Acts of power in the
Governours of the Plantations."[52] In the background, of course, was
McCulloh's concern with the French threat to the British colonies.

Instead of disparaging French government in America, McCulloh
suggested that it be emulated.[53] He was particularly impressed with the
French administrative organization, which provided a regular plan of
control for colonial officials and made the crown the unchallenged
center of colonial government. The British constitution had been formed
before colonies existed, and therefore "provision for the Government
of our distant Colonies . . . was left to be done by us—according as the
nature and circumstance of our Affairs require the same to be Amended
or Altered." McCulloh saw many weaknesses in the administration of
British America. Governors ignored royal instructions and could not
easily be brought to answer for their actions. Charter colonies had
assumed "Powers altogether inconsistent with that dependance which
they owe to their Mother Country." The absence of an "established
Rule of Action," and limitations on the rights of colonial assemblies
generally, produced a situation in which "the Governours have too
often formed themselves with particular parties in Order by their
Interest and Support to enlarge his prerequisites and profits, and the
moment he becomes the head of such a Party he must then enter into
their Views and Measures, and if needfull, make the business of the
Crown, Subservient thereto." The result was that colonial governments
were frequently prompted "to Act in Opposition to His Majesties
measures."[54]

McCulloh's analysis was not simply critical; he also had some positive
suggestions. Colonial administration and trade regulation needed reform
by act of Parliament. Regular rules and proceedings through a Council
of Trade should be adopted, following the French system. Suggesting
that the sugar duty be reduced by one-third to increase trade and provide
revenue for colonial defense, McCulloh also recommended parliamentary
enactment of a stamp tax to raise a fund which would "be Applyed
only to the Security and Advantage of the Colonies under the Manage-

---

[52] Add. MSS, 11514, 11, 12, 13-14, Brit. Museum.
[53] *Ibid.*, 17. This was an important theme in the writings of the 1750s which I
hope to expand in another piece.
[54] *Ibid.*, 70-71, 85, 109, 123-126.

ment of the said Council of Trade."[55] Part of the justification of these measures was military. If England acted through parliamentary reform, said McCulloh in 1751, France could be beaten.

In later publications McCulloh linked the French menace to the dangers of colonial union and independence. Attributing the information to an unnamed French officer, he wrote in 1755 of a French scheme "to use their utmost endeavours to make themselves Masters of the *English Islands* in the *West-Indies,* and to encourage the *English Colonies* on the Continent of *America* to unite and form a Republican Government; . . . Such Schemes appear at present to be wild and extravagent, yet there are many things in the Womb of Time, which may favour the ambitious Views of *France* in such Enterprises." Unless abuses were corrected, prophesied McCulloh, the result would be the "Foundation of a kind of Independency in the Colonies on the Continent of *America.*"[56]

Although no "Commonwealthman," McCulloh was not an unyielding supporter of the royal prerogative. In his 1751 manuscript and in a subsequent pamphlet he emphasized that

Experience hath shown, that it is extremely difficult to enforce the Execution of any Law made contrary to the general Bent and Disposition of the People; but how much more so must it be to enforce a Law made here, and to put in Execution in *America,* not only contrary to the general Bent and Disposition of the People, but likewise contrary to the very Genius and Constitution of some of their Governments; wherefore, in passing Laws of this Nature, 'tis most humbly submitted, whether it may be more proper, and better answer the End thereby proposed, so to form the law, as that the People there should not have too great a Temptation to resist, and act contrary to it.[57]

McCulloh thought he understood what Americans were willing to

---

[55] *Ibid.,* 163, 173, 179. While any effort to attribute specific colonial reforms to particular individuals is fraught with danger, it is worth emphasizing that McCulloh was pushing for the principal provisions of both the Sugar Act and the Stamp Act as early as 1751. Recent efforts to reduce the importance of McCulloh's later influence upon these measures—Franklin B. Wickwire, *British Subministers and Colonial America, 1763-1783* (Princeton, N. J., 1966), 111-113, for example—have not recognized the early date of McCulloh's first proposals.

[56] *The Wisdom and Policy of the French,* 127-129. Ellis Huske, *The Present State of North-America* (London, 1755), 63, refuted such fears. Malachy Postlethwayt, *Britain's Commercial Interest Explained and Improved* . . . (London, 1757), 517, picked up this report and recirculated it.

[57] Add. MSS, 11514, Brit. Museum; *Miscellaneous Essay,* 86.

accept in the 1750s, and perhaps he was right.[58] He sought reform to mitigate the threat of American independence.

The mid-1750s brought a new sense of urgency to imperial matters, and continued uncertainty among imperial politicians. The French were challenging Britain in the Ohio backcountry and elsewhere in America. Many reformers were calling for colonial unification, and the Albany Congress of 1754 produced a specific proposal. One of the major reasons for British lack of enthusiasm for the Albany Plan of Union was the concern, voiced to Newcastle by the Speaker of the House of Commons, that a bill for colonial union would encourage considerable debate over the "ill consequence to be apprehended from uniting too closely the northern colonies with each other, an Independency upon this country to be feared from such an union."[59] Such fears of colonial independence soon made their way to America. A London correspondent reported in the *Maryland Gazette* that "some persons have been apprehensive, that our Colonies and Plantations in America might in Time shake off their Dependence upon us, and set up for themselves." Another London observer whose comments were printed in America explained the British dilemma well: "The Americans are doubtless too thirsty after power; and perhaps we are too suspicious of its uses. . . . Could we not upon mature consideration find some method of arming them with power without alluring them by the specious bait of independence?"[60]

Those who advocated an all-out military effort against the French sensed that the mother country was constrained by fear lest the colonies become too powerful. When he pressed for an invasion of Canada in 1755, Governor Shirley attempted to assuage such concerns:

Apprehensions have been entertain'd, that they [the colonies] will in time unite to throw off their Dependency upon their Mother Country,

[58] McCulloh opposed the Stamp Act as finally promulgated, partly because it failed to meet his specifications. See Jack P. Greene, " 'A Dress of Horror': Henry McCulloh's Objections to the Stamp Act," *Huntington Library Quarterly*, XXVI (1962-1963), 253-262.

[59] Alison Gilbert Olson, "The British Government and Colonial Union, 1754," *WMQ*, 3d Ser., XVII (1960), 31. As Olson points out, "1754 was a year in which English fear of an American revolt was enjoying one of its periodic revivals." *Ibid.* William Knox subsequently saw 1755 as the date when "a general disposition to independence of this country prevailed throughout the whole." *Extra Official State Papers*, II (London, 1789), 11.

[60] *Maryland Gazette*, July 10, 1755; *New York Gazette, or Weekly Post-Boy*, Jan. 19, 1756.

and set up one General Government among themselves; But if it is consider'd, Sir, how different the present Constitutions of their respective Governments are from each other; how much the Interests of some of them clash, and how opposite their Tempers are; such a Coalition among them will seem highly improbable, at all Events, they could not maintain súch an Independency, without a Strong Naval Force, which it must forever be in the Power of Great Britain to hinder them from having.[61]

Most of the same arguments were employed by the anonymous author of *The State of the British and French Colonies in North America,* published in London that same year.

315

The author of the *State* was appalled by colonial selfishness and disunity. "The colonies have, in reality, in many cases," he wrote, "acted as if they thought themselves so many independent states, under their respective charters, rather than as provinces of the same empire: which consideration necessarily requires a union of the parts, for security of the whole." If the colonies would not themselves unite, it was in the power of Parliament to unite them. Why, indeed, had not Parliament acted already? His answer was that disunion was part of a continuing British policy of *divide et impera* initiated by former administrations for fear of "the danger, in an united state, of their throwing off dependence and setting up for themselves." This would not happen, however, unless the colonies were rich, united in their interests, and "driven to that extremity, by usage which would make Britons themselves impatient of subjection." Even under these conditions, rebellion could not succeed as long as the colonies lacked a fleet and Britain had "one to restrain them." In such circumstances, however, the situation would be highly dangerous, for if the colonies did revolt, they would not do so "with design to set up for themselves," but "would be under a necessity to seek the protection of some other power." The unidentified other power obviously was France. Genuinely independent former colonies would continue to trade with Britain, but if they were to fall under French "protection," Britain would be deprived "intirely of those rich branches of commerce, and both their wealth and power would be turned against her."[62] All this fit very well with the scheme of McCulloh's anonymous French officer.

According to the author of the *State,* nothing more confirmed the colonies in the opinion that Britain sought to "keep them low" than

---

[61] Beer, *British Colonial Policy,* 171n.
[62] *State of the British and French Colonies,* 57-58.

the governors and other officers sent to America. Needy persons had filled their purses and enriched themselves in trade, while acting prejudicially to the colonies and sending home false information. The anonymous writer cited Father Charlevoix and Cadwallader Colden in support of his charges, which had overtones of both Cato and McCulloh. Adopting the family metaphor, the author concluded that "want of care in the parents begat want of care in the children: and this was the rise of the present disorders in the colonies." Harmony between Great Britain and her colonies was essential, and "a good mother seldom fails to have good children." The colonists did not think of themselves as aliens who had forfeited their British rights by removal to America; they acknowledged the king and enriched the power and dominion of Britain, so that "they ought not to be thought presumptuous, if they consider themselves upon an equal footing with us, or treated the worse, because they will be Englishmen." As happened so often, the family metaphor and political vocabulary became confused. What sort of family did the author envision, where "good children" dependent upon their parents were also equals? In the end, the concept of the family dominated over the "rights of Englishmen." The author of the *State* employed the metaphor to provide an ultimate perspective on the colonial situation:

Britain the political parent of her colonies (like a natural one, who intends to raise a progeny for advantage, strength and power) in their infancy should indulge, nourish, and support them. As they encrease and become capable of helping themselves and benefiting their mother country, they should be taught the obligations they owe her: that all their particular and heriditary rights and privileges, are derived from her: that they are bound to obey her laws; and that restraints laid on them are intended for mutual advantage.[63]

The concept, while perhaps muddled, was clearly paternal.

Like Henry McCulloh, the author of the *State* wanted colonial union by act of Parliament and increased colonial revenues from sugar duties or a land tax to support the war effort. Citing an unnamed American correspondent, he argued that "none of these taxes . . . would be much disliked in America." The French must first be subdued, but after victory the British should "apply seriously to reform abuses within, and put the Colonies on a footing which may prevent their falling into the same unhappy circumstances any more."[64]

[63] *Ibid.*, 59-64, 129.
[64] *Ibid.*, 146-147.

Discussion of potential American independence was not confined within the British Empire. Between 1753 and 1761 the Swedish botanist Peter Kalm, who had toured America in the late 1740s, published his three-volume *En Resa Til Norra America* in Stockholm. Kalm saw British restrictions on colonial commerce and the increasing number of non-British colonists, who had "no particular attachment to Old England," as centripetal influences. "I have been told by Englishmen, and not only by such as were born in America but also by those who came from Europe," wrote Kalm, "that the English colonies in North America, in the space of thirty or fifty years, would be able to form a state by themselves entirely independent of Old England." He saw the French menace as the principal factor preventing "the connection of the colonies with their mother country from being quite broken off," and questioned whether England ever seriously intended to conquer Canada, as the proximity of the French deterred the colonies from seceding.[65] As Kalm indicated, most of these observations reflected opinions given him by the colonials whom he had met in his travels.

One of Kalm's hosts (and undoubtedly one of his informants) was Dr. John Mitchell, whose *The Contest in America between Great Britain and France* was published in London in 1757. Like many another physician in America in the eighteenth century, Mitchell was a Scotsman with an Edinburgh education.[66] He had considerable intellectual and scientific pretensions, and an extended acquaintance with others who shared them. It was he who had recommended Kalm to Benjamin Franklin.[67] Given such intellectual interchange, it was hardly surprising that many colonials could agree on what constituted critical imperial issues, including the fear of American independence. In the preface to *The Contest* Mitchell criticized "the false and groundless notion that seems to influence many people's opinions and conduct with regard to the colonies, . . . the fear of their rebelling, and throwing off their dependance on Britain." He cited Joshua Gee on this point and added some more contemporary arguments. Current experience invalidated

317

[65] Adolph B. Benson, ed., *Peter Kalm's Travels in North America*, I (New York, 1966), 138-140.
[66] For biographical details on Mitchell (1690?-1768) see Raymond Phineas Stearns, *Science in the British Colonies of America* (Urbana, Ill., 1970), 539-554; Lyman Carrier, "Dr. John Mitchell, Naturalist, Cartographer, and Historian," *Annual Report of the American Historical Association*, I (1918), 201-219; and Theodore Hornberger, "The Scientific Ideas of John Mitchell," *Huntington Lib. Qtly.*, X (1946-1947), 277-296.
[67] Benjamin Franklin to Cadwallader Colden, Sept. 29, 1748, in Labaree et al., eds., *Franklin Papers*, III, 319.

fears of American independence. How could the colonists withstand "the whole force and naval power of Britain" if they could not successfully resist "a few ragamuffians in Canada"? British concern over possible American independence, which Mitchell assumed to be global, was most "dangerous," especially when coupled with a policy which permitted the continuation of French power in order to keep the colonies "in awe." In perhaps the first direct refutation of the argument that it was in Britain's best interest to let France retain Canada, Mitchell disparaged the view that the French would "become an auxiliary to Britain, to preserve its colonies, trade and commerce!" Much more likely, "if our colonies were inclinable to rebel, France would both encourage them to it, and support them in it; which she may easily do by having an influence over them." Mitchell did not object to the presence of France in North America, however, so long as it was kept within bounds.[68]

Although he denied the possibility of American separation in the foreseeable future, Mitchell was quite prepared to produce arguments that fit with British fears. He was also willing to suppose that the Americans might eventually seek independence. Therefore, the colonies must be established on "such a footing, as to secure their dependance hereafter, when it may be in danger perhaps." Power was not the source of jealousy, but manufactures were critical. Manufacturing competition, Mitchell insisted, would be "the first cause of a rupture between Britain and her colonies, if ever any such thing happens." The conclusion that Mitchell drew from this assertion was an interesting one, anticipating in part the position Franklin would take three years later in his famous Canada pamphlet. The colonies would grow in population, and so some other employment besides manufacturing must be provided. Mitchell suggested encouragement of raw materials such as hemp, flax, silk, and naval stores. This would give Britain what it needed, promote colonial prosperity, and keep the colonies in a dependent economic status. Lurking in the background as a clinching argument, but not taken by Mitchell to its logical conclusion, was the notion that since manufactures were the product of labor, and commodities were the product of land, the more land America had the better. Mitchell went so far as to contend that the French not be permitted to prevent the Americans from expanding, but he did not insist that Britain's true interest was to acquire all of Canada.[69] Franklin and others would add that refinement later.

---

[68] *Contest in America*, xxi-xxii.

[69] *Ibid.*, xxiii-xxvii. William Franklin, accompanying his father in England, sent Isaac Norris a copy of Mitchell's book in late 1757. Labaree *et al.*, eds., *Franklin*

Mitchell's work was only one of a number of tracts on America published in London at this time.[70] To most Englishmen, the colonies were the reason for the French war and were expected to be a central theater of it. Clearly the colonies had to be defended, and justifications for defending them were often linked with proposals for reforming them. One example among many was *A Letter to a Member of Parliament, on the Importance of the American Colonies, and the Best Means of Making Them Most Useful to the Mother Country,* published in London in 1757. Although the *Letter's* main aim was to justify the expense of settlement in Nova Scotia, the writer made a number of wide-ranging observations and suggestions on American affairs. None of these was original, and their appearance in this pamphlet indicates the wide currency of certain ideas. Instead of a "pernicious" duty on foreign molasses, the author wanted a reasonable one, which he was sure would be met by Americans with "a Chearful Obedience." A penny sterling per acre tax on waste lands in America would prevent land speculation. Reform in Nova Scotia particularly and in America generally was necessary, he concluded, "to eradicate the unnatural Suspicion of their [the colonies] becoming one Time or other independent; with as much Reason, a Man may refuse to build or repair a valuable House, etc, for fear of its being burned."[71]

Discussion of potential American independence had become so commonplace that when teen-aged Arthur Young produced a potboiler on America in 1759 in return for £10 credit from his bookseller, all the old arguments were trotted out. Young particularly cannibalized Mitchell's *The Contest.* An expanded and secure American territory should be encouraged to grow needed agricultural produce rather than engage in manufacturing, and Young's list of suggested products improved even on Mitchell's lengthy one. With a proper commercial policy, Young added, British fears of American independence would prove foolish.[72]

The year 1759 saw the British victorious everywhere. Quebec and Guadeloupe both fell, stimulating debate on the nature of the impending

319

Papers, VII, 281n. Martin Bladen had earlier made this argument for Nova Scotia. See n. 27.

[70] For a general discussion of the publications see Lawrence C. Wroth, *An American Bookshelf 1755* (Philadelphia, 1934), esp. 20-32.

[71] *Letter to a Member of Parliament,* 12, 17, 23.

[72] Arthur Young, *Reflections on the Present State of Affairs at Home and Abroad* (London, 1759), 10ff. For Young's dealings with his bookseller see M. Betham-Edwards, ed., *The Autobiography of Arthur Young with Selections from his Correspondence* (London, 1898), 24.

peace and the future of the Empire in America. The wide-reaching discussion in the British press from 1759 to 1761, which has usually been labeled the "Canada-Guadeloupe" debate, provided an opportunity to collect and focus all the arguments of the past century relating to America. The leading pamphleteers and polemicists did not miss their opening, and most self-styled colonial experts had their say either in print or in memorials to the ministers. It is simply untrue, therefore, that in the years immediately preceding the Stamp Act the British had not given serious thought to the American colonies and to colonial policy. Nor is it true that the British thinking proceeded in naive ignorance of the explosive possibilities in America. A number of pamphleteers dealt in the years 1759 to 1761 with the subject of potential American separation. Most still denied the possibility, but there were open predictions of independence, and the denials often conveyed a new spirit of American defiance.

Although not the opening shot of the debate over Canada, the work that triggered the discussion of American independence appeared in January 1760 as *Remarks on the Letter Address'd to Two Great Men.*[73] The *Letter Addressed to Two Great Men, on the Prospect of Peace* (1759) had insisted that since North America had been the center of the war, all territory taken there by the British should be retained at the peace. More important, the *Letter* had argued that Canada was essential to colonial security and that the bartering of territory on the American continent for European advantage would be strongly criticized by the colonies. Although written by a dependent of a leading politician out of power, the *Letter* seems to have reflected fairly accurately the leanings of the ministry.[74]

The authorship of the answering *Remarks on the Letter* is uncertain. Contemporaries attributed it either to William Burke, a courtesy "cousin" of Edmund and since September 1759 secretary and register for Guade-

[73] For a brief summary of the issues see John M. Bumsted, "Thomas Jefferys's *History of the French Dominions*," in Leder, ed., *Colonial Legacy*, II, 141-161, esp. 154-157. The generalizations on the debate which follow are based on my full-length study of it, currently in preparation.

[74] The standard bibliography of the debate is Clarence Walworth Alvord, *The Mississippi Valley in British Politics: A Study of the Trade, Land Speculation, and Experiments in Imperialism Culminating in the American Revolution*, II (Cleveland, 1917), 253-264, supplemented by C. E. Fryer, "Further Pamphlets for the Canada-Guadeloupe Controversy," *Mississippi Valley Historical Review*, IV (1917-1918), 227-230. These bibliographies are extremely limited, hardly reflecting the extent of the debate. Alvord's listing of 65 pamphlets can be more than doubled, and both he and Fryer omitted all consideration of the newspaper and periodical controversies.

loupe, or to Charles Townshend, the brilliant but erratic young politician who was known as an American specialist.[75] Whoever the author, he responded vehemently to the insistence of the *Letter to Two Great Men* that the colonies would oppose a decision to return Canada to the French. He hoped this opinion was misinformed, but if it were correct—"if our *American* Colonies should be so absurd and ungrateful to tell us, after all the Blood and Treasure expended in their Cause, that we do nothing, if we do not make Conquests for them"—then, the author added truculently, "they must be taught a Lesson of greater Moderation." He then advanced arguments for retaining the sugar islands rather than the continental territory. The basic thrust of the position was commercial; the West Indies produced goods not in competition with Britain, while the continental colonies produced the same goods as Europe, and a continual unfavorable trade balance would eventually lead them to manufacturing in competition with the mother country. Almost as an afterthought, the author added a point that was evidently in general circulation. As the American colonies prospered, he said, "the Necessity of a Connection with *England*, with which they have no natural Intercourse by Reciprocation of Wants, will continually diminish." The ultimate result was obvious, and to retain Canada would only contribute to "the risque, and that perhaps in no very distant Period, of losing what we now possess." Even if Britain could retain all Canada, it should not do so, for a "Neighbour that keeps us in some Awe, is not always the worst of Neighbours."[76]

321

By the spring of 1760 three basic positions had emerged on the issues of British conquests and the forthcoming peace treaty. One emphasized territorial gains in North America. The nation had gone to war over American questions, and the French had to be eliminated from the continent for the security of the colonies. A second position focused on the Caribbean. Its arguments were largely commercial and naval, based upon traditional mercantilist notions of the value of colonies for their

[75] The *Letter* was probably penned by John Douglas (1721-1807), later bishop of Salisbury, who at this time was in the employ of William Pulteney, the earl of Bath. See *DNB* s.v. "Douglas, John." For ministerial views see the duke of Newcastle's letter to the earl of Hardwicke, Oct. 31, 1759, in Philip C. Yorke, *The Life and Correspondence of Philip Yorke, Earl of Hardwicke*, II (Cambridge, 1913), 242, and Max Savelle, *The Diplomatic History of the Canadian Boundary, 1749-1763* (New Haven, Conn., 1940), 92-98. The problem of the authorship of the *Remarks* and subsequent pamphlets expanding its arguments is a complex one with which I hope to deal in another place. For an attribution to Burke see *London Chronicle*, May 15-17, 1760; for one to Townshend see *Sentiments Relating to the Late Negotiation* (London, 1761), 12.
[76] *Remarks on the Letter*, 26, 29-43, 50-51.

raw materials and upon concern about the possibility of American manufacturing. It less dismissed the concern for American security than turned the argument on its head; to eliminate the French would be dangerous to the Empire. Advocates of a third position, not yet well defined, wanted all conquests retained. Whatever the argument, the discussants displayed a good deal of hostility, latent and overt, to the American continental colonies.[77]

The time seemed ripe for a strong statement from an American perspective, and this Benjamin Franklin sought to provide. Franklin had some assistance from Richard Jackson, a wealthy Englishman who served as agent for several colonies and in 1762 entered Parliament.[78] In England as agent for the Pennsylvania Assembly in its dispute with Thomas Penn, Franklin had for some months been publicly although anonymously concerned over the willingness of many Englishmen to sacrifice North American victories to other considerations.[79] Privately, he was also disturbed by "the Prevailing Opinion . . . among the Ministers and great Men here" that "the Colonies have too many and too great Privileges; and that it is not only the Interest of the Crown but of the Nation to reduce them."[80] Closely connected with the concern about possible American separation, this "prevailing opinion" had found expression in the debate over the conquered territories. Franklin was therefore anxious not only to argue for the security of North America, but to counter America's critics, whose charges, if not checked, could provide the rationale for attempts at tighter and more systematic imperial control. The pamphlet Franklin produced in 1760 clearly recognized a relationship between fears of separatism and future imperial policy.

As an answering pamphlet in an ongoing controversy, *The Interest of Great Britain Considered, With Regard to her Colonies* used arguments that were to some extent predetermined. Franklin had to respond to a number of deftly made points, many of them implicitly or explicitly hostile to the American colonies. He began by taking notice of the comments

[77] This paragraph will be fully elaborated in my forthcoming study of the debate.

[78] For the authorship of *The Interest of Great Britain Considered. With Regard to her Colonies* . . . (London, 1760) see Labaree *et al.*, eds., *Franklin Papers*, IX, 53-58. For Jackson (1722-1787) consult Michael G. Kammen, *A Rope of Sand: The Colonial Agents, British Politics, and the American Revolution* (Ithaca, N. Y., 1968), 22-25, and Sir Lewis Namier and John Brooke, *The History of Parliament: The House of Commons 1754-1790*, II (London, 1964), 669-672.

[79] Verner W. Crane, "Franklin's Political Journalism in England," *Journal of the Franklin Institute*, CCXXXIII (1942); Verner W. Crane, ed., *Benjamin Franklin's Letters to the Press, 1758-1775* (Chapel Hill, N. C., 1950), 9-17.

[80] Franklin to Isaac Norris, Mar. 19, 1759, in Labaree *et al.*, eds., *Franklin Papers*, VIII, 293.

of the *Remarks on the Letter* regarding security. North America was different from Europe because it was thinly settled, and therefore European rules could not be applied. If Canada were returned to France, forts would prevent French conquest but not the depredations of Indians or the expense of defending America in yet another war. Only retention of Canada could assure complete security. Franklin insisted that the colonies were at present perfectly contented, but "the safety of a considerable part of the state, and the interest of the whole are not to be trusted to the wisdom and vigor of future administrations, when a security is to be had more effectual, more constant, and much less expensive." Moreover, he suggested, "They who can be moved by the apprehension of dangers so remote as that of the future independence of our colonies" could scarcely be relied upon for sound decisions. To those who feared the rise of American manufactures, Franklin answered that "a people spred thro' the whole tract of country on this side the Mississippi, and secured by Canada in our hands, would probably for some centuries find employment in agriculture, and thereby free us at home effectually from our fears of American manufactures." Only the poor without land provided cheap labor for manufacturing.[81]

Franklin then addressed himself to an argument that obviously bothered him, although it had taken up little space in the *Remarks on the Letter*. As he summarized it, the claim was that "our present colonies are large enough and numerous enough, and the French ought to be left in North America to prevent their increase, lest they become not only *useless* but *dangerous* to Britain." Franklin agreed that America would increase greatly in population, perhaps outnumbering the British in a century. Until then, however, Britain would supply the colonies with manufactures and thus increase its trade and naval power. Repudiating the corporate metaphor, Franklin insisted that the human body and the body politic were different, since the human body had finite limits of growth, while the state could grow indefinitely. The conclusion he reached from this argument was expressed, almost inevitably, in terms of the family: "The mother being of full stature, is in a few years equal'd by a growing daughter: but in the case of a mother country and her colonies, it is quite different. The growth of the children tends to encrease the growth of the mother, and so the difference and superiority is longer preserv'd."[82] Equality of population would occur sooner but for the fact

323

---

[81] The pamphlet is printed in its entirety *ibid.*, IX, 59-100, and for convenience citations will be to this reprint. Quotations on pp. 71, 73. See also 61-62, 66-69, 71-72, 73-74.

[82] *Ibid.*, 77, 78-79.

that American expansion would stimulate British growth as well.

Having disposed of the argument of inutility, Franklin denied that the growth of the colonies would make them dangerous. The continental colonies were fourteen separate states with "different forms of government, different laws, different interests, and some of them different religious persuasions and different manners." Unity had been unattainable in the face of a common enemy; what reason then to fear lest the colonies unite to oppose a nation they loved so well and with which they had so many ties of "blood, interest and affection"? So far Franklin sounded like a typical colonial. He then turned, however, to "Commonwealthman" arguments. Only the "most grievous tyranny and oppression" could bring about colonial union. He cited European cases where this had happened, leaving the implication that the British had better not be oppressive. "While the government is mild and just, while important civil and religious rights are secure," he wrote, "such subjects will be dutiful and obedient." If checking American population growth were to become a goal of British policy, Franklin added sarcastically, why not an act of Parliament "enjoining the colony midwives to stifle in the birth every third or fourth child"?[83] This echo of Swift was hardly in the best spirit of dutiful obedience to the British government.

In his most famous aphorism from the Canada pamphlet Franklin wrote, "The waves do not rise, but when the winds blow." Eight years later he used the phrase as motto for a piece on the causes of the American discontents.[84] But in a sense it might equally well have been the motto for *The Interest of Great Britain* itself. In the course of countering the *Remarks on the Letter,* Franklin only increased the apprehensions of his English readers, for he converted a relatively brief reference to American independence into a major issue in the crucial debate over Canada. The length and sheer virtuosity of his defense of the Americans against the charge of separatism gave credence to the accusation. And Franklin's arguments were not designed to assuage British fears of the growth of colonial population and power. Franklin not only emphasized growth, but defiantly appended to the pamphlet his "Observations concerning the Increase of Mankind, Peopling of Countries, etc." As a subsequent pamphleteer (probably the author of *Remarks on the Letter*) legitimately commented, Franklin did not "seem in any part of his long treatise to disown what I all along advance, that Canada joined to what we have in America will prove our destruction, but he only shifts it off to a greater

[83] *Ibid.,* 90, 91, 94.
[84] *Ibid.,* 91 and n.

distance." In this sense, *The Interest of Great Britain* became virtually an antidefense of the American position.[85]

Franklin was quickly answered by a pamphlet attributed to William Burke. *A Copy of a Letter from a Gentleman in Guadaloupe, to his Friend in London* focused almost exclusively on the independence issue, showing that denials like Franklin's only stimulated greater anxieties. *A Copy of a Letter* fully recognized the ambiguity of Franklin's argument, and turned it against the American full force. If Canada could make the American colonies as rich and powerful as Franklin insisted, they would soon rival Great Britain. The author waxed lyrical about the extent, climate, soil, lakes and woods, and raw materials of America. "Such a Country at such a Distance could never remain long subject to Britain," he insisted. The colonists had been taught the art of war, "and they can furnish themselves with every thing in a few Years, without the Assistance of Britain." Even in the face of the French menace, the Americans had grumbled and complained against Britain, and without the French to check them, "you must keep 'a numerous Standing Army to over awe them." Everything strengthened the ability to revolt of "a People who must become more licentious from their Liberty and more factious from the Distance of the Power that rules them." The pamphlet concluded its jeremiad in ringing phrases:

> . . . One must be very little conversant in History, and totally unacquainted with the Passions and Operations of the human Mind, who cannot foresee those Events as clearly as any Thing can be discovered, that lyes concealed in the Womb of Time; it is no Gift of Prophesy, it is only the natural and unavoidable Consequence of such and such Measures, and must appear so to very Man whose Head is not too much affected with popular Madness or political Enthusiasm.[86]

A later extension of this pamphlet dealt with other issues, but reiterated the fear of independence.[87]

[85] *Reasons for Keeping Guadaloupe at a Peace, Preferable to Canada, Explained in Five Letters, from a Gentleman in Guadaloupe, to his Friend in London* (London, 1761), 60. For examples of scholarly discussion of *The Interest of Great Britain Considered* see Verner W. Crane, "Certain Writings of Benjamin Franklin on the British Empire and the American Colonies," *Papers of the Bibliographic Society*, XXVIII (1934), 1-27; Gerald Stourzh, *Benjamin Franklin and American Foreign Policy* (Chicago, 1954), 68-80; and Labaree *et al.*, eds., *Franklin Papers*, IX, 47-59. Because the importance of the independence theme is not usually stressed, the provocative nature of the pamphlet is frequently missed.

[86] (London, 1760), 8-9.

[87] See n. 85.

A final defense of the Americans was presented in 1761 in John Rutherfurd's *The Importance of the Colonies to Great Britain, with some Hints towards Making Improvements to their Mutual Advantage: And upon Trade in General.*[88] Like Henry McCulloh a Scotsman, Rutherfurd had been a collector of quitrents in North Carolina, and was in Britain seeking reinstatement to that office from which Gov. Arthur Dobbs had suspended him four years earlier. Unlike McCulloh, however, Rutherfurd was less concerned with political than with commercial arrangements. He dealt with commerce in terms of the threat of American independence, putting all Franklin's arguments into this effort. Rutherford denied that if Canada were retained, the Americans would manufacture for themselves "and throw off their dependence on the mother country." Such a possibility, he said, was "an object at too great a distance to be dreaded" and not so easily accomplished as some imagined. The colonies were jealous of each other, and while interest on money was high and land cheap, labor would be expensive. Moreover, "we can be certain, that so long as the American planter can find vent for the produce of his lands to enable him to purchase British manufactures, it will never occur to him to manufacture, because in every respect it will be contrary to his interest." The ready availability of inexpensive land was essential. Rutherfurd argued that the poor in Europe learned trades because land was dear and employment scarce, and admitted that "when the Americans come to be in the same situation, that their lands (whatever be the extent thereof) are so much improved, that their poor in order to get bread must also manufacture, there will be an end of their dependance."[89] Inducements to the colonists to grow agricultural products were required, and Rutherfurd appended to his pamphlet a translation of a French essay on hemp production.

The Importance of the Colonies to Great Britain was the last significant statement on general imperial policy in the public debate over Canada and the forthcoming peace treaty. After Rutherfurd, the pamphleteers and journalists turned to domestic politics and to consideration of the proposed terms of peace. But the Canada debate had provided a final synthesis of a century of concern over American independence on the eve of British efforts to rationalize the administration of their newly enlarged empire.

[88] Published in London, 1761, and reprinted in "Some North Carolina Tracts of the 18th Century," ed. William K. Boyd, *N. C. Hist. Rev.*, II (1925), 351-376. See pp. 351-354 for biographical information on Rutherfurd.
[89] *Ibid.*, 360-361, 371-372.

326

It is impossible to reconstruct completely the frame of mind of either Britons or Americans on the relationship of colonies and metropolis in the early 1760s. But one important strand in their attitudes was clearly a product of common sense deductions from commonly held assumptions of the time. Considerations of the balance of power, of changes in economic patterns, of population growth, of legislative autonomy—particularly when viewed in the personal terms of metaphors such as that of the family—made eventual American independence quite conceivable. Certainly a good many colonial "experts" in Britain had the possibility in the back of their minds as new American policy was being formulated. The earl of Shelburne, for example, was greatly influenced by the economic opinions of Josiah Tucker, and Shelburne's personal secretary, Maurice Morgann, advocated strong measures to avoid separation by putting the colonies in their place.[90] Men involved in the construction of the Stamp Act, particularly Henry McCulloh, also had clear notions of potential American independence. McCulloh and Morgann had both proposed general imperial reforms not unlike those actually put into practice immediately after 1763 for the express purpose of preventing American separation.[91] Charles Townshend feared ultimate independence.[92] And even colonials who had denied the possibility had anticipated the later American perception of British policy in suggesting British repression as the principal condition for secession or revolt.

Those who wrote on the American question did not consciously intend to promote independence. But the discussion of the possibility and even the eventuality of independence—a discussion that began in the seventeenth century and culminated in the spate of writings of the 1750s and early 1760s—would provide an important frame of reference for interpreting the events of the crisis toward which the Empire was swiftly moving. American colonials would find it easy to explain British policy, however pragmatically developed, as part of a consistent program, long in the making, for keeping America dependent. And British statesmen—even when they did not envision reform for that purpose—would readily discover in American responses to their actions the very tendencies toward

[90] John Norris, *Shelburne and Reform* (London, 1963), 32; Wickwire, *British Subministers*, 90-95.

[91] Maurice Morgann, "On American Commerce," and "Plan for securing the future Dependence of the Provinces on the Continent of America," Shelburne Papers, William L. Clements Library, University of Michigan, Ann Arbor, Mich.; McCulloh proposals discussed above; McCulloh, "Miscellaneous Representations relative to our concerns in America," submitted in 1761 to the earl of Bute (reprinted, with an introduction by W. A. Shaw, London, 1905).

[92] Namier and Brooke, *Charles Townshend*, 147.

separatism that had been fearfully postulated for over a century. More-over, by accepting the metaphor of the family and taking it seriously, both sides made conflict between the mother country and the colonial children far more likely.[93]

The difficulty was not that men failed to consider the nature of the im-perial relationship, but that their consideration of it had made it a prob-lem for which they could find no solutions and had generated prophecies that could only be fulfilled.

[93] Burrows and Wallace, "The American Revolution," *Perspectives*, VI (1972), *passim*.

The Origins of Civil Millennialism in America: New England Clergymen, War with France, and the Revolution

Nathan O. Hatch*

N O doubts clouded the Reverend Samuel Sherwood's assessment of the impending war between Great Britain and the American colonies. "God Almighty, with all the powers of heaven, are on our side," he declared to his Connecticut audience early in 1776. "Great numbers of angels, no doubt, are encamping round our coast, for our defence and protection. Michael stands ready, with all the artillery of heaven, to encounter the dragon, and to vanquish this black host." With a confidence almost prophetic, Sherwood announced the coming defeat of the "antichristian tyranny" which the British government represented; because the king's chief ministers had sipped the golden cup of fornication with "the old mother of harlots," they faced the imminent doom reserved for the wicked, persecuting tyrants of the earth. In building the climax of his address, which translated the conflict into a struggle of cosmic significance, Sherwood predicted that the British attack on America was one "of the last efforts, and dying struggles of the man of sin." From this apocalyptic point of view America's victory would initiate Christ's millennial kingdom.[1]

Sherwood was by no means the only American minister whose millennial hopes were fired by the Revolutionary struggle. The cosmic interpretation of the conflict—God's elect versus antichrist—appeared as a significant pattern in the intricate tapestry of ideas used by New England clergymen to explain the war's purpose. Moreover, by the time American victory seemed assured, the rhetoric of New England sermons was brimming with euphoric images of America's role in hastening the kingdom. The prospects for this blessed age had not seemed so bright since the founding

* Mr. Hatch is a post-doctoral fellow, Department of History, The Johns Hopkins University. He would like to thank John M. Murrin and J. G. A. Pocock for their advice and criticism.
[1] Samuel Sherwood, *The Church's Flight into the Wilderness: An Address on the Times* (New York, 1776), 39-49, quotations on pp. 46, 15, 49.

of New England. "Vice and immorality shall yet here, become . . . banished," proclaimed George Duffield, chaplain to the Continental Congress,
"and the wilderness blossom as the rose."[2]

Certainly the most striking feature of this millennial language in the
Revolutionary era is the way it adapted the framework of apocalyptic history to commonly held political ideas. Sermons during the war stressed
repeatedly that American liberty was God's cause, that British tyranny
was antichrist's, and that sin was failure to fight the British. With the
coming of peace many ministers envisioned Christ's thousand-year reign
on earth as an extension of the civil and religious liberty established in
America.[3] This amalgam of traditional Puritan apocalyptic rhetoric and
eighteenth-century political discourse I have chosen to call "civil millennialism," a term warranted by the extent to which these themes were directed by the society's political consciousness. Under the aegis of civil
millennialism ministers of varying theological persuasions came to do
homage at the same shrine, that of liberty, and expressed their allegiance
in projections about the future which were as novel as they were pervasive.[4]

The language of civil millennialism has a strange ring to an ear accustomed to that of Puritan apocalyptic thought, but not because the political dimension of millennialism was itself a novelty. Englishmen since
the Reformation had often been willing to oppose civil governments
deemed to be under the control of antichristian power. They assumed
that the frustration of French and Spanish hegemony abroad and Catholic

---

[2] George Duffield, *A Sermon Preached in the Third Presbyterian Church* . . .
(Philadelphia, 1784), 17.

[3] For sermons that interpret the Revolution as the struggle of the elect versus
antichrist see Abraham Keteltas, *God Arising and Pleading His People's Cause* . . .
(Newburyport, Mass., 1777), and Samuel West, *A Sermon Preached before the
Honorable Council* . . . (Boston, 1776). For good examples of ministers whose
millennial hopes were aroused by American victory see Ezra Stiles, *The United
States elevated to Glory and Honor* . . . (New Haven, Conn., 1783), and Benjamin
Trumbull, *God is to be praised for the Glory of his Majesty* . . . (New Haven,
Conn., 1784).

[4] I have described this apocalyptic orientation as "civil" rather than "civic" or
"political" because this was the adjective most frequently used by ministers to define
those privileges of citizenship which increasingly occupied their attention. Several
scholars who have written about millennial interpretations of the Revolution have
recognized a fundamental change from earlier apocalyptic understanding. See
Ernest Lee Tuveson, *Redeemer Nation: The Idea of America's Millennial Role*
(Chicago, 1968), 24; John G. Buchanan, "Puritan Philosophy of History from
Restoration to Revolution," *Essex Institute Historical Collections*, CIV (1968), 342-
343; and J. F. Maclear, "The Republic and the Millennium," in Elwyn A. Smith, ed.,
The Religion of the Republic (Philadelphia, 1971), 183-194.

political influence at home played a major role in realizing the day when swords would be beaten into plowshares. Across the Atlantic, New Englanders for a century also had watched political developments for signs of the coming times. What *does* give civil millennialism its distinctive quality is the new configuration of civil and religious priorities in the minds of the clergy. In a subtle but profound shift in emphasis the religious values that traditionally defined the ultimate goal of apocalyptic hope —the conversion of all nations to Christianity—became diluted with, and often subordinate to, the commitment to America as a new seat of liberty. Although its rhetoric was conventional, this new form of millennialism, channeled in the direction of prevailing political values, stood in marked contrast to traditional New England apocalyptic hopes.

331

Nothing makes this point clearer than the differences between civil millennialism and the apocalyptic expectations of the Great Awakening. Jonathan Edwards may have resembled Sherwood or Duffield in the application of apocalyptic ideas to his own times and in his post-millennial view of the future, but such similarities are less significant than the fundamental contrasts between the two perspectives. The New Light confidence in the progressive course of history was based on the spread of vital piety; Christ's kingdom advanced toward its completion by the effusion of God's spirit in widespread revivals. The Revolutionary millennialist, on the other hand, based his apocalyptic hopes on the civil and religious liberty that American victory over Britain would insure. His vision of the future inspired him to attempt to thwart the precipitate advance of power rather than to advocate the conversion of sinners. Edwards saw the Concert of Prayer as the primary institution for promoting the kingdom; praying bands of pious saints were the avant-garde who would drive back the forces of darkness. In contrast, ministers such as Abraham Keteltas or Samuel Langdon welcomed to the cause of God anyone who would take up the sword against the antichrist of British tyranny. The spontaneous defense of liberty in America encouraged them to interpret existing American society as the model upon which the millennial kingdom would be based. Inspired by the complex of ideas here called civil millennialism, New England ministers of the Revolutionary era resisted tyranny in God's name, hailed liberty as the virtue of the "New American Israel," and proclaimed that in sharing these values with all mankind America would become the principal seat of Christ's earthly rule.[5]

[5] For an excellent example of the striking contrast between the millennium of Edwards and that of the Revolution cf. Edwards, *Some Thoughts Concerning the*

In view of the substantial differences between these two interpretations of prophecy it is necessary to reexamine the origins and development of civil millennialism in order to explain more adequately how it became so ingrained in the minds of New England ministers. Put another way, the intention is to rethink the assumption common in recent literature that the origins of civil millennialism can be traced directly to the piety of the Great Awakening. According to this interpretation, the revivals of the 1740s aroused a new, potent sense of American destiny—expressed by the millennialism of such New Lights as Edwards—which flowered into the intense religious patriotism of the young Republic. In his massive study of the mind of eighteenth-century New England Alan Heimert attributes the fervor of the Revolutionary clergy to an excited millennial expectancy that flowed from the Awakening.[6] Heimert recognizes certain characteristics of civil millennialism but sees them only as modifications of the dynamic postmillennialism of New Light ministers. In emphasizing the dominant imprint of the Awakening on the intellectual activity of the mid-eighteenth century, he not only dismisses the heritage of pre-Awakening Puritanism but also jumps quickly from the Awakening to the Revolution, assuming that the imperial wars of the period were "incidental, even irrelevant" to the clergy's definition of New England identity. Within this framework the ideas that developed before and after the Awakening had little bearing on the shifting patterns of religious patriotism. Edwards and his successors rekindled the torch of American mission and destiny lit by the founders of the "city on a hill" and passed it directly to the patriots who fought for a new republic.[7] Although not all scholars would accept Heimert's stress on the New Light origins of the Revolution, few would doubt that the piety of the Awakening was the main source of the civil millennialism of the Revolutionary period.[8]

332

Revival of Religion in New-England . . . in C. C. Goen, ed., *The Works of Jonathan Edwards,* IV (New Haven, Conn., 1972), 348-370, with the sermon by Ebenezer Baldwin, *The Duty of Rejoicing under Calamities and Afflictions* . . . (New York, 1776).

[6] Alan Heimert, *Religion and the American Mind: From the Great Awakening to the Revolution* (Cambridge, Mass., 1966), 59, 413-509.

[7] According to Heimert, the Awakening shattered "the social assumptions inherited from the seventeenth century [and] allowed the evangelical ministry to offer the American people new commitments, political as well as ethical." After 1740 little of intellectual significance remained outside of the issues posed by the "two parties" formed in the Awakening. *Ibid.,* 14, 3. For Heimert's discussion of the insignificance of developments between the Great Awakening and the Revolution, particularly the Anglo-French wars, see *ibid.,* 84-85.

[8] A complete historiographical essay could be written to explain the current

This interpretation is open to serious question. In the first place, if the roots of civil millennialism are to be found primarily in New Light enthusiasm, it is strange that its rhetoric was employed by Old Lights such as Langdon, Jeremy Belknap, and Samuel West, as well as the rationalist John Adams. The prevalence of this way of thinking among men of contrasting theologies can hardly be explained simply by reference to the New Light intellectual tradition.[9] Secondly, while recent scholarship has focused on the exultant hopes that characterized the Awakening, it has conspicuously avoided the same careful analysis of New Light thought in the years of the revival's demise. There has been little effort to examine the influence of an increasingly secular society upon the millennial perspective derived from the Awakening. Scholars have not adequately considered the significance of the decline of apocalyptic hope in the later 1740s, when Americans concentrated on concerns other than vital religion.[10] The third and most basic flaw is the almost total neglect of the apocalyptic categories used by the clergy to explain their intense interest in the Anglo-French wars. Assuming that after the Awakening the clergy's sense of history included a moral distinction between the Old World and America—an incipient American nationalism—many scholars slight the importance of the conflict with France for New England thought. Looking only for signposts pointing in the direction of Americanization, they have made an easy detour around many issues, significantly imperial in

333

---

scholarly paradigm of tracing the origins of American patriotism and nationalism primarily to the Great Awakening. See Sacvan Bercovitch, "Horologicals to Chronometricals: The Rhetoric of the Jeremiad," in Eric Rothstein, ed., *Literary Monographs*, III (Madison, Wis., 1970), 81; Darrett B. Rutman, ed., *The Great Awakening: Event and Exegesis* (New York, 1970), 4-5, 70; Conrad Cherry, ed., *God's New Israel: Religious Interpretations of American Destiny* (Englewood Cliffs, N. J., 1971), 29-30; and Cedric B. Cowing, *The Great Awakening and the American Revolution: Colonial Thought in the 18th Century* (Chicago, 1971), 203.

[9] When numerous opposers of enthusiastic religion discuss the Revolution using a millennial paradigm, how can scholars assume that the Great Awakening was their common source? It would seem far more reasonable that a viewpoint prevalent among both Old and New Lights would have its intellectual origins in their shared heritage and experience rather than in the source of their theological division.

[10] Few authors who discuss religion and its relation to the Revolution fathom the profound intellectual shift that Edmund S. Morgan has captured so poignantly in one sentence: "In 1740 America's leading intellectuals were clergymen and thought about theology; in 1790 they were statesmen and thought about politics." It is necessary to reconsider what happens to New Light millennial confidence when society at large substitutes politics for religion "as the most challenging area of human thought and endeavor." "The American Revolution Considered as an Intellectual Movement," in Arthur M. Schlesinger, Jr., and Morton White, eds., *Paths of American Thought* (Boston, 1963), 11.

character and scope, which profoundly influenced New England ministers in the two decades before the Stamp Act.[11]

In 1742 Edwards anticipated with excitement the dawning of the millennium. In his defense of the Great Awakening, *Some Thoughts Concerning the Revival of Religion,* he suggested that this "very great and wonderful, and exceeding glorious work" surpassed any that had ever been seen in New England or in other lands. The great increase in seriousness, the new conviction of the truth of the gospel, and the unusual changes in young people throughout New England were convincing signs that God would soon transform the world into the "Latter-day Glory." Edwards was so encouraged by the progress of piety that he announced that the millennium would probably begin in America.[12]

Edwards did not stand alone in interpreting the renewal of vital religion as a foretaste of Christ's kingdom. *The Christian History,* published by Thomas Prince and his son to propagate the Awakening, reflected widespread assurance that the kingdom was making significant advances. Typical was the report of Peter Thacher, pastor at Middleborough, Massachusetts: "I desire to rejoice to hear that the Lord Christ is carrying on his own Work with such a mighty Arm in so many Places. . . . If it be the Dawn of the glorious Gospel-Day; I trust the whole earth shall soon be filled with the Knowledge of the *Saviour*."[13] In the summer of 1743 almost seventy New England ministers signed *The Testimony and Advice of an Assembly of Pastors,* supporting the revivals and declaring that these effusions of the Spirit confirmed the expectations "of such as are *waiting for the Kingdom of God,* and the coming on of the . . . latter Days."[14] These New Lights saw the millennium as a culmination of processes

[11] For Heimert nothing can be of real intellectual significance in 18th-century New England unless it encouraged Americanization. The Awakening was "in a vital respect an American declaration of independence from Europe." The "guiding light" of subsequent Calvinism was "a delight in the New World itself." Thus New Lights found little to interest them in the conflict with France because the drama of history no longer included foreign characters. *Religion and the American Mind,* 14, 86-87, 98, 267-269. For a conflicting interpretation that sees New England intensely caught up in the French wars "as another battle to make the world safe for Protestantism and purified of popery," see Kerry A. Trask, "In the Pursuit of Shadows: A Study of Collective Hope and Despair in Provincial Massachusetts during the Era of the Seven Years War, 1748 to 1764" (Ph.D. diss., University of Minnesota, 1971), 223-286.

[12] Edwards, *Some Thoughts Concerning the Revival,* in Goen, ed., *Works,* IV, 343-344, 353.

[13] Thomas Prince, Jr., ed., *The Christian History* (Boston, 1743-1745), II, 95.

[14] *Ibid.,* I, 158, 163-164, 182.

at work in the revival. They pictured the imminent age of peace in images that expressed the realization of revival hope. It would be a time of vital religion, when holiness of life rather than empty profession would prevail. Confident that these ends would be accomplished by a "wonderful *revival and propagation* of religion," Edwards identified the Awakening as "the earnest," "the dawning," "the prelude," "the forerunner" of that blissful age which was swiftly approaching.[15] In *The Christian History* Daniel Putnam made the connection between vital religion and the millennium even more explicit when he encouraged his fellow clergymen to pray for revival in order that "the *Kingdoms of this World* may become the *Kingdom* of OUR BLESSED LORD AND SAVIOUR JESUS CHRIST."[16]

For Edwards the revival impulse greatly overshadowed any political means of overthrowing antichrist and initiating the thousand years of peace. "The authority of princes" could never accomplish the goal of the Spirit, nor could political and military activities in themselves sound the knell for Satan's empire. This could only be done by "multitudes flocking to Christ."[17] Later, during the French wars, Edwards was often encouraged by God's providential defeat of the enemy, who fought on the side of antichrist, but these defeats he interpreted as "temporal mercies," incentives to the more important works of repentance and revival. Even in the political realm Edwards's primary vision was of the day when "vital religion shall then take possession of kings palaces and thrones; and those who are in highest advancement shall be holy men."[18]

To their dismay Edwards and the other revivalists did not see their dreams fulfilled in the immediate dawning of the new age. As early as the summer of 1743 indications began to appear in *The Christian History* that all was not well with the revival. While the pastors explained with

[15] Jonathan Edwards, *The Works of President Edwards* (reprint ed., New York, 1968 [orig. publ. London, 1817]), V, 239; Edwards, *Some Thoughts Concerning the Revival*, in Goen, ed., *Works*, IV, 353-358.

[16] *The Christian History*, I, 182.

[17] Edwards, *Works*, V, 239, 241.

[18] *Ibid.*, II, 480; V, 253. In a letter to William M'Culloch, Sept. 23, 1747, Edwards reconfirmed his subordination of political and military affairs to the issue of vital religion: "New-England has had many other surprising deliverances from the French and Indians. . . . These deliverances are very wonderful . . . but there are no such effects of these mercies upon us that are the subjects of them, as God requires, and most justly expects. The mercies are acknowledged in words, but we are not led to repentance by them; there appears no such thing as any reformation or Revival of religion in the land." S. E. Dwight, *The Life of President Edwards . . .* (New York, 1830), 243-244.

a touch of nostalgia the earlier spiritual movings in their churches, they wondered unhappily why the Spirit had withdrawn. "*Manna* grows taste-less and insipid after a Year or two's Enjoyment," one minister lamented, "and too many are for making a Captain, and returning to *Egypt*."[19] Throughout 1744 the clergy's dejection deepened. While not a single minister reported a fresh revival, many expressed anxiety at the "melan-choly abatements" of divine grace. A letter signed by ten ministers in eastern Connecticut depicted the situation with imagery drawn not from the hopeful visions of St. John's Apocalypse but from the humble prayer of Isaiah that in the midst of wrath God would remember mercy.[20] Even Edwards had to confess that "the work is put to a stop every where, and it is a day of the Enemy's triumph."[21]

If the Great Awakening was the catalyst that transformed post-millennialism into a dynamic paradigm to explain current events, what happened when the fires of the revival flickered and went out? How did the New Lights respond to the increasingly difficult problem of relating millennial hope to historical reality? By the spring of 1745 this problem had become acute. *The Christian History* collapsed early that year for at least the obvious reason that there were simply no revivals to report. As New Englanders challenged the French at Louisbourg later that spring, their attention was further distracted from the concerns of vital piety. A new tour by George Whitefield went almost unnoticed amid the frenzied activity inspired by the "mad scheme" to seize Cape Breton Island.[22]

Several options, all rather unpleasant, faced the minister who had anticipated that the Awakening would issue directly into the millennium. The fact that the kingdom's advance was checked, at least temporarily, led to deferred hope among some and outright pessimism among others. The writings of Edwards, Aaron Burr, and Joseph Bellamy expressed three different responses to the pressing need to forge new links between an optimistic tradition of providential history and the discouraging facts of day-to-day experience in a society increasingly unsympathetic to the millennial message.

One solution was to take celebrational note of revivals wherever they

[19] *The Christian History*, I, 259.
[20] *Ibid.*, II, 114, 168, 311-312.
[21] Dwight, *Life of Edwards*, 212.
[22] John E. Van de Wetering, "The *Christian History* of the Great Awakening," *Journal of Presbyterian History*, XLIV (1966), 129; Edwin Scott Gaustad, *The Great Awakening in New England* (New York, 1957), 79.

might be found. The decline of piety in New England had no necessary counterpart in Europe or in other parts of the British Empire. In this context we can understand Edwards's increasing involvement in transatlantic affairs after 1745. His extensive correspondence with Scottish ministers reflected an interest in the success of awakened Protestantism that went far beyond any provincial commitment to New England or America. Never again did he assert that America would have a special role in the coming of the millennium. Thus in his *Humble Attempt* of 1747, written in response to a proposal by Scottish ministers for extensive networks of Christians who would pray regularly for new revivals, Edwards showed no inclination to draw a moral distinction between the Old World and the New. In lamenting the spiritual decadence of the whole British Empire he manifested a pessimism about America no less pronounced than for the British Isles.[23] On other occasions, in numerous letters to friends in Scotland, he contrasted the woeful decay of religion in America—"at present very sorrowful and dark"—with comforting evidences of divine activity elsewhere in the Empire. In one of these letters he expressed the hope that recent news from Britain would excite New Englanders to seek God's face, if they were not too far "buried in ignorance, or under the power of a lethargic stupor." Edwards could no longer find signs of the coming millennium exclusively in America; the decline of experimental religion there forced him to look beyond the Atlantic to see God at work.[24]

337

Edwards's solution to the problem of relating history to millennial theory was at best a holding action that avoided the major question: How could one anticipate the millennium in a society unaffected by revivalism? What happened, for instance, when revival fires were extinguished not only in New England but also throughout the Empire? This was the problem that Edwards's son-in-law, Aaron Burr, faced in the 1750s. Finding that both England and America were afflicted by irreligion and infidelity, and fearing the spiritual destruction of the whole British people,[25] Burr maintained Edwards's postmillennialism but reshuffled his categories to develop a millennial vision that can only be called pessimistic.[26] Thus

[23] Edwards, *Works*, II, 476.
[24] Dwight, *Life of Edwards*, 262, 278, 287, 412.
[25] Aaron Burr, *A Discourse Delivered at New-Ark* . . . (New York, 1755), 23, 28. In his interpretation of this sermon Heimert singles out Burr's denunciations of Great Britain as an indication of the increasing American dissatisfaction with Old World Protestantism. Apparently he overlooks the fact that Burr directed this criticism as much to America as to England. *Religion and the American Mind*, 85-86.
[26] James W. Davidson has made the excellent point that postmillennialism was

in his sermon *The Watchman's Answer*, Burr developed a view of history and the apocalypse that Edwards would hardly have recognized. According to Burr, the course of history since the Reformation had not progressed in a millennial direction. Not only had the initial break with Rome fallen far short of the hopes it had raised, but in more recent times the night of antichristian domination had continued and even deepened. Burr climaxed this pessimistic argument by disagreeing explicitly with Edwards's interpretation of the slaying of the witnesses in Revelation 11. Whereas for Edwards this worst time of persecution for the church had already taken place, Burr confessed his belief that the "sorest Calamity and Distress" were yet tó come. The church should prepare itself to suffer cheerfully in an era of "Heresy and Wickedness, Tumults and Corruptions." Instead of sounding a trumpet of hope, Burr issued an exhortation to endurance; instead of projecting a vision of progress, he renewed the jeremiad theme.[27] He saw the millennium as the ultimate extrication of the church from its plight of "Midnight Security." Like Cotton Mather, whose chiliasm envisioned no interruption of the downward course of the church until God supernaturally intervened, Burr articulated a postmillennialism in which only a cosmic reordering would defeat the evil forces rampant among men.[28]

Both Edwards and Burr related their apocalyptic hopes to the events of contemporary history. The failure of the Awakening thus left them no choice but to alter their views of the future. Edwards maintained his optimism by broadening his vision to include the Empire; for Burr even that panorama failed to inspire hope. In contrast to both, another New Light leader, Joseph Bellamy, maintained his millennial expectations by disassociating the millennial future from contemporary history. He was thus able to speak optimistically of Christ's eventual kingdom without regard to its current record of success or lack thereof. His 1758 sermon *The Millennium*, without mentioning a single contemporary event, either religious or political, offered Christians only the timeless hope that some-

---

not a constant "which affected the behavior of people in different times and situations in any consistent manner." He effectively demonstrates that a postmillennial framework did not necessarily imply an imminent millennium, an unclouded optimism, or an intense activism to bring on the kingdom. "Searching for the Millennium: Problems for the 1790's and the 1970's," *New England Quarterly,* XLV (1972), 241-261, esp. 250-255, quotation on p. 255.

[27] Aaron Burr, *The Watchman's Answer* . . . (Boston, 1757), 19-22, 34-40, quotations on pp. 22, 39.

[28] For Cotton Mather's views on the second coming of Christ see Robert Middlekauff, *The Mathers: Three Generations of Puritan Intellectuals, 1596-1728* (New York, 1971), 320-349, esp. 335.

day Christ would prevail.[29]

The New Light millennial vision could never have provided the intellectual foundation for the historical optimism prevalent among ministers of the Revolutionary era. Based on the success of awakened piety, it could not sustain the interest of a generation whose infatuation with revivalism faded as quickly as it had flowered. When society ceased to march to the revival's cadence, the New Light drummers faced the necessity of developing a more compelling beat. The Anglo-French conflicts that claimed New England's attention after 1745 provided just such an opportunity. In the wars with France the New England clergy found a broader basis for a millennial hope that could encompass all of society.

339

In July 1745 the New England press reported what must have been for its readers the most astounding news story in memory: the French fortress of Louisbourg had been captured by New England arms! In reactions that were almost ecstatic, newspapers, firsthand accounts, and sermons told how four thousand undisciplined "Land-Men unused to War" had sailed to Cape Breton Island in a makeshift fleet without British naval support or heavy artillery and there had besieged and reduced the most awesome military bastion in North America. Poetic descriptions compared the feat to the greatest victories of Marlborough, and ministers were inspired to proclaim that God had "triumphed gloriously over his and our antichristian enemies." This mighty blow to the Man of Sin evoked numerous expressions of millennial hope from the clergy and pointed to the new concerns that would preoccupy them in the subsequent years of imperial war.[30]

In the years between the "crusade" against Louisbourg in 1745 and the signing of the Peace of Paris in 1763 the conflict with France gripped New England society with an overriding intensity. Villages had to be defended against unpredictable attack and forces marshaled for offensive

[29] Joseph Bellamy, *The Millennium*, in Alan Heimert and Perry Miller, eds., *The Great Awakening: Documents Illustrating the Crisis and Its Consequences* (Indianapolis, Ind., 1967), 609-635. In other sermons Bellamy displays the same exclusively religious and apolitical concern. See *A Blow at the Root of the refined Antinomianism of the present Age* (Boston, 1763); *An Essay on the Nature and Glory of the Gospel of Jesus Christ* . . . (Boston, 1763); and *The Half-Way-Covenant* (New Haven, Conn., 1769).

[30] Thomas Prince, *Extraordinary Events the Doings of God* . . . (Boston, 1745), 20; Joseph Sewall, *The Lamb Slain* . . . (Boston, 1745), 29. There is no adequate analysis of the psychological impact of the Louisbourg campaign upon New Englanders. Francis Parkman, *A Half-Century of Conflict*, II (Boston, 1892), is as helpful as anyone.

engagements. The urgency of other public affairs faded for those who experienced the anxiety of battle, the despair of defeat, the joy of victory.[31] New Englanders in general, and clergymen in particular, perceived the "Gallic peril" as a massive, insidious threat to their religion and liberties. John Mellen warned his countrymen in 1756: "Our enemies may yet triumph over us, and the gospel taken from us, instead of being by us transmitted to other nations. It is possible, our land may be given to the beast, the inhabitants to the sword, the righteous to the fire of martyrdom, our wives to ravishment, and our sons and our daughters to death and torture!"[32] Similarly, Ebenezer Pemberton declared that "the fires of *Smithfield*, which burnt with such *unrelenting* fury in the days of *Queen Mary*," should remind New England of the *"inhuman* barbarities" and the "methods of *torture* and *violence"* that characterized French rule.[33] Mellen and Pemberton joined a host of their colleagues who vented their anxiety by picturing the grim consequences of French victory. Images of enslavement, prisons, galleys, and horrible tortures expressed the clergy's fear that life under the yoke of France would be "lingering Death." To French tyranny, Solomon Williams preferred that New England be destroyed by an earthquake.[34]

The ministers' rhetoric associated France inseparably with "the merciless Rage of *Popish* power" and evoked images of the inquisition, the fury of Queen Mary, the schemes of the Stuarts, and the more recent suppression of Protestants in France. Roman Catholicism represented for New Englanders not only their ancestors' most hated foe but also an immediate conspiracy against the liberties of all mankind.[35] Typical of

---

[31] For discussions of New England's intense involvement in the French wars see John M. Murrin, "Anglicizing an American Colony: The Transformation of Provincial Massachusetts" (Ph.D. diss., Yale University, 1966), 118-119, and Trask, "In the Pursuit of Shadows," 13, 223-286.

[32] John Mellen, *The Duty of all to be ready for future impending Events* (Boston, 1756), 19-20.

[33] Ebenezer Pemberton, *A Sermon Delivered at the Presbyterian Church in New-York, July 31, 1746* (New York, 1746), 19.

[34] Gad Hitchcock, *A Sermon Preached in the 2d Precinct in Pembroke* . . . (Boston, 1757), 19; Solomon Williams, *The Duty of Christian Soldiers* . . . (New London, Conn., 1755), 33-34; Isaac Stiles, *The Character and Duty of Soldiers* . . . (New Haven, Conn., 1755), 2.

[35] William McClenachan, *The Christian Warrior* (Boston, 1745), 5; Thomas More Brown, "The Image of the Beast: Anti-Papal Rhetoric in Colonial America," in Richard O. Curry and Thomas More Brown, eds., *Conspiracy: The Fear of Subversion in American History* (New York, 1972), 1-20; Sister Mary Augustina Ray, *American Opinion of Roman Catholicism in the Eighteenth Century* (New York, 1936).

this mood was the fear expressed by Prince that "our inveterate and *popish* Enemies both without and within the Kingdom, are restless to enslave and ruin us." If France won the struggle, "Cruel *Papists* would quickly fill the *British Colonies,* seize our Estates, abuse our Wives and Daughters, and barbarously murder us; as they have done the like in *France* and *Ireland.*"[36]

These perceptions of a massive French-Catholic conspiracy were linked directly to an apocalyptic interpretation of history in which the French were accomplices in Satan's designs to subjugate God's elect in New England. According to John Burt, the conduct of the French "bespeaks them the Offspring of that *Scarlet Whore, that Mother of Harlots,* who is justly *the Abomination of the Earth.*"[37] In the years of the French wars the ministers' constant use of such highly charged images as "the Man of Sin," "the North American Babylon," "the Mother of Harlots," and "the Romish Antichristian Power" expressed their sense of the cosmic significance of the conflict and showed that the traditional apocalyptic view of history retained great power.[38]

341

In delineating this moral dichotomy between themselves and the French, New Englanders altered the patterns of apocalyptic thought. Turning from spiritual introspection, they began to underscore their collective role in the last decisive struggle with Satan. Rather than becoming "indifferent to and weary with" this interpretation of history, clergymen at mid-century manifested an intensity of interest in antichrist's overthrow unknown since the time of John Cotton and Edward Johnson.[39] Vivid perceptions of an external foe confirmed their sense of identity as God's elect people living in the end times and linked their lives to the cosmic war between good and evil. In the minds of Old Lights images of antichrist shifted from "enthusiasm" to the French menace,

[36] Thomas Prince, *A Sermon Delivered At the South Church in Boston . . .* (Boston, 1746), 12, 18.

[37] John Burt, *The Mercy of God to his People . . .* (Newport, R. I., 1759), 4.

[38] Nathaniel Appleton, *A Sermon Preached October 9 . . .* (Boston, 1760), 36; Williams, *Duty of Christian Soldiers,* 26; Sewall, *The Lamb Slain,* 34.

[39] Heimert, *Religion and the American Mind,* 85. For a concise discussion of New England's collective introspection in the late 17th and early 18th centuries see Perry Miller, "Errand into the Wilderness," in his *Errand into the Wilderness* (Cambridge, Mass., 1956), 1-15. This literature of the jeremiad stands in marked contrast to the European orientation of both New England's first settlers and that generation which after 1745 was preoccupied with imperial conflict. Aletha Joy Gilsdorf discusses the important role that antichrist played in the thought of early New Englanders in "The Puritan Apocalypse: New England Eschatology in the Seventeenth Century" (Ph.D. diss., Yale University, 1965).

and New Lights ceased to be preoccupied with the dangers of an unconverted ministry. More concerned with the common struggle than with
divisive questions relating to the spread of vital piety, the clergy found
remarkable solidarity in a renewed sense of apocalyptic history.[40]

The response of New England ministers to French defeat reveals the
power of this apocalyptic perspective. Had the clergy, burdened by the
anxiety of war, used the imagery of prophetic scripture as mere rhetoric
to stir their countrymen to fight, one would expect this form of discourse
to have ended with the cessation of conflict. Yet British victories, far from
signaling the demise of the apocalyptic vision, gave rise to an unprecedented outpouring of hope that Christ's kingdom was imminent. When
Louisbourg fell, ministers overcame their theological differences to join
in a harmonious chorus of millennial rejoicing. Not only would the Man
of Sin no longer rule as vice-regent in the area of Cape Breton, but the
conquest of Louisbourg was a sign that the day was not far off when
it would be proclaimed that "Babylon the Great is fallen."[41] Less than
a year later the defeat of the Pretender at Culloden evoked even greater
displays of millennial expectancy.[42] Not since the rousing times of the
Awakening had the ministers been so sure that the new age was about
to dawn.

For the duration of the French wars the apocalyptic dimensions of
the conflict became even more pronounced in the minds of the clergy.
By the mid-1750s references associating France with antichrist had increased significantly.[43] Nor was this perspective limited to New England.
For the Virginian Samuel Davies the contest of an all-Catholic French
alliance with an all-Protestant British coalition suggested nothing less
than "the commencement of this grand decisive conflict between the Lamb
and the beast." Without qualification he pictured the consequence of

342

---

[40] The intensity of Old Light hatred of factionalism can be seen in Charles
Chauncy, *Seasonable Thoughts on the State of Religion in New-England* (Boston,
1743), 175, and Isaac Stiles, *A Prospect of the City of Jerusalem* . . . (New London,
Conn., 1742), 45. There was remarkable unanimity, for instance, in the Old and
New Light reactions to the Louisbourg campaign. Cf. the thanksgiving sermons
given on the same day by Prince, *Extraordinary Events,* and Charles Chauncy,
Marvellous Things done by the right Hand and holy Arm of God . . . (Boston, 1745).

[41] Sewall, *The Lamb Slain,* 34; Chauncy, *Marvellous Things,* 21.

[42] Hull Abbot, *The Duty of God's People to pray for the Peace of Jerusalem* . . .
(Boston, 1746), 25-26; Prince, *Sermon Delivered At the South Church,* 37.

[43] Trask notes that there were more publications with eschatological themes
during the 1750s than in any other decade of the colonial period. "In the Pursuit of
Shadows," 199.

French victory as the slaying of the witnesses when antichrist would establish his reign. French defeat, on the other hand, would introduce the most significant revolution in history, namely, *"a new heaven and a new earth."*[44]

When the long-awaited news of French downfall in Canada reached New England millennial optimism knew no limits. In sermon after sermon ministers celebrated the removal of the last and greatest obstruction to the coming kingdom. Typical was the thanksgiving sermon of Nathaniel Appleton, who delighted in God's judgment upon the French— "a Vial of his Wrath [poured] upon this Part of Antichrist"—and anticipated the "greater and more marvellous Works" that God was about to accomplish. Samuel Langdon anticipated the "final ruin of that spiritual tyranny and *mystery of iniquity."* The time was at hand for the shout of general joy: *"Babylon the great is fallen, is fallen!"*[45] Jonathan Mayhew, reversing his pessimistic estimation of the course of history prompted by the earthquake of 1755, expressed elation that God was revealing His purpose to destroy the Beast; in confounding the antichristian forces by a succession of judgments He would initiate "a most signal revolution in the civil and religious state of things in this world; and all the kingdoms thereof are to become the kingdoms of our Lord."[46] Only such acts of divine intervention as the Reformation, the defeat of the Armada, the overthrow of the Stuarts, the founding of New England, and the accession of the Hanoverians could be compared with the remarkable conquest of Canada, a victory that Solomon Williams declared to be "of more Importance than has ever been made by the *English,* since *England* was a Nation."[47]

In light of this rhetoric the suggestion that New England ministers had disengaged from the French and Indian War or saw it as "incidental, even irrelevant, to the central theme of history" seems as unbelievable as

343

[44] Davies presented this apocalyptic interpretation of the war in a fast sermon at Hanover, Va., in Oct. 1756. See Samuel Davies, *The Crisis: or, the Uncertain Doom of Kingdoms at Particular Times,* in his *Sermons on Important Subjects,* V (Philadelphia, 1818), 239-266, quotations on pp. 257, 258.

[45] Appleton, *Sermon Preached October 9,* 1-6, 26, 36; Samuel Langdon, *Joy and Gratitude to God* . . . (Portsmouth, N. H., 1760), 42-43. See also Andrew Eliot, *A Sermon Preached October 25th 1759* . . . (Boston, 1759), 42.

[46] Jonathan Mayhew, *Two Discourses Delivered October 25th. 1759* . . . (Boston, 1759), 49, 61.

[47] Solomon Williams, *The Relations of God's People to him* . . . (New London, Conn., 1760), 19. See also Thomas Barnard, *A Sermon Preached before his Excellency Francis Bernard* . . . (Boston, 1763), 36-44.

eighteenth-century Harvard College requesting the Pope to give the Dudleian Lecture. Far from withdrawing from the imperial conflict, New Englanders translated it into genuinely cosmic categories. Fighting the French became the cause of God; marching to battle hastened the destruction of antichrist; victory proclaimed a "Salvation, a Deliverance, by far superior to any—nay to all that *New-England* ever experienced."[48] If there were still some clergymen who in 1760 could not discern the progress of providential history in the French defeat and who still found their spirits uplifted solely by the Concert of Prayer, they were few and insignificant. With rare exceptions the clergy saw the war's end as unequivocal evidence that the kingdom of darkness could no longer restrain the latter-day glory. "What a Scene of Wonder opens to our View!" exclaimed Mather Byles, almost breathless with anticipation. "Good God! what an astonishing Scene of Wonders! Methinks, a universal Transport animates every Countenance, and sparkles in every Eye."[49]

By 1760 New England clergymen appear to have lost a clear distinction between the kingdom of God and the goals of their own political community. Military victories of Protestants over Catholics, which for earlier New Englanders had been means to the end of worldwide revival, now pointed toward a different end. The idea of a millennium of liberty both civil and religious had captured the clergy's imagination. During the two decades of war with France ministers had continued the long-established practice of aligning their own cause with that of God, but these years had worked a reordering of the clergy's values and priorities. Yet because the French wars were not the only cause of this pervasive shift, one must trace other, no less crucial intellectual changes by which antichrist became much more a symbol of tyranny than of heresy and the millennium much more an age of liberty than of piety.

Rarely did New Englanders tire of building myths about the heroic acts of the founders of "the city on a hill." For the historian these myths are important because they reflect their authors' values and were used by them to express their concerns.[50] In analyzing the rhetoric of the jere-

---

[48] Heimert, *Religion and the American Mind*, 85; Eli Forbes, *God the Strength and Salvation of his People* . . . (Boston, 1761), 9.
[49] Mather Byles, *A Sermon, Delivered March 6th 1760* . . . (New London, Conn., 1760), 13.
[50] Wesley Frank Craven, *The Legend of the Founding Fathers* (New York, 1956), 1-65; Carl Bridenbaugh, *Mitre and Sceptre: Transatlantic Faiths, Ideas, Personalities, and Politics, 1689-1775* (New York, 1962), 171-206.

miad Perry Miller has shown how second- and third-generation New England ministers reproached their contemporaries by constructing exalted myths of the early settlers. Similarly, by tracing the formulation of myths during the two decades after 1740 we can more easily grasp the changing values and interests of the eighteenth-century ministers who created them.[51]

Although the Great Awakening shattered the traditional language of the jeremiad, it did not replace it with an alternative paradigm by which ministers interpreted the mission of early New England. Rather, it bisected the earlier myth so that each side in the dispute over enthusiastic religion inherited a facet of the older interpretation. In contrasting the exemplary first generation with the declension of their own age, both Old and New Lights focused on the particular characteristics of the founders that confirmed their own points of view. While New Lights exalted the "Power of Religion among the primitive Planters" and lamented its subsequent decay, Old Lights dwelt upon the love and unity of the first settlers and bemoaned the "Unscriptural Separations and Disorderly Practices" that disturbed their own day.[52] Most important, neither of these myths about early New England differed in substance from the interpretation that characterized the traditional jeremiad. Both the New Light emphasis on vital religion and the Old Light stress on unity and charity were fragments of the same earlier myth that had honored the forefathers for both their piety and their harmony.[53]

During the French wars this religious mythology underwent a massive change. As early as 1736 Prince pointed in the new direction when he called for imitation of the "worthy Fathers" not only for their vital and pure Christianity, but also for their "LIBERTY both *Civil* and *Ecclesiastical*."[54] Reflecting the increasing concern of New Englanders for the

[51] Perry Miller, *The New England Mind: From Colony to Province* (Cambridge, Mass., 1953), 27-39.

[52] *The Christian History*, I, 37; Stiles, *Prospect of Jerusalem*, 46. For New Light statements that idealized the power of vital religion among the first generation see *The Christian History*, I, 1, 72, 98, 106. Old Light jeremiads, which emphasized the unity of New England's founders, are seen in William Worthington, *The Duty of Rulers and Teachers in Unitedly Leading God's People* . . . (New London, Conn., 1744), 23-24, and Nathaniel Appleton, *The Great Blessing of Good Rulers* . . . (Boston, 1742), 42.

[53] Both of these themes are evident in such earlier jeremiads as that of Samuel Danforth, *A Brief Recognition of New Englands Errand into the Wilderness* (1671), in A. W. Plumstead, ed., *The Wall and the Garden: Selected Massachusetts Election Sermons 1670-1772* (Minneapolis, Minn., 1968), 65-67.

[54] Thomas Prince, *A Chronological History of New England* (Boston, 1736), I, "Dedication," ii.

privileges confirmed to them by the Glorious Revolution and the Massachusetts Charter of 1691, this new emphasis began to appear in numerous sermons on the nature of good government, but it was only after the Awakening that the myth of the forefathers as stalwarts of liberty became a dominant theme, revealing the clergy's changing concerns.

In 1754 Mayhew articulated the form of this myth, which would become standard for the following generation. "Our ancestors," he declared, "tho' not perfect and infallible in all respects, were a religious, brave and vertuous set of men, whose love of liberty, civil and religious, brought them from their native land, into the American deserts."[55] By the end of the French and Indian War this grafting of whig political values into the traditional conceptions of New England's collective identity was virtually complete. In his thanksgiving sermon for the victory at Quebec Samuel Cooper reflected on New England's history and surmised that his progenitors had transplanted themselves into the wilds of America because they were "smitten with a Love of Liberty, and possessed with an uncommon Reverence to the Dictates of Conscience."[56] In repeating this interpretation of the myth New England ministers did not argue for a more secular interpretation of their own origins. Instead, they incorporated certain prevailing political values into a framework that still idealized the religious motivations of their ancestors. It was not piety alone but also the sacred cause of liberty that had inspired migration to the New World.[57]

The new terms of this myth indicate the evolution of the clergy's definition of their society's meaning and purpose as with greater frequency and intensity they attributed religious significance to commonly held political values. This quest for "civil and religious liberty" became the social ideal of clergymen who in many cases made a virtual identification of piety and whiggery. Benjamin Stevens expressed the sentiment of a growing number of ministers when he proposed that "liberty both civil and religious is the spirit and genius of the sacred writings."[58]

This new pattern of identity found expression in distinctly apocalyptic categories. The civil and religious liberty of British Protestants became the divine standard against the antichristian foe of French popery and

[55] Jonathan Mayhew, *A Sermon Preach'd in the Audience of His Excellency William Shirley* . . . (Boston, 1754), 28.
[56] Samuel Cooper, *A Sermon Preached before His Excellency Thomas Pownall* . . . (Boston, 1759), 28.
[57] Eliot, *Sermon Preached October 25th*, 17.
[58] Benjamin Stevens, *A Sermon Preached at Boston* . . . , *May 27, 1761* . . . (Boston, 1761), 8.

346

slavery. In a sermon to soldiers in 1757 James Cogswell indicated the civil priorities that had come to evoke a religious reaction: "I would entreat you to see to it that *you engage in so noble a Cause for right Ends.* Let your principal Motives be the Honor of God, and the Defence of your Country. Fight for Liberty and against Slavery. Endeavour to stand the Guardians of the Religion and Liberties of *America;* to oppose Antichrist, and prevent the barbarous Butchering of your fellow Countrymen." Cogswell urged the troops to be "inspired with an unconquerable Aversion to Popery and Slavery and an ardent Love to Religion and Liberty." In this new eschatology the French were identified with cosmic evil as much for their civil tyranny as for any other reason, and, as Samuel Davies admitted, "the Art of War becomes a Part of our Religion."[59]

As the ministers more closely identified religion and liberty, it was not uncommon for them to attribute to antichrist a plot between "the *scepter* and the *surplice* for enslaving both the *bodies* and *souls* of men."[60] The civil dimension of Satan's designs became a major theme both in the development of myths about the past and in the depiction of the French threat. In this way New Englanders moved in the direction of equating the war of the dragon against the woman with the threat of "slavery" common to whig ideology.[61] Thus when John Adams in 1765 pictured the course of history as a progressive, if embattled, advance of civil and religious liberty against the tyranny of antichrist represented in the canon and feudal law, he was expressing a pattern of thought that was prevalent among New England intellectuals.[62]

Perceiving that popery and slavery had struck a bargain for their destruction, New Englanders grounded their collective identity solidly in the ideals of British Protestantism and the British constitution. Far from developing in the twenty years before the Stamp Act a sense of America's moral superiority to England, the clergy identified Great Britain as the bastion of freedom and the bulwark against antichrist. For

347

[59] James Cogswell, *God, the pious Soldier's Strength and Instructor* . . . (Boston, 1757), 26, 11; Samuel Davies, *The Curse of Cowardice* . . . (Woodbridge, N. J., 1759), 2, 304. See also John Ballantine, *The Importance of God's Presence with an Army* . . . (Boston, 1756), 18-19.

[60] Jonathan Mayhew to Experience Mayhew, Oct. 1, 1747, Jonathan Mayhew Papers, Boston University Library, Boston.

[61] Charles W. Akers, *Called unto Liberty: A Life of Jonathan Mayhew, 1720-1766* (Cambridge, Mass., 1964), 81-97.

[62] John Adams, *A Dissertation on the Canon and Feudal Law,* in Charles Francis Adams, ed., *The Works of John Adams* . . . , III (Boston, 1851), 447-452.

most ministers the corollary of abhorring the superstition and idolatry of popish religion was "Loyalty to the Crown . . . Attachment to the Protestant Succession in the illustrious House of *Hanover* . . . and . . . Establishment in Protestant Principles."[63] New Englanders had never been more proud of their birthright as British subjects because increasingly the liberties they most valued were perceived as those of freeborn Britons. By the end of the French wars the preachers often referred to God's British Israel and included Britons among God's covenanted people.[64]

The clearest indication of the clergy's anglicization is the new dimension of their myth-building. During the two decades after the Great Awakening they not only altered the purposes for which their ancestors settled New England but enlarged their myths to include Great Britain. It is fair to say, in fact, that during the French wars New England ministers gave far more time to creating a usable British past than to formulating myths about the New World. Tracing providential history as the continuous battle of liberty versus tyranny, they centered their attention on the British constitution—"the admiration and Envy of the World."[65] In sermon after sermon they lifted up the standard of British liberty against the aggressive tyranny of Roman Catholicism. Assuming that popery and slavery were inseparably connected, they discovered that all Britain's past evils were attributable to Catholicism and France.[66] According to Thomas Prince, King Charles I "married a *French Papist,* Sister of King *Lewis* XIII of *France,* which was the pernicious Fountain of almost all the Miseries of the *British* Nations ever since." Similarly, the arbitrary government of James II could be linked to his "popish and despotic Principles," as could the futile designs of Charles the Pretender, whose outlook was characterized by *"Popish* Tyranny, Superstition, Bigotry, and cruel Principles."[67]

Although the ministers did include the founding of New England among the great acts by which providence had secured their rights as free men, they focused their myth-making on the Glorious Revolution and the accession of the Hanoverians. It was King William, "the Deliverer of the Nation, and the Shield of its Liberty," who more than anyone else protected succeeding generations from popish enslavement. Ministers

---

[63] Abbot, *Duty of God's People,* 17-18.

[64] Thomas Foxcroft, *Grateful Reflections on the signal Appearances of Divine Providence* . . . (Boston, 1760), 10, 12; Langdon, *Joy and Gratitude,* 23-24.

[65] Barnard, *Sermon Preached before Bernard,* 37.

[66] Charles Chauncy, *The Counsel of two confederate Kings* . . . (Boston, 1746), 26; Foxcroft, *Grateful Reflections,* 12-20.

[67] Prince, *Sermon Delivered At the South Church,* 8, 12.

repeatedly exalted the Glorious Revolution as the fountainhead of the privileges enjoyed by eighteenth-century Britons.[68] In similar fashion the standard myth portrayed the Hanoverians as preservers of liberty and Protestantism. According to Thomas Foxcroft, if George I had not come to the throne, events "might have involved *Britain,* and these Colonies with it, in Blood and Ruin, and might have entail'd Chains and Misery on the latest Posterity."[69] In another sermon Foxcroft summed up this myth of the British past:

Now to single out a few very memorable Times, and not go back beyond the Memory of many yet alive:—Never to be forgotten is that glorious *Year* 1688, signalis'd as a *Year of the Right Hand of the most High,* by that most seasonable Interposition of Divine Providence in the wonderful REVOLUTION; delivering us from the Perils we were in of *Popery* and *Slavery,* two of the most comprehensive Mischiefs, and securing to us our invaluable Laws and Liberties, the Rights of Conscience, and the Religion of Protestants.—Again, Never to be forgotten is that glorious Year 1714, signalis'd as a *Year of the Right Hand of the most High,* by the happy and most seasonable *Accession* of the illustrious House of HANOVER to the *British* throne; Preventing that imminent Danger the *Protestant Succession* (in the Fate of which all our valuable Interests must be involv'd) was in at that Juncture, when deep-laid Plots of Papal Enemies and false Brethren threatened to subvert it.[70]

349

This idealization of British liberty, both civil and religious, came to maturity in the 1740s and 1750s. Although the Anglo-French wars were by no means the single determinant of this development, the conflict brought into the forefront of religious thinking certain whig political ideals which since the seventeenth century had been latent in New England thought. Against the onslaught of popery and slavery the sacred cause of liberty became the banner under which New Englanders rallied. The clergy expressed this new feeling of identity in the themes that reflected their sense of the past and view of the future. Not only had the course of providential history followed the rise of liberty, but the triumph of liberty would be realized in the coming of the millennium. Just as New

[68] Foxcroft, *Grateful Reflections,* 20. See also Chauncy, *Counsel of two confederate Kings,* 26, and Barnard, *Sermon Preached before Bernard,* 38.
[69] Foxcroft, *Grateful Reflections,* 23.
[70] Thomas Foxcroft, *A Seasonable Memento for New Year's Day* (Boston, 1747), 70.

Lights in the 1740s had seen the past and future in terms of the concerns of vital piety, so clergymen at war with France expressed their allegiance to liberty in the framework of civil millennialism.

Understandably exhilarated by the expulsion of France from North America, New Englanders anticipated the total destruction of the power of antichrist. They had scarcely savored victory, however, when the grasping hand of tyranny reappeared in a new and dangerous form. What is remarkable about the ministers' response both to the Stamp Act and to the attempt to create an American bishopric is their application of the compelling ideology of civil millennialism to these unexpected challenges.[71] Although the threats now came from England, they represented a continuation of the Man of Sin's assault on liberty. Thus when Sherwood attributed the Quebec Act to "the flood of the dragon that has been poured forth . . . for the establishment of popery," or when Langdon suspected that British taxation originated in popish religion, they were speaking from the same perspective of providential history that had fired New England's opposition to French tyranny.[72] Attempting to identify the Image of the Beast (Rev. 13), Sherwood in the mid-1770s gave an illuminating demonstration of how civil millennialism could be mobilized against the British:

Whether that persecuting power be intended, that has in years past, been so cruelly and barbarously exercised in France, and other popish countries, against the humble followers of Christ, to the massacre and destruction of so many thousands of protestants; or whether there be a reference to the

350

[71] In his thanksgiving sermon on the repeal of the Stamp Act Joseph Emerson viewed this taxation in the same historical framework in which New Englanders had seen the threat of French oppression. It was another in a long succession of attempts by popery and slavery to subvert liberty. The purpose of the taxation was "to support the pride and vanity of diocesan Bishops, and it may be by and by making us tributary to the See of Rome." Emerson feared that the conflict between England and the American colonies would weaken both so that the French or the House of Stuart might come to power. *A Thanksgiving Sermon, Preach'd at Pepperrell* . . . (Boston, 1760), 11-21. In similar fashion William Patten suggested that the sponsors of the Stamp Act were "perhaps no enemies to France, and not very friendly to Christian liberty," while Stephen Johnson feared the tyranny of "a corrupt, Frenchified party in the nation." *A Discourse Delivered at Hallifax* . . . (Boston, 1766), 21. See also Stephen Johnson, *Some Important Observations* . . . (Newport, R. I., 1766), 15.

[72] Sherwood, *The Church's Flight*, 33; Samuel Langdon, *Government Corrupted By Vice* (Boston, 1775), 28-29.

corrupt system of tyranny and oppression, that has of late been fabricated and adopted by the ministry and parliament of Great-Britain, which appears so favourable to popery and the Roman catholic interest, aiming at the extension and establishment of it, and so awfully threatens the civil and religious liberties of all sound protestants; I cannot positively determine. But since the prophesies represent this wicked scheme of antichristian tyranny, as having such an extensive and universal spread over the earth . . . it need not appear strange or shocking to us, to find that our own nation has been, in some degree, infected and corrupted therewith.[73]

351

The civil millennialism of the Revolutionary era, expressed by rationalists as well as pietists, grew directly out of the politicizing of Puritan millennial history in the two decades before the Stamp Act crisis. In marked contrast to the apolitical millennial hopes of Jonathan Edwards, which had been based on the success of the revival, civil millennialism advanced freedom as the cause of God, defined the primary enemy as the antichrist of civil oppression rather than that of formal religion, traced the myths of its past through political developments rather than through the vital religion of the forefathers, and turned its vision toward the privileges of Britons rather than to a heritage exclusive to New England.

During the Revolutionary crisis, when ministers once again emphasized the moral distinction between the Old World and the New, ironically they did so because in the previous years their own identity had become shaped in the image of British culture.[74] The sacred cause of liberty of which the patriot clergy were so enamored was not the flowering of an incipient American nationalism planted by the Awakening, nor did the initial volley of American muskets transform the millennialism of Edwards into that of Sherwood or Langdon. Instead, the religious patriotism that animated the Revolution had intellectual roots far more British than American. In the early 1770s, however, the intellectual and emotional force of civil millennialism, incorporating whig political values, was brought to bear against England itself, as ministers linked apocalyptic vision to the cause of American liberty, identified the "fixed plan to enslave the colonies" with Satan's continuing conspiracy against God's people, and detected in the growth of arbitrary power, the corruption of placemen, and the ominous threat of standing armies the unabated malice

---

[73] Sherwood, *The Church's Flight*, 14-15.
[74] For a full description of the British orientation of 18th-century American culture see Murrin, "Anglicizing an American Colony."

of the Man of Sin. It was this redefinition of the terms of providential history that constituted the distinctive contribution of the New England clergy to Revolutionary ideology. In picturing the struggle of liberty versus tyranny as nothing less than the conflict between heaven and hell, the clergy found their political commitments energized with the force of a divine imperative and their political goals translated into the very principles which would initiate the kingdom of God on earth.[75]

[75] An adequate understanding of the clergy's role in the Revolution awaits a thorough analysis of the relationship between traditional ideas of providential history and the prevailing mood of "country" ideology. The most helpful work in this direction is Bernard Bailyn, "Religion and Revolution: Three Biographical Studies," *Perspectives in American History*, IV (1970), 85-169.

Revolution and Reform:
An Interpretation of Southern Taxation,
1763 to 1783

Robert A. Becker*

ALTHOUGH it has been nearly half a century since J. Franklin
Jameson suggested that the American Revolution was a social as
well as a political movement, some of his ideas have not yet been
fully explored. Among them is the proposition that seemingly lesser
changes in law and custom which affected the daily lives of ordinary
Americans were as important in determining the nature of the Revolution as the vast constitutional changes worked by prominent men acting
on a continental stage.[1] The world of most eighteenth-century Americans
was, after all, not continental but local. Their families, their lands, their
crops—these were what occupied their time from day to day. Lawyerly
pronouncements from Philadelphia or Charleston on the nature of the
British constitution were important to them. But so was the question of
how big the poll tax would be this year, and whether poor land would
be taxed as high as good land, for of all the different ways in which the
common citizen came in contact with his government, few were more
sensitive than the regular confrontation between taxpayer and tax collector.
Unlike the Stamp Tax or the Townshend revenue duties, internal taxes
had to be paid year after year, on the coasts and in the backlands, in good
times and bad, no matter what the condition of Anglo-American relations, and tax questions were often at the brawling center of colonial
politics.[2] In the southern colonies a characteristic pattern of taxation had
emerged by the 1760s. Independence and the Revolution changed that

* Mr. Becker is a member of the Department of History, Louisiana State University. He wishes to thank the Research Council of Louisiana State University
for research support.

[1] J. Franklin Jameson, *The American Revolution Considered as a Social Movement* (New York, 1926).
[2] See Robert Arthur Becker, "The Politics of Taxation in America, 1763-1783"
(Ph.D. diss., University of Wisconsin, 1971).

pattern, and the newly independent states levied taxes that were, on the whole, less regressive and more equitable than they had been before.

The politics of colonial taxation was extremely complex. The tax system in each southern colony by 1763 was the result of long development reaching back (except in Georgia) nearly a century and a half, and each system reflected the particular political and economic conditions of the colony involved. The interests of settlers in the piedmont and mountain South often clashed with the interests of those who lived in the lowcountry areas. Large planters and small farmers, no matter where they lived, often disagreed about what constituted fair taxation. Occasionally the "country" interest would unite against the commercial interest, ranging farmers and planters, large or small, east or west, against the merchant community. At other times, merchants and backcountry farmers made common cause against the large planters of the tidewater regions. In the eighteenth century the distinction between "planter" and "merchant" sometimes became unclear as many of the larger planters, particularly in Virginia and Maryland, regularly purchased the crops of their smaller neighbors and operated as planter-merchants.[3]

It is hardly surprising, then, that by 1763 each southern colony relied on a different mixture of poll, property, and commercial taxes to meet the ordinary expenses of government and the extraordinary expenses of fighting Indians and Frenchmen, or dealing with natural disasters. But this diversity concealed an underlying uniformity: throughout the South, the tax laws overburdened the politically impotent in general and the poor in particular, and favored the interests of the men of established landed wealth who normally dominated the southern legislatures.[4] Some colonies achieved this by relying heavily on poll taxes which were regressive in that they required all free white males above a certain age

354

[3] *Ibid.*, Chaps. 4-5; L. C. Gray, "The Market Surplus Problems of Colonial Tobacco," *Agricultural History*, II (1928), 19-21.

[4] On the domination of southern legislatures by men of landed wealth see Jack P. Greene, "Foundations of Political Power in the Virginia House of Burgesses, 1720-1776," *William and Mary Quarterly*, 3d Ser., XVI (1959), 485-506; Charles Albro Barker, *The Background of the Revolution in Maryland* (New Haven, Conn., 1940), 180-183; William A. Schaper, "Sectionalism and Representation in South Carolina," *Annual Report of the American Historical Association for the Year 1900*, I (1901), 345-354; and Jack P. Greene, *The Quest for Power: The Lower Houses of Assembly in the Southern Royal Colonies, 1689-1776* (Chapel Hill, N. C., 1963), Chap. 2.

to pay an equal tax, regardless of their wealth or income. Elsewhere, acreage land taxes (as distinct from ad valorem land taxes) which were discriminatory in that they taxed each acre equally, without regard to location, quality, productivity, or market value, worked to the low-country planters' advantage. Some colonies employed both types of discriminatory taxation.

Although tax discrimination took different forms in different colonies, the pattern was evident everywhere. In North Carolina, the system was simplicity itself: nearly three-quarters of the colony's revenues were collected by poll taxes, levied on every white male sixteen or older, regardless of his ability to pay, and on all blacks, slave or free, male or female, over the age of twelve.[5] In effect, the poll tax on slaves operated as a property tax paid by their owners, but landed and commercial wealth escaped virtually untapped. There were special penalties for those who were too poor to pay their poll taxes. Their personal property could be auctioned off, and if the auction failed to raise enough to clear the tax, the delinquent might be jailed for a month and then sold as an indentured servant for what he owed plus the cost of keeping him in jail "to such Person who for the shortest Time of Service will pay the Same."[6]

North Carolina's tax system was not only the most regressive in the South but also the least efficient and the most corrupt. Sheriffs and collectors falsified tax lists, piled fines on those who failed to obey arbitrary regulations, and arranged hasty auctions for overdue taxes so that their friends might bid valuable properties in cheaply.[7] Governor William

355

---

[5] Marvin L. Michael Kay, "The Payment of Provincial and Local Taxes in North Carolina, 1748-1771," *WMQ*, 3d Ser., XXVI (1969), 222-225; Marvin L. Michael Kay, "Provincial Taxes in North Carolina During the Administrations of Dobbs and Tryon," *North Carolina Historical Review*, XLII (1965), 440-441; "A Table of North Carolina Taxes, 1748-1770," in William K. Boyd, ed., *Some Eighteenth Century Tracts Concerning North Carolina* (Raleigh, N. C., 1927), 413ff. In 1760 ratable polls also included "all Persons of Mixt Blood to the Fourth Generation, of the Age of Twelve Years and upwards, and all white Persons intermarrying with any Negro, Mulatto, Mustee, or other Person of Mixt Blood, while so intermarried." Walter Clark *et al.*, eds., *The State Records of North Carolina* (Winston, Raleigh, and Goldsboro, N. C., 1895-1914), XXIII, 526-531, hereafter cited as *N. C. State Recs.* The volume numbers for the *N. C. State Recs.* begin with XI; Vols. I-X are William L. Saunders, ed., *The Colonial Records of North Carolina* (Raleigh, N. C., 1886-1890), hereafter cited as *N. C. Col. Recs.*

[6] *N. C. State Recs.*, XXIII, 526-531. Although the laws also provided that paupers might under some circumstances be excused from taxes, sheriffs apparently violated those laws with impunity. See, for example, "An Act directing the Duty of Sheriffs, with Respect to Insolvent Taxables," 1774, *ibid.*, 970, and Julian P. Boyd, "The Sheriff in Colonial North Carolina," *NCHR*, V (1928), 164-165.

[7] Herman Husband, "An Impartial Relation of the First Rise and Cause of

Tryon estimated in 1767 that only about half the money collected at the county level ever found its way into the treasury.[8]

Such corruption was among the primary causes of the Regulator troubles of the late 1760s, but the Regulators' criticisms of North Carolina taxes went much deeper. They, or at least their spokesmen, understood that even if all the grafting sheriffs and collectors were replaced by scrupulously honest men, the colony's revenue system would continue to be discriminatory and regressive as long as general poll taxes remained a substantial part of it. Is it just, asked a resident of Mecklenburg, that a man "worth 10,000 £ pays no more than a poor back settler that has nothing but the labour of his hands to depend upon for his daily support?"[9] A few shillings in taxes might seem trifling to gentlemen "Rowling in affluence," complained petitioners from Rowan and Orange counties in 1768, but "to Poor People who must have their Bed and Bedclothes yea their Wives Petticoats taken and sold to Defray [taxes], how Tremenious [sic] judges must be the Consequences: an only Horse, to raise Bread or by Only Cow, to give Milk to an helpless Family by which in a Great Measure are Otherwise Supported seized and sold."[10] To end oppression of "poor Inhabitants . . . by reason of disproportionate Taxes," Anson County petitioners demanded that an income tax be instituted so that each man might pay "in proportion to the proffits arising from his Estate." Herman Husband made the point graphically in 1770. "The Publick taxes," he wrote, "is an unequal burden on the poor of this

356

the Recent Differences, in Public Affairs, In the Province of North Carolina . . . ," in Boyd, ed., Tracts, 260-262, 318-319; George Sims, "An Address to the People of Granville County," June 6, 1765, ibid., 182-192; "The Request of the Inhabitants of the West Side of Haw-River, to the Assembly-men and Vestry-men of Orange County," Mar. 22, 1768, ibid., 264-266; Orange County instructions to representatives [Dec. 1773], N. C. Col. Recs., IX, 699-706. See also Kay, "Payment of Provincial and Local Taxes," WMQ, 3d Ser., XXVI (1969), 222-225; Kay, "Provincial Taxes," NCHR, XLII (1965), 440-453; Boyd, "The Sheriff," ibid., V (1928), 161-172; and John S. Bassett, "The Regulators of North Carolina (1765-1771)," Annual Report of the American Historical Association for the Year 1894 (1895), 150-155.

[8] Gov. William Tryon to Lord Shelburne, 1767, quoted in Lawrence Henry Gipson, The Coming of the Revolution, 1763-1775 (New York, 1954), 144. Kay, "Provincial Taxes," NCHR, XLII, 441, n. 2, estimates that 25% of all poll taxes collected between 1754 and 1770 were embezzled by sheriffs and notes that it is impossible to determine how much more was embezzled at higher levels.

[9] "A Letter from Mecklenburg in North Carolina," Boston Chronicle, Nov. 7, 14, 1768, reprinted in William S. Powell et al., comps. and eds., The Regulators in North Carolina: A Documentary History, 1759-1776 (Raleigh, N. C., 1971), 195-196.

[10] "Petition of Citizens of Rowan and Orange Counties," Oct. 4, 1768, ibid., 187-188.

province, by reason the poorest man is taxed as high as the richest. Allowing the taxes to be all necessary, yet there ought to be some regard had
to the strength of the beast, for all asses are not equally strong. We ought
to be taxed accordingly to the profits of each man's estate."[11]

During the summer of 1768 the Regulators from Orange County
offered Governor Tryon their aid in wresting financial reforms from an
assembly that was "too hard for your Excellency as well as for us" to
handle. But Tryon chose to avoid a long, costly battle with his assembly
over tax reform, and by 1771 the Regulation had been crushed.[12] Demands
for a more equitable distribution of taxes went unanswered in North
Carolina before the Revolution. Yet the Regulator movement in general,
and the unsuccessful efforts to reform the colony's revenue system in
particular, convinced many discontented North Carolinians that the source
of their most pressing problems lay in Edenton, not London. It is not
"any reflection on the king, to say, the poor are oppressed," explained
Husband in 1770, "for he don't make our laws."[13] Some were beginning
to see that the principles colonial legislatures invoked so freely against
parliamentary taxation could have internal applications as well.[14]

In Virginia, tobacco export taxes, supplemented by quitrents and
occasional minor poll taxes, paid the ordinary costs of running the colony.
When frontier war with the French began in 1754 and the House of
Burgesses had to raise money for defense, however, the pattern of discrimination in favor of landed wealth emerged clearly. The Burgesses
looked on a land tax—any land tax—as an inconvenient, unpleasant, and
above all temporary expedient. In 1755, after a year of new poll taxes
had failed to raise enough revenue, they reluctantly imposed the first
provincial land tax Virginians had known for over a century. This was
an acreage tax that fell on all land equally, regardless of its productivity
or location, and thus benefited those well-established planters in the tidewater and eastern counties who owned the best land and enjoyed
relatively easy access to the sea.[15] Furthermore, the amount raised annually

357

[11] "The Petition of the Inhabitants of Anson County," Oct. 9, 1769, N. C. Col.
Recs., VIII, 75-80; Husband, "Impartial Relation," in Boyd, ed., Tracts, 318. See
also Orange County instructions, N. C. Col. Recs., IX, 701.
[12] Francis Dorset et al. to Tryon, 1768, N. C. Col. Recs., VII, 801-803. The 8
signers of the letter were described as "persons stiling themselves Regulators."
Tryon's reply is ibid., 804-806. See also Kay, "Provincial Taxes," NCHR, XLII, 447-
453.
[13] Husband, "Impartial Relation," in Boyd, ed., Tracts, 318.
[14] For an internal application of arguments commonly used by colonial legislatures against parliamentary taxes see "Inhabitants of the West Side of Haw-River,"
ibid., 264-266.
[15] William Zebina Ripley, The Financial History of Virginia, 1609-1776 (New

by land taxes from the first in 1755 to the last in 1768 never equaled the amount raised by the poll taxes. The Burgesses expected the wartime poll tax to bring in £10,000 in its first year. The new land taxes raised less than £4,000 in their first two years.[16] The Burgesses planned to raise £24,000 annually from poll taxes between 1763 and 1765 to retire the colony's paper money, but they expected to raise only £19,000 annually during the same period from all other sinking-fund taxes combined (which included the land tax and some tobacco export duties, slave import taxes, and carriage taxes). From 1766 through 1768 they planned to raise £30,000 a year by increasing poll taxes while reducing the yield from all other sinking-fund taxes to £15,000 per year.[17] These figures do not take into account either the extra poll tax (forty-six pounds of tobacco per poll) levied in 1764 to pay for suppressing Pontiac's rebellion or other supplementary poll taxes levied in 1766, 1769, and 1772.[18]

The Burgesses showed their preference for poll taxes again in 1765. For several years, treasurer of the colony and Speaker of the House John Robinson had been quietly lending to his associates and to himself more than £100,000 in paper money that had been taxed out of circulation and that Robinson, as treasurer, should have destroyed.[19] In April 1765, six

---

York, 1893), 32-39; Percy Scott Flippin, *The Financial Administration of the Colony of Virginia*, The Johns Hopkins University Studies in Historical and Political Science, XXXIII (Baltimore, 1915), 79-80. The appropriate laws are in William Waller Hening, ed., *The Statutes at Large; Being a Collection of All the Laws of Virginia* . . . (Richmond, Va., 1819-1823), VI, 435-438, 522-530, VII, 69-87, 163-169, 171-179, 255-265, 347-353, 357-363, 495-502. Unlike some northern colonies, Virginia did not distinguish for tax purposes between cultivated and wild land or between "located" (surveyed) and unlocated land. The impact of the new taxes on land speculators is unclear. It is very doubtful that taxes were collected on unsurveyed tracts on or beyond the frontier, although those who held surveyed land farther east did pay, whether or not their land was under cultivation.

[16] Ripley, *Financial History*, 40-41. As in North Carolina, slaves were ratable polls and to that extent the poll taxes operated as a property tax on slave owners. *Ibid.*, 36-38.

[17] Journals of the Virginia House of Burgesses, May 24, 1763, hereafter cited as Va. House Journals. Colonial and early state legislative journals are available as "Records of the States of the United States; a Microfilm Compilation Prepared by the Library of Congress in Association with the University of North Carolina," William S. Jenkins, ed. Poll taxes were therefore expected to produce over 55% of the sinking funds for 1763-1765, 66% for 1766-1768, and 68% by 1769 (£24,000 on polls against £6,250 on land and £5,000 on tobacco exports).

[18] Hening, ed., *Statutes of Va.*, VIII, 38-41, 273-275, 340-342, 533-534. Paid in currency at rates established by law in 1761, the 46 pound poll tax came to about 8s. per poll. *Ibid., VII*, 385. Poll taxes levied by counties and parishes made the disparity between poll and property taxes even greater. See Ripley, *Financial History*, Chap. 4.

[19] On the Robinson scandal see David John Mays, *Edmund Pendleton, 1721-*

months after they had complained to Parliament and the king that further parliamentary taxes would reduce the colony to "desolation," the Burgesses proposed to tax the money in again in order to cover Robinson's peculations, which were well known to many Burgesses but had not yet become public knowledge, and they proposed doing it by poll taxes.[20] The Burgesses hoped to borrow £240,000 sterling from English merchants: £100,000 of this sum would be used to redeem the illegally circulating currency that Robinson had loaned out, and a loan office would be opened with the remainder. But English merchants, who were having difficulty collecting debts from Virginians, doubted the integrity and credit of the colony, and the Burgesses therefore agreed to back their borrowing with the colony's most dependable source of revenue, the tobacco export tax.[21] They planned to increase it from 3s. sterling a hogshead to 10s. between 1766 and 1775, and then lower it to 6s. for four years after that. As matters stood, however, the bulk of the new taxes would have been paid by the larger tobacco planters—directly if they marketed their crops under the old consignment system or exported them on their own account, indirectly in the form of lower prices if they sold to the Scottish merchants in Virginia who were beginning to dominate the tobacco trade.[22] To correct this, the Burgesses prepared a plan designed to shift the whole burden from tobacco exports to polls. They proposed that the colony repay every planter and exporter an amount equal to the new tax on every hogshead exported, the money to be raised by a new poll tax of 3s. from 1767 to 1769 and 3s. 6d. from 1770 to 1779.

The plan failed in the council where it ran into a strong prejudice against new taxes and the loan office plan. In May 1766 Robinson died, and the following month reports of large unexplained shortages at the treasury appeared in the Virginia papers.[23] The taxes imposed during

1803: A Biography, I (Cambridge, Mass., 1952), Chaps. 11, 12, and Joseph Albert Ernst, "The Robinson Scandal Redivivus: Money, Debts, and Politics in Revolutionary Virginia," *Virginia Magazine of History and Biography*, LXXVII (1969), 146-173.

[20] Va. House Journals, Nov. 14, 1764, May 24, 1765; Thomas Jefferson to William Wirt (enclosure), Apr. 12, 1812, in Paul Leicester Ford, ed., *The Works of Thomas Jefferson*, XI (New York, 1905), 228-229. The details of the Burgesses' plan described below are from Va. House Journals, May 24, 1765.

[21] Petition of merchants trading in and to Virginia, Va. House Journals, Nov. 2, 1764.

[22] For the marketing practices of Virginia planters see Gray, "Market Surplus Problems," *Ag. Hist.*, II (1928), 13-21, and Richard L. Morton, *Colonial Virginia*, II (Chapel Hill, N. C., 1960), 510-511.

[23] Virginia Council Journals, May 28, 1765; Robert Carter Nicholas to the

the French and Indian War had weighed heavily on people's pockets and on the public mind as well. "Taxes on taxes are multiplied," James Maury of Louisa County had complained in 1756, adding that they were especially burdensome to the "lower ranks of people." When the Robinson scandal broke a decade later, it seemed to many that little had changed: taxes were still high and there was in addition a critical currency shortage.[24] Some sheriffs refused even to try to collect taxes, and several counties found it impossible to hire anyone who would collect them.[25] The news of mysterious shortages at the treasury provoked an uproar. Aspiring politicians like Robert Carter Nicholas, who had been appointed temporary treasurer after Robinson's death and was politicking hard to win the job permanently, found it prudent to speak publicly of money "squeezed from the people for their taxes."[26] The Stamp Act crisis had focused public attention on the distinction between just and unjust taxes, and discussion soon spread (as it had in North Carolina) from the narrow topic of malfeasance to the broader issue of fundamental tax reform. A writer in the *Virginia Gazette*, for example, denounced poll taxes as oppressive and demanded that they be replaced by property taxes so that "none but those possessed of slaves, and other estates, will pay the levies and taxes. They are best able and they ought."[27]

After the Robinson scandal the Burgesses separated the offices of treasurer and Speaker of the House, and created a watchdog committee to audit the public accounts every six months and to publish its findings, so that, as one irate correspondent put it, we "may be fully satisfy'd how the Money raised by heavy Taxes, and (by most of us) in the Sweat of our Brows, is disposed of."[28] In the winter of 1766 the Burgesses also ap-

---

Printer, Purdie and Dixon's *Virginia Gazette* (Williamsburg), June 27, 1776; Ernst, "Robinson Scandal," *VMHB*, LXXVII (1969), 155. The exact details of Robinson's embezzlements and the names of those involved never became fully public, but by the fall of 1766 the fact that large sums were unaccounted for could no longer be effectively denied. *Ibid.*, 161-166.

[24] James Maury to John Fontaine, June 15, 1756, in Ann Maury, ed., *Memoirs of a Huguenot Family* (New York, 1853), 400-408. In a letter that was typical of the times Peter Fontaine of Hanover County complained that "things wear but a gloomy aspect." This country, he continued, "is so excessively poor, that even the industrious, frugal man can scarcely live, and the least slip in economy would be fatal. There is no money . . ." Peter Fontaine to J. Fontaine, July 8, 1765, *ibid.*, 374.

[25] Hening, ed., *Statutes of Va.*, VIII, 178-182; Va. House Journals, Dec. 12, 1766.

[26] Nicholas to the Printer, Purdie and Dixon's *Va. Gaz.*, June 27, 1766.

[27] "Consideratus," *ibid.*, July 11, 1766.

[28] Hening, ed., *Statutes of Va.*, VIII, 211-214; "A Planter," Rind's *Va. Gaz.*,

proved a new tax on slaves and earmarked the proceeds for "lessening the levy by the poll." The following spring they proposed a new loan office plan that did not include taxes to bail out Robinson's estate and that would have been supported by a variety of means other than poll taxes. In 1768, on the same day they asked George III and Parliament to relieve them of the Townshend revenue duties, the Burgesses also resolved that "so much of the several acts of assembly imposing the land and poll tax on the inhabitants of this colony, as requires taxes to be collected in the present and succeeding year, be repealed."[29] When frontier troubles and floods forced new taxes the next year, these taxes were laid on legal processes, tobacco exports, tavern licenses, slaves, and carriages. "It hath been found by experience," the Burgesses intoned, that these were "easy to the people, and not so burthensome as a poll tax."[30]

The elimination of land and poll taxes for the sinking fund by 1770 made the question of what constituted an equitable tax less pressing for the moment. Nevertheless, the Burgesses had not rejected the principle of poll taxes or the principle of taxing land by the acre, nor had they publicly committed themselves to taxation in proportion to ability to pay. But the Robinson scandal and the continuing dispute with England over taxes made it inevitable that the question of tax equity would come up the next time Virginia had to raise large sums rapidly.

South Carolina's tax system was far more comprehensive than either Virginia's or North Carolina's, and far less regressive. It included, among other things, rates on imported slaves, spirits, and some food items, a poll tax on free blacks (but none on whites), and taxes on money-at-interest, on annuities, on the "wares merchandize and book debts of persons in trade, shop keepers and others," and on "profits of all faculties, professions, (the clergy excepted,) factorage and handicraft trades throughout this Province." In addition, land and slaves were taxed, but in ways that favored the wealthy lowcountry planters who dominated the legislature.

361

Aug. 8, 1766.
[29] Hening, ed., *Statutes of Va.*, VIII, 237-238, 295-298; Va. House Journals, Apr. 11, 1767, Mar. 21, Apr. 7, 1768; Va. Council Journals, Apr. 13, 1768. This action was justified by a report from the committee auditing public accounts. It revealed that £170,420 of the treasury notes issued between 1754 and 1762 were still circulating. Counting the £109,335 the Robinson estate owed the public (plus about £60,000 more in various tax arrears) as assets, the committee concluded that the tobacco and carriage taxes and license fees would be more than sufficient to redeem the remaining £294 within two years. The purpose and result of the measure were to keep the old treasury notes circulating still longer. In 1772 over £88,000 worth were still out. Va. House Journals, Apr. 17, 1768, Mar. 6, 1772.
[30] Hening, ed., *Statutes of Va.*, VIII, 343.

Of the different kinds of property taxed—land, slaves, town lots and buildings, wharves or other improvements on town lots, money-at-interest, and merchants' stock-in-trade—all except the first two paid ad valorem. Land other than town lots was taxed equally by the acre regardless of its location, productivity, or value, and the value of slaves for tax purposes was fixed by law at a level substantially below that of their current market value.[31]

The system worked to the disadvantage of backcountry settlers. South Carolina's Regulators, for example, demanded that "the tax upon lands up on the frontiers, which are of very little value, ought not to be as great as upon lands of great value near a market." Although the legislature responded to several Regulator complaints, it ignored all demands that land taxes be levied ad valorem.[32]

South Carolina was unique among the southern colonies in having an important commercial city, Charleston. The colony's tax laws discriminated blatantly against city residents in general and the commercial community in particular. Before 1759 Charleston was required by law to raise 20 percent of the general provincial tax revenues. In 1759 the city's share rose to 25 percent. By 1765 it stood at 28 percent. City residents complained that they and only they paid an ad valorem tax on their property. Merchants objected that they paid a tax on their property and slaves as well as a tax on the income derived from them "under the head of profits in trade, faculties, etc.," while "the planter in the country pays no tax at all on the profits of his own labor . . . or the profits of his Negroes however great such annual profits may be." A man who had £7,000 invested in property or stock-in-trade in Charleston in 1770, complained one petitioner, paid 10s. tax for each £100 value, or a total of £35. But

[31] Thomas Cooper and D. J. McCord, eds., *The Statutes at Large of South Carolina* (Columbia, S. C., 1836-1841), IV, 128-144, 150-151, 189-198, 238-248, hereafter cited as *S. C. Statutes;* W. Roy Smith, *South Carolina as a Royal Province, 1719-1776* (New York, 1903), 238; South Carolina House Journals, Feb. 22, 1770, Early State Records microfilm. For domination of legislative proceedings by lowcountry representatives see Schaper, "Sectionalism and Representation," *AHA Annual Report for 1900,* I, 345-353. From tax records for 1786-1787 Jackson Turner Main, *The Social Structure of Revolutionary America* (Princeton, N. J., 1965), 57-58, concludes that in the prosperous rice-growing parishes of St. Paul's and St. James's "one-third of the taxpayers had 1,000 acres and more and one-fourth had fifty slaves." It was just such areas that were heavily overrepresented in the pre-Revolutionary legislature.

[32] Petition of Thomas Bell *et al.,* S. C. House Journals, July 4, 1768; petitions of "several inhabitants living on the frontier and interior parts of this province," *ibid.,* July 5, 11, 1769; Richard Maxwell Brown, *The South Carolina Regulators* (Cambridge, Mass., 1963), 139; S. C. House Journals, Nov. 25, 1769.

a man who invested £7,000 in land outside Charleston might pay as little as £7 property tax.[33]

Poor relief made Charleston's tax burden heavier still. After 1763, poor rates soared as indigent persons drifted into the city from all parts of South Carolina and from North Carolina and Georgia. The city had spent £1,200 on poor relief in 1747; the cost rose to £6,100 in 1763 and £6,500 in 1766, much of the money raised by special taxes in addition to what Charlestonians paid in common with the rest of the colony for the support of the transient poor.[34] City spokesmen often demanded that poor relief be put "on such a Footing that every Part of the Province may bear an equal Proportion thereof."[35] When a seven-man committee, containing four city representatives, reported in 1767 that Charleston's poor rates were "intolerable" and recommended that poor relief costs be supported by the colony as a whole, the rural-dominated assembly decided that the problem needed more study. It appointed a new committee of seven, this time including only one city representative, which ultimately made several recommendations that did not include support of Charleston's poor by means of a colony-wide general property tax. The one recommendation that threatened to cost the country parishes substantial sums—that paupers arriving in Charleston be swiftly returned to their parish of origin—was defeated by the house.[36]

Led by Christopher Gadsden, city petitioners repeatedly and unsuccessfully asked for essentially the same reform that backcountry Regulators were demanding: a colony-wide property tax based on value rather than on acreage.[37] By the end of 1770 it was clear that substantive tax reform would have to await either a redistribution of power within the

363

---

[33] S. C. House Journals, Apr. 16, 1767, Feb. 22, 27, 1770. The percentages for Charleston are *ibid.*, Apr. 16, 1767. See also Smith, *South Carolina*, 282, and M. Eugene Sirmans, *Colonial South Carolina: A Political History, 1663-1763* (Chapel Hill, N. C., 1966), 244.
[34] Petition of Charleston Vestrymen and Churchwardens, S. C. House Journals, Nov. 25, 1766; report of a committee to consider the problem of poor relief in Charleston, *ibid.*, Apr. 6, 1767.
[35] Presentment of the Grand Jurors, Charleston, Jan. 21, 1771, printed in *South-Carolina Gazette* (Charleston), Feb. 7, 1771; S. C. House Journals, Feb. 22, 1770; presentment of the Grand Jurors, Charleston, Jan. 15, 1770, printed in *South-Carolina Gazette; and Country Journal* (Charleston), Jan. 23, 1770.
[36] S. C. House Journals, Mar. 4, 12, 13, Apr. 6, 8, 1767. The legislature did agree to extend the time necessary to establish residency (and therefore a claim on the public for support) from 3 months to 12, and to finance a new poorhouse and hospital out of import duties on wine, rum, and other consumables. *S. C. Statutes*, VII, 90-92.
[37] S. C. House Journals, Feb. 22, Mar. 2, 15, 1770.

colony or a crisis severe enough to force the dominant political interests to barter reform in one area for public support in another.

The tax system of sparsely populated Georgia, which enjoyed what amounted to a subsidy from Parliament, resembled that of South Carolina. Georgia imposed an acreage land tax and a head tax on slaves, but ad valorem rates on town lots, buildings, money "lying at Interest by Choice," and all "Goods Wares and Merchandize" imported into the colony "with Intent to Sell again by any Merchant, Factor, Store keeper or other person whatsoever."[38] The laws discriminated most heavily against free blacks. They alone paid colony poll taxes, commonly 15s. a year for most of the period from 1763 to 1770. By contrast, the tax on each slave and on each one hundred acres of land was usually only 2s. 6d. In 1773, when land and slave taxes were at a ten-year low of 1s. 6d. per slave or hundred acres, the free black poll tax reached a peak of 20s.[39]

Of all the southern colonies, proprietary Maryland had the most clearly defined system of party politics, and its tax system was shaped by party strife. A proprietary (court) party battled an antiproprietary (country) party for control of the legislature. The court party dominated the council, and country party leaders, excluded from the proprietor's favor and opposed to his supporters for a variety of political, personal, economic, and religious reasons, struggled to maintain a majority in the lower house.[40] They constantly sought popular issues on which to attack the proprietorship and win public support, and in taxation they found an issue made to order to do exactly that. But the subject had to be handled delicately, for no matter how much leaders of the two factions were at odds, they shared an important characteristic: virtually all of them were substantial landowners. A sizable majority of the assemblymen owned more than 500 acres each, and many measured their holdings in thousands of acres. Among the councillors, the average holding was over 8,000 acres in 1758 and over 7,800 acres in 1771. Leaders of both factions and both houses were included among Maryland's leading land-

[38] Allen D. Candler, comp., *The Colonial Records of the State of Georgia,* XIX, Pt. I (Atlanta, 1911), 163. The tax acts of 1770 and 1773 are *ibid.,* 161-198, 449-505. For the period 1763-1768 the relevant Georgia tax laws are available on the Early State Records microfilms as Georgia Session Laws. Sources for Georgia taxation in the colonial period are limited compared to those available for the other southern colonies.

[39] See Becker, "Politics of Taxation," 134-136.

[40] Barker, *Background of the Revolution,* Chaps. 4, 5, 7; J. Thomas Scharf, *History of Maryland from the Earliest Period to the Present Day* (Baltimore, 1879), I, 501-502; J. Hall Pleasants, "Introduction" to W. H. Brown *et al.,* eds., *Archives of Maryland* (Baltimore, 1890-   ), LV, xxxii-xxxiii, hereafter cited as *Md. Arch.*

holders.[41] Neither group had much desire to see land taxes, in particular ad valorem land taxes, adopted colony-wide. During most of the Seven Years' War, the problem facing country party leaders was to avoid passing new land taxes, but to do it in such a way that the proprietor and his supporters would be blamed for any ill consequences.

They found a solution: they saw to it that every land tax bill that cleared the lower house between 1758 and 1764, when attempts to impose new land taxes were abandoned, included provisions that were designed to rally popular support to the country party, but that guaranteed that the bills would never become law. The proposed tax bill of 1762 may be taken as an example, since acts virtually identical with that bill were passed by the house and rejected by the council twice annually beginning in 1758.[42] The 1762 bill proposed taxing improved land, together with undeveloped land "yielding no present annual profit" because it was "daily increasing in value." All land, cultivated and wild, would be taxed at 5 percent of the "yearly value," which was fixed at 5 percent of the current market value as estimated by tax assessors. Declaring it "reasonable and just" that the proprietor's land be taxed "in equal Proportion" with everyone else's, the bill taxed proprietary quitrents and unleased lands. Other kinds of property, including "sterling money in Great Britain," slaves, servants, merchants' stock-in-trade, carriages, ships, and a variety of agricultural commodities, were to be taxed 5s. on each £100 of assessed value. The salaries of "all and every Person or Persons, ecclesiastical or civil, within this Province, having or exercising any Benefice, Publick Office or Employment of Profit" would be taxed at 5 percent of the "clear annual . . . Profit of such Benefice; Office or Employment"—a provision aimed directly at proprietary appointees.[43]

The idea of taxing proprietary lands and appointees was popular enough in itself, but the bill of 1762 contained other provisions to make it even more appealing. It exempted anyone with three or more children

365

[41] Barker, *Background of the Revolution*, 22-24, 181-183. Barker examined the estates of 125 members from 1740 to 1771 and found only 16 that totaled under 500 acres. See also Ronald Hoffman, "Economics, Politics and the Revolution in Maryland" (Ph.D. diss., University of Wisconsin, 1969), 80-81.

[42] The act is in *Md. Arch.*, LVIII, 525-571. Councillor Daniel Dulany described the proposed law as "essentially the same" as that of 1758. Dulany to Cecil Calvert, Sept. 10, 1764, "The Calvert Papers," Maryland Historical Society, *Publications*, XXXIV (1894), 231-233, hereafter cited as "Calvert Papers." Spurred on by the shock of Braddock's defeat, the assembly in 1756 had passed an acreage land tax that was to continue for 5 years. *Md. Arch.*, LII, 480-521. But this was the last land tax adopted before the Revolution.

[43] *Md. Arch.*, LVIII, 548-550, 544-545.

who was receiving public charity or whose personal estate was valued at less than £50 from paying the taxes. Leaseholders whose contracts ran seven years or less would be excused from land taxes and their landlords required to pay these taxes instead, as "if no such Lease . . . had been made." Any debtor could subtract 5s. from the interest on every £100 he owed in order to pay taxes; creditors were required to absorb the loss or face prosecution for usury.[44]

All involved understood that these proposals were totally unacceptable to the proprietor and his supporters. The council knew all too well that granting tax assessors virtually unlimited power to decide property values (as the bill proposed) could result in the manipulation of assessments to build country party support and empty proprietary pockets. That was happening in Pennsylvania, and the Maryland councillors did not intend to grant "so great a Latitude" to the "partiality of the Assessors."[45] The council's nine consecutive rejections of the plan can have surprised no one. Indeed, the plan's proponents never expected it to become law; its purpose was political, not financial. Its supporters, Gov. Horatio Sharpe explained accurately, had "nothing in view but by offering such Laws as they knew would not pass to lay a foundation for Popularity against the ensuing Election."[46]

The country party also used popular aversion to poll taxes as an antiproprietary weapon.[47] The house repeatedly insisted that the council's real desire was to institute a "grievous unequal and unnecessary" poll tax to pay the salaries of proprietary appointees. The councillors understood the popular distaste for poll taxes. They loudly denied the house's allega-

[44] Ibid., 549.
[45] Council to Gov. Horatio Sharpe, Apr. 24, 1762, ibid., 45. Sharpe commented several times on the country party's disturbing tendency to "adopt Pennsylvania Politics." Sharpe to Calvert, May 8, 1764, ibid., XIV, 156-158; Sharpe to John Sharpe, May 27, 1756, in Scharf, History of Maryland, I, 488-490. For proprietary tax problems in Pennsylvania see Becker, "Politics of Taxation," Chap. 2.
[46] Sharpe to Calvert, Feb. 15, 1762, Md. Arch., XIV, 24; Dulany to Calvert, Sept. 10, 1764, "Calvert Papers," 227-247.
[47] See, for example, Md. Arch., LXI, 264-275, and Sharpe to Shelburne, May 14, 1767, C.O. 5/113, Public Record Office. Except for a poll tax to support the Anglican clergy (commonly 30 pounds of tobacco paid by all inhabitants over 16 except white women) which raised about £8,000 a year by 1766, Maryland's reliance on poll taxes for colony expenses during the late colonial period was minimal. But county and local poll taxes carried the heavy burden of poor relief. For example, of 118,513 pounds of tobacco raised on polls in Worcester County in 1766, less than 1,500 pounds was earmarked for delivery to the provincial government, while 40% of the total went to local poor relief. Md. Arch., LXI, cvii, 505-513. See also John A. Kinnaman, "The Internal Revenues of Colonial Maryland" (Ph.D. diss., University of Indiana, 1955), 59.

tion and accused it of making "forced Constructions" and "unfair Deductions" from council messages "in order to mislead others."[48]

As a result, Maryland had no effective land taxes in force from 1763 to 1775.[49] Judged by the goals of the country party leaders—that taxes, particularly land taxes, be kept at a minimum and that popular discontent with proprietary rule be increased—the policy succeeded. During the final years before independence the country party continually presented itself as the taxpayers' friend. Such tactics had the advantage of consistency: they were not dependent on parliamentary blunders like the Stamp Act to arouse popular support. Internal taxation was an issue that had constant political impact on all Marylanders; it could be hammered at again and again, year after year, no matter what the state of Anglo-American relations. Thus the country party insisted that tavern license fees go into the public treasury instead of the proprietor's pocket;[50] thus it battled for lower fees for public officers and a reduced poll tax for support of the clergy until it won a decisive electoral victory in 1773 in large part on those issues.[51] By playing on popular opposition to England's colonial policy and by fanning popular discontent over taxes and fees, the country party rose to its peak of influence shortly before the war for independence began. As long as a king and a proprietor were available against whom that discontent could be directed, its tactics were well chosen. But with independence, country party leaders found themselves the new establishment and faced the uncomfortable necessity of having to make good on their former commitments.

The demand for tax reform varied from colony to colony. Protests were strongest in North Carolina, where the system was especially regressive and tax oppression was one of several grievances that drove western set-

367

48 "Remarks upon a Message, sent by the Upper to the Lower House of Assembly of Maryland," [Apr. 24], 1762, Md. Arch., LIX, 386-388; Maryland House Journals, Nov. 25, 1763, Maryland Council Journals, Apr. 24, 1762, Nov. 26, 1763, Early State Records microfilm. The house's suspicions regarding the poll tax had some basis in fact. Gov. Sharpe had suggested poll taxes in lieu of land taxes as early as 1757. Sharpe to Calvert, Nov. 9, 1757, in Scharf, History of Maryland, I, 500.

49 Even the acreage land tax of 1756 raised only £11,200 between Apr. 1758 and Nov. 1763. Md. Council Journals, Apr. 24, 1762, Nov. 23, 1763.

50 See, for example, Lord Baltimore to Gov. Sharpe, Feb. 7, 1765, Md. Arch., LIX, 359-360, and "An Act for licensing Ordinary Keepers Hawkers Pedlars and Petty Chapmen," ibid., LXI, 473-482.

51 Hoffman, "Revolution in Maryland," Chap. 6; Scharf, History of Maryland, II, 125-126; Gov. Robert Eden to Lord Hillsborough, Apr. 4, 1771, Maryland Historical Magazine, II (1907), 242-244; Md. Arch., LXIV, 254-256. The dispute over fees and clergy support can be followed in the House and Council Journals, 1770-1773, ibid., LXII-LXIV.

tlers into open rebellion. The push for reform was less urgent in South Carolina, with its more inclusive revenue system, and in tiny subsidized Georgia. The strength of the reform movements in Virginia and Maryland fell somewhere between the extremes of North Carolina and Georgia. In the two Chesapeake colonies the structure of government and politics operated to dissipate demands for reform that ran counter to the interests of the dominant elites. This was achieved in Maryland when the leadership of the country party coopted the reform effort, blunted it, and turned it to their own uses. It was accomplished in Virginia by the patchwork relief measures that followed the Robinson scandal but left the revenue system fundamentally the same. Throughout the South, those who sought to reform the colonies' discriminatory tax systems met with little success between 1763 and 1775. But independence created unexpected opportunities for changing society and government, and these regressive tax systems were among the institutions that did not survive the shock of revolution intact.

As rebellion became revolution and provisional revolutionary governments were formed, the new southern states faced a common problem: how to retain and build popular support while at the same time raising the unprecedented sums of money necessary to establish and defend independence. Initially they all met the problem by issuing large amounts of paper currency while postponing the taxes necessary to support it. But by 1777 it was clear throughout the South that effective taxation could not be reasonably delayed much longer. By that time it was also clear that the Revolution had created the potential for fundamental reform in a variety of institutions. New constitutions had been debated, drafted, and adopted, laws redrawn and revised, and policies reformulated, and at every step there were opportunities for change, not least in the area of taxation. Grappling with the problem of taxing an independent people, southern legislators wrote laws that redressed grievances long complained of, laws that altered the basis of southern taxation.

The problem of maintaining public support was especially urgent in North Carolina, where the collapse of the Regulation had left a large reservoir of discontent in the back areas that loyalists hoped to exploit. Governor Josiah Martin predicted in 1775 that any attempt by the rebelling colonists to collect a tax would be widely opposed and would work to the loyalists' advantage.[52] Wisely, the new provincial govern-

[52] Gov. Josiah Martin to earl of Dartmouth, Oct. 16, 1775, N. C. Col. Recs.,

ment decided not to push the matter of war taxes too soon. More important, when new tax laws were written they responded to long-standing complaints and redressed some long-standing grievances.

The provincial congress that convened in August 1775 decided to emit $125,000 in paper and to support the emission by poll taxes beginning in 1777. In May 1776 the provincial congress ordered an additional emission of £500,000, with taxes (again on polls) not to start until 1780.[53] At the same time North Carolinians were becoming aware of the potential for widespread change inherent in revolution, and some began to echo old Regulator grievances and to demand a variety of reforms. Mecklenburg County instructed its delegates to the state constitutional convention that "in fixing the fundamental principles of Government" they should "oppose everything that leans to aristocracy or power in the hands of the rich and chief men exercised to the oppression of the poor." Specifically, the county instructions demanded that poll taxes be replaced by "a General and equal land tax . . . throughout the State" so that all would pay "according to their estates."[54]

Before any taxes could be collected under the provincial congress's proposed poll taxes, a state convention adopted a constitution that substantially decreased the overrepresentation of the lowcountry counties, whose representatives had shown little interest in reforming the tax laws.[55] When the first legislature met under the new constitution in 1777, it quickly became clear that on matters of public finance at least there had indeed been a revolution in North Carolina. The state's first tax law substituted an ad valorem property tax for the pervasive prewar poll taxes. Levying "a tax on property by general assessment will tend to the ease of the inhabitants of this State," the legislators explained, "and will greatly relieve the poor people thereof." In November 1777 they reaffirmed their commitment to a "general Tax, in Proportion to the Ability of each individual" to pay.[56] Subsequent laws incorporated clauses favoring some

369

X, 270; William Hooper to Robert Morris, May 27, 1777, New-York Historical Society, *Collections,* XI (1878), 428-429.

[53] Journals of the North Carolina Provincial Congress, Sept. 5, 6, 1775, May 9, 1776, *N. C. Col. Recs.,* X, 192-195, 572-573.

[54] "Instructions to the Delegates from Mecklenburg to the Provincial Congress at Halifax in November, 1776," *ibid.,* 870a-870f.

[55] Elisha P. Douglass, *Rebels and Democrats: The Struggle for Equal Political Rights and Majority Rule During the American Revolution* (Chapel Hill, N. C., 1955), 131-132. The constitution of 1776 granted every county 2 representatives, ending the preferential system under which several lowcountry counties had 5 representatives in the late colonial period. *N. C. Col. Recs.,* X, 106-113.

[56] "An Act for levying a Tax by General Assessment . . . ," *N. C. State Recs.,* XXIV, 6-9; "An Act for Levying a Tax . . . ," *ibid.,* 134-135. The tax was one

special interest groups, but the basic provisions of the tax law of 1777 were repeated in the rest of North Carolina's wartime tax acts, and the commitment to taxation according to value remained firm.[57] The Revolution had provided the opportunity to win tax reforms that had long been denied.

In 1775 the provincial government of Virginia also faced the problem of raising funds without alienating loyalties, and it resolved the problem, as did North Carolina, by the simultaneous emission of paper money and the postponement of taxes to support it. The provincial convention issued £350,000 in the summer of 1775 and £100,000 more the following spring. Funding taxes (poll and acreage land taxes) were not to take effect until 1777.[58] By the fall of 1776 Virginia had a new constitution and a new state legislature that promptly pushed the starting date for tax collections back to 1778, explaining that people in many parts of the commonwealth would be "unable to pay" if collections began as scheduled in 1777. The legislators also authorized the state to borrow or emit an additional £400,000, with taxes to sink the debt not slated to take effect until 1784. When they authorized borrowing another $1,000,000 in May 1777 and committed the state to paying it back by December 1784, they made no specific provisions for funding beyond a promise to levy property taxes in the future.[59]

Delay also permitted the convention, and later the legislature, to sidestep the troublesome question of tax reform. Once early hopes that in-

---

half penny for each "pound value of all the Land, Lots, Houses, Slaves, Money, money at interest, Stock in trade, Horses and Cattle in this State." The sole remnant of the poll tax fell on freemen whose estates were worth less than £100 assessed value.

[57] *Ibid.*, 109-113, 134-135, 200-204, 221-222, 317-318, 344-347, 390-394, 429-439. The following is an example of special interest legislation. In 1781 the tax on money-at-interest was lowered to a level far below that of taxes on other property, and the next year it was abolished altogether, prompting special interest groups like the Edenton merchant community to demand that stock-in-trade be similarly exempted. *Ibid.*, 390-394, 429-434; resolves of an Edenton town meeting, Aug. 1, 1783, in Griffith J. McRee, ed., *Life and Correspondence of James Iredell*, II (New York, 1857), 60-62.

[58] Journals of the Virginia Provincial Convention, July 17, Aug. 26, 1775, June 12, 1776, Early State Records microfilm. The convention hoped to postpone the beginning of taxation to 1779, but George Mason and others urged "the necessity of immediately laying such taxes as the people could bear, to sink the sum emitted as soon as possible." They were able to reduce the delay but not eliminate it. Mason to George Washington, Oct. 14, 1775, in Robert A. Rutland, ed., *The Papers of George Mason, 1725-1792*, I (Chapel Hill, N. C., 1970), 255-256.

[59] Hening, ed., *Statutes of Va.*, IX, 219-225, 286-289.

dependence could be swiftly and cheaply won collapsed and it became clear that heavy war taxes were inevitable,[60] the clamor for reform began. "I need only tell you of one definition that I heard of Independency," wrote a worried Landon Carter to George Washington in the spring of 1776: it was expected to result in a government "independent of the rich men." Some irresponsible candidates, he explained, were stooping so low as to seek election to the assembly by denouncing taxes that had been passed largely, they asserted, to serve the needs of the rich. Worse yet, Carter continued, the appeal seemed to work and such men were getting elected.[61] Petitions to the new assembly conceded the need for effective taxation, but insisted that the burden be distributed more equitably than in the past. Culpeper County petitioners denounced acreage land taxes because such taxes ignored "the very great difference in the value thereof, arising from its situation and fertility." Others denounced the poll taxes as inherently unjust and demanded that taxes be distributed "in proportion to [the value of] . . . real and personal estate."[62]

The imminence of invasion made unified public support a matter of urgent necessity, and demands for reform could not be shunted cavalierly aside. According to Edmund Pendleton, it took "long debate," sprinkled with "much Altercation," but in January 1778 the assembly approved a tax law that provided a good measure of the way revolution altered political priorities in Virginia.[63] Equal acreage land taxes, the tax haven of larger tidewater planters that had been successfully protected even through the brief spasm of reform that followed the Robinson scandal of 1766, were eliminated. For them the law substituted an annual tax of 10s. for each £100 value of all land, plate, slaves, horses, mules, and of "all salaries, and . . . the neat income of all officers of profit," continental military officers excepted. Assessors were to rate property "as the same would in their judgment sell for in ready money, having regard to the

---

[60] For the hope that the war could be financed without major new taxes see Richard Henry Lee to Patrick Henry, Apr. 20, 1776, in James Curtis Ballagh, comp., *The Letters of Richard Henry Lee*, I (New York, 1911), 176-179.

[61] Landon Carter to Washington, May 9, 1776, in Peter Force, ed., *American Archives*, 4th Ser., VI (Washington, D. C., 1846), 390. Mason shared Carter's low opinion of the kind of men being elected to the Virginia legislature. Mason to R. H. Lee, May 18, 1776, in Rutland, ed., *Mason Papers*, I, 271.

[62] Petitions from Orange, Culpeper, and Monongahela counties, Va. House Journals, Nov. 3-4, 11, 1777; Fairfax County instructions to delegates, Aug. 20, 1777, in Rutland, ed., *Mason Papers*, I, 347.

[63] Edmund Pendleton to William Woodford, Jan. 16, 1778, in David J. Mays, ed., *The Letters and Papers of Edmund Pendleton, 1734-1803*, I (Charlottesville, Va., 1967), 246; Va. House Journals, Dec. 13, 1777, Jan. 10, 19-23, 1778.

371

local situation of lands and other circumstances." Reform did not extend
to the elimination of the poll tax, which was set at 5s.[64] Nevertheless, the
crisis forced on the new state by independence created the conditions
under which reforms long demanded and long denied were enacted.
Revolutionary Virginia's legislature committed itself to the idea that taxation should be tied much more closely to a standard of ability to pay than
it had been in the past.

Problems developed. Assessors at first had almost complete freedom
in estimating property values, and assessments varied greatly as a result.
Pendleton reported that the assessed value of similar slaves ranged between £70 and £1,590, so that one man might pay 21s. and another more
than £22 for similar property. Some assessors based their judgments on
what land would sell for in specie, others on what it would sell for in
paper currency. Still others rated land on the basis of what it would sell
for if *all* the land in a county were put on the market simultaneously—a
stretched interpretation of the law aimed at reducing land taxes to a
level far below that intended by the legislature. These evasions cut deeply
into the expected revenues, and by the end of 1778 the assembly, reluctantly
admitting that "the taxes collected . . . are not sufficient to answer the purposes of the said act," raised taxes across the board.[65]

In the fall of 1778 Virginia legislators began looking for some way
to make the system operate uniformly across the state while retaining
ad valorem taxes. One possibility involved "classing" land—that is,
dividing land into several categories or classes according to location and
quality, and then fixing by law the assessed value of all land within a
particular class. John Tyler, for example, proposed dividing the state into
two regions, one east and one west of the Appalachian Mountains, with
higher assessed values for the former than for the latter. Within each
region land would be divided into three classes according to quality, and
each of those would in turn be broken down into three smaller classes,
with maximum assessed values for each class fixed in the law. All told,
Tyler suggested eighteen distinct categories of land. Thomas Jefferson

<hr/>

[64] Hening, ed., *Statutes of Va.*, IX, 349-368. Additional taxes on money, interest
payments, spirits, and a tobacco export duty rounded out the revenue program.
Rutland credits Mason with drafting the reformed tax proposal. Rutland, ed.,
Mason Papers, I, 375n-377n.
[65] Pendleton to Woodford, May 24, 1779, in Mays, ed., *Letters of Pendleton*,
I, 286; Hening, ed., *Statutes of Va.*, IX, 547-552. The rationalizations for low assessments appear in "An act to explain and amend the acts of General Assembly,
providing a supply of money for public exigencies," May 1779, *ibid.*, X, 9-10.

prepared a similar plan that provided for six different categories.[66] In the end, however, the assembly elected to increase revenues by increasing taxes rather than by restricting the power of local assessors.[67]

But the problem of wildly varying assessments remained, and by the spring of 1779 the assembly was again ready to reconsider the tax laws. An attempt to roll back all the wartime reforms and return to the pre-independence system of acreage taxes was beaten down, for not even Pendleton, who had earlier described taxation based on property assessments as "disgusting where it has been tried," was willing to return completely to the old ways. "It would be most unjust," he now thought, for someone to pay no more for valuable land bordering the Rappahannock River than Pendleton paid for his "black Jack barrens." The assembly in 1779 adopted Jefferson's plan for dividing land into six categories.[68] Through the remainder of the war, the state continued to tinker with its taxes, but all the tinkering that was done after 1777 and all the different plans put forth to rationalize assessments were in the end merely variations on a common theme—that taxation in Virginia would henceforth be based on the value of estates, and thus would be bound more closely to the ability to pay principle than it had been before independence.[69]

South Carolina's provincial government also began the Revolution with a policy of fighting first and paying later. In June 1775 the provincial congress ordered £1,000,000 in currency issued, but decided to proceed cautiously with taxes because, said David Ramsay, of "a fear of alarming the people." A time of "civil convulsion," explained William Henry Drayton, was no time to levy heavy new taxes on the people, particularly not in a state that had, like North Carolina, a history of Regulator discontent that tories might exploit.[70] The provincial congress

373

[66] The various plans described are in Julian P. Boyd et al., eds., The Papers of Thomas Jefferson, II (Princeton, N. J., 1950), 221n-224n.

[67] Hening, ed., Statutes of Va., IX, 547-552. The new law promised to rectify the "great inequality and injustice" that resulted from varying assessments, but it merely admonished tax officials to find "some general mode" for making assessments within each county.

[68] Pendleton to Woodford, Jan. 31, 1778, May 24, 31, 1779, in Mays, ed., Letters of Pendleton, I, 246, 286, 290; Hening, ed., Statutes of Va., X, 9-14.

[69] Hening, ed., Statutes of Va., X, 501-517, XI, 140-145.

[70] "Extracts from the Journal of the First Provincial Congress," June 14, 1775, in William Edwin Hemphill and Wylma Anne Wates, eds., Extracts from the Journals of the Provincial Congresses of South Carolina, 1775-1776 (Columbia, S. C., 1960), 51; David Ramsay, History of South Carolina, from Its First Settlement in

emitted £120,000 more in November 1775 and another £750,000 in March 1776 without initiating taxes, and the new state government, organized in the spring of 1776, continued the policy of the old provisional government. Not until January 1777 did South Carolina pass a general property tax to support the war.[71]

In South Carolina, however, tax delay was not followed by major tax reforms as it was in North Carolina and Virginia. The new state constitution did little to reapportion the legislature; majority control remained firmly in the hands of the lowcountry planter aristocracy, and their interests continued to prevail in the new tax laws. The law of January 1777 left the prewar tax system virtually unchanged, and it remained substantially unchanged throughout the Revolution, a result unique among the southern states.[72] Even modest attempts to distribute taxes according to ability to pay were regularly defeated. Thus a move to lay a special tax on anyone possessing more than £10,000 in cash failed in 1780, as did a later effort by Gadsden to have taxes doubled on all land over 20,000 acres owned by one man.[73] But even in South Carolina, reform came shortly after the war ended. In 1784 the legislature abolished acreage taxes and replaced them with ad valorem rates, adopting the most comprehensive plan of any state that classed land according to value. The laws created twenty-four distinct categories with land values ranging from twenty-six dollars to twenty cents an acre. The justice of the changes had long been conceded, noted Ramsay, but the lowcountry planters were only "very slowly convinced" to put them into effect.[74]

The royal governor of Georgia, James Wright, reported in January 1775 that the Georgia provincial congress would probably levy a tax of £150,000 sterling to support opposition to England, but the members of the provincial congress itself had no such delusions. They resolved to emit £10,000 in paper as an emergency measure and bound all Georgians to contribute by an "equal and general tax" toward sinking the money, but that was all. The date of collection and the method of apportioning

---

1670 to the Year 1808, II (Charleston, S. C., 1858), 102; John Drayton, *Memoirs of the American Revolution*, I (Charleston, S. C., 1821), 264-265.

[71] "Extracts," Nov. 15, 1775, Mar. 6, 1776, in Hemphill and Wates, eds., *Extracts*, 130, 225; *S. C. Statutes*, IV, 361-363, 365-374.

[72] *S. C. Statutes*, IV, 635-674; Douglass, *Rebels and Democrats*, 43-44.

[73] S. C. House Journals, Feb. 8-9, 23, 1780; Jerome Joshua Nadelhaft, "The Revolutionary Era in South Carolina, 1775-1788" (Ph.D. diss., University of Wisconsin, 1965), 117-119.

[74] *S. C. Statutes*, IV, 627-637; Ramsay, *History of South Carolina*, II, 107-108.

the tax were both left comfortably vague.[75] British invasion soon reduced rebel Georgia to a few upland areas and scattered its officials as far as North Carolina, but the rebel government had time enough to write a constitution, and there was also time for the new legislature to pass a tax law that altered the prewar pattern, although hardly in the direction of greater equity. Land continued to be taxed equally by the acre, but poll taxes now became an important part of the revenue system as well. It is doubtful, however, that much was collected under the new system since within a year the state was invaded and within two it was virtually an English colony again. Only a handful of rebel officials remained in the back areas to keep up a pretence of American authority with the aid of rump assemblies that were chosen irregularly and met sporadically.[76]

375

Not until January 1782 did an effective American legislature reconvene in Georgia, and not until July 1783 did it pass a new tax law. Acreage taxes remained, but the poll taxes instituted in 1778 were dropped, except for unemployed men over twenty-one. The legislators clearly intended the law as an interim measure since they also ordered a complete survey of all kinds of taxable property so that a future session could "lay an equitable tax on the inhabitants." And they made clear their intention to tax land in the future by value, not acreage, and to resume poll taxes.[77] Georgia thus ended the war on an ambiguous note with respect to tax reform.

There was no ambiguity at all about the impact of the Revolution on Maryland taxation. Leaders of Maryland's "patriot party" (for the most part leaders of the old antiproprietary party)[78] found themselves forced to make important concessions to popular pressures, concessions that fundamentally altered the colony's tax system. Reforms that country party leaders had championed earlier, safe in the knowledge that the proprietor would never permit them, now had to be implemented. The overthrow of the proprietary government had removed all excuses for not doing so. Thus Anne Arundel County instructed its delegates to the

[75] Gov. James Wright to Lord Dartmouth, Jan. 3, 1775, Georgia Historical Society, *Collections*, III (1873), 229-230; "Journal of the Georgia Provincial Convention," July 8, 12, 1775, in Allen D. Candler, ed., *The Revolutionary Records of the State of Georgia*, I (Atlanta, 1908), 243, 251-252.

[76] *Ga. Col. Recs.*, XIX, Pt. 2, 87-99; Kenneth Coleman, *The American Revolution in Georgia, 1763-1789* (Athens, Ga., 1958), 155-165.

[77] *Ga. Col. Recs.*, XIX, Pt. 2, 263-278; Coleman, *American Revolution in Georgia*, 163-164, 190-191.

[78] Philip A. Crowl, *Maryland During and After the Revolution: A Political and Economic Study*, The Johns Hopkins Univ. Studies, LXI (Baltimore, 1943), 19-29.

state constitutional convention in 1776 to insist that "all monies to be raised on the people be by fair and equal assessment in proportion to every person's estate; and that the unjust mode of taxation by the poll, heretofore used, be abolished."[79] These and other demands for fundamental reforms in Maryland's government filled some of the old country party leaders with deep misgivings. Charles Carroll of Carrollton feared a plot to "introduce a levelling scheme" under the "cloak of providing great privileges for the people." Although he and those who thought like him at the state constitutional convention succeeded in staving off many reforms (such as the elimination of property qualifications for voting), they were nevertheless forced by fear of a popular rebellion against their leadership to make a number of concessions.[80]

The convention dealt with taxation by abolishing all poll taxes and by adopting taxation based on wealth. These reforms were not left to mere statute: the new principles were embedded in the state bill of rights, which declared that "the levying taxes by the poll is grievous and oppressive, and ought to be abolished; that paupers ought not to be assessed for the support of government, but every other person in the state ought to contribute his proportion of public taxes for the support of government according to his actual worth in real or personal property within the state."[81] Two tax laws passed in April 1777 established the state's first tax system in accordance with the constitutional mandate. Subsequent laws refined and expanded the definition of taxable property but did not materially weaken the basic reforms incorporated into the bill of rights.[82] Carroll thought the new policies unjust, unwise, and certain to be very costly to Maryland's wealthiest men, himself included. But, he explained to his father, who was similarly outraged, no matter how heavily the taxes bore on the rich, it would be fruitless, even hazardous, to oppose them too strongly. "There is a time," he explained later, "when it is wisdom to yield to injustice and to popular heresies and

376

---

[79] *Maryland Gazette* (Annapolis), Aug. 22, 1776.
[80] Charles Carroll to his father, Aug. 20, Oct. 4, 1776, Carroll Papers, Maryland Historical Society, Baltimore; Hoffman, "Revolution in Maryland," Chaps. 9-10; Douglass, *Rebels and Democrats*, Chap. 4.
[81] *A Declaration of Rights, and the Constitution and Form of Government, Agreed to by the Delegates of Maryland, in free and full Convention assembled* (Annapolis, [1776]).
[82] Maryland Session Laws: Feb. 1777, Chaps. XXI, XXII, Mar. 1778, VII, Oct. 1778, VII, Mar. 1779, XI, July 1779, V, Oct. 1779, XXV, Nov. 1782, VI, Early State Records microfilm; Md. House Journals, Jan. 9, 1781; Hoffman, "Revolution in Maryland," 305-308.

delusions," particularly when such "unjust proceedings are popular."[83]

Other prewar commitments on taxes now had to be honored as well. Clauses requiring landlords to pay the property taxes of their tenants, and allowing debtors to deduct money from the interest they owed their creditors and to use that money to pay taxes, had been confidently inserted in pre-independence bills that were never expected to take effect. In 1777 these measures were enacted into law. The new laws required owners of leased land to pay all taxes on their lands, regardless of any prior agreements included in their tenants' leases. They authorized debtors to deduct 10s. from the interest payments on each £100 they owed and to use the money to pay taxes; creditors had to absorb the loss regardless of the terms of their contracts. After 1780 debtors could withhold a flat rate of one-sixth of their interest payments in order to pay taxes.[84] But these changes were less significant than those won at the state constitutional convention. By eliminating all poll taxes and by embedding in the bill of rights the idea that taxation should be based on the ability to pay, Maryland joined North Carolina, Virginia, and, to a lesser extent, South Carolina as an example of the way the Revolution provided the opportunity to reform formerly regressive tax systems.

Long before independence the idea that taxes ought to be proportional to wealth or income was current in the southern colonies among those whose interests were not effectively represented in the legislatures. The idea underlay many of the reforms such people demanded unsuccessfully before the Revolution, as it did many of the calls for reform that followed independence. Not all the resulting attempts at reform succeeded, and of those that did, not all were permanent.[85] But in the contest between those who fought against reform of the South's colonial tax systems and those who fought for it, victory lay wholly with the former before independence but substantially with the latter after it. By the end of the

377

---

[83] Carroll to his father, Apr. 4, Nov. 13, 1777, Carroll Papers.

[84] Maryland Session Laws: Feb. 1777, XXI, XXII, Mar. 1778, VII, Mar. 1779, XI, July 1779, V, Oct. 1780, XXV, Nov. 1782, VI.

[85] In Apr. 1784 the North Carolina legislature reinstated poll taxes and replaced ad valorem property taxes with acreage rates. Not until 1786, when the state began classing land according to location, would at least some of the wartime reforms be reenacted. "An Act to amend an Act, intitled, An Act for ascertaining what property in this State shall be deemed taxable property, . . ." *N. C. State Recs.,* XXIV, 543-546; "An Act for Levying a Tax for the Support of Government. . . ," *ibid.,* 802-803.

war or shortly thereafter, four of the southern states had taken long steps in the direction of fundamental tax reform. The pattern of those reforms lends support to the thesis set forth by Jameson in 1926: that the Revolution not only severed ties with England, but that the "transforming hand of revolution" set free many economic desires and social aspirations, and that American society was "altered by the forces thus let loose."[86]

[86] Jameson, *American Revolution*, 9.

Religion, Communications, and the Ideological Origins of the American Revolution

Harry S. Stout

... I saw before me a Cloud or fogg rising; I first thought it came from the great River, but as I came nearer the Road, I heard a noise something like a low rumbling thunder and presently found it was the noise of Horses feet coming down the Road and this Cloud was a Cloud of dust made by the Horses feet; it arose some Rods into the air over the tops of Hills and trees and when I came within about 20 rods of the Road, I could see men and horses Sliping along in the Cloud like shadows and as I drew nearer it seemed like a steady Stream of horses and their riders, scarcely a horse more than his length behind another, all of a Lather and foam with sweat, their breath rolling out of their nostrils every Jump; every horse seemed to go with all his might to carry his rider to hear news from heaven for the saving of Souls, it made me tremble to see the Sight ...

NATHAN Cole's description of George Whitefield's appearance before four thousand avid listeners in Middletown, Connecticut, in 1740 captures our attention at least partly because Cole's voice is one that is rare in early American literature.[1] The crude spelling and syntax signal a vernacular prose composed by an ordinary man, whose purpose is less to analyze the theological issues of the revival than to describe an exhilarating event. Lacking the literary refinements of a classical education, Cole portrayed his experience in the form of a "realistic narrative" framed against a concrete social background.[2] Although common in setting, the

---

Mr. Stout, a member of the Department of History at the University of Connecticut, is currently a Mellon Fellow in the Humanities at the University of Pennsylvania. He presented an earlier version of this article at a colloquium sponsored by the Newberry Library in September 1976.

[1] Michael J. Crawford, ed., "The Spiritual Travels of Nathan Cole," *William and Mary Quarterly*, 3d Ser., XXXIII (1976), 93. The crowd estimate at Middletown is taken from *George Whitefield's Journals* (Philadelphia, 1960), 479.

[2] Hans W. Frei distinguishes a "realistic narrative" in the following terms: "Realistic narrative is that kind in which subject and social setting belong together, and characters and external circumstances fitly render each other.... [R]ealistic narrative, if it is really seriously undertaken and not merely a pleasurable or hortatory exercise, is a sort in which in style as well as content in the setting forth of didactic material, and in the depiction of characters and action, the sublime or at least serious effect mingles inextricably with the quality of what is casual, random, ordinary, and everyday" (*The Eclipse of Biblical Narrative: A Study in Eighteenth and Nineteenth Century Hermeneutics* [New Haven, Conn., 1974], 13-14).

passage is hardly trivial, for it brings to life the impassioned world of the
common people and conveys, in their own words, a sense of the irrepressible
spontaneity that marked the revivals throughout the colonies. Thunderous
noise, clouds of dust, horses in a lather, and unrecognizable shadowy figures
dominate a vocabulary that manages to express, as no official account could
possibly do, the powerful emotions evoked by the Great Awakening.

With Whitefield's celebrated speaking tours of the colonies there appeared an innovative style of communications that redefined the social
context in which public address took place. The sheer size and heterogeneity
of the audience exceeded anything in the annals of colonial popular assembly.
To organize the mass meetings, both speaker and audience altered the roles
and language they customarily adopted in public worship. In the process, a
new model of social organization and public address developed—a model
which could be applied to a broad range of social, political, and religious
contexts.

Contemporary and historical accounts agree that the Awakening was the
most momentous intercolonial popular movement before the Revolution.
Indeed, the parallel between the popular engagement and "enthusiasm"
evidenced alike in the revivals and the rebellion merits close attention.
Unfortunately, however, attempts to explain the meaning those two movements had for their participants must confront the fact that the documentary
evidence originates overwhelmingly from an elitist "rhetorical world" that
excluded the common people from the presumed audience.[3] Although the
informed writings of the Founding Fathers provide the official revolutionary
vocabulary, they do not render in a realistic narrative form the ideological
arousal of the common people, who, by the very rhetoric of those documents,
were excluded from the message. How were revolutionary sentiments communicated with ideological force to an audience unversed in the rhetorical
forms of the literature? And, conversely, how did the active popular self-
consciousness manifested in the popular movements energize a republican
vocabulary and push it in egalitarian directions the leaders had never
intended? The documents are of little help here. More to the point, they
actually create the problem of interpretation.

Cole's description of the popular enthusiasm of the revival suggests a
different approach to the problem of popular culture and republican ideology.
If *what* was communicated is qualified by the restrictive rhetoric through
which the ideas were intended to be transmitted, it may help to ask instead
how communications were conducted and how they changed during the
second half of the eighteenth century? There could be no egalitarian culture

---

[3] The term "rhetorical world" is taken from Gordon S. Wood, "The Democratization of Mind in the American Revolution," in *Leadership in the American
Revolution*, Library of Congress Symposia (Washington, D.C., 1974), 72.

as we know it today without an ideological predisposition toward the idea that the vulgar masses ought to be reached directly. By examining the changing style of communications in the revivals it is possible to gain insights into the nature of an egalitarian rhetoric through which, and only through which, republican ideas could be conveyed to an unlettered audience.

David Ramsay, a noted participant in and historian of the Revolution, recognized that, to understand the meaning of the Revolution, "forms and habits" must be regarded.[4] Before a republican vocabulary could communicate radical social meanings, a new rhetoric had to appear in which familiar terms were used to express unfamiliar thoughts. And this, it is argued here, is precisely what happened in the mass assemblies inaugurated by preachers like Whitefield. Despite the differences in intellectual substance between the revivals and the rebellion, those movements exhibited a close rhetorical affinity that infused religious and political ideas with powerful social significance and ideological urgency.

381

The point of departure for this article is Alan Heimert's study of *Religion and the American Mind*.[5] Published in 1966, the book had a generally cool reception. Critical essays by Edmund S. Morgan and Sidney E. Mead pointed out conceptual shortcomings in the work but failed to recognize its value in suggesting a method of historical analysis that focuses on the context of communications.[6] This failure had the unfortunate effect of foreclosing a line of inquiry into the subject of religion and the ideological origins of the Revolution.

Heimert's foreword states his central thesis: religious "Liberalism was profoundly conservative, politically as well as socially, and . . . its leaders, insofar as they did in fact embrace the Revolution, were the most reluctant of rebels. Conversely, 'evangelical' religion, which had as its most notable formal expression the 'Calvinism' of Jonathan Edwards, was not the retrograde philosophy that many historians rejoice to see confounded in America's Age of Reason. Rather Calvinism, and Edwards, provided pre-Revolutionary America with a radical, even democratic, social and political ideology, and evangelical religion embodied, and inspired, a thrust toward American

[4] David Ramsay, *The History of the American Revolution* (1789), in Edmund S. Morgan, ed., *The American Revolution: Two Centuries of Interpretation* (Englewood Cliffs, N.J., 1965), 8.
[5] Alan Heimert, *Religion and the American Mind: From the Great Awakening to the Revolution* (Cambridge, Mass., 1966).
[6] Edmund S. Morgan's review in *WMQ*, 3d Ser., XXIV (1967), 454-459, and Sidney E. Mead, "Through and beyond the Lines," *Journal of Religion*, XLVIII (1968), 274-288. The prominent exception to the negativity of the reviews is William G. McLoughlin's "The American Revolution as a Religious Revival: 'The Millennium in One Country,'" *New England Quarterly*, XL (1967), 99-110.

nationalism."[7] This assertion diverged dramatically from the conventional wisdom regarding the relations of religion and the Revolution. In demonstrating his thesis Heimert contended, in now notorious words, that it was necessary to read the sources "not between the lines, but, as it were, through and beyond them."[8] Only by doing this would it be possible to cut through the immediate idiom of political discourse that dominated the official Revolutionary debates and discover the underlying "relationship of ideology and political commitment to modes of persuasion."[9] In Heimert's view, these "modes of persuasion" were derived from the Evangelical rather than the Liberal tradition.

382

Against this thesis, and the method upon which it rests, Morgan and Mead launched an impressive assault. The conceptual framework they impose on early America, and their way of reading historical documents, were molded largely by Perry Miller, and it was as an extension of Miller's work that they interpreted Heimert.[10] To them, Heimert's tactic of reading "beyond" the content of the documents to the styles they expressed smacked, in Morgan's word, of "fantasy."[11] They contended that the method not only detached the historian from the security of objective reference (that is, the content of the documents) but also ignored social and intellectual connections between revivalism and republicanism that were neither as sharp nor as consistent as Heimert supposed.

Influential as these criticisms have been in stifling consideration of *Religion and the American Mind*, we must ask whether in fact Heimert wrote the book the critics reviewed. If Heimert's study is simply an extension of Miller, then the problems with the book become insurmountable because,

---

[7] Heimert, *Religion and the American Mind*, viii.

[8] *Ibid.*, 11. Heimert's terminology is not meant to imply that one reads beyond the documents by ignoring documentation (as nearly 2,000 footnotes fully attest). Rather, it is the recognition, recently articulated by Gene Wise, that to get at the meaning of verbal statements "one would have to go beyond the documents to the original experience they came out of" (*American Historical Explanations: A Strategy for Grounded Inquiry* [Homewood, Ill., 1973], 73).

[9] Heimert, *Religion and the American Mind*, vii.

[10] Mead is most explicit here in the opening comments of his review: "Essentially Mr. Heimert's work seems to me to be a 639-page expansion, with massive footnoting of some suggestions imaginatively adumbrated in 1961 by Perry Miller.... The voice seems to be that of Jacob, but the hand that tapped the typewriter was that of Esau" ("Through and beyond the Lines," *Jour. of Religion*, XLVIII [1968], 274).

[11] Morgan states in his review: "The world he offers us has been constructed by reading beyond the lines of what men said; and what he finds beyond the lines is so far beyond, so wrenched from the context, and so at odds with empirical evidence, that his world, to this reviewer at least, partakes more of fantasy than of history" (*WMQ*, 3d Ser., XXIV [1967], 459).

as the critics demonstrate, there is no clear and consistent link between revivalism and republicanism at the level of ideas. But if the book is viewed in a different context altogether—if Heimert was not seeking to establish direct intellectual links between religious thought and political rebellion—then the entire effort needs to be revaluated.

Perry Miller's fullest statement on religion and the ideological origins of the Revolution appeared in his essay "From the Covenant to the Revival," published in 1961.[12] Addressing the role of "Calvinistic" Protestantism (a term he applied indiscriminately to Liberals and Evangelicals) in the Revolution, Miller insisted that, with the exception of a few hopelessly optimistic Anglicans, the American people shared a religious tradition articulated in the Reformed vocabulary of "federal" theology.[13] Under the influence of this austere covenantal tradition the colonists could never be moved by self-congratulatory appeals to natural rights and enlightened self-interest. Rather, the dynamic for revolution issued from a deep sense of moral corruption and degradation that found a target in English oppression but, more important, spoke to the sins of colonial society itself. For generations of colonists schooled in the language of covenant, judgment, and collective accountability, the jeremiad functioned as the "form of discourse" capable of driving them to a moral revolution. Considered as an intellectual movement, the Revolution represented a spiritual purge administered to a corrupt established order in the interest of restoring a pure order that would both free the colonists from a decadent oppressor and cleanse their own society. The Revolution was inspired by this highly unstable compound of pious contrition and political rebellion, moral reformation and patriotic resistance.

Miller's essay came to exert an enormous influence on assessments of the role of religion in the Revolution.[14] Yet nowhere did it reflect a recognition of the social dislocations and divisions which we now know proliferated in eighteenth-century America.[15] Miller's framework fails to show how Ameri-

[12] In James Ward Smith and A. Leland Jamison, eds., *The Shaping of American Religion* (Princeton, N.J., 1961), 322-368.

[13] *Ibid.*, 325.

[14] See, in particular, Edmund S. Morgan, "The Puritan Ethic and the American Revolution," *WMQ*, 3d Ser., XXIV (1967), 3-43, and Bernard Bailyn, *The Ideological Origins of the American Revolution* (Cambridge, Mass., 1967), 7, 32, 140, 193, 250. It is instructive to note exactly where Miller's "From the Covenant to the Revival" fits in Heimert's work. In *Religion and the American Mind* the essay is cited only three times, and never expanded on. Even more revealing, in his introductory essay to the volume of Great Awakening documents jointly edited with Miller (*The Great Awakening: Documents Illustrating the Crisis and Its Consequences* [Indianapolis, 1967]), Heimert includes Miller in every historiographical citation, but not one of those citations is to "From the Covenant to the Revival."

[15] See Kenneth A. Lockridge, "Social Change and the Meaning of the American Revolution," *Journal of Social History*, VI (1973), 403-439, and Jack P. Greene,

cans sharing the "Puritan Ethic" could have been so sharply divided over the issue of independence or why, among the patriots, such confusion and contradiction raged over the question of what the Revolution was all about.[16] Finally, it is impossible in Miller's terms to account for receptivity to rebellion on the part of a populace of limited literacy.[17] To focus solely on the ideas set forth in surviving documents as the source of ideological change is to confuse a deep cultural transformation with its subsequent manifestation in a self-conscious, theoretical vocabulary.

In opposition to Miller, Heimert describes two clearly separate and distinctive revolutionary styles in eighteenth-century America, each originating in opposing "rhetorical strategies" that crystallized after the mass revivals.[18] On the one hand, there was the rebellion itself—the movement for independence from England, which Heimert concedes may well have proceeded from Liberal assumptions. On the other hand, there emerged with the rebellion an egalitarian impulse that pointed toward the creation of a society fundamentally incompatible with traditional conceptions of order, hierarchy, and deference.[19]

384

"The Social Origins of the American Revolution: An Evaluation and Interpretation," *Political Science Quarterly*, LXXXVIII (1973), 1-22.

[16] See John R. Howe, Jr., "Republican Thought and the Political Violence of the 1790s," *American Quarterly*, XIX (1967), 147-165.

[17] Drawing upon a sampling of colonial will signatures, Kenneth A. Lockridge concludes that "the literacy of that American generation which took the colonies into the Revolution was less than perfect. It seems probable that one-quarter of the generation born around 1730 . . . was totally illiterate. Including New England in the total would not much alter the level of enduring illiteracy since two-thirds of the population lived outside of New England" (*Literacy in Colonial New England: An Enquiry into the Social Context of Literacy in the Early Modern West* [New York, 1974], 87).

[18] I use the term "mass revival" here intentionally to distinguish multi-community meetings addressed by itinerating preachers, who were often uneducated and of low social origins, from local revivals conducted by a settled pastor. Heimert's concentration on Jonathan Edwards and the established New England ministry tends, I believe, to work at cross-interests to his point concerning the stylistic innovation of the revivals. Historians would do better to concentrate on Whitefield and the awakening he inspired through his public addresses to unprecedented thousands of auditors. The fundamental problem raised by the revivals was not Edwards's treatises but the itinerants' practices.

[19] Heimert, *Religion and the American Mind*, 14, 532. To avoid terminological confusion I will use the term "rebellion" to refer to independence from England and "revolution" to describe the radical internal impulse to reorder American society in an egalitarian direction. Similarly, the classical (deferential) theory of republicanism richly described in Gordon S. Wood, *The Creation of the American Republic, 1776-1787* (Chapel Hill, N.C., 1969), 3-124, and J. G. A. Pocock, "The Classical Theory of Deference," *American Historical Review*, LXXXI (1976), 516-523, must be distinguished from the more radical egalitarian "republicanism" that ultimately

Approaching the problem of popular receptivity and concentrating on the verbal forms through which ideas were presented, Heimert locates the sources of this animating egalitarianism in the Great Awakening but concludes that it can be understood only by reading beyond the religious content of evangelical ideas to the new forms of public address established in the revivals. At some point prior to the popular reception of a revolutionary vocabulary, a new rhetoric must appear in which familiar terms can be used to mean something different—and this change in the *form*, as distinguished from the *content*, of communications marks the moment of a fundamental transformation of popular consciousness. Any revolution in world-view requires an new rhetoric. The most conspicuous and revolutionary product of the revivals was not to be found in doctrine, in the creation of new ecclesiastical or academic institutions, or even in resistance to the tyranny of established religion or monarchy. Evangelicalism's enduring legacy was a new rhetoric, a new mode of persuasion that would redefine the norms of social order. In Heimert's words, "quite apart from the question of Revolution, the contrasts between Liberal and Calvinist social thought were possibly of less ultimate significance than the remarkable differences between their oratorical strategies and rhetorical practices."[20]

385

Heimert's recognition of the revolutionary potentialities of the revivals suggests a closer look at evangelical oratory, particularly in relation to the forms of public worship that prevailed before the revivals. Despite differences in style and substance between Puritanism and southern Anglicanism, all churchmen believed traditionally with Samuel Willard that God did "Ordain Orders of Superiority and Inferiority among men."[21] This hierarchical world-view presupposed a society of face-to-face personal relationships in which people identified themselves with reference to those around them and acted according to their rank in the community. Forms of attire, the "seating" of public meetings, and patterns of speech were among the more conspicuous indications of a pervasive social stratification that separated the

---

came to mean, in Wood's terms, "nothing less than a reordering of eighteenth-century society and politics as they had known and despised them . . ." (*Creation of the American Republic*, 48).

[20] Heimert, *Religion and the American Mind*, 18.

[21] Perry Miller and Thomas H. Johnson, eds., *The Puritans* (New York, 1938), 251. For a discussion of the inherited social ethic which the revivals challenged see especially William G. McLoughlin, *Isaac Backus and the American Pietistic Tradition* (Boston, 1967), 1-22; Rhys Isaac, "Religion and Authority: Problems of the Anglican Establishment in Virginia in the Era of the Great Awakening and the Parsons' Cause," *WMQ*, 3d Ser., XXX (1973), 3-36; and Isaac, "Evangelical Revolt: The Nature of the Baptists' Challenge to the Traditional Order in Virginia, 1765 to 1775," *ibid.*, XXXI (1974), 345-368.

leaders from the rank and file. As Stephen Foster observes, "mutuality, subordination, and public service constituted a kind of sacred trinity of all respectable societies, Puritan or otherwise."[22]

The social institutions of colonial America were designed to sustain this prevailing perception of proper social organization. In this traditional social ethic, itinerancy was inconceivable because, in Increase Mather's words, "to say that a Wandering Levite who has no flock is a Pastor, is as good sense as to say, that he that has no children is a Father."[23] What made a pastor was not simply the preaching of the Word but also a direct, authoritarian identification with a specific flock. To ignore the personal and deferential relationships of a minister with his congregation would be to threaten the organic, hierarchical principles upon which both family and social order rested.

That ministers be "settled" was no idle proposition but rather an insistence carrying with it responsibility for the whole social order. An institution as critically important as the church could deny the forms of social hierarchy only at the peril of undermining the entire organization of social authority. In terms of communications this meant that speaker and audience were steadily reminded of their *personal* place in the community; in no context were they strangers to one another, for no public gatherings took place outside of traditional associations based upon personal acquaintance and social rank.[24]

Within this world of public address Liberals and Evangelicals alike realized that something dramatically different was appearing in the revivalists' preaching performances. The problem raised by the revivals was not their message of the new birth. Indeed, it was the familiar message of regeneration that lulled leaders into an early acceptance and even endorsement of the revivals. The problem, it soon became clear, was the revolutionary setting in which the good news was proclaimed. The secret of Whitefield's success and that of other evangelists (no less than of Patrick Henry in the 1770s) was not simply a booming voice or a charismatic presence. It was a new style: a rhetoric of persuasion that was strange to the American ear. The revivalists sought to transcend both the rational manner of polite Liberal preaching and the plain style of orthodox preaching in order

---

[22] Stephen Foster, *Their Solitary Way: The Puritan Social Ethic in the First Century of Settlement in New England* (New Haven, Conn., 1971), 18.

[23] Quoted in Cedric B. Cowing, *The Great Awakening and the American Revolution: Colonial Thought in the Eighteenth Century* (Chicago, 1971), 23.

[24] On the cultural implications of a face-to-face traditional society see Rhys Isaac, "Dramatizing the Ideology of Revolution: Popular Mobilization in Virginia, 1774 to 1776," *WMQ*, 3d Ser., XXXIII (1976), 364-367. I am indebted to Professor Isaac for sharing his article with me prior to its publication and for clarifying many of the points raised in this essay.

to speak directly to the people-at-large.[25] Repudiating both the conventions of the jeremiad and the ecclesiastical formalities, they assaulted the old preaching style no less devastatingly than they attacked the doctrines of covenant theology. Their technique of mass address to a voluntary audience forced a dialogue between speaker and hearer that disregarded social position and local setting.

Immensely significant were the separation of the revivalists from local ministerial rule and their unfamiliarity with the audience. Until then, preachers, like political leaders, had to know whom they were addressing. Because the very act of public speaking signified social authority, they were expected to communicate through the existing institutional forms. When public speakers in positions of authority communicated outside of the customary forms, they set themselves, by that act itself, in opposition to the established social order. The eighteenth-century leaders' obsession with demagogy and "enthusiasm" can only be understood in the context of a deferential world-view in which public speakers who were not attached to the local hierarchy created alternative settings that represented a threat to social stability. The frenzy raised by the itinerants was not born of madness but was derived from the self-initiated associations of the people meeting outside of regularly constituted religious or political meetings and, in so doing, creating new models of organization and authority. As the Harvard faculty clearly recognized in their censure of Whitefield, the "natural effect" of his preaching was that "the People have been thence ready to despise their own Ministers."[26]

In gathering their large and unfamiliar audiences the revivalists utilized the only form of address that could be sure to impress all hearers: the spoken word proclaimed extemporaneously in everyday language. As historians immersed in printed documents, we scarcely recognize the dominance of speech and oratory in aural cultures—an orality that, by definition, never survives in the written record. Alphabetic writing and print emerged, after all, as an *imitation* of spoken words, and so they have remained ever since. Recognition of the powerful social and psychological imperatives of direct oral address has led Walter Ong to observe that "writing commits the words to space. But to do so, it makes words less real, pretends they are something they are not: quiescent marks."[27] Print and typographic culture create highly

387

---

[25] Although Puritan rhetoric rejected the ornamental tropes and "witty" figures common to classical (Ciceronian) rhetoric, the New England plain style remained a literate rhetoric born in the schools and designed to instruct a reading public. The plain style was not intended to persuade essentially illiterate audiences unused to the logic of rational discourse. See Walter J. Ong, *Ramus: Method, and the Decay of Dialogue* (Cambridge, Mass., 1958), 212-213.
[26] Heimert and Miller, eds., *Great Awakening*, 352.
[27] Walter J. Ong, *Why Talk? A Conversation about Language* (San Francisco, 1973), 17.

visual, sequential, and analytic patterns of thought which aural cultures, attuned to easily remembered forms of speech, cannot readily comprehend.[28] Unlike print, which is essentially passive, reflective, and learned, sound is active, immediate, and spontaneously compelling in its demand for a response. Speech remains in the deepest sense an event or psychological encounter rather than an inert record—an event that is neither detached from personal presence nor analyzed, but is intrinsically engaged and calculated to persuade. Print cannot match the persuasive power of the spoken word whose potential audience includes everyone who can understand the language. It is no wonder that literate elites have feared persuasive orators from Plato condemning the sophists to Charles Chauncy damning the demagogues of the revival. Once orators are allowed the opportunity to address the people, there is, in Chauncy's words, "no knowing how high it [their influence] may rise, nor what it may end in."[29]

To portray the word as event, as a vital indwelling principle, the revivalists employed what Miller termed a "rhetoric of sensation"[30]—a new rhetoric that, through its recognition of the singular power of the spoken word delivered to a mass audience, differed fundamentally from the Old Light or rational preaching which was written out like a lecture and was more concerned, in the revivalists' words, with "ornament" than with the "affections." The animadversions of Liberals against what they called the revivalists' "mighty noise," which not only stimulated enthusiasm but also challenged the social order, were certainly justified from their perspective.[31] Ong makes the important point that "script, and particularly the alphabet, provides a heightened experience of order. The world of thought is itself a beautifully intricate world, and the world of words is likewise impressively, if mysteriously, organized. . . . To attack the printed word would be to attack *the* symbol of order."[32]

Looking to the New Testament as their model, the revivalist rediscovered

[28] On the relationship of literacy and analytical thought see Jack Goody and Ian Watt, "The Consequences of Literacy," *Comparative Studies in Society and History*, V (1963), 304-345, and Jack Goody, "Evolution and communication: the domestication of the savage mind," *British Journal of Sociology*, XXIV (1973), 1-12.
[29] Heimert and Miller, eds., *Great Awakening*, 256.
[30] Perry Miller, *Errand into the Wilderness* (Cambridge, Mass., 1956), 167-183. Heimert brilliantly develops this theme in his chapter on "The Danger of an Unconverted Ministry," which he singles out as the "principal hinge" of his study (*Religion and the American Mind*, 159-236).
[31] John Caldwell, *The Nature, Folly, and Evil of rash and uncharitable Judging. A Sermon Preached at the French Meeting-House in Boston . . .* (1742), in Richard L. Bushman, ed., *The Great Awakening: Documents on the Revival of Religion, 1740-1745* (New York, 1969), 159.
[32] Walter J. Ong, *The Presence of the Word: Some Prolegomena for Cultural and Religious History* (New Haven, Conn., 1967), 136.

the effectiveness of extemporaneous address in their struggle against the Standing Order. Recent analyses of New Testament rhetoric demonstrate the prevailing orality of the gospel. Amos Wilder, for example, notes that "Jesus never wrote a word. . . . In secular terms we could say that Jesus spoke as the birds sing, oblivious of any concern for transcription. Less romantically we can say that Jesus' use of the spoken word alone has its own theological significance."[33] Throughout the gospels the Word is the oral word, and the Good News is uttered through ordinary speech. In his classic study of the Western literary tradition Eric Auerbach pointed out that "in the last analysis the differences in style between the writers of antiquity and early Christianity are conditioned by the fact that they were composed from a different point of view and for different people."[34]

389

Returning not only to the social doctrine of the gospel but to its rhetoric as well, the evangelists excited the people to action by "calling them out" and exhorting them to experimental Christianity. Radical attacks on an "unconverted ministry" that acted more like "Letter-learned . . . Pharisees" than preachers of the Word take on additional meaning in the social context of eighteenth-century established religion.[35] The danger that the Liberals sensed in the revivals was rhetorical as well as doctrinal. The Anglican commissary Alexander Garden correctly, and sarcastically, identified this threat: "*What went you out*, my Brethren, *to see*, or rather to *hear?* Any *new* Gospel, or message from Heaven? Why, no? but the *old* one explained and taught in a *new* and better Manner."[36] Pointing to the spirit of this new manner, one opponent of the revivals observed that "it abhors Reason, and is always for putting out her Eyes; but loves to reign Tyrant over the Passions, which it manages by Sounds and Nonsense."[37] The identification of sight with reason, and of sound with the passions, is here obvious and comes very near to the center of the raging controversy surrounding the itinerants. At stake was nothing less than the rules and conventions governing public address and social authority.

The revivalists' repudiation of polite style and their preference for extemporaneous mass address cut to the very core of colonial culture by attacking the habit of deference to the written word and to the gentlemen

[33] Amos N. Wilder, *Early Christian Rhetoric: The Language of the Gospel* (Cambridge, Mass., 1971), 13.

[34] Eric Auerbach, *Mimesis: The Representation of Reality in Western Literature*, trans. Willard R. Trask (Princeton, N.J., 1953), 46.

[35] Gilbert Tennent, *The Danger of an Unconverted Ministry, Considered in a Sermon on Mark VI. 34* (1741), in Heimert and Miller, eds., *Great Awakening*, 73.

[36] Alexander Garden, *Regeneration, and the Testimony of the Spirit. Being the Substance of Two Sermons . . .* (1740), *ibid.*, 58.

[37] *A true and genuine Account of a WANDERING SPIRIT, raised of late . . .*, *ibid.*, 149.

who mastered it. Evangelical rhetoric performed a dual function: it proclaimed the power of the spoken word directly to every individual who would hear, and it confirmed a shift in authority by organizing voluntary popular meetings and justifying them in the religious vocabulary of the day. Partly through doctrine, but even more through the rhetorical strategy necessitated by that doctrine, the popular style of he revivals challenged the assumption of hierarchy and pointed to a substitute basis for authority and order in an open voluntary system.

390

The popular rhetoric of the evangelists contrasted sharply with the much more formal modes of address preferred by upholders of established authority. Nowhere were the social divisions of American society more clearly reflected than in the leaders' utilization of a printed form of discourse that separated the literati from the common people. Throughout the eighteenth century, public communications were not only increasingly printed but were tuned to a genteel European literary style governed by canons of correct usage. As George Philip Krapp observed in his seminal history of the English language, "pronunciation, grammar and spelling were not then tests of respectability [in the seventeenth century] . . . in the degree to which they have since become. What seems now like illiterate speech, the speech of persons who do not reflect how they speak, was then merely the normal speech of the community."[38] With no printed dictionaries to provide authority for correct spelling and usage, seventeenth-century vernacular literature exhibited a high degree of variability. As the spread of printing in the eighteenth century gave increased importance to writing, however, there emerged a concomitant movement toward standardization of spelling and usage. Following the appearance of Samuel Johnson's dictionary in 1755, language came to be thought of as written rather than spoken, and educated elites on both sides of the ocean adopted a written style intended to communicate with their literate peers.[39] Linguistic divisions between the well-bred and the vulgar became increasingly clear to both sectors of the colonial society. One revealing example of a distinctive lower-class style is a radical essay, *The Key of Libberty,* written (though never accepted for publication) in 1797 by James Manning, an untutored Massachusetts farmer who "neaver had the advantage of six months schooling in my life." In organization, spelling, and grammar the essay stands in stark contrast to the

[38] George Philip Krapp, *The English Language in America,* I (New York, 1925), ix.
[39] See, for example, H. L. Mencken, *The American Language: An Inquiry into the Development of English in the United States,* 4th ed. (New York, 1936), 380, and James Root Hulbert, *Dictionaries: British and American,* rev. ed. (London, 1968), 10.

polished style of the whig patriots. It was, as Manning recognized, "not in the language and stile of the Larned for I am not able."[40]

Linguistic uniformity conspired with classical education to establish a learned discourse that effectively separated the literate elite from the common folk. Hugh Blair, whose handbook, *Lectures on Rhetoric and Belles Lettres,* came to epitomize the style for aspiring gentlemen, averred that the educated class "is now so much accustomed to a correct and ornamental style, that no writer can, with safety, neglect the study of it."[41] To encourage such a style Blair pointed to the patrician cultures of classical Greece and Rome, and urged his fellow literati "to render ourselves well acquainted with the style of the best authors. This is requisite, both in order to form a just taste in style, and to supply us with a full stock of words on every subject."[42] The classical heritage provided a vocabulary and mode of discourse which leaders had to learn if they were to communicate through the proper forms.[43]

Classical learning inculcated a set of social and cultural attitudes about the nature of speaker and audience that went far beyond the content of literature. A formal, analytical style conveyed social as well as literary prerogatives. For centuries, masters of print and the written word enjoyed social power and prestige partly because the people were awed by a sequential form of communications they could not understand. The eighteenth-century rise in learned treatises, tightly argued pamphlets, and belletristic writing reflected an effort, in Mather Byles's words, to "cultivate *polite* Writing, and form and embellish the Style of our ingenious Countrymen.—"[44] But Byles's "ingenious Countrymen" did not include the common folk.

391

---

[40] Samuel Eliot Morison, ed., "William Manning's *The Key of Libberty,*" *WMQ,* 3d Ser., XIII (1956), 202-254.

[41] Hugh Blair, *Lectures on Rhetoric and Belles Lettres,* I (Philadelphia, 1862), 215. Blair's lectures and essays were gathered together for publication in 1783.

[42] *Ibid.,* 214.

[43] Walter Ong observes in "Latin and the Social Fabric," that "using Latin was like playing a game whose rules could never be changed. . . . Latin was not merely one subject among many or even among several . . . Latin effected the transit from ignorance to tribal or communal wisdom. . . . Youngsters were given to understand that the treasures of all understanding were stored in the ancient tongues" (*The Barbarian Within* [New York, 1962], 206, 215). For descriptions of the classical grounding of colonial thought and education see Richard M. Gummere, *The American Colonial Mind and the Classical Tradition* (Cambridge, Mass., 1963); Robert Middlekauff, "A Persistent Tradition: The Classical Curriculum in Eighteenth-Century New England," *WMQ,* 3d Ser., XVIII (1961), 54-67; Meyer Reinhold, ed., *The Classick Pages: Classical Reading of Eighteenth-Century Americans* (University Park, Pa., 1975); and Wood, *Creation of the American Republic,* 48-53.

[44] Miller and Johnson, eds., *The Puritans,* 689. For a description of the increasingly high incidence of colonial borrowing from polite British culture see T. H. Breen, *The Character of the Good Ruler: A Study of Puritan Political Ideas in New*

The eighteenth-century shift in the direction of print and polite style was reflected in the growing appeal of rational religion among the educated elite. Cotton Mather typified this shift as early as 1726 in his *Manuductio ad Ministerium*, which, as Miller recognized, "in its catholicity of taste and urbanity suggests the spirit of current periodical essays rather than the utilitarian aim of a preaching manual."[45] Followers of deism, which carried the Liberal print-centered rationalism to an extreme, tended, in Ong's words, "to think of God himself as no longer a communicator, one who speaks to man, but as a Great Architect . . . , a manipulator of objects in visual-tactile space."[46] Treating communications as written rather than spoken, and locking words in printed space, rational Protestantism was incapable of penetrating the soul of an aural society; its ideas set forth in printed sermons and treatises could never inform a popular mentality attuned to the spoken word.

Attached to the elitist typographic culture were social imperatives. As long as social identities depended on a traditional social order for context and location within a finely graded hierarchy, communications had to be transacted through an elitist rhetoric. Power became so closely tied to print that advanced literacy and a classical education were virtually prerequisite to authority, and a college education guaranteed rapid advance in the social hierarchy.[47] By 1776 there were nearly three thousand college graduates in the colonies who, through the remarkable improvements in post and press, were able to communicate with one another on a scale and with a frequency unimaginable in the seventeenth century.[48] The cosmopolitan "better sort" formed a close-knit community that provided both authors and audience for

England, 1630–1730 (New Haven, Conn., 1970), 203-239, and Jack P. Greene, "Search for Identity: An Interpretation of the Meaning of Selected Patterns of Social Response in Eighteenth-Century America," *Jour. Soc. Hist.*, III (1970), 189-200.

[45] Miller and Johnson, eds., *The Puritans*, 669. See also Johnson's discussion of Puritan rhetoric, *ibid.*, 64-79.

[46] Ong, *Presence of the Word*, 73. The same print-centered ("visual") mode of perception is apparent in the Lockean epistemology that underlay Liberal assumptions in both religious and political contexts. See Ernest Tuveson, "Locke and the 'Dissolution of the Ego,'" *Modern Philology*, LII (1955), 164-165.

[47] On the social meaning and political significance of a classical education in the colonies see James Axtell, *The School upon a Hill: Education and Society in Colonial New England* (New Haven, Conn., 1974), 201-244; James J. Walsh, *Education of the Founding Fathers of the Republic: Scholasticism in the Colonial Colleges* . . . (New York, 1935); and Robert M. Zemsky, "Power, Influence, and Status: Leadership Patterns in the Massachusetts Assembly, 1740-1755," *WMQ*, 3d Ser., XXVI (1969), 511-512.

[48] Axtell, *School upon a Hill*, 213. For classic descriptions of the expanding networks of communications in 18th-century America see Frank Luther Mott, *American Journalism: A History of Newspapers in the United States Through 250 Years, 1690-1940* (New York, 1941), 3-110, *and* Wesley Everett Rich, *The History of the United States Post Office to the Year 1829* (Cambridge, Mass., 1924), 3-67.

the wave of printed literature that began to surge in the late eighteenth century. Pamphlets written by educated gentlemen, primarily lawyers, merchants, ministers, and planters, were addressed to their peers.[49] The common people were not included in the audience, but it was assumed that they would continue to defer to the leaders. There was no recognition that the pamphleteers' impassioned celebration of republicanism would require a new rhetoric of communications reflecting a profound shift in the nature of social authority—a rhetoric, in brief, that threatened to undermine the exclusive world in which the pamphlets were originally conceived.

With the coming of independence the American leadership could congratulate itself on the creation of a unique republican world-view through their publications. At the same time, however, these leaders could neither anticipate nor appreciate an egalitarian rhetoric that would soon compel them to relinquish their traditional claims to power and authority in the new republic. As a model of society, the neoclassical world of the colonial gentlemen was essentially stable; their exclusion of the common people meant that their writings could not reflect a changing self-consciousness initiated from below. The very outlook that created a learned and articulate "Republic of Letters" served, at the same time, to limit the writers' historical consciousness. Quite simply, the people were neither heard nor understood in their own terms.

The creation of an egalitarian rhetoric owed nothing to the classical heritage. If we are to understand the cultural significance of the Revolution, we must move beyond the rhetorical world of informed publications to the social world of popular assembly. We must *listen* as the "inarticulate" would have listened and determine to what extent religious and political meetings had a common rhetorical denominator that reached a revolutionary crescendo in the movement for independence.[50] For Philip Davidson, whose

393

[49] Gordon S. Wood observes that "even more indicative of the limited elitist conception of the audience was the extraordinary reliance on personal correspondence for the circulation of ideas. It is often difficult to distinguish between the private correspondence and the public writings of the Revolutionaries, so much alike are they" ("Democratization of Mind," *Leadership in the American Revolution,* 67-72).

[50] That the revivals did, in fact, continue to grow is most clearly reflected in the rapid growth of the dissenter movements in the colonies. Thomas Jefferson, for example, observed that by the time of the Revolution "two-thirds of the people [of Virginia] had become dissenters" (*Notes on the State of Virginia,* ed. William Peden [Chapel Hill, N.C., 1955], 158). More generally, Isaac Backus noted that, by 1795, the number of Separate Baptist preachers had grown to 1,125 (*A History of New England with Particular Reference to the Baptists,* ed. David Weston, 2d ed. [Newton, Mass., 1871], 401).

work continues to stand as the best general description of communications in the Revolutionary period, there was an unmistakably oral orientation to patriot "propaganda."[51] Throughout the colonies there existed a broad range of dramatic and oral communications in which, in William Eddis's words, "the busy voice of preparation echoes through every settlement."[52] The mobilization of the people was accomplished through extra-institutional mass meetings which, Merrill Jensen recognizes, were "of even greater long-range importance than mob action."[53]

The Founding Fathers were reluctant, for obvious reasons, to dwell on the oral dynamic unleashed in the course of rebellion; the same cannot be said of the loyalist opposition. Jonathan Sewall recognized both the evangelical and oral connections with republicanism: "there is an Enthusiasm in politics, like that which religious notions inspire, that drives Men on with an unusual Impetuosity, that baffles and confounds all Calculation grounded upon rational principles. Liberty, among Englishmen, is a Word, whose very Sound carries a fascinating charm."[54] Loyalist literature is replete with complaints that American towns were increasingly "filled with mock orations and songs, which for composition and sentiment would disgrace the most stupid and abandoned . . ."[55]

Whigs and loyalists used against one another the same arguments from constitution, law, and natural rights, but the charge of demogogic orality was

[51] Philip Davidson, *Propaganda and the American Revolution, 1763-1783* (Chapel Hill, N.C., 1941). Despite his penetrating description of Revolutionary communications, Davidson failed to recognize that the sort of mass society in which a manipulative propaganda could flourish did not exist in pre-Revolutionary America. What made the pamphlets significant was not the writers' intent to hoodwink the people but rather their exclusion of the people from the presumed audience. Both the term and the practice of mass propaganda originated after the Revolution. See David Hackett Fischer, *The Revolution of American Conservatism: The Federalist Party in the Era of Jeffersonian Democracy* (New York, 1965), 144-149.

[52] William Eddis, *Letters from America*, ed. Aubrey C. Land (Cambridge, Mass., 1969), 100.

[53] Merrill Jensen, "The American People and the American Revolution," *Journal of American History*, LVII (1970), 15. For suggestive descriptions of how these "mass meetings" aroused "popular enthusiasm" for independence see Davidson, *Propaganda and the American Revolution*, 173-208; Isaac, "Dramatizing the Ideology of Revolution," *WMQ*, 3d Ser., XXXIII (1976), 357-385; and Robert Middlekauff, "The Ritualization of the American Revolution," in Stanley Coben and Lorman Ratner, eds., *The Development of an American Culture* (Englewood Cliffs, N.J., 1970), 31-43.

[54] "A Letter from Jonathan Sewall to General Frederick Haldimand," May 30, 1775, in Jack P. Greene, ed., *Colonies to Nation, 1763-1789: A Documentary History of the American Revolution* (New York, 1975), 267.

[55] Margaret Wheeler Willard, ed., *Letters on the American Revolution* (New York, 1925), 81. See also Ramsay, *History of the American Revolution*, 16-17.

a one-way criticism. The loyalist opposition never mustered a counterattack until after 1773; and when it finally appeared, it was almost exclusively printed. Like earlier Liberal rhetoric, that of the loyalists disdained the "wild uproars" of the whigs which culminated in nothing less than a "Yell of Rebellion," and concentrated instead on pen and press.[56] In Davidson's words, "the Tory appeal was a written appeal; the dearth of oral, dramatic, and pictorial suggestions is striking."[57]

Insofar as the whig gentlemen favored traditional modes of public address, they failed to plumb the depths of a popular revolutionary spirit that was oral and egalitarian rather than printed and elitist. Bernard Bailyn, who has examined the ideological origins of the Revolution more deeply than any other scholar, relies almost exclusively on printed sources as a sufficient explanation for the development of a Revolutionary mentality. It was "the opposition press, as much as any single influence," Bailyn argues, "that shaped the political awareness of eighteenth-century Americans."[58] Although this is true for the informed populace, the link between print culture and the people, between pamphlets and popular ideology, is assumed, not demonstrated. Despite the rhetorical incompatibility of a popular culture and tightly reasoned pamphlets, the existence of a distinctive popular ideology is denied.[59] But as Patrick Henry pointed out, "the middle and lower ranks of people have not those illumined ideas which the well-born are so happily

395

[56] Daniel Leonard, "To the Inhabitants of the Province of the Massachusetts-Bay," (1775), in Leslie F. S. Upton, ed., *Revolutionary Versus Loyalist: The First American Civil War, 1774-1784* (Waltham, Mass., 1968), 39.

[57] Davidson, *Propaganda and the American Revolution*, 298, 301.

[58] Bernard Bailyn, *The Origins of American Politics* (New York, 1967), 38-39. Bailyn attributes many of the ideas presented in the "opposition press" to the English "real whig" tradition. This is of some importance because, like the American whigs, the English libertarian persuasion was almost exclusively print-centered. As Caroline Robbins observes, "the Real whigs, the liberals, seem to have been associated in certain areas and institutions around a few persuasive men. They were related by a bewildering series of marriages. . . . They relied on conversation, on letters among themselves or occasionally in the public press, on the dissemination of the printed word. . . . [T]hey followed a hit-and-miss method, consistent only in their determined faith in the printed tracts and treatises continually produced by them" (*The Eighteenth-Century Commonwealthman: Studies in the Transmission, Development and Circumstance of English Liberal Thought from the Restoration of Charles II until the War with the Thirteen Colonies* [Cambridge, Mass., 1959], 381, 382, 383).

[59] Bernard Bailyn argues that "the outbreak of the Revolution was not the result of social discontent. . . . Nor was there a transformation of mob behavior or of the lives of the 'inarticulate' in the pre-Revolutionary years that accounts for the disruption of Anglo-American politics" ("The Central Themes of the American Revolution: An Interpretation," in Stephen G. Kurtz and James H. Hutson, eds., *Essays on the American Revolution* [Chapel Hill, N.C., 1973], 12).

possessed of—they cannot so readily perceive latent objects."[60] Henry's refusal to enter into "the labyrinths of syllogistic [Latin] argumentative deductions" in his public address may well account for the power of his oratory, which more than one commentator has likened to that of the revivalists in style and impact.[61]

The problem with Bailyn's analysis is not that it is wrong in the way it portrays ideology; indeed, it represents a brilliant plea for the late eighteenth century as an "age of ideology." The problem is pamphlets: although central to the rebellion and to the articulation of classical republican theory in the colonies, they are not sufficient to explain the process of an egalitarian cultural transformation. Bailyn concentrates on the pamphlets and the "real whig" country ideology as the formative sources of the rebellion. Having set the ideological background for rebellion, he describes some of the manifestations of the "transforming radicalism" unleashed by the Revolution.[62] But the instances of transforming radicalism which Bailyn isolates are described far more effectively than they are explained in terms of their cultural sources. Pamphlets could never represent the primary source of radical republicanism, any more than the revivals could have issued from printed sermons or the loyalist critique of the rebellion organize itself through oral popular appeals.

Recognizing the failure of pamphlets to capture the growing revolutionary sentiment in America, a writer for the *Pennsylvania Packet* argued in 1776 that "our cause will never appear to advantage in a pamphlet. . . . When you write a pamphlet you are expected to say the best, if not all that can be said on the subject, and if it contains [only] a few weighty arguments the author is despised and the subject suffers."[63] The writer was referring, of course, to pamphlets generally. Not every pamphlet was limited by the rhetorical constraints of a classical style. What made Thomas Paine's *Common Sense* so unlike the prevailing pamphlet literature of the day was its scorn for the best literary canons and its repudiation of the language and

[60] William Wirt Henry, ed., *Patrick Henry: Life, Correspondence and Speeches*, III (New York, 1891), 462.

[61] Heimert, *Religion and the American Mind*, 232, 233; Rhys Isaac, "Preachers and Patriots: Popular Culture and the Revolution in Virginia," in Alfred F. Young, ed., *The American Revolution: Explorations in the History of American Radicalism* (DeKalb, Ill., 1976), 152-154.

[62] Bailyn states that "the radicalism the Americans conveyed to the world in 1776 was a transformed as well as a transforming force. . . . Institutions were brought into question and condemned that appeared to have little if any direct bearing on the immediate issues of the Anglo-American struggle" (*Ideological Origins of the American Revolution*, 161, 232).

[63] Quoted in Thomas R. Adams, *American Independence, the Growth of an Idea: A Bibliographic Study of the American Political Pamphlets Printed Between 1764 and 1776 . . .* (Providence, R.I., 1965), xiv-xv.

396

forms of classical discourse. Coming from a lower-class Quaker background, Paine lacked the formal Latin education common to other pamphleteers; in its place he managed to establish a new style that anticipated the wave of nineteenth-century literature intended for the people generally.[64]

Another major atypical pamphlet to appear in the colonies before independence was *An Oration on the Beauties of Liberty*, published in 1773 by the Baptist minister and linen-draper John Allen. Like Paine, Allen was a recent arrival from England at the time *An Oration* was printed, and, like *Common Sense*, the tract enjoyed immense popularity in the colonies.[65] In style it bears repeated resemblances to the "enraged" language which scholars have found throughout *Common Sense*.[66] Also, as in *Common Sense*, the references and quotations are not drawn, as in the other pamphlets, from classical republicanism or British constitutional theory, but rather from the Bible. There is not one page of *An Oration* that does not supply biblical precedent or injunction for the assault on privilege and tyranny. Ahab, the golden calf, Zedekiah, Cain, Abel, and Rehoboam constituted a familiar vocabulary that was "opened up" and explained repeatedly in colonial sermons. To liken a ruler to Ahab or a social order to Babylon was to call for a revolution.

397

Perhaps the most important aspect of *An Oration* is that it was obviously meant to be heard as well as read.[67] Its full impact can be felt only when one *listens* to the rhetoric. Addressing the common people, Allen repeatedly relied on a coarse prose, rather than on logical syllogisms or authorities from a printed past. Reminding the people that rulers and ministers were "servants" who must "hear" a free and "affectionate" people, Allen demanded, "Has not the voice of your father's blood cry'd yet loud enough in your ears, in your hearts? . . . Have you not heard the voice of blood in your own streets . . . ?"[68] In striking contrast to virtually all the other pamphleteers, but like Paine later, Allen aimed his rhetoric beyond the literate elite to the rank and file.

If action proceeds from a cultural perception of public events in terms of symbolic forms, then analyses of the mobilization of ideas into ideology and

[64] This point is effectively developed in Eric Foner, *Tom Paine and Revolutionary America* (New York, 1976), xv-xvi, 80-87.

[65] *An Oration Upon the Beauties of Union* (Boston, 1773) was exceeded in separate editions by only two pamphlets including the "runaway best seller" *Common Sense*. For tabulations see Adams, *American Independence*, xi-xii.

[66] See, for example, Bernard Bailyn, "Common Sense," in *Fundamental Testaments of the American Revolution*, Library of Congress Symposia (Washington, D.C., 1973), 7-22.

[67] John M. Bumsted and Charles E. Clark, "New England's Tom Paine: John Allen and the Spirit of Liberty," *WMQ*, 3d Ser., XXI (1964), 570.

[68] Allen, *An Oration on the Beauties of Liberty*, 19, 27.

action must recognize, at least in part, the cultural preconditions for receptivity, particularly on the popular level. A discontinuous ("revolutionary")
cultural change could, by definition, never emerge from a continuing intellectual tradition; there must be a break somewhere. Where are the sources
of such a radical ideology to be discovered?

Without denying the influence of typographic culture on the leaders of
the rebellion and in the formation of the new governments, it might be
helpful to think of republicanism in a pluralistic context as absorbing both
traditional and egalitarian perceptions of social order. The theoretical work
of J. G. A. Pocock builds upon an understanding of the unavoidable
"multivalency" of language that derives from the different experiences of
speakers and hearers.[69] Recognizing the truism that words do not necessarily
mean what either the speaker or the historian believe they mean, Pocock
does not examine language and ideas as fixed entities, but rather insists that
language and communications not be separated from the circumstances and
comprehension of their individual users. When "conceptual and social
worlds" are placed in conjunction, no singular "constellation of ideas" or
"climate of opinion" appears to have embodied an identical meaning for all
social ranks.[70] To get at the popular meaning of republican ideology requires
moving beyond the verbal content of the documents themselves to the social
world in which they were transmitted.

Pocock's insights, placed in the context of the American Revolution,
reveal that not one but two ideological explosions propelled the colonies into
a new nation. Both leaders and followers were possessed of an extraordinarily
powerful ideology that at points converged on common antagonists and a
common vocabulary, and at other points diverged dramatically. No ideology
that is pieced together solely from the literate world of print can fully
comprehend the radical dynamic of the Revolution. It is incapable of
accounting for the enormously creative power of *vox populi* to organize a
social order bound together in voluntary associations based on discussion and
public address. Resisting John Adams and others who located the Revolution's *raison d'être* among the classical world view of the elite, Benjamin
Rush issued the following advice to historians: "I hope with the history of
this folly, some historian will convey to future generations, that many of the
most active and useful characters in accomplishing this revolution, were
strangers to the formalities of a Latin and Greek education."[71]

[69] See, especially, J. G. A. Pocock, *Politics, Language and Time: Essays on
Political Thought and History* (New York, 1971), 3-41.

[70] *Ibid.*, 15.

[71] Quoted in Meyer Reinhold, "Opponents of Classical Learning in America
during the Revolutionary Period," American Philosophical Society, *Proceedings,*
CXII (1968), 230.

The social conditions that allowed for the popular upsurge in the revivals and rebellion did not permit unstructured public address to degenerate into "anarchy" and mass rebellion, as the Standing Order had always feared. Perhaps the enduring legacy of the Revolution lay in its demonstration that distinctive ideologies *could* work in concert. The typographic ideology of the real whig tradition was, as Bailyn and others demonstrate, an "inner accelerator" of a transforming radicalism, but only in the sense that the aroused elite were compelled by the logic of their argument for rebellion to create, in law and politics, an egalitarian vocabulary, and, in communications, the secular equivalents of the revival in voluntary political parties and free presses.[72] Beneath that impulse, however, we must also recognize typographic ideology and the rebellion as accelerating a movement *already in progress*, a movement that originated among the lower rather than the upper strata of colonial society, and that, combined with profound social strains which increased throughout the eighteenth century, opened the way for the "enchanting sound" of mass public address.[73]

399

While the whig justification of the rebellion pointed to an "invisible government" of ministers, cliques, and venal officials, another conspiracy, recognized as early as 1773 by the loyalist Boucher, was equally "invisible" and far more powerful. Attacking the foundations of traditional social order, this conspiracy derived its "invisibility" from its essentially extemporaneous nature. In Boucher's words: "as though there were some irrefutable charm in all extemporaneous speaking, however rude, the orators of our committees and sub-committees, like those in higher spheres, *prevail with their tongues.* To public speakers alone is the government of our country now completely committed. . . . An empire is thus completely established within an empire; and a new system of government of great power erected, even before the old one is formally abolished."[74] An empire premised on talk, wholly lacking in the formal coercive structure that kings, churches, aristocracies, standing armies, and mercantile controls provided, did indeed represent a revolutionary departure in the principles of government and social order. Voluntaryism, the very linchpin of social, religious, and political organization in the new republic, was perhaps the clearest manifestation of this revolutionary system

---

[72] Bailyn, *Ideological Origins of the American Revolution*, 95.

[73] Garden, *Regeneration, and the Testimony of the Spirit*, in Heimert and Miller, eds., *Great Awakening*, 47.

[74] Jonathan Boucher, *A View of the Causes and Consequences of the American Revolution in Thirteen Discourses* . . . (New York, 1967 [orig. publ. London, 1797]), 320, 321. See David Ammerman's discussion of "government by committee," in *In the Common Cause: American Response to the Coercive Acts of 1774* (Charlottesville, Va., 1974), 103-124, and Wood, *Creation of the American Republic*, 319-328.

of authority.[75] Of course, public address did not replace print, nor was the populace hostile to print and literacy *per se*, but only to a print culture that was elitist and hierarchical. Still, it is no accident that early republicanism represented the "Golden Age of Oratory," because mass address was, for a time, the most effective means of reaching the new audience and utilizing the egalitarian style seized upon by republican orators and revivalists as the creative force within the popular ideology.[76]

The rhetorical transformation in the revivals signified an emerging popular culture asserting itself against a paternalistic social ethic. In the course of the Revolution, the social order prefigured in evangelical assemblies was suffused with secular and political meanings articulated in the world-view of republicanism. This new order, in Michael Kammen's description, was not so much a "seamless web" as an "unstable pluralism" defying reduction to any one ideology or social system.[77] The rhetorical division resulting from the revivals played a major role in generating subsequent tensions and conflicts in American society. These tensions, moreover, reflected not so much opposing ideas with conflicting literary traditions as entirely different social outlooks and attitudes toward social authority, all deriving legitimacy from the individualism implicit in a mass democratic society. Evangelical attacks on a settled and educated ministry may have expressed a pristine "anti-intellectualism" in the colonies,[78] but it was an anti-intellectualism that was positive and creative—indeed, revolutionary. Without it there would have been no creation of an egalitarian American republic.

The oral explosion and egalitarian style evidenced in the revivals were

[75] On the frontier the essentially oral, voluntary association was most clearly manifested in the revivals which, as Donald G. Matthews suggests, represented a critical "organizing process" in the new nation. See Matthews, "The Second Great Awakening as an Organizing Process, 1780-1830," *Am. Qtly.*, XI (1969), 23-43. Similarly, Leonard L. Richards points out how, in the voluntary reform efforts of the "evangelical crusade," evangelical abolitionists effectively utilized the "revolution in communications and the creation of mass media" to bypass traditional social channels and organize voluntary associations within "impersonal, large-scale organizations" (*"Gentlemen of Property and Standing": Anti-Abolition Mobs in Jacksonian America* [New York, 1970], 167).

[76] Wood points this out in *Creation of the American Republic*, 621-622, and "Democratization of Mind," in *Leadership in the American Revolution*, 78-82. Perhaps not sufficiently emphasized in studies of early American literature is the abrupt decline in public significance of pamphlets, letters, treatises, and printed sermons after the Revolution.

[77] Michael Kammen, *People of Paradox: An Inquiry Concerning the Origins of American Civilization* (New York, 1972), 89-96. The social ramifications of this cultural pluralism are treated in Robert H. Wiebe, *The Segmented Society: An Introduction to the Meaning of America* (New York, 1975).

[78] Richard Hofstadter, *Anti-Intellectualism in American Life* (New York, 1962), 55-141.

not limited to religion, nor was the articulation of a radical ideology the conscious objective of itinerant evangelists. The primary concern of the revivals was the saving of souls, and the rhetorical innovations that lent force to the movement were not fully perceived or verbalized for what they could come to represent: a revolutionary shift in world-view. As a movement initiated from below, the social experience of the revivals existed in fact before the emergence of a literate rationale. This does not mean that the experience proceeded from irrational impulses but, rather, that the terms necessary for rational comprehension and formal legitimation had to be invented. What opponents of the revivals termed a "spirit of superstition" was, for Jonathan Edwards, a new "sense" that could not easily be rendered into the existing forms of speech: "Some Things that they are sensible of are altogether new to them, their Ideas and inward Sensations are new, and what they therefore knew not how to accommodate Language to, or to find Words to express."[79] Edwards's concern was to fit the new social experience of the revivals to its proper spiritual vocabulary, while acknowledging that no language could fully express the essence of religious faith.

What Edwards and other churchmen failed to recognize was that the "spirit of liberty" manifest in the revivals would not be contained in religious categories. In the movement for independence both leaders and followers adopted a political vocabulary that expressed the egalitarian impulse in the secular language of republicanism. This vocabulary was largely provided, as Bailyn and Caroline Robbins demonstrate, through the Commonwealth tradition. But the ethos and ideological fervor of republicanism did not derive so much from the injection of Commonwealth vocabulary into colonial pamphlets as from the translation of the evangelical experience into a secular theoretical vocabulary that more adequately embodied, for some, the revolutionary thrust first widely experienced in the revivals. Words that were abstracted from their restrictive, deferential context came to mean something else. In Tocqueville's observation, Americans had a penchant for abstract words because only by using a vocabulary lacking specificity could they communicate radical ideas that destroyed a conventional style. "An abstract word," Tocqueville noted, "is like a box with a false bottom; you may put in it what ideas you please and take them out again unobserved."[80] The "country" publicists did not provide the textbook of revolution, so much as a lexicon of revolution, the meaning of which could be grasped only within a persuasion that celebrated the sovereignty of the new political audience.

[79] Jonathan Edwards, *The Distinguishing Marks of a Work of the Spirit of God* . . . (1741), in Bushman, ed., *Great Awakening*, 123. On Edwards's use of language see Harold P. Simonson, *Jonathan Edwards: Theologian of the Heart* (Grand Rapids, Mich., 1974), 91-118.

[80] Alexis de Tocqueville, *Democracy in America*, eds. J. P. Mayer and Max Lerner (New York, 1966), 482. See also Robert E. Shalhope, "Toward a Republican Synthesis: The Emergence of an Understanding of Republicanism in American Historiography," *WMQ*, XXIX (1972), 72-73.

401

The Tax Man Cometh: Ideological Opposition to Internal Taxes, 1760-1790

Thomas P. Slaughter

In the arguments occasioned by the Stamp Act, a distinction had been taken between *internal* and *external* taxes; by the former were meant *taxes* on things out of the immediate power of commerce; by the latter, *taxes* on such as were *within* it. These (being paid at the ports) were more generally called *duties*. The former had been denied upon the principle (among others) that such a power of taxing subjected the whole of every American's property to the power of Parliament; by which means he could not be said to have any that was absolutely *his own*.

James Iredell, unpublished pamphlet, June 1776.[1]

OPPONENTS of the proposed national Constitution in 1786 and 1787 were appalled by its surrender of the very principles for which they had fought the Revolution. "In this new Constitution," a South Carolinian wrote, "every thing is transferred, not so much power being left us as Lord North offered to guaranty to us in his conciliatory plan."[2] Antifederalists were especially shocked by the Constitution's

Mr. Slaughter is a member of the Department of History at Rutgers University, New Brunswick, N.J. Acknowledgments: This project was completed with the assistance of grants from the American Association for State and Local History, the American Bar Foundation, and the Research Council of Rutgers University. I thank all three organizations for their support. I presented a version of this article at the Philadelphia Center for Early American Studies and thank those who attended for their helpful comments, especially Richard R. Beeman, Paul G. E. Clemens, J. William Frost, and P.M.G. Harris. I also gratefully acknowledge the assistance of Joyce Appleby, Douglas Greenberg, Stephen Innes, Rhys Isaac, Stanley Katz, Christopher Lee, Jackson Turner Main, Louis Masur, Edmund Morgan, John Murrin, Jack Rakove, Denise Thompson, and Gordon Wood.

[1] Griffith J. McRee, *Life and Correspondence of James Iredell . . .* , 2 vols. (New York, 1857), I, 287.

[2] Jonathan Elliot, ed., *The Debates in the Several State Conventions on the Adoption of the Federal Constitution, as Recommended by the General Convention at Philadelphia, in 1787*, 2d ed. (Washington, D.C., 1861), IV, 289. For a similar statement by Amos Singletary of Massachusetts see *ibid.*, II, 101.

taxation clause. "By sect. 8 of article 1," a Massachusetts Antifederalist argued, "Congress are to have the unlimited right to regulate commerce, external and *internal*. . . . They have also the unlimited right to imposts and all kinds of taxes, as well to levy as to collect them. They have indeed very nearly the same powers claimed formerly by the British parliament. Can we have so soon forgot our glorious struggle with that power, as to think a moment of surrendering it now?"[3]

Antifederalist pamphleteers despised far more than the Constitution's taxation clause. Theirs was a broad attack on the document's philosophy and the entire system of government designed to implement its principles.[4] They saw themselves as defending the ideal of local rule against potential encroachments of an ambitious central government, just as, they believed, Revolutionaries had defended America against Great Britain. In this light, Antifederalists were especially enraged by the proposal to entrust a national congress "with every species of *internal* taxation."[5] They could not comprehend how men who so recently had shed blood to secure individual liberty and local control over taxation could turn around and give both away. "When I recollect," one lamented, "how lately congress, conventions, legislatures, and people contended in the cause of liberty, and carefully weighed the importance of taxation, I can scarcely believe we are serious in proposing to vest the powers of laying and collecting internal taxes in a government so imperfectly organized for such purposes."[6]

This article focuses on the ideological concept of "internal taxes." It relates part, but only part, of the story of ideological conflict in late eighteenth-century America. For those Americans who divided the world of taxes into internal and external spheres, the distinction was only one of many principles that shaped their views of the political world. Their

403

---

[3] "Agrippa" [James Winthrop?], No. 9, *Massachusetts Gazette* (Boston), Jan. 14, 1788, in Cecelia M. Kenyon, ed., *The Antifederalists* (Indianapolis, Ind., 1966), 142-143.

[4] On Antifederalist thought see Herbert J. Storing, ed., *The Complete Anti-Federalist*, Vol. I: *What the Anti-Federalists Were* For (Chicago, 1981); Kenyon, ed., *Antifederalists;* and Jackson Turner Main, *The Antifederalists: Critics of the Constitution, 1781-1788* (Chapel Hill, N.C., 1961).

[5] "Centinel," *Independent Gazetteer, or Chronicle of Freedom* (Philadelphia), Oct. 5, 1787, in Kenyon, ed., *Antifederalists*, 9.

[6] "Letter from the Federal Farmer," No. 3, Oct. 10, 1787, in Kenyon, ed., *Antifederalists*, 225. Gordon S. Wood has contested the common attribution of this pamphlet to Virginian Richard Henry Lee. Although he does not identify the real author, Wood argues from internal evidence that he was possibly a New Yorker. See "The Authorship of the *Letters from the Federal Farmer*," *William and Mary Quarterly*, 3d Ser., XXXI (1974), 299-308. For a dissenting reply see Steven R. Boyd, "The Impact of the Constitution on State Politics: New York as a Test Case," in James Kirby Martin, ed., *The Human Dimensions of Nation Making: Essays on Colonial and Revolutionary America* (Madison, Wis., 1976), 276n.

arguments about the justice and constitutionality of these two sorts of taxes were intimately tied to beliefs about representation, sovereignty, and the relationship between local and central governments. Nonetheless, for reasons of clarity and coherence, this article must eschew the temptation to try to weave the entire fabric of this ideology as well as refrain from devoting much space to others. As a first step toward these grander goals, however, it isolates this one central thread of "localist" ideology.[7] It attempts to define the meanings of the internal-external distinction at two points in time—the 1760s and 1780s—and to suggest, though not to trace, the role of the distinction in the conflicts that racked America after the Revolution.

404

The article does not offer a continuous history of opposition to centrally imposed internal taxes between 1766 and 1786, when the controversy was not a lively one at the intercolonial or national level. Localist sentiment persisted during those years. Opposition to internal taxes was deep and unappeased but dormant. During the two decades after repeal of the Stamp Act, few Americans articulated this fear. Other menaces occupied their energy.

Discussion of internal taxes in the era of the Revolution must first confront a historiographic whirlwind that was unleashed by Edmund S. Morgan in a 1948 article and that he and Helen M. Morgan restated in the book that is still the standard account of the Stamp Act controversy.[8] The Morgans argued, contrary to virtually unanimous agreement among historians, that Americans denied the authority of Parliament "to tax the colonies at all" in 1765 and consistently maintained that position through 1776. According to the Morgans, the "official statement of belief" adopted by "the formally elected representatives" in every colony except Georgia and North Carolina "almost universally" acknowledged Parliament's authority "to legislate for the whole empire in any way that concerned the common interests of all the members of the empire . . . , but they denied that Parliament's legislative authority extended either to the internal polity of the colonies or to taxation." The Morgans contended that scholars had been misled by the distinction between internal and external taxation in newspapers, pamphlets, and resolutions adopted "by informal gatherings of small groups." These unrepresentative documents, as the Morgans defined them, had led historians to mistake "the views of

---

[7] I use "localist" to denote a person whose fundamental ideology or political world view is more provincial than national or international. The term also describes a range of values sometimes labeled "country" to distinguish them from "court" or "cosmopolitan" persuasions. For a different and more precise definition of "localist" and "cosmopolitan" see Jackson Turner Main, *Political Parties before the Constitution* (Chapel Hill, N.C., 1973), 32-33.

[8] Morgan, "Colonial Ideas of Parliamentary Power, 1764-1766," *WMQ*, 3d Ser., V (1948), 311-341; Morgan and Morgan, *The Stamp Act Crisis: Prologue to Revolution* (Chapel Hill, N.C., 1953; rev. ed., New York, 1963).

factions or the idiosyncracies of a single man" for the beliefs of most colonists.[9]

This thesis is still a prominent interpretation of Revolutionary ideology, although it has not gone unchallenged.[10] Perhaps the most telling criticism came from Bernard Bailyn, who, like the Morgans, considered constitutional principles a cause of the Revolution, but who relied for his evidence on the pamphlets they dismissed as unrepresentative. Bailyn rejected the significance of the Morgans' distinction between taxation and legislation and the one they sought to supplant as well. According to Bailyn, it was Americans' interpretation of divided sovereignty—of "internal" and "external" spheres of government—that led them to take up arms in the 1770s. "In the perspective of the fundamental problem of sovereignty," he argued, "whether the colonists did or did not admit Parliament's right to impose 'external' taxes is less important than that they universally thought in terms of 'internal' and 'external' spheres of government, and that this distinction, of which the taxing issue was a specification, provided them with the means of discriminating among and qualifying the sovereign powers of Parliament."[11]

In fact, what the Morgans and Bailyn identified by their disagreement and by their reliance on different types of sources was a conflict among Americans about representation, sovereignty, and lawful types of taxation. Neither the Morgans nor Bailyn saw it that way, though; neither posited

[9] Morgan, "Colonial Ideas," *WMQ*, 3d Ser., V (1948), 314, 315, 325-326; Morgan and Morgan, *Stamp Act Crisis*, 9, 50, 152-154. For examples of the credibility of the external-internal distinction the Morgans wrote about it see Carl Becker, *The Declaration of Independence: A Study in the History of Political Ideas* (New York, 1922), 90; Lawrence Henry Gipson, *The Triumphant Empire: Thunder-Clouds Gather in the West, 1763-1766*, The British Empire before the American Revolution, X (New York, 1961); and Samuel Eliot Morison and Henry Steele Commager, *The Growth of the American Republic*, 2 vols. (New York, 1930), I, 155. These historians agreed that Americans invoked the internal-external distinction to justify opposition to the Stamp Act but then abandoned it during resistance to the Townshend duties, which were external taxes.

[10] See, for example, the exchange between Curtis P. Nettels and Morgan in *WMQ*, 3d Ser., VI (1949), 162-170; Bernhard Knollenberg, *Origin of the American Revolution: 1759-1766* (New York, 1960); Jack M. Sosin, *Agents and Merchants: British Colonial Policy and the Origins of the American Revolution, 1763-1775* (Lincoln, Neb., 1965), 48-57; Ian R. Christie, "William Pitt and American Taxation, 1766: A Problem of Parliamentary Reporting," *Studies in Burke and His Time*, XVII (1976), 167-179; and Gipson, *Triumphant Empire*. For evidence of the continuing influence of the Morgans' interpretation see, for example, Paul R. Lucas, *American Odyssey, 1607-1789* (Englewood Cliffs, N.J., 1984), 215-216; Robert Middlekauff, *The Glorious Cause: The American Revolution, 1763-1789* (New York, 1982), 70-126, esp. 123-125; and Jerome R. Reich, *Colonial America* (Englewood Cliffs, N.J., 1984), 259-264.

[11] Bailyn, *The Ideological Origins of the American Revolution* (Cambridge, Mass., 1967), 198, 211-213, esp. 213n.

much conflict among the colonists who supported the Revolutionary movement. But read together, their sources drew the lines that would matter when Americans battled over political philosophy and practice during the 1780s and 1790s. Both the Morgans and Bailyn were basically correct about what their documents reveal, although, as argued below, alternative interpretations of the Morgans' legislative resolutions are equally plausible. Bailyn and the Morgans were unduly confident, however, about the representativeness of their samples.

The article must also address the relevant portion of Gordon S. Wood's *Creation of the American Republic*, which carried Bailyn's study of "sovereignty" forward in time through the ratification of the Constitution. Peripherally to the central concerns of his analysis, Wood observed that with the enforcement of the Townshend duties the distinction between internal and external taxes, "never surely grasped, at once dissolved." The distinction was abandoned, Wood implied, and was never reclaimed, at least through 1787. The section below that examines the Antifederalist distinction between internal and external taxes dissents from this implication. The article seeks to demonstrate the centrality of the discrimination between internal and external taxes in Antifederalist ideology and to demonstrate the continuity over time of a distinction that played a dynamic role in political conflicts of the 1760s, the 1780s, and the 1790s. In this, it intends to establish the relationship of ideological continuities so ably investigated by whig and neo-whig historians with the conflict that has generally been the province of heirs to the Progressive school. All have overlooked the recurrent role played by this distinction in the ideological battles of the late eighteenth century.[12]

According to the Morgans, then, the distinction between internal and external taxes was never popular in America. Wood posited that whatever significance the distinction held in America at the time of the Stamp Act crisis evaporated before the Revolution, never to appear again. Bailyn argued that the distinction existed only as part of a larger configuration of ideas outside of which it had no particular relevance. The Morgans, Wood, and Bailyn all agreed, however, that there was little dissent within the patriot camp from the ideas they each described, at least during the 1760s—that all Revolutionaries shared the same ideology.

This essay takes issue with the interpretation of the internal-external dichotomy offered by each of these historians. It dissents from the Morgans' dismissal of the distinction's importance. It questions Bailyn's and the Morgans' consensual portrayal of Revolutionary ideology. It

[12] Wood, The Creation of the American Republic, 1776-1787 (Chapel Hill, N.C., 1969), 349. This article does not, however, challenge Wood's overall interpretation of the 1780s, especially where he shares Charles A. Beard's understanding of the role of conflict and where he surpasses Beard's comprehension of the role of competing ideologies in that conflict. See Beard, An Economic Interpretation of the Constitution of the United States (New York, 1913).

challenges Wood's assertion that by the 1770s the internal-external configuration had lost any importance it once had. On the contrary, this article contends that the ideological distinction was significant in the 1760s and in post-Revolutionary America, and that by the 1780s it was important precisely because Americans who had agreed about the need for revolution disagreed about the necessity of dividing sovereignty over internal and external taxes.[13]

When Parliament met in the early months of 1766 to discuss the Stamp Act rebellion, its members focused on the argument used by Americans to contest the act's constitutionality. A year earlier, M.P.s had dismissed the "strange language" of colonists who did "not think an internal and external duty the same."[14] Now, in the face of unprecedented colonial resistance to a law of Parliament, its members were more inquisitive about what North Americans were saying.

William Pitt tried to explain. According to Pitt, the colonists believed that *"the House had no right to lay an internal tax upon America, that country not being represented"* in Parliament. Barlow Trecothick made essentially the same point to his peers when he observed that "the Americans think that the imposition of internal taxes ought to be confined to their own assembly." The North Americans thought "this law unjust in its original," Richard Hussey told the Commons, because it was constitutionally novel. No previous act of Parliament had "laid an internal tax, at least no internal tax which can so fairly be called so as this Act."[15] Colonists, according to

407

[13] In fact, my engagement with the noted neo-whig historians mentioned above partially obscures the degree to which my interpretation builds on theirs. Their demonstration of the central role played by ideology in the American Revolution is my inspiration. In this sense and in the sense that I find consistency over time in the thought of Americans, I have more in common with the interpretations of Bailyn and the Morgans than with neo-Progressives who dismiss or ignore the relevance of ideology as anything more than evolving propaganda. Since I focus on conflict among Revolutionaries, however, I depart from the consensual vision of the neo-whigs. Like the Progressives, I see conflict as central to the Revolutionary experience. Like Wood (who is something of a bridging figure between the two schools) and Beard, both of whom are inspirations for my analysis, I recognize conflicting ideologies and interests as the center of America's political universe during the 1780s.

[14] William Beckford, Feb. 6, 1765, in R. C. Simmons and P.D.G. Thomas, eds., *Proceedings and Debates of the British Parliaments Respecting North America, 1754-1783* (New York, 1983), II, 11, hereafter cited as *Proceedings*. For Parliament's discussion of internal taxes during 1765 see also the speeches of George Grenville, Isaac Barré, and Rose Fuller, *ibid.*, 10, 12, 13.

[15] *Ibid.*, 82, 86, 87, 91, 285, 298. See also the 1766 speeches of Henry Conway, Hans Stanley, Charles Yorke, William Blackstone, Alexander Wedderburn, Isaac Barré, George Grenville, and Lord Strange (Stanley Smith), *ibid.*, 135, 136, 139, 140, 143, 144, 145, 294. According to Grenville and others, there was precedent for Parliament's assessing internal taxes on America. They considered the Post Office Act of 9 Anne an internal tax (*ibid.*, 10).

their British interpreters, maintained that sovereignty was constitutionally divided between Parliament and their local assemblies. They held that internal taxes could be levied justly only by local, representative institutions—not by a remote Parliament in which they were not represented.

Some members of Parliament were still not sure they comprehended the American position or that it made any sense. "I cannot understand the difference between external and internal taxes," George Grenville asserted in response to Pitt's explanation. William Blackstone and Lord Mansfield, the two reigning experts on such matters, could find no such distinction in law, either common or statute. Blackstone also denied that under British law "the right of imposing taxes arises from representation." Lord North, perhaps most subtly of all, later argued that "in point of right there is no difference [between internal and external taxes]; in point of operation there certainly is: external might not go further, internal might."[16]

North's comment is most helpful for understanding Parliament's confusion. It seems odd to find Grenville, for example, claiming not to comprehend the distinction between internal and external taxes since he had used the adjectives himself for years prior to this confrontation. North, Townshend, and other M.P.s also commonly distinguished between internal or interior taxes on the one hand and external taxes or customs duties on the other.[17] But North's distinction between "right" and "operation" helps clarify how Grenville and other British politicians could use the internal-external configuration at one moment and then deny understanding it the next. They apparently perceived the difference between the two types of taxes in operation but were surprised and honestly befuddled by the argument against Parliament's constitutional right to lay internal taxes. Americans had apparently taken a commonplace operational description, invested it with ideological significance, and turned it into a constitutional argument.

The ideological distinction that Parliament was hearing for the first time

---

[16] In other words, the kinds of internal taxes—excise, stamp, poll—could go "further" in the ways in which they were collected and reach deeper into people's lives. British politicians who remembered Walpole's excise scheme and Bute's cider tax might also have recalled that protests against internal taxes tended to go a good deal "further" as well. *Ibid.*, 86, 87, 129, 132, 140, 145. North's observations came in his speech of Dec. 8, 1768, Cavendish Diaries, Egerton MSS, 215, fol. 302, British Library, quoted in John L. Bullion, *A Great and Necessary Measure: George Grenville and the Genesis of the Stamp Act, 1763-1765* (Columbia, Mo., 1983), 204. See also P.D.G. Thomas, *British Politics and the Stamp Act Crisis: The First Phase of the American Revolution, 1763-1767* (Oxford, 1975), esp. chap. 12, and Thomas P. Slaughter, "The Empire Strikes Back: George Grenville and the Stamp Tax," *Reviews in American History*, XII (1984), 204-210.

[17] See, for example, *Proceedings*, II, 11, 14, 35, 136, 145; Thomas, *British Politics and the Stamp Act Crisis*, chap. 12; and Thomas, ed., "The Parliamentary Diaries of Nathaniel Ryder, 1764-1767," *Camden Miscellany*, No. 23, Camden 4th Ser., VII (1969), 233-238, 253-276, 291-300.

in the mid-1760s was made frequently by theorists of American rights. In 1764, before the Stamp Act rebellion, Massachusetts Lt. Gov. Thomas Hutchinson informed a Connecticut correspondent that "your distinction between duties upon trade and internal taxes agrees with . . . the opinion of most People here." There is no reason to question his assessment. American witnesses called before Parliament in 1766 told its members the same thing. Testimony from residents of Massachusetts, Rhode Island, New York, Pennsylvania, and Virginia agreed; Parliament heard that crowds, newspapers, pamphlets, politicians, and private citizens in each of these colonies "make the distinction between internal and external duties." It was the understanding of most American witnesses, even those who did not share the sentiment, that colonists opposed the Stamp Act because it was an internal tax, that they would predictably resist any other internal tax, but that there was less danger of violent protest against external taxes, at least on ideological grounds.[18]

409

In America, the distinction had reached the level of popular song by 1765. On August 29, a crowd paraded through the streets of Newport, Rhode Island, and constructed a gallows for the effigy of a "Stampman." On one of the gallows posts they hung a copy of a ditty heard on the streets of American towns that summer. The pertinent stanza read as follows:

> Those Blessings our Fathers obtain'd by their blood,
> We are justly oblig'd as their Sons to make good;
> All internal Taxes let us then nobly spurn,
> These Effigies first—next the Stamp Paper burn.[19]

The language of the ideological distinction between internal and external taxes had penetrated beyond the intellectually rarefied world of pamphlet literature. We might even surmise, as Hutchinson and others did, that crowds mouthing such words had some understanding of their meaning.

---

[18] Hutchinson quoted in Edmund S. Morgan, "Thomas Hutchinson and the Stamp Act," *New England Quarterly*, XXI (1948), 476. Morgan argued that if Hutchinson really meant "most people" in Massachusetts, "he was lying" (p. 478). Morgan's point was that the lieutenant governor's statement contradicted the evidence of colonial views located by Morgan in the assembly petitions of 1765-1766. This article identifies a body of evidence vindicating Hutchinson's observation. See the testimony of Col. George Mercer, William Kelly, Thomas Moffatt, Martin Howard, Barlow Trecothick, James Balfour, and Benjamin Franklin in *Proceedings*, II, 113-121, 134-135, 166, 194, 199-218, 228-233. When asked whether Americans made the same objections to external taxes that they were making against an internal one in 1765, Trecothick replied, "only to the weight of the taxes, none to the authority laying them" (*ibid.*, 191). Trecothick contradicted himself and the other witnesses when he testified that Americans opposed all taxes. Howard agreed with this latter statement.

[19] *Boston Evening-Post*, Sept. 2, 1765.

Those who sang this song apparently shared a hatred of the stamp tax. They expressed a disdain for internal taxes of all sorts and saw this internal tax as a threat to the liberties hard-won by their ancestors. They were also, it appears, distinguishing between two types of taxes and making an ideological argument against only one.

Such popular expressions of ideology tell us little more about the particulars of this distinction. Other sources are needed to define the terms of debate and to isolate the fears shared by Americans. Pamphlets, newspaper articles, private correspondence, and resolutions of legislative assemblies are all helpful for understanding ideological conflict and agreement among the colonists.

The 1760s can be considered as a unit for discussing internal taxes. All the ingredients of the distinction were present before the Stamp Act rebellion.[20] All remained potent spices in America's ideological stew thereafter. What changes occurred were those of precision and definition. Under the pressure of conflict in 1765, proponents of the distinction were forced to articulate previously unexamined beliefs more clearly and perhaps more consistently. They did not, however, modify or retract any significant component of their ideology.

At the heart of the distinction were theories about the relationship between representation and freedom, about the constitutional necessity for dividing sovereignty between Parliament and colonial assemblies, and about the role played by taxes in all of these theories. In each case the distinction between internal and external taxes seemed crucial to some Americans.

Definition of terms, although not always the prime concern of colonial theorists, must be the next step for us. It is not always as clear as it might be—in the case of the song posted by the Newport crowd, for example—exactly what colonists meant when they attached the limiting modifier "internal" to "taxes." Few bothered to explain so familiar a term. Several contemporary definitions do survive, however, that help to translate the shorthand language of popular protest. Charles Carroll of Carrollton, for one, explained the distinction between internal and external taxes to a British correspondent in September 1765. "England restrains our trade,"

[20] Richard Bland, Thomas Hutchinson, Benjamin Franklin, and the legislatures of Connecticut and Massachusetts were among those making the distinction before 1765. See Bland, *The Colonel Dismounted* . . . (Williamsburg, Va., 1764), 22, in Bernard Bailyn, ed., *Pamphlets of the American Revolution* (Cambridge, Mass., 1965), 320; Hutchinson to Richard Jackson, July 23, 1764, quoted by Morgan, "Hutchinson and the Stamp Act," *NEQ*, XXI (1948), 485-486; Franklin to Jackson, May 1, 1764, and Jackson to Franklin, Jan. 26, 1764, in Leonard W. Labaree *et al.*, eds., *The Papers of Benjamin Franklin* (New Haven, Conn., 1959-), XI, 186, 35; Malcolm Freiberg, ed., *Journals of the House of Representatives of Massachusetts*, XLI (Boston, 1971), 76; Thomas Fitch *et al.*, *Reasons Why the British Colonies in America Should Not Be Charged With Internal Taxes* . . . (New Haven, Conn., 1764), 4-5, in Bailyn, ed., *Pamphlets*, 386-387.

Carroll wrote, "she appoints our Governors, lays duties on our exports and imports; and the exertion of this power or right, as a necessary consequence of our dependence on the mother country, has all along been admitted and acquiesced in by the colonies. It was in this sense I admitted the propriety of her taxing us."[21] Carroll clearly and forthrightly conceded Parliament's right to tax the colonies, but not in the form of internal taxes. When he denied Parliament's right to tax the colonies, according to Carroll, what he meant was Parliament's authority to tax the colonies internally. For him, sovereignty was necessarily divided between Parliament and colonial assemblies; only the assemblies could constitutionally assess internal taxes on their constituents.

Representation was the key. As Benjamin Franklin defined the terms for Parliament, an American theory of representation lay at the heart of the distinction colonists were making. "I think the difference [between internal and external taxation] is very great," Franklin testified. "An external tax is a duty laid on commodities imported; that duty is added to the first cost, and other charges on the commodity, and when it is offered to sale, makes a part of the price. If the people do not like it at that price, they refuse it; they are not obliged to pay it. But an internal tax is forced from the people without their consent, if not laid by their own representatives."[22] A majority of the Massachusetts assembly had advanced this same theory of representation in a November 1764 petition to Parliament. The assemblymen pointed out in this official communication that the colonies "have always judged by their representatives both of the way and manner, in which internal taxes should be raised within their respective governments."[23] According to this argument, garnering the consent of the people through their chosen representatives was a necessary precondition for the just exaction of internal taxes. Colonists differed about what it would take to represent them adequately, but Stamp Act resisters, with few exceptions, could agree that Americans were not represented in Parliament. In other words, they did not accept the notion of virtual representation.

While American opponents of the Stamp Act concurred that there was a necessary link between representation and authority to assess internal taxes, they disagreed profoundly about what constituted adequate representation for the task. Some maintained that tensions between the colonies and Britain would be eased by acceptance of M.P.s elected by colonists. "If you chuse to tax us," Franklin wrote to Richard Jackson,

411

[21] Carroll to Henry Graves, Sept. 15, 1765, in Thomas Meagher Fields, ed., *Unpublished Letters of Charles Carroll of Carrollton* . . . (New York, 1902), 89.

[22] *The Examination of Doctor Benjamin Franklin, before an August Assembly, relating to the Repeal of the Stamp Act &c.* (Philadelphia, 1766), in Labaree *et al.*, eds., *Franklin Papers*, XIII, 139. In a letter of Mar. 13, 1768, to his son William, Franklin again affirmed Parliament's authority to lay duties on imported goods but not "internal taxes" (*ibid.*, XV, 76).

[23] Freiberg, ed., *Mass. House Journals*, XLI, 76.

"give us Members in your Legislature, and let us be one People."[24] Other Americans were not so sanguine: the geographical remoteness of Parliament would always, under any conceivable electoral arrangement, deny them adequate representation in Parliament for the purpose of assessing internal taxes. Thomas Fitch, for example, thought the colonies were "subordinate jurisdictions or governments which by distance are so separated from Great Britain that they are not and cannot be represented in Parliament."[25] According to Stephen Hopkins, the colonies were "at so great a distance from England" that Parliament could never truly know American conditions and could not become sufficiently representative to levy internal taxes.[26] During the 1760s this ideological quarrel among Americans had little impact on the organization of intercolonial opposition to Great Britain. It was not the sort of issue that would prevent Fitch and Franklin—or others who had different standards of representation— from uniting against Parliament and its internal stamp tax. By either standard, colonists were not represented in Parliament.

The terms of another potential ideological clash were also defined during the 1760s but submerged on an intercolonial or national level beneath other concerns until the 1780s. Some Americans contended during the 1760s that sovereignty could be divided between Parliament and colonial assemblies but not shared—that divided sovereignty in fact described traditional relationships within the empire. Those who embraced this critical distinction separated authority over internal taxes from authority over external taxes. Writing before the Stamp Act revolt, Richard Bland pointed out that Virginians were "in every instance . . . of our EXTERNAL government . . . subject to the authority of the British Parliament, but in no others." Since Bland maintained that colonial legislatures had exclusive right to legislate matters relating to their "INTERNAL government," it seemed to him that "any tax respecting our INTERNAL polity which may hereafter be imposed on us by act of Parliament is arbitrary . . . and may be opposed."[27] The Connecticut legislature drew the line dividing sovereignty in the same place, as revealed in the title to its 1764 pamphlet: *Reasons Why the British Colonies in America Should Not Be Charged with Internal Taxes*.[28] Thomas Hutchin-

[24] Franklin to Jackson, May 1, 1764, in Labaree *et al.*, eds., *Franklin Papers*, XI, 186.

[25] Fitch *et al.*, *Reasons Why*, 4-5, in Bailyn, ed., *Pamphlets*, 386-387.

[26] [Stephen Hopkins], *The Rights of Colonies Examined* (Providence, R.I., 1765), in Bailyn, ed., *Pamphlets*, 513. Hopkins was not consistent, however, in that he protested the external taxes imposed by the Sugar Act in 1764. Mack E. Thompson, "The Ward-Hopkins Controversy and the American Revolution in Rhode Island: An Interpretation," *WMQ*, 3d Ser., XVI (1959), 363-375; David S. Lovejoy, *Rhode Island Politics and the American Revolution, 1760-1776* (Providence, R.I., 1958).

[27] Bland, *Colonel Dismounted*, 22, in Bailyn, ed., *Pamphlets*, 320.

[28] Fitch *et al.*, *Reasons Why*, in Bailyn, ed., *Pamphlets*, 378-407.

son expressed to one of its authors his estimate that most people in his acquaintance agreed.

Even before the Stamp Act it seemed clear to Franklin that "two distinct Jurisdictions or Powers of Taxing cannot well subsist together in the same Country. They will confound and obstruct each other." He reasoned that sovereignty could be divided between different levels of government, but that authority over internal and external taxes, for example, could not be shared. In the case of the North American colonies, which were an ocean away from Parliament, the division of authority over taxation was traditional, practical, and necessary. "When any Tax for America is propos'd in your Parliament," Franklin wrote, "how are you to know that we are not already tax'd as much as we can bear? If a Tax is propos'd with us, how dare we venture to lay it, as the next Ship perhaps may bring us an Account of some heavy Tax impos'd by you."[29] Franklin, Bland, and the Massachusetts assembly in its 1764 petition to Parliament all argued that this traditional arrangement of divided sovereignty should continue as long as the colonies were not represented in Parliament.

Some Americans rejected this vision of divided sovereignty in 1765, as others would during the 1780s. James Otis, for one, denied any limitation on Parliament's authority. He believed that "the Parliament of Great Britain has a just and equitable right, power, and authority *to impose taxes on the colonies, internal and external, on lands as well as on trade.*" Even in dissent, however, Otis communicated in the language of America's popular protest. Even those who denied the validity of the ideological distinction in 1765 recognized its vitality and thus legitimized the terms of its argument. Rhode Island physician Thomas Moffatt did not like it, but he read the distinction "in the newspapers." William Kelly, of New York, did not understand it, but he knew colonists made "a distinction between internal taxes and some others which I did not quite comprehend." Virginia merchant James Balfour reported that "the distinction between internal and external duties" was common in his colony, and his fellow Virginian Col. George Mercer agreed that "the Stamp Act being an internal tax was one of the great objections to it."[30]

413

[29] Franklin to Jackson, May 1, 1764, in Labaree *et al.*, eds., *Franklin Papers.* XI, 186.

[30] Otis, *The Rights of the British Colonies Asserted and Proved* (Boston, 1764), 38, 42, in Bailyn, ed., *Pamphlets*, 447, 450-451, and *A Vindication of the British Colonies* . . . (Boston, 1765), 5, *ibid.*, 555; *Proceedings*, II, 119, 201, 207, 209, 210. Rhode Island lawyer Martin Howard and Boston merchant Barlow Trecothick offered testimony contradicting the other witnesses. They thought Americans objected to all taxes levied by Parliament (*ibid.*, 121, 190). There were other significant dissents from the external-internal distinction in America during the 1760s. These included the New York assembly's acknowledgment that Parliament had the authority "to model the Trade of the whole Empire," while contesting Parliament's decision to tax the colonies at all since "all Impositions, whether they be internal Taxes, or Duties paid, for what we consume, equally diminish the Estates upon which they are charged." New York Assembly, Petition to the House

Understandably, given the plethora of contradictory information before it, Parliament remained confused about what colonists thought. American witnesses testified to the ideological force of the internal-external distinction throughout the colonies. Private correspondence, newspaper excerpts, and pamphlets reaching London all provided supporting evidence. But the official protests of several colonial assemblies made no explicit distinction of that kind, while the resolutions of other assemblies seemed to deny Parliament's authority to levy taxes of any sort for America.

The colonists interrogated before Parliament were put on the spot to explain this apparent discrepancy in the "American" position. They clearly felt obliged to paper over some of the disagreements among colonists on the issue of taxation. They were also trying to minimize American claims in order to placate Parliament and assure repeal of the Stamp Act. Nonetheless, the official resolutions of the assemblies and Franklin's testimony explaining them help us to understand better some of the difficulty historians have had in interpreting the colonial positions—usually depending upon which sources they credit—and some of the problems associated with translating the language of two hundred years ago.

The position of Rhode Island's legislature was the clearest. This assembly's official protest against the Stamp Act forthrightly limited its own claim to authority over internal taxes. The "Rhode Island Resolves" stated plainly that "his Majesty's liege People, the Inhabitants of this Colony, are not bound to yield Obedience to any Law or Ordinance, designed to impose any internal Taxation whatsoever upon them, other than the Laws or Ordinances of the General Assembly aforesaid."[31]

The case for other colonies—Connecticut, Maryland, and Virginia—is more complex. It is a matter of interpretation over which historians may reasonably disagree. The official Maryland and Virginia Stamp Act protests referred respectively to "Taxes and internal Polity" and "internal Polity and Taxation."[32] Connecticut's assembly asserted exclusive jurisdiction over "taxing and internal Police."[33] Each of these phrases explicitly made the "internal" distinction. None specifically attached the adjective to taxes. The drafters certainly understood and accepted the common belief in an exclusive authority over "internal" affairs for their bodies. They all said that sovereignty was divisible but could not be shared by two distinct

---

of Commons, Oct. 18, 1764, in Edmund S. Morgan, "The New York Declaration of 1764," *Old South Leaflets*, No. 224 (1948), 7-15.

[31] Edmund S. Morgan, ed., *Prologue to Revolution: Sources and Documents on the Stamp Act Crisis, 1764-1766* (Chapel Hill, N.C., 1959), 50-51.

[32] "Maryland Resolves," Sept. 28, 1765, *ibid.*, 52-53. The Virginia Resolves were printed in the *Maryland Gazette* (Annapolis), July 4, 1765, and elsewhere. Morgan included the different versions in *Prologue to Revolution*, 46-50.

[33] Connecticut Resolves, Oct. 25, 1765, in Morgan, ed., *Prologue to Revolution*, 54-56.

legislative bodies—that one assembly could legislate externally and another internally but that two legislatures could not share power over either category of taxes, and each writer remained vague about where (in which category) to place import duties. The authors of all three protests believed that Parliament acted constitutionally only in the "external" sphere. And, finally, all three saw the Stamp Act as a novel and insidious type of legislation. It was the first time Parliament had ever "taxed" them.

To these legislatures, "taxation" was apparently synonymous with the "internal taxation" of Rhode Island's assembly and of other Americans during the 1760s. To embrace their position, the drafters of the resolves must either have seen previous customs duties as "external" taxes or not as taxes at all but perhaps only as regulations of trade. In either case they came close to making the same distinction and endorsing the same constitutional relationship as those who specifically used "internal" and "external" to describe two types of taxation and two legislative sovereigns. Possibly because the Chesapeake colonies and Connecticut had no major molasses trade, they were better able to concentrate their fury against the Stamp Act while overlooking the Sugar Act. But this explanation can hardly apply to Rhode Island.

415

The intercolonial Stamp Act Congress also chose to imply rather than assert the distinction between types of taxes, as Carl Becker pointed out over sixty years ago. This assembly described the Stamp Act as "imposing Taxes" having "a manifest tendency to subvert the rights and liberties of the colonies," while it referred to the Sugar Act only vaguely as one of "several late acts" imposing "duties" that "will be extremely burthensome and grievous." The Congress thus implied, without ever using the words "internal" and "external," that there was a distinction to be made between the ideologically invidious (internal) Stamp Act and the economically odious (external) Sugar Act.[34]

---

[34] Becker, *Declaration of Independence,* 90-91. The practical effect of the Stamp Act Congress's two lines of logic was opposition to all taxes, as some members of Parliament recognized before many Americans did. It is this sort of colonial reasoning that best fits the interpretations of the Morgans, who took the constitutional arguments seriously, and those of the Progressive historians, who have not credited Revolutionary ideas with any consistent motive force. The Morgans contended that Americans opposed all taxes levied by Parliament as early as 1765. Progressives have generally viewed constitutional arguments as propaganda or rationalizations for perceived pecuniary interest. One ground for reconciliation lies in the position adopted in this article. The colonists' ideas should be taken seriously, not because they were consistently embraced by "most" Americans who marched off to Revolution to the tune of constitutional opposition to all taxation without representation, but because there was profound disagreement among Americans, as the Progressives have told us all along, and because the language of politics records some of the competing themes sounded by America's different drummers. American Revolutionaries disagreed about the theory and practice of politics, and they did not all perceive their interests in the same way. These disagreements had a profound impact on American politics during the two decades

The assemblies of Connecticut, Maryland, and Virginia were not alone in using "taxation" and "internal taxation" synonymously. Charles Carroll of Carrollton, Daniel Dulany, Thomas Fitch, Benjamin Franklin, and Stephen Hopkins also employed the terms interchangeably.[35] And, according to Franklin, so did other Americans. During his examination it was pointed out to Franklin that the resolutions of several assemblies, including that of his own colony of Pennsylvania, said that "all taxes," not just "internal" taxes, lay outside the bounds of Parliament's authority over America. "If they do," Franklin replied, "they mean only internal taxes; the same words have not always the same meaning here and in the Colonies. By taxes they mean internal taxes; by duties they mean customs; these are their ideas of the language."[36]

Thus we must be careful not to dismiss the internal-external distinction even in those cases where it does not explicitly appear. The difference was apparently so common that it was assumed by many of its users. At least two witnesses to William Pitt's pleas for repeal of the Stamp Act, for example, heard him make the distinction. At least one witness, on the other hand, neglected to record it in his notes on Pitt's speech. All three notices appeared in the *Virginia Gazette* without comment, raising the possibility that the differences in the language used to report the speech may not even have struck some Americans, because they used "taxation" and "internal taxation" interchangeably. This understanding of internal taxes may have been so common among the colonists that we anachronistically impose precision on their words by demanding the appearance of the distinction before we recognize its validity. By focusing only on the presence or the absence of a word we may misconstrue their meaning.[37]

There can be no confusion, however, about the range of fears shared by Americans who embraced an ideology imbued with the distinction between internal and external taxes. Theirs were embellishments of radical whig horrors conjured for the education of a public at risk of losing its liberty. "It is seldom," wrote a contributor to the *Boston Evening-Post* in

416

---

after the Revolution. Conflict, not consensus, was the distinctive mark of those years.

[35] Fitch *et al.*, *Reasons Why*, 4-5, 15, and *passim*, in Bailyn, ed., *Pamphlets*, 386-387, 389, and *passim*. Daniel Dulany, *Considerations on the Propriety of Imposing Taxes in the British Colonies* . . . ([Annapolis, Md.], 1765). Dulany argued that the colonists were not and could never be represented in Parliament because of its distance from and inaccessibility to North Americans. He used the terms "taxes" and "internal taxes" interchangeably just as Fitch *et al.* did. Like Franklin, he understood sovereignty to be divided between colonial legislatures and Parliament. Bailyn, ed., *Pamphlets*, 618-620, 626, 652, and *passim*. See references to Franklin and Carroll in notes 20, 21, 22, 24, and 29.

[36] Labaree *et al.*, eds., *Franklin Papers*, XIII, 156. Virginian James Balfour understood his colony's resolutions in the same way (*Proceedings*, II, 201).

[37] *Virginia Gazette* (Williamsburg), Apr. 11, 18, 1766. See Christie, "Pitt and American Taxation," *Burke Studies*, XVII (1976), 167-179.

February 1765, "indeed very seldom, that any people have had more at stake than we at Present have."[38] "The parliament of Great Britain have no right to level an internal tax upon the colonies," another writer stormed.[39]

What were these rights at stake in 1765? Stephen Hopkins thought that when Parliament sought "to establish stamp duties and other internal taxes" for the colonies, it threatened to reduce Americans to "the miserable condition of slaves." Linking the issue of representation to his fears, Hopkins argued that a legislature too remote to appreciate American conditions and interests could not possibly "determine with confidence on matters far above their reach." In all likelihood, such policy would compel Americans "to go naked in this cold country" or else clothe themselves in animal skins. Property, civilization, even the physical survival of the colonists seemed at risk. Expanded jurisdiction for admiralty courts to enforce the new tax would inflict cruel punishments— in costs, time, and anxiety—even on those found innocent of charges. Remote, unrepresentative legislatures and remote, inaccessible courts of law threatened colonial prosperity, according to Hopkins. Local legislative bodies and local courts knew local conditions. They could, therefore, better dispense justice and more equitably assess internal taxes.[40]

417

The British justification of the Stamp Act as necessary to raise funds for American defense seemed to Hopkins similarly fallacious: "To take the money of the Americans . . . and lay it up for their defense a thousand leagues distance from them when the enemies they have to fear are in their own neighborhood, hath not the greatest probability of friendship or prudence." Again Hopkins was expressing a localist argument and fears. He would leave laws, justice, and even defense (despite its external connotations) to those who knew local conditions from experience. Since circumstances varied widely among the colonies, each, according to Hopkins, should administer its own affairs; otherwise, central authority would threaten the property, the lives, and hence the freedom of colonists. "They who have no property," Hopkins concluded, "can have no freedom, but indeed are reduced to the most abject slavery."[41] Here

---

[38] *Boston Evening-Post*, Feb. 4, 1765, 1.

[39] *Ibid.*, May 13, 1765. See also Aug. 13, 26, 1765, and the *Connecticut Gazette* (New Haven), Sept. 9, 1765, reprinted in the *Boston Gazette*, Sept. 9, 1765.

[40] [Hopkins], *Rights of the Colonies Examined*, in Bailyn, ed., *Pamphlets*, 508, 512, 513, 515-517. Hopkins's exaggerated fears were, of course, a classic example of the radical whig ideology described so ably by Bailyn in *Ideological Origins;* Caroline Robbins in *The Eighteenth-Century Commonwealthman: Studies in the Transmission, Development and Circumstance of English Liberal Thought from the Restoration of Charles II until the War with the Thirteen Colonies* (Cambridge, Mass., 1959); and J.G.A. Pocock in *The Machiavellian Moment: Florentine Political Thought and the Atlantic Republican Tradition* (Princeton, N.J., 1975).

[41] [Hopkins], *Rights of the Colonies Examined*, in Bailyn, ed., *Pamphlets*, 516.

was a classic summary of localist logic and fears for any decade in the second half of the eighteenth century.

Some Americans did not endorse the concept of divided sovereignty in the 1760s. They disagreed about the meaning of "representation," and the disagreement was already an important ideological quarrel. Other Americans demanded division of authority over internal and external taxes between local and central governments and denied in principle the right of a central government to tax their property. By "taxes" they may have meant "internal taxes," but by "representation" American localists did not mean sending several delegates hundreds of miles to be outvoted by politicians with interests alien from theirs.

418

The riots stopped with repeal of the Stamp Act. There were few protests against the Revenue Act of 1766, a blatant revenue-raising measure but an external one. Efforts to organize intercolonial resistance to the Townshend duties after 1767 were divisive and far less successful than the Stamp Act protests. Never again before the Revolutionary War would Americans—outside of Boston—achieve the same sort of unanimity against British taxes that they enjoyed during Stamp Act resistance. And that was due at least in part to Parliament's de facto respect for the constitutional distinction Americans had made during the 1760s. In the absence of the ideological dimension of internal taxation, it was clearly difficult to unite Americans of diverse economic interests against British external taxes. It would take the presence of British soldiers in Boston after 1768, "customs racketeering," and the Coercive Acts to ignite again the localist fires fueled by the Stamp Act.[42]

The principle of divided sovereignty—of divided authority over internal and external taxes—was not abandoned by localists during the 1770s.

[42] Standing armies, corrupt collectors of external taxes, and such repressive measures as the Boston Port Act were also perceived as threats to localist ideals. See, for example, Oliver M. Dickerson, *The Navigation Acts and the American Revolution* (Philadelphia, 1951), chap. 9. Some Americans also opposed external taxes for ideological reasons. John Dickinson, for one, equated all taxation with representation. Even Dickinson, though, was understood at the time to argue that Americans should accept external taxes levied by Parliament. See Becker, *Declaration of Independence*, 118; David L. Jacobson, *John Dickinson and the Revolution in Pennsylvania, 1764-1776* (Berkeley, Calif., 1965); Milton E. Flower, *John Dickinson: Conservative Revolutionary* (Charlottesville, Va., 1983); and *The Farmer's and Monitor's Letters, to the Inhabitants of the British Colonies* (Williamsburg, Va., 1769). Even Morgan, whose major interpretive points concern the colonists' dedication to principle and the consistency of their principles over time, must acknowledge that colonial resistance to British taxes after 1766 was never again so dedicated or interregionally united. "It is of course impossible to tell why men act as they do," Morgan concludes, but that should not lead us to "attribute to the men of previous ages an extraordinary simple-mindedness and demand of them a standard of righteousness which only an angel or a fanatic could meet" (*The Birth of the Republic, 1763-89* [Chicago, 1956], 49-51).

Since the concept was never challenged, there was no perceived need to articulate or defend it. Americans did not reach a consensus about this principle during those years. They still disagreed about the validity of divided sovereignty as a description of the British constitution and as an eternal verity for political society. When the issue of Parliament's authority emerged in the first Continental Congress, according to John Adams, "some were for a flat denial of all authority; others for denying the power of taxation only; some for denying internal, but admitting external, taxation."[43] In other words, Americans still differed about the ideological significance of internal taxes and about the localist description of divided sovereignty within the empire. But this dispute was a secondary issue of intercolonial affairs in 1774, one that could again be ignored as Americans united to confront more pressing threats to their liberties.

For over twenty years after the Stamp Act controversy few Americans ever explicitly mentioned internal taxes as an immediate threat to liberty. Those who did were usually only explaining to foreigners or to posterity— or reminding themselves—what had happened in 1765 and why.[44] Financier Robert Morris, for one, certainly would have liked to invest the Continental Congress with the sovereign power to exact internal taxes.[45] Nonetheless, Congress posed no widely perceived threat to those who believed in divided sovereignty or to those who denied any remote central government's authority to levy internal taxes.

This ideological fissure among Americans continued to exert a subterranean influence on American politics; it was a component of political conflict, and one that probably reflected social-structural and interregional strains. Conflicting views of representation would become even more critical on a national level, though, when Americans organized their own central government and considered levying internal taxes in a national legislature some still considered remote and inadequately representative. This then became one key place to draw the defining line between localists or provincials and those who shared a more national or cosmopolitan ideology.

As we have seen, Americans who challenged Parliament's authority to impose internal taxes based their claims on a localist theory of representation and an ideology that assumed the impossibility of assigning concurrent jurisdiction to two independent governments. Since colonists were

419

---

[43] Charles Francis Adams, ed., *The Works of John Adams*. 10 vols. (Boston, 1850-1856), II, 374.

[44] See, for example, the epigraph to this article.

[45] On the designs of Robert Morris and other nationalists see E. James Ferguson, "The Nationalists of 1781-1783 and the Economic Interpretation of the Constitution," *Journal of American History*, LVI (1969), 241-261, and Jack N. Rakove, *The Beginnings of National Politics: An Interpretive History of the Continental Congress* (New York, 1979).

not represented in Parliament—and some believed they never could be—British politicians had no right to tax them. Since the colonies taxed themselves internally, Parliament could not possibly share that right.

When they established their own central government under the Articles of Confederation, Americans reserved all tax-making authority to the states. Because the Continental Congress possessed no independent power over taxes, the latent disagreement over divided sovereignty never became a divisive issue within that body, at least from a localist perspective. Granted, when the impost seemed a genuine possibility, some in Congress insisted that the states retain control over collectors. This certainly was a variant of localist fears of tax collectors appointed by remote central governments. Congress, however, with its circumscribed powers, never posed the same sort of threat as Parliament. The danger of this central government enacting internal taxes never materialized, but a public outcry would certainly have met an amendment to the Articles vesting the Congress with such authority. Given the fate of the much less ideologically controversial impost, it is unimaginable that the states would have approved any internal tax.[46]

When delegates gathered to reorganize the central government in 1787, the voices of Americans who cared deeply about divided sovereignty and the ideological distinction between internal and external taxes were not heard.[47] The Constitution proposed by the Philadelphia convention granted a national congress the unlimited "power to lay and collect taxes, duties, imposts, and excises."[48] The document thus gave the central government taxing authority in both internal and external realms as defined during the 1760s. The Constitution also denied the states power to act independently in the external sphere; it reserved for the central government exclusive control over customs duties, regulation of interstate trade, international treaties, and other portions of the parliamentary sovereignty that localists acknowledged in the 1760s.[49] The taxing authority of the proposed national government would be no less, and was

[46] Rakove, Beginnings of National Politics, 157-158, 170, 303, 306-309, 315, 362, 380, 399.

[47] The fact that controversy over the internal-external distinction never arose in the Continental Congress or the Constitutional Convention may indicate the unrepresentative character of those bodies. The isolation of each from the pressures of public opinion is well known. See, for example, Charles Warren, The Making of the Constitution (Cambridge, Mass., 1948), 627, and Rakove, Beginnings of National Politics. Absence of such debates does not demonstrate, as the rest of this article argues, that the issue was no longer volatile.

[48] U.S., Constitution, Art. 1, sec. 8, par. 1.

[49] Ibid., Art. 1, sec. 10, par. 2. The New Jersey Plan also proposed giving the central government authority to raise both internal and external taxes. The internal tax specifically authorized in the New Jersey Plan was a stamp tax. See Max Farrand, ed., The Records of the Federal Convention of 1787, 4 vols. (New Haven, Conn., 1911-1937), I, 242-245.

420

certainly designed to be even greater, than anything attempted by the British government during the 1760s and 1770s.

Localists—now pejoratively termed Antifederalists by proponents of the Constitution—discovered and passionately denounced parallels between British claims in the 1760s and powers granted by the document to the central government. Most shocking of all was the renunciation of local control over internal taxes so soon after the war to secure such rights from Britain. A Pennsylvania writer had not forgotten the "glorious struggle" with Great Britain; he was appalled that the proposed national congress would be "vested with every species of *internal* taxation," and he feared that the collection of such taxes would be enforced by that bane of all radical whigs, "the standing army."[50]

This anonymous author and others believed, as some colonists had in the 1760s, that "there is a strong distinction between external and internal taxes."[51] William Goudy of North Carolina feared that the taxation clause of the proposed constitution "will totally destroy our liberties."[52] He and the majority of North Carolina's ratifying convention thought Article 1, section 8 should be amended to substitute a quota system for authority to lay internal taxes. Only if the quota remained unfilled by the states should the national congress be permitted to enact excises and other internal taxes.[53]

Localists in 1787 shared a more precise understanding of what they meant by external and internal taxes than colonists had displayed during the 1760s. The "Federal Farmer" saw clear differences between the two sorts of taxes. "External taxes," he wrote, "are import duties, which are laid on imported goods; they may usually be collected in a few seaport towns, and of a few individuals, though ultimately paid by the consumer; a few officers can collect them, and they can be carried no higher than trade will bear, or smuggling permit—that in the very nature of commerce, bounds are set to them."[54] For these reasons—the natural and fixed limitations on the amounts assessed, the few places where the taxes could be collected, the few officers employed in collection, and the limitation of taxes to items produced by foreigners—localists believed that external

421

[50] "Centinel," *Independent Gaz.*, Oct. 5, 1787, in Kenyon, ed., *Antifederalists*, 9.

[51] "Letter from the Federal Farmer," No. 3, Oct. 10, 1787, in Kenyon, ed., *Antifederalists*, 223.

[52] Elliot, ed., *Debates in State Conventions*, IV, 93.

[53] *Ibid.*, 245. Similar amendments were offered in several other state conventions, including New York, Virginia, and Pennsylvania. See, for example, *ibid.*, II, 331. These proposals were quite close to Lord North's of 1775. On opposition to internal taxes see also Merrill Jensen, ed., *The Documentary History of the Ratification of the Constitution*, Vol. II: *Ratification of the Constitution by the States: Pennsylvania* (Madison, Wis., 1976), 162, 307, 445, 447, and Storing, ed., *Complete Anti-Federalist*, III: *Pennsylvania*, 41.

[54] "Letter from the Federal Farmer," No. 3, Oct. 10, 1787, in Kenyon, ed., *Antifederalists*, 223.

taxes might be assessed legitimately and collected by a republican central government.

Taxes laid on property, produce, manufactures, and commerce were different matters. The "Federal Farmer" thought that only the states should act in these realms. "Internal taxes," he wrote, "as poll and land taxes, excises, duties on all written instruments, &c. may fix themselves on every person and species of property in the community; they may be carried to any lengths, and in proportion as they are extended, numerous officers must be employed to assess them, and to enforce the collection of them." Localists agreed that the result must be a proliferation of taxes on every species of property in order to keep the collectors engaged, and that the resulting "disorder and general dissatisfaction" with the national government would ultimately provoke violent suppression by a national army.[55]

Others foresaw a similar result for the system proposed in the Constitution. The new government would immediately lay excise and other "internal taxes upon your lands, your goods, your chattels, as well as your persons at their sovereign pleasure," and "the produce of these several funds shall be appropriated to the use of the United States, and collected by their own officers, armed with a military force, if a civil aid should not prove sufficient."[56] First would come a raft of internal tax laws; then tax collectors would follow shortly behind. "The tax-gatherers will be sent," warned Joseph M'Dowall of North Carolina, "and our property will be wrested out of our hands." "If the tax-gatherers come upon us," he predicted, "they will, like the locusts of old, destroy us."[57] But not all Americans would simply roll over and submit to such oppression. In some regions, at least, the locusts M'Dowall warned of would be met by armed men determined to defend their hard-won liberties. Robert Livingston of New York thought the result must be either abdication of duties and office by the tax collectors or "an internal war."[58]

This civil war was perhaps what localists feared most from the internal taxing power of the proposed central government. Patrick Henry warned: "Look at the part which speaks of excises, and you will recollect that those who are to collect excises and duties are to be aided by military force. . . . Suppose an excise-man will demand leave to enter your cellar, or house, by virtue of his office; perhaps he may call on the militia to enable him to go."[59] Americans had not submitted to such intrusions in the past, and they would not do so now. Blood would flow.

Lack of knowledge of and sympathy for, the conditions and views of

[55] *Ibid.*, 223-224.

[56] "John De Witt," "To the Free Citizens of the Commonwealth of Massachusetts," letter No. 2, *American Herald* (Boston), Oct.-Dec. 1787, in Kenyon, ed., *Antifederalists*, 100. "Agrippa," No. 9, *Mass. Gaz.*, Dec. 28, 1787, *ibid.*, 137.

[57] Elliot, ed., *Debates in State Conventions*, IV, 87, 88.

[58] *Ibid.*, II, 344.

[59] *Ibid.*, III, 411-412.

many regions would make the national legislature the wrong institution to
enact internal tax laws.[60] As in 1765, it was hardly certain that the whole
people could ever be represented in a national legislature. Since only
experience would tell, localists believed that powers of internal taxation
must be reserved to the states, at least for the time being. "If a proper
representation be impracticable," reasoned the "Federal Farmer," "then
we shall see this power resting in the states, where it at present ought to
be, and not inconsiderately given up."[61] For now, it was at least certain
that the legislative branch of the central government would have "but very
little democracy in it."[62] Compared to the states, then, the central
government would be freer to ignore the desires of a large portion of the
citizenry and would possess the financial and military might to enforce its
will—to the possible extinction of the states and individual liberty.

423

Pennsylvania localists not only decried the weakness of the democratic
element in the Constitution, but in their ratifying convention they even
doubted the good will and intentions of those who would represent them
in the national legislature. Not just lack of knowledge about many
constituents, but an actual contempt for some citizens, would lead the
national representatives to enact oppressive taxes *deliberately*. Thus "that
strongest of all checks upon the conduct of administration, *responsibility to
the people*, will not exist in this government." Because of the imprecise
election methods and the length of terms served by representatives under
the proposed system, "they will consist of the lordly and high minded; of
men who will have no congenial feelings with the people, but a perfect
indifference for, and contempt of them; they will consist of those harpies
of power that prey upon the very vitals, that riot on the miseries of the
community."[63]

Pennsylvania localists could not trust the system embodied in the
Constitution, or the sort of men who would run it, with internal taxing
power under any circumstances. The Constitution seemed almost to
ensure a wave of economic repression and political violence. To them it
appeared certain that the "same force that may be employed to compel
obedience to good laws, might and probably would be used to wrest from
the people their constitutional liberties."[64] They foresaw use of state
militias "to enforce the collection of the most oppressive taxes"; they

[60] See *ibid.*, II, 335, and IV, 80, 88. On the desirability of keeping the central
government impoverished see *ibid.*, II, 74, 531. On the linkage between representation and internal taxation see "Philadelphiensis," No. 10, *Independent Gaz.*, Feb.
21, 1788, in Kenyon, ed., *Antifederalists*, 79.
[61] "Letter from the Federal Farmer," No. 3, Oct. 10, 1787, in Kenyon, ed.,
Antifederalists, 225.
[62] *Ibid.*, 217.
[63] "The Address and Reasons of Dissent of the Minority of the Convention of
the State of Pennsylvania to Their Constituents," *Pennsylvania Packet, and Daily
Advertiser* (Philadelphia), Dec. 18, 1787, in Kenyon, ed., *Antifederalists*, 55-56.
[64] *Ibid.*, 56.

predicted the marching of Pennsylvania militiamen to New England or Virginia to "quell an insurrection occasioned by the most galling oppression."[65] Ultimately, they believed, the death of state governments would certainly follow adoption of this constitution with its authority to levy internal taxes and raise armies to enforce the laws.

Localists contended in 1787, as colonists had in 1765, that to assign concurrent taxing powers to both local and central governments was to assure the demise of local political institutions. It was a hard-and-fast rule of the political world, they maintained, that the strong devour the weak—as power consumes liberty—if wealth and might are not isolated and caged. According to William Findley of Pennsylvania, "the powers given to the federal body for imposing internal taxation will necessarily destroy the state sovereignties for there cannot exist two independent sovereign taxing powers in the same community, and the strongest will, of course, annihilate the weaker."[66] Some foresaw the state governments gliding "imperceptibly and gradually out of existence."[67] Others anticipated the end coming quickly and violently with the state governments being "totally annihilated."[68] But all localists agreed that it was fanciful to trust that the state and national governments would cooperate in the collection of internal taxes.[69]

Some localists portrayed the Constitution's advocates as well intentioned but misguided.[70] Others were more suspicious and saw in the taxation clause an active conspiracy to destroy the states and create a consolidated government. The minority at the Pennsylvania ratifying convention predicted that the national government would "monopolize every source of revenue [and] indirectly demolish the State governments." Were the states "to impose taxes, duties or excises on the same articles with Congress," the Pennsylvania localists believed that the national government would "abrogate and repeal the laws whereby they are imposed."[71] In Virginia, Patrick Henry was also quick to discover

---

[65] Ibid., 57, 58.

[66] Jensen, ed., Documentary History, II, 448. A "Federal Republican" argued that the internal taxing power of the national government under the new constitution would "reduce the several states to poverty and nothing" (A Review of the Constitution Proposed by the Late Convention by A Federal Republican [Philadelphia, 1787], in Storing, ed., Complete Anti-Federalist, III, 74).

[67] Elliot, ed., Debates in State Conventions, III, 149.

[68] Ibid., II, 337.

[69] [Robert Yates], "Brutus," No. 6, New York Journal and Weekly Register (New York City), Dec. 27, 1787, in Kenyon, ed., Antifederalists, 325. See also "Brutus," No. 5, in Storing, ed., Complete Anti-Federalist, II, 392; "Letter from the Federal Farmer," No. 2, Oct. 9, 1787, in Kenyon, ed., Antifederalists, 213. On the same point see "A Manifesto of a Number of Gentlemen from Albany County," New York Jour., Apr. 26, 1788, in Kenyon, ed., Antifederalists, 363.

[70] William Grayson, Debates in the Virginia Convention, in Kenyon, ed., Antifederalists, 285, 289; Elliot, ed., Debates in State Conventions, II, 333.

[71] "Address and Reasons of Dissent," Pa. Packet, Dec. 18, 1787, in Kenyon, ed., Antifederalists, 41.

conspiracy afoot. "Your rich, snug, fine, fat, Federal offices—The number of collectors of taxes and excises will outnumber any thing from the States," Henry prophesied. These excise men would graze the states clean, leaving nothing but a consolidated national government behind. Henry had no doubt who would win the inevitable battle between the state and national authorities. "If we are to ask which will last the longest," he argued, "the State or the General Government, you must take an army and a navy into the account." Clearly, the central government would triumph. "Can, then, the State Governments look it in the face?" he queried. "You dare not look it in the face now, when it is but an *embryo*."[72] Indeed, a New York delegate believed that this talk of concurrent jurisdiction over taxation was ludicrous in the light of claims for the supremacy of laws adopted by the proposed national congress. He argued that if state and national taxes conflicted, Congress would simply "abolish the state governments."[73]

425

For Antifederal localists, then, the issues and the stakes had changed little from the 1760s. The constitutional conflict over internal and external taxation had at least as much meaning for Americans in 1787 as in 1765. In both cases some saw the reservation of internal taxation to the colonies/ states as crucial to the survival of liberty. In each case they predicted violent conflict and consequent loss of liberty as the likely results of granting the central government authority to assess internal taxes. It made little difference that the central government after 1787 would be managed by elected Americans rather than British politicians over whom they had virtually no influence. The problems of representation remained largely the same. Whether elected or not, men who shared no sympathy for the needs of some regions could not represent all their constituents' interests adequately to tax them. In 1787 as in 1765, localists believed that internal taxing authority must be left to local representatives who lived among their constituents and knew their wants and needs. Under the proposed system this would not be possible. Each congressman would represent as many as 30,000 people, and districts would grow even larger. A senator from Philadelphia, Boston, or Charleston, for example, could never truly appreciate or represent the unique problems and needs of frontiersmen. Furthermore, as a matter of logic and political theory, localists strongly resisted the idea that two sovereign governmental bodies could coexist,

---

[72] Patrick Henry, Debates in the Virginia Convention, in Storing, ed., *Complete Anti-Federalist*, V, 244.

[73] Elliot, ed., *Debates in State Conventions*, II, 339. "Aristocrotis" satirically advised friends of the new constitution on the subterfuges they should use to delude people into supporting the document. Among other lies, "the people must be told, that the revenue of the nation will be chiefly raised by impost under the new constitution, and that internal taxation will seldom if ever be recurred to" (*The Government of Nature Delineated or An Exact Picture of the New Federal Constitution by Aristocrotis* [Carlisle, Pa., 1788], in Storing, ed., *Complete Anti-Federalist*, III, 210).

share concurrent jurisdiction, cooperate, and survive. They believed that sovereignty could be divided but not shared. To give both the central government and the states authority to lay internal taxes was to decree the virtual death of the states. The larger and stronger government would inevitably overwhelm the states with taxes, tax collectors, and, if necessary, soldiers to enforce its laws. In the face of such might, state governments would be compelled to repeal tax laws or simply leave an overburdened populace alone and not collect taxes at all. In the end, the states would either fade to shadows or be violently annihilated by a national army. However the end came, the fate of the citizen, the state, and the nation would ultimately be the same. Discontent, resistance, repression, violence, tyranny, and death would be the short and brutal history of the American republic.

As subsequent events showed, the localists of 1787 were only partially correct in their predictions. The state governments were not annihilated, nor did they glide out of existence. The national government did not dissolve in a cauldron of tyranny and anarchy. On the other hand, the nationalists' assurances—which localists interpreted as promises—that a direct excise would only be a tax of last resort proved false. One of the earliest fiscal measures of the new Congress was the whiskey excise of 1791. Localists were also correct in predicting that passage of internal taxes by a remote central government would bring the nation to the brink of "internal war." The Pennsylvania militia would not march to New England or Virginia to "quell an insurrection occasioned by the most galling oppression." The militias of Pennsylvania, New Jersey, Maryland, and Virginia would march west, however, to suppress an excise-tax revolt on the other side of the Appalachian Mountains in 1794. The Whiskey Rebellion would result from precisely the sorts of tensions foreseen by localists in 1765 and 1787-1788.[74]

Localists of the 1780s and 1790s were also heirs to a consistent pattern of beliefs. There was more continuity than change in the ideology that had the internal-external distinction at its heart. The theories of constitutionalism, sovereignty, representation, and taxation embraced by some Americans altered little, except in achieving greater clarity and precision, from 1765 through 1787 and beyond. And the Antifederalists' defense of this ideology in 1787 is one clear case where their claims to recognition as true defenders of the principles of the 1760s and 1770s can be vindicated.

Looking forward in time, we can define America's "court" and "country" political factions in part by their respective stands on the ideological distinction between internal and external taxes.[75] Federalist or "court"

[74] Thomas P. Slaughter, *The Whiskey Rebellion: Frontier Epilogue to the American Revolution* (New York, forthcoming).

[75] Joyce Appleby, "Commercial Farming and the 'Agrarian Myth' in the Early Republic," *Journal of American History,* LXVIII (1982), 833-849, and "What is Still American in the Political Philosophy of Thomas Jefferson?" *WMQ,* 3d Ser.,

administrations during the 1790s would propose and enforce the internal taxes that provoked the Whiskey Rebellion and Fries's Rebellion. The Washington administration's justification for its proposed excise tax on whiskey would bear a remarkable resemblance to the Grenville ministry's rationale for the Stamp Act. George Washington's armed enforcement of the law at the head of a 15,000-man army—a force comparable in size to the one he led against Great Britain in the Revolution—was a militant defense of law and order equal in spirit to Great Britain's attempts in Boston after 1768 and throughout America beginning in 1775. And it was more successful.

"Country" opponents of the whiskey excise began in 1790 to articulate the same ideology, in the same language, as anti-Stamp Act pamphleteers. They explicitly resurrected the Stamp Act as symbol and example of their cause. They defined their philosophy of divided sovereignty between central and local governments in the same way as Stamp Act rebels and Antifederalists had done; they shared the same attitudes toward representation; and they divided the world of taxes into internal and external spheres. Localist fears had not changed, but the threat to liberty once perceived to emanate from London now seemed to localists to reside in the national capital of Philadelphia. The Washington administration's militant enforcement of the excise and the resulting bloodshed seemed to localists of 1794 horrific vindication of their ideology.[76]

When the Jeffersonian Republicans emerged victorious in 1800, one widely celebrated consequence was repeal of the whiskey excise. The "country" party of America's first party system remained loyal to its ideological roots and never adopted a peacetime internal tax. Only in war—James Madison's excise during the War of 1812—would the Republicans invoke what they saw as the emergency taxing power of the Constitution. Only for the duration of an extraordinary threat, localists agreed, might an exception be made to their ideological demand that remote central governments refrain from intrusion on local control over internal taxes.

427

XXXIX (1982), 287-309; John M. Murrin, "The Great Inversion, or Court versus Country: A Comparison of the Revolution Settlements in England (1688-1721) and America (1776-1816)," in J.G.A. Pocock, ed., *Three British Revolutions: 1641, 1688, 1776* (Princeton, N.J., 1980), 368-453; Robert E. Shalhope, "Republicanism and Early American Historiography," *WMQ*, 3d Ser., XXXIX (1982), 334-356; and James H. Hutson, "Country, Court, and Constitution: Antifederalism and the Historians," *ibid.*, XXXVIII (1981), 337-368.
[76] Slaughter, *Whiskey Rebellion.*

The publisher and editor gratefully acknowledge the permission of the authors and the following journals and organizations to reprint the copyright material in this volume; any further reproduction is prohibited without permission:

The University of Toronto Press for material in *The Canadian Historical Review*; *The William and Mary Quarterly*; the Academy of Political Science for material in the *Political Science Quarterly*; the *American Quarterly*; *The New England Quarterly*; the *Journal of the History of Ideas*.

CONTENTS OF THE SET